DATE DUE

CONTEMPORARY MUSICIANS

K

ISSN 1044-2197

CONTEMPORARY MUSICIANS

PROFILES OF THE PEOPLE IN MUSIC

LEIGH ANN DeREMER, Editor
LUANN BRENNAN, Contributing Editor

VOLUME 27
Includes Cumulative Indexes

GALE GROUP

Detroit
New York
San Francisco
London
Boston
Woodbridge, CT

STAFF

Leigh Ann DeRemer, *Project Editor*
Luann Brennan, *Contributing Editor*
Pauletta Hightower, *Outside Editor*

Carol Brennan, Gloria Cooksey, Melissa Walsh Doig, Lloyd Hemingway, Laura Hightower, Ann Schwalboski, Geri Speace, Jane Spear, Julie Sweet, Nathan Sweet, *Sketchwriters*

Bridget Travers, *Managing Editor*

Maria L. Franklin, *Permissions Manager*
Margaret Chamberlain, *Permissions Specialist*

Mary Beth Trimper, *Composition Manager*
Dorothy Maki, *Manufacturing Manager*
Stacy Melson, *Buyer*

Robert Duncan, *Imaging Specialist*
Randy Bassett, *Image Database Supervisor*
Pamela A. Reed, *Imaging Coordinator*
Michael Logusz, *Graphic Artist*
Cover illustration by John Kleber

Printed in the United States of America

ISBN 0-7876-3252-X
ISSN 1044-2197

10 9 8 7 6 5 4 3 2 1

Contents

Introduction ix

Cumulative Subject Index 271

Cumulative Musicians Index 295

June Anderson ... 1
Operatic superstar

Martha Argerich ... 5
Award-winning Argentine pianist

Harold Arlen ... 9
Immigrant's son turned lyricist and composer

Atari Teenage Riot ... 13
Makes a statement with hardcore punk

The Atomic Fireballs ... 17
Revived swing in the nineties.

Bauhaus ... 19
Goth rock showmen

Thomas Beecham ... 23
Unparalled influence on 20th century music

Eric Benét ... 26
R&B music with integrity

The Beta Band ... 29
Radical combination of music genres

Blink 182 ... 32
Music speaks of Southern California lifestyle

Blondie ... 35
Legendary punk group

Caspar Brötzmann ... 39
Guerilla punk guitarist

Built to Spill ... 42
Secret of underground alternative rock

Cake ... 45
New rock with familiar sentiment

Hoagy Carmichael ... 49
Popular composer with privileged start

Citizen King ... 53
Alternative rock band resists being pigeonholed

Colin Davis ... 56
Renound British conductor

Banco De Gaia ... 59
Cerebral multi-instrumentalist

Joe Diffie ... 62
Man with the golden voice

Sara Evans ... 66
Returned to music of country legends

Everlast ... 69
American as apple pie

Fear Factory ... 73
Nu metal rockers

Fuel ... 76
An un-alternative rock band

Gene Loves Jezebel ... 79
Mystery men of eighties alternative rock

Alvin Youndblood Hart ... 82
Self-taught multi-instrumentalist

Dave Holland ... 85
Key jazz man

Enrique Iglesias ... 89
Latin sensation follows own footsteps

Natalie Imbruglia ... 92
Australian soap star turned pop sensation

The Jam 96
Enduring British punk band

Kid Rock 99
Diverse music stands alone

Diana Krall 102
Canadian jazz glamour girl

Jonny Lang 106
Teenage blues prodigy

Limp Bizkit 109
Rap and rock hybrid

Lit 113
Modern classic rock band

Lo Fidelity All Stars 116
Eclectic British rock band

Jack Logan 119
Garage-style low fidelity

Lonestar 122
Traditional country and swing

Jennifer Lopez 125
Multi-talented Latin entertainer

Luscious Jackson 128
Female band softens and matures

M People 132
Dance group wins critical acclaim

Madness 136
British ska revivalists

Russell Malone 140
Jazz guitarist plays to common fan

Manic Street Preachers 143
Modern glam-rock band

Amanda Marshall 147
Canadian songstress

Mary Martin 151
Broadway's brighest star

Mase 155
Rapper seeks spiritual pursuits

Matchbox 20 158
Driven by fraternal momentum

MC Eiht 162
Founding West Coast rapper

Susannah McCorkle 165
Jazz standard singer

The McGuire Sisters 168
Popular female singing group of the fifties

Brad Mehldau 171
Dynamic jazz force

Ethel Merman 174
Broadway diva

Moby 178
Techno genre leader

Mogwai 182
Profound instrumental rockers

Randy Newman 186
Grammy award-winning musician

Orgy 190
Old school meets state-of-the-art

Leon Parker 193
Explores soul of jazz

Nicholas Payton 195
Young lion of jazz

Pennywise 198
Energetic punk band

Bernadette Peters 201
Zany Broadway and film actress

Placebo 205
Provocative punk group

The Roots 208
Groundbreaking hip-hop group

Sawyer Brown 211
High energy band

Ron Sexsmith 214
Critically acclaimed Canadian songwriter

Woody Shaw 217
Significant influence on American jazz

Sheep On Drugs 221
Techno-infused rock and roll

Skunk Anansie 224
Perfect metal/punk outfit

Slick Rick 227
Rap success behind bars

Smash Mouth 230
More than a one-hit wonder

Social Distortion 233
Edgy eighties punk band

Kay Starr 236
Diverse vocalist of the fifties

Sun Ra 239
Unearthly jazz musician

David Sylvian 243
Gained success with Japan

Texas 247
Scottish group with modern rock feel

Type O Negative 250
'Gothadelic' rock group

Tom Waits 253
Beatnik singer and songwriter

Rick Wakeman 257
Busy pop musician

The Waterboys 261
British Celtic folk-rock band

Wilco 264
Maintained country roots

Mark Wills 267
Unassuming, exuberant performer

Introduction

Fills the Information Gap on Today's Musicians

Contemporary Musicians profiles the colorful personalities in the music industry who create or influence the music we hear today. Prior to *Contemporary Musicians,* no quality reference series provided comprehensive information on such a wide range of artists despite keen and ongoing public interest. To find biographical and critical coverage, an information seeker had little choice but to wade through the offerings of the popular press, scan television "infotainment" programs, and search for the occasional published biography or exposé. *Contemporary Musicians* is designed to serve that information seeker, providing in one ongoing source in-depth coverage of the important names on the modern music scene in a format that is both informative and entertaining. Students, researchers, and casual browsers alike can use *Contemporary Musicians* to meet their needs for personal information about music figures; find a selected discography of a musician's recordings; and uncover an insightful essay offering biographical and critical information.

Provides Broad Coverage

Single-volume biographical sources on musicians are limited in scope, often focusing on a handful of performers from a specific musical genre or era. In contrast, *Contemporary Musicians* offers researchers and music devotees a comprehensive, informative, and entertaining alternative. *Contemporary Musicians* is published three times per year, with each volume providing information on about 80 musical artists and record-industry luminaries from all the genres that form the broad spectrum of contemporary music—pop, rock, jazz, blues, country, New Age, folk, rhythm and blues, gospel, bluegrass, rap, and reggae, to name a few—as well as selected classical artists who have achieved "crossover" success with the general public. *Contemporary Musicians* will also occasionally include profiles of influential nonperforming members of the music community, including producers, promoters, and record company executives. Additionally, beginning with *Contemporary Musicians 11,* each volume features new profiles of a selection of previous *Contemporary Musicians* listees who remain of interest to today's readers and who have been active enough to require completely revised entries.

Includes Popular Features

In *Contemporary Musicians* you'll find popular features that users value:

- **Easy-to-locate data sections:** Vital personal statistics, chronological career summaries, listings of major awards, and mailing addresses, when available, are prominently displayed in a clearly marked box on the second page of each entry.

- **Biographical/critical essays:** Colorful and informative essays trace each subject's personal and professional life, offer representative examples of critical response to the artist's work, and provide entertaining personal sidelights.

- **Selected discographies:** Each entry provides a comprehensive listing of the artist's major recorded works.

- **Photographs:** Most entries include portraits of the subject profiled.

- **Sources for additional information:** This invaluable feature directs the user to selected books, magazines, newspapers, and online sources where more information can be obtained.

Helpful Indexes Make It Easy to Find the Information You Need

Each volume of *Contemporary Musicians* features a cumulative Musicians Index, listing names of individual performers and musical groups, and a cumulative Subject Index, which provides the user with a breakdown by primary musical instruments played and by musical genre.

Available in Electronic Formats

Diskette/Magnetic Tape. *Contemporary Musicians* is available for licensing on magnetic tape or diskette in a fielded format. The database is available for internal data processing and nonpublishing purposes only. For more information, call (800) 877-GALE.

Online. *Contemporary Musicians* is available online as part of the Gale Biographies (GALBIO) database accessible through LEXIS-NEXIS, P.O. Box 933, Daton, OH 454012-0933; phone: (513)865-6800, toll-free:800-543-6862.

We Welcome Your Suggestions

The editors welcome your comments and suggestions for enhancing and improving *Contemporary Musicians*. If you would like to suggest subjects for inclusion, please submit these names to the editors. Mail comments or suggestions to:

The Editor
Contemporary Musicians
Gale Group, Inc.
27500 Drake Rd.
Farmington Hills, MI 48334-3535

Or call toll free: (800) 347-GALE

June Anderson

Opera singer

Photograph by Malcolm Clark. AP/Wide World Photos. Reproduced by permission. ©

Considered one of the most talented performers in opera, soprano June Anderson has amassed a wide following throughout Europe and the United States, ranking among the most important singers in the international opera and concert world today. Those within the opera community compare her flawless, seemingly effortless vocal qualities to those of legendary soprano Joan Sutherland. One of her most notable achievements includes winning the prestigious Bellini d'Oro prize, the first non-Italian to do so, and she sang the voice of Queen of the Night in the Milos Forman film *Amadeus.* Despite her stunning performances and undeniable talent, some directors remain reluctant to work with Anderson because of her sense of perfectionism, her desire to work by her own terms, and her reputation as "difficult" to work with. However, Anderson, who prefers to concentrate on performing at her best rather than indulging in the business of money available to contemporary opera stars through mass and popular music recordings, contends that she only strives for the best for herself as well as for her colleagues. She told David J. Baker of *Opera News,* in response to critics who denounce her personality and accuse her of acting too demanding, "People don't take things seriously. I don't do the political niceties, I don't do the schmoozing, I don't play the games. I'm too straight. I think my singing should speak for itself—we don't need anything else." Those close to Anderson further dispute her tough reputation. Instead, they claim, Anderson enjoys her privacy, admits to suffering from stage fright, and at times feels shy around strangers.

Likewise, many music and opera directors appreciate Anderson's serious approach to her work, in addition to her well-projected, flexible voice and movie star appearance. Composer Leonard Bernstein deeply admired her singing and acting technique, and Eve Queler, Opera Orchestra of New York director, told Baker that she welcomes working with the impressive soprano. "She's very smart and very, very serious," said Queler. "I've seen her refuse parts if she couldn't identify with the person. She won't do a role just for the sake of the job or for the composer. I considered myself very lucky to work with her. She's such a positive force." Furthermore, director Francesca Zambello commented to Baker that because Anderson holds to such high standards, some of her colleagues often perceive her demands as difficult. Moreover, Zambello described Anderson as one of only a few performers "who are willing to collaborate and who are not afraid of process, not afraid to really dig in and inspire everybody around you. It's difficult, but it's rewarding."

June Anderson was born in Boston, Massachusetts, on December 30, 1952. Anderson enjoyed singing and

For the Record . . .

Born December 30, 1952, in Boston, MA. *Education:* Graduated *cum laude* from Yale University, 1974; majored in French; studied with vocal instructor Robert Leonard from 1974 until mid-1990s.

Started taking private singing lessons at age 11; became youngest finalist ever, at age 17, in the Metropolitan Opera National Auditions; made professional debut with the New York City Opera in Mozart's *The Magic Flute,* 1978; gave European debut performance in Rossini's *Semiramide* at the Rome Opera, 1982; debuted at the Paris Opera in *Robert le Diable,* 1985; recorded *Candide* with Leonard Bernstein and the London Symphony Orchestra, sang in Berlin at concert celebrating the fall of the Berlin Wall, 1989; won critical praise for role of Lucia in Donizetti's *Lucia di Lammermoor,* 1986 at the Royal Opera House in Covent Garden (London), 1992 with the Metropolitan Opera of New York; sang leading part for first time in Bellini's *Nora* at the Lyric Opera of Chicago, 1997; gave first performance as the lead, Leonora, in *Il Trovatore* by Verdi, 1998.

Awards: First non-Italian singer to win the Bellini d'Oro Prize.

Addresses: *Home*—Paris and New York City.

dancing around the family home as a child, and she decided to take private voice lessons at age 11. Anderson told Kathy Petrere in an interview for the Lyric Opera in Chicago, "My mother had wanted me to dance, and singing seemed to come naturally because I sang all the time. She says that I just wandered around the house, my life was 'en recitatif.'" Within a few short years, at age 17, she became the youngest finalist ever at the Metropolitan Opera National Auditions. Although this success demonstrated her obvious talent, Anderson remained unsure about pursuing professional singing as a career. Thus, in the meantime, she enrolled at Yale University as a French major, graduating *cum laude* in 1974.

Determined to Succeed

After college, she began to contemplate a career in opera and took instruction from Robert Leonard, a teacher who continued to work with Anderson until his death in the mid-1990s. According to the June Anderson website, she noted, "I decided to go to New York and thought that if in two years' time I was not famous I would go to Law School. Well, at the end of about nine months I was *not* famous, I'd run out of all my money and it was at that point that I would be a singer if it *killed* me." However, Anderson, although driven by the challenge to prove herself to the opera world, soon realized that achieving success would not come to fruition so easily as it had in her childhood. "As a youngster and a teenager, studying privately, everything had been easy and I was always being told I was wonderful. All of a sudden, nobody thought I was wonderful any more. So I thought, 'Damn it, I'll show them; I'll prove to them that I am!'"

Eventually, Anderson's determination paid off, and she made her professional debut with the New York City Opera in *The Magic Flute* in 1978, followed by her European debut in Rossini's *Semiramide* at the Rome Opera in 1982. Since the time of her debut in New York, Anderson went on to appear in every major opera house across Europe and the United States. Some of her stage appearances include performances with the opera companies of Vienna, Paris, Hambourg, Madrid, Florence, Geneva, La Scala, the Royal Opera House at Covent Garden, Venice, Rome, Bologna, Metropolitan Opera (New York), Chicago, San Francisco, and Philadelphia. And Anderson has collaborated with some of the most notable conductors, such as Leonard Bernstein, James Colon, Charles Dutoit, Daniele Gatti, James Levine, and many others.

Repertoire Spoke for Itself

By the 1990s, Anderson's extensive operatic repertory spoke for itself; she had mastered nearly 50 roles in various operas, from Mozart to Puccini. One of her most celebrated, as well as most challenging, performances arose from singing the lead (Norma) in Vincenzo Bellini's *Norma,* an opera known for its emotionally intense range of both music and drama. Following the premiere of *Norma* at the Lyric Opera in Chicago on February 6, 1997, *Chicago Tribune* reviewer John von Rhein wrote that the soprano's "clear, bright upper range was at its clarion best" and "dramatically, Anderson was exceptional, drawing out all the conflicting emotions with an intensity tempered by dignity." Anderson herself felt an affinity to the role also, as the told Baker, "Working on Norma has been the greatest experience of my life, because it's the most extraordinary role. It's hard to do anything after Norma, because everything else pales." Moreover, Anderson's success with *Norma* provided a much needed boost to her career, which had suffered after the 1992-93 season; during a series of shows for a production of

Gaetano Donizetti's *Lucia di Lammermoor* with the Metropolitan Opera, the director dropped Anderson from the title role and replaced her with another singer. Although some critics blamed Anderson's less than perfect performances and ill temperament for her leaving the show, Anderson pointed to the director's reinterpretation of the opera as the cause of her inability to grasp the role and thought that the Metropolitan production strayed too far from the original work. And in support of Anderson's claim, a significant number of critics noted her performance as Lucia as one of her greatest accomplishments.

Upon the success of *Norma,* Anderson planned to tackle another demanding role in 1998, again with the Metropolitan Opera for a production of *Il Trovatore,* an opera composed by Giuseppe Verdi. Anderson took the lead, playing Leonora, a role for which she won favorable reviews. Directors, such as Queler, expressed no doubt in Anderson's ability to master Leonora, as she told Baker, "She is growing, maturing, and she always had the top notes.... For the top voice, which is very strong, there's no challenge." However, Anderson, although thrilled at the opportunity to return to the Metropolitan Opera, continued to prefer tackling her personal favorite, *Norma.* Leonora lacks what she called, as quoted by Baker, "the incredible double whammy of Norma," meaning the music combined with the drama.

Remained Independent

Throughout her professional career, Anderson remained truly independent in promoting her talent. She preferred to manage her own affairs and lacked exclusive recording contracts or any personal connections with opera companies or directors. Rather, she determined her own schedule and operatic direction. In addition, since the death of her former teacher, Anderson chose to coach herself, believing that most modern-day voice instructors fail to hand down valuable traditions and performance practices to their students. Anderson, who remains single and lives alone, keeps apartments in both Paris and New York City. Her hectic travel schedule, which takes her to cities around the globe, leaves her little time for leisure activities, and she admits to often feeling lonely, although not bored.

When Anderson does finds time away from preparing for her next role, she enjoys shopping, exercising, spending time with friends, and dining at a designer McDonalds restaurant in New York City for the french fries, one of her favorite foods. She also collects opera memorabilia, especially old musical manuscripts and paintings of famous opera singers, and considers herself an avid film buff, boasting an enormous video collection of classic Hollywood movies. "If I could have been anything in the world," she told Baker, "I would have been a movie star in the thirties." But with this dream not likely to come true for Anderson, she plans to continue to perfect her singing and add a new dimension to every role she undertakes. Undoubtedly, the gifted diva has achieved her desire to rise to the top of the opera world—by her own terms.

Selected discography

Operas (with others)

Rossini: *Mose in Egitto* (Anderson is Elcia), Philips, 1981.
Albinoni: *Il Nascimento dell'Aurora* (Anderson is Dafne), Erato Num, 1983.
Rossini: *Maometto* (Anderson is Anna), Philips, 1983.
Thomas: *Hamlet* (Anderson is Ophelie), EMI, 1983.
Wagner: *Die Feen* (Anderson is Lora), Orfeo, 1983.
Adam: *Le Postillion de Lonjumeau* (Anderson is Madeleine), EMI, 1985.
Bizet: *La Jolie Fille de Perth* (Anderson is Catherine), EMI, 1985.
Meyerbeer: *Robert le Diable* (Anderson is Isabelle), Legendary, 1985.
Auber: *La Muette de Portici* (Anderson is Elvire), EMI, 1986.
Donizetti: *La Fille du Regiment* (Anderson is Marie), EMI CMS, 1986.
Halevy: *La Juive* (Anderson is Princess Eudoxie), Philips, 1986 and 1989.
Bernstein: *Candide* (Anderson is Cunegonde), Deutsche Grammophon, 1989.
Verdi: *Rigoletto* (Anderson is Gilda), London, 1989.
Massenet: *Cherubin* (Anderson is L'Ensoleillad), RCA, 1991.
Mozart: *Die Zauberflote* (Anderson is Queen of the Night), Telarc, 1991.
Rossini: *La Donna del Lago* (Anderson is Elena), Philips, 1992.

Recitals and concerts

June Anderson Dal Vivo In Concerto, Bongiovanni, 1984.
Bellini Opera Arias, EMI, 1987.
Rossini—Soirees Musicales, Nimbus Records, 1987 and 1988.
June Anderson and Alfred Kraus Live from the Paris Opera, EMI, 1987.
French Opera Arias, EMI, 1989.
Rossini Scenes, London, 1991.

Vocal music

(with others) Orff: *Carmena Burana,* Deutsche Grammophon, 1984.
(with others) Beethoven: *Symphonie Nr. 9 d-moll op. 125—"Ode an die Freiheit,"* Deutsche Grammophon, 1989.

(with Cecilia Bartoli) Pergolesi: *Stabat Mater and Salve Regina,* London, 1991.
(with Cecilia Bartoli) Scarlatti: *Salve Regina,* London, 1991.

Sources

Periodicals

Opera News, February 14, 1998, pp. 20-25, p. 48.
Time International, December 21, 1992, p. 52; May 31, 1993, p. 58; February 21, 1994, p. 48.

Online

"An Hour with June Anderson," http://members.iquest.net/-kpetrere/june.htm, (June 21, 1999).
June Anderson website, http://www3.sympatico.ca/balza/junecara.htm, (June 21, 1999).
"OperaWeb Singers: June Anderson," http://www.opera.it/English/Cantanti/Anderson.html, (August 6, 1999).

—*Laura Hightower*

Martha Argerich

Piano

If admirers of Argentine pianist Martha Argerich could ask the award-winning musician for one wish, they would most likely try to persuade her to perform and record solo more often. Fans and classical music critics alike often express their frustration with the virtuoso, but not because they feel she lacks talent; critics repeatedly compare her sound, energy, and passion to that of piano legend Vladimir Horowitz. Rather, Argerich, one of the world's most exciting and expressive musicians to see and hear perform, appears on stage alone only on rare occasions, preferring to share the spotlight with other musicians. Likewise, her recordings as a soloist remain rare in comparison to those of other great classical pianists, although her discography includes works by Bach, Bartók, Beethoven, Brahms, Chopin, Falla, Franck, Hayden, Liszt, Paganini, Prokofiev, Rachmaninoff, Ravel, Schubert, Schumann, and Tchaikovsky. "Any recording involving Martha Argerich is to be treasured," wrote Allen Linkowski for *American Record Guide.* "Her discography is much too small for a pianist of her stature, and public appearances become rarer and rarer with the passing of time." She enjoys playing the piano, but feels uncomfortable within the business of music and working as a "pianist." An always gracious performer, she collaborates with orchestras and ensembles "first among equals," as quoted by Bob Cowan in *Independent.*

The reluctant, yet not entirely reclusive, Argerich has presented the music world with just a portion of the masterpieces she knows and loves. Perhaps her reluctance could stem from wanting to always play to perfection and the pressures of turning professional at an early age, as illustrated by her description of one of the most defining moments from her childhood to Jura Margulis of the *Call Project:* "When I was very young, about eight or so, I was to perform a Mozart concerto, and before the concert I went to the bathroom, knelt down, and told myself that if I missed a single note, I would explode. I don't know why I believed that, but I didn't miss a single note. It's terrible for a young person, and that explains something about me today, I think."

Born in 1941 in Buenos Aires, Argentina, Martha Argerich displayed an interest in music at the tender age of about two years and eight months old. An extremely gifted child, her mother had enrolled her in kindergarten early, and most of the children were much older than Argerich. One of her classmates, an older boy around five years old, insisted on teasing Argerich, telling her that she was not old enough to do certain things. Nevertheless, the determined Argerich would always do exactly what her classmate said she couldn't, including playing the piano. "Once he got the idea of telling me I couldn't play the piano," Argerich related to Dean Elder in a 1979 interview for *Clavier.* "I still remember it. I immediately got up, went to the piano, and started playing a tune that the teacher was playing all the time. I played the tune by ear and perfectly. The teacher immediately called my mother and they started making a fuss. And it was all because of this boy who said 'You can't play the piano.'"

Recognizing her daughter's inborn musical ability, Argerich's mother decided to enroll her child in private lessons. And Argerich began playing the piano seriously at the young age of five, taking instruction from a renowned Italian teacher named Scaramuzzo. Argerich's mother, while not a musician herself, insisted on the best for her daughter and forced Argerich to practice. She commented to Elder that "I had the type of teacher and parents who used to tell me when I was a little girl that my fiancé was the piano. I didn't have much freedom as a child." Although Scaramuzzo flaunted a despotic and sometimes sadistic approach to teaching, he had taught some of the greatest pianists from Argentina. "When he would say mean, caustic things, he would do it very calmly, very coolly, such things as one was an idiot, and one shouldn't come to the lesson, and I had to concentrate on the mole next to his nose in order not to cry.... He was quite unpredictable, irrational, but a great teacher," Argerich told Margulis. "He said a student is like iron or steel, if you bend iron it breaks, and the sooner the better. If you bend steel, it regains its original shape." Thus Argerich, able to withstand the demands of her instruc-

For the Record . . .

Born in 1941 in Buenos Aires, Argentina. *Education:* took private lessons from age five to ten with renowned Italian instructor Scaramuzzo; later studied in Europe with other notable instructors, including Madame Dinu Lipatti, Nikita Magaloff, Arturo Benedetti Michelangeli, and Friedrich Gulda.

Made professional debut at age eight in Buenos Aires; gave U.S. debut performance for Lincoln Center's Great Performers Series in New York, 1966; performed as guest soloist with numerous North American orchestras, such as the Boston Symphony, Chicago Symphony, Los Angeles Philharmonic, Montreal Symphony, National Symphony, New York Philharmonic, Philadelphia Orchestra, and Toronto Symphony; appeared on stage and recorded with other classical musicians, including violinist Gidion Kremer, cellist Mischa Maisky, pianist Nelson Freire, and pianist/conductor Alexandre Rabinovitch..

Awards: First prize at the Geneva Invitational Competition and the Ferruccio Busoni International Competition in Bolzano, Italy, 1957; became first musician from the Western Hemisphere to win first prize at the Chopin Competition in Warsaw, Poland, in 1965.

Addresses: *Record company*—Deutsche Grammaphon, 825 Eighth Ave., New York, NY, 10019, (212) 333-8000.

tor, continued to develop her musical talent. In just a few years, at only eight years old, Argerich made her first professional appearance in Buenos Aires, displaying her mastery of both the Mozart D minor and the Beethoven C major Concertos. And by the age of 11, now studying with one of Scaramuzzo's assistants who taught her much about sight reading, the child prodigy had mastered concertos by Schumann as well.

Argerich continued to dazzle audiences throughout Argentina after her debut. Then around the age of 12, she left the guidance of Scaramuzzo's assistant for Europe to study with other notable instructors, including Madame Dinu Lipatti, who also used a harsh teaching style; Nikita Magaloff, who adored Argerich's playing; Arturo Benedetti Michelangeli, who insisted his students strive for perfection; and Friedrich Gulda, who Argerich considered one of her most important influences. Because Argerich, who spoke Spanish, and Gulda, who spoke German, could not communicate in the same language, they spoke instead through music, as well as in a made-up language they used together, which Gulda called "pan-Romanic." Argerich told Margulis that during one of her first lessons in Vienna, Austria, with Gulda, "he tried to transmit a certain emotion in the music to me, and since he couldn't find words, he grabbed me and pulled me in the bathroom, picked up a wet sponge, and dampened his face. Pointing to his soaked face, he said 'Like that! Like that!'" Gulda also would record his lessons with Argerich and make his young student listen to the recordings with him, so that she could criticize her own work. "This was very interesting because it was very democratic," Argerich said to Elder. "He liked to know what I had to say, what I thought. It was not this thing that usually happens between pupil and teacher. It was fantastic." He believed that a musician needed a bit of talent, instruction, and a sort of arrogance or vanity in order to rouse an audience. Argerich, one of his prized students, seemed to radiate all of these qualities.

In Europe, Argerich's skills steadily improved, and in 1957 at age 16, during the span of three weeks time, she won both the Geneva International Competition and the Ferruccio Busoni International Competition in Bolzano, Italy. For these competitions, the teenage pianist performed the Liszt Sixth Hungarian Rhapsody. Amazingly, she had never played a piece by Liszt before, as she confided to Elder, "At that time I was very superstitious so I wouldn't play a piece all the way through even for myself. I was afraid that something... so I just waited until I passed to the next round to learn the next pieces." Subsequently, these achievements brought even more prestige to her already legendary career. However, Argerich, feeling overwhelmed with her schedule, decided to retreat from making appearances for awhile, but emerged again in 1965 and became the first musician from the Western Hemisphere to win first prize at the ChopinCompetition in Warsaw, Poland. Following this, she made her United States debut in 1966, performing for Lincoln Center's Great Performers Series in New York. With her reputation secured in North America, she then went on to perform as guest soloist with numerous orchestras such as the Boston Symphony, Chicago Symphony, Los Angeles Philharmonic, Montreal Symphony, National Symphony, New York Philharmonic, Philadelphia Orchestra, and Toronto Symphony.

As Argerich's career progressed into the 1970s and 1980s, she declined more and more opportunities to give solo recitals. In addition, Argerich realized that the life of a professional musician had its down sides as well as its rewards. She confessed to Elder, "I love very much to play the piano, but I don't like being a pianist. I don't like the profession. And when one plays, of course, it is important to practice. But the profession itself—the traveling and the way of life—all this has nothing to do with playing or with music, absolutely nothing! This is what I do not enjoy about being a concert pianist. You never know when you are are very young, when you are studying, what the profession is about." However, she did not turn into a musical recluse. Rather, Argerich altered her schedule to include numerous chamber performances, ranging from the works of Bach to Mozart, in addition to the master works of Beethoven, Schumann, Chopin, Bartók, Janacek, and Messiaen. She most often appeared for recorded work and on stage with partners such as violinist Gidion Kremer, cellist Mischa Maisky, pianist Nelson Freire, and pianist/conductor Alexandre Rabinovitch. She enjoyed sharing the limelight with other talented musicians who, in turn, inspired her to delve into each piece.

Argerich also took inspiration from watching other musicians perform. One of her most memorable experiences includes attending a Vladimir Horowitz concert in January of 1978 with her piano partner Freire. The event marked Horowitz's first appearance with an orchestra in 25 years, as well as Argerich's first time to see him in person. Regarding Horowitz, Argerich said to Elder, "The strength of his expression, the sound, and this incredible violence he has inside which is so strange, weird, and frightening. That he can express it. He's like possessed. I've read about this, but this was the first time that I saw on stage someone who has that!" Later, though, critics would compare Argerich's playing to that of the legendary Horowitz. As Cowan noted in a 1999 review of her performance at Tokyo's Suminda Triphony Hall, "Argerich thunders the keys with as much energy and passion as Vladimir Horowitz did 22 years earlier at Carnegie Hall."

The remarkable artist continued to make guest appearances, give chamber performances, and release recordings well into the 1990s, all of which won critical praise. Further, she received two Grammy Award nominations for chamber music in 1997, one for an album of piano pieces by Strauss, and the other for her recording with Kremer featuring Beethoven violin sonatas. In 1998, John Ardoin of the *Dallas Morning News* named Argerich's two-day concert at Carnegie Hall on October 24 and 25 as one of the ten best classical performances of the year; for the event, the standard-setting pianist played concertos of Chopin and Liszt with the Montreal Symphony.

As an adult Argerich made time for other interests in addition to her music, a freedom she lacked throughout her upbringing. She confided to Elder that "I have long periods without touching the piano, and I don't miss it. And then I can get possessed by the piano for a while as well." During these times away from playing, she enjoys taking walks, spending time and talking withnon-musicians, and experiencing different atmospheres unrelated to music.

Selected discography

Bach: English Suite #2 in a, BWV, 1979.

Bach: Partita for Piano #2 in c, BWV, 1979.

Bach: Toccata in c, BWV, 1979.

Beethoven/Haydn: Piano Concertos (2/11), EMI, 1983.

(with Maisky) *Bach: Cello Sonatas,* Deutsche Grammaphon, 1987.

(with Kremer) *Beethoven: Violin Sonatas nos. 1-3,* PGD/Deutsche Grammophon, 1987.

(with Rabinovitch) *Brahms: Haydn Variations, etc.,* 1987.

Schubert: Sonata for Arpeggione; Schumann: Fantasiestücke, 1987.

Schumann: Kinderszenen, Kreisleriana, PGD/Deutsche Grammophon, 1987.

(With Abbado and Dutoit) *Tchaikovsky: Piano Concerto 1; Prokiev: Piano Concerto 3,* PGD/Deutsche Grammophon, 1987.

(with Kremer) *Beethoven: Violin Sonatas nos. 4 & 5,* PGD/Deutsche Grammophon, 1988.

(with Leonard Bernstein) *Stravinsky: Les Noces, Mass,* 1988.

(with Kremer and the Orpheus Chamber Orchestra) *Mendelssohn: Violin and Piano Concerto in D Minor, etc.,* 1989.

(with Abbado and the London Symphony Orchestra) *Ravel: Piano Concerts, Menuet antique, etc.,* reissued 1989.

(with Ricci) *50th Anniversary Concert,* Etcetera, 1991.

Chopin Compact Edition—Préludes, Etc., 1991.

(with Rostropovich) *Chopin Compact Edition—Sonata for Cello and Piano, etc.,* 1991.

(with Kremer) *Tchaikovsky Compact Edition—Piano and Violin Concertos,* 1991.

(with Rabinovich and others) *Rachmaninoff: Suites Op. 5 & 17, Symphonic Dances Op. 45,* reissued 1992.

(with Kremer) *Prokofiev:Violinsonaten, 5 Melodien,* 1993.

(with others) *Strauss: New Year's Eve Concert 1992,* 1993.

(with Maisky) *Beethoven: Cellosonaten Op. 69 & 102, etc.,* Deutsche Grammophon, 1994.

(with Rabinovitch) *Mozart: Sonatas,* 1994.

(with Abbado and Berliner) *Prometheus—The Myth in Music,* 1994.

(with Kremer) *Schumann: Piano Concerto, Violin Concerto,* WEA/Atlantic/Teldec, 1994.

(with Chailly and Kondrashin) *Argerich—Rachmaninoff 3, Tchaikovsky 1,* Philips, 1995.

(with Sinopoli) *Beethoven: Piano Concertos 1 & 2,* DG, 1995.

(with Kremer) *Beethoven: Violin Sonatas nos. 6-8,* PGD/Deutsche Grammophon, 1995.

(with others) *Duo Piano Extravaganza: Martha Argerich and Friends,* PGD/Philips, 1995.
Shostakovich, Hayden: Piano Concerti, 1995.
(with Kremer) *Beethoven: Violin Sonatas nos. 9 & 10,* PGD/Deutsche Grammophon, 1996.
(with Abbado and the London Symphony Orchestra) *Chopin, Liszt: Piano Concertos,* 1996.
(with Abbado and others) *Prokofiev, Ravel: Piano Concerti,* DG, 1996.
Schumann, R.: Fantasie in C, Op. 17/Fantasiestuecke Op. 12 nr. 1-8, EMI, reissued 1996.
(with Rabinovich) *Schumann: Klavier quartett, etc.,* 1996.
(with Abbado) *Tchaikovsky: Piano Concerto 1, etc.,* 1996.
(with others) *Centenary Edition Vol. 10 (1988-1997),* 1997.
(with others) *Complete Beethoven Edition Vol. 7—Violin Sonatas,* 1997.
(with others) *Complete Beethoven Edition Vol. 8—Cello Sonatas,* 1997.
Martha Argerich Collection, DG, 1997.
Great Pianists of the 20th Century—Martha Argerich Vol. 1, Philips, 1998.
(with Dutoit) *Piano Concertos: Prokofiev (#1, #3)/ Bartók (#3),* EMI, 1998.
Chopin—The Legendary 1965 Recording, EMI, 1999.
(with Charles Dutoit and the Montreal Symphony Orchestra) *Chopin: Piano Concertos Nos. 1 & 2,* EMI, 1999.
(with Horowitz and others) *Great Pianists of the 20th Century,* Brilliant Classics, 1999.
Great Pianists of the 20th Century—Martha Argerich Vol. 2, Philips, 1999.
(with Rabinovich and Faerber) *Mozart: Piano Concertos no. 10, 19 & 20,* Teldec, 1999.
(with Kremer and Maisky) *Shostakovich, Tchaikovsky: Trios,* Deutsche Grammophon, 1999.

Sources

Periodicals

American Record Guide, January 11, 1996, p. 156(1); September 19, 1996, p. 210(1); May 1, 1997.
Daily Telegraph, March 26, 1999.
Dallas Morning News, February 23, 1997, p.7C; July 29, 1998, p. 29A; October 28, 1998, p. 33A; December 29, 1998, p.23A; July 6, 1999, p. 19A.
Independent, March 4, 1994; October 12, 1998, p. 11; July 30, 1999, p.18.
New Statesman, April 2, 1999.
Newsday, December 1, 1996, p. C27; October 28, 1997, p. B09.
USA Today, August 29, 1995.

Online

"Argerich Biography," http://www.peabody.jhu.edu/~juragaga/Argerichbio.htm (August 9, 1999).
"Argerich—Discography," http://www.andrys.com/argerich.html (August 11, 1999).
"Argerich—Interview excerpts, 1978," http://www.andrys.com/arg-1979.html (August 10, 1999).
Amazon.com, http://www.amazon.com (August 12, 1999).
CDnow, http://www.cdnow.com (August 12, 1999).
"Interview with Martha Argerich," http://www.peabody.jhu.edu/~juragaga/Argerich.htm (August 9, 1999).
"Pianist: Martha Argerich," http://www.geocities.com/Vienna/Strauss/2914/artists/argerich.html (June 6, 1999).

—Laura Hightower

Harold Arlen

Piano, composer, arranger, vocalist

AP/Wide World Photos. Reproduced by permission. ©

For more than a century, a large number of immigrant Jews from Poland, Germany and Russia fled to the United States to avoid persecution. Many a son of a Jewish cantor became a singing star, or one of America's top lyricists and composers. Harold Arlen was such an example. He was the son of immigrants from the Vilna section of Poland, who wrote many of the top musical "standards" that will remain the favorite music of many generations. Born Hyman Arluck on February 15, 1905 to Samuel Arluck and Celia Orlin, he changed his name after he quit high school and began to perform professionally.

Arlen first learned to sing in his father's synagogue choir but most of his musical training and background was gained from his mother. By the time he was seven, he was regularly singing in Buffalo's Pine Street synagogue choir. At nine he studied piano with Arnold Cornelisson, who was an organist, composer and conductor of the Buffalo String Orchestral Society.

Arlen dropped out of Hutchinson Central High School and later Technical High School when he was sixteen. Afterwards, he began to earn his living playing the piano in silent movie houses as well as performing in a vaudeville act. He formed the Snappy Trio with two other teenagers and regularly performed in the brothel district in Buffalo. Two additional members were added and the group was renamed the Southbound Shufflers. The group was hired to play on Great Lakes' steamers. He was soon asked to joined the Yankee Six, another dance band that soon grew to twelve pieces and later renamed The Buffalodians. He served as the band's arranger, pianist, and sometimes singer. The Buffalodians became a favorite of the area townspeople and their engagements took them to downtown ballroom restaurants as well as college and other societal functions. Th group became so popular, they appeared in Cleveland and Pittsburgh. In 1925, they were given the opportunity to perform at various Broadway clubs in New York City

Arlen was noticed by Broadway and popular music composer Vincent Youmans, who gave him a part in the 1929 musical "Great Day" as rehearsal pianist. . It was there that Arlen established a long time collaboration with composer and lyric writer Ted Koehler. During a rehearsal they combined to write "Get Happy" and soon convinced the financial backers of the program that Arlen had great potential as a songwriter. "Get Happy" was subsequently used in *9:15 Revue* and was made a major hit by singer Ruth Etting in 1930. "Get Happy," Arlen's first song, still remains a standard today.

In the early thirties, Arlen joined the music publishing house of J. H. Remick and also recorded as a vocalist

For the Record . . .

Born Hyman Arluck, February 15, 1905 Buffalo, NY, (died April 23, 1986 New York, NY of Parkinson's disease); son of Samuel Arluck, a Jewish cantor and Celia (born Orlin); married Anya (died March 9, 1973); children: Samuel Arlen. *Education:* Studied piano with Arnold Cornelisson, Conductor of the Buffalo String Orchestral Society

Made his debut as a rehearsal pianist on Broadway in 1929 in the show *Great Day;* employed as a songwriter for the J. H. Remick Publishing Company early 1930s; worked as a singer with notables such as Benny Goodman, Red Nichols, Joe Venuti and Eddie Duchin; wrote musical scores for Broadway and film scores for Hollywood including *The Wizard of Oz*, 1939; *At the Circus*, 1939; *Up in Arms*, 1944; *A Star is Born*, 1954; *The Country Girl*, 1954; and *Gay Purr-ee*, 1961; later returned to Broadway; credited with having composed over thirty standards.

Awards: Academy Award for Best Song, "Over the Rainbow" from the *Wizard of Oz,* 1939; received ASCAP/ Richard Rodgers Award for distinguished contributions to the musical theater; inducted into Songwriters Hall of Fame.

with the big bands fo Joe Venuti, Eddie Duchin , Red Nichols, and Benny Goodman. He continued his collaboration with Ted Koehler and they combined to write revues for New York's Cotton Club. Arlen also served as the club's musical director. Classic standards were introduced during this time including, "Between the Devil and the Deep Blue Sea," "Stormy Weather," "I Gotta Right to Sing the Blues," "I Love a Parade," "I've Got the World on a String," and "Kickin the Gong Around." "Stormy Weather" was received so favorably, it led to Arlen receiving his first film contract.

Arlen wrote the music for three Broadway musicals from 1930-34. He departed for Hollywood where he continued for a decade to concentrate on motion pictures with the exception of one Broadway show "Hooray for What?". In Hollywood, he began his new collaboration with Johnny Mercer and they received Academy Award nominations for "Blues in the Night," "That Old Black Magic," "and 'My Shining Hour." One of Arlen finest screen songs was "Last Night When We Were Young" and was written for the motion picture "Metropolitan" with lyrics written by Harburg. But the song was deleted as a vocal number and used instrumentally as background music. In later years it was recorded by Judy Garland and other vocalists but did not become a major hit until the 1950's when Frank Sinatra released it on the Capitol Record label.

On January 8, 1937, Harold Arlen married a former Powers model and show girl, Anya "Annie" Taranda, who had previously appeared in the 1932 edition of "Earl Carroll's Vanities." The wedding was held the day after he had handed her a note telling her that they were getting married the next day and didn't she think it was about time. He was a dapper figure and often was seen dressed sporting a cane as well as a flower in his buttonhole. The *New York Times* reported that, "he was known to get his ideas for songs in many places, while being driven in Los Angeles or while strolling around the Central Park Reservoir with his dog".

In 1939, Arlen was hired by Arthur Freed of MGM and joined E. Y. "Yip" Harburg for his biggest film success, *The Wizard of Oz.* The film featured such songs as "We're Off to See the Wizard," "Ding Dong, the Witch is Dead," "Follow the Yellow Brick Road, "and it's most famous song, "Over the Rainbow,". Arlen and Harburg were given a two month window to complete the score before filming and many years later he expressed how troubled he had been with the short amount of time to complete the musical score. In his biography of Harold Arlen, Edward Jablonski revealed that "Over the Rainbow" had come to Arlen "out of the blue" when Arlen and his wife had driven to a Graumann's Chinese movie theater on Sunset Boulevard in Los Angeles. She drove because he was too worried that he had not yet written a ballad for the film. When they reached a spot where the original Schwab's Drug Store was, the long lined melody came to Arlen. He quickly jotted it down in the car and the next day wrote both the bridge and the middle and presented it to Harburg to complete.

Harburg disliked it and remarked, "that's for Nelson Eddy and not for a little girl from Kansas." With advice from songwriter Ira Gershwin, Harburg changed it to a quicker tempo and a thinner harmonic texture and titled the song "Over the Rainbow." "Over the Rainbow" was presented to executives at Metro Goldwyn Mayer Studios (MGM); they remained largely unenthusiastic and three times tried to have the song cut from the motion picture. But each time producer Arthur Freed insisted the song be restored to the film. "Over the Rainbow" t received the Academy Award for best song in 1939. It also became a huge hit and signature song for fourteen year old Judy Garland. In 1963, "Over the Rainbow" was one of sixteen songs selected by the American Society of Composers, Artists and Publishers (ASCAP) as being one of the top songs of the first half of the twentieth century. Eileen Farrell sang it on the soundtrack of "Interrupted Melody" in 1955 and a decade later it was again used in the Metro Goldwyn Mayer (MGM) motion picture "Patch of Blue" that starred Sidney Poitier and Shelley Winters.

In 1941, Arlen and Savannah, Georgia native Johnny Mercer, and the grandson of a Confederate Army Colonel joined forces to write "Blues in the Night" for the film by the same name. It was a huge success and was vocalist Dinah Shore's first recording to sell over a million copies. It appeared on "Your Hit Parade" for 13 weeks, twice in the number one position. "Blues in the Night" was also nominated for an Academy Award but lost out to Jerome Kern's and Oscar Hammerstein II's "The Last Time I Saw Paris". Kern strongly felt that Arlen's song should have won the Academy Award and influenced the Academy's governing body to change the laws governing the nomination of songs. He was so successful that future considerations included focus on songs written for motion picture screen plays.

In 1942 Arlen and Johnny Mercer wrote "That Old Black Magic" for Broadway's *Star Spangled Rhythm*. The song became popularized by Billy Daniels and sold over two million copies. By 1943, "That Old Black Magic" had been recorded by many orchestras and vocalists including Charlie Barnet, Judy Garland, Frank Sinatra, Glenn Miller, Fred Waring and Margaret Whiting. That same year it appeared on the Hit Parade fifteen times and has been performed in many motion pictures including *Here Comes the Waves* in 1944, *Meet Danny Wilson* in 1952, *Bus Stop* in 1956. In 1958, Louis Prima/Keely Smith recorded the song and it received a Grammy Award.

1943 brought another standard to the popular music field when Arlen and Mercer again combined to write "One For My Baby" (And One More For the Road) for the Fred Astaire starred motion picture *The Sky's the Limit*. Frank Sinatra recorded it three different times and he sang it in the motion picture *Young at Heart*. It was also a major hit for Tony Bennett, Harry Belafonte, Fred Astaire, and Johnny Mercer. Lena Horne also made it a regular selection in her performances.

Arlen again teamed with Koehler for the 1944 Oscar nominee "Now I Know." He returned to Broadway on October 5, 1944 and worked with Harburg. *Bloomer Girl* was introduced at the Shubert Theater with Arlen completing the musical score. The show ran for over 650 performances and starred Celeste Holm, Dooley Wilson and David Brooks. *Bloomer Girl* was followed by two additional shows that both flopped including *St. Louis Woman* with Johnny Mercer. It was originally planned as a folk play using an all black cast but was rewritten and became a melodrama that concentrated on the affair of a jockey and a St. Louis woman , for whose love for her drives him to murder. "Come Rain or Come Shine" came out of the play and remains a standard today.

Arlen continued to concentrate on Broadway but never fully abandoned Hollywood and he received Academy Award nominations for "Ac-cent-tchu-ate the Positive" in 1944 with Mercer, "For Every Man There's a Woman" with Leo Robin in 1948, and "The Man That Got Away" with Ira Gershwin in 1954 . "The latter, a bluesy ballad Judy Garland performed in the remake of *A Star is Born*, was another classic song Arlen wrote for the silver screen. It proved to be Garland's second signature song and was frequently included in her repertoire that also included Arlen's "Over the Rainbow."

In 1959 his Broadway career came to an end with the failure of *Saratoga*. The cast was comprised of some of Broadway's finest with Howard Keel and Carol Lawrence in the leading roles and ran for only 80 performances before the lights dimmed for good. New York theatercritic John Chapman wrote "My suggestion for the best enjoyment of *Saratoga* is that you stop trying to follow the plot before it starts and concentrate on the really good things."

In addition to the "standards" listed throughout, additional classic compositions include: "Happiness is a Thing Called Joe", "Hit The Road to Dreamland", "I've Got A Right to Sing the Blues," "Ill Wind," "It's Only a Paper Moon," "Let's Fall in Love", and the lovely song "A Sleepin' Bee" that is based on the Haitian folk belief from a story by novelist Truman Capote. All in all, Arlen composed music for over 25 films. He once confessed, "I wanted to be a singer. Never dreamed of songwriting." Harold Arlen died on April 23, 1986; he suffered from Parkinson's disease. On the day he was buried, it was reported by the *New York Times* that a strange phenomenon was sighted by several people: spectacular rainbows in the sky. "All the rainbow reporters mentioned two facts: that they hadn't seen a rainbow in a long, long time and that April 25th was also the day that Harold Arlen was buried."

Selected discography

Harold Sings Arlen, Columbia.

Harold Arlen: American Songbook Series-The Smithsonian Collection of Recordings, RD.

Ella Fitzgerald Sings the Harold Arlen Songbook - Volume I, Verve.

Ella Fitzgerald Sings the Harold Arlen Songbook - Volume II, Verve.
Lee Wiley Sings the Songs of Rodgers and Hart and Harold Arlen, Audiophile.
Harold Arlen - American Negro Suite, Premier.
Peggy Lee: Love Held Lightly, Angel.
Rosemary Clooney Sings the Music of Harold Arlen, Concord.
Over the Rainbow:- The Music of Harold Arlen, DRG Records.
Eileen Farrell Sings Harold Arlen, Reference Recordings.
The Song is Harold Arlen, ASV Living Era.

Broadway Original Cast Recordings

Bloomer Girl.
Jamaica, RCA.
St. Louis Women, Angel.
The Wizard of Oz, CBS Records.
The Wizard of Oz, Turner Classic Movies Rhino.
Star Spangled Rhythm, Sandy Hook.
A Star is Born, Columbia.
The Great Songs from the Cotton Club, Mobile Fidelity.
Rhythmic Moments (American Piano Volume IV), Premier.
Harold Sings Arlen, Columbia.

Selected Films with Songs by Harold Arlen

The Wizard of Oz, MGM/US Home Video, 1939.
At the Circus, MGM/UA Home Video, 1939.
Up in Arms, Embassy Home Entertainment, 1944.
A Star is Born, Warner Home Video, 1954.
The Country Girl, Paramount, 1954.
Gay Purr-ee, Warner Home Video, 1961.

Sources

Books

Barrett, Mary Ellin, *Irving Berlin, A Daughter's Memoir*, Simon & Schuster 1994.
Bennett, Tony, *The Good Life,* Pocket Books, 1998.
Bering, Rudiger, *Musicals*, Barron's Educational Series Inc., 1998.
Ewen, David, *American Songwriters*, H. W. Wilson and Company 1987.
Ewen, David, *American Popular Songs: From the Revolutionary War to the Present*, Random House, 1966.
Gammond, Peter, *The Oxford Companion to Popular Music*, Oxford University Press 1993.
Green, Stanley, *Broadway Musicals, Show by Show*, Hal Leonard Corporation, 1996.
Harrison, Nigel, *Songwriters, A Biographical Dictionary with Discographies*, McFarland and Company, 1998.
Jablonski, Edward, *Harold Arlen, Rhythm, Rainbows and Blues*, Northeastern University Press, 1996.
Lax, Roger and Frederick Smith, *The Great Song Thesaurus,* Oxford Univ. Press 1989.
Maltin, Leonard, *Movie and Video Guide 1995,* Penguin Books Ltd., 1994.
Musiker, Reuben and Naomi Musiker, *Conductors and Composers of Popular Orchestral Music*, Greenwood Press 1998.
Osborne, Jerry, *Rockin Records,* Osborne Publications 1999.
Stambler, Irwin, *Encyclopedia of Popular Music*, St. Martin's Press, 1966.

Periodicals

New York Times, April 24, 1986.

Online

"HaroldArlen," www.mplcommunications.com/MBR/harold_arl, (September, 1999).
"Harold Arlen, Selections from *The Wizard of Oz*", *G. Schirmer, Inc.*, www.schirmer.com/composers/arlin wizard.html, .(September, 1999).
"Johnny Mercer Biography," *Johnny Mercer home page*, www.johnnymercer.com, (September, 1999).

—Francis D. McKinley

Atari Teenage Riot

Electronic punk rock group

Photograph by Tibor Bozi. Corbis. Reproduced by permission. ©

The German-based, hardcore punk group Atari Teenage Riot rightfully admits to jolting audiences with more than an earful of heavy guitar riffs and samples, thundering drum beats, and screeching shouts. Front man Alec Empire, along with Carl Crack, Hanin Elias, and Nic Endo, make even the popular techno band Prodigy seem timid. In fact, creating as much noise as possible is of primary concern to Atari Teenage Riot. "We wanted to make a statement, and we knew that by using a lot of noise, people would pay attention" Empire told Michael Mehle in the *Denver Rocky Mountain News.* The band's statement, a primarily political one, calls for an end to the communist and capitalist systems, both of which, according to the band, lead to government control and conformity. Instead, Atari Teenage Riot screams for a society based on self-responsibility, racial and cultural diversity, and tolerance.

Empire explained to Mehle, "We formed Atari Teenage Riot because of the political situation in Europe, especially the situation in Germany. When we put out the single 'Kill the Nazis,' ['Hetzjagd Auf Nazis'] we brought the whole subject of racism to the techno scene. Now the music is being played at demonstrations and has created this vibe where people want to change." Moreover, Atari Teenage Riot attacked such social and political issues like no other band prior. "With phasers set to kill, the band pointed out social injustices and pulled the proverbial trigger to set them right," commented Eric Bensel of *Magnet* magazine. "Few artists have been this musically volatile and downright shocking." Since the group's explosive start in 1992, they successfully conquered their home of Germany, where most clubs and record stores initially refused to play or sell their music, and then moved beyond Europe to bring their terrifying, cutting-edge sound to the rest of the world.

Before Atari Teenage Riot stormed Europe, Asia, and the United States, the concept for the anti-establishment uproar was just taking shape in the young mind of Alec Empire, the main force behind the group. Born on May 2, 1972, in West Berlin, Germany, Empire picked up his first guitar at age eight. By age ten, he considered himself one of the city's best break dancers, and at age 11, Empire witnessed rap music, the first style of music he really liked. But as rap grew more popular and commercialized, Empire turned to the punk scene already spreading across Great Britain and the United States. At this time still an adolescent, Empire formed his own punk band, Die Kinder, which lasted until the group's breakup in 1988. Disillusioned because "we found that punk was dead," Empire wrote for Digital Hardcore's website, the 16-year-old isolated himself from friends for several months, listening to nothing but classical works by composers such as Debussy, Schoe-

For the Record . . .

Members include **Carl Crack** (born in Swaziland in southeast Africa), MC, DJ; **Hanin Elias** (born in Damascus, Syria), vocals; **Alec Empire** (born May 2, 1972, in West Berlin, Germany), guitar, vocals, programming; and **Nic Endo** (joined band c. 1999), vocals.

Empire formed punk group Die Kinder (disbanded in 1988); formed Atari Teenage Riot, early 1992; signed with and left Phonogram label, 1993; formed Digital Hardcore Recordings (DHR), c. 1994; released debut album, *Delete Yourself,* March 1995; signed with Grand Royal Records for American distribution, 1996; released second album, *Burn, Berlin, Burn!,* toured with pop sensation Beck, 1997; released third album, *60 Second Wipeout,* spring 1999.

Addresses: *Home*—Berlin, Germany. *Record company*—DHR, 30 Dean St., London, U.K. W1V 5AN; Grand Royal Records, P.O. Box 26689, Los Angeles, CA 90026. *Website*—www.digitalhardcore.com; www.grandroyal.com.

nberg, and Bartók, playing video games, and recording tapes of his guitar effects.

Longed for Alternatives

Looking back on his teen punk days, Empire described this period as both rewarding and tiresome. The downside of punk, according to Empire, comes from its restrictiveness. He told Bensel, "The negative stuff that I learned—I had to learn it at some point—was that scenes can become a creative prison where certain worlds are created. And it's really hard to step out of that.... A lot of punk is just about fashion or buying a certain product, which is maybe differentfor a lot of other people, but it's the same process." Nonetheless, Empire thought he learned a positive lesson from his experience with Die Kinder. He realized "how to be creative by destroying something," as quoted by Bensel. "Destruction, most of the time, is connected to something negative. But I think for me it's a positive process because it includes the chance of creating something new."

With Die Kinder behind him, Empire longed for an alternative creative outlet. Then, while staying in Nice in the south of France during the summer of 1988, he attended his first acid-rock party, and the new psychedelic sound quickly influenced Empire's next musical direction. When he returned to Germany for the next school year, he immediately started working to earn enough money to buy a sampler. Like many young Germans at this time, after the Berlin Wall came down in 1989, Empire was drawn to the new music played at the raves, techno parties held in the cellars of East Berlin's condemned houses. The atmosphere and music at the parties reminded him of the energy he found in acid-rock.

However, by 1991 the techno underworld had changed. Many party-goers took to harder drugs like heroin, a substance that often leads to addiction (Empire, who never tried drugs himself, only accepts drug use in moderation); the music itself now seemed lethargic, mainstream, and restrictive; and neo-Nazis and their racist rhetoric had permeated the rave scene as well. One night, Empire witnessed a Frankfurt rave club refusing to admit a group of young Turks, and he concluded that the culture that had previously inspired him had come to accept right-wing behavior. Thus Empire, whose grandfather had perished in a German concentration camp during World War II, decided to create a new type of music, along with other young Berliners who shared his values, in resistance to the current rave culture.

Believed in Diversity

Consequently, Empire formed Atari Teenage Riot in early 1992, a group that, not surprisingly, took strong offense when labeled as "techno." He wanted to express his belief of the importance of diversity, so he made an effort to select band members from different backgrounds. The resulting ensemble consisted of Empire, Hanin Elias, a native of Damascus, Syria, with an aggressive feminist agenda, and Carl Crack, an MC and DJ originally from Swaziland in southeast Africa. Together, the group's music broke off in a new direction from progressive rock, techno, and jungle to include hardcore and punk influenced break beats. By the fall of the same year, Atari Teenage Riot released their first single, "Hunt Down [Kill] the Nazis." Nevertheless, many record shops, especially those specializing in techno music, initially boycotted the single, and most DJs refused to play the record at dance clubs. Refusing to let this lack of support dissuade them, Atari Teenage Riot's uniquely violent sound eventually reached the youth culture of Berlin and caught the attention of record companies.

Hoping to spread their message to a wider audience, Atari Teenage Riot signed to a major European label,

Phonogram, in 1993. However, Phonogram tried to leash the group's political attack and hard-hitting music, and record company executives wanted to turn Atari Teenage Riot into just another marketable techno supergroup. Therefore, Empire and his band mates left the label to strike out on their own after releasing two EPs, *Atari Teenage Riot* and *Kids Are United.* Then, with the leftover advance money given to the group by Phonogram for an unreleased album, Empire formed his own label called Digital Hardcore Recordings (DHR).

With the freedom to control their own musical interests, Atari Teenage Riot released their debut album, *Delete Yourself,* in March of 1995, followed by the *Speed* EP. Soon thereafter, underground support swelled, and Atari Teenage Riot played for sold out shows throughout Berlin. As their reputation spread across Europe, the group received an invitation from British radio legend John Peel to record a BBC session. Then in early 1996, Grand Royal Records (a label formed by the Beastie Boys) approached Atari Teenage to distribute DHR's records in the United States. Empire accepted the offer, and Grand Royal released a series of seven-inch singles later that fall, which American fans received with enthusiasm. Grand Royal's website reported that "the audience was subsequently confused, amazed, assaulted and won over."

Accepted by American Audiences

By December of 1996, Atari Teenage Riot received the opportunity to perform live in record stores and clubs in New York City, as well as other venues up and down the Easy Coast. The group earned positive press and shocked audiences with their abrasive onslaught, despite the maternity absence of Elias. Empire expressed to Mehle his surprise at how well American audiences had accepted the group and further commented, "Even in America, we thought maybe people are just into us because the music is strange. But we met so many people at the shows who say they've been waiting for a band to have these messages." Other artists took notice of Atari Teenage Riot as well, and Beck asked them to open for his United States tour of 1997. That year also saw the release of Atari Teenage Riot's second album, *Burn, Berlin, Burn!* In addition, they performed opening stints for rock group Rage Against the Machine that same year and went on to play live with such bands as Dinosaur Jr., Wu-Tang Clan, and the Disposable Heroes of Hiphoprisy.

In the spring of 1999, Atari Teenage Riot added a new member to the band, Japanese-American Nic Endo, and returned with their third album entitled *60 Second Wipeout,* considered a more ambitious, yet also more politically and musically aggressive, effort. First, Empire opted to use only original studio sounds and all his own guitar work, rather than including samples, for this record. "Empire's guitar-playing values speed-thrash malevolence, and when paired with Endo's painful skronkage, the album is decidedly denser than its predecessor," concluded Bensel. Second, well-known singer Kathleen Hanna, formerly of the punk group Bikini Kill, added vocals to the track "No Success."

Finally, Atari Teenage Riot asked New York City rappers the Arsonists to contribute to the project after seeing them perform at a show in Berlin. However, convincing the rap artists to accept the offer took some persuading, as Arsonist member D-Story explained to Bensel. "Nicky (Endo) came up to me," said D-Story, "and I thought that she was trying to hook up with me. I didn't know who they were. So the whole night I'm performing, and she's smiling at me, and I'm like, 'Cool, I know what this is about.'" Then, to D-Story's surprise, Empire showed up alone after the show at the Arsonists' hotel room to pick them up. Although puzzled, D-Story, Q-Unique, and Freestyle went with Empire to Atari Teenage Riot's studio. D-Story continued, "So we went to their crib, and it was like a big vampire-setting type shit. If wings had come out of somebody's back, I would've said, 'All right, cool.' We were petrified and ready to expect anything. We all had our fists clenched tight." However, their worries subsided when Atari Teenage Riot played their music. The Arsonists immediately accepted Empire's offer, and the two groups met in New York to record three tracks together, including "Your Uniform (Does NotImpress Me)," "No Success," and "Anarchy 1999." Like Atari Teenage Riot's previous album, *60 Second Wipeout* fared well with both fans and critics.

As for the band's future, Empire, now an avid fan of Wilson Pickett and jazz great Otis Redding, told Rodd McLeod in an interview for Rollingstone.com, "Atari Teenage Riot is a spontaneous thing, it could end any day," but added that "We'll [DHR] have a big impact in the coming years." And when asked whether he thought kids who listen to Atari Teenage Riot could possibly feed off the music's violent energy and ignore the group's revolutionary aspect, Empire replied, "A lot of people ask me that, but strangely enough I've never come across people who take the music as just entertainment. In America we met lots of 16-year-olds whose first contact with these ideas is Atari Teenage Riot, so it's a different situation. I don't want to judge people in the audience. But it's not like people are having a nice dance party to a track like 'Start the Riots' or 'Death of a President D.I.Y.!"

Selected discography

Albums

Delete Yourself, DHR, 1995.
The Future Of War, DHR, 1997.
Burn, Berlin, Burn!, DHR/Grand Royal, 1997.
60 Second Wipeout, DHR, 1999.

EPs

Atari Teenage Riot, Phonogram, 1993.
Kids Are United, Phonogram, 1993.
Speed, DHR, 1995.
Kids Are United, DHR, 1995.
Sick To Death, DHR, 1997.
Destroy 2000 Years Of Culture, DHR, 1997.

Singles

"Hetzjagd Auf Nazis," Riot Beats, 1992.
"Raverbashing," DHR, 1994.

Sources

Periodicals

Dallas Morning News, March 15, 1997.
Denver Rocky Mountain News, December 5, 1997.
Entertainment Weekly, November 15, 1996; October 3, 1997.
Independent, November 6, 1998.
Magnet, June/July 1999.
Washington Post, July 16, 1999.

Online

Digital Hardcore Recordings, http://www.digitalhardcore.com (August 4, 1999).
Rollingstone.com, http://www.rollingstone.com (August 4, 1999).
Grand Royal Records, http://www.grandroyal.com (August 4, 1999).

—Laura Hightower

The Atomic Fireballs

Swing band

The Atomic Fireballs were one of several 1990s bands that helped rekindle American swing or jump blues, which peaked in popularity during the mid-1930s through the 1940s. Artists such as Cab Calloway and Duke Ellington defined the genre's golden age. Like other "neo swing" groups, including the Cherry Poppin' Daddies, Royal Crown Revue, and the Brian Setzer Orchestra, the Atomic Fireballs from Detroit, Michigan, came from another musical realm. While the above mentioned groups infused their music with hints of rock and roll, the Atomic Fireballs brought something more to their style of jump blues, namely the onstage energy and musical influences of ska and punk music.

Some modern swing fans say that the Atomic Fireballs aren't really "swing" at all, claiming that the group plays too fast for them to dance to the songs. However, lead singer John Bunkley refused to let such criticisms stand in his way, as he told John Farinella in a Launch.com: Discover New Music website feature story. "Basically it's too bad if the swing dancers don't accept us, because we never really got together for them, we got together for us." Therefore, although the swing revival seemed just another passing fad by the end of the 1990s, the Atomic Fireballs, armed with their own version of the jump blues, were just heating up. After releasing a self-produced album in 1997 entitled *Axen* (distributed by Steeple-Chase), the band embarked on their first national tour and released *Birth of the Swerve* on the independent label Orbital in 1998. Their major-label debut, *Don't Torch This Place,* arrived in 1999 on Lava, a subsidiary of Atlantic Records.

Lead singer Bunkley and jazz trumpeter James Bostek formed the group in Detroit in 1996, hiring guitarist Duke Kingins, drummer Geoff Kinde, trombone player Randy "Ginger" Sly, upright bassist Shawn Scaggs, and tenor saxophonist Eric Schabo to complete the lineup. Neither of the two knew much about the swing craze at the time; Bunkley, for one, had been a member of a ska band called Gangster Fun that had just broken up, while Bostek had substantial training in jazz. Nevertheless, they set out to take the jumping blues of the 1940s and bring it up to date with a more contemporary element. They borrowed ideas from the music of groups such as Funkadelic, Fishbone, X, Minor Threat, the Dead Kennedys, the Mighty Mighty Bosstones, and INXS to figure into their overall sound.

Because the Atomic Fireballs used punk, ska, and rock and roll as influences, they never intended to fit into the same category as the other swing revivalists. "We were just trying to put some roots-rock band together, so we always approached it with a harder edge," Bunkley explained to Farinella. "Everyone started putting us in the swing genre, so we checked it out and saw whatthe other bands were doing show-wise. I was like, 'Well, we sweat a lot more than them.' We don't care how neat we are onstage."

The band started performing in public in 1997 after releasing *Axen,* with their first show scheduled for Valentine's Day of that year. Moreover, the event was highly publicized around Detroit, and several members of the press were in attendance. Adding to the pressure also included the fact that the Atomic Fireballs never had prior opportunity to perfect their live act, as they were set to headline the concert. "At our first gig there were a lot of people and we had to be on our toes," Bunkley told Farinella.

Despite the group's nervousness, their energetic show struck a chord with the audience that night, and before long, the group piled into a beat-up 15-passenger van to take their music to towns across the Midwest. Playing in clubs and converting fans from Chicago, Pittsburgh, St. Louis, and their hometown, the Atomic Fireballs's popularity swelled, and the band accepted an offer to make a record with the independent label Orbital. Released in 1998 and produced by Charlie Baby, dB, and the Atomic Fireballs, *Birth of the Swerve* captured the recording birth of the newest rock/jump blues band to step into the swing scene at the time. Five songs from the album would show up on the group's subsequent album.

For the Record . . .

Members include **John Bunkley** (former member of Gangster Fun), vocals; **James Bostek** (studied jazz), trumpet; **Duke Kingins**, guitar; **Geoff Kinde**, drums; **Randy "Ginger" Sly**, trombone; **Shawn Scaggs,** upright bass; **Eric Shabo**, tenor saxophone.

Released debut *Axen*, SteepleChase, 1997; performed for the fist time in public on Valentine's Day, 1997; released *Birth of the Swerve* on Orbital, 1998; toured the U.S., performed with the Vans Warped Tour, 1998; released first album with Lava/Atlantic, *Torch This Place,* 1999.

Addresses: *Home*—Detroit, MI. *Record company*—Atlantic Recording Corp., 1290 Avenue of the Americas, New York City, NY 10104, (212) 707-2000, fax (212) 405-5507.

The same year, the Atomic Fireballs embarked on their first national tour of the United States. They also performed as part of the Vans Warped Tour, a concert series formed in 1995 featuring bands playing a range of music from metal and punk to progressive hip-hop and swing. Considered a catalyst for propelling bands to greater fame, the Warped Tour boasted future well-known outfits such as No Doubt, Sublime, Limp Bizkit, and the Mighty Mighty Bosstones. In addition to music, the festivities at the concert events included skateboarding, BMX bike racing contests, and famous snowboarders.

Amid the atmosphere of skateboarders and surfers, the Atomic Fireballs said they felt right at home. "It was really fun to play right before or after [the hard-core, San Francisco Bay area punk band] Rancid. Those people gave us our shakes, man. They looked at us in the first couple songs and then their heads started bobbing," Bunkley recalled to Farinella. "By the end they asked for more. I take that as a great compliment." During the band's own tour of the southern United States, the Atomic Fireballs received compliments as well. After one performance, a couple of African American women approached Bunkley, telling the 140-pound singer that they thought the group had a lot of soul. "They told me I could dance and I could sing, and they said 'Those white boys in your band can dance and sing, too.' They might not have much soul offstage, but when you put a mic or horn in their hands ... That's where it all counts."

After proving that the Atomic Fireballs could appeal to a variety of audiences rather than exclusively to swing enthusiasts, the band received several offers from big-label record companies. Signing with Lava/Atlantic, the band worked with producer Bruce Fairbairn to release the twelve-track album *Torch This Place* in the late spring of 1999. The release captured the excitement of the group's live performances with authenticity and received overwhelming support from critics and fans alike. For example, Gary Graff concluded in *MusicHound Swing!: The Essential Album Guide* that "tracks such as 'Spanish Fly,' 'Caviar & Chillins,' 'Mata Hari,' and 'Man With the Hex' will give any Brian Setzer or Cherry Poppin' Daddy a run for his money."

Backed by their promising new release, the band left Detroit for another national tour, where they enjoyed seeing sights they had never seen before. Bunkley especially admired the Georgia O'Keeffe Museum in Santa Fe, New Mexico, as well as the Cadillac Ranch in Texas. The Atomic Fireballs also made their first television appearance, performing their upbeat interchanges on the *Late Night with Conan O'Brien Show.*

Selected discography

Axen, SteepleChase, 1997.
Birth of the Swerve, Orbital, 1998.
Torch This Place, Lava/Atlantic, 1999.

Sources

Books

Knopper, Steve, editor, *MusicHound Swing!: The Essential Album Guide,* Visible Ink Press, 1999.

Periodicals

Billboard, April 17, 1999, p. 14.
University Wire, June 1, 1999.

Online

"The Atomic Fireballs Great Balls of Fire," Launch: Discover New Music, http://www.launch.com, (June 18, 1999).
Modern Music Showcase—The Atomic Fireballs, http://www.imusic.com/showcase/modern/atomicfireballs.html, (October 14, 1999).
"The Atomic Fireballs," *Rolling Stone.com*, http://www.rollingstone.tunes.com, (August 4, 1999).

—Laura Hightower

Bauhaus

Rock group

Often referred to as the "godfathers" of goth-rock because of their sometimes dark music and frightening stage show theatrics, Bauhaus served as an inspiration to later gothic outfits such as Christian Death, Alien Sex Fiend, and Marilyn Manson. However, confining Bauhaus to the category of goth-rock ignores the group's sense of humor, uniqueness, and desire for musical experimentation. "Their music was dark rock 'n' roll," asserted the Official Bauhaus Web Site, "owing more to Elvis Presley's 'Heartbreak Hotel' than to their imitator's pompous epics which gave the Gothic genre a bad name." After the members of Bauhaus went their separate ways in 1983, they continued to find commercial and critical acclaim with acts such as Love and Rockets. And into the later 1990s, Bauhaus songs still sounded contemporary, the group's albums sold better than ever, and the band's live shows remained legendary.

Bauhaus formed in 1978 in Northampton, England; the group's founding members included bassist and vocalist David J (born David Jay Haskins), his brother Kevin Haskins, a drummer, guitarist Daniel Ash, and vocalist Peter Murphy. David J, Haskins, and later Ash all played together prior to Bauhaus under various names such as The Craze, The Submerged Tenth or Jack Plug, and The Sockettes. However, all of these relatively unknown outfits seemed to lack a certain chemistry. In an attempt to salvage the threesome's pursuits, Ash decided to call upon Murphy, an old school friend who shared the trio's musical tastes, and asked him to join the band. This decision proved beneficial from the start, for within just a couple of weeks, Ash and Murphy had written an astounding number of songs, including "Dark Entries," "In the Night," "Boys," "Harry," and many more.

A month later, after David J and Haskins joined the pair to further develop lines for the collection of songs, and the four musicians officially named themselves Bauhaus 1919 after the German art movement (the suffix 1919 was later dropped in 1979 from the group's namesake). On New Year's Eve, 1978, they made their first public debut in England. Soon thereafter, Bauhaus recorded in just one take a 12-inch single on the Small Wonder label that included the track "Bela Lugosi's Dead." The epic, nine minute-long song, released in August of 1979, would later become a Bauhaus classic and goth-rock anthem. While the song never reached the pop charts, it remained on the United Kingdom independent charts for several years. At the band's request, the 12-inch version of "Bela Lugosi's Dead" never appeared on an album until the release of the Bauhaus compilation *Crackle* in 1998.

With just one single to their name, Bauhaus quickly gained attention for their live performances held in small clubs. Using videos projected onto a small screen and a single white strobe light, the band produced a startling and hypnotic show. "You may not care to have the fear of God instilled in you at a gig, partially from the band," wrote *Melody Maker,* as quoted by the band's website, "but Bauhaus proved an exhilarating exception. Audience communication is never broached, more a sense of intimidation that immediately demands you take an interest—deeply explosive drums, throbbing basses and a never ending variety of guitar sounds which never resort to conventional methods of attack."

After performing almost non-stop and just three months after releasing their first single, Bauhaus signed with the Beggars Banquet's subsidiary label 4AD. In January of 1980, the group released their second single, "Dark Entries." Later in the summer of the same year, after touring Europe, they released the single "Terror Couple Killed Colonel," another independent chart hit. In September of 1980, Bauhaus arrived in the United States for their first American tour, releasing another single, a cover of the 1970s glam-rock group T-Rex's "Telegram Sam," toward the end of the month.

Upon returning to England, Bauhaus released their debut album, the psychedelic, dark, and original *In the Flat Field,* in October of 1980. An immediate success,

For the Record . . .

Members include **Daniel Ash,** guitar, vocals; **David J** (born David Jay Haskins), bass, vocals; **Kevin Haskins**, drums; **Peter Murphy** (born in Northampton, England), vocals.

Group formed in Northampton, England, developed legendary yet simple stage shows, 1978; released classic single "Bela Lugosi's Dead,"Small Wonder, 1979; released debut album, *In the Flat Field,* 4AD, 1979; released *Mask,* Beggars and Banquet, 1980; released first U.K. Top 20 hit, "Ziggy Stardust," which reached number 15 and *The Sky's Gone Out,* Beggars Banquet, both in 1982; released *Burning from the Inside,* Beggars Banquet/A&M, 1983; reunited for worldwide tour; released compilation album *Crackle,* 1998.

Addresses: *Record company*—Beggars Banquet Records, 580 Broadway, Ste. 1004, New York City, NY 10012; phone: (212) 343-7010; fax: (212) 343-7030. *Website*—The Official Bauhaus Web Site, http://www.bauhausmusik.com.

although the album originally contained none of Bauhaus's previous singles, the record peaked at number one on the independent charts and number 72 on the pop charts. (In the 1990s, all of the 4AD singles were remastered and included in an expanded CD of *In the Flat Field.*) Unlike any other band prior, Bauhaus on their debut introduced listeners to the dense, raw force that would become their own unique style.

February of 1981 took Bauhaus back to the United States for a second, 16-date tour. Also that year, Bauhaus, by now gaining a wider audience, transferred to the Beggars Banquet label. Subsequently, they released the single "Kick in the Eye," which introduced a more commercial sound through its dance rhythms, soon followed by "The Passion of Lovers," which Bauhaus composed and recorded in one day. Both singles made the British top 60 in 1981. Also this year, Ash formed a group outside of Bauhaus called Tones on Tale.

An Ambitious Follow-up

In October of 1981, Bauhaus released their second album entitled *Mask,* marking a shift in musical direction for the group. More ambitious, accessible, and mature than the group's debut effort, *Mask* featured other musical elements such as metal and electronic textures. However, the broader collection of songs also retainedthe experimental edge and the dark, foreboding core of Bauhaus's earlier music. Bob Gulla in *musicHound Rock: The Essential Album Guide* defined the work as "Bauhaus's finest, showing a variety of styles and extremes in both musicianship and verse." Likewise, the album succeeded in terms of commercial appeal as well, reaching number 30 on the British charts.

Despite the group's intense touring schedule that led them across Europe and abroad, a significant breakthrough record continued to elude Bauhaus. Nonetheless, the band headed back to the studio to record the EP *Searching for Satori* (released in March of 1982), which also included a remix of "Kick in the Eye" and reached number 45 on the British charts. The next single, "Spirit," appeared later that summer, making the British top 50. For this song, Bauhaus used an outside producer for the first and last time. Unhappy with the arrangement and final outcome of "Spirit," the group recorded a longer, more complete version that showed up on their next album.

In the meantime, Bauhaus experienced a bit of mainstream recognition when Murphy took on an acting job and starred in a series of television commercials advertising Maxell tapes. Filmed by a renowned director named Howard Guard (who later made the video for a Bauhaus song entitled "She's in Parties"), the trend-setting commercials drew acclaim from the advertising industry. Moreover, the popularity of the ads resulted in Bauhaus receiving a cameo appearance in the film "The Hunger." In the movie, a vampire myth set in New York City starring David Bowie and Catherine Deneuve, the group performed "Bela Lugosi's Dead" in a club frequented by the film's leading characters.

Provoked the Press

In the fall of 1982, Bauhaus made a connection of sorts with Bowie again by releasing a cover of the musician's song "Ziggy Stardust," followed by a version of pop/electronic innovator Brian Eno's "Third Uncle." Throughout the group's career, and especially since their recording of "Telegram Sam," some members of the English press accused Bauhaus of sounding similar to Bowie or mimicking the glam-rock style with their elaborate stage shows. Fully realizing that a remake of a Bowie song would invite an abundance of media protest, Bauhaus decided to provoke the press even more by adding "Third Uncle" to the release of "Ziggy Stardust." For the 12-inch version, the group further included a live cover of the Velvet Underground's "Waiting for the Man," featuring the vocals of former Velvet Underground member Nico. And while the project began out of Bauhaus's sense of humor, the popular single finally earned the group their first United Kingdom Top 20 hit as "Ziggy Stardust" ascended to number 15.

Propelled by the pop chart success of the single, *The Sky's GoneOut,* Bauhaus's next album also released in 1982, entered the album charts at number four. To show their gratitude to record buyers, the group included free with the first 30,000 copies a live album consisting of live performances from late 1981 and early 1982. The free album was released later that year independently as *Press the Eject and Give Me the Tape.* Although *The Sky's Gone Out* gave the group their greatest mainstream recognition, the album nonetheless lacked the lyrical humor of Bauhaus's earlier work.

In early 1983, with the band already booked for studio time to work on their next album, Murphy contracted viral pneumonia. The other members of Bauhaus, though, opted to start recording without the lead singer, whose serious illness prevented him from participating. By the time he recovered, the bulk of the record was completed, leaving Murphy the opportunity to reinterpret the vocals for only four songs. Consequently, 1983's *Burning from the Inside* consisted of greater contributions from Ash and David J, who sang on most of the album's tracks and added a more acoustic sound to the music. Despite the fact that all the members of Bauhaus did not contribute equally to writing and recording *Burning from the Inside,* the album proved yet another critical and popular achievement, climbing to number ten on the pop charts, and spurred the successful single "She's In Parties." However, the diverse album also prompted the breakup that would come in July of 1983, as the members of Bauhaus displayed an obvious interest in pursuing other musical avenues.

Bauhaus Split Up

Bauhaus promoted the album with a tour of Japan, returning to the British for a tour of England from June 11 until July 5. During Bauhaus's last performance held at Hammersmith Palais in England, Ash exited the stage with the words "Rest in peace," as quoted by the group's website. (A recording of the live show entitled *Rest in Peace: The Final Concert* was later released in 1992.) Shortly thereafter, a press release confirmed rumors that Bauhaus had broken up. Feeling that fan club members who had already paid their annual subscription deserved compensation, Bauhaus sent out 325 copies of a single the band had decided not to release on an album called "The Sanity Assassin." The song was later made available to the general public as a track on *Crackle.*

After Bauhaus split apart, all of the group's members went on to enjoy commercially successful careers. Murphy first formed a band called Dali's Car with Mick Karn (formerly of the group Japan) and then released a string of solo projects. His more noteworthy albums included *Deep* (1990) and *Cascade* (1995). Ash continued playing with Tones on Tail, joined by Haskins after Bauhaus's breakup, and David J released some solo records in addition tojoining the group the Jazz Butcher for a short time. In 1985, Ash, David J, and Haskins reunited as Love and Rockets after a proposed Bauhaus reunion fell through. Love and Rockets, embracing the diversity and creativity evident on *Burning from the Inside,* earned both critical acclaim and commercial acceptance throughout the remainder of the 1980s and into the 1990s.

In 1998, with Love and Rockets and Murphy at a recording standstill, Bauhaus reformed for several live shows in Los Angeles, followed by a series of summer concerts across the United States and a fall tour in Europe. In celebration of the reunion, the band released the "best of" album *Crackle* on the Beggars Banquet label. During their visit to Chicago while on tour, Bauhaus booked some studio time and even began work on a new song, leading to rumors that a new release was in the making. Although 15 years had passed since the Bauhaus breakup, the group's reunion and tour of sold-out performances established the notion that the legacy and influences of Bauhaus remained as strong as ever.

Selected discography

as Bauhaus

"Bela Lugosi's Dead," (12-inch single), Small Wonder, 1979.
In the Flat Field, 4AD, 1980.
Mask, Beggars Banquet, 1981, reissued, 1995.
Lagartija Nick, (EP), Beggars Banquet, 1982.
Press the Eject and Give Me the Tape, Beggars Banquet, 1982.
Searching for Satori, (EP; includes "Kick in the Eye"), Beggars Banquet, 1982.
The Sky's Gone Out, Beggars Banquet/A&M, 1982.
Ziggy Stardust, (EP), Beggars Banquet, 1982.
4AD, (EP), 4AD, 1983.
Burning from the Inside, Beggars Banquet/A&M, 1983, reissued, 1989.
The Singles 1981-1983, Beggars Banquet, 1983.
1979-1983, Beggars Banquet, 1985.

1979-1983, Vol. 1 and Vol. 2, Beggars Banquet, 1986.
Swing the Heartache: The BBC Sessions, BBC/Beggars Banquet, 1989.
Rest in Peace: The Final Concert, Nemo/Beggars Banquet, 1992.
Crackle, Beggars Banquet, 1998.

as Love and Rockets

Seventh Dream of Teenage Heaven, UK Beggars Banquet, 1985, reissued, Beggars Banquet/RCA, 1988.
Express, Beggars Banquet/Big Time, 1986.
Earth, Sun, Moon, Beggars Banquet/Big Time, 1987.
Love and Rockets, Beggars Banquet/RCA, 1989.
Hot Trip to Heaven, American, 1994.
This Heaven, (EP), UK Beggars Banquet, 1995.
Body and Soul, (EP), American, 1995.
The Glittering Darkness, (EP), UK Beggars Banquet, 1996.
Sweet F.A., American, 1996.

Peter Murphy solo

Should the World Fall Apart, UK Beggars Banquet, 1986, reissued, Beggars Banquet, 1996.
Love Hysteria, Beggars Banquet/RCA, 1988, reissued, Beggars Banquet/Atlantic, 1995.
Deep, Beggars Banquet/RCA, 1990, reissued, Beggars Banquet/Atlantic, 1995.
Holy Smoke, Beggars Banquet/RCA, 1992, reissued, Beggars Banquet/Atlantic, 1995.
You're So Close, (EP), Beggars Banquet/RCA, 1992.
The Scarlet Thing in You, (EP), Beggars Banquet/Atlantic, 1995.
Cascade, Beggars Banquet/Atlantic, 1995.

Sources

Books

Graff, Gary and Daniel Durchholz, editors, *musicHound Rock: The Essential Album Guide,* Visible Ink Press, 1999.
Robbins, Ira A., editor, *Trouser Press Guide to '90s Rock,* Fireside/Simon and Schuster, 1997.

Periodicals

Atlanta Journal and Constitution, September 11, 1998, p. P04.
Dallas Morning News, September 24, 1998, p. 43A.
Toronto Star, September 4, 1998.

Online

All Music Guide website, http://www.allmusic.com, (September 26, 1999).
The Official Bauhaus website, http://www.bauhausmusik.com, (September 26, 1999).
RollingStone.com, http://www.rollingstone.tunes.com, (September 26, 1999).

—Laura Hightower

Thomas Beecham

Conductor

AP/Wide World Photos. Reproduced by permission. ©

Sir Thomas Beecham's influence on classical music during a span of several decades across the twentieth century was unparalleled. Founder and principal conductor of the London Philharmonic Orchestra, Beecham depleted much of his own fortune to present before British audiences orchestral works and operas that had heretofore been considered daring, avant-garde, or even too "foreign"; as a result, he introduced a generation of London music-lovers to some outstanding composers, especially the lighter French artists of the previous century. Beecham was known for a legendary wit and his cutting manner, but many of the artists who worked with him recalled him as a delightful taskmaster.

Beecham was born in St. Helens, a town in the Lancashire area of England, on April 29, 1879. He was the namesake of his grandfather, who had created a tremendous family fortune with his own brand of digestive pills that also bore the name Beecham. The young boy enjoyed close ties with the elder Beecham; relations with his own parents were never wholly amiable during his adult life. His gift for music was evident at a young age to his father, a collector of rare musical instruments, and formal instruction at the piano began at the age of six. For several years he attended a Lancashire school where he was also able to indulge in his second love—athletics—but enrolled in Wadham College at Oxford University to study music in 1897. He considered becoming a concert pianist.

That same year, Beecham had founded the St. Helens Orchestral Society, where he first practiced the art of conducting. When in 1899 the Hallé Society Orchestra appeared in St. Helens for a scheduled engagement, its conductor became unavailable, and Beecham took the podium instead. This debut was deemed a success, though he and the musicians had not been able to rehearse the program beforehand. The following year, he moved to London and began to study music composition privately with a series of teachers.

Beecham was still working toward a career as a pianist, but a 1904 injury to his wrist ended these hopes. Though still in his mid-twenties, Beecham had already traveled extensively in Europe to further his musical education, attending opera performances at some of the continent's most famous venues. He made his London conducting debut with the Queen's Hall Orchestra in December of 1905, but the performance was given mixed reviews by critics. Beecham had been disheartened by the difficulty of the experience as well. With the support of a clarinetist named Charles Draper, he founded the New Symphony Orchestra in 1906, and Beecham began selecting its sixty-five members according to his own high standards.

For the Record . . .

Born April 29, 1879, in St. Helens, Lancashire, England; (died March 8, 1961 in London, England); son of Joseph (a chemist) and Josephine (Burnett) Beecham; married Utica Celestia Welles, 1903 (divorced, 1943); married Betty Humby Thomas (a pianist), 1943 (she died in 1957); married Shirley Hudson, 1959; children: Adrian Welles (one of two sons from his first marriage). *Education:* Attended Wadham College, Oxford, 1897-98; studied musical composition privately after 1900.

Founder, St. Helens Orchestral Society, 1897; made first appearance as an orchestra conductor with the Hallé Orchestra, St. Helens, 1899; founded New Symphony Orchestra, 1906; founded London Philharmonic Orchestra, 1932; founded Royal Philharmonic Orchestra, 1946.

Awards: Named Companion of Honour, 1957.

Performances of the New Symphony Orchestra, with Beecham at the podium, met with a more favorable reception from critics. "This time Beecham's arresting style triumphed,and it was obvious that Britain had an important young conductor," assessed the *British Dictionary of National Biography.* His newfound acclaim brought him into contact with the relatively unknown English composer Frederick Delius, and Beecham began to debut new orchestral works written by Delius with the New Symphony. Delius, of German parentage, was influenced by Norwegian composer Edvard Grieg, and created works that blended the styles of Romanticism and Impressionism beginning with his first success, 1907's *Brigg Fair.*

In 1903, during a period of family strife, Beecham wed the daughter of an American diplomat, Utica Celestia Welles. Together they had two sons, and traveled across Europe, but the union disintegrated within a few short years. They did not divorce, however, until 1943. By 1910, Beecham and his father had mended their differences, and the latter provided financial backing for the son's plan to mount a program of operas at London's Covent Garden. Over the next several years, Beecham and his British National Opera Company presented some striking, altogether grand productions of works from the canon of European composers, some of which had not yet been performed in Britain. Richard Strauss's *Elektra, Feuersnot,* and *Der Rosenkavalier,* Richard Wagner's *Tristan und Isolde,* and even Sergei Diaghilev's famed Ballets Russes from Paris all appeared before London audiences, led by Beecham's baton. Already a celebrated London figure, the press loved to report some of his more pithy utterances. He once told his orchestra, "We must ensure that we start and stop together—what happens in between is of no great consequence."

The Covent Garden seasons were annual financial losses, however, and the outbreak of World War I and England's belligerent relationship with Germany further curtailed Beecham's plans. So Beecham founded a small touring company, and with it staged operas across the British Isles during the war years; the programs were notable for their affordable ticket prices, making the whole endeavor quite an egalitarian one. In 1916, Beecham's father died, and he inherited a baronetcy, but financial woes began to plague him. His 1920 season of Covent Garden operas sustained heavy losses, and he nearly went bankrupt. As the *British Dictionary of National Biography* noted, "until 1923 he was almost absent from the musical scene. From then until 1929 his life seems to have been a gradual climb back to the pinnacle he had achieved so early."

The composer Delius, who suffered from paralysis and encroaching vision problems with age, was feted with a festival in his honor presented by Beecham in 1929; the series, which became an annual event, marked the beginning of a more widespread recognition for Delius's works. By 1932, after several years of exacting negotiations, Beecham entered into an agreement with the British Broadcasting Corporation and the London Symphony Orchestra to create the London Philharmonic Orchestra. Several seasons of distinguished performances followed, but the onset of world war once more brought an abrupt change to Beecham's fortunes.

Beecham spent much of the war years touring the United States and Australia, perhaps the result of lingering problems in Britain as a result of his 1936 tour of Nazi Germany with the orchestra group. Furthermore, an expatriate German woman, Berta Geissmar, served as his personal secretary at both home and on tour. At one performance, German chancellor Adolf Hitler was the guest of honor, and as customary, the entire hall was expected to rise and salute him upon his entrance. Beecham avoided this by adamantly entering the concert hall after the Führer had been seated. On another night, Beecham and the Philharmonic played at a concert hall in Ludwigshafen belonging to the chemical giant BASF, who also manufactured recording equipment. The evening's program was recorded, the first time in history that a live orchestra's performance was duplicated on tape.

Beginning in 1940, Beecham, like other European masters, made a number of guest appearances with the Metropolitan Opera of New York. Divorced in 1943, he remarried pianist Betty Humby Thomas, and wrote an autobiography of his early life, *A Mingled Chime,* that was published in 1944. He returned to London in 1944, and became immersed in artistic and other arguments with the London Philharmonic. As a result, he broke with the organization and formed the Royal Philharmonic Orchestra in 1946. With that body he honored the eighty-three-year-old Richard Strauss with a momentous London festival in 1947. In 1950, the Royal Philharmonic made a successful tour of North America, and Beecham led the orchestra through several stellar recordings as well. He also wrote a biography of Delius that appeared in 1958.

Among the recordings that preserve Beecham's legacy, critics have cited *Puccini: La Bohéme* with Jussi Bjoerling and Victoria De Los Angeles, issued on RCA in 1956 and reissued by the EMI's Seraphim label, as exemplary. "What makes this recording unique?" posited *Opera News* writer Walter Price, who termed it "one of the few opera albums deserving to be called 'great.'" Price listed its exceptional features: "It unites a British conductor, a Swedish tenor, a Spanish soprano, a Swiss bass ... and four Americans in major parts ... not an Italian in hearing distance." As with the lighthearted operatic romp of *La Bohéme,* Beecham was partial to the works of French composers such as Bizet, Debussy, and Saint-Saëns; the entire Mozart repertoire was also a personal favorite.

Beecham's second wife died in 1957, the same year he received the Companion of Honour designation from the British crown. He married his personal secretary, Shirley Hudson, in 1959, but fell ill the following year while touring the United States with the Royal Philharmonic. He died in London in March of 1961. As a conductor and orchestra director, Beecham had a reputation for a rather formidable style of management. He disliked rehearsals very much, and made certain that his musicians knew their parts well before he appeared before their assemblage with his baton. "Orchestral players will long remember him as not only a great conductor, but a witty and stimulating person who could inspire them to produce their best and showed obvious pleasure in what he heard,"noted the *British Dictionary of National Biography.* He left behind an extensive musical library, which in 1997 was acquired by England's University of Sheffield.

Selected discography

Beecham Conducts Delius, 1987.

Lollipops, 1992.

Brahms: Symphony No. 1; Wagner/Horenstein, London Symphony Orchestra, 1996.

Beecham Conducts Handel, 1997. *Mozart: Symphonies No. 39, 40 and 41/Beecham, London Philharmonic Orchestra,* 1997.

Beecham Favorites: Bizet, Greig, Chabrier, et al./London Philharmonic Orchestra, 1998.

Beecham Conducts Schubert: Symphony No. 5; Franck: Symphony, 1998.

Great Recordings of the Century: Schubert: Symphonies Nos. 3, 5, & 6/Beecham, Royal Philharmonic Orchestra, 1999.

Haydn: Symphonies No. 104, 99 & 93/Beecham, London Philharmonic Orchestra, 1999. *Beecham Conducts Wagner - Die Meistersinger, etc.,* 1999.

Mozart: Symphonies No. 29, 35 & 38/Beecham, Royal Philharmonic Orchestra, 1999. *The 1959 Royal Festival Hall Concert/Beecham, Royal Philharmonic Orchestra,* 1999. *The Beecham Edition: Delius: A Village Romeo & Juliet,* 1992.

Bizet: Symphony in C, etc., EMI Classics.

Bizet: Carmen, EMI Classics.

Borodin: Prince Igor, Polovtsian Dances, etc., EMI Classics.

Grieg: Peer Gynt, Suite, etc., EMI Classics.

Mendelssohn: Violin Concerto, etc./Jascha Heifetz, EMI Classics.

Mozart: Clarinet & Bassoon Concertos, EMI Classics.

Mozart: Clarinet Concerto, etc., EMI Classics.

Mozart: Die Entführung aus dem Serail, etc., EMI Classics.

Mozart: Die Zauberflöte, EMI Classics.

Puccini: La Bohème, EMI Classics.

Rimsky-Korsakov: Scheherazade, etc., EMI Classics.

Schubert: Symphonies Nos. 3, 5 & 6, EMI Classics.

Sibelius: Symphonies Nos.4 & 6, EMI Classics.

Sibelius: Violin Concerto, etc./Jascha Heifetz, EMI Classics.

Sources

Books

Williams, E. T., and C. S. Nicholls, editors, *British Dictionary of National Biography, 1961-1970*, Oxford University Press, 1963-64, pp. 87-90.

Periodicals

American Record Guide, May/June 1999.

Opera News, March 18, 1995; July 1, 1995.

—*Carol Brennan*

Eric Benét

Singer, songwriter

Photograph by Pacha. Corbis. Reproduced by permission. ©

The music industry often uses terms like "retro-soul" or "alternative R&B" to describe the music of Eric Benét, one of a new generation of African American artists, such as D'Angelo, Maxwell, and Grammy award winner Tony Rich, who create music without the use of samples. However, Benét declines to categorize his music as alternative."The term 'alternative R&B' does kind of bug me a little bit because I feel that what we're doing is pure R&B or a closer representation," stated Benét in an interview for the *Philadelphia Tribune.* "I just think that for the past fifteen years or so, the masses have just been so hungry and starving for some music with some integrity, some lyrical depth and with some substance to it.... So much of what was happening then [during the 1960s and 1970s] sounds so similar to what they're calling alternative R&B. It's just a strange term."

Since his debut effort in 1996, *True To Myself,* followed by 1999's *A Day In The Life,* the young purveyor of contemporary soul ranks among the most innovative singers and songwriters of the 1990s. A musician who always remains true to the roots of R&B while adding his own modern flair, Benét said on the Warner Brothers website, "I like the idea of making music that transcends time and history. Ella Fitzgerald, Nat King Cole: people will be playing their records 100 years from now. I hope to make music like that." And with two critically successful albums to his name thus far, Benét could likely achieve such a lofty goal.

Eric Benét Jordan, named after poet and author Stephen Vincent Benét, was born in 1970 in Milwaukee, Wisconsin, and continues to make his home there as an adult. Growing up in a household always filled with music, Benét, a self-taught musician, seemed destined to gravitate toward singing and songwriting. For example, instead of telling her children what to do, Benét's mother would sing her words, such as "Go and clean your roooom!," he recalled in an interview with the iMusic website. His other musical inspirations came from singing in church, as well as listening to the popular R&B artists of the 1960s and 1970s throughout his childhood. Together with his brother and two sisters, Benét displayed an interest in and obvious talent for music and harmonizing that would one day lead him to the top of the R&B charts.

In the meantime, the aspiring singer, along with his sister Lisa and cousin George Nash, Jr., an accomplished guitarist, formed a band called Benét and released their first collection of songs in 1992 on EMI Records. However, because the label was in the midst of a corporate reorganization during the time, the album went largely unnoticed. Consequently, the group felt devastated by the blow, but Benét would soon realize that a

For the Record . . .

Born Eric Benét Jordan, 1970, in Milwaukee, WI: one brother, two sisters; children: one daugher, India, born 1992.

Released debut album, *True To Myself,* Warner Bros. Records, (single "Spiritual Thang" became a top ten hit on the R&B charts), 1996; released album *A Day In The Life,* Warner Bros. Records, 1999.

Addresses: *Home*—Milwaukee, WI. *Record company*—Warner Brothers Records, 3300 Warner Blvd., Burbank, CA 91506; 75 Rockefeller Plaza, New York City, NY 10019. *Website*—Warner Brothers Records, http:www.wbr.com; Eric Benét—The Official Site, http://www.ericbenet.com.

series of tragic events would prove much more difficult for him to recover from than the failure of his group.

Within an 18-month period in 1995, Benét witnessed his father's demise from cancer and endured the death of former girlfriend Tami. The young woman, also the mother of Benét's daughter India, born in 1992, suffered extensive injuries from a car accident and laid unconscious in a coma for five days until she finally passed away. Benét, torn apart emotionally by Tami's death, fell into a two-year depression. Only his daughter, at the time still a toddler, prevented himfrom giving up completely. "It really was the hardest thing I've ever gone through," Benét admitted to an interview with Chris Wells in *Independent.* "Even losing my father, as traumatic as that was, didn't hurt as much because... well, at least when we knew he was dying we all—my mom, two sisters, my brother—got the chance to say goodbye. Tami and I weren't actually together at the time she died—I was just seeing India every weekend—but the feelings of guilt, remorse, bereavement, depression just took over. Hearing India call my name when I came home from work at the end of the day felt like all I had to hang on."

Thus Benét, now a single parent, took on the responsibility of raising his daughter alone. With his music career on hold because of his mental state, he worked shifts at UPS (United Parcel Service) and helped local Milwaukee musicians record demos in the studio. Eventually, Benét started to write songs again, most of them reflecting on his recent experiences. Then, with the help of Nash and friend Demonte Posey, a keyboard player and programmer, he recorded a demo tape of three songs and sent them to Warner Brothers Records. Soon thereafter, Warner Brothers responded with an offer for a record contract.

With his enthusiasm about music restored, Benét released his debut album, *True to Myself,* in 1996. The album, co-produced with Nash and Posey, drew on his childhood influences, early 1970s soul musicians like Al Green, Sly Stone, and Stevie Wonder. Nonetheless, Benét managed to blend his own contemporary artistry in with the forms he borrowed from his contemporaries, earning him critical recognition for his edgier take on R&B. Moreover, whereas most R&B artists usually adhere to one particular style of music, Benét also attempts to incorporate aspects of other genres into his songs as well. "They [other artists] kind of have the same vibe throughout the whole record. With my record, on one song, I might do something a little rocky, in another song I might do something kind of Beatleish and in another song, I might do something gospel/bluesy—it's kind of hard for people to take sometimes," Benét told the *Philadelphia Tribune.* The record's first single, "Spiritual Thang," became a top ten hit on the R&B charts, and the single "Let's Stay Together" was featured in the Martin Lawrence film *A Thin Line Between Love and Hate.* The album also included a song about his late girlfriend called "While You Were Here," which tallied up the aspects of their relationship taken for granted.

Despite the success of Benét's first single, his debut effort lacked support in record sales. The young singer blamed some of the lower than expected numbers on the fact that his music did not fit in with the typical urban radio format. "Urban radio has become this thing, with so many songs sounding alike," Benét commented in the *Philadelphia Tribune.* "If you deviate from that then it's really hard to be accepted. If you put any other influences of any other genres of music in your particular vibe, you're not Black enough or you're selling out. I think it's a very narrow minded view of music, urban audiences have gotten so used to a certain kind of thing... everyone's doing the same runs vocally, the same kick sound, the same snare, something that's flexing creativity, throwing a couple of chord progressions in there and it's kind of hard to get embraced." Nevertheless, even without the support of radio play, the determined singer forged ahead with a world tour to promote *True to Myself,* drawing fans into his music wherever he traveled.

After completing his worldwide tour, Benét returned to Milwaukee to write new songs for afollow-up release. For this collection of work, he teamed with other talented writers and producers, in addition to Nash and Posey; the album featured the vocals of singer Tamia and collaborations with producers Wyclef Jean and Ali Shaheed from the rap/hip-hop group A Tribe Called Quest, as well as a duet with hip-hop artist Faith Evans for a remake of "Georgy Porgy" by the 1980s pop group Toto. After a year of arranging and recording music with producers, Benét released *A Day In The Life* in 1999, considered by critics as his best work to date. In addition, Warner Brothers witnessed a marked improvement in record sales over Benét's debut release. Benét himself felt *A Day In The Life* illustrated that he had matured as a writer and performer, and said he took time to come up with the right body of work. The album, more grounded in classic R&B, was largely inspired by Benét's real life experiences. "I keep a journal," he said, as quoted by the Warner Brothers website. "The album title came from re-reading passages in my diary. As a songwriter, I just opened myself up to whatever came out of my heart."

Although Benét strives to achieve recognition for his music, his most important undertaking remains caring for his daughter. Therefore, he continues to live in Milwaukee so his mother can help take care of India, enabling him to record and tour. "I record in Philadelphia... Los Angeles... play all over the world, but when I get back home I like to keep all the things that surround her as calm and uneventful as possible." he said to Wells. "OK, sometimes—not often—I have just taken her out of school for a week and done lessons with her just so we could be together. But, y'see, the older she gets, the more evident it is that she's the single most important thing that's happened to me."

Selected discography

Albums

True To Myself, Warner Brothers Records, 1996.
A Day In The Life, Warner Brothers Records, 1999.

Singles

"Let's Stay Together," Warner Brothers Records, 1996.
"Spiritual Thang," Warner Brothers Records, 1996.
"True To Myself" (Maxi Single), Warner Brothers Records, 1996.
"Georgy Porgy" (Maxi Single), Warner Alliance, 1999.
"Spend My Life With You," Warner Alliance, 1999.

Compilations

A Thin Line Between Love And Hate, Warner Brothers Records, 1996.
Batman & Robin, Warner Brothers Records, 1997.
Ride, Tommy Boy, 1998.

Sources

Periodicals

Dallas Morning News, March 20, 1997, p. 39A.
Independent, April 23, 1999, p. 13.
People, May 24, 1999, p. 41.
Philadelphia Tribune, May 30, 1997, p. PG.
Toronto Sun, May 9, 1999, p. S13; May 21, 1999, p. 77.

Online

Eric Benét—The Official Site, http://www.ericbenet.com (August 24, 1999).
iMusic Urban Showcase, http://www.imusic.com (August 24, 1999).
Launch: Discover New Music, http://www.launch.com (August 24, 1999).
RollingStone.com, http://www.rollingstone.com (August 4, 1999).
Warner Brothers Records, http://www.wbr.com (August 24, 1999).

—*Laura Hightower*

The Beta Band

Hip-hop group

The British quartet known as the Beta Band quickly earned the reputation as one of the hottest new acts in music after the release of their first EP, 1997's *Champion Versions.* Their unique sound, which defies classification, combines an array of musical styles, from hip-hop, rap, and soul to psychedelic rock, pop, punk, and folk. Although critics often compared the Beta Band's music to that of American pop star Beck, they also noted a distinct, original quality about their work. For example, David Daley of *Magnet* magazine noted, "While they share a basic indie-rock sensibility with musical deconstructivists like Beck—embracing skewed melodies, tape loops, hip-hop beats and garage-sale electronica—everything the Betas record manages to sound radically different." After the Beta Band's first release, they produced two more EPs in 1998, which were later combined into a single album, followed by the group's first full-length album in 1999. Like the first EP, their subsequent recordings only added more fuel to their rising popularity. Even multi-platinum selling bands like the Verve and Oasis looked to the Beta Band as one of their favorite groups, and the Beastie Boys personally requested the Betas to DJ an after show party in England. In addition, the gritty-voiced jazz singer from New Orleans, Dr. John, called on two of the foursome to contribute to his album *Anutha Zone.*

While most newcomers only dream of the hype, critical attention, and loyal flock of disciples collected by the band in just two short years, the Betas insisted that their music, not the media game, remained the sole purpose of the band. Nonetheless, the young Brits were sure to draw attention to themselves, if not for their rhythms punctuated by bongos, pots and pans, a brass car horn, "whistles, bells, cheers, trotting horses and sounds not unlike a cuckoo clock," commented Neil Strauss of *The Times* (London), then for their wildly entertaining live shows. During a typical performance, complete with their homemade short films, poetry readings, potted plants, and festive costumes amid skillful gospel piano and rock guitar melodies, the Beta Band switches instruments and swaps roles while creating tunes which they call dance music. "We're always playing things we don't know how to play," drummer Richard Greentree told Daley. "We just want to get a noise out of it and see what it sounds like. The thing is, you can get soul across in a song if you mean it, even if you're not able to play the instrument."

The foursome, made up of Steve Mason (a former automobile mechanic and guitarist, John McLean (a former art student and DJ), Robin Jones (a former art student and drummer), and Richard Greentree (a former carpenter and bassist from the coastal town of)—all except Greentree are from Edinburgh, Scotland, Greentree is from Portsmouth, England— decided to create the Beta Band in 1996 while sharing a cramped flat together in London. Although they owned few instruments to work with, primarily an old acoustic guitar and some pans, as well as a massive record between them, the group managed to use these sparse belongings to compose songs for their first EP, *Champion Versions,* which included the stand-out opening track "Dry the Rain." To their surprise, the record, then available on vinyl only, received radio air play, and the Beta Band's alluring music immediately caught the attention of listeners and critics.

However, Mason, McLean, Jones, and Greentree, taken aback by the sudden recognition, seemedunsure about diving into the pop scene right away, claiming that they "weren't really a band," as quoted by Ben Thompson in *Independent,* and repeatedly dodging reporters for interviews. Jones remarked to Matthias Clamer of *Spin* magazine, "We didn't fancy being in a band and we didn't want to play live. It just kind of crept up on us." For about one year after their 1997 release, they played just three London shows and two low-profile tours around Great Britain. Then, rather than meeting the expectations of fans and the press by finally recording a full-length album, the Betas, almost in defiance, instead opted to release two more EPs, *The Patty Patty Sound* and *Los Amigos Del Beta Bandidos,* both in 1998. Like the Beta Band's first release, the subsequent recordings of

For the Record . . .

Members include **Richard Greentree** (born in Portsmouth, England, former carpenter), bass, percussion; **Robin Jones** (born in Edinburgh, Scotland, former art student), drums, percussion; **Stephen Mason** (born in Edinburgh, Scotland, former automobile mechanic), vocals, guitar, percussion; **John McLean** (born in Edinburgh, Scotland, former art student), decks, samples, percussion.

Group formed in 1996 in London, England; released first EP, *Champion Versions,* Regal, 1997; released EPs, *The Patty Patty Sound* and *Los Amigos Del Beta Bandidos,* Regal, 1998; combined EPs into a single album, *The Three E.P.'s,* and released debut full-length album, *The Beta Band,* both on Astralwerks, 1999.

Addresses: *Home*—London, England. *Record company*—Astralwerks, 104 W. 29th St., Flr. 4, New York City, NY 10001. *Website*—http://www.astralwerks.com. Official Beta Band website: http://www.compsoc.man.ac.uk/~jimhobbs/betaband/main.htm.

long, intricate songs earned critical praise as well. The track "Inner Meet Me," for example, from *The Patty Patty Sound,* "is a joyous whirl with trippy synth effects, a funky scratch beat and a good-time energy about it." Likewise, "Push It Out," a song from *Los Amigos Del Beta Bandidos,* "is weird and otherworldly, a Bernie Worrell-ish deep groove," wrote Colin Berry in *Magnet.*

By this time, record buyers in Britain and even in the United States were scrambling to pick up copies of the three EPs, driving retail prices to well over fifty dollars for each record. Therefore, in order to remedy the inflated costs, Regal Recordings and the Astralwerks label (who distributes the Beta Band for the American market) combined the three EPs into one album in 1999, appropriately titled *The Three E.P.'s,* which highlighted the numerous styles the Beta Band had assimilated into a cohesive body of work. Still, despite the enthusiasm surrounding the release, the band continued to ignore the media and industry spectacle. As McLean later explained to Daley, "We just don't care about image or fashion. We're tired of hype and trendiness. You look around at the other bands getting the same hype, listen to their music and it sounds awful. It's all just nonsense." Eventually, though, the Beta Band started to lose the race in trying to distance themselves from the mounting pressure and hype. Thus, the Betas gave way in 1999 when their record company pleaded with them to begin work on an album. However, in order to thwart the music press, they pretended as if they composing songs for another series of EPs. The journey began when the foursome set off for a remote location in the northwest corner of Scotland near the ocean. They camped in a small hut that belonged to McLean's grandfather and packed the tiny cabin with their equipment and instruments, leaving them not even room enough for a place to sleep. Just six day later, the Beta Band emerged from their retreat with several hours worth of music and headed back to England to record four sets of songs in four different studios. "We tried to make it easy on ourselves. And there's only so much time you can spend in one place. So we treated (all the sessions) as separate projects," Greentree told Daley.

The end result, 1999's *The Beta Band,* again proved an instant success, although McLean admitted to *Music Week* that "Because of the time limit, we didn't really have the opportunity to rip tracks apart as we'd like to have done." Nevertheless, he continued, "The finished album sounds pretty diverse because we have so many ideas. If we share anything it's eclecticism but we converge on certain things. Steve Mason, our guitarist, is the man with the reggae influences, I'm more from a hip-hop background." Critics, too, seemed to agree with McLean's assessment. "The Beta males layer warped voices, pastoral guitars and random sound effects over slow-motion loops to evoke a chance meeting between King Crimson circa 1969 and HappyMondays 1989," concluded Rob Sheffield in *Rolling Stone.* "Of course, it's not all gold, but the funniest tunes will give you fits—try 'The Cow's Wrong,' which features singer Stephen Mason intoning bovine poetry until the drum machine's batteries wear down."

With no plans of slowing down, the three Scotsmen and lone Englishman, somewhat more at ease with their popularity, planned a more extensive club tour in support of *The Beta Band.* "The live side of things is also an important part of the puzzle," McLean assured *Music Week.* "People will see the progress we've made." Therefore, during the summer of 1999, the Beta Band made their first trip to New York City and kicked off their stay in the United States at the trendy Joe's Pub, a venue frequented by celebrity patrons such as magician David Blaine and actor Leonardo Dicaprio, in the East Village. But the laid back Betas refused to change their usual show for the hip New York crowd. Instead, as Daley described the scene, "they're simply slapping down hip-hop records as they feel like it. There's silence. There's confusion. There's chaos."

Furthermore, the quartet, after gaining more studio knowledge through work on *The Beta Band,* intended to use technology more with future projects. "Hopefully, we've stumbled along a way of recording that will help us move away from guitars. The sound changes so much because we're still learning all the things you can do in a studio. The house engineers always tell us, 'You can't do it that way.' Well, sure you can. We're just doing things most people don't even bother to try," Greentree said to Daley.

The always inventive Beta Band pursued other creative avenues, in addition to their own special concoction of British pop. They published a pamphlet of original artwork called *The Flower Press,* and Mason also released a solo project in 1999 entitled *King Biscuit Time Sings Nelly Foggit's Blues in "Me and the Pharaohs,"* a record full of "Chipmunk-style" vocals. Although some critics described the group as obscure, purposefully weird, or mysterious, the Beta Band claimed that their projects simply reflect who they are. As Jones explained to Clamer, "Folks thought *The Flower Press* was mysterious. To us it was a perfectly normal thing to do."

Selected discography

Champion Versions (EP), Regal, 1997.
Los Amigos Del Beta Bandidos (EP), Regal, 1998.
The Patty Patty Sound (EP), Regal, 1998.
The Beta Band, Astralwerks, 1999.
The Three E.P.'s, Astralwerks, 1999.

Sources

Calgary Sun, July 4, 1999, p 38.
Entertainment Weekly, January 22, 1999, p.100.
Independent, September 18, 1998, p. 13; October 2, 1998, p. 15.
Independent on Sunday, June 20, 1999, p. 5.
Indieworld, December 9, 1997.
Magnet, April/May 1999, pp. 63-64; June/July 1999, pp. 60-61, 92.
Rolling Stone, July 8-22, 1999.
Select, September 1998.
Spin, June 1999.
The Times (London), July 9, 1999.

—*Laura Hightower*

Blink 182

Punk band

David Atlas. Reproduced by permission. ©

Blink 182, a pop-punk group native to the San Diego, California, area, found an audience first with the extreme sport crowd and the suburban youth of the United States and Australia, then went on to claim a worldwide, mainstream following with the 1999 album *Enema of the State.* Guitarist and singer Tom Delonge, bass guitarist Mark Hoppus, and drummer Travis Barker (who replaced Scott Raynor on drums around 1997), all avid skaters and snowboarders, play Southern California punk rock, a form whose roots trace back to 1960s surfer music. The same style influenced such bands as the Descendents, from the Los Angeles punk explosion of the 1980s, and Pennywise, another 1990s Southern California band who played warp-speed punk music to intelligent and positive-thinking lyrics.

However, Blink 182 took a departure from other punk bands, primarily political-minded acts like Rancid or Green Day. And instead of singing about social problems or rebellion, Blink 182 spoke of the everyday life of adolescents and performing lewd acts. "We're one of the few bands that encompass a full lifestyle," Delonge told Michael Mehle of the *Denver Rocky Mountain News.* "A band like Black Crowes, they write a bunch of songs about nothing, and who really cares? We bring along a whole Southern California lifestyle, about running around naked and having fun. But we take our music seriously, and we have a lot of thoughts about relationships and what not. It takes an educated listener to know that we're not just singing about (flatulence) and masturbation. At least not all of the time."

Blink 182 started to take shape in 1991 when Hoppus's sister introduced her brother to Delonge, who at the time worked loading and delivering concrete bags but also possessed a knack for writing "faulty songs about zits and girls not liking me," he recalled to Jeffrey Rotter in *Spin* magazine. The two quickly became friends, and later asked Raynor to play drums with them in a band. By 1993, they officially named Blink 182 and built a reputation that surrounded their naughty stage shows. The group's performances, held in clubs in and around San Diego, often included wet t-shirt and wet-pants contests.

However, the three men also gained attention for their clean-cut, all-American looks and for playing upbeat punk music. After releasing a cassette-only collection of songs on the independent Kung Fu label, they received and accepted a contract offer from Cargo Music. In 1995, Blink 182 released their first full-length album entitled *Cheshire Cat* on the Grilled Cheese label, a division of Cargo. *Map of the Universe,* released on Lime/Parloplan, followed later that year, and in 1996 the band signed a joint venture record deal with Cargo Music and MCARecords.

For the Record . . .

Members included **Travis Barker** (born Travis Landon Barker on November 14, 1975; joined band c. 1997; former drummer and percussionist for The Aquabats), drums; **Tom Delonge** (born Thomas Delonge on December 13, 1975,), vocals, guitar; **Mark Hoppus** (born Markus Allen Hoppus on March 15, 1972, in Ridgecrest, CA), vocals, bass; **Scott Raynor** (left band c. 1997), drums.

Formed group 1993; released debut album *Cheshire Cat*, Grilled Cheese/Cargo, 1995; joined the Vans Warped Tour for the first time, 1995; released platinum-selling album *Dude Ranch,* Cargo/MCA, 1997; released *Enema of the State,* MCA, 1999; *Enema of the State* entered the *Billboard* album chart at number nine, 1999.

Addresses: *Home*—Blink 182, P.O. Box 500901, San Diego, CA 92150-0901. *Record company*—MCA, 70 Universal City Plz., Universal City, CA 91609; (818) 777-4000; fax (818) 777-1407. *Website*—Blink 182 Official Web Site, http://www.blink182.com.

Also that year and again in 1997-99, Blink 182 joined the Vans Warped Tour, a concert series formed in 1995 featuring bands playing a range of music from metal and punk to progressive hip-hop and swing. Considered a catalyst for propelling bands to greater fame, the Warped Tour boasted future well-known outfits such as No Doubt, Sublime, Limp Bizkit, and the Mighty Mighty Bosstones. In addition to music, other events at the concert events included skateboarding, BMX bike racing contests, and snowboarders. Introducing the extreme sport lifestyle and music to countries abroad as well, the tour regularly traveled to Europe, Asia, and Australia.

During this time, Blink 182 also toured the United States extensively and made two trips to Australia, where the group's live acts became especially popular. The band's popularity soared, though, with the release of 1997's *Dude Ranch,* which eventually went platinum in both the United States and Australia and earned gold status in Canada. Mostly appealing to listeners under 20, as well as to those who enjoyed skating and snowboarding, the catchy collection of songs included Blink 182'a first *Billboard* chart single "Dammit (Growing Up)." The adolescent, whining hit examined the typical jitters and worries of suburban, middle-class teenage life.

Beginning in the summer of 1997 and lasting through late December of 1998, the group toured non-stop to support *Dude Ranch.* Within this time, Blink 182 lost Raynor, who left the band on good terms to pursue other interests; Barker stepped in as his replacement. After touring, the band returned to San Diego to begin work on their next album at Signature Sound studios in January of 1999. Working with a new producer, Jerry Finn, who also produced albums with Green Day, Rancid, and Pennywise, Blink 182 completed the record within two months.

In the spring of 1999, Blink 182 found mainstream success with the release of *Enema of the State,* which debuted on the *Billboard* album charts at number nine. Although the band continued to please their adolescent and high school fans with singles like "What's My Age Again?," "Going Away to College," and "All the Small Things," as well as by featuring an adult film star on the album's cover, they also explored a greater musical and lyrical depth with tracks such as "Adam's Song," which examined the suicidal state of the world. However, keeping true to Blink 182 form, the music video for "What's My Age Again?" followed the band running naked through the streets of San Diego, while the band chose to spoof the Backstreet Boys in making the video for "All the Small Things." That summer, the band completed a headlining North American Tour, made a cameo appearance in the film *American Pie,* and joined the Warped Tour for show in North America and Europe. In addition, Hoppus and Delonge were asked to record Jan and Dean's (a 1960s surfer pop group) "Dead Man's Curve" for the CBS miniseries *The History of Rock 'n' Roll.*

Despite the record's popular success, their offers for media tie-ins, and the band's attempts to add more thoughtful lyrics to some of their songs, Blink 182 would not escape without facing some criticism, most of which centered upon the group's stage show antics. As Rotter explained, "Blink's leering, puerile patter would've been pretty common fare at a Motley Crüe show... but punks aren't to say 'Show us your tits!' and get such a warm response." Even though Delonge insisted that his group was simply "keeping it real" and acting "just like those kids out there," the more righteous punk bands and outspoken female punkers refused to see Delonge's logic. Both believe the sexism displayed by Blink 182 and other such groups, especially those who played on the Warped Tour of 1999, give punk music a bad name. Jessica Hopper, a publicity representative for several punk acts and editor of *Hit It or Quit It,* expressed her concern for the damage done to the punk scene in general. "Every time Blink is called a punk band, or even a pop-punk band," she said to Rotter, "we all get associated with that—we all get painted with that big, gross brush."

Moreover, Tristin Laughter of Lookout! Records, former home of Green Day, wrote in a 1999 *Punk Planet* (an influential music magazine) article, as quoted by Rotter "The treatment of women that [a female fan] is seeing reinforces her own sense that she exists to amuse and be exploited... boys who go see the punk bands on the Warped Tour may be inspired to start their own punk bands. Girls may be inspired to think they could actually be pretty enough to be cheered on when they remove their shirts." Likewise, Billy Spunke of the punk band the Blue Meanies told Rotter, "I think they [Blink 182] are just trying to get in the mindset of a teenager, which means a lot of curiosity about sex. But there are issues of responsibility that go with that."

Nonetheless, Blink 182 seemed unscathed by their critics as the band continued to gain even more fans. Besides music, the trio enjoys skateboarding and snowboarding when they find time, as well as creating and launching a new website. The site, which sells skate products over the internet, eventually grew into an enterprise involving 40 different merchandising companies.

Selected discography

Cheshire Cat, Grilled Cheese/Cargo, 1995.
Dude Ranch, Cargo/MCA, 1997.
Enema of the State, MCA, 1999.

Sources

Books

Graff, Gary and Daniel Durchholz, editors, *musicHound Rock: The Essential Album Guide,* 1999.

Periodicals

Business Wire, October 19, 1997.
Denver Rocky Mountain News, July 9, 1999, p. 15D.
Newsday, July 15, 1999, p. C01.
Rolling Stone, July 8-22, 1999, pp. 149-150; September 16, 1999, p. 46.
Spin, November 1999, pp. 116-118.
Washington Post, July 21, 1999, p. C05.

Online

Blink 182 Official Website, http://www.blink182.com, (September 29, 1999).
"Blink 182" (published in *Heckler Magazine,* 1997), http://www.bayinsider.com/partners/heckler/old_heckler/4.6/blink1
82.html, (September 29, 1999).
RollingStone.com, http://www.rollingstone.tunes.com, (September 30, 1999).

—Laura Hightower

Blondie

Rock band

One of the most successful American groups to emerge as part of the late 1970s New Wave sound, Blondie formed in the midst of New York City's legendary punk scene. They rose to stardom, though, not with the hard and loud sound of such New York punk legends as the Ramones, but by expressing the attitude behind that sound through a wide variety of pop music styles. Lead singer Deborah Harry embodied that attitude in her performances, which rock critic Steve Huey of the *All Music Guide* described as "imitating and inverting clichés about musical styles and personae associated with women."

Their unique sound resulted in a string of albums and singles that all reached number one on the charts, starting with the disco hit "Heart of Glass" from *Parallel Lines* in 1978 and ending with the calypso-flavored "The Tide Is High" from *Autoamerican* in 1980. These years of uninterrupted success came to an end in 1982 due to illness and infighting. Even in their absence, the music of Blondie remained popular and, after sixteen years apart, most of the band members reunited to put together

David Atlas. Reproduced by permission. ©

For the Record . . .

Members include **Clem Burke** (born November 24, 1955, in New York; joined group c. 1975), drums; **Paul Carbonara** (joined group 1998), guitar; **Jimmy Destri** (born April 13, 1954), keyboards; **Leigh Foxx** (joined group 1998), bass; **Nigel Harrison** (band member 1978-82), bass; **Deborah Harry** (born July 1, c. 1945, in Miami, FL), vocals; **Frank Infante** (band member 1977-82), guitar, bass; **Billy O'Connor** (left group 1975), drums; **Fred Smith** (left group 1975), bass; **Chris Stein** (born January 5, 1950, in Brooklyn, NY), guitar, vocals; **Gary Valentine** (band member 1975-77), bass.

Group formed c. 1974, in New York City; signed with Private Stock label and released debut *Blondie,* 1976; signed to Chrysalis Records, 1977, and released *Parallel Lines,* 1978; contributed "Call Me" to *American Gigolo* soundtrack, 1980; Stein became ill and group disbanded, 1982; group reunited and released new studio album, *No Exit,* 1999.

Harry appeared in films *The Foreigner,* 1978, *Union City,* 1979, *Videodrome,* 1982, *Hairspray,* 1988, and *Copland*, 1997, in stage production *Teaneck Tanzi: The Venus Flytrap,* 1983, and in television program, *Mother Goose Rock 'n' Rhyme,* 1989; Harry released first solo album, *Koo Koo,* 1981; Stein founded Animal Records, 1982, before being stricken with *pemphigus vulgaris* (a skin disease); Destri released solo album *Heart on the Wall,* 1982; Harry and Stein co-authored book *Making Tracks: The Rise of Blondie,* 1982; Stein wrote music for cable television program *Fifteen Minutes* and material for Harry's 1986 album, *Rockbird;* Harry dueted with Iggy Pop on *Red Hot + Blue* anthology, 1990; Burke played drums with Eurythmics, Dramarama, and others; Harry was sued for song-publishing income by former manager Peter Leeds, 1993; Harry sang with the Jazz Passengers, 1998.

Awards: Platinum awards for albums *Parallel Lines,* 1979, *Eat to the Beat,* 1980, and *Autoamerican,* 1981, and for single "Call Me," 1980.

Addresses: *Record company*—Beyond Music, P.O. Box 18524, Beverly Hills, CA 90209. *Website*—www.blondie.net.

a new album. As if they had never gone away, Blondie had a hit album in *No Exit* and a hit single with "Maria" in 1999.

The core of the band that became Blondie first played together in The Stilettoes, which featured Harry and two other female vocalists. Guitarist Chris Stein came on board after attending one of their shows, impressed by The Stilettoes' take on the music of such 1960s girl groups as the Shangri-Las. In 1975 a series of further changes transformed the band into Blondie. Another girl group aficionado, drummer Clem Burke, joined, bringing with him his friend, bass player Gary Valentine. That same year, Jimmy Destri brought his Farfisa organ to the band. On top of the personnel changes, Harry decided the group needed a new name, and she chose one that she often heard from truck drivers who passed her in the street.

While Harry would come to be the face and voice of Blondie, Stein and Burke would come to drive the band's distinctive sound. In *Guitar Player* Michael Molenda wrote, "[T]he muted rhythm figures—typically with a hint of slapback—and moody singlenote lines of guitarist Chris Stein broadcast a Blondie song even before Harry enters the mix." Although Stein jokingly told Molenda that he had "adapted a certain way of playing to Clem's crappy timing," many credited Burke's drums as a driving force for the band. In describing Blondie's songs, critic Greg Kot wrote in *Rolling Stone* that "Burke made them explode."

Lived and Worked Together

The distinctive Blondie sound didn't develop overnight. In their early years, the whole group roomed together in the same loft near legendary punk club CBGB, where New York's punk scene was coming to life. They honed their mix of innocent pre-punk pop styles with songs about the tough life of the city streets, which Harry sang with an ironic glamour that drew on her past as a Playboy Bunny. In 1976, Blondie cut their first single, "X Offender," toning down the titlefrom "Sex Offender" out of fear of controversy. They then issued their debut album, *Blondie*, on the Private Stock label. Their 1977 follow-up, *Plastic Letters,* gave the band their first taste of success, spawning two Top Ten singles in Great Britain. In spite of the hits in England, this was a tumultuous time for the band. One of the hits, "Denis," was a cover of the 1963 song "Denise," by Randy and the Rainbows. While such a song fit nicely with the interests of Harry, Stein, and Burke, Valentine found it too commercial and refused to play it. He left the band, but not before writing the other British hit on the album, "(I'm Always Touched by Your) Presence, Dear."

The year 1978 proved to be a milestone, as personnel changes and a new label brought incredible commercial success in the U.S. Frank Infante had joined the band to play bass when Valentine left, but now he moved to guitar as Nigel Harrison came aboard as the bassist. This version of Blondie signed with a larger label, Chrysalis, and began recording their next album with noted New Wave producer Mike Chapman. The resulting album, *Parallel Lines,* propelled the band into the limelight, where they would remain for the next three years. The album also showed the group's adeptness with diverse styles, with both the disco "Heart of Glass" and the punkish "One Way or Another" climbing to number one on the charts.

Blondie continued to gain momentum when their 1979 album *Eat to the Beat* yielded the hit "Dreaming." Their next single proved to be one of their biggest hits, but it came from a movie soundtrack instead of one of their albums. Collaborating with German disco producer Giorgio Moroder, Blondie had a smash in 1980 with "Call Me," from the *American Gigolo* soundtrack. Then they went back to the studio to record another album. The result, *Autoamerican,* repeated their success while again highlighting their innovative use of widely different musical styles. "Rapture" was yet another number-one hit, a rap-tinged song at a time before rap music had come to the attention of most of the popular music world. Not to be tied to one kind of beat, they also released the calypso-influenced hit "The Tide Is High" from the same album.

Illness and Fighting Took Center Stage

Blondie had reached their peak, and now internal tensions threatened to pull them down. For one thing, they had to fight the perception that Blondie was Harry's stage name and that she was the whole act. Publicists concocted a promotional campaign featuring the slogan "Blondie Is a Group" in an attempt to educate the public. Although officially still a group, by 1981 individual band members had started working on projects outside Blondie. That year Harry released her first solo album, *Koo Koo,* which went gold. Around this same time, Stein began to struggle with a rare and debilitating genetic illness, *pemphigus vulgaris.* Harry, Stein's partner offstage as well as on, devoted time to caring for him. Amidst all this turmoil, Blondie's 1982 album *The Hunter* failed to yield the commercial or critical success of their earlier work. It did, however, yield a moderately successful single, "Island of Lost Souls." A tour in support of the album proved extremely difficult for Stein and, in October of 1982, the band broke up.

Yet Blondie maintained a presence even in the absence of new material. Their songs remained popular in dance clubs and appeared on several compilations targeted at that audience, overshadowing Harry's solo albums. While Harry was recording on her own and acting inmovies, most notably *Hairspray* in 1988, the rest of the band worked farther away from the limelight, variously trying their hands at record production and playing with other bands. But even after a decade, Blondie would not go away. Their music gained exposure to whole new audiences in the 1990s, with covers of "One Way or Another" appearing on the soundtracks of *The Rugrats Movie* and *Sabrina: The Teenage Witch* television show. Now the children of Blondie's original fans experienced the music.

Interest in Blondie would not fade. In 1997 the album *Essential Blondie: Picture This Live* was released, featuring stage performances from 1978 and 1980. This occasion gave critics the opportunity to assess the band's work and legacy. Writing in the *Village Voice,* Robert Christgau called the album a "memento mori for fans who loved them to the bone and forensic evidence against fools who mistook their flesh for plastic." Still, the album had a limited-edition release, targeted at hardcore Blondie fans wishing to remember the past instead of at potential new audiences.

Reunited and Rejuvenated

But it turned out that Blondie wasn't done yet. Upon being approached to record two new songs to add to a greatest hits collection, the band that hadn't performed together in sixteen years decided to put out an album of all-new material. The result was the 1999 release *No Exit,* which found surprising commercial and critical success for an album by a band reuniting after nearly twenty years. This version of the group brought Harry, Stein, Burke, and Destri back together. Valentine toyed with the idea of rejoining, but decided against doing so. Infante and Harrison never even received an invitation, so they sued over Blondie's recording and performing without them. In the meantime, guitarist Paul Carbonara and bassist Leigh Foxx joined the lineup. The album reunited more than just the band members; two producers from Blondie's past joined in the project. Mike Chapman helped them record demos for the album, and then the group's first producer, Craig Leon, came in to put together the final product.

No Exit received a warm reception from both the public and critics. The album debuted at number 18 on the Top 200 chart and maintained strong sales. Meanwhile, reviewers expressed surprise at the quality of new material from a band that hadn't recorded together in almost twenty years, applauding them for reuniting for the sake of music, not money. Christgau wrote, "[H]ere the commitment is as palpable as such ironic formalists can make it." Harry told Lyndsey Parker of *Launch,* "We're trying to see the album as a continuation—trying to pick up where we left off. I certainly didn't want to hybridize the old stuff and just do a rehash; I wanted to integrate it with a little bit of modernity." Indeed, the collaboration with rapper Coolio on the title track showed that the group still had the same willingness to experiment with new styles, keeping Blondie's sound as fresh as ever in spite of their long separation.

Selected discography

On Chrysalis, except where noted

Blondie, Private Stock, 1976, reissued, Chrysalis, 1977.
Plastic Letters, Private Stock, 1977, reissued, Chrysalis, 1977.
Parallel Lines (includes "Heart of Glass" and "One Way or Another"), 1978.
Eat to the Beat (includes "Dreaming"), 1979.
Autoamerican (includes "Rapture" and "The Tide Is High"), 1980.
(Contributors) *American Gigolo* (film soundtrack; includes "Call Me"), 1980.
The Best of Blondie, 1981.
The Hunter (includes "Island of Lost Souls"), 1982.
Once More into the Bleach, 1988.
The Complete Picture: The Very Best of Deborah Harry and Blondie, 1991.
Blonde & Beyond, 1993.
The Ultimate Collection, 1994.
Atomic (12-inch dance remix), 1995.
Remixed, Remade and Remodeled (also known as Remix Project), 1995.
Essential Blondie: Picture This Live, Capitol, 1997.
No Exit (includes "Maria"), Beyond, 1999.

Solo recordings by Deborah Harry

Koo Koo, 1981.
Rockbird (includes "French Kissin' in the USA"), Geffen, 1986.
Def, Dumb and Blonde, Geffen, 1989.
(With Iggy Pop) "Well Did You Evah," *Red, Hot + Blue,* Chrysalis, 1990.
Debravation, Sire/Reprise, 1993.

Solo recordings by Jimmy Destri

Heart on the Wall, 1982.

Videos

Best of Blondie: The Videos, Pacific Arts, 1981.
Live in Concert (also known as *Blondie: Live*), MCA, 1987.

Sources

Periodicals

Guitar Player, April 1999, pp. 58-64.
Melody Maker, March 9, 1991; July 10, 1993.
New York Times, December 22, 1978.
Rolling Stone, April 15, 1993; October 14, 1993; January 9, 1999; February 9, 1999; April 12, 1999.
Village Voice, January 27, 1998, p. 83; March 23, 1999, p. 120.

Online

"Blondie," *All Music Guide*, http://www.allmusic.com (June 18, 1999).
"Blondie: Still Golden," *Launch,* http://www.launch.com (June 18, 1999).

—Lloyd Hemingway

Caspar Brötzmann

Guitar

From his first recording, *The Tribe,* it was clear that Caspar Brötzmann was something more than a mere guitarist, he was a guerilla, prepared to use any means necessary to free his instrument for unknown purposes. Listening to the awesome wall of guitar sound he creates, turbulent forces and frightening beings emerge and struggle to free themselves, to find a shape. All in all, Brötzmann is probably the greatest unknown guitarist in the world—and maybe the greatest known one too. As Neil Kukarni wrote in *Melody Maker,* "Let's see Brötzmann is God scrawled on a few walls."

The intensity, and volume, of Caspar Brötzmann's music may be partially genetic—his father Peter Brötzmann is one of the world's leading free jazz players and his explosive saxophone is the reed equivalent of Caspar's guitar. Caspar was weaned on the music of his father. As a child, his mother frequently took him and his sister to see his dad's shows. Over 30 years later, it was the atmosphere rather than the music that remained clearest in his memory. And he says the constant presence of musicians of various cultures in their house in Wuppertal, Germany had the most lasting effect: "Growing up, from the time I was three or so, there were always black people sitting in the kitchen, talking in French, or English, or Dutch. That helped make my understanding of the world a lot more open. I learned to respect other people."

When Caspar was 13, he heard Led Zeppelin's single, "Communication Breakdown." It was his first guitar epiphany. He was captivated by the sound an electric guitar could produce. It wasn't long before he got his first instrument, an acoustic guitar. But, eventually, he began hanging out at the *Jugendclub* in town, a local activities center for teenagers, that had electric instruments. He started jamming with other kids, and by the time he was 16, he had formed his first band, the Caspar Brötzmann Band. On his 18 birthday, when he was legally of age to enter a contract, he signed the papers for the bank loan, went down to a local music store and bought his first electric guitar. That guitar, a beautiful Fender Stratocaster, was his first official act as an adult. A clerk at the store gave Brötzmann the only guitar instruction he ever had—a quick tour of the controls, strings, body, electronics and neck of his new instrument. Otherwise he is completely self-taught. "I can't even read music," he said, "[but] it's not important. I've always played with my ears and my feelings."

By the late 1970s, Brötzmann had acquired a reputation as one of the hot, up and coming guitarists in Wuppertal. Punk was the rage throughout Europe at the time and when he was 18 he was asked to join a punk band there, *Die Alliierten.* Punk music wasn't exactly what Brötzmann was looking for, but he was proud that he was able to persuade the band to perform political songs, "about the war, about skins and punks living together like human beings." *Die Alliierten* played about thirty shows and cut a seven-inch single entitled "Die Alliierten," but after a year Brötzmann was ready for something else.

He realized clearly for the first time, on the evening of his second guitar epiphany, that he could find his own musical voice. "I was alone in the band's rehearsal room, playing by myself. Suddenly, I said to myself,' That's it, Caspar!' I knew I had to find my own freedom in music, to make my own name, to work on expressing my own emotions. I really remember that night!" As he began to find his own sound he knew next to nothing about Jimi Hendrix. Ironically, Hendrix is the guitarist with whom he would most often be compared. When he listened to him for the first time—the *Isle of Wight* concert recording given to him by his mother—he didn't especially like the music!

In 1981, when he was 20, he moved to West Berlin. The city had numerous advantages for a young musician: for one thing, while Brötzmann had exhausted the possibilities Wuppertal offered, Berlin had a thriving underground music scene. Berlin was full of musicians, new wave was taking off, Einstürzenden Neubauten were becoming popular, and Nick Cave was starting to spend time in

For the Record . . .

Born October 13,1962, in Wuppertal, Federal Republic of Germany.

Acquired first guitar, age 13, 1975; formed Caspar Brötzmann Band 1978; took out loan to purchase first electric guitar, October 13, 1980; joined Die Alliierten, c. 1980; moved to West Berlin and formed Caspar Brötzmann and the Bunkers, 1981; formed Massaker, 1986; released *The Tribe*, ZENSOR Musikproduktion, 1987; released*Black Axis*, ZENSOR Musikproduktion, 1989; signed with Rough Trade, 1991; released *Home*, 1994; toured USA with Massaker, 1994-96; released *Mute Massaker*, 1999.

Addresses: *Home*—Berlin, Germany; *Record company*—Zomba Records, Eicklerstrasse 25, 44651 Herne, Germany.

the city. Another incentive was that the West German military could not draft a young man living in West Berlin. But Brötzmann had another reason: he was in love and his girlfriend was living in Berlin. Within a year he had formed another band, Caspar Brötzmann and the Bonkers. He made his first European tour with the band, a guitar-bass-drum trio and won a Berlin rock award. Soon afterward, the band broke up. "The bass player and drummer were interested in a funky sound," Brötzmann recalled. "I wanted something else."

For a while he played solo gigs. For Brötzmann, playing solo means playing solo—just him and his guitar on stage, with no back-up at all. In 1986 he formed Massaker, another stripped-down power trio, anchored by Eduardo Delgado Lopez and Frankie Neumeier. "Massaker was the first *real* band of my own. I came into my own with that band, " he said, "everything up till then was just development." The band recorded its first album for Zensor in 1987, *The Tribe.* It was a powerful blend of punk and Berlin New Wave, heavy metal, and the trademark style Brötzmann was still perfecting—the wall of guitar sound that mocked the boundary between musical tones and white noise. The next album, 1989's *Black Axis*, was the first pure Caspar Brötzmann record. All the vestiges of punk and heavy metal are gone and recognizable riffs and normal rock chords are nonexistent. Instead his droning open strings and fierce hammers and slides up and down the neck created layer upon layer of guitar sound—or so it seemed, because everything on Massaker albums was played inreal time.

Audiences at their concerts heard all the pyrotechnics of Massaker's recordings, charged with Brötzmann's energy and sheer volume. Caspar continued to play solo in Massaker's early days. Concerts around the time of *Black Axis*'s release would open with the mounting sound of Brötzmann's guitar in the darkened hall followed by his appearance, unlit at the side of the stage. The guitar rose, screamed over the audience, blanketed it, two, five, ten minutes, before the drone and thump of Massaker sounded and the curtain finally rose on Delgado Lopez and Neumeier. Brötzmann's solo sound was so overwhelming you were left wondering why he even needed a band.

Brötzmann signed with Rough Trade in 1991. *Black Axis* was followed by *Der Abend der schwartzen Folklore* and *Koksofen* in 1993. Preparing for its first tour of the United States, Massaker went into the studio in March of 1994 and cut *Home*, a collection of five pieces that originally appeared on *The Tribe* and *Black Axis,* records that were never released in America. The new recordings benefitted from greatly improved studio quality as well as six years of playing together. *Home* presented a mature, confident Brötzmann. He had found the freedom he first glimpsed in *Die Alliierten*'s practice room fifteen years earlier. Massaker spent most of the next two and a half years touring the United States, visiting every state along the way except Alaska, Hawaii, and Florida, playing all of the big cities a couple times. "We made five tours, four of them by car. It was difficult. The toughest trip was driving from New York City all the way to Austin, Texas and going straight on stage as soon as we arrived."

Brötzmann didn't limit himself to playing with Massaker. He has performed with a number of artists from various genres. Soon after he formed Massaker he toured with Henry Rollins and Lydia Lunch on the *Spoken Word* Tour in Europe. He has recorded with his father Peter Brötzmann, once as a duo on *Vodka King*, and once as part of the März Combo. He has performed with Pigface, Les Tambours de Bronx, and drummer/percussionist Hamid Drake. He accompanied vocalist Diamanda Galas on a piece on F.M. Einheit's *Stein*, and recorded *Zulutime* with Page Hamilton after Massaker toured with Hamilton 's band Helmet. He has worked most frequently with Einheit of Einstürzende Neubauten, including the CD *Merry Christmas.*

In July of 1999, Brötzmann released a CD, *Mute Massaker*, that shows the guitarist exploring a new sound. With drummer Robert Dämmig and bassist Ottmar Seum—a member of The Bunkers fifteen years earlier—backing him up, Brötzmann sounds more like Hendrix than ever before. The rough-hewn jackhammer sculpting is toned down in favor of long-lined, liquid improvisations that Hendrix might have used in one of his blues explorations. Nonetheless itis neither blues nor jazz nor even rock—none of the familiar structures are there—it is just Brötzmann, creating his own structures. He describes the CD as "a guitar record." Not that he means his older records weren't, just that on *Mute Massaker* he does not sing at all. His concentration on playing guitar could lead him back to occasionally playing solo again—something he gave up in the mid-nineties.

Ideas for new projects abounded—Brötzmann says he had enough material leftover from *Mute Massaker* for three follow up CDs. The only thing holding him back was money. The market for challenging music is a small one; he couldn't even find a record company willing to release *Mute Massaker* in thc United States. You get the feeling though that for Brötzmann the most important thing is that he's able to play. "I've been paying guitar 23 years now and it's like a little baby," he said. "I really care for my work. Sometimes I feel like I could be a good painter, but I'm not! So I paint with music. It's a kind of love situation—to find a way to talk to the people."

Selected discography

The Tribe, Zensor Musikproduktion, 1987.
Black Axis, Zensor Musikproduktion, 1989.
(with Peter Brötzmann) *Last Home,* Deutsche Pathological, 1990.
Der Abend der schwartzen Folklore, Our Choice/Rough Trade, 1992.
Koksofen, Homestead Records/Rough Trade, 1993.
(with F.M. Einheit) *Merry Christmas,* Rough Trade, 1994.
Home, thirsty ear, 1995.
(with Page Hamilton) *Zulu Time,* Atavistic, 1996.

Sources

Periodicals

Billboard, December 3, 1994.
Melody Maker, March 4, 1995; August 24, 1996.

Telephone interviews with Caspar Brötzmann, July 3 and July 12, 1999 contributed to this article.

—Gerald E. Brennan

Built to Spill

Rock band

Built to Spill, one of several projects created by musician Doug Martsch, always took pride in its reputation as one of the best kept secrets of the underground, alternative rock scene. Martsch, considered by critics as one of independent rock's most striking songwriters and guitarists, felt compelled to maintain his anonymity; a shy and humble person, he never wanted to live the life of a pop star. Reflecting on life and love with intellectual angst, Martsch's songs "are divided into sections that go beyond verse-chorus-verse form, with pop ditties that stop halfway and turn into glorious landscapes of mangled guitar strings," as stated in the *Trouser Press Guide to '90s Rock.* However, since signing with a major label, Warner Brothers, for 1997's *Perfect From Now On,* the band has progressively emerged into the mainstream. Subsequently, the group's 1999 release, *Keep It Like A Secret,* brought Martsch and his partners an even broader fan base and critical acclaim. The release also marked Built to Spill's first collaborative effort.

Previously, Martsch would rotate and replace band members and write the music and lyrics by himself, believing that such an approach would keep his songs from growing stale. But for the band's first two major label albums, Martsch kept the participating band members consistent, with plans of holding on to the lineup, guitarist Brett Nelson (of Butterfly Train) and drummer Scott Plouf (of the Spinanes), for future work. To his surprise, Martsch had found greater rewards in playing with others who also held a stake in the music. Moreover, Built to Spill had finally produced a commercially appealing, but still artistically satisfying record. "A lot of it had to do with the last record," Martsch told David Daley of *Magnet* magazine. "Just how much work it was, how I was kind of unsure about it. Basically, I just got burned out on doing things myself. Also, I realized the things I like to listen to, my favorite things, tend to be collaborative things. I just thought more interesting music could be made with other people involved in writing and stuff." Thus, with Built to Spill's new creative direction, speculators predict that the rock world will continue to hear the tedious guitar playing and unforgettable music of Martsch for some time to come.

Doug Martsch's musical career began in Boise, Idaho, with his first band, a little-known yet influential group called Treepeople. Described as "Boise's rock heroes" by the official Built to Spill website, Treepeople consisted of Martsch and friend Scott Schmaljohn (now of Stuntman), in addition to a rotating cast of bassists and drummers. In order to attract a wider audience, Martsch and Schmaljohn relocated the group to Seattle, Washington, where they released two albums, *Guilt, Regret and Embarrassment* in 1990 on Westworld Records (re-released on K Records in 1998) and *Just Kidding* on C/Z Records; two EPs, *Time Whore* in 1989 and *Something Vicious* in 1991, both on C/Z; and numerous seven-inch singles. Then, despite the band's success, Martsch decided to leave Treepeople in 1992 to pursue his own musical interests. His former partners stayed together for awhile, but without Martsch, the group split up for good in 1993.

Martsch, a native of Boise, returned to his hometown in 1993 to escape city life in Seattle and contemplate his next career move while working odd jobs, writing music, and playing musicwith friends. Soon thereafter, Martsch helped form Built to Spill and released the band's first album, 1993's *Ultimate Alternative Wavers,* which introduced the band's jam-oriented, post-punk style of pop. Although all of the songs either reached or exceeded the nine-minute mark, the *Trouser Press Guide to '90s Rock* noted that Martsch "manages to endow each jagged, twisted guitar line with the emotion of the song, whether it be anger, introspection or love." The initial Built to Spill lineup included Martsch, Raif Youtz, and Brett Netson (not the later Brett Nelson), but Martsch's band mates were at the same time members of other groups as well. Youtz, a member of Sone, and Netson of Caustic Resin performed only a couple of live shows with Martsch in support of Built to Spill's debut before the initial group disbanded.

For the Record . . .

Members include **Doug Martsch** (born in Boise, ID; girlfriend, Kanena Youtz; children: one son, Ben), guitar, vocals; **Brett Nelson** (of Butterfly Train), bass; and **Scott Plouf** (formerly of the Spinanes), drums. Former members include **Andy Cappos**, **James Dillon**, **Brett Netson** (of Caustic Resin), and **Raif Youtz** (of Halo Benders and Sone).

Martsch joined Treepeople c. 1988, left group 1992; formed Built to Spill and released first album, *Ultimate Alternative Wavers* on C/Z, 1993; toured with Lollapalooza and the Foo Fighters, signed contract with Warner Brothers Records, 1995; released major label debut *Perfect From Now On,* 1997, followed by *Keep It Like A Secret,* 1999.

Addresses: *Home*—Boise, ID. *Record company*—Warner Brothers, 3300 Warner Blvd., Burbank, CA 91505; 75 Rockefeller Plaza, New York, NY 10019. *Websites*—www.wbr.com, www.builttospill.com.

After the breakup, Martsch signed with friend and producer Chris Takino's UP Records and traveled to Seattle to record Built to Spill's next record with help from K Records proprietor Calvin Johnson. For this session, the band's lineup included the members of Farm Days, a band that Martsch, Andy Cappos, and Brett Nelson had formed during their high school days. The resulting three, two-song singles were released by Atlas/Face The Music, K, and Saturnine, and appeared again later on the album *The Normal Years.* Next came the album *There's Nothing Wrong With Love* on UP Records with help from producer Phil Elk in 1994, featuring more of Martsch's intricate guitar work. With shorter tracks, about three to four minutes each, the album centered on deconstructed pop songs about growing up. One of the songs entitled "Cleo," named after Martsch's son Benjamin Cleo, gives an account of the world from the point of view of a newborn baby, followed by songs that tell the frustration of adolescence and young adulthood.

While continuing to develop ideas for Built to Spill, Martsch found time to work with other musicians as well. Martsch and Johnson had formed a friendship while recording back in 1994 and decided to record together as the Halo Benders. Other participants in the project included Steve Fisk (who helped produce the Treepeople albums), Ralph Youtz, and Wayne Flower. The primarily "Basement Punk" album, as described by Built to Spill's website, entitled *God Don't Make No Junk,* hit stores in 1995 on the K label. Around the same time, he teamed with acid-rock band Caustic Resin to record some tracks. During his career, Martsch released two albums with Caustic Resin: *Body Love Body Hate* on C/Z Records in 1993 and *Fly Me to the Moon* on Up Records in 1995. In addition, he recorded with the group Butterfly Train for 1994's *Building Trust from Trust* and 1996's *Distorted, Retarded, Peculiar,* both for Up Records.

By now, critics and rock enthusiasts began to take notice of Built to Spill, and Martsch asked two musicians from the band Lync to join him for a tour. After appearing on second stage for Lollapalooza in the summer of 1995 and in Europe that winter as the opening act for the Foo Fighters, Built to Spill received offers from several major recording labels. Martsch, who ultimately signed a contract with Warner Brothers Records, then prepared Built to Spill for their first major release. In the meantime, Martsch released the *Built to Spill Caustic Resin* EP (1995) from a session earlier that year. The participants for this project included Martsch and James Dillon as Built to Spill, as well as Netson and Tom Romich of Caustic Resin. He also found time in 1996 to work on and release a second project by the Halo Benders entitled *Don't Tell Me Now.* Built to Spill then released *The Normal Years* in 1996, a ten-song rarities compilation featuring every band lineup between 1993 and 1995.

Finally, Built to Spill's major label debut neared completion, and on January 28, 1997, the band (now consisting of Martsch, Nelson, and Plouf) released *Perfect From Now On* for Warner Brothers, a serene, sprawling epic containing only one song shorter than five minutes. As a whole, the new songs were more melodic, yet less pop-oriented and upbeat. Critics responded with praise for the work and noted Built to Spill's resolution to continue to swim against the mainstream in spite of their major label contract. "If he [Martsch] wanted to keep Built to Spill a secret, it worked," wrote Daley, for the album sold just about 40,000 copies. Subsequently, Martsch recorded again with the Halo Benders, releasing *The Rebels Not In* in 1998 on K Records, before teaming again with Nelson and Prouf to work on Built to Spill's sophomore album.

The result of the collaborative effort between the threesome, 1999's *Keep It Like A Secret,* "is the punchy, direct and radio-ready collection that people had hoped Martsch would deliver, thus allowing the Warner Bros. machinery to turn him into a star," Daley surmised. The album's central theme comes through in the track "You Were Right," which references songs from the classic rock era. For example, Built to Spill quotes reggae legend Bob Marley in the opening verse with "You were wrong when you said everything's going to be all right," followed with lyrics by other rock idols who had the right idea, Kansas, Pink Floyd, and Bob Seger respectively. With the powerful release behind them, Built to Spill mounted a cross-country tour of the United States, playing with bands such as Sleater-Kinney and 764-HERO, as well as making an appearance on television's *Late Night with Conan O'Brien,* before taking their sound to Europe for a tour with Modest Mouse.

Martsch, who Teresa Gubbins of the *Dallas Morning News* described as "an anti-hero whose modesty and down-to-earth demeanor have an almost bewitching effect," continued to make his home in Boise with girlfriend Karena Youtz (who contributed lyrics for *Keep It Like A Secret*) and their son Ben. As of the summer of 1999, he planned to head back to the studios for another incarnation of the Halo Benders, and admirers hoped a new record from Built to Spill would soon follow.

Selected discography

Singles

"So And So So And So," Saturnine, 1994.
"Joyride," K, 1994.
"Car," Atlas/Face The Music, 1994.
"Distopian Dream Girl," Up, 1995.
"In The Morning," City Slang (U.K.), 1995.
"Untrustable," Warner Brothers, 1997.

Albums

Ultimate Alternative Wavers, C/Z, 1993.
There's Nothing Wrong With Love, Up, 1994.
(With Caustic Resin) *Built To Spill Caustic Resin* (EP), Up, 1995.
The Normal Years, K, 1996.
Perfect From Now On, Warner Brothers, 1997.
Keep It Like A Secret, Warner Brothers, 1999.

Compilations

Bite Back: Live At The Crocodile Cafe, PopLlama, 1995.
Stacked Up!, Up, 1995.
Up In Orbit!, Up, 1997.
Spunk #7, Spunk, 1998.
Yoyo A Go Go: Another Live Compilation, Yoyo, 1999.

Sources

Books

Robbins, Ira A., ed., *Trouser Press Guide to '90s Rock,* Fireside/Simon & Schuster, 1997.

Periodicals

Dallas Morning News, March 19, 1999.
Magnet, April/May, 1999; June/July, 1999.

Online

"Built To Spill. com—The Story," official website, http://www.builttospill.com (August 5, 1999).
"Built To Spill," *Launch: Discover New Music,* http://www.launch.com (August 16, 1999).
"Built To Spill," *Rolling Stone.com,* http://www.rollingstone.tunes.com (August 16, 1999).

—*Laura Hightower*

Cake

Rock band

In 1997 Cake's popularity exploded and their shows sold out across the United States with the release of *Fashion Nugget,* proving that a modern rock band who performed melancholy pop songs mixed with funk, folk, country, and a mariachi country could succeed in the music industry. Throughout the group's rise to the top since its formation in 1991, Cake experienced repeated lineup changes. Nonetheless, at moments when most bands would crumble, Cake continued to forge ahead, and the group's subsequent album, 1998's *Prolonging the Magic,* was considered by critics as their most ambitious collection of songs to date. More than just a trendy alternative rock group, Cake exhibited a uniqueness on all three of their full-length albums with a full-time trumpeter, country-inspired guitar melodies, and the poetic, eclectic, and sometimes sarcastic lyrics of lead singer and chief songwriter John McCrea. The group's songs, though they sound modern, also exhibit an older and familiar feeling and tell stories of hard luck and lost love.

McCrea, born around 1965 in Sacramento, California, spent most of the 1980s in his hometown of Sacramento,

Photograph by Tim Mosenfelder. Corbis. Reproduced by permission.

For the Record . . .

Members include **Greg Brown** (left group 1998), guitar; **Victor Damiani** (joined group 1994, left group 1997), bass; **Vince di Fiore,** trumpet; **Frank French** (left group 1994), drums; **John McCrea** (born c. 1965 in Sacramento, CA), chief songwriter, vocals, guitar; **Xan McCurdy** (joined group 1998), guitar; **Sean McFessel** (left group c. 1991), bass; **Gabe Nelson** (joined group c. 1991, left group 1994, rejoined group 1997), bass; **Todd Roper** (joined band 1994), drums.

McCrea formed Cake, 1991; released debut album *Motorcade of Generosity* on their own without a distributor, 1993; group signed with Capricorn Records, who released Cake's debut in original form, single "Rock 'n' Roll Lifestyle;" released sophomore effort, *Fashion Nugget,* which contained first hit single "The Distance," 1996; opened for Counting Crows on their East Coast Tour, 1997; released *Prolonging the Magic,* considered Cake's most ambitious album, began first European tour, 1998, followed by headlining tour of the United States, 1999.

Addresses: *Record company*—Capricorn Records, 1100 Spring St. NW, Ste. 103, Atlanta, GA 30309-3918, (404)873-3918. *Management*—Absolute Artists, San Francisco, CA (415)241-7015. *Website*—Cake (official website): http://www.cakemusic.com. Capricorn website: http://www.capri.corn.com.

where he played solo as well as with various bands. Besides rock, McCrea held an interest in other musical styles as well. In the late 1980s, McCrea moved to Los Angeles, believing that his chances of succeeding in music would improve in the larger city. Once in here, he played solo acoustic music at various coffee shops around the Los Angeles area. As a solo artist, McCrea performed many of the songs that would eventually make Cake a well-known name, such as "I Bombed Korea," "Haze of Love," "Sheep Go to Heaven," and "Jesus Wrote a Blank Check."

By 1991, McCrea realized that living in Los Angeles had done little to improve his career. Therefore, he moved back to Sacramento and formed Cake. He recruited Frank French on drums, Vince di Fiore on trumpet, Greg Brown on guitar, and Sean McFessel on bass. McFessel left the band the same year to attend college. Regarding his decision to add a trumpet player to the group, McCrea told Joe Schaeffer of the *Washington Times,* "When the band was first put together, we didn't have a trumpet for the first month. I knew we didn't want a searing, soaring, brave, white lead guitar making its way through the clouds. And I was listening to a lot of mariachi music, and it struck me that the trumpet didn't have such a stigma." Subsequently, needing a new bassist, McCrea replaced McFessel with Gabe Nelson. Two years later in 1993, Cake released their first record, a seven-inch single called "Rock 'n' Roll Lifestyle," which also included the song "Jolene" on the flip side.

After this, the group headed to the studio to work on their first album, the self-produced *Motorcade of Generosity,* an albumapplauded for its superb songwriting as well as for it's airy, low production quality. The members of Cake worked on the album in between their day jobs: driving cabs, working for courier services, and waiting tables. Determined to make a record even in the absence of record company support, Cake paid for the entire project themselves, recorded the songs by themselves, and designed all of the artwork for the album. Upon the completion of their debut, they sold *Motorcade of Generosity* on their own without distribution.

Soon, though, Cake and *Motorcade of Generosity* caught the attention of Capricorn Records, and in 1994, the group signed with the label and reissued their debut in its original form. Despite this achievement, Cake saw two more members leave the group that year; French and Nelson left the band, and drummer Todd Roper and bassist Victor Damiani joined as their replacements. The reshaped quintet started touring the United States in smaller venues, selling their own t-shirts on stage to earn extra money. In the meantime, later that year, Capricorn released the group's 1993 single "Rock 'n' Roll Lifestyle," which received air play on college and alternative radio stations across the country. In addition, McCrea co-produced a video for the song that aired sparingly on the cable channel MTV (Music Television). While the band's popularity continued to grow, Capricorn released two more singles from Cake's debut: "Ruby Sees All," followed by "Jolene."

As soon as Cake completed their first national club tour, they returned to Sacramento to work on their follow-up album. In the same Sacramento studios they used to record their debut, Cake recorded the more refined *Fashion Nugget* in late 1995 and early 1996. Later that year, Capricorn released the album, which featured the group's first hit single "The Distance." The song peaked at number three on modern rock charts, and the song's video climbed to number three on MTV as well. In December of 1996, while Cake made another tour, Capricorn released the next single from the album entitled "I Will Survive," a cover of Gloria Gaynor's self-promoting 1970s disco anthem. Instead of playing the song as a modern rock-infused disco remake, Cake opted to perform a serious, straight version that adhered to Gaynor's original spirit, with di Fiore's trumpet weaving through stringed instruments. Again, radio listeners and music video viewers reacted with enthusiasm.

As Cake's popularity continued to soar upon the release of *Fashion Nugget,* the group accepted an invitation to open for the rock band the Counting Crows on their East Coast Tour. In the spring of 1997, another popular single from the record, "Frank Sinatra," hit store shelves, and Cake saw another change in the group's lineup. Damiani said goodbye to Cake in order to pursue other interests, and the band persuaded bassist Nelson to return in his place. By this time, though, the fast pace of recording and touring caught up with McCrea, who was forced to cut the band's tour short because of extreme exhaustion. Thus, McCrea and Cake returned to Sacramento to rest before working on the next project.

Subsequently, another band member left Cake in January of 1998. This time, the group lost guitarist Brown, who formed a new group called Deathray with Damiani. Roper, Cake's drummer, admitted that personality conflicts plagued the group since the single "The Distance," written by Brown, propelled the group into mainstream acceptance. As he told Ken Micallef in an interview for the Launch.com website, "John can be difficult to be around. That Greg [Brown] wrote the hit and John received all the attention created a lot of tension in the band. We would often travel across the country in our van and not say a word to each other for six hours straight. That was normal for us."

Despite the group's internal strife, McCrea nonetheless regretted the loss of his band mate. "It wasn't easy," said McCrea in an interview with Michael Mehle published in the *Denver Rocky Mountain News.* "Mostly, what wasn't easy was having a sense of faith that everything was going to work out. It really didn't seem like it would. I was really contemplating disbanding and starting something new. Greg was a really big part of the band. However, I'm really glad that we kept going." After Brown's departure, the band needed a new guitarist, but McCrea decided not to replace him right away. Instead, he chose to use a variety of guitarists for Cake's third album, *Prolonging the Magic,* completed by August and released in September of 1998.

The more tight-knight *Prolonging the Magic* marked the peak of Cake's recording career with the album's groove beats, weaving guitar and mariachi trumpet lines, and obvious country influences. "The trumpet work of Vincent di Fiore slips in and out of the songs, punching up the choruses and adding wistful undertones to the verses. McCrea delivers a string of poetic non sequiturs in his delightful deadpan [voice], exploring deceivingly dark subjects about one-way relationships, the emptiness of Sunset Strip, the allure of evil and the power of greed," concluded Mehle. The album also contained the group's most successful hit single, "Never There," an older song that McCrea originally wrote and arranged when he was 18. The single made it's way to the number one spot on *Billboard* magazine's alternative rock charts and maintained this position for three weeks. The song's critical acclaim and radio popularity surprised McCrea and the rest of the band, because they experienced trouble recording the track in the studio. Moreover, the single sounded different, as well as more impressive, than Cake's prior radio successes.

Other noteworthy singles on *Prolonging the Magic* included catchy tunes such as "Daria" and "Friend Is a Four Letter Word," the sing along "Satan Is My Motor," and the Hawaiian guitarinfluenced "Mexico." In reference to the group's third release, Brown professed, "It's about John's great songs and his vision," as quoted by Micallef. "Some of these are his oldest songs, but they are also some of his best. I may criticize him, but it's done in a spirit of love." Prior to the album's release date, back in August, Cake held auditions to find a permanent guitarist and hired Xan McCurdy to fill the opening. That fall, Cake arrived overseas for their first European tour, followed by a tour beginning in the spring of 1999 in the United States.

After promoting *Prolonging the Magic,* McCrea intended to take some time off to write for awhile, although fans were already asking when Cake would release their next record, and record company executives worried that if Cake took a break, the public might forget about the group. "They [Capricorn] haven't given me much time to write new songs," McCrea conceded to Mehle. "What happens, when you're in a band, is that you release a record, put everything you have into that record, go on tour for a year and a half, trying to introduce it to people. You get off the road and people ask: 'Where the hell is your next album? It's been a year and a half, where's you're next album?' You just want to say, 'Give me a break.'"

Selected discography

Motorcade of Generosity, Capricorn, 1994.
Fashion Nugget, Capricorn, 1996.
Flirting With Disaster (soundtrack), Geffen Records, 1996.
An American Werewolf In Paris (soundtrack), Hollywood, 1997.

Live From 6A:... With Conan O'Brien (compilation), Mercury, 1997.
MTV Buzz Bin Vol. 2 (compilation), Mammoth Records, 1997.
Prolonging the Magic, Capricorn, 1998.

Sources

Books

Graff, Gary and Daniel Durchholz, editors, *musicHound Rock: The Essential Album Guide,* 1999.

Periodicals

Arizona Republic, February 11, 1999, p. 40.
Columbian, February 21, 1999.
Dallas Morning News, March 13, 1997, p. 35A; February 8, 1999, p. 23A.
Denver Rocky Mountain News, July 2, 1997, p. 19D; February 8, 1999, p. 5D.
Gannett News Service, December 20, 1996.
Independent, April 23, 1991, p. 12.
St. Louis Post-Dispatch, February 27, 1997, p. 10.
Washington Times, November 12, 1998, p. M2.

Online

"Cake, A Band from Sacremento," *Cake* (official website), http://www.cakemusic.com, (September 7, 1999).
"Cake: Dilemma in the Frosting," *Launch.com: Discover New Music*, http://www.launch.com, (September 7, 1999).

—Laura Hightower

Hoagy Carmichael

Songwriter, actor

AP/Wide World Photos. Reproduced by permission. ©

Most of the popular music composers of the first half of the twentieth century were born into homes of wealthy parents. The State of Indiana produced two of the most prominent composers, Cole Porter, a Yale graduate, whose grandfather had made millions of dollars in the Western timber industry. The other was Hoagland Howard Carmichael, (later nicknamed Hoagy by a college sweetheart), born November 22, 1899 in Bloomington, Indiana, the son of Howard Clyde Carmichael, an itinerant laborer and Lida Mary Robinson. Hoagy's father frequently moved his family around the Midwest in search of steady work, but always returned to Indiana. The elder Carmichael had served in the Spanish American War and was a middle-weight regimental boxing champion and nicknamed "Cyclone." Hoagy's mother helped supplement the family income by playing piano in the local silent movie house, social functions and at university dances. In 1944 she was named the State of Indiana Mother of the Year.

Carmichael learned to play the piano at an early age by his mother and when he was sixteen the family moved to Indianapolis where he further studied with a black ragtime pianist, Reggie Duval. He dropped out of high school in 1915 and worked as a cement mixer on a twelve hour shift. Always fascinated with jazz sounds, he returned to Bloomington in 1919 to complete his high school education and study ragtime composition with Duval.

In 1920, Carmichael entered the University of Indiana where he earned a Bachelor's Degree and then a Law Degree in 1926. It was also here where he formed his own small band calling it Carmichael's Collegians. The band helped him become a campus celebrity. The next several years brought him close to many jazzmen including the legendary cornet player, Bix Beiderbecke, who would remain a close friend and an enormous musical inspiration for many years. His first song to be recorded was "Riverboat Shuffle. It was written in 1922 for Beiderbecke.

After graduating from law schoool, he began a long time relationship with the New York music publisher, Mills Music and wrote "Boneyard Shuffle" and "Washboard Blues." By 1927, he had joined the Florida Law Firm of Carmichael and Carmichael—no relation— in West Palm Beach. While struggling as a young lawyer, he scribbled a song on the front pages of a law book waiting for business. He once remarked that he went to Florida to start a law career because of the real estate boom in those days. "I figured there ought to be work for a good lawyer there because of all that selling and reselling going on," Carmichael recalled in an interview some years later. "There probably was, too—only I wasn't a

For the Record . . .

Born Hoagland Howard Carmichael November 22, 1899 in Bloomington, IN, (died December 27, 1981 Rancho Mirage, CA after a heart attack); son of Howard Clyde Carmichael and Lida Mary Robison; married Ruth M. Meinardi in NY, 1936, (divorced 1955); children: Hoagland Bix Jr., born 1938, Randy Bob, born1940 ; married Dorothy Wanda McKay in June 20, 1977. *Education*: Graduated from the University of Indiana at Indianapolis with a Bachelors Degree and a Law Degree; studied with Reggie Duval, Ragtime Musician..

First published work was "Riverboat Shuffle," 1926; "Washboard Blues" and "Barnyard Shuffle" followed in 1927; wrote his greatest hit, "Stardust" with lyrics added two years later by Mitchell Parish; is credited with writing over 500 songs including over fifty classic "standards;" appeared in ten Hollywood films.

Awards: Academy Award, Best Song, "In the Cool Cool Cool of the Evening," 1951; elected to Songwriters Hall of Fame, 1971; awarded an Honorary Doctorate Degree from Indiana University, 1972; Star Dust Trail Award by the Newport Jazz Festival at Carnegie Hall, NY, 1979.

good lawyer. A note to me was something that belonged on a musical staff."

Carmichael loved music and enjoyed composition and not long after arriving in Florida, Carmichael heard Red Nichol's version of his "Washboard Blues" and concluded he was not suited for the legal profession. He resigned from the firm and returned to Bloomington after unsuccessfully making it on New York's Tin Pan Alley. For the next two years Carmichael performed with Jean Goldkette's band and musician Don Redman learning to read music, as wellas continuing to compose with "Stardust" gathering dust. It would later be named the all time favorite song.

"Stardust" was not recorded until several years later as a ragtime piece by Don Redman and the McKinney Cotton Pickers, a black jazz ensemble. The song made little impression and it was later changed to a slower tempo at the advice of arranger Jimmy Dale. Carmichael soon realized the potential of the newly arranged song and with the recommendation of his publisher, Irving Mills, Mitchell Parish was brought in to write lyrics. By 1929, Carmichael had gone to Hollywood but the gates to the big silver screen studios were also firmly closed to him. He returned to New York by hitch-hiking across the country and worked as a song plugger for Mills Music. During this time the melody for "Stardust" was completed and he returned to New York and organized another band. "Stardust" had been conceived when Carmichael had made a visit to his old alma mater at the University of Indiana in 1927. He recalled a girl he had once loved and lost as he sat on the campus "spooning wall" one evening. He went to the university "Book Nook,", which had a piano and wrote the first version of the melody as a piano instrumental. A classmate, Stuart Gorrell, named the composition when he heard it because "it sounded like dust from stars drifting down through the summer sky." Gorrell later became an executive with the Chase Manhattan Bank and co-wrote the classic "Georgia on My Mind" with Carmichael. In 1929, lyrics were added by Mitchell Parish at the urging of Carmichael's publisher, Irving Mills and, that same year, it was introduced at the Cotton Club in New York. The big break for Carmichael came when Isham Jones recorded the song. Subsequent renditions by other artists including Artie Shaw in 1940 sold over two million copies and helped make it a classic "standard." Walter Winchell, the syndicated New York columnist thought it was gorgeous and lyricist Mitchell Parish recalls, "He was so crazy about it that he plugged it almost daily in his column. Even years later I recall sitting in the; Copa [Copa Cabana Night Club in New York City] one night and listening to Nat King Cole. Nat sang 'Stardust' to a beautiful arrangement by Gordon Jenkins and everybody in the place, including Winchell, had a tear in his eye. I've heard the song done thousands of times, but I remember Nat's rendition above all others."

"Stardust" has also been recorded over five hundred times in over fifty arrangements for every possible instrument or combination of instruments. Its lyrics have been translated into over forty different languages. It may be the only song recorded on both sides of a phonograph record by two different bands. One side was a presentation by Tommy Dorsey and on the flip side a recording by Benny Goodman and his orchestra. It has become the most recorded American popular musical composition and in 1964 the American Society of Composers, Authors and Publishers (ASCAP), celebrating its 50th Anniversary, released its all time Hit Parade and "Stardust" was included.

In 1930, Carmichael again joined with classmate Stuart Gorrell to write the ever popular "Georgia on My Mind." Its first recording was made on September 15, 1930 by a band led by Carmichael that included Bix Beiderbecke in one of his last recording sessions. Contrary to popular belief, Carmichael did not write "Georgia on My Mind" with reference to the State of Georgia" but to his sister Georgia, who was going through a terrible divorce at the time the song was being written. It was written by Carmichael to entice his publisher to pay him $35 a week against "Stardust" royalties. "Rockin Chair" was also written in 1930 and ten years laterCarmichael was sitting in Billy Berg's Club, at Hollywood's Vine Street night club when an unknown singer sang "Ol Rockin Chair". Carmichael was so impressed at the young singer, he went to the stage and served as his mentor by obtaining immediate work for him at $75.00 a week. The singer Francesco Lo Vecchio later changed his name to Frankie Laine and launched a career that has spanned sixty years. "Ol Rockin Chair" and "Georgia on My Mind" were both released successfully by singer Mildred Bailey and the former became her theme song. "Georgia On My Mind" was revived by singer Ray Charles in the 1950's and has remained a big hit ever since.

From 1931-34 Carmichael added additional "standards" that included "Lazy River, "co-written with Sidney Arodin, a New Orleans clarinetist, and "In the Still of the Night." The warm and gentle flow of its melody comes from the relaxed easy going sounds that were typical of many New Orleans great clarinetists of the time He also collaborated with struggling lyricist Johnny Mercer to issue "Lazybones", which they claim was written in only twenty minutes. Another song that was very popular in 1934 was his song called "Judy." Although it never became a standard, it was so popular at the time that Ethel Frances Gumm took the stage name, Judy Garland.

In 1937 Carmichael married Ruth M. Meinardi, a young model in New York City; he joined Paramount Pictures as a staff songwriter that same year. He appeared in his first of many films, *Topper*, and performed his composition "Old Man Moon" which starred Cary Grant and Constance Bennett. That same year he added another classic "standard" to his repertoire in "The Nearness of You" in collaboration with Ned Washington. This song was later added to the Paramount motion picture *Romantic in the Dark*. 1938 brought three more standards, "Heart and Soul," "Two Sleepy People," and "Small Fry." "Heart and Soul" was written by Carmichael and lyricist Frank Loesser for Paramount Pictures, and Carmichael once remarked the song was kicked around the rooms of the studio so much that the best use it got was for actor Anthony Quinn's voice practice. However, it became a big hit in 1938 when Bea Wain performed it with the Larry Clinton Orchestra and it was revived by the Four Aces in the mid fifties and became a hit again.

When Carmichael was still in school at the University of Indiana, a friend gave him a poem on a scrap of paper with the notion of turning it into a musical piece. Carmichael wrote the melody for it but put it aside and forgot about it. Years later he came across it and decided it was good enough to be published. Unfortunately, he had no idea who the lyricist was other than the initials "J. B. penned on the original poem. He recruited his friend Walter Winchell to read a few lines on the air and asked that the person who wrote it come forward. Forty eight people claimed to have written the lovely poem but all proved to be fakes. Finally, he received word that the poem had once appeared in an old issue of Life Magazine and the authorship was traced to Jane Brown-Thompson of Philadelphia. The song, "I Get Along Without You Very Well" was introduced on the radio by Dick Powell on January 19, 1940. The day before Jane Brown-Thompson died never knowing that the beautiful poem she had written when she was a young widow had become a hit. Frank Sinatra's version in the mid-1950's helped resurrect his slipping career.

In 1940 Carmichael and Johnny Mercer introduce the Broadway Musical, *Walk With Music*, at the Ethel Barrymore Theater; it closed after only three weeks. They would later combine to write two "standards", "Skylark" and "Baltimore Oriole". In 1942 Frank Sinatra recorded his first solo, "The Lamplighter's Serenade", a product of Carmichael and Paul Francis Webster. "Hong Kong Blues," "How Little We Know," and "Old Master Painter," were three more "standards" added over the next three years and the first two were added into the film, *To Have and To Have Not*, starring Humphrey Bogart and Lauren Bacall. *To Have and To Have Not* also marked Carmichael's film debut as an actor. Over the next three years he appeared in a number of films and his song "Ole Buttermilk Sky" was nominated for an Academy Award in the film *Silver Saddle*.

Throughout the forties and fifties, Carmichael continued to appear in motion pictures and wrote over five hundred musical compositions including "In the Cool Cool Cool of the Evening" that won an Academy Award in 1951 with Johnny Mercer. The song was performed by Bing Crosby in the Paramount motion picture *Here Comes the Groom*. In 1955, he divorced his first wife, Ruth Menardi. In addition his voice became familiar to millions through radio with a Sunday evening show entitled *Open House at Hoagy's* and *Tonight at Hoagy's* on the Mutual Network in 1944. *The Hoagy Carmichael Show* was introduced on the Columbia Broadcasting System (CBS) in 1946; he also made other guest appearances on radio and later on television programs.

In 1965 he published his second book of memoirs, *Sometimes I Wonder*. Singer Peggy Lee was riding on a plane with him at the time and suggested the title before it was published. Carmichael received a series of awards and honors over the next few years including the initial induction into the Songwriters Hall of Fame with Duke Ellington and eight others. In 1977 he married actress Dorothy Wanda McKay after a fifteen year courtship.

Carmichael appeared in ten motion pictures, the western television series *Laramie* and his songs have been heard in over a hundred motion pictures from the 1930's through much of the 1990's. He also appeared in the RKO Academy Award winning motion picture, *The Best Years of Our Lives*, in 1946 and frequently appeared as a singer/pianist and as a character actor. Prior to his death, he spent a great deal of time playing golf, collecting rare coins and making guest appearances on television. He continued to write compositions but none rivaled his earlier writings.

He passed away after suffering at heart attack at his home in Rancho Mirage, California on December 27, 1981 and was returned to his native Bloomington, Indiana and buried on January 4, 1982. The University of Indiana maintains a lively memorial to their famous songwriter and performing artist, which contains a large collection of memorabilia donated by the Carmichael family including photographs, a piano, music manuscripts, scrapbooks and paintings housed in the Hoagy Carmichael Room in Bloomington.

Selected discography

Stardust and Much More, RCA BMG Bluebird 8333-2-RB.

In Hoagland, DRG 5197.

The Music of Hoagy Carmichael, Audiophile Records ACD-220.

The Song Is Hoagy Carmichael, Academy of Sound and Vision LTD

Stardust: Capitol Sings Hoagy Carmichael, Volume 15, Gold Rush 32592.

Hoagy Carmichael: Ole Buttermilk Sky, Collectors Choice Music.

The Hoagy Carmichael Songbook, RCA 2148.

Great American Composers: Hoagy Carmichael, Columbia C21-22 8105.

The Jazz Greats Play Hoagy Carmichael, Prestige Records PRCD 24191-2.

Carmichael Sings Carmichael, Aero Space Records 51011.

Hooray for Hoagy!, Audiophile ACD-251.

Sources

Books

Carmichael, Hoagy and S. Longstreet, *Sometimes I Wonder Why*, Farrar, Staus and Giroux 1965.

Ewen, David, *American Popular Songs: From the ;Revolutionary War to the Present*, Random House, 1966.

Ewen, David, *American Songwriters*, H. W. Wilson Company, 1987.

Feather, Leonard, *Encyclopedia of Jazz*, Horizon Press, 1960.

Gammond, Peter, *The Oxford Companion to Popular Music*, Oxford Univ. Press 1993.

Harrison, Nigel, *Songwriters, A Biographical Dictionary With Discographies*, McFarland and Company Inc. 1998.

Jablonski, Edward, *Harold Arlen Rhythm Rainbows And Blues*, Northeastern University Press 1996.

Lax, Roger & Frederick Smith, *The Great Song Thesaurus*, Oxford Univ. Press 1989.

Maltin, Leonard, *Movie and Video Guide 1995*, Penguin Books Ltd., 1994.

Simon, W. L., *Readers Digest Treasury of Best Loved Songs*, Readers Digest, 1972.

Stambler, Irwin, *Encyclopedia of Popular Music,* St. Martins Press, 1966.

Periodicals

Los Angeles Times, December 28, 1981.

New York Times, December 28, 1981.

Online

Hoagy Carmichael, www.hoagy.com (September 1999).

Additional information was obtained through two interviews with Frankie Laine in October and November 1998.

—Francis D. McKinley

Citizen King

Rock band

Photograph by David C. Deal. Corbis. Reproduced by permission©

Flamboyant frontman Matt Sims, who provides vocals and plays bass guitar for Citizen King, asserted, "We are going to be, hopefully, the band people think of that is not a rock 'n' roll band, not a funk band, not a hip-hop act with live instrumentation," according to Warner Brothers Records. "We are trying to break a bunch of pigeonholes." The tavern-funk/alternative rock band, whose members also include drummer DJ Brooks, keyboardist Dave Cooley, records man Malcolm Michiles, and guitarist Kristian Riley, hail from Milwaukee, Wisconsin, the same Midwestern city famous for its bratwurst and beer.

However Milwaukee also gave the world a host of talented artists, like pianist Liberace, architect Frank Lloyd Wright, guitarist Les Paul, and the soul band Harvey Scales and the Seven Sounds, one of Sims's favorite live acts. Hoping to add the name Citizen King to the list of well-known Milwaukee natives, the group released their first album, *Brown Bag,* in 1995 for the independent label Don't Records. Then, after signing with Warner Brothers, the band returned with *Mobile Estates* in 1999. The album, which included the single "Better Days (And the Bottom Drops Out)" that entered the *Billboard* modern rock chart, brought Citizen King a wider audience outside their hometown.

Before joining forces to play music, the members of Citizen King spent most of their free time during high school at a Milwaukee bowling alley, the place where they first met. "We're the bombast bowlers this side of the Mason Dixon," Sims boasted to Carrie Bell of *Billboard* magazine. "In fact, we challenge any band that thinks they can beat us. They will go down." The five young men became fast friends, discovering that in addition to being bowlers by nature, they also loved listening to the same styles of music.

One night in 1988, they attended a concert featuring the Beastie Boys, Run-DMC, LL Cool J, and Fishbone (a group Citizen King would later tour with). "That was the show where I said, 'Hey, I know what I want to be doing,'" Sims recalled to Mac Randall in a feature story for the Launch: Discover New Music website. "And everyone in the band felt the same way. Between those four acts, we knew exactly what we wanted to do, no matter what." In addition to the aforementioned outfits, the members of Citizen King became huge fans of the Los Angeles punk legends Fear; samples from two of that band's songs would later appear on tracks for *Mobile Estates.*

According to Warner Brothers, Sims also remembered going to see Harvey Scales "bumpin' bellies with all the women in the audience, singin' about a 'Disco Lady'," during shows at a localclub called Boobie's Place. His performances inspired the band to create danceable

For the Record . . .

Members include **DJ Brooks** (son of a saxophonist who played with Sly and the Family Stone; took lessons from James Brown drummer Clyde Stubblefield), drums; **Dave Cooley**, keyboards; **Malcolm Michiles**, records; **Kristian Riley**, guitar; **Matt Sims**, vocals, bass.

Formed band and started playing in clubs across the Midwest, 1993; released debut album *Brown Bag*, Don't Records, 1995; released first major-label album, *Mobile Estates*, Warner Brothers Records, 1999; toured the U.S. and Europe, 1999.

Addresses: *Home*—Milwaukee, WI; *Management*—Case Management, Milwaukee, WI. *Booking agent*—Monterey Peninsula Artist. *Record company*—Warner Brothers Records, 3300 Warner Blvd., Burbank, CA 91505-4694, (818) 953-3223, fax (818) 953-3699. *Website*—Citizen King Official Website, http://www.citizenking.com.

tunes that often had a tavern-funk vibe. Brooks, Citizen King's drummer, drew inspiration from soul, blues, and funk music first-hand. Growing up, he took lessons from legendary drummer Clyde Stubblefield, who played with James Brown's band. Brooks's father, who played saxophone with Sly and the Family Stone for awhile, was a friend of Stubblefield.

Thus, in full agreement regarding the style of music they wanted to play, Sims and his comrades formed Citizen King in 1993. Before this, they worked with a group called Wild Kingdom that broke up. The name Citizen King refers to "that old Orson Welles movie, that French king who used to go out dressed in rags to see what his subjects were sayin' about him and that former Governor of Louisiana, Huey "Kingfish" Long, whose slogan was 'Every Man a King'," reported Christina Cramer for the *Rolling Stone* website.

The band started out performing their break-beat vibes at local clubs in their hometown, as well as throughout the Midwest. Soon thereafter, the buzz surrounding Citizen King's music and live shows caught the attention of Speech (born Todd Thomas) of the alternative hip-hop group Arrested Development. Speech produced several tracks on Citizen King's debut album entitled *Brown Bag,* released on Don't Records in 1995. The record sounded much like the major-label album to follow, but more low-tech. "I didn't do as much rhyming, and it's not sample-based because we didn't have the gear back in the day—we couldn't afford it," said Sims to Randall. "Malcolm made loops by putting little pieces of tape on a record player, and when he played a record, he'd make it so the groove would skip really smoothly. That's how we got away without using a sampler."

The following year, the band released and EP, *Count the Days,* and toured with the funk/rock group Fishbone. Around the same time, Citizen King traveled to Austin, Texas, to play at the South by Southwest convention. Here, executives from 510, a Warner Brothers subsidiary, liked what they heard and signed the band to the major label. Taken by surprise, Sims told Bell, "We love music, but we goof around a lot, so we never expected a record company to take us seriously. Our music is all over the place style-wise. Plus, we live in Milwaukee, which isn't given props as a cultural center very often." They were also skeptical of signing with a major label for fear of losing their artistic freedoms. "We were afraid about signing ... because of all the horror stories you hear. But they basically let us do what we want, and you can't ask for more than that," Sims admitted to Billboard magazine's Catherine Applefeld Olson.

Nonetheless, *Mobile Estates* took off following its release in the spring of 1999 after nine months in the making. A labor intensive yet fun process for the band saw them experimenting with all types of music. Olson described the group's first major-label effort as a "fitting blend of hip-hop, rock, and fresh melodies;its songs are laden with samples and immediately danceable beats." When not laying down his rhymes, Sims vocals sound much like a cross between alternative rockers Beck and Lenny Kravitz, as well as classic rock star Steve Miller. Meanwhile, guitarist Riley and keyboardist Cooley weaved melodic sounds through Brooks's drumming, Sims's bass lines, and the record wizardry of Michiles. *Mobile Estates,* produced by Eric Valentine (known for producing records for both Smash Mouth and Third Eye Blind), was recorded at Bionic, the band's own studio located in the basement of an abandoned warehouse.

Although the album contains a musically diverse collection of songs, Citizen King decided to play it safe with the first released single, "Better Days (And the Bottom Drops Out)," which sounded similar to what other bands were playing at the time. "The song is fresh-sounding and kind of reminiscent of Beck; that seems to do well for us," Mary Shuminas of a Chicago radio station commented to Olson. Like most of their other songs, the country blues meets modern day sampling technology "Better Days" was inspired by Citizen King's real life experiences. Sims explained to Bell, "It's a narrative about where our band was three years ago. I was working at a dollar store. I had no money and wasn't happy. I decided music had to be all or nothing. I don't miss those dollar store days, although I do miss stealing stupid trap from there. Not that much has changed though. I'm still pinching pennies." Other notable tracks included the mellow soul of "Jalopy Style," the guitar-riffed, space-aged punk "Safety Pin," and the upbeat, drum and samples "Bill-hilly."

Riding upon the success of *Mobile Estates,* Citizen King started an extensive tour of the United States and Europe in the late spring of 1999. Later that summer, Citizen King made a soundtrack appearance for the film "Mystery Men," playing a cover of the Specials' song "Gangsters." Over the years, Citizen King amassed an enormous record collection—nearly 25,000 vinyl albums in all stored in a vault in their rehearsal studio. Michiles packs up the ones he needs for specific concert performances. Sims said that the group begged radio stations for vinyl, as most switched to an all-electronic format, every time they appeared for a radio show.

Selected discography

Brown Bag, Don't Records, 1995.
Count the Days, (EP), 1996.
Mobile Estates, Warner Brothers Records, 1999.
(With others) *Mystery Men,* (soundtrack), Interscope Records, 1999.

Sources

Periodicals

Billboard, February 6, 1999, p. 20; March 27, 1999, p. 91.
Rolling Stone, May 27, 1999, p. 61.

Online

Citizen King Official Website, http://www.citizenking.com (October 6, 1999).
All Music Guide website, http://www.allmusic.com (October 6, 1999).
Launch: Discover New Music, http://www.launch.com (October 6, 1999).
"Citizen King: They Rock, They Bowl,*" Rolling Stone.com,* http://www.rollingstone.tunes.com (October 5, 1999).

Additional information provided courtesy of Warner Brothers Records.

—Laura Hightower

Colin Davis

Conductor

AP/Wide World Photos. Reproduced by permission. ©

Critics deem Sir Colin Davis one of Britain's greatest living conductors. His career is noteworthy for long associations with the Symphony Orchestra of the British Broadcasting Corporation (BBC) and Royal Philharmonic Orchestra. He is also particularly renowned in classical circles for his work with opera companies, such as Milan's La Scala, on heady new productions from among the repertoire of great operas by the likes of Wolfgang Amadeus Mozart and Giuseppe Verdi. North American audiences have encountered and found favor with Davis and his talents since the 1950s, and he has recorded with both his own orchestras as well as with some of Europe's most illustrious ensembles over the course of several decades since.

Davis was born Colin Rex Davis on September 25, 1927, in Weybridge, a town in England's Surrey countryside. A brood of seven children depended on his father's salary as a bank clerk, but Reginald and Lillian Davis imparted to their children the more invaluable gift of music appreciation. Classical records were commonplace in the home, and Davis went on to play clarinet in the band at his school, Christ's Hospital Boys' School in Sussex. At the Royal College of Music, he continued in his study of the instrument, and even played it in the band of the Household Cavalry when he was drafted into military service in 1946.

After two years in the Cavalry, Davis came to realize that his overwhelming desire was not to play, but to conduct. He practiced in his apartment to recorded music, read the formal manuals for the art, and took a sole lesson with a professional. He was still playing the clarinet, however, and in the pit of the Glyndbourne Orchestra, he was able to observe a famed conductor, Fritz Busch, and his movements. Davis then began conducting with small orchestras, such as the Kalmar in 1949, and small vocal ensembles like the Chelsea Opera Group in 1950. His professional debut came during the ballet season at London's Royal Festival Hall in 1952.

Over the next five years, Davis continued to perfect his craft, and in 1957 was hired by the BBC's Scottish Orchestra as its assistant conductor. He spent two years with it in Glasgow, while also accepting the Scottish National Orchestra's invitation to serve as guest conductor. In 1959, he was appointed conductor of Sadler's Wells Opera, a London outfit. Within a few months of his return to the capital, a fortuitous opportunity came Davis's way: the legendary conductor Otto Klemperer fell ill before a scheduled engagement with the London Philharmonic, and officials at the Royal Festival Hall asked Davis if he would like to take Klemperer's place. The performance was Don Giovanni, the Mozart opera, and boasted a celebrated array of

For the Record . . .

Born September 25, 1927, in Weybridge, Surrey, England; son of Reginald George (a bank clerk) and Lillian Constance (Colbran) Davis; married April Rosemary Cantelo (a singer; divorced, 1964); married Ashraf Nani, 1964; children: on son, Kurosh. *Education*: Attended Royal College of Music, mid-1940s.

Professional clarinet player with the Glyndbourne Orchestra; made professional conducting debut at the Royal Festival Hall, 1952; assistant conductor, British Broadcasting Corporation (BBC) Scottish Orchestra, Glasgow, 1957-59; conductor, Sadler's Wells Opera, London, 1959; principal conductor, Sadler's Wells Opera, London, 1960-65; chief conductor, BBC Symphony Orchestra, 1967-71; musical director, Royal Opera House at Covent Garden, London, 1971-83; principal conductor and music director, Bavarian Radio Symphony Orchestra, Munich, Germany, 1983-92; honorary conductor, Dresden Staatskapelle, 1990–; principal conductor, Royal Philharmonic Orchestra, London, 1990–.

Awards: Commander of the Order of the British Empire, 1965, knighted, 1980; Grand Prix du Disque Mondiale, 1967, for recording of Handel's *Messiah;* Gold Medal, Royal Philharmonic Society, 1995.

Addresses: *Office*—Royal Philharmonic Orchestra, 16 Clerkenwell Green, London EC1R 0DP, England.

performers; Davis's guidance over them and the outstanding orchestra over those two nights cemented his reputation as one of Britain's new generation of conductors. He was just thirty-two. That same year, he embarked upon what would be the first of several lengthy tours of the North American continent, and conducted the Canadian Broadcasting Corporation Symphony Orchestra for a series of broadcasts across Canada.

Davis remained with Sadler's Wells, and was named principal conductor in 1960. That same year, when another celebrated conductor became ill, Davis was asked to substitute for an ailingSir Thomas Beecham, founder of the Royal Philharmonic, at the Glyndbourne Festival. In 1961, he made his professional debut on American soil with the Minneapolis Symphony, and returned to the country in 1964 to conduct at New York's Carnegie Hall with a fellow maestro Georg Solti on a tour commemorating the sixtieth anniversary of the London Symphony Orchestra. New York critics extolled Davis's talents in the next day's papers.

Davis remained principal conductor with Sadler's Wells until the end of 1965, and then came to be professionally affiliated with the London Symphony Orchestra for the next few years. He made a recording for the Philips label with it and the LSO Chorus of Handel's Messiah during 1966, which won France's Grand Prix du Disque Mondiale the following year. Davis and the Orchestra even spent a month in Daytona Beach, Florida, as part of the inaugural festivities for the newly created Daytona International Music Festival. He also conducted the LSO's impressive performance at London's Royal Festival Hall of an opera from French romantic composer Louis-Hector Berlioz, The Trojans, in December of 1966. Just a month later, he returned to the United States and conducted a contemporary opera by twentieth-century English composer Benjamin Britten. Peter Grimes was a tremendous success, and Davis earned wholehearted critical plaudits for his talents at the podium.

In the fall of 1967 Davis was named chief conductor of the BBC Symphony Orchestra, and for some time it was rumored that he would be tapped to fill American conductor Leonard Bernstein's place when the latter retired from the New York Philharmonic. Davis's extensive tour engagements, as well as a month-long guest stint with the New York Philharmonic in 1968, seemed a likely portent of a post with a major North American orchestra. But instead he was named musical director of the Royal Opera at Covent Garden in 1971, where he spent the next dozen years. In 1983 he was appointed principal conductor and music director of the renowned Bavarian Radio Symphony Orchestra in Munich, Germany. He remained there until the early 1990s, when he returned to England to accept the position of principal conductor for the Royal Philharmonic Orchestra. He became the principal guest conductor of the Dresden Staatskapelle in 1990, and of the New York Philharmonic in 1998.

Davis's first marriage ended, and in 1964 he married a student of Persian heritage, Ashraf Nani, with whom he had a son. The British crown honored him in 1966 with its Commander of the Order of the British Empire medal in 1966, and he was knighted in 1980. Over the course of his long and distinguished career, Davis has made numerous recordings for the Philips and BMG Classics labels. Live performances of his work with the Bavarian Radio Symphony Orchestra are also noteworthy examples of his musical leadership. A recording of Gustav Mahler's Eighth Symphony was reviewed by Stephen D. Chakwin Jr. in American Record Guide, who gave it effusive praise. "Davis takes broad but not slow-sounding tempos, gets his players to give full value to every note, lays down a solid bass line, and shapes the phrases with sure control and lyric splendor," opined Chakwin.

Davis has become particularly associated with the repertoire of Berlioz, and of the nationalist Finnish composer Jean Sibelius. On two occasions he has made recordings of the entirety of Sibelius's music—once in the 1960s with the Boston Symphony, and again in the mid-1990s with the London Symphony Orchestra. This latter work was critiqued by American Record Guide contributor Philip Haldeman, who found the recording of Tapiola particularly noteworthy. "Every shadowy secret and poetic nuance of Sibelius's dark forest is revealed in lush detail," Haldeman wrote. "Davis builds the piece from a relatively unpretentious beginning, then draws us inevitably along the wispy paths and deep into the fairy grottos."

On the occasion of a Sibelius Festival with the New York Philharmonic, Davis spoke with American Record Guide writer Wynne Delacoma about the Scandinavian composer, who died in 1957, and the affinity he feels with Sibelius. "I'm basically schizophrenic—like most people, only they don't admit it," Davis declared. "There are all kinds of dark, ghastly things in the dark wood of the human soul. And [Sibelius] brings them out. He's a very complicated man. He was a huge drinker, riddled with self-doubt. He was a very, very difficult man but he had the intellect to get all this down on paper, thank God. It's the conflict in oneself that is evident in Sibelius at all times."

Selected discography

Complete Mozart Edition Vol. 37: Idomeneo/Davis, 1991.
Brahms: Choral Works/Davis, Stutzmann, Bavarian Radio, 1993.
Britten: A Midsummer Night's Dream/Davis, McNair, Asawa, 1996.
Wagner: Lohengrin, RCA Victor, 1996.
Berlioz: Complete Orchestral Works/Sir Colin Davis, 1997.
Berlioz: L'Enfance du Christ, etc./Davis, Morison, Pears, 1997.
Mahler: Symphony 8, RCA, 1997.
Britten: Peter Grimes/Davis, Vickers, Harper, et al., 1999.
Berlioz: Symphonie Fantastique/Colin Davis, et al., 1999.
Sibelius: Karelia Suite, The Oceanides, Finlandia, Valse Triste, Tapiola, Night Ride, Sunrise, RCA, 1999.

Sources

American Record Guide, July/August 1997; March/April 1998; September/October 1999.
Stereo Review, February, 1996, p. 152.

—*Carol Brennan*

Banco De Gaia

Multi-instrumentalist

The British electronic music pioneer and multi-instrumentalist Toby Marks, known in the music business as Banco De Gaia, utilizes musical samples from all over the world to create a danceable, yet still cerebral, body of work with an obvious international flavor. He entered the electronica scene in 1991 when he issued a collection of cassette-only releases that focused mainly upon ambient textures and sounds. In addition to music, Marks also participated in numerous environmental and Tibetan freedom support groups. He is regarded not only as a talented composer, but also as a person with a deep-rooted social consciousness. Thus, his social and political convictions often informed the themes of his music, leading many critics to label his work as "intelligent techno." In 1999, Marks took a new musical direction when he produced *The Magical Sounds of Banco De Gaia* under his own record label. Instead of focusing mainly on ambient sounds, he chose to create a more upbeat, lively collection of songs that brought him greater mainstream success.

Born Toby Marks in 1964 in South London, England, De Gaia experienced a typical middle-class British upbringing, attending a traditional boys' school in the town of his birth. He took to playing a variety of instruments early on, and by 1978, Marks joined a heavy metal band, serving as the group's drummer. His musical interests started to shift, though, during the 1980s when electronic music exploded in Great Britain's acid-house nightclubs.

During his teens and twenties, Marks also began reading about the Buddhist religion and other related subjects in an attempt to discover a deeper meaning of life; he believed that the Western culture he was raised in had not provided him with a sense of spirituality. In his study of Buddhism, he repeatedly came upon the subject of Tibet, a country invaded and taken over by China in 1950. After the invasion, the Chinese government set out to destroy the traditions and spiritual culture of Tibet, killing and torturing millions of Tibetans as well as their spiritual leaders. Touched and angered by the Tibetan peoples' struggle to regain their freedom from the Chinese since the time of the hostile takeover and subsequent human rights abuses, Marks decided to support the Tibetan cause. He remained an activist for Tibet's freedom, in addition to environmental preservation, throughout his adulthood. Moreover, Eastern cultures and music such as that of Tibet would find a place in his own work.

Around 1986, Marks moved to Portugal where he performed mostly Beatles songs in bars for tourists in order to earn a living. While living in Portugal, Marks also adopted his recording persona, Banco De Gaia, the name of one of the country's banks. Then in 1989, Marks bought his fist sampler, which furtherignited his interest in electronic music, and soon recorded his first song entitled "Maxwell House." Subsequently, he returned to London, spending the early 1990s releasing cassette-only albums distributed through Planet Dog, a network of clubs and electronic/ambient artists. These albums, now out of print, included *Medium* (1991), *Freeform Flutes & Fading Tibetans* (1992), and *Deep Live* (1993).

Marks put a different spin on his brand of electronica in comparison to other ambient artists. Rather than only drawing upon the influences of Western musical culture, Marks, through his spiritual connections to other cultures, included elements of Eastern and Arabic music, which he tied in with ambient and dance rhythms. "You can sample anything," Marks told Tony Fletcher in an interview for *Newsday,* "so why limit yourself to western sounds? I'm not consciously bringing in world music elements. It's just that some elements are coming from parts of the world further away than ours."

Eventually, Planet Dog transformed into a record label, and Marks released his first record on compact disc in 1993, the *Desert Wind* EP. In early 1994, Marks released his debut album entitled *Maya,* followed by *Last Train to Lhasa* in 1995. Although the debut contained some of Marks's favorite tracks, such as "Mafich Arabi" and "Heliopolis" (released as a single in 1994), songs he continued to play during live shows throughout his career, his sophomore effort sounded more refined

For the Record . . .

Born Toby Marks in 1964 in South London, England; married.

Began musical career in 1978 as a drummer in a heavy metal band; inspired by acid-house music, as well as Buddhism and Tibetan culture during the 1980s; moved to Portugal, performed Beatles songs in clubs to tourists, 1986; recorded "Maxwell House," 1989; returned to London, released series of cassette-only albums: *Medium*, 1991; *Freeform Flutes & Fading*, 1992; *Deep Live*, 1993; released, *Desert Wind* EP, 1993; released debut CD, *Maya*, Planet Dog, 1994; released *Last Train to Lhasa*, Planet Dog, 1995; issued rare concert recording, *Live at Glastonbury*, Planet Dog, 1996; released *Big Men Cry*, Planet, 1997; toured U.S. with Moby, moved to English countryside, formed own label, Gecko Records, released *The Magical Sounds of Banco De Gaia*, 1999.

Addresses: *Home*—Cheddar, U.K. *Record company*—Gecko Records, P.O. Box 1195, Cheddar, BS27 3YE, U.K. *Website*—http://www.banco.co.uk. *E-mail*—toby@banco.co.uk.

because of his improved production skills. Furthermore, the entire album dealt with the plight of Tibet, and Planet Dog released the title track as a single. Most critics agreed that *Last Train to Lhasa,* infused with trance-like beats and spiritual chants, represented one of Marks's best works.

The following year, 1996, brought a rare concert recording entitled *Live at Glastonbury* that captured one of Marks's most renowned live performances. Compared to his prior albums, this release focused less on serene, ambient textures and more on upbeat, groove-oriented sounds and bass rhythms. "A very good recording of possibly the most vibey gig I did in '95, definitely makes you feel like you're there," wrote Marks on his website regarding the live album. "Well, obviously it doesn't really, but it definitely sounds like a good gig, which it was."

In 1997, Marks released the album *Big Men Cry* and returned to his mellow tones, although the album still contained some danceable tracks. A variety of live instruments added to Marks's inspiring songwriting ability and sampling and production skills made the collection a worthwhile accomplishment. Nonetheless, Marks admitted to suffering from writers' block the previous year, a frustration that the prolific musician had never suffered from before. Moreover, working in a dark studio some twenty miles away from his home made the creative process even more difficult forMarks. However, after hearing the recordings made during his 1995 show in Glastonbury, the musician felt more inspired. He was not aware that the performance had been taped by the man running the stage, but because Marks liked the recording so well, he immediately agreed to it's release. Suddenly, the process of creating songs for *Big Men Cry* seemed to fall into place.

Despite his triumph, though, the release of *Big Men Cry* led to problems between Marks and his record label. As the last album Marks was under contract to produce for Planet Dog, the work lacked commercial appeal, and the label refused to promote *Big Men Cry* as heavily as they had promoted his prior records. Therefore, Marks, feeling that his interests and Planet Dog's interests had grown apart, decided to start anew.

After a disappointing United States tour with techno artist Moby in an attempt to promote the album himself, Marks returned to London and took a retreat with his wife to an area of England called the New Forest in Somerset. Taken by the peaceful, serene landscape, he relocated from London to a town in Somerset called Cheddar. Here he bought a home, remodeled the garage into a studio, and formed his own label imprint, Gecko Records. By 1999, with his faith restored and the freedom to work by his own terms, Marks released *The Magical Sounds of Banco De Gaia,* an album that demonstrated a whole new side of the musician. As a whole, the songs were more upbeat and fun, giving the record more commercial appeal than any of his previous releases. Nevertheless, Marks continued with the ambient structures of his past, retaining the ability to please older Banco De Gaia fans as well as new listeners.

Critics praised the album with reviews like "Toby takes you on a journey... The opening track ['I Love Baby Cheese'] immediately grabs you with its catchy vocal snippets and breakbeats, and is a great opening statement," as Tom Harding of *Future Music* concluded. Other tracks such as "Harvey And The Old Ones" and the blissful "Sinhala" continued the beating rhythms, even though an apparent touch of classic ambient influences remained. "When I started writing the album it was a breeze, the easiest of all the albums," Marks told Harding. "We had a new place to live and I love the countryside so that definitely shows through. The album is much more uplifting and light-hearted."

Following the success of *The Magical Sounds of Banco De Gaia*, Marks began a tour to further promote his new album. In the past, his live performances featured a five-piece band that included drums, percussion, bass, saxophone, and guitar, the instruments that Marks played himself for recorded work. For the 1999 tour, Marks opted for a simpler lineup that consisted of a rhythm section to complement his guitar playing and handling of the technical equipment. However, he managed to maintain the excitement of his previous concerts by adding more specialeffects lighting and a slide show that he described to Fletcher as a "personalized rave."

Selected discography

Maya, Planet Dog/Mammoth, 1994.
(compilation)*One A.D.,* Waveform Corporation, 1994.
(compilation)*Trance Europe Express 3,* Volume, 1994.
Last Train to Lhasa, Planet Dog/Mammoth, 1995.
Live at Glastonbury, Planet Dog/Mammoth, 1996.
Big Men Cry, Planet Dog/Mammoth, 1997.
(compilation)*Pi,* Sire, 1998.
"I Love Baby Cheesy" (single), Gecko/Six Degrees, 1999.
The Magical Sounds of Banco De Gaia, Gecko/ Six Degrees, 1999.

Sources

Books

Graff, Gary, Daniel Durchholz, editors, *musicHound Rock: The Essential Album Guide,*, Visible Ink Press, 1999.

Periodicals

Dallas Morning News, September 4, 1997, p. 5C.
Esquire, December 1, 1995, p. 56.
Future Music, August 1999, pp. 60-62.
Newsday, November 17, 1999, p. B23.

Online

"Banco De Gaia," *All Music Guide* website, http://www.allmusic.com, (September 13, 1999).
"Banco De Gaia," *Launch.com: Discover New Music*, http://www.launch.com, (September 13, 1999).
The Official Banco De Gaia Website, http://www.banco.co.uk, (September 13, 1999).
"Banco De Gaia," *Rolling Stone.com Artists A to Z*, http://www.rollingstone.tunes.com, (September 13, 1999).

—Laura Hightower

Joe Diffie

Singer, songwriter

Ken Settle. Reproduced by permission.©

Acceptance of a gift should not be difficult. However, when that gift is not perfect, acceptance is not easy—especially when that gift is a child. In 1989, Joe Diffie, who country legend Vern Gosdin, according to *The News-Times* called, "the man with the golden voice," had to accept an imperfect gift when his son, Tyler was born with Down's syndrome. "I was just devasted," Diffie told *People*. "I remember thinking, 'How could I have something imperfect?' I was just so hurt. I heard Down's and thought the world had ended." But the world had not ended—a new world had just begun. Fans of the "golden voice" began to bring their Down's children to Diffie's concerts. Diffie also told *People*, "I think parents think; 'Well if I take my kids to this guy's show, it's not going to be an embarrassment because he has a child like mine'." Thus, while Diffie's fans continued to sell out his concerts and push his albums to number one, Diffie accepted his imperfect gift, stating to *People*, "Tyler's a beautiful child. I couldn't be prouder."

Joe Logan Diffie was born on December 29, 1958, in Tulsa, Oklahoma. He grew up in a musical family with his two sisters, Meg and Monica. Diffie's mother, Flora loved to sing, while his father, Joe Riley, played the guitar. In fact, according to his web site, Diffie first learned how to play guitar on his Dad's F-hole Airline from Sears & Roebuck. But, it was in a car where Diffie first began to sing. "I remember singing at around three or four years old," he recalled to imusic.com. "My mother and dad, me and my two sisters—we'd take trips and we'd all sing harmony while my dad was driving." Diffie recollected listening to country legends Merle Haggard and George Jones. But, as Diffie told *New Country* reporter Brian Mansfield, it was another country legend that sang Diffie to sleep: " my mom and dad say; I wouldn't go to sleep unless they put a Johnny Cash record on."

Diffie's first public performance came at the ripe old age of four when he sang, "You Are My Sunshine" with his aunt's country band. By high school, Diffie had joined, as stated on countrystars.com, a "four-song ... garage band" as well as a gospel ensemble. However, being a country music star wasn't Diffie's dream job; he wanted to become a doctor. He wanted to be a heart surgeon, but after a football injury, he decided to become a chiropractor. Yet, he kept part of his heart in music by playing with Higher Purpose, a gospel group, and Special Edition, a bluegrass band. After graduation, Diffie attended Cameron University and married Janise Parker. When the reality of having to make a living started to sink in, Diffie curtailed his plans to become a chiropractor as well as his musical gigs and found "real" jobs—first in a Texas oil field, then in an iron foundry. Diffie told *Tennessean*'s reporter Thomas Goldsmith that working in an oil field was, "nasty, nasty work; you had oil all over you all the

For the Record . . .

Born Joe Logan Diffie on December 29, 1958 in Tulsa, OK; son of Joe Riley (a teacher, rancher, and welder) and Flora Diffie; married Janise Parker (divorced in 1986); married Debbie Jones in 1988; children: Parker and Kara (from first marriage) and sons: Tyler and Drew (from second marriage). *Education*: Attended Cameron University.

Worked in Texas oil field as well as in a foundry throughout the late 1970s and mid-1980s; began rededicating himself to music by singing with bluegrass group, Special Edition; landed job at Gibson Guitar Company in Nashville, TN to pay the bills; contracted songwriter for Forest Hills Music publishers, 1987; became professional demo record singer; co-penned Holly Dunn's hit "There Goes My Heart Again;" signed to record deal with Epic Records, 1990; released debut album, *A Thousand Winding Roads*, album yielded four number one singles: "Home," "If You Want Me To," "If the Devil Danced in Empty Pockets," and "New Way to Light Up an Old Flame;" released second album, *Regular Joe*, 1992; album included the number one single, "Is It Cold in Here (Or Is It Just You)" as well as earned Diffie a Country Music Association nomination for Male Vocalist of the Year; recorded duet with Mary-Chapin Carpenter "Not to Much to Ask," 1993, released *Honky Tonky Attitude* released *Third Rock from the Sun*, 1994; released *Life's So Funny* and *Mr. Christmas* , both in 1995; released *Twice Upon a Time*, 1997; created Third-Rock a show business/entertainment company; released *Greatest Hits*, 1998; released *A Night To Remember*,1999.

Awards: *CashBox* magazine's Male Vocalist of the Year and *Billboard* magazine's Top Singles Artist of the Year, both 1990; Country Music Association Award for his vocal collaboration with George Jones on "I Don't Need Your Rocking Chair," 1992; Country Radio Broadcasters Humanitarian Award, 1997; Grammy for "Same Old Train," 1999.

Addresses: *Record company*—Epic Records, 550 Madison Ave. 22nd Fl., New York, NY 10022-3211, (212) 883-8000. fax (212) 883-4054. *Publicist*—Stephanie Kidd, Third Rock Entertainment, Nashville, TN; *Website*—www.joediffie.com.

time." Working as a machinist in an iron foundry, he further told Goldsmith, was not much better. "I hated every second of that foundry job, just detested it." Yet, he spent eight years at the foundry until finally, in 1986, he was laid off which according to imusic.com, "proved to be Diffie's blessing in disguise." He and Janise also divorced that same year.

Re-ignited Musical Spark

Throughout the mid-1980s, Diffie not only played shows with his aunt and sister, he also concentrated on songwriting and ran an eight-track recording studio. "Of course, it didn't do well financially; most small studios didn't," Diffie told imusic.com. "But I had to work on my guitar, and learn a bit of bass and drums to help out on sessions." This practice created a successful Hank Thompson hit, "Love On the Rocks." However, it wasn't Diffie's musicianship, but his songwriting that led him to Nashville. Diffie heard that country superstar Randy Travis may record one of his songs. Encouraged by this news and with money from his parents, Diffie, in December of 1986, packed up and headed to Music City. He explained to imusic.com, "I was real naïve when I arrived. It was scary. But I knew I'd kick myself if I didn't try."

In Nashville, Diffie quickly found work at the Gibson Guitar Company, not designing or playing guitars, but loading and unloading them. Yet, he remembered his Dad's advice, "Do something every day to work toward your goal." Diffie worked hard toward his goal of becoming a country singer, but he was also helped by a little luck. After rooming with a bluegrass musician, Diffie discovered their next-door neighbor was Johnny Neal, a popular songwriter. "I showed him some demos," Diffie further commented to imusic.com, "and, by helping me get a publishing deal, he got me started." Soon after, Diffie quit his job at the Gibson Guitar Company, and signed on as a songwriter at Forest Hills Music. Country superstars such as Charley Pride and Conway Twitty as well as up-and-comers Tracy Lawrence and Doug Stone began recording Diffie's songs. In 1988, not only was Diffie's professional career hot, but so was his personal life. He married Debbie Jones, a nurse technician. In 1989, "There Goes My Heart Again," a tune co-written by Diffie, became a smash hit for Holly Dunn. At the same time, Diffie also sang on demo tapes including harmony for a then unknown Tim McGraw. His vocal contribution helped get McGraw signed to a recording contract, and, in return, McGraw recorded Diffie's "Memory Lane," his second single. Record labels soon began seeking out the popular songwriter and finally, in 1990, Epic Records signed Diffie.

Combined Ballads and Wit for Success

In 1990, Diffie's debut album, *A Thousand Winding Roads,* leapt onto country music charts and produced four smash number one singles: "Home," "If You Want Me To," "If the Devil Danced in Empty Pockets," and "New Way to Light Up an Old Flame." According to imusic.com, Diffie was "the first country singer to be accorded a #1 hit his first time at bat" with "Home." It was also the first single in country music history to top the charts of all major music-business magazines simultaneously. Yet, Diffie was not only gaining recognition for his booming tenor so evident on ballads like "Home," but also for his, "once so clever, yet so down-home and so sincere [song writing]," *Country Music* stated. "[Song writing] that ... could have come straight from the pens of honky-tonk poet laureates of yesteryear."

In 1992, Diffie released his second album, *Regular Joe,* which produced four more smash hits including the jukebox favorite, "Is It Cold in Here (Or Is It Just You)" and, according to Diffie's web site, one of his favorite songs to perform live, "Ships That Don't Come In." *Regular Joe* earned Diffie a Country Music Association (CMA) nomination for Male Vocalist of the Year. He was also nominated for his duet, "Not Too Much to Ask" with Mary-Chapin Carpenter, the CMAFemale Vocalist of the Year that same year. Carpenter had chosen Diffie for this duet, because she felt he combined an understanding of classic country singing with a uniquely modern interpretation. That same year, Diffie won a CMA award for "I Don't Need No Rocking Chair," his vocal collaboration with the legendary George Jones. Yet, smash hits were not the only contribution he made in 1992. Inspired by his son Tyler, he also organized the First Steps concert and golf tournament—an annual event which raises money for disabled children.

In 1993, Diffie, with his third album, *Honky Tonk Attitude,* began to a blend a bit of humor into his ballads. Witty songs such as "Prop Me Up Beside the Jukebox (If I Die)," showed fans Diffie's funny bone. Also, critics such as *Country Music*'s Rich Kienzle felt the album as a whole pushed Diffie "further into that idiom where he shows the gutsiness that many younger singers never quite catch. It's New Traditionalism without compromise, but music that fans of certain more modern-sounding singers can enjoy as well." Such critical accolades would make any country singer happy. However, Diffie was offered the highest praise from his peers when he was asked to become a member of Nashville's cherished Grand Ole Opry.

Diffie released his fourth album, *Third Rock from the Sun,* in 1994. This album once again showed Diffie's two sides. The hard rocking title tune offered a humorous story about a meteor hitting the earth, while "So Help Me Girl," another number one single, once again presented a tender love story. In 1995, Diffie continued his hot streak by releasing his fifth and sixth albums: *Life's So Funny* and *Mr. Christmas.* With *Life's So Funny,* Diffie, "turns a little more personal and emotional," @Country asserted. Yet, Diffie maintained his cleverness with the single, "Bigger Than The Beatles." This song, described by @Country, "is a novelty pop-rocker with Fab Four-like "yeah, yeah, yeahs," as Diffie sings about a lounge performer and a waitress who both dream of stardom from a Holiday Inn." Diffie's Christmas album, *Mr. Christmas,* was reviewed by @Country and, "offers a new take on some past and soon-to-be holiday favorites," according to the website. Diffie's "Leroy the Redneck Reindeer," as the lyrics describe, is a "down-home party animal two-steppin' across the sky" who is "delivering toys to all the good ol' boys and girls along the way." This funny twist on a classic has become a fan favorite, while the album "is warm and fuzzy," @Country stated, "and will be cherished just like that worn stocking hanging about the hearth."

Singer Turned Businessman

In 1996, after five years and six albums, Diffie became worn-out by the constant stress to produce hit singles. It did seem, however, that television and movies were just catching on to Diffie's popularity. Ford Motor Company chose Diffie's hit single, "Pickup Man," as their national jingle, "She Ain't Comin' Back" provided a theme for the blockbuster movie *Twister,* and Diffie acted opposite one of his idols, Johnny Cash, in a television movie. Nevertheless, these pursuits didn't quite revive Diffie's creative spirit, so he created Third Rock Entertainment. "I was feeling a bit of staleness, both in my career and my everyday life," explained Diffie on his web site. "I felt like it was time to make some kind of move." Some people thought that he "wouldn't stick with running his own show business company. "But it's been so good for me; man, I enjoy it. I'm at the office everyday. It's been so refreshing and has helped me in so manyways. I feel like I've got my finger on my own pulse," he further explained. However, show business was not Diffie's only work. He also continued organizing events and raising money for First Steps, and in 1997, Country Radio Broadcasters awarded Diffie its Humanitarian Award for his years of charitable work. "It is, he says, the highest honor he has ever received."

After a year of rejuvenation, Diffie returned to hit making with the release of his seventh album, *Twice Upon a Time.* For this album, Diffie told imusic.com he "looked for songs that dealt with everything about being human." In turn, imusic.com called this album, "a true aural page-turner, well-paced, and irresistible." Once again, Diffie had successfully blended wit and heart. In "Houston We Have a Problem," the song's unlucky narrator finds himself, according to imusic.com, 'hoping for romantic assignation in the cheap seats at the end zone' [only to find] himself 'sitting here crying in the parking lot of the Astrodome'." Nevertheless, it is the album's final song, "One More Breath" that is, as imusic.com further stated, "an affirmation of not only love, but of life itself."

In 1998, Diffie released *Greatest Hits*, an album that collected 12 of his most popular songs, including "Home," "John Deere Green," and "Ships That Don't Come In," as well as previously unreleased songs such as "Texas Size Heartache," "Poor Me," and "Hurt Me All The Time." The website countrystars.com hailed this album as "a 12 song testament—written in platinum and solid gold—to a man who has established his place as one of the definitive country artists of this decade." In 1999, Diffie also became a two-time Grammy winner for his vocal performance on "Same Old Train."

Diffie's ninth album, *A Night to Remember*, released in 1999, offered something new not only to Diffie's long-time fans, but also to country music. "I wanted to record an entire album of lyrics that had messages," Diffie told countrystars.com. "Every song had to have something to say. I think for a while now Country music has been afraid to play a song with any substance to it. What I'm trying to do there is present some songs that I feel have some depth." Diffie reached his goal to create songs with messages especially with the single, "You Can't Go Home." The song's message, "I came looking for a feeling/But the feeling's gone/You can go back/But you can't go back home." *Los Angeles Times* reviewer John Roos remarked that the song is "a more realistic bookend to Diffie's warmly nostalgic first hit, 'Home.'" And countrycool.com praised Diffie's effort as "an album to remember." Despite such favorable reviews, Diffie felt he had not reached all of his goals. As he told rockvillage.com, "I would like [to write a song] ... about my son Tyler who has Down's syndrome."

Thus, Diffie has been given the gift of acceptance—from country music and from his fans. He has also learned not only how to accept an imperfect gift, but how to learn from that imperfect gift as well. Perhaps that lesson has influenced how he would like to be remembered: "I hope I'd always be known as a great singer," he explained to countrystars.com, "but that's really secondary. If people could say, 'He was a good friend ... a nice guy ... someone you could trust,' I'd be really satisfied. Strip everything else away, and those are the things that matter the most."

Selected discography

A Thousand Winding Roads, Epic, 1990.
Regular Joe, Epic, 1992.
Honky Tonk Attitude, Epic, 1993.
Third Rock From The Sun, Epic, 1994.
Life's So Funny, Epic, 1995.
Mr. Christmas, Epic, 1995.
Twice Upon A Time, Epic, 1997.
Greatest Hits, Epic, 1998.
A Night To Remember, Epic, 1999.

Sources

Periodicals

Country Music, May/June 1991; July/August 1993.
Los Angeles Times, October 13, 1999.
News-Times, May 17, 1997.
People, Fall 1994.
Tennessean (Nashville), January 5, 1991.

Online

"CHAT-A-LOG: Joe Diffie," http://www.rockvillage.com (November 16, 1999).
Country, http://www.cdnow.com (November 16, 1999).
"Get to Know Joe," *Official Joe Diffie Web Site*, http://www.joediffie.com (November 16, 1999).
"Joe Diffie, *A Night To Remember*," *The World of Country Music*, http://www.countrycool.com (November 16, 1999).
"Joe Diffie," *Great American Country Joe Diffie Page*, http://www.countrystars.com (November 16, 1999).
"Joe Diffie," *iMusic Country Showcase*, http://www.imusic.com (November 16, 1999).
"Making Hit Records Is No Joke For Joe Diffie," *New Country: Joe Diffie*, available at http://www.cciweb.com (November 16, 1999).

—Ann M. Schwalboski

Sara Evans

Singer, songwriter

Throughout her life, Sara Evans only held but one dream: to sing and compose country songs. "God put me on this earth to be a singer," said Evans, as quoted by John Meroney of *American Enterprise.* "It's what I love to do more than anything, and I'm going to make it." Moreover, Evans wanted to succeed by returning to the traditional country songs brought to life by legendary stars such as Patsy Cline, Hank Snow, Tammy Wynette, George Jones, and Patty Loveless, musicians Evans considered her greatest influences. During the late 1990s, an era when most aspiring country musicians turned to contemporary, pop radio-friendly tunes, Evans made her initial mark by performing country songs that looked to the past, exemplified by her 1997 debut entitled *True Lies.* But despite critical acceptance and a nomination by the Academy of Country Music in 1998 for best new female vocalist, *True Lies* made little impact. Thus, for her follow-up release, 1999's *No Place That Far,* Evans bowed to producers, who persuaded the artist to update her repertoire, and finally earned the popular recognition she had longed for since her childhood.

Sara Evans was born February 5, 1971, in Columbia, Missouri. She spent her early years, along with her six brothers and sisters (sister Ashley later sang backup for Evans, and sister Allyx, born around 1989, started performing with a Missouri-based band at about nine years of age), on a farm outside Franklin, Missouri, where her family raised corn, beans, tobacco, and livestock for a living. Although the family remained poor, Evans nevertheless enjoyed a happy upbringing, recalling fond memories of the stories her grandfather used to tell her about the Grand Ole Opry, the longest-lived radio show in the United States. Established in Nashville, Tennessee, on November 28, 1925, the live program brought the songs of legendary performers to homes across America and established Nashville as the undisputed center of the country music industry.

Hearing tales of the stars who graced the stage of the Grand Ole Opry struck a chord with the Evans children, and by the age of four, Evans and her two older brothers started traveling on weekends and during the summer months as the Evans Family Band. Inspired by the underlying foundation of country music, the group performed gospel and bluegrass music at festivals and church revivals. Before long, word spread of the young girl's awe-inspiring talent, leading the band to rename itself the Sara Evans Show. As the band's popularity grew, the Sara Evans Show eventually brought in about fifty dollars for each performance, but the extra money failed to uplift the family's meager income; Evans's mother once resorted to trading firewood for Levi jeans in order to give the children Christmas presents. Another unfortunate incident occurred when Evans, eight years old at the time, suffered a debilitating injury when a speeding car hit her as she crossed a highway. The accident left her with two shattered legs, cracked wrists, and countless stitches. Doctors told her she would probably walk with a limp for the rest of her life. Determined to make a full recovery, Evans spent a full year in physical therapy and healed completely, except, as she noted to *Country Music,* "my left leg looks a little odd. It's got this little bow in it that protrudes above the knee."

Evans longed to see Nashville since first hearing of the Grand Ole Opry and made her first trip to the city at age eleven. Accompanied by her father, Evans made the journey in order to record a single, "What Does a Nice Girl Do in the Meantime," with the song "I'm Going to Be the Only Female Fiddle Player in Charlie Daniels' Band" on the record's flip side. While the single went unnoticed, Evans continued to hold the dream of making it in Nashville. Therefore, after graduating from high school and a short stint at college, Evans returned to Nashville with serious plans of breaking into country music. "I skipped college, and had no other aspirations but to sing," Evans told Meroney. "So I came here with my older brother, started waiting tables at the Holiday Inn on Briley Parkway, and tried to meet whomever I could."

The person who inspired Evans the most was Craig Schelske, a musician from Oregon whom she would later marry. "He was a room service waiter trying to do the

For the Record . . .

Born February 5, 1971, in Columbia, MO; daughter of Pat Boggs (mother), Jack Evans (father), and Melvin Boggs (stepfather); two brothers: Jay and Matt; four sisters: Lesley, Ashley (sings backup for Evans), Erin, and Allyx (born c. 1989); married musician Craig Schelske; one son: Jack Avery (born August 21, 1999).

Started performing with older brothers as the Evans Family Band (later renamed the Sara Evans Show) at age four; recorded first single "What Does a Nice Girl Do in the Meantime?" in Nashville, TN, at age eleven; signed with RCA Records, 1996; released debut *Three Chords and the Truth,* 1997; released follow-up effort, *No Place that Far,* RCA, 1998.

Addresses: *Home*—Springfield, TN. *Record company*—RCA Records, 1540 Broadway, New York City, NY 10036, (212) 930-4000, fax (212) 930-4468. *Fan Club*—Sara Evans Fan Club, P.O. Box 509, Knoxville, TN 37901.

same thing," the singer revealed to Meroney. "We started dating, fell in love, and he asked me to go to Oregon with him and sing in his band." Evans accepted her companion's offer and spent the next three years performing with Schelske's band throughout the Pacific Northwest. For the first time in her career, Evans finally met some of the biggest names in country music as the band opened for such renowned performers as Willie Nelson, Tim McGraw, and Clay Walker. Evans earned decent money as well, usually performing six nights per week. Nevertheless, she felt that returning to Nashville would provide her with a more certain chance at success.

Upon her return to Nashville, Evans soon realized that most artists had turned away from traditional country and toward a style that appealed to a wider, mainstream audience, a transition accelerated by country superstar Garth Brooks in the early 1990s. Thus, traditional country and its use of fiddles, mandolins, and rhythm instruments (like the acoustic guitar and bass) were often replaced by a more neutral, pop sound recorded with rock and roll production elements. Progressive country revealed more complexity as well, often abandoning the use of just three chords per song in favor of more adventurous guitar work. By the mid 1990s, country music—fueled by contemporary artists—had surpassed both pop and urban contemporary formats as the number one music choice of music behind rock.

Although excited by such changes, Evans had always felt partial to the traditional style and sought out entertainment lawyer Brenner Van Meter, who by coincidence was considering leaving her law practice to manage talent, for advice. Taken by Evans's gifted singing and songwriting ability, as well as by the singer's preference to perform traditional country, she arranged for Evans to meet her husband, John Van Meter, an executive at Sony Tree Publishing Company. The couple believed that the time might be right for a gritty country singer to break into the business, and Evans accepted a job recording songs for writers to submit to major artists as potential album tracks. Soon, established songwriters were seeking out Evans's vocals to give their music a test run.

Eventually, Evans met well-known songwriter Harlan Howard, who wanted to sell his 1964 classic "I've Got a Tiger By the Tail"—written with Buck Owens, who also recorded the song—to a major female singer. Believing that Evans's voice would help to promote the song, the Van Meters invited Howard to sit in during recording. "I went in, sang the song, came out of the singing booth, and there's Harlan Howard on the couch," recalled Evans, according to Meroney. "He said, 'Are you that little girl in there singing? You're great. I've been looking for you for years to sing my music. I can't believe how country you are.' I had never even thought about it before." With Howard's help and encouragement, Evans and her management felt confident enough to approach RCA Records about her own singing career. To Evans's amazement, RCA's chairman, Joe Galante, offered the singer a contract the same day of her audition.

Evans released her debut for RCA, *Three Chords and the Truth,* in the fall of 1997. Produced by Pete Anderson, her first full-length album included the Howard/Owens single in addition to the understated ballad "Unopened," the Patsy Cline-inspired "Imagine That," and her own co-written "The Week the River Raged." Although the album failed to bring in substantial revenues—Chuck Eddy of *Rolling Stone* declared *Three Chords and the Truth* "Nashville's Most Unjustly ignored debut" that year—critics hailed the record and Evans a major success. "Sara Evans is so good she's scary," concluded Paul Verna for *Billboard* magazine. "At once a preserver of the best of country's history and a progressive writer and singer forging a timeless contemporary country sound, she invites favorable comparisons to the best country divas.... Evans is a considerable country talent." The impressive debut also led the Academy of Country Music (ACM) to nominate Evans in 1998 as the year's best new female vocalist.

Despite sluggish sales, the ACM and critical recognition helped Evans forge ahead, and the following year brought forth *No Place that Far,* the singer's follow-up album. Regarding her debut, most radio stations grumbled at the fact that, in addition to the record's lack of progressive tracks, Evans and Anderson had set up studio in California rather than in Nashville. Therefore, for her second project, RCA hired Nashville-based producers Norro Wilson and Buddy Cannon. Her label also encouraged the singer to collaborate with Nashville songwriters such as Tom Shapiro, Tony Martin, Billy Yates, and Mantraca Berg. "It was a difficult process," Evans told Chet Flippo in *Billboard,* "but I feel we did it without being too contemporary. I think it's what radio is really wanting. The song search was extremely difficult. You want songs that are country but also songs that radio will accept.... Joe [Galante] had to very gently pull me more in that contemporary direction. Because, the bottom line is, if we can't get on radio, we can't do anything. That's just the way it is right now. Eventually, it will happen. I just have to stay in that frame of mind."

The album's title-track and second radio single, written by Evans along with Shapiro and Martin and featuring the vocals of Vince Gill, travels through uplifting gospel territory as well as into depressing rural harmonies reminiscent of the Carter Family. The song became Evans's first hit, climbing to the number one position on *Billboard*'s Hot Country Singles and Tracks chart in March of 1999. Evans's favorite song, though, was one written by Howard and Beth NielsonChapman entitled "Time Won't Tell." "Garth [Brooks] and Trisha [Yearwood] wanted it for their duet project, but Harlan gave it to us," she revealed to Flipp. "He's always been very big about helping new artists, going all the way back to Patsy Cline. That was a great catch. It's got to be heard. That one of the greatest songs Harlan's ever written."

No Place that Far, with its stylistically varied songs, also fared well with critics. Eddy, for example, applauded Evans's ability to perform both contemporary and traditional songs. The reviewer further added, "Evans' real forte is brisk commercial stuff, mainly about women starting over: a rockabilly duet with George Jones that hints at his old Fifties white lightning; a heading-out-of-New Orleans-with-Rand McNally divorce waltz in which both the knot and (if you trust her pronunciation) the night come untied; and an album-opening hoedown where her big, brave alto yearns for a corner in Winslow, Arizona." Country music fans approved of Evans's effort as well, and the release rose to the top of the *Billboard* country album chart in early 1999. That same year, the musician earned additional honors as the Country Music Association (CMA) nominated her for two awards: video event of the year and the CMA's Horizon award, both for her work in 1998. After marrying Schelske, Evans made her home in Springfield, Tennessee. The couple had one son, Jack Avery, born August 21, 1999.

Selected discography

Three Chords and the Truth, RCA, 1997.
No Place that Far, RCA, 1998.

Sources

Periodicals

American Enterprise, March/April 1998, pp. 52-57.
Billboard, October 11, 1997, p. 83; September 26, 1998, p. 32; March 6, 1999, p. 114.
Country Music, June/July 1999, p. 44.
Rolling Stone, December 1, 1998, p. 128.

Online

"Country Singer Sara Evans Gives Birth," *CDNOW,* http://www.cdnow.com/cgi-bin/mserver/redirect/leaf=allstararticle/fid=16030, (October 24, 1999).
Today: theEnews, http://www.theenews.com/bms/tdn-slug82499_saraevans.html, (October 24, 1999).

—Laura Hightower

Everlast

Singer, songwriter, guitar

Hip-hop singer Everlast, born Erik Schrody, makes a forceful case for claiming that despite being white and growing up in the suburbs, his gravitation toward the rap and hip-hop culture was as American as apple pie. "If you go by that little inscription on the Statue of Liberty, the purest idea of America is complete cultural chaos," he told *Spin* magazine's Charles Aaron. "Why don't we have a national culture? Because we have *all* cultures. America has its fingertips into everything, and so does hip-hop, that's why it makes so much sense." Taking this notion to heart, the tattooed singer/rapper who converted from Catholicism to the Muslim faith and built an enormous collection of baseball cards over the years released his first album, the unimpressive *Forever Everlasting,* in 1990. That same year, he put his solo aspirations aside to form the Gaelic rap/hip-hop trio House of Pain with Danny Boy, born Daniel O'Connor, and DJ Lethal, born Leor DiMant, who later joined the rap/metal band Limp Bizkit.

Although the group found success, proving that hip-hop and rap had grown beyond the confines of African American neighborhoods, Everlast announced his departure from the trio the day House of Pain's third album came out in 1996. In 1998, after suffering through financial difficulties and a painful breakup with his former girlfriend, Everlast released the acclaimed *Whitey Ford Sings the Blues*—named after Whitey Ford, a New York Yankees pitcher during the 1950s and 1960s—considered a more mature and ambitious effort than any work he had done with House of Pain. And by early 1999, the single "What It's Like," a series of hard luck stories set to acoustic blues guitar and a lazy breakbeat became a radio hit. Like the characters in the song, Everlast lived through hard times in his own life as well, forcing him to approach life with a more grown-up outlook. For example, Everlast viewed his conversion to Islam as a serious undertaking and thus prays daily, practices fasting, and regrets his sacrilegious tattoos. Moreover, the same day he completed *Whitey Ford Sings the Blues,* Everlast suffered a near-fatal heart attack—brought on by a birth defect, in addition to a lifetime of smoking, drinking, and stress—that he continued to recover from throughout 1999.

Everlast was born into a family of Irish descent in Hempstead, Long Island, New York in 1970. His grandfather was a "red-headed singing bartender from Brooklyn," Everlast's mother, Rita Mulligan, told Aaron. Everlast's father, a construction worker, moved the family to Southern California when he was around 11 years old. The Schrody family's finances fluctuated throughout Everlast's childhood, and during the early 1980s, Everlast and his sister Cassandra (born around 1973) were bounced back and forth from Los Angeles to New York as his father chased jobs.Eventually, the family settled in the upscale suburb of Woodland Hills, located in the San Fernando Valley near Los Angeles. Here, Everlast found himself one of the few working-class kids among a group of wealthy kids with little direction and started smoking marijuana.

However, Everlast's interests suddenly shifted as soon as he heard the rap group Run-D.M.C.'s "Rock Box" for the first time. "I stopped hanging out with all those hesher/stoner kids, and got into hip-hop full-blown," recalled Everlast to Aaron. "I still loved my Led Zeppelin and Black Sabbath, but that first Run-D.M.C. album blew me away." During his late teens at Taft and Canoga Park high schools, the area school system incorporated busing, an event that significantly altered the racial make-up of students. Before long, Everlast started rebelling against suburban life, often ditching school to take the bus to Los Angeles with his new Latin and African American friends. Around this time he also met future House of Pain band member Danny Boy, his only significant white friend. Everlast later recalled these adventures as the happiest times in his life, even overshadowing the success he achieved with House of Pain.

With friend Divine Styler, who later released three albums, including 1999's *Directrix: World Power 2,* Everlast started rapping and making tapes produced by good

For the Record . . .

Born Erik Schrody in 1970 in Hempstead, Long Island, NY; son of a construction worker father and mother Rita Mulligan, a restaurant franchise manager; one sister, born c. 1973.

Released unimpressive debut, *Forever Everlasting*, Warner Bros. Records, 1990; formed group House of Pain, 1990; House of Pain released platinum-selling, self-titled debut on Tommy Boy Records, 1992; left House of Pain, 1996; released comeback solo album, *Whitey Ford Sings the Blues,* survived life-threatening heart attack, 1998.

Awards: Double platinum for *Whitey Ford*, 1999.

Addresses: *Record company*—Tommy Boy Music, 902 Broadway, 13th Flr., New York City, NY 10010, (212)388-8300.*Home*—Los Angeles, CA. *Website*—Official Everlast Website, http://www.forevereverlasting.com.

friend DJ Bilal Bashir. He lived with the Bashir family for a short time when his mother kicked him out of the house for neglecting his schoolwork. Several of Everlast's friends knew rap artist Ice-T, one of the founding fathers of the gangsta rap genre. And after Ice-T heard one of Everlast's demos, the legendary rapper expressed an immediate interest. "Ice-T said he'd like to meet me," Everlast told Julian Dibbell in an interview with *Details.* "Then they told him I was white, and he said he *really* wanted to meet me."

After meeting Ice-T, the 17-year-old Everlast joined Ice-T's crew, the Rhyme Syndicate, and recorded his debut album for Warner Brothers Records. Released in 1990 and produced under the auspices of the Rhyme Syndicate, the record made little or no impression, and Dibbell noted that "the rapper was packaged as a boxer with a Sean Penn pout and greased back locks." Nevertheless, Everlast would later express gratitude for the album's failure. As he told Aaron, "I thank God every day that record flopped. I could have been Vanilla Ice, dude. Then it really would've been over."

Indeed, Everlast's story would have ended there if not for his embrace of a different sort of ethnic undertaking and meeting DJMuggs of the interracial rap trio Cypress Hill. Joined by Danny Boy and producer DJ Lethal in 1990, Everlast created House of Pain as the first Gaelic hip-hop group, draping the group carelessly in Irish imagery more as a marketing scheme than a cultural identity, especially given the fact that DJ Lethal was the son of Jewish Latvian immigrants. Needless to say, touting their "Irishness" angered many, who felt that the gimmick reinforced negative stereotypes. Nonetheless, House of Pain adopted a three-leafed logo along with orange and green colors to symbolize Irish pride. And references to the pub life culture were scattered throughout tracks like "Shamrocks and Shenanigans" and "Top of the Morning to Ya," though House of Pain made certain to avoid the political reality of Ireland.

The group's platinum-selling self-titled debut, released in 1992, contained the popular hit single "Jump Around." Embraced by hip-hop and pop music fans alike, the song became a college party anthem and even prompted a hard-core rap following in Ireland. Although Everlast insisted that the song was never meant for pop radio, he confessed to *Billboard* magazine's Gil Griffin, "When I was watching MTV and saw our video as one of the top five, then saw our single in the Top Five on the pop charts, I bugged." Following *House of Pain*'s success, Everlast landed a small role in the independent film *Judgment Night.*

House of Pain's next two albums,1994's *Same As It Ever Was*, and 1996's *Truth Crushed to Earth Will Rise Again*, failed to recapture the frenzy inspired by the first album, and Everlast struggled to grow musically with rap and hip-hop. Not to mention, his close friendship with Danny Boy and DJ Lethal had become mired in substance-abuse and was almost nonexistent. Therefore, Everlast, feeling that his happiness and mental state were in jeopardy, made a difficult decision to quit the band on the release date of the third album. "I felt like, if I didn't just get away from everything that was around me at the time that something really bad would have happened," he commented in a 1999 interview for the Totally LA website. "I was like the lead guy, so it was almost like there was a pressure on me sometimes to do things I didn't want to do because the other two guys wanted them done, and I felt that I had been friends with these guys for so long that if I didn't quit, I wouldn't be friends with them now, which I am. I'm better friends with Lethal than I've ever been and Danny Boy I haven't seen in a while, but I still got tremendous love for him."

Little did he know at the time, circumstances would become much worse after leaving House of Pain before they would improve. Everlast was sued by his record company, sold his Hollywood Hills dream home, almost went bankrupt—at one point he had but $12 in his bank account—fell out with his management, lost his Screen Actors Guild (SAG) card, and was placed under house arrest for trying to carry a gun aboard an airplane. Then he endured a painful breakup with his girlfriend, which he later documented in a song from *Whitey Ford Sings the Blues* entitled "The Letter." After a seven-year relationship, Everlast's girlfriend was fed up with his constant infidelities. "I was an asshole, bottom line," he regretfully admitted to Aaron.

Humbled by these events, he traded a life of booze, women, and insensitivity for one of spirituality, sincerity, and social awareness. After selling his home, Everlast became roommates with his mother, who battled cancer in the mid-1980s, and the two shared a Los Angeles condominium which also doubled as Everlast's new studio. His parents divorced when he was 20, but Everlast, who learned to play guitar listening to his father's Neil Young records as a child, never fully forgave his father. In spite of these feelings, Everlast said he still loved his father and continued to maintain a relationship with him out of respect for the teachings of Islam, which tells its followers to honor both parents.

Determined to make a career comeback as well as a personal one, Everlast started the five-month process of writing and recording music for *Whitey Ford*, intended at first to be "a straight-up hip-hop album," he told *Entertainment Weekly*'s Tom Sinclair. However, he ended up recording the atypical "What It's Like," at the urging of his producer Dante Ross. "I've been playing guitar for a long time, but I never thought of putting guitars on a hip-hop record," said Everlast. "But I was in the studio strumming that song one night, and Dante said, 'Yo, that's dope. We've got to record that.'" And because "What It's Like," sounded so well set to a moody acoustic guitar and an understated string section, Everlast decided to record a few more tracks with the instrument.

In addition to giving a bluesy, acoustic feel to hip-hop, Everlast also brought a sense of social concern to the album. "What It's Like," for example, tells the stories of three individuals suffering through hard times—a homeless alcoholic, a woman seeking an abortion abandoned by her unborn child's father, and an ill-fated gangster—for whom Everlast empathizes in a line from the chorus, "God forbid you ever had to walk a mile in their shoes." As Everlast told Sinclair, "It's about empathy. It's saying, don't judge ... because you've got as much dirt under your fingernails." Likewise, another song called "Ends" condemns greed.

Feeling self-fulfilled with his accomplishment, Everlast believed his personal troubles were finally behind him. But on the sameday he wrapped up recording, he suffered another wake-up call, this time the event proved life threatening. That night, after eating dinner at his home in February of 1998, he felt his chest tighten and at first thought indigestion was the cause of his pain. Producer John Gamble, watching Everlast struggle for several hours to breath normally, finally decided to call for an ambulance, and within moments of arriving at Cedars-Sinai Hospital, Everlast's heart failed, his aorta was torn and he lost large amounts of blood. Born with a heart defect, a bicuspid aortic valve, doctors had predicted Everlast would need surgery when he reached his 50s. However, heavy smoking and drinking combined with nervousness and stress had sped up the process.

Everlast awoke four days later to the relieved faces of his parents, as well as to a ticking sound, a prosthetic heart valve. "Every time it closes, that's the sound it makes," he explained to Alona Wartofsky of the *Minneapolis Star Tribune.* "It's soothing. I fall asleep to it every night. If it stopped making this sound now I'd be a little worried." Everlast spent the remainder of the year and 1999 recovering from his heart attack. He released *Whitey Ford* (produced by Ross and Gamble) in mid-1998, but the record failed to earn recognition right away. Then several months later, MTV started airing the video for "What It's Like" on a regular basis, helping to bring the album out of obscurity. Subsequently, radio stations started to embrace the single as well, and soon thereafter, "What It's Like" hit number one on both modern rock and mainstream charts. By the summer of 1999, the album achieved double platinum status.

While continuing to recover, Everlast also toured in 1999 to support his record. Furthermore, he landed another acting role as police officer O'Maley in an upcoming film by hip-hop producer "Prince" Paul Huston entitled *A Prince Among Thieves.* One of his favorite recording artists is Lauryn Hill, and he concluded to Aaron that people who "don't feel her record [the single "Ex-Factor"]—I mean *feel* it— inside, there's something wrong with them." He also admires Outkast, Miles Davis, Tom Waits, Hank Williams, and newcomer Fiona Apple.

Selected discography

with House of Pain

House of Pain, Tommy Boy, 1992.
Same As It Ever Was, Tommy Boy, 1994.
Trutyh Crushed to Earth Will Rise Again, Tommy Boy, 1996.

Solo

Forever Everlasting, Warner Brothers Records, 1990, reissued, Rhino Records, 1999.
Whitey Ford Sings the Blues, Tommy Boy, 1998.

Sources

Periodicals

Billboard, October 31, 1992.
Dallas Morning News, February 11, 1999, p. 45A.
Details, November, 1992.
Entertainment Weekly, February 19, 1999.
Minneapolis Star Tribune, March 5, 1999, p. 03E.
Newsday, May 27, 1999, p. C01.
Spin, June 1999.
Toronto Star, February 25, 1999.
Toronto Sun, February 27, 1999, p. 38.

Online

"Everlast Interview," *Totally LA Website,* http://www.totallyla.com/Interviews/Everlast/Text.htm, (October 17, 1999).
"Everlast," *Official Everlast Website,* http://forevereverlasting.com, (October 17, 1999).

—Laura Hightower

Fear Factory

Metal rock band

Photograph by Joe Giron. Corbis. Reproduced by permission. ©

After Fear Factory's second consecutive sell-out concert at London's Astoria in 1999, Ben Myers of *Melody Maker* declared the rock band "the kings of nu metal." Myers further added, "While Korn and Deftones operate on the hip hop crossover axis, these chaps take the dynamics of what was once speed metal and weld it to the best electronica—from band associate Gary Numan to Nine Inch Nails' monolithic beats. Only, somehow, it sounds surprisingly fresh, almost ... ground-breaking.... To see a band so focused, consistent and minimal still sounding like God punching sheet metal in a cathedral can't fail to excite." The Los Angeles-based band became one of the most popular speed metal/industrial acts of the1990s, gathering a loyal following of fans largely by grassroots touring. By the middle of the decade, with the release of 1995's *Demanufacture,* the band finally earned greater radio airplay and gained worldwide mainstream attention.

Fear Factory emerged in 1990 in Los Angeles, California, when members Burton C. Bell on vocals, Dino Cazares on guitar and bass, and Raymond Herrara on drums decided to form a band. Bell, known for his dry, guttural vocal delivery, and Cazares had been friends for years and lived in a large house together with other roommates in Los Angeles. "He was right into death metal," Bell told Australia's *Rebel Razor* magazine in an article on the band's website. "He introduced death metal to me and I introduced Godflesh to him, bands like that." Bell was a member of a local Los Angeles band called Hateface prior to forming Fear Factory. He compared their sound to early metal rock bands like Helmet and White Zombie. It was during his upbringing in Houston, Texas, that Bell became an avid fan of metal rock.

The group started out playing local gigs in Los Angeles, where they established a grassroots following, before landing a record deal with Roadrunner Records. In 1992, the band released their debut album, *Soul of a New Machine.* Soon thereafter, because of Fear Factory's endless touring schedule, the group recruited bassist Andrew Shives. The additional bass guitarist enabled Cazares to play guitar full-time and allowed the band to tour more easily. From the onset, Fear Factory appealed to rock enthusiasts "who don't like metal, but who still like their rock in violent, disruptive doses," according to Paul Hampel of the *St. Louis Post-Dispatch.* "Punks who eschew the likes of hair bands such as Iron Maiden (Fear Factory's unlikely tour mates [in 1996]) are some of the band's most ardent supporters." In 1993, Fear Factory released a second album, *Fear Is the Mindkiller,* also issued by Roadrunner. Unlike the group's debut, which focused on speed metal rock, Fear Factory's follow-up effort incorporated techno/industrial elements into the overall sound. At the same time, the popularity of techno

For the Record . . .

Members include **John Bechdel** (born August 23, 1964; guest musician), keyboards; **Burton C. Bell** (born c. 1969; raised in Houston, TX; son of a National Public Radio correspondent [father] and an artist [mother]), vocals; **Dino Cazares** (born September 2, 1966), guitar, bass; **Raymond Herrera** (born December 18, 1972, in Mexico), drums; **Christian Olde-Wolbers** (born August 5, 1972, in the Netherlands; also lived in Belgium; joined group, 1994), bass; **Andrew Shives** (joined band 1992, left band 1994), bass.

Formed band in 1990 in Los Angeles, CA; signed with Roadrunner Records, released debut *Soul of a New Machine,* 1992; released *Demanufacture*, 1995; toured as part of Ozzfest concert series, 1997; single "Cars" from the album *Obsolete* crossed over to modern rock charts, 1999.

Addresses: *Home*—Los Angeles, CA. *Record company*—Roadrunner Records, 536 Broadway, New York, NY 10012, (212) 274-7500, fax (212) 334-6921. *Website*—Fear Factory Official Website, http://www.fearfactory.com.

music was growing across Europe and the United States. The addition of electronic ingredients further increased the group's fanbase.

Personal conflicts led to the replacement of Shives by Christian Olde-Wolbers in 1994. After recruiting Olde-Wolbers, Fear Factory recorded their third album, *Demanufacture,* issued in 1995 by Roadrunner. According to Bell, the album surrounded the concept of stripping down society's laws, government, servitors, religion, and death. "The whole disc is the story of ananonymous man of the future," the vocalist informed Hampel. "He has lived in the stultifying, hateful atmosphere of a society ruled by the iron hand of a totalitarian system. One day, he snaps, sees the light of non-conformity and the importance of individuality."

For example, "Pisschrist," a song inspired from a photograph by Andres Serrano that drew outrage from religious groups, questioned the power of religion. Regarding his own religious beliefs, Bell commented, as quoted by *Rebel Razor,* "I'm agnostic really.... I believe in personal spirituality, but letting a group of people tell you how you should worship or what your spirituality is, is wrong." The lead singer also professed that one should believe in himself first and search for spiritual power from within. Expressing his satisfaction with the record, Bell added, "I like listening to it myself, which says a lot because I didn't really listen to *Soul Of A New Machine* or *Fear Is The Mindkiller* that much. But I'm really proud of this record 'cause we worked very hard and even if I weren't in the band I'd probably buy the record." Following the release of *Demanufacture,* Fear Factory finally had greater radio airplay and continued to tour non-stop. As the band gained even more fans, they toured with big-name acts such as Biohazard, Iron Maiden, and Korn.

In the meantime, around 1995, Bell joined a side project with Geezer Butler of Black Sabbath. Butler formed a new band and enlisted Bell as the lead singer. "There's the Fear Factory element in there, but I'm doing a lot more different things," Bell told *Rebel Razor.* "There's a couple of samples but there's no keyboards on the album. There's four of us in the band—Geezer, myself, Dean Castranova who plays drums for Ozzy [Osbourne], and a guy named Petro Howse who's been a friend of Geezer's for a long time."

In the midst of exhaustive touring, Fear Factory found time to record a remix EP entitled *Remanufacture,* released in 1997. That same year, the group also joined the Ozzfest tour. Ozzfest '97, a hard rock and heavy metal road show assembled by former Black Sabbath singer Ozzy Osbourne, toured 21 cities that year and also featured bands such as Marilyn Manson, a reunited Black Sabbath, Pantera, Type O Negative, and Machine Head.

Fear Factory toured for the next two years and released the album *Obsolete* in 1999, which featured a cover version of Gary Numan's classic single "Cars." "We're really big fans of the original," Cazares told Carrie Bell of *Billboard.* "Fear Factory is brutal and heavy, but we still have a lot of melodic elements in our records and keyboards. So Gary [who appeared as guest vocalist for the remake] was a huge influence." By July of that year, the single reached number 40 on *Billboard*'s Modern Rock chart, marking the first time Fear Factory had crossed over to an alternative audience. Nevertheless, the group held mixed feelings about the song's success. "Our record company saw it as a way to market Fear Factory to a new audience, and people ate it up," added Cazares. "Which, in itself, is a cool thing, but we would be more excited if we bridged that gap with one of our own songs. We don't want to be known as a cover band."

The group resisted comparisons to other rock bands who caught the attention of alternative radio, feeling that Fear Factory's music provided a unique sound all its own. "Our band is definitely still growing in America, but we didn't do this to get popular quick or copy some other band. We aren't jumping on the Limp Bizkit [the popular rock/hip-hop band] tip," noted Cazares to Bell. "We created our own style and intend to use it."

Selected discography

Soul of a New Machine, Roadrunner, 1992.
Fear Is the Mind Killer, Roadrunner, 1993.
Demanufacture, Roadrunner, 1995.
Remanufacture, (EP), Roadrunner, 1997.
Obsolete, Roadrunner, 1999.Sources

Sources

Periodicals

Billboard, August 7, 1999, p. 69.
Boston Globe, April 9, 1997.
Los Angeles Times, June 17, 1997; July 1, 1997.
Melody Maker, January 16, 1999; October 2, 1999.
St. Louis Post-Dispatch, February 29, 1996, p. 12; March 8, 1996, p. 06E.
Washington Post, August 18, 1999.

Online

Fear Factory Official Website, http://www.fearfactory.com (November 24, 1999).
Rolling Stone.com, http://www.rollingstone.tunes.com (November 19, 1999).

—Laura Hightower

Fuel

Rock band

While it is not unusual for a band to produce and finance a record in an attempt to gain an audience and a record contract, Fuel took such an initiative a step further. After relocating to the mid-sized Pennsylvania town of Harrisburg rather than to a large American city, the band ultimately distributed their self-made EP entitled *Porcelain* to radio stations and record stores across the United States. Before long, Fuel accepted a recording offer with Sony subsidiary 550 Music, recorded their major-label debut, released the hit single "Shimmer," earned critical accolades, headlined stadium concerts, and toured with various acts from the rock band the Foo Fighters to the punk outfit Green Day. "It was a big job," said guitarist and songwriter Carl Bell in an interview with Wendy Hermanson for Launch.com. "We had the record stores designing and hanging up displays for us! They were so supportive. Some of the stores were part of [national] chains, so they'd distribute [our record] for us by sending it to other stores along with the shipments!"

Lead guitarist and vocalist Carl Bell, along with boyhood friend and bas guitarist Jeff Abercrombie, grew up in

Photograph by Joshua Kessler. Sony Music Entertainment Inc. Reproduced by permission.

For the Record . . .

Members include **Jeff Abercrombie**, bass; **Carl Bell**, guitar, vocals; **Kevin Miller**, drums; **Brett Scallions**, lead vocals, guitar.

Abercrombie, Bell, and Scallions formed band in Kenton, TN, and recorded first demo tape, c. 1995; relocated to Harrisburg, PA, 1995; released self-produced, self-financed EP *Porcelain,* 1996; signed with Sony 550 Music and released major-label debut *Sunburn*, 1998; recorded single for *Godzilla* soundtrack, 1998.

Addresses: *Home*—Harrisburg, PA. *Management*—Media Five. *Record company*— Sony 550 Music, 2100 Colorado Ave., Santa Monica, CA 90404, (310) 449-2100, fax (310) 449-2932.

Kenton, Tennessee, located in the western part of the state near the Kentucky border. "There was nothing much to do there," Bell informed *Billboard* magazine's Mark Marone. "It's just soybeans and cattle, pretty barren. Some great people, but as far as activities, you're not going to find any." Growing up without television in a town with only two stoplights and a population of around 2,000 people, Bell resorted to other forms of entertainment, mainly listening to a collection of 500 rock and roll albums that his brother won from a Memphis radio station contest. "I inherited the complete [Led] Zeppelin and everything coming out at the time," Bell told Noah Tarnow of *Rolling Stone.* "Instead of flipping on the TV, I'd just open up the console stereo system and throw on a [Rolling] Stones record."

Although both Bell and Abercrombie started out playing guitar, Bell slyly convinced his pal to switch to bass "cause it was cooler," recalled Abercrombie, according to the band's record label. Throughout the years, though, the young men experienced trouble finding other musicians to form a band with. Eventually, Abercrombie met singer and guitarist Brett Scallions, who lived in the nearby town of Brownsville and performed in small venues with other musicians. While the young singer worshipped the vocals of the Cult's Ian Astbury, Scallions's own voice resonated with an expressive energy. Soon thereafter, Scallions agreed to join Bell and Abercrombie on lead vocals and rhythm guitar, and the group began to crystallize.

After rehearsing together for a short time, Fuel recorded their first piece of music, an eight-song demo tape that sold close to 5,000 copies at local stores and live gigs. Encouraged by this initial success, Fuel decided to take their music more seriously and move to a larger town in 1995. But instead of relocating to one of the more recognized cities for hopeful musicians, such as New York, Los Angeles, Seattle, or Nashville, the group opted to move to Harrisburg, Pennsylvania, a town not usually considered a springboard for rock bands. However, Fuel chose the town for two reasons. First, Harrisburg was central to a host of larger cities, including Washington, D.C., New York, Baltimore, and Philadelphia. And second, Fuel had already amassed a cult following of fans in Harrisburg. "Actually, local radio would play local music, and we knew we'd get gigs," Bell said to Tarnow. Scallions further added, "We began to build a loyal following. The fan base supported us from day one, and it just grew and grew," as quoted by the band's record label.

In fact, Fuel found not only a receptive audience in their adopted hometown, but also discovered that local radio stations and record stores seemed eager to help the band with the promotion and distribution of their first EP, the self-produced and self-financed *Porcelain,* 1996. Record stores designed displays for Fuel and distributed the EP by sending it to other stores in their respective national chains, while radio stations began to play an early version of the single "Shimmer" from *Porcelain.* Soon after their first gig at the Electric Factory in Philadelphia, Fuel had sold-out shows, positive press, and calls from various record companies. Before long, Fuel signed a recording contract with 550 Music, a division of Sony Music.

In 1998, Fuel released their major-label debut *Sunburn,* produced by Steve Haigler (noted for his work with the Pixies, Quicksand, and Local H) and engineered by Tom Lord-Alge (known for his work mixing songs with the Dave Matthews Band and the Wallflowers). All of *Sunburn*'s eleven songs were written by Bell. The prolific songwriter explained, "Writing is like therapy for me," as quoted by 550 Music. "It helps you decode what's going on in your life." Bell admitted to at times spending several hours searching for the most compelling word to match the melodies in his head. "There has to be something that hooks me. You have to find it quickly, then slowly flesh out the details." His attention to detail both musically and lyrically paid off with *Sunburn.* Edgy, explosive tracks that unexpectedly switch to introspective moments included "Untitled" as well as "Jesus or a Gun," while the song "It's Come to This" centered around a drum and bass approach. The album's most successful single, in terms of popular attention, was "Shimmer," described by Tarnow as "super premium plus," and a good mix of "breezy melodies with full-out metallic aggression." By September of 1998, "Shimmer" reached number five on the *Billboard* Modern Rock chart, and in December, *Radio & Records* ranked the single as the number one modern rock track of the year. The album overall went certified gold, selling over 500,000 copies, and also hit the number one slot on *Billboard*'s Heatseakers chart.

In the meantime, the trio befriended drummer Kevin Miller, a member of another East Coast band who grew up in Allentown, Pennsylvania, near Harrisburg. After recording *Sunburn* with an outside sessions drummer, Fuel asked Miller to join the group. The quartet rehearsed just six hours before playing onstage together for the first time—a high-profile show at New York's C.B.G.B.'s nightclub. "It was my first show, and they threw me right into the melting pot," Miller remembered, according to 550 Music. "I figured that I had honed my skills for years and years for a moment like this, so it was either put up or shut up!" Also in 1998, Fuel recorded a single for the platinum-selling *Godzilla* soundtrack entitled "Walk the Sky" with Pearl Jam producer Brendan O'Brien and appeared for the first time on television on *Late Night With Conan O'Brien.* In addition, the band toured with well-known acts such as the Foo Fighters and Green Day.

With their hit radio songs and widely-televised videos, Fuel quickly became one of the most popular up-and-coming bands of the year. In September of 1998, the band set out on their first headlining tour, including dates overseas, arena shows, and an enthusiastic performance at the Bumbershoot Festival in Seattle, Washington. All four musicians claimed that while they enjoywriting and recording music together, they find the greatest adrenaline rush during live performances. During one performance in Sacramento, California, in late 1998, the onstage excitement led to a trip to the hospital. "We were rockin' out," Bell told Tarnow. "and my guitar hit [lead singer] Brett Scallions and he needed eight stitches in his face. He was, like, snorting and blowing blood and chunks out of his nose. The hospital report said, 'Assault with guitar.'"

Despite Fuel's acceptance by modern rock fans and radio, the group remained adamant about the correct genre to place their music under. "We're a rock band," Bell confessed to Hermanson. "If you want to call it alternative, so be it, and we're glad of the alternative airplay. But we like to just think 'Rock.'"

Selected discography

Porcelain, (EP), 1996.
"Shimmer," 550 Music, 1998.
Sunburn, 550 Music, 1998.
"Walk the Sky," *Godzilla: The Album,* Epic Soundtrax, 1998.

Sources

Periodicals

Billboard, April 4, 1998, p. 7.
Rolling Stone, September 17, 1998, p. 29.

Online

Launch.com: Discover New Music, http://www.launch.com (November 23, 1999).

Additional information provided by 550 Music, a division of Sony Music.

—*Laura Hightower*

Gene Loves Jezebel

Rock band

In the midst of a surge of popularity in the mid-1980s, Gene Loves Jezebel remained among the least understood of the barrage of bands that comprised the musical genre called alternative rock. The band and its music in many ways reflected a cult-like persona, and conflicting reports concerning the origins and membership of the band dealt the group an aura of mystery that successfully enhanced the appeal of Gene Loves Jezebel. The band, which was heavily influenced by the gothic music movement, initially emerged as a trio and expanded later into a quintet. Their unique style, characterized by a high degree of experimentation, garnered significant support from broad-minded audiences including collegiate radio listeners. Despite a virtual disbanding of the group's membership in the mid-1990s, Gene Loves Jezebel regrouped with relentless persistence and expanded its experimental evolution into the late 1990s.

Conflicting accounts detail the specific origins of Gene Loves Jezebel. Among those, many popular stories maintain that the twin siblings, Jay (born John) and Michael Aston of South Wales, originally formed a group by the name of Slav Arian. Some sources cited the group's name as Slav Arian and others reported the group's name as Slay Arian. Still other reports indicated that the group was called Slavorian. As with the precise name of the band, little else was clearly documented about the early Slav Arian group. Reports concur nonetheless that Slav Arian was a forerunner to Gene Loves Jezebel, and that musicians Michael Aston and Jay "J" Aston, identical twins from a working class family in Porthcawl, Wales, were deeply involved in the roots and history of both bands. According to one version of the account, the twins, who sang and played guitar, moved to London, England in 1980, and there they re-christened their Slav Arian band under the name of Gene Loves Jezebel. Another mainstream version holds that Michael Aston initially moved from Porthcawl to London on his own and established the Slav Arian band while his brother remained in Wales, and that the two rejoined forces later in London. In the wake of conflicting details as to whether one or both twins initially went to England, it was nonetheless evident that the brothers "surfaced" on the British music underground sometime around 1980. Also clear was the fact that Gene Loves Jezebel was a reinvention of the earlier Slav Arian group of 1980 or 1981.

Prior to the name change, one or both of the Astons established a professional relationship with guitarist and songwriter Ian Hudson; Hudson later joined with the twins to form a trio. A short-lived association with a drummer named James Chater predated the initial formation of the group as a trio; thus their earliest performances did not include a drummer and utilized a drum machine as an interim solution for rhythm. Gene Loves Jezebel appeared in a live performance for the first time on December 30, 1981 and performed their London debut at the Convent Garden Rock Garden.

In keeping with the group's unaffected and characteristically unrehearsed music style, the name of the band was not an issue for some time until the trio sought to come up with a billing name for themselves. All the while the twins were popular frequenters of a club called the St. Martins, where the other patrons dubbed J with the nickname of "Jezebel" because of his long and flowing-hair. Michael Aston, who limped from a badly healed broken leg, received the nickname "Gene," evocative of the late bop musician, Gene Vincent, who was crippled in a motorcycle accident in the 1950s. Historical details notwithstanding, the trio adopted the name of Gene Loves Jezebel no later than 1982 in London, England and achieved a peak of popularity in the mid-1980s. In 1982 the group secured a booking at the Institute of Contemporary Art Rock Week Festival, and the performance led to a record deal with Situation 2 Records. When the new group assembled to begin its first commercial recording session, it had expanded to a quartet, with the addition of Julianne Regan on piano and vocals. Also in the very early days of Gene Loves Jezebel's recording history, they were joined by well-respected guitarist, Albi Deluca, for the taping of the 1983 single release, "Screaming for Emmalene." Although Hudson was heard on bass for that

For the Record . . .

Members include **Jay "J" Aston** (born John Aston in Porthcawl, Wales, twin brother of Michael Aston), vocals and guitar; **Michael Aston** (born in Porthcawl, Wales, twin brother of Jay Aston), vocals and guitar; **Chris Bell,** (replaced Marcus Gilvear, 1986); **Marcus Gilvear,** (on *Immigrant,* 1985-86); **Steve Goulding,** (briefly replaced Dick Hawkins in the early 1980s); **Richard (Dick) Hawkins,** drums; **Ian Hudson**, guitar; **Steve Marshall**, bass; **John Murphy,** drummer; **Julianne Regan,** (joined after first single demo, 1982-1984), bass, piano, and vocals; **Peter Rizzo,** (replaced Julianne Regan, 1984), bass; **James Stevenson** (replaced Ian Hudson, 1986), guitar.

Signed with Situation 2, 1982; U.S. tour, 1985; signed with Geffen, 1986; signed with Beggars Banquet, 1986; signed with Robison Records Ltd., 1998; U.S. tour, 1999.

Addresses: *Record company*—Monte Robison, Robison Records Ltd; *Email*— Morobison@aol.com.

tape, the group's 1983 British debut album called *Promise* featured Hudson in his regular position on rhythm guitar following the introduction of bassist Steve Marshall into the group. Drummer Richard "Dick" Hawkins joined the group as well for that album. *Promise* was later released in the United States on Geffen in 1987.

In 1984 the twins brought the band to the United States, and it was there that Gene Loves Jezebel established its greatest concentration of listeners. The band members collaborated with fellow Welshman, John Cale, on the 1984 release, *Immigrant,* which became a classic. The album was released on three separate labels over the course of the next two years. Beggars Banquet released the disc in 1984, and Situation 2 (a Beggar's Banquet subsidiary) released it in the United Kingdom in 1985. Also in 1985, the album appeared in the United States under the Relativity label. Cale, who produced the album, appeared with Gene Loves Jezebel during their first United States tour near the end of 1985. The mid-1980s also saw the demise of Hawkins and the addition of Marcus Gilvear as drummer. Gilvear was intermittently replaced by Chris Bell, to the point where both drummers, Gilvear and Bell, are credited for the drum accompaniments on *Immigrant.* Reportedly the two drummers switched turns even mid-song on certain cuts of that album.

Gene Loves Jezebel signed with Geffen in 1986 and with Beggars Banquet that same year. Also in 1986 guitarist Ian Hudson, who was a member of the original trio, left the music industry altogether. The group's ensuing release was *Discover,* featuring guitarist James Stevenson of Chelsea and Generation X fame. Stevenson, a master of guitar heroics, brought a new flamboyance to the group, and the band's popularity soared. The artistic content of Gene Loves Jezebel's work at times spawned debate, although classic Gene Loves Jezebel albums such as *Discover* came to be prized on college radio broadcasts, where freedom of expression ruled the airwaves. "Motion of Love," "Desire," and the group's 1990 single, "Jealous," each surfaced in the top 100 of the *Billboard* charts, and Gene Loves Jezebel sold over one million records on the Geffen Label.

Young female fans swooned at every stop as Gene Loves Jezebel toured and performed to sellout crowds, most frequently in the United States where, according to Jay Aston in *Musician's Monthly,* "[H]ere they celebrate the otherness, they love what's different about the group." Surprisingly, in the estimation of the Aston's, the group was preceded by a media image that presented it as the paradigm of the cold and dark gothic bands that permeated the British alternative rock scene at the time. In reality, the group's members espoused lightheartedinnocence, frolic, and fun; they were neither introspective nor morose. In actuality they were the antithesis of the contemporary gothic movement.

The dichotomy of image led to hesitancy among the band members as the 1980s drew to a close. In 1987, Gene Loves Jezebel founder Michael Aston quit the group and moved to Los Angeles, California to pursue a career as a solo recording artist. In 1992 he formed a group called the Immigrants and reinvented that band under the name Edith Grove in 1994. His twin brother remained in London for the duration, occupied in propelling the momentum of Gene Loves Jezebel. The band released the album *Kiss of Life* in 1990; that disc featured the hit single, "Jealous," that reached number 68 on the United States music charts in August of 1990. Another album, *Heavenly Bodies,* followed in 1993; and in 1995 Michael Aston returned to the Gene Loves Jezebel circle to collaborate on an anthology that was released in September of 1995. The band at that time included "J" Aston, guitarist Stevenson, drummer Chris Bell, and bass player Peter Rizzo. Gene Loves Jezebel then severed its ties with Beggars Banquet, refused a contract offer from Atlantic Records, and signed with Avalanche Records to produce the reprise album, *Some of the Best of Gene Loves Jezebel.* After the best of album, the group aligned briefly with Savage Records before essentially disbanding for approximately three years. Michael Aston went on to record with Scenic and as a solo act on *Why Me, Why This, Why Now,* in 1995. J meanwhile also went solo and Stevenson joined another band, called the Cult.

A new and more focused band emerged in 1998 when J assembled Stevenson and Rizzo for a resurrection of Gene Loves Jezebel. They recorded a new album called *VII* in 1999 under the newly formed record label, Robison Records Ltd. *VII* featured a dozen new songs created through the mixology and production talents of industry specialist Peter Walsh, whose technical expertise was a well-known component behind U2 and Peter Gabriel. In April of that same year the group toured the United States and the Americas to promote the album. Although traditional critics remained largely at a loss to extol the musical virtue of Gene Loves Jezebel and despite persistent personnel changes and other inconsistencies, the band's 20-year staying power served to validate the Aston twins and their cohorts in bringing an experimental musical genre to the forefront.

Selected discography

Singles

"Shavin' My Neck," 1982.
"Screaming For Emmalene" (with Albi Deluca), 1983.
"Bruises," Canadian Beggars Banquet (Canada)/Vertigo, 1983.
"Influenza," Relapse, 1984.
"Shame," Whole Heart Howl, 1984.
"Cow," 1985.
"Heartache," 1985.
"Desire," 1985.
"Sweetest Thing," 1986.
"Motion of Love," 1987.
"Gorgeous," 1987.
"Jealous," 1990.
"Tangled Up In You," 1990.
"Josephina," 1993.

Albums

Promise, Situation 2 (United Kingdom), 1983.
Immigrant (with John Cale), Beggars Banquet (Canada), 1984.
Immigrant (with John Cale), Situation 2 (United Kingdom), 1985.
Immigrant (with John Cale), Relativity, 1985.
Desire (with James Stevenson), Relativity, 1985.
Discover (with James Stevenson), Beggars Banquet, 1986.
Glad To Be Alive, (limited edition included with *Discover),* 1986.
Discover (with James Stevenson), Geffen, 1986.
Promise, Geffen (re-release, United States), 1986.
The House of Dolls (includes "Motion of Love"), Beggars Banquet (Canada), 1987.
The House of Dolls (includes "Motion of Love"), Geffen, 1987.
Suspicion, Geffen, 1988.
Kiss of Life (without Michael Aston, includes "Jealous"), 1990.
Josephina, Savage, 1992.
Heavenly Bodies (without Michael Aston), 1993.
From the Mouths of Babes, AV, 1995.
Some of the Best of Gene Loves Jezebel, Avalanche, 1995.
Desire: Greatest Hits Remixed, Cleopatra, 1998.
VII, Robison Records Ltd., 1999.
Voodoo Dollies: The Best of Gene Loves Jezebel, Beggars Banquet, 1999.
Love Lies Bleeding, Robison Records Ltd., 1999.
Live in Voodoo City, Robison Records Ltd., 1999.

Sources

Periodicals

Melody Maker, September 1987.

Online

All Music Guide, http://www.allmusic.com/cg/x.dll?UID=3:28:37[PM&p=amg&sql=B13035--~C (December 6, 1999).
"Boss Booking Agency—Michael Aston of Gene Loves Jezebel," http://www.thebossbookingagency.com/Aston.html (December 6, 1999).
"Gene Loves Jezebel," http://rollingstone.tunes.com/sections/artists/text/bio.asp?afl=rsn&LookUpString=740 (December 6, 1999).
"Gene Loves Jezebel," http://dspace.dial.pipex.com/goth/glj.htm (December 6, 1999).
"Influential English rock Group Gene Loves ...," http://www.businesswire.com/webbox/bw.030199/190600370.htm (December 7, 1999).

—Gloria Cooksey

Alvin Youngblood Hart

Guitar

Photograph by Ann Katzenbach. Reproduced by permission. ©

Alvin Youngblood Hart (born Gregory Edward Hart), a self-taught guitarist, songwriter, and multi-instrumentalist, helped lead a younger generation of creative blues artists during the 1990s. Similar to artists such as Keb' Mo' and Corey Harris, the free-spirited, Memphis-based musician with a solid foundation in the blues wrote and performed songs personalized with his own insights and experiences. Moreover, Hart's musical influences extended beyond the confines of the blues, as did those of blues veteran Taj Mahal, who viewed the blues as a world music rather than an American genre. Borrowing techniques from an array of artists such as rock guitarist Jimi Hendrix to alternative bluesman Captain Beefheart, Hart developed an eclectic blues style that included elements of western swing, pop, reggae, and rock.

Hart's 1996 debut album *Big Mama's Door* earned the singer and guitarist the W.C. Handy Award (he was nominated for a total of five) for best new artist in 1997. In 1999, *Downbeat* magazine named Hart's 1998 follow-up album, the acclaimed *Territory,* as blues album of the year. With two successful records to his name at just 35 years of age, critics predicted that, like his predecessor Taj Mahal, Hart would prove an important inspiration to contemporary blues musicians for years to come. "Using mandolin, 12-string and lap steel guitars, Hart cuts straight through the soul of the music," commented Michael Point in *Downbeat,* "transcending simple labels like 'blues' in favor of something more universal and all-encompassing." Likewise, *Downbeat*'s Frank-John Hadley added, "Hart is a fine, discriminating singer and multi-instrumentalist whose interpretations of country blues and other African-American folk song are among the most involved anywhere." And Hart himself further explained, "To me blues is all about personal expression and musical adventure, and that's what I strive for when recording."

Hart's musical adventure began far from the cultural heart and soul of blues music, which originated in the southern United States. Although Hart would later live in Chicago as a teenager and serve time in the U.S. Coast Guard stationed on the Mississippi River, two areas known for influencing blues artists, Hart's first introduction to the blues occurred during his early childhood in California. Born on March 2, 1963, in Oakland, Hart said blues music always filled the family home, as both his parents had roots in rural Mississippi. "I just came upon the blues, what, just hearing it every day in the house," Hart explained to Renee Montagne in an interview for the National Public Radio (NPR) broadcast *Morning Edition.* "My dad used to walk around the house singing, 'Momma killed a chicken, thought it was a duck, put him on the table with his legs sittin' up, got to bottle up and go,' you know. I've been hearing that since day one. Playing in

For the Record . . .

Born Gregory Edward Hart, March 2, 1963, in Oakland, CA; *Education:* Studied guitar with Clarence "Gatemouth" Brown.

Released debut album, *Big Mama's Door,* Columbia/Okeh, 1996; released *Territory,* Hannibal, 1998; toured with alternative rock bands, including the Afghan Whigs and Son Volt, 1999.

Awards: W.C. Handy Award for best new artist, 1997; *Downbeat* magazine award for best blues album of the year for *Territory,* 1999.

Addresses: *Home*—Memphis, TN. *Record company*—Hannibal/Rykodisc, Shetland Park, 27 Congress St., Salem, MA 01970; phone: (888) 2-EARFUL. *Website*—http://www.rykodisc.com.

the house, playing in my head, you know, from day one." In addition, family vacations to Carroll County, Mississippi, where Hart's grandparents lived, further strengthened his admiration for the blues.

From Oakland, the Hart family moved to Los Angeles, then to Ohio, before settling in Chicago, a city rich in the blues culture. Here, Hart met and played music on the streets with other blues artists like the late Maxwell Street Jimmy and Lucky Lopez, who remained relatively unknown outside Chicago, and earned his middle name "Youngblood" from the older musicians. In order to entice them to let him sit in and play, Hart used to put extra money in their tip boxes.

As a young adult, Hart spent seven years with the Coast Guard. For three and a half of those years, he was based on a buoy boat in the town of Natchez, located on the Mississippi River. During the day, the crew set up buoys in the river to mark the deep water for commercial boats and also built navigational lights along the river bank. But at night, with the crew's ship tied to a tree in the middle of the river, Hart usually concentrated on playing blues. "I'd get a chance to practice music a little bit on the bow of the boat, you know, where nobody was, if the mosquitoes weren't too bad." One of Hart's later instrumental songs, "Underway at 7," was inspired by his time spent on the Mississippi. "We used to have breakfast at 6:30 and get underway at 7," Hart told Montagne, explaining the song's title.

After serving with the Coast Guard, Hart turned to music. In 1996 at age 33, he released his 14-track debut album, *Big Mama's Door,* with producers Michael Nash and Carey Williams on the Columbia/OKeh label; "Big Mama" refers to Hart's grandmother from Mississippi. Beginning with the first song, the album's title track, and continuing throughout the record, Hart explored his country blues side and the acoustic blues tradition through his own expressive interpretations. Critics often complain that most younger blues artists seem overly studied when they take on the rich blues heritage. However, Hart displayed a comfortable ease and sense of authority in his singing, finger picking, and playing slide guitar. On his original song "Joe Friday," Hart sounded much like one of blues music's icons, the Mississippi Delta legend Robert Johnson. He also covered other artist's tunes, including Charley Patton's "Pony Blues," Leadbelly's "When I Was a Cowboy," and Willie McTell's "Hillbilly Willie's Blues." In 1997, Hart received five W.C. Handy Award nominations for his debut and won the title for best new artist.

Around the same time Hart released *Big Mama's Door,* he was one of six slide guitarists chosen to participate in sessions with Junior Wells, known as one of the creators, along with Little Walter, the two Sonny Boy Williamsons, and James Cotton, of Mississippi Delta/Chicago-style harmonica playing. The sessions resulted in the 1996 release of *Come on in This House,* produced by John Snyder on the Telarc label. For the album, Hart performed on both 12-string dobro and National steel guitar.

Two years later in 1998, Hart released his sophomore effort, *Territory,* this time with Hannibal (a division of Rykodisc), a label that appeared to give the artist a broader range of creativity. Continuing to illuminate the blues tradition, Hart performed a haunting version of a lesser-known song by Skip James (1902-1969) entitled "Illinois Blues," as well Bukka White's (1909-1977) backwoods-inspired "Mama Don't Allow." For both songs, he heightened the drama with his skillful slide guitar playing. Hart also performed the age-old folk song "John Hardy," adding his own personal touch by playing acoustic guitar and concertina, while Taj Mahal stepped in to play mandolin and provide vocal support for "France Blues." But unlike Hart's first album, *Territory* traveled beyond traditional blues. An admitted fan of singing cowboys Roy Rogers and Gene Autry during his childhood, Hart paid tribute to western swing music through his original song "Tallacatcha," featuring the lap steel guitar and fiddle. He also performed a remake of Captain Beefheart's blues-rocker "Ice Rose," a Jamaican, ska groove entitled "Just About to Go," and the lamentful Tin Pan Alley number "Dancing With Tears in My Eyes."

"One of the ways for me to keep music enjoyable is to cover a lot of ground or play whatever I feel I can get away with at the time," Hart explained to Hadley, recollecting the lessons he learned while studying for a short time with the musically versatile multi-instrumentalist Clarence "Gatemouth" Brown, considered one of the foremost architects of modern blues guitar. "He was always telling me to forget about what labels people want to put on you and just try to have a good time playing music." Taking Brown's advice in recording *Territory* obviously paid off for Hart, as the acclaimed collection won the blues album of the year award in 1999 from *Downbeat* magazine.

Making a more diverse record also brought Hart fans from outside the blues scene, and by the spring of 1999, the artist opened for alternative rock acts such as the Afghan Whigs and Son Volt. "It's kind of loud, so I'm playing electric guitar as opposed to doing my regular acoustic gig," he told Hadley. In addition to playing guitars, Hart also enjoyed repairing and restoring, buying, selling, and trading the instruments. For his next project, he hoped to record a harder-edged album because, as he recalled, "I grew up on all that early-to mid-'70s Frank Zappa music." In the future, Hart also wanted to work with his older brother, a funk base player who lives in Japan, on a tribute album to Sonny Sharrock (1940-1994), a well-known experimental, free-jazz guitarist.

Selected discography

Big Mama's Door, Columbia/OKeh, 1996.
(With others) *Come on in This House,* Telarc, 1996.
Territory, Hannibal, 1998.
(With others) *Every Road I Take: The Best of Contemporary Acoustic Blues,* Shanachie, 1999.

Sources

Books

Rucker, Leland, editor, *musicHound blues: The Essential Album Guide,* Visible Ink Press, 1998.
Swenson, John, editor, *Rolling Stone Jazz and Blues Album Guide,* Random House, 1999.

Periodicals

Downbeat, September 1998, p. 55; March 1999, pp. 22-25; April 1999, p. 64; August 1999, p. 42.
Independent, July 3, 1998, p. 17.
Morning Edition (NPR), July 21, 1998.
Newsday, August 27, 1998, p. C07.
St. Louis Post-Dispatch, July 25, 1996, p. 08; August 21, 1998, p. E4.
Village Voice, September 15, 1998, p. 62.

—*Laura Hightower*

Dave Holland

Double bass, cello

British bassist and cellist Dave Holland established his reputation as a key figure in jazz back in 1968 when he moved to New York City to perform and record with jazz legend Miles Davis and his band. In 1972, Holland became the leader of his own group for the first time and released the stunning *Conference of the Birds,* considered one of the best works in contemporary jazz. Although Holland continued to record with other jazz musicians and bands, lead and record with his own groups, and release solo albums, he was not able to recapture the intensity of his debut album until 1998's *Points of View.* In response to the album, Holland received a Grammy Award nomination for best jazz instrumental performance, and *Downbeat* magazine named him jazz bassist of the year. Dedicating himself to music at a prolific and continuous pace throughout his career, Holland always made certain to share the credit with his collaborators.

Born on October 1, 1946, in Wolverhampton, England, Holland discovered his musical talent at an early age and started out playing the ukelele at age four. At ten years old, Holland started learning the guitar, concentrating on the bass guitar and forming his first band with a group of friends by the age of 13. The group, with Holland performing in public for the first time, played at local clubs and dances. Two years later, now 15 years old, Holland joined another band. When his new group started to perform on a regular basis, he decided to leave school in order to devote himself to a career in music and to expand his ideas on bass guitar. Although he took piano lessons for a short time, throughout his childhood he mostly taught himself how to play the era's popular music from song books and by listening to the radio.

Around this time, Holland discovered jazz music after hearing recordings of Ray Brown and Leroy Vinnegar, two legendary bassists. Inspired by their music, Holland purchased his first double bass and practiced along with the records. Continuing to play popular tunes as a bass guitarist, he also frequented jazz clubs with his double bass, often sitting in on stage with other local jazz musicians. At the age of 17, in the summer of 1963, Holland accepted an offer to play double bass with a dance band working at a resort for the season, leaving his bass guitar work behind. When his stint for the summer ended, he joined a big band accompanying singer Johnny Ray for a short tour, then moved to London to play music in a restaurant.

This move would change Holland's musical direction for the remainder of his career, as he immediately started studying with James E. Merritt, at the time the principal bassist for the London Philharmonic Orchestra. Merrit, also a teacher at the Guildhall School of Music and Drama, convinced Holland in thespring of 1964 to apply to Guildhall's three-year program. After taking the entrance exam and receiving a full scholarship, Holland started attending the school that fall. Holland studied with intensity, and by his second year, he earned the position of principal bassist with the school's orchestra. In the meantime, Holland began to work with other jazz artists around London, performing first with bands that played King Oliver, New Orleans style jazz and Louis Armstrong. Before long, he could adapt to ensembles playing every jazz style from swing to modern.

Influenced by the innovations of contemporary jazz, Holland in 1966 began playing with other artists who held similar interests like multi-instrumentalist John Surman, John McLaughlin, Evan Parker, Kenny Wheeler, John Taylor, Chris MacGregor, and others. His influences during this time included well-known jazz bassists such as Charles Mingus, Scott LaFaro, Jimmy Garrison, Ron Carter, and Gary Peacock, while his studies in school introduced him to contemporary composers, including the works of Bela Bartók. Concurrently, Holland played with various chamber orchestras and started to record music for film, television, and radio.

Holland's career continued to escalate, and 1967 saw him on stage with such jazz greats as Coleman Hawkins, Ben Webster, and Joe Henderson. One night in July of 1968,

For the Record . . .

Born October 1, 1946, in Wolverhampton, England; *Education:* Studied with bassist James E. Merrit and at Guildhall School of Music.

Joined first jazz band, 1963; moved to New York City and played with Miles Davis, 1968; released first album as bandleader, *Conference of the Birds,* 1972; forms group called Gateway, 1975; released first solo bass album, *Emerald Tears,* 1977; released first solo cello album, *Life Cycle,* 1981; released *The Razor's Edge* as bandleader of his own quintet, 1987; formed a new quartet, released *Extensions,* 1989; released *Dreams of the Elders* with subsequent quartet, 1995, followed by *Points of View,* 1998; all released on ECM label.

Awards: *Downbeat* magazine's 1989 album of the year for *Extensions; Downbeat* magazine's 1998 acoustic bassist of the year.

Addresses: *Home*—New York City, NY; *Management*—Vision Artist Management and Consultation, contact: Louise Holland, phone: (718) 857-5727, fax: (718) 623-1404, e-mail: HollandL13@aol.com. *Booking*—Sala Enterprises, contact: Anna Sala, 805 Seventh Ave., Ste. 1100, New York City, NY 10019, phone: (212) 262-4481 ext. 243, fax: (212) 397-5973, e-mail: AMSala@aol.com. *Record company*—ECM, 1540 Broadway, 40th flr., New York City, NY 10036, phone: (212) 930-4996. *Website*—ECM, http://www.ecmrecords.com; Dave Holland—Official Website, http://www.jazzcorner.com/holland.

Miles Davis came to Ronnie Scott's, a well-known jazz club in London where Holland often appeared. When Davis heard him play, he asked Holland to join his band. Within two weeks of that night, Holland moved to New York City and spent two years touring and recording with Davis, as well as performing with other musicians within New York's jazz community. He appeared on a number of Davis's albums, including *Filles de Kilimanjaro,* September of 1968, *In a Silent Way,* February of 1969, and *Bitches Brew,* August of 1969.

In late 1970, Holland left Davis's group to form a band called Circle with Chick Corea, Anthony Braxton, and Barry Altschul. In Circle, Holland played both cello and bass. The group broke up after just one year together, and Holland, in early 1972, took a job playing with Stan Getz and his band. Around this time, he worked briefly with Thelonious Monk, began a musical relationship with Sam Rivers, and worked as a guest teacher at the Creative Music Studio in Woodstock, New York. The same year also marked Holland's first recorded album as a bandleader with the release of *Conference of the Birds* in November on the ECM label. The title song was inspired by the singing birds outside Holland's London flat, according to the musician, rather than by the classic poem by Attar as some reviewers and critics often suggest. With Braxton and Rivers playing flute and reeds, alongside Altschul on drums and percussion, Holland produced a record that would become a jazz classic.

In 1973, Holland left Getz's group to focus on performing with Braxton, as well as with Rivers. Two years later, in 1975, he participated in forming a trio named Gateway with guitarist John Abercrombie and drummer Jack DeJohnette, a fellow member of Davis's group; Gateway continued to tour and record together throughout the 1990s. After working with singer Betty Carter for a few months in 1976, Holland spent the remainder of the 1970s playing and recording with Rivers, in addition to releasing a solo bass album entitled *Emerald Tears* in August of 1977. The record led Holland to hold solo concerts for the first time in his career.

In 1981, Holland left Gateway and Rivers for a time in order to make plans for his own band and released a solo cello album called *Life Cycle* later that year in November. Although more consistent than his previous solo effort, many critics believed that the album needed further development. Following the completion of *Life Cycle,* Holland assembled his first full-time band. The original members included Wheeler on trumpet and flügelhorn, Julian Priester on trombone, Steve Coleman on alto saxophone and flute, and Steve Ellington on drums; later members included Marvin "Smitty" Smith, replacing Ellington on drums, and Robin Eubanks, who substituted for Priester on trombone. The group recorded three albums together: *Jumpin' In* (released in October of 1983), *Seeds of Time* (released in November of 1984), and the much celebrated *The Razor's Edge* (released in February of 1987).

After the release of *The Razor's Edge* and an extensive tour, Holland disbanded the quintet to work with a trio again. In March of 1988, he released *Triplicate* with DeJohnette and Coleman, then performed and recorded two albums with pianist Hank Jones and others: *The Oracle* (released in March of 1989) and *Lazy Afternoon* (released in July of 1989). Later that year, he formed a new quartet with Coleman, Eubanks, and Smith, and in September of 1989, the group released *Extensions,* a recording voted album of the year by *Downbeat* magazine.

Since accepting his teaching position with the Creative Music Studio, Holland continued to instruct others throughout the 1980s. He became artistic director of a summer jazz workshop held at the Banff School in Banff, Canada, from 1983 until 1990. He also joined the faculty of the New England Conservatory of Music in Boston, Massachusetts, as a full-time instructor in 1987 and taught at the school until 1990.

During 1990, Holland toured worldwide with DeJohnette's group called Parallel Realities. The group—also featuring pianist/keyboardist Herbie Hancock and guitarist Pat Metheny—appeared on a Grammy nominated album, Metheny and Roy Haynes's *Question and Answer.* In 1992, Holland appeared as a regular with Hancock's trio and performed on Joe Henderson's *So Near, So Far,* an album that won a Grammy Award. Holland then spent 1993 touring Europe to give solo concerts, recording his second solo bass album entitled *One's All,* and later touring with a project also consisting of Carter, Geri Allen, and DeJohnette. The musicians released a live recording of a concert held at the Royal Festival Hall in London called *Feed the Fire* in 1994.

Early that same year, Holland brought together a new quartet, this time made up of vibraphonist and composer Steve Nelson, saxophonist Eric Person, and drummer Gene Jackson. During the summer of 1994, Holland toured with Gateway and recorded an album with the trio in December under the title *Homecoming,* released by ECM. In the meantime, he toured Europe and the United States with his new quartet. Then in early 1995, they recorded *Dream of the Elders.* A subtle yet powerful album, Ken Micalleff in *Audio* described the work as "a sublime example of Holland as bandleader, composer and bassist.... another peak in the bass legend's mountain of music." Subsequently, Holland toured with his own quartet and as a member of Hancock's group through the end of the year.

1996 proved a busy year for Holland, as he continued to tour as a part of Hancock's quartet, again with Gateway, and with his own band. Active in the studio as well, Holland participated in the recording of three Grammy-nominated albums, including saxophonist Michael Brecker's *Tales from the Hudson,* Hancock's *The New Standard,* and pianist Billy Child's *The Child Within.*

In 1997, the musician decided to disband his previous group, forming another quintet composed of alto saxophonist Steve Wilson (replaced by Chris Potter in June of 1998), Eubanks, Nelson, and drummer Billy Kilson. After performing on stage together, the group headed for the studio to record the Grammy-nominated album *Points of View,* released in March in Europe and in September in the United States in 1998. The critically well-received effort led *Downbeat* in 1999 to award Holland for a second time, this time by naming him 1998's acoustic bassist of the year.

In addition to performing with his quintet in 1998, Holland toured with Hancock's *The New Standard* group, as well as with Brecker's *Tales from the Hudson* lineup and a *Porgy and Bess* (the musical) project headed by Henderson, who Holland often performed with earlier in his career. His other live performances includedplaying with Gateway, as a member of Wheeler's group, in a duo with guitarist Jim Hall, and in a trio with Anouar Brahem and Surman. The same year, Holland appeared on various releases by other artists, two of which included saxophone player Joe Lovano's *Trio Fascination* and vibraphone player Gary Burton's *Like Minds.* Performing almost non-stop with his quintet and others the following year, Holland planned to continue his busy pace. By the end of 1999, Holland had already recorded with albums with numerous artists such as vocalist Cassandra Wilson, saxophonist Charles Lloyd, vocalist Dominique Eade, and saxophonist Andy Middleton. In March of 2000, Holland scheduled a series of trio concerts also featuring Brahem and Surman.

Selected discography

Conference of the Birds, ECM, 1972.
Emerald Tears, ECM, 1977.
Life Cycle, ECM, 1982.
Jumpin' In, ECM, 1983.
Seeds of Time, ECM, 1984.
The Razor's Edge, ECM, 1987.
Triplicate, ECM, 1988.
Extensions, ECM, 1989.
One's All, ECM, 1993.
Dream of the Elders, ECM, 1995.
Points of View, ECM, 1998.

Sources

Books

Cook, Richard and Brian Morton, editors, *The Penguin Guide to Jazz on CD,* Penguin Books, 1998.
Swenson, John, editor, *The Rolling Stone Jazz and Blues Album Guide,* Random House, 1999.

Periodicals

Audio, July 1996, p. 84; August 1994, p. 75.
Billboard, July 20, 1996, p. 56; February 8, 1997, p. 1; August 16, 1997, p. 33; November 21, 1998, p. 43; February 13, 1999, p. 40.
Downbeat, December 1998, pp. 74-75; January 1999, pp. 52-53; February 1999, p. 67; August 1999, p. 38.
Stereo Review, June 1997, p. 85.

Online

Dave Holland—Official Website, http://www.jazzcorner.com/holland (October 8, 1999).
ECM Records: Biography, http://www.mediapolis.com/ecm-cgi-bin/bio?282 (October 8, 1999).

—Laura Hightower

Enrique Iglesias

Singer, songwriter

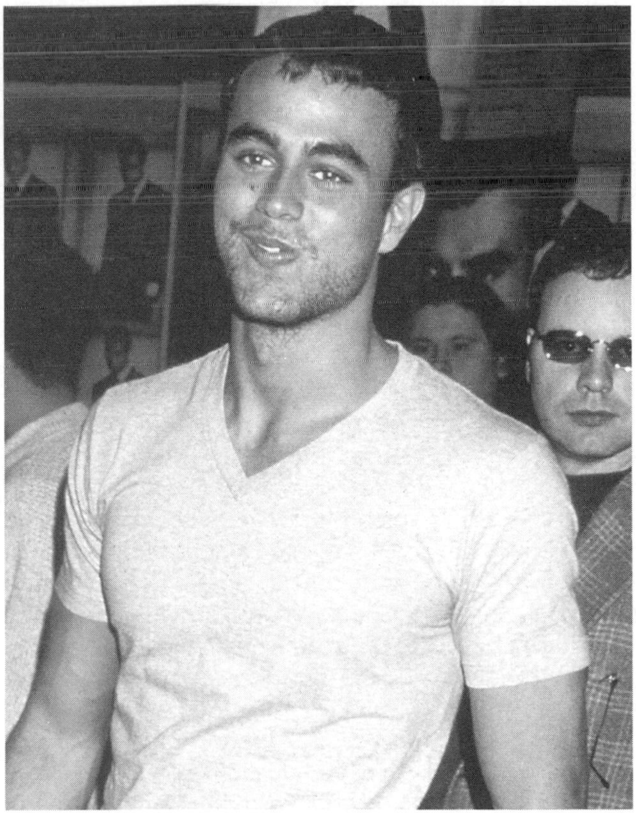

Photograph Mitch Gerber. Corbis. Reproduced by permission. ©

Romantic balladeer, Enrique Iglesias, prayed as a child to become a popular singer, but his superstar father never knew about the young boy's ambition. When Iglesias was old enough to make an audition tape, he mailed the samples to prospective record companies under an assumed name, fearful of prejudice in light of his father's prominence in the recording industry. Talent and desire won out for Enrique Iglesias, and he signed a recording contract exclusively on his own merits, secure in the knowledge that he succeeded on talent and charisma, and without the use of his well-connected surname. Iglesias's famous paternity became evident on the occasion of his first recorded release in 1995 under his true name of Iglesias. Regardless, the popular singer and songwriter settled into his career, confident at his ability to establish name recognition as Enrique (not Julio) Iglesias, through his personal musical style and appeal.

Enrique Iglesias was born Enrique Iglesias Preysler in Madrid, Spain, on May 8, 1975. He was the youngest of six siblings, three boys and three girls. His parents, Isabel Preysler and Julio Iglesias, divorced in 1979. Enrique Iglesias continued to live in Madrid with his mother, a Philippine-born journalist, until the early 1980s when Preysler received kidnap threats against her children. Reluctantly she sent the youngsters to the United States to live in Miami, Florida, with their superstar father. In Florida, Enrique Iglesias became enamored with water sports, especially wind-surfing; he also loved to water ski and scuba dive. By the time he was in his early teens he made regular summer trips to Hawaii where he lived a humble existence in a shack and spent his days windsurfing. Although the circumstances of his childhood kept him physically apart from his parents, the family nonetheless stayed in touch as much as was reasonably possible. His mother remained in Spain, while his father, an international singing idol, was seldom at home. In Miami the children were raised almost exclusively by a nursemaid, Elvira Olivares, who took the family under her wing and loved the children as her own. Later, when Enrique Iglesias released his first record album, he dedicated the work lovingly to Olivares.

When Iglesias was grown, according to his parents' wishes, he enrolled at the University of Miami as a business administration student, but his career goal since childhood was to become a singer. Iglesias spent his free time practicing singing with friends and, eventually, made a demo tape and sent it to recording studios. Iglesias, well aware of his father's notoriety in the music industry, sent the audition tapes under the name of Enrique Martinez, in order to insure that he would be assessed on his own merit rather than on the basis of his famous father's reputation. When executives at Fonovi-

For the Record . . .

Born Enrique Iglesias Preysler, May 8, 1975, in Madrid, Spain; son of Madrid Preysler (a journalist) and Julio Iglesias (a singer). *Education:* Attended University of Miami.

Signed with Fonovisa Records, 1994; released "Si Tu Te Vas (If You Leave)" (a single), fall 1995; released "Bailamos (We Dance)" his first English-language single, 1999; signed with Universal Music Group/Interscope, 1999.

Awards: Best Latin Pop Performance, National Academy of Recording Arts and Sciences, 1997; American Music Award; Hot Latin Tracks Artist of the Year, Latin Music Awards, *Billboard,* 1997, 1998; Ace Award; Premios Lo Nuestro; Premios Eres.

Addresses: *Record company*—Interscope Records, 10900 Wilshire Blvd., Los Angeles, CA 90024, phone (310) 208-6547, fax (310) 208-7343.

sa Records heard Iglesias's audition tape in 1994, they signed him to a contract to record three albums. He subsequently abandoned his studies at the university, to his father's dismay, and it was only after the deal was finalized that Julio Iglesias learned of his son's impending career as a recording artist. The younger Iglesias was nonetheless gratified in the knowledge that he secured the contract on his own initiative.

He set a bustling pace during the ensuing years and released six albums in less than five years, each of which sold in phenomenal numbers. A songwriter as well as a crooner, Iglesias wrote many of the songs that he recorded. Fonovisa released Iglesias's debut album of romantic balladsin October of 1995. The Spanish-language album, entitled *Enrique Iglesias,* was a number one best seller in the Latin music arena and sold nearly three million copies within a matter of weeks. By the end of 1997 worldwide sales figures for the album were reported at six million copies, including sales of nearly one-and-one-half million copies in the United States alone.

The debut album featured a hit single, "Si Tu Te Vas (If You Leave)," that zoomed into a top-ten position on the record charts. Although Iglesias preferred to distance himself from the legacy of his father, it was an unavoidable issue for critics to compare the two; and comparisons resounded more freely because a song by the elder Iglesias was on the record charts simultaneously with that of the younger. Julio Iglesias's song was far less popular, however, and held a slot at number 17 while "Si Tu Te Vas" held the number six position. In the light of critical comparison, Enrique Iglesias asserted that but for the surname and familial relationship, his own singing bore no resemblance to that of his father. Nevertheless, an undeniable reality surfaced—that both singers possessed extraordinary romantic appeal for female audiences. Belinda Luscombe of *Time* commented further that the father-and-son pair shared a "certain musk-scented vocal quality," while the younger Iglesias struggled to assert himself as an individual. Peter Castro quoted him in *People,* "I'm very proud of my father, but when you read *Billboard* now, you see Enrique Iglesias."

Enrique Iglesias's second album, *Vivir,* was released in the fall of 1997 and sold four million copies by the end of that year, including 1.1 million in the United States. Also in 1997 Iglesias toured the Americas and Spain. His third album (and third Spanish-language release), *Cosas Del Amor,* appeared in music stores on September 22, 1998. Despite his hesitation to record in English, Iglesias's popularity suffered no handicap due to language barrier. He received extensive media coverage in the United States as well as in other non-Spanish-speaking countries. While the largest base of his popularity remained in Mexico and Argentina, he secured guest spots on both the "Late Show with David Letterman" and "Tonight Show with Jay Leno," and released an Italian-language recording in 1996. By the time Iglesias released an English-language recording he had in fact made 190 television appearances in 23 countries and had sold 13 million albums worldwide.

Iglesias released "Bailamos (We Dance)," his first English-language release, in 1999 as part of the soundtrack to a movie starring Will Smith and Kevin Kline called *Wild Wild West.* When Smith solicited a recorded contribution from Iglesias for the Overbrook/Interscope movie soundtrack, Iglesias turned to an earlier recording that he had never released to any record label. Iglesias offered the recording to Universal Music Group/Interscope for the movie soundtrack and the record company not only liked the song, but proceeded to sign Iglesias to a six-album recording contract, including three Spanish albums and three in English. That episode was a milestone in Iglesias's career, marking the point where he crossed over effectively from the Latino musical genre and into the generic popular styles. Additionally, the $44 million contract, for six albums, moved Iglesias into the forefront among the highest-paid Latino artist of the times. "Bailamos," released as a single, rapidly sped its way to number one on the *Billboard* Hot 100 chart in early September of 1999.

By the end of the decade, eleven of Iglesias's single releases held a spot at number one among a totalof 19 countries. He secured 116 platinum records and 26 international awards, including a Grammy for Best Latin Pop Performance in 1997, plus an American Music Award; and he was a two-time recipient of *Billboard*'s Latin Music Award as the Hot Latin Tracks Artist of the Year. He was not yet 30, but his image had appeared on 250 magazine covers.

In 1998 Iglesias secured the title of *People en Espanol's* "sexiest man," yet for all his charm he maintained that he wrote his best song material when he was mooning over a romantic breakup. Although he earned a reputation as a sloppy dresser—complete with five-o'clock shadow and oftentimes grungy attire—press relations notwithstanding there was nothing that hampered his image as a ladies' man. Iglesias's managers meanwhile bemoaned the fact that their client was somewhat given to risk-taking, especially when he required 40 stitches in his head following a water-skiing accident in 1998 when he slammed into a mangrove tree.

Emphatic in his likes and dislikes, Iglesias professed that he harbored a sympathetic heartstring for Loony Tunes' Wile E. Coyote, and Iglesias's own personal taste in music runs to other popular singers including Michael Jackson, Bruce Springsteen, Billy Joel, and the group Dire Straits. He professed that his interest in women veers toward talent over beautiful looks. He openly shunned the playboy image that pursued his father over the years and aspired to settle into a comfortable and monogamous relationship. In response to the suggestion that Julio Iglesias and Enrique Iglesias might one day record a duet together, the latter responded without malice that he would prefer to sing in duet with pop star Michael Jackson.

Selected discography

Singles

"Si Tu Te Vas (If You Leave)," 1995.
"Éxperiencia Religiosa (Religious Experience)," 1996.
"Bailamos (We Dance)," Overbrook Music, August 10, 1999.

Albums

Enrique Iglesias (includes "Si Tu Te Vas"), Fonovisa, 1995.
Version En Italiano, Fonovisa, 1996.
Vivir, Fonovisa, 1997.
Cosas Del Amor, Fonovisa, 1998.
Bailamos, Fonovisa, 1999.
Enrique, Interscope Records, 1999.

Sources

Periodicals

Billboard, April 11, 1998; July 10, 1999; September 9, 1999; September 11, 1999.
Maclean's, September 2, 1996.
People, April 22, 1996; May 11, 1998; August 16, 1999.
Rolling Stone, August 19, 1999.
Time, November 6, 1995.
Variety, December 8, 1997.

Online

"About Enrique Iglesias," http://www.enriqueiglesias.com/about1.htm (August 3, 1999).
"Enrique Iglesias," http://rollingstone.tunes.com/sections/artists (August 13, 1999).
"Straight Talk: Advice from Enrique Iglesias," http://www.usaweekend.com/97_issues/970601/970601talk_iglesias.html (August 3, 1999).

—Gloria Cooksey

Natalie Imbruglia

Singer, songwriter

S.I.N./Corbis. Reproduced by permission. ©

Australian soap opera star turned pop/alternative rock sensation Natalie Imbruglia made headlines across Europe and the United States, gracing the cover of *Spin* magazine and turning into an MTV (Music Television) superstar upon the release of her debut album *Left of the Middle.* Containing the hit single "Torn," Imbruglia's first recording effort eventually sold close to six million copies. As of early late 1997, "Torn" had already hit number one in most European countries, including the United Kingdom, and *Left of the Middle* had sold millions of copies. All the while, American music fans eagerly awaited the release of Imbruglia's debut in the United States. In a phenomenon usually unheard of in the music industry, Imbruglia appeared on the MTV cable network to release her video for "Torn," and performed on the American television show *Saturday Night Live* nearly a week prior to the release of *Left of the Middle* in the United States in early March of 1998.

Imbruglia's exquisite looks and singing/songwriting skills brought her international stardom that seemed to occur almost overnight. Elysa Gardner of *Entertainment Weekly,* describing the artist's physical appeal, noted, "in the video for 'Torn,' she sulks gracefully in a worn T-shirt and baggy pants—that suggest a young Audrey Hepburn as refashioned for the post-grunge crowd." Despite her appearance, though, the petite (at five feet, two inches tall), youthful, and innocent-looking musician with large blue eyes, enjoyed the recognition she received for her singing and songwriting abilities rather than her beauty.

The second eldest of four girls, Imbruglia was born February 4, 1975, to the son of an Italian expatriate and his schoolteacher wife. Imbruglia (pronounced Im-BROO-lia, the "g" being silent) grew up in a coastal town located just north of Sydney, Australia. She described her upbringing to Nick Compton in *Independent on Sunday* as "real Brady Bunch." The four girls formed close bonds, and Imbruglia's parents have enjoyed a successful marriage. Nonetheless, Imbruglia always felt different in certain ways from the rest of her family. Displaying a seemingly inborn desire to perform, the future actress/singer started taking dance lessons around age two and developed an interest in theater during her early teens. A self-described "drama queen," Imbruglia conceded to Compton, "you can always find your own turmoil, a way to isolate yourself.... I felt different and isolated, just in the sense that I was so ambitious, much more than anyone else in the family."

Short-lived Acting Career

This desire to add a sense of angst to her life led to rebellious periods, and Imbruglia developed a knack for

For the Record . . .

Born February 4, 1975, near Sydney, Australia; father was son of an Italian immigrant; mother, a schoolteacher; second eldest of four daughters. *Education*: Studied at a performing arts school in Sydney.

Started acting in commercials at age 14; joined cast of Australian soap opera *Neighbours* at age 17; left show two years later; moved to London to further pursue acting career, 1995; spent two years unemployed and began writing songs before releasing 1997 debut *Left of the Middle* (released in 1998 in the U.S.); recorded songs for two soundtracks including *Go!* and *Stigmata*, both released in 1999.

Awards: 1998 Australian Recording Industry (Aussie) Awards for best single and best debut single for "Torn," best debut album and best pop release for *Left of the Middle,* and best female artist; 1998 Brit Awards for best international newcomer and best international female artist.

Addresses: *Home*—London, England. *Record company*—RCA Records, 1540 Broadway, New York City, NY 10036, (212) 930-4000; fax (212) 930-4468.

beach bumming with the popular crowd and getting into trouble in school. One time, she was suspended from her Catholic school in Sydney for getting drunk while staying at a monastery for a school-sponsored religious excursion. But in the midst of seeking out trouble, Imbruglia had also been taking singing lessons for two years, in addition to dancing and acting in school musicals. At age 14, Imbruglia sought out an agent in Sydney and landed some parts in television commercials. Her mother was against this because she felt that six nights of dance lessons was more than enough theatrical training for her daughter. Around this time, she also earned a scholarship to attend a performing arts school in Sydney, but soon dropped out to try to find a professional acting job. Within six months of leaving school at age 16, she landed her first role.

At age 17, Imbruglia joined cast of a popular Australian soap opera (which also aired in the United Kingdom) called *Neighbours,* the same show that gave the world pop singer Kylie Minogue, known for her cover of the song "Loco-Motion." On the series, Imbruglia played the more or less trashy, man-eating Beth Brennan. However, the young actor found little creative fulfillment on the show and left two years later. In 1995 at age 19, Imbruglia moved to London with hopes of finding more substantive opportunities.

To Imbruglia's dismay, making the transition to London was not as easy as she expected. In Australia, the young actor entered the entertainment field with ease, but in London, she floundered in unemployment for nearly two years, at times existing on nothing but beans and rice for food. In addition to experiencing difficulty obtaining United Kingdom work permits, Imbruglia's name and face, now attached to the soap opera stigma, further prevented the determined performer from meeting other professionals who would take her seriously. Left without direction for the first time in her life, Imbruglia spent most of this period partying wildly in the London club scene and later sank into a deep depression.

Discovered Songwriting

In order to combat the sadness over her lack of success, Imbruglia began writing songs, with no intentions of ever letting anyone hear them. The last thing the admittedly pessimistic and sometimes insecure Imbruglia wanted was for people to make fun of her work or compare her to former cast mate Minogue. Nevertheless, when Imbruglia met her future manager Anne Barrett, her music career started to take shape. Barrett, who thought Imbruglia's songs had potential, hooked her client up with a host of highly respected, yet not entirely mainstream writers and producers, including Phil Thornalley (a former member of the pop group the Cure), Nigel Godrich (who worked on Radiohead'sacclaimed album *OK Computer*), and singer/songwriter Mark Goldenberg (who penned a hit song for the Eels called "Novocaine For The Soul"). Soon thereafter, Imbruglia gave a demo tape to RCA Records U.K., who like what they heard. She later accepted the record company's contract offer.

Before long, RCA released Imbruglia's debut album, *Left of the Middle,* in late 1997 in the United Kingdom. The album's first single, "Torn" quickly topped the British charts, even nudging out Elton John's Princess Diana tribute "Candle in the Wind" in October of 1997 for the number one spot. Although the record and single were not released in the United States until the spring of 1998, Imbruglia was already gaining attention with the American alternative/pop audience. Radio stations began playing "Torn" weeks before the album's official debut in the United States. Then Imbruglia performed live on MTV for the debut of her "Torn" video on March 6, 1998, followed the next night by an appearance on the television comedy show *Saturday Night Live.*

The following week *Left of the Middle* hit store shelves in the United States and entered the *Billboard* chart at number ten, selling more than 84,000 copies in seven days. The album went certified platinum just five weeks after its release date, making it the fastest album to break that mark in RCA history. Moreover, by March 18, 1998, Imbruglia's first album became the largest debut for a new, alternative pop-rock female artist in history, selling more in its first week than records by Alanis Morissette, Meredith Brooks, and Fiona Apple combined.

While some critics and fans are quick to dislike or typecast television stars turned musicians, Imbruglia's first collection of inspiring songs spoke for themselves. She took pains to separate herself from the commercially-minded soap star Minogue, who released sugar-coated pop tunes, and co-wrote ten of the twelve songs on her debut, including the British hit single "Wishing I Was There." Although Imbruglia's album remained suitable for pop audiences, she also embraced lyrical depth and attitude. Musically, the singer's collection revealed references to the folk overtures of American singer Shawn Colvin, Imbruglia's strongest influence. And unlike Minogue, who continued acting after embarking on a singing career, Imbruglia, who experienced a greater creative excitement with music, opted to concentrate solely on her singing and songwriting. "The only way I'm gonna get better at what I do is to stay focused," she told Gardner. "I don't believe in spreading yourself too thin."

Fell Prey to British Tabloids

Imbruglia, like most celebrities, was not immune to criticism. In England, not long after the release of *Left of the Middle,* controversy erupted in January when tabloids discovered that anearlier version of "Torn," which Imbruglia's frequent songwriting partner and producer Thornalley cowrote with members of the American alternative rock group Ednaswap in 1995, had been a hit in Norway for singer Trine Rein. Imbruglia explained to Gardner, "What happened was, [the British tabloid] *The Sun* tried to make a big story out of it.... I was 'Naughty Natalie.' But I never said I wrote ['Torn'], and I never said it was written for me.... [Rein's record company] had the choice to release 'Torn' in the United Kingdom, but they didn't, and so now they're kicking themselves because another artist had success with it." Fortunately, the tabloids proved unsuccessful in their attempts to bring Imbruglia's reputation into question, and the more "credible" British press received her version of the song with stellar reviews. Other standout tracks from *Left of the Middle* included "Intuition," "City," and "One More Addiction."

After this, the British tabloids delved into Imbruglia's personal life. While recording her debut in Los Angeles, Imbruglia met and dated American television star David Schwimmer (from the television series *Friends*). The relationship ran its course, but Imbruglia admits that her involvement with Schwimmer helped boost her confidence while making the record. She also learned to guard her privacy more closely through the experience. Sill, some critics labeled Imbruglia as just another record company puppet, carefully groomed to fit into the pop star image. However, Imbruglia vowed not to go down in music history as another forgotten one-hit wonder, and the majority of the media acknowledged her as a serious musician. For example, the British magazine *Melody Maker* described her debut effort, according to the website RollingStone.com, as "intelligent songs full of an inner strength, a powerful voice projected with knowing confidence."

First Worldwide Tour

With the controversy behind her, Imbruglia set out on a tour to support her album, beginning in the United Kingdom during the late spring of 1998, followed by an American tour later that fall. One important date Imbruglia accepted included performing at the annual installment of the Princes In The Park Concert, commonly known as the Prince's Trust Concert, in London's Hyde Park. Other performers such as All Saints, Simple Minds, Simply Red, Eternal, and Boyzone, also joined the event, with all proceeds benefiting the Prince's Trust Charity, held on July 5, 1998.

Later that fall, Imbruglia met and cowrote songs with musician Dave Stewart (of the Eurythmics). Their collaborative efforts came about by chance after Imbruglia heard one of Stewart's demo tapes while driving in Germany with a German record company executive. Subsequently, Imbruglia happened to see Stewart in a London restaurant and told him how much she liked the tape shehad heard. "We ended up back at my apartment, which was just around the corner from the restaurant," Stewart told MTV. "I was playing acoustic guitar and she was singing and it sounded really great. Natalie and I have written about six songs, and I'll probably finish them in the studio when we both have time." Music industry insiders unofficially predicted that at least some of the songs could surface on an Imbruglia's follow-up effort.

Toward the end of the year, Imbruglia not surprisingly was up for several music awards. She received three nominations for the 1998 MTV Europe Music Awards for best female artist, best breakthrough artist, and best song for "Torn," as well as three Grammy Award nominations for best new artist, best pop album for *Left of the Middle,* and best female pop vocal performance for "Torn." In October of 1998, Imbruglia left the big winner from the Australian Recording Industry Awards, known as the Aussie Awards, taking home five awards out of her nine nominations. These included best single and best debut single for "Torn," best debut album and best pop release for *Left of the Middle,* and best female artist. Imbruglia also received honors at the Brit Awards in February of 1999. That night, she took home two awards for best international newcomer and best international female artist.

After a whirlwind year, Imbruglia spent most of 1999 relaxing and writing songs for a second album, although she found time to contribute to film soundtrack recordings. She first recorded a track for the *Go!* soundtrack, released in April of 1999. Other well-known artists such as No Doubt, Fatboy Slim, and Eagle Eye Cherry also appeared on the album. Imbruglia then sang a breathtaking, experimental number called "Identify" written by Smashing Pumpkins front man Billy Corgan for the film *Stigmata,* released in September of 1999.

The year before, Imbruglia bumped into Corgan while making a video in Los Angeles for her debut. Corgan, responsible for writing and producing the *Stigmata* soundtrack, told Imbruglia about a song he had written for the record with her in mind to sing. Imbruglia immediately said yes, although she remained unsure if the project would truly come about. So when the deal officially came through months later, Imbruglia felt elated. "I just couldn't believe it," she commented to MTV. "I hadn't even seen the movie, and I didn't care. I was like, 'I want to do this song.' Partly because of Billy, and because I love the song and wanted to sing it." After recording "Identify" and filming the supporting video for the single, something she loves to do because it gives her the opportunity to use her acting skills, Imbruglia planned to give her full attention to completing songs for her next release.

Selected discography

Left of the Middle, RCA, 1998.

(with others) *Go!* (soundtrack), 1999.

(with others) *Stigmata: Music From the MGM Motion Picture Soundtrack,* EMD/Virgin, 1999.

Sources

Books

musicHound Rock: The Essential Album Guide, Visible Ink Press, 1999.

Periodicals

AAP General News (Australia), February 25, 1999.

Business Wire, March 18, 1998; May 6, 1998; September 30, 1998.

Daily Telegraph, November 29, 1997; May 21, 1998, p. 30.

Entertainment Weekly, March 20, 1998, p. 42.

Independent, November 20, 1998, p. 13.

Independent on Sunday, February 8, 1998, p. 2.

People, December 28, 1998, p. 114.

USA Today, March 23, 1998, p. 03D.

Online

Launch: Discover New Music, http://www.launch.com (September 24, 1999).

MTV Online, http://www.mtv.com (September 24, 1999).

RollingStone.com, http://www.rollingstone.tunes.com (September 24, 1999).

—Laura Hightower

The Jam

Punk band

Next to the Clash, the Jam are considered one of the most enduring band to emerge from the British punk scene. Gradually earning the respect and admiration of the British press, a huge following in the United Kingdom and Europe, and a cult following in the United States, the Jam were eventually dubbed by Vic Garbarini of *Musician* "*the* British pop phenomenon of the early 80s." Contemplating the group's rise to prominence, Weller commented in an April 1979 interview with Ian Birch of *Melody Maker,* "It's taken four years of hard work and believing in ourselves and not listening to other people saying we're shit or something. It's a question of maturing, growing up fast," asserted the songwriter. "I tell you ... a great quote I saw in the paper the other day comes from Stevie Wonder's song 'Uptight.' The line says 'No one is better than I, but I know I'm just an average guy.' That really sums it up, as far as I'm concerned. It's a question of saying we're just the same as everyone else, but we have our pride and self-respect and we know we're good. As far as I'm concerned, we're the best ... but anyone can do it."

However, unlike many of their contemporaries, the Jam stretched beyond the social idealism and angst of the punk scene. Ultimately, the music and songs themselves, rather than the issues, mattered most, and Weller, the primary songwriter, penned tunes drawn from such unlikely and diverse influences as the Small Faces and Curtis Mayfield. For these reasons, the group enjoyed enormous success in its homeland, and many believed the Jam to be the only British rock band since the Beatles to define its times so well. From the group's debut release in 1977, the Jam displayed an increasing versatility and were well on the way to embracing worldwide acceptance. "The band don't *want* to be 'big'; they *crave* it," insisted Birch in 1979. Therefore, it came as a surprise in 1982 when Weller abruptly broke up the Jam at the peak of the band's popularity. Subsequently, Buckler formed the Time in the United Kingdom with guitarist Kenny Kustow (former member of the Tim Robinson Band) and released a number of singles during the 1980s, while Foxton made an attempt at a solo career which produced the album *Touch Sensitive* for Arista Records in 1984. In 1986, he founded the short-lived group 100 Men. Weller, however, continued to stretch his artistic development, forming the soul-funk-jazz group the Style Council soon after leaving the Jam and enjoying a successful solo career beginning in 1992.

Throughout their time together, media attention centered around the Jam's lead singer and guitarist, Paul Weller, born John William Weller on May 25, 1958, in the working-class town of Woking, Surrey, England. Raised in the place of his birth on Stanley Road, Weller years later wrote poetry and lyrics that commented on the strong sense of community that reigned in the neighborhood. Without many opportunities for formal training, Weller, inspired by the rock music of the day, was nonetheless drawn to music early on. "The whole reason I started playing music when I was 12 or 13 was because of the Beatles," he told Adam Sweeting of *Melody Maker* in 1984, "so I was brought up on all that and I did believe in it."

The roots of the Jam can be traced back to1972, when Weller started playing with school friend Steve Brooks at local working men's clubs. By 1973, the band also included Nigel Harris and Dave Waller. However, between the years of 1975 and 1976, the lineup was significantly altered,and Weller remained as the only original member. After Brookes, Harris, and Waller left the Woking-based foursome, Rick Buckler and Bruce Foxton stepped in as replacements. The new trio, now consisting of Weller (who performed most of the lead guitar and vocals and wrote most of the songs), Buckler, and Foxton, were the Jam for the next six years. Around 1976, at the dawn of the punk era, the band moved to London and broke into a circuit of clubs that nurtured the growing scene. In 1977, in the wake of the Sex Pistols' rise in popularity, the Jam secured a contract with Polydor Records and embarked on their first major tour,

For the Record . . .

Members include **Steve Brookes** (left band c. 1975); Rick Buckler (joined band c. 1975), drums; **Bruce Foxton** (joined band c. 1975), bass, vocals; **Nigel Harris** (left band c. 1975), drums; **Dave Waller** (left band c. 1975), bass; **Paul Weller** (born John William Weller on May 25, 1958, in Woking, Surrey, England; married Dee C. Lee, 1986; children: John), guitar, vocals.

Formed band in Woking, Surrey, England, 1973; group moved to London and started playing club circuit, 1976; signed with Polydor Records and released debut album *In the City*, 1977; released last studio effort, *The Gift*, and disbanded, 1982; Polydor released all of the Jam's 13 singles on the album *Compact Snap!*, 1983.

Addresses: *Record company*—Polydor Records, 1416 N. La Brea Ave., Hollywood, CA 90028.

opening for the Clash. Although the tour was a washout, the Jam issued their first single, "In the City," in the spring of 1977, which reached the United Kingdom top 40. Following this, the Jam hastily recorded and released their full-length debut, also entitled *In the City.* Despite criticism that the album sounded too much like the Who, *In the City* peaked at number 20 on the United Kingdom charts, and by August of 1977, the band released a second single, "All Around the World," which rose to number 13.

Following a sold-out headlining tour in their native United Kingdom, the Jam released their second album, *This Is the Modern World,* in December of 1977, and kicked off another British tour. Unfortunately, American fans were less enthusiastic. The Jam's first American tour went ignored, while their second American tour turned into a disaster; they were made to open for the hard rock outfit Blue Oyster Cult and were often booed off the stage. Upon their return to England, the Jam nevertheless found themselves firmly solidified in the "mod revival" landscape of Great Britain and witnessed a string of hits over the next few years. In late 1978, the band released a more pop-based album, *All Mod Cons,* which reached number six in their homeland, but failed to chart in the United States. They followed this up with a more lyrically political collection entitled *Setting Sons.* The album, released in1979, hit the number four position in the United Kingdom, and finally charted in the United States at number 137. The group had two number one United Kingdom singles: "Start!" and "Going Underground," in 1980.

In 1981, the Jam released the album *Sound Affects,* a more rhythm and blues, soul-influenced work than previous albums. Instead of focusing on social commentary, Weller lightened up his songwriting and developed such noteworthy tracks as "Boy About Town" and "But I'm Different Now." Despite the shift in musical and lyrical direction, the band retained their loyal following in the United Kingdom and gained a wider audience in Japan, though American support continued to allude them. In 1982, the Jam released their final studio effort, *The Gift,* on which the group merged rhythm and blues with funk and included highlights like "Town Called Malice," "Precious," and "Happy Together." But just as the trio reached the peak of their career and soon after the release of *The Gift,* Weller informed Foxton and Buckler that he was tired of the Jam. Fans and the music industry were surprised when the band announced they planned to break up. Following an emotional farewell tour in the United Kingdom, Weller immediately formed a new funk-jazz group, the Style Council, then went on to enjoy an acclaimed solo career beginning in 1992. Although Foxton and Buckler continued playing with other bands and pursuing solo projects, they remained embittered that Weller had abandoned his longtime friends and had taken most of the credit for the Jam's prosperity. In 1983, following the disbanding of the Jam, Polydor released all of the Jam's 13 United Kingdom singles on *Compact Snap!*; all 13 songs re-charted in the United Kingdom top 100. Still unable to earn anything more than a cult following in America, the Jam remained popular and highly influential overseas.

Selected discography

In the City, Polydor, 1977.
Peel Sessions, Strange Fruit, 1977.
This Is the Modern World, Polydor, 1977.
All Mod Cons, Polydor, 1978.
Setting Sons, Polydor, 1979.
Sound Affects, Polydor, 1980.
Dig the New Breed, Polydor, 1982.
The Gift, Polydor, 1982.
Compact Snap!, Polydor, 1983.
Greatest Hits, Polydor, 1991.
Extras: A Collection of Rarities, Polydor, 1992.
Wasteland, Pickwick, 1992.
Live Jam, Polydor, 1993.
Beat Surrender (collection), Karussell, 1993.

Jam Collection, Polydor, 1996.
Direction Reaction Creation, Polydor, 1997.

Sources

Books

Contemporary Musicians, volume 14, Gale Research, Inc., 1995.
musicHound Rock, Visible Ink Press, 1999.

Periodicals

Melody Maker, April 28, 1979, pp. 24-25; October 30, 1982; March 24, 1984.
Musician, April 1984; October 1992.

Online

Rolling Stone.com, http://www.rollingstone.tunes.com (December 9, 1999).

—*Laura Hightower*

Kid Rock

Rap/rock artist

David Atlas. Reproduced by permission. ©

Part old school rap, part metal rock, and likened to rap artist Eminen for his often profane lyrics, as well as for his roots near Detroit, Michigan, Kid Rock proved that he stood apart from the hip-hop crowd with his wild and diverse music. In fact, Rock (born Robert Ritchie), with his skillful heavy metal guitar playing, shares more in common musically with metal assault groups such as Rage Against the Machine and Limp Bizkit. For example, as described by Mark Seliger in *Rolling Stone* magazine, the single "Bawitdaba" from 1998's *Devil Without a Cause* "mixes cries of 'up jump the boogie' with guitar aggression, coming off like a White Zombie [rock metal band] cover of a Grandmaster Flash [funk group] song." And the Atlantic Records website concluded, "Kid Rock unleashes the full-on motherlode: a rambunctious cocktail shaker of blue-eyed hip-hop, freestyle rap, spaced-out funk, psychedelic rock, jazz, blues and everything else under the sun up to and including the proverbial kitchen sink."

When the rap/rock star boasted "I'm going platinum" in the title track of *Devil Without a Cause* (a phrase that record company executives tried to persuade him to remove), he must have somehow known that this confident statement would become a reality. Moreover, the success of *Devil Without a Cause* eventually surpassed this prediction, going triple platinum following his crowd-pleasing show for the music festival Woodstock and headlining with Limp Bizkit for a worldwide tour in 1999. After this, his music was featured on popular television shows such as MTVs Beach House, ESPN's X-Games, and ABC's Wild World Of Sports. Prior to the success of album "My big feat before that had been selling 14,000 records out of my basement," he admitted to Seliger. Furthermore, Rock became the first white hip-hop artist to embrace and glorify "white trash" culture and to gain the respect of several African American rap artists, namely Sean "Puffy" Combs and Ice Cube, as well as heavy metal bands like as Metallica.

While Kid Rock seemed to personify the so-called white trash culture, his true background proved otherwise. He actually grew up in a more affluent environment, far away from the trailer park world he glorifiedsin his songs. Rock, born Robert Ritchie (known as Bob to friends) around 1972, spent his childhood in the rural town of Romeo, Michigan, near Detroit, in a lakefront home with six acres of land. Rock's chores at home included mowing the lawn, picking apples from the family orchard, and feeding the horses. His mother, Susan Ritchie, stayed at home with her three children: Rock, older brother Billy, and older sister Carol. And his gregarious father, Bill Ritchie, owned a successful business.

Nonetheless, Rock's childhood was not as happy as one might expect. Throughout his upbringing until the time he

For the Record . . .

Born Robert (Bob) Ritchie in Romeo, MI, c. 1972; son of Bill and Susan Ritchie; two siblings: older brother Billy and older sister Carol; children: son Robert Ritchie, Jr. (known as Junior).

Started as DJ at parties and clubs throughout high school in and around Detroit, MI; made demo tape, signed with Jive Records, released first album, *Grit Sandwiches for Breakfast,* 1990; toured with Ice Cube and Too $hort, 1990; debut record failed in sales and Jive dropped Rock from label, c. 1991; released two albums and one EP on independent labels, including *The Polyfuze Method*, 1992; *Fire It Up* EP, 1994; *Early Mornin' Stoned*, 1996; signed with Atlantic Records, c. 1997; released *Devil Without a Cause,* which later reached triple-platinum status, 1998; performed at music festival Woodstock, toured worldwide with Limp Bizkit, 1999.

Addresses: *Home*—Royal Oak, MI. *Record company*—Atlantic Records, 9229 Sunset Blvd., Ste. 900, Los Angeles, CA 90069; 1290 Avenue of the Americas, New York City, NY 10104. *Website*—http://www.atlantic-records.com, Kid Rock Official Website: http://www.kidrock.com.

succeeded as a musician, Rock had a troubled past with his father, as documented in his song "My Oedipus Complex" from the EP *Fire It Up.* He described his father as a workaholic and an often distant and demanding parent who never approved of Rock's lifestyle and musical pursuits. When his father sold his profitable Lincoln-Mercury car dealership in 1999, he tried one last time to persuade Rock to take over the business and leave music for the weekends. However, Rock and his father, who became less judgmental after Rock's success, finally made peace sometime later that year. With their relationship more or less amended,Rock's father proudly wears a *Devil Without a Cause* t-shirt and calls himself "Daddy Rock."

As Rock grew older, he started to develop more urban interests, like break dancing and listening to hip-hop records, and often backed out of his duties around the family home. "How can I say it? He was original," sister Carol, who manages Rock's finances, told Seliger. "He always did what he wanted to do. When Michael Jackson was on TV with his white socks up to here, Bob was upstairs the next day having my mom hem his pants. Music was all he cared about." In addition to hip-hop and dance music, Rock also enjoys rockers such as Bob Seger, Ted Nugent, and Lynyrd Skynyrd, as well as the music of country legends Dwight Yokam and Hank Williams, Jr. Then at around the age of 13 or 14, Rock received his first set of turntables for Christmas from his mother, and soon thereafter, he went to his first party in Detroit with some African American girls from Romeo High School.

At the party, the DJ noticed the only white kid at the party, Rock, eyeing his equipment and let him join in. Consequently, Rock's self-taught scratching so impressed an amateur promoter that he offered Rock a gig to DJ in the Detroit suburb of Mt. Clemens, and before Rock knew it, he was spinning records for all-black crowds around the Detroit area. "At first people would be like, 'Who is this white guy?'" Rock's friend Chris Pouncy recalled to Seliger. "But once they heard him scratch, he always got love in the neighborhood." Inspired by the overwhelming acceptance, Rock earned enough money picking apples at home to upgrade his equipment and also added rapping to his DJ shows.

By now a well-known name around Detroit, some local dealers helped Rock finance a demo tape on the condition that he mention their names in his songs. Subsequently, he signed a deal with Jive Records and released his first album in 1990, *Grit Sandwiches for Breakfast,* a Beastie Boys-sounding record with explicit lyrics. The exposure also landed him spots to perform with rap artist Ice Cube and the rap group Too $hort. Although Rock thought he had broken into the music industry, the release failed to sell, and Jive dropped the young rapper from the label.

Much of the remainder of the 1990s saw Rock making albums for independent labels, including 1992's *The Polyfuze Method,* which featured Rock's growing musical ability with country-inspired rapping alongside rock guitar riffs; 1994's *Fire It Up* EP, a predominantly metal rock release; and 1996's *Early Mornin' Stoned,* which included contributions from Black Crowes keyboardist Eddie Harsch and the vocals of soul singer Thornetta Davis. This album, financed by a loan from Rock's father, drew critical acclaim and caught the attention of the major label Atlantic Records. When company executives came to see one of Rock's shows, they signed him immediately. During this time, Rock also added more rock influences to his songs and assembled his backing group called the Twisted Brown Trucker Band, which featured guitarists Kenny Olson and Jason Krause, keyboardist Jimmie Bones, drummer Stefanie Eulinberg, and Rock's midget sidekick Joe C. In addition, his best friend, Matt Shafer learned to use the turntables from Rock and later joined the group as DJ Kracker.

Enthusiastic about his major label contract, Rock then set out to write and record his next release. But from the start, Rock experienced problems with writers block and in working with Atlantic, who wanted him to focus more on rock rather than rap, for the *Devil Without a Cause* album."Even though they were tellin' me I could do anything I wanted, they still wanted it a certain way," he revealed to Hobey Echlin in *Alternative Press.* "The first time I turned in 'Cowboy,' I said, 'This is the best song I've ever written.' I sent it in, and they [Atlantic] told me they didn't hear it." As a result of Atlantic's lack of support, Rock's writer's block persisted and worsened. After traveling with pal DJ Cracker to Memphis and New Orleans in search of musical inspiration and arriving back in Detroit with nothing, Rock was left with just one more week to complete the album.

In spite of the battle between Rock and Atlantic, he finally determined to make the music he wanted, as he told Echlin. "I thought about everything I'd been through in the last 10 years; all the music I'd made. And I thought, 'Well, what the label wants is something I can do.' But I made what I wanted to." Therefore, with his intentions set, he completed the music in the remaining week, complete with a sample from classic rock group Fleetwood Mac for the track "Wastin' Time." And although his label again thought the finished product seemed too "all-over-the-place" and pleaded with him to cut out the line "I'm going platinum" from "Devil Without a Cause," Rock stood by his former decision, and the album reached record stores in the late summer of 1998.

After songs from *Devil Without a Cause,* including the hits "Bawitdaba" and the country-rap influenced "Cowboy,"played on the radio and videos aired on MTV, millions of kids across the United States became instant followers of Rock. Soon, Rock saw his platinum dream come true, followed by sales reaching double platinum, then triple platinum levels after his notable performance at Woodstock in the summer of 1999. Many agreed that Rock stole the show at Woodstock as he took the stage with a fur coat, covered Creedance Clearwater Revival's "Fortunate Son," and played guitar riffs from Lynyrd Skynyrd's "Sweet Home Alabama" during "Cowboy." Rock told Seliger, "Everyone's trying to do something special for Woodstock. I covered every base I thought I was good at. It solidified ten years of hard work for me." During Rock's worldwide tour with rock group Limp Bizkit beginning in the late summer of 1999, his flamboyant shows would continue to turn heads and promote further sales of *Devil Without a Cause.*

Even with his fame and fortune, Rock declined to change his lifestyle, and those who know him insist that his real-life persona doesn't match the swaggering rock star image he displays in public. Instead, Rock made his home in the Detroit suburb of Royal Oak, where Rock, a single parent, shares a bungalow with his young son, Robert Ritchie, Jr. (known as "Junior" or "June Bug"). His sister, Carol, cares for Junior, who was born out of a relationship during Rock's teenage years, when Rock tours. Rock still drove around town in his souped-up 1983 Coupe de Ville and admitted to Seliger that he does feel like "white trash" in certain ways, regardless of his more privileged upbringing. "I guess I just want to let everybody know it's all right to be who you are, it's all right where you come from. I *do* feel like white trash.... I am technically. I like to drink beers, smoke ... I'm not trying to date the prom queen."

Selected discography

Grit Sandwiches For Breakfast, Jive, 1990.
The Polyfuze Method, Continuum, 1992
Fire It Up (EP), Continuum, 1994.
Early Mornin' Stoned, Top Dog, 1996.
Devil Without a Cause, Atlantic, 1998.

Sources

Periodicals

Alternative Press, August 1999, pp. 51-58.
Rolling Stone, July 8-22, 1999, p. 98; September 2, 1999, pp. 69-72.

Online

"Kid Rock," *Atlantic Records,* http://www.atlantic-records.com (August 27, 1999).
Kid Rock Official Website, http://www.kidrock.com (August 27, 1999).

—Laura Hightower

Diana Krall

Singer, piano

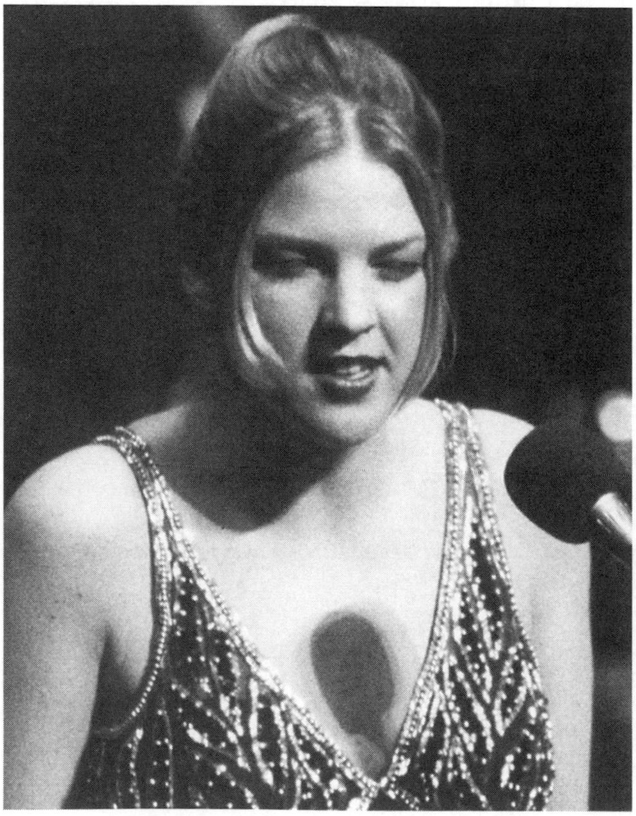

Photograph by Jack Vartoogian. Reproduced by permission. ©

Often referred to as the "glamour girl of jazz" for her stunning appearance, Canadian jazz pianist and singer Diana Krall became the toast of the international jazz scene, as well as to more mainstream audiences, during the mid-1990s. "Whenever anyone who would be considered a jazz musician hits in this way, it's a little bit of a strange alchemy that we can't figure out," editor-in-chief of *Jazziz* magazine Larry Blumfield told reporter Steve Dollar of the *Atlanta Journal and Constitution.* "In the terms of her appearance and the way she uses jazz tradition, she's more accessible to a broader audience than a lot of other artists are, without necessarily dumbing things down. One thing that really works in her favor is she's able to straddle that fence between what a real jazz fan wants and what a popular audience needs." Moreover, the tall musician with long, straight blond hair and green eyes proved that her artistry, rather than her looks, led her to attract fans from around the world. The *New York Times* called her "a superb jazz pianist and an even better singer," as quoted by David Hayes in *Chatelaine,* although she would humbly describe her piano technique as limited and never thought she had a good voice. Once when she was nine years old, she tried out for a local youth choir and was rejected because the teacher thought her voice was too low. Chastened by the rejection, she rarely sang in public until more than a decade later. In spite of this, Krall would later draw attention as much for her sultry singing as for her accomplished piano playing. "Krall's style is a Canadian accent with excellent time and a voice that is inherently lovely," remarked Gene Lees in *Jazz Times.* A modest yet commanding performer, Krall plays mostly her own interpretations of the old jazz standards accompanied by her relaxed, intimate singing style.

Despite Krall's undeniable talent as a serious pianist and singer, her success drew attack from some jazz critics and fans who accused her of selling out to the popular culture (In 1998, she appeared on two episodes of television's *Melrose Place* playing herself as a performer at a local bar and toured with Sarah McLachlan's all-female Lillith Fair concert.) "Too many jazz fans don't want anyone else to like it, and when someone breaks into huge sales, the only-I-understand this music group draws its snickersnees" commented Lees. And Krall herself felt somewhat uneasy about her sudden fame. "Well, I'm shy. And I'm embarrassed," she admitted to Lees. "I feel like that when I walk out on stage and everybody claps. When we finish a show ... and people give me a standing ovation, I feel like saying, 'No, it's okay, sit down and don't bother.' I'm not comfortable with it. I love to make people happy but I'm not comfortable with that." Furthermore, Krall, who never wanted to rise to the top of jazz and who just wanted to play the piano, found that standing in the limelight included it's draw-

For the Record . . .

Born November 16, 1964, in Nanaimo, British Columbia, Canada; daughter of an accountant father and teacher, librarian mother; one sister. *Education:* Attended Berklee College of Music in Boston, MA; also studied with Alan Broadbent, Mike Renzi, and Jimmy Rowles.

Began playing piano in local bars at age 15; earned scholarship at age 17 to Berklee College of Music; attended jazz camp in Port Townsend, WA; discovered by drummer Jeff Hamilton and legendary bassist Ray Brown, earned grant from Canada Arts Council to study in Los Angeles with Broadbent and Rowles, 1983; moved to New York City to study under Renzi, joined jazz trio in Boston, 1990; released first album, *Stepping Out,* 1993; released All For You, a tribute album to Nat King Cole; released *Love Scenes*, 1997; toured with Lillith Fair concert, 1998; released *When I Look In Your Eyes*, 1999.

Addresses: *Home*—New York City, NY. *Record company*—Verve Music Group (distributes Verve, GRP, and Impulse), 555 W. 57th St., New York City, NY 10019. *Website*—http://www.vervemusicgroup.com.

backs, adding, "I think I put a lot of pressure on myself where it isn't necessary. I'm trying to handle it. I'm happy for my success, and I'm trying to enjoy it."

Diana Krall was born on November 16, 1964, in Nanaimo, British Columbia, Canada, a town located west of Vancouver across the Strait of Georgia on Vancouver Island. As a child, Krall, the oldest of two daughters (her sister later became a police officer in Nanaimo), enjoyed a home always filled with music. Her father, an accountant, accumulated over the years an enormous record and sheet music collection and Krall's mother Adella, an elementary school teacher andlibrarian who later earned a master's degree in educational administration, played the piano and sang. Both parents loved music and old television and radio shows. In addition, the future jazz musician's great, great aunt performed in Vaudeville in New York City. "I couldn't have had more supportive parents," Krall related to Lees. "The most important thing for me is my family." Nevertheless, Krall's parents at first held other hopes for their daughter's future. When one of her piano teachers told her mother that Krall possessed the potential to play jazz or pop music as a professional, Krall's mother recalled to Hayes, "I just smiled and thought, well, that's nice of her to say but Diana's going to university. I didn't want her playing in bars. I didn't have much regard for music as a career."

In many ways, though, Krall experienced a typical middle-class, small-town upbringing. She spent summers at the beach and winters on the ski slopes, listened to rock stars like Peter Frampton and the group Supertramp, and held dreams of exploring space as an astronaut, building model rockets with friend Bob Thirsk. (While Krall never made it to Canada's space program, Thirsk did, and he even took one of her CD s on the space shuttle with him.) However, Krall, who began playing the piano at age four, was also drawn to the music handed down from her father's record collection, including recordings of Fats Waller and Bing Crosby. She started taking piano lessons and singing with her grandmother, on her father's side; Krall said she sounds a lot like her as an adult with her low, sultry voice. Every day after school, she would go to her grandmother's house to play piano and sing, but Krall would never sing at home because she never thought she had a good enough voice. By 15, she played in a local bar and restaurant, singing as little as possible. At age 17, she won a scholarship to attend the Berklee College of Music in Boston, Massachusetts. She studied in Boston for 18 months before returning to Nanaimo.

Krall's big break came two years later in 1983, when her parents sent her to jazz camp in Port Townsend, Washington. Through the camp director, Bud Shank, she met several of her future friends, including drummer Jeff Hamilton, a member of an influential west coast jazz quartet called the L.A. 4. A few weeks later, when his quartet was playing a show in Krall's hometown, Hamilton brought legendary jazz bassist Ray Brown (the first husband of singer Ella Fitzgerald who Krall would later record with) to hear her perform at a bar down the street. Like Hamilton, Brown was impressed by the young pianist's talent. During their stay in Nanaimo, she invited the two musicians to her family's home for dinner, and Hamilton convinced Krall's mother that her daughter could "make it in jazz." Although her mother had previously disapproved of Krall pursuing a career in jazz, an industry often known for disappointments and drug use, she changed her mind after spending time with Hamilton and Brown. She remembered thinking, "These musicians have distinguished careers. They're pretty real people," as she told Hayes.

Thus, with her parents' blessing, Hamilton encouraged Krall to move to Los Angeles to study, and she earned a grant from the Canada Arts Council to do so. There, she first studied with Alan Broadbent, but she found her most important influence and teacher in pianist Jimmy Rowles (1918-1996), who played with singers such as Billie Holiday and Peggy Lee. The first time Krall went over to his house to meet him, she ended up spending most of the day. He conducted .informal lessons and told Krall old stories about Holiday, Sarah Vaughan, and other jazz legends. "It was just as important to me to hang out and listen to stories as it was to practice andplay," Krall told Lees. "He'd play for me, and then I'd play for him. But most of the time was spent with me listening to him play. And we'd listen to records. We'd listen to Ben Webster, Duke Ellington." Furthermore, Rowles, also a singer noted for his passionate, stylish vocals, pressed Krall to develop her voice. With his encouragement, and because she realized she would earn more opportunities to play if she sang, Krall conceded and started performing in Los Angeles piano bars. Three years later, she moved to Toronto, then to New York in 1990, where she studied with Mike Renzi and for awhile commuted to Boston to work with a jazz trio.

By now, critics, jazz fans, and record labels were taking note of Krall's soulful voice and confident piano skills. In 1993, she released her debut album on the Canadian label Justin Time entitled *Stepping Out,* a forceful trio work with bassist John Clayton and friend Hamilton on drums. Following her debut, the record company GRP, one of North America's foremost jazz labels, signed Krall, and she released her second album in 1995. Her former mentor Brown also appeared with fellow bassist Christian McBride for the record entitled *Only Trust Your Heart.* In addition, tenor saxophonist Stanley Turrentine contributed to the recording as a special guest, adding more variety to the ensemble.

After a Canadian summer jazz-festival tour with guitarist Russel Malone and bassist Paul Keller in 1995, Krall made her next album, 1996's *All For You,* a tribute to jazz great Nat King Cole. Again, Krall illustrated the way in which she allows her music to breathe and encourages musical conversation within her band. "Alternately happy-go-lucky and smokey, *All For You* features Krall's single-malt vocals and accomplished piano playing (backed by guitar and acoustic bass) on a collection of mainly lesser-known standards (the classic jazz repertoire of songs written by the great Broadway show tune composers of the 1930s and '40s). A highlight: 'Frim Fram Sauce,' a novelty tune recorded by Cole in 1945," commented Hayes. The album, nominated for a Grammy award that year, topped the jazz charts in the United States for over two years and broke sales records (for a jazz recording) around the world. Jazz artists, especially newcomers, rarely see their albums appeal to such a wide audience.

Krall's next release in 1997, *Love Scenes,* further exemplified her continuing maturity and her band's cohesiveness with a more relaxed tone than her previous albums. Joined by Malone and McBride, the record built upon jazz standards of artists such as Irving Berlin, Harry Warren, Percy Mayfield, and George and Ira Gershwin. This release was also nominated for a Grammy award. Then in 1998, Krall released a collection of favorite Christmas songs entitled *Have Yourself a Merry Little Christmas.* This year also saw Krall's popularity skyrocket, aided by her hit single, a Fats Waller tune called "Peel Me a Grape." She appeared on two episodes of the Fox network's *Melrose Place,* accompanied pop singer Celine Dione on her Christmas album, recorded a duet with alternative artist Sarah McLachlan, and joined McLachlan and a host of other female musicians for the Lillith Fair concert. Krall told Dollar, regarding her playing Lillith Fair, "It was wonderful to hear teenage girls (yell for) 'Peel Me a Grape' and 'Go Russell!' I was sitting at the press conference with these women (Sarah McLachlan and others), going, 'Oh my God, these people are just as serious about what they do as we are.'"

Krall followed these successes with 1999's *When I Look In Your Eyes,* this time on the Verve label. John Ephland of *Down Beat* magazine noted that like her prior releases, Krall's most recentalbum continued her focus on "sultry standards, bouncin' swingers, a contemporary tune thrown in for fun." Other musicians featured for the album included Malone, Ben Wolfe and Clayton sharing duties on bass, Hamilton, Lewis Nash on drums, and Larry Bunker on vibes. The noted orchestrater Johnny Mandel also worked with Krall for *When I Look In Your Eyes* as director.

Krall now lives in New York City and continues to focus on her jazz career, keeping an apartment in Manhattan's Union Square neighborhood. Because her family always remains central to Krall's life, she travels back to her hometown in Canada to visit about once a month. Krall, a pianist and singer who mainly reinterprets the music of the past, says she only writes her own music when she feels she has something to say. Instead, the jazz artist finds creative fulfillment in taking an old standard and arranging it and performing with her own style. To those critics who accuse Krall of "going pop," the talented musician told Dollar, "I'm not out to please the jazz police, nor am I out just to win an audience. I'm just out to make the kind of record that I would love to put on and listen to."

Selected discography

Stepping Out, Justin Time, 1993.
Only Trust Your Heart, GRP, 1995.
All for You, Impulse, 1996.

Love Scenes, Impulse, 1997.
Have Yourself a Merry Little Christmas, Impulse, 1998.
When I Look In Your Eyes, Verve, 1999.

Sources

Books

Swenson, John, editor, *Rolling Stone Jazz and Blues Album Guide,* Random House, 1999.

Periodicals

Atlanta Journal and Constitution, December 6, 1998, p. L01.
Chatelaine, September 1, 1997, pp. 52-55.
Down Beat, September 1999, p. 52.
Edmonton Sun, June 9, 1999, p. 11.
Gannett News Service, March 8, 1999.
Independent on Sunday, November 8, 1998, p. 10.
Jazz Times, September 1999, pp. 34-39.
London Free Press, November 21, 1998, p. C5.
Minneapolis Star Tribune, October 30, 1996, p. 04B.
Newsday, August 7, 1996, p. B07.
Newsweek, June 14, 1999, p. 68.
St. Louis Post-Dispatch, November 27, 1993, p. 08D; March 17, 1995, p. 08E; September 19, 1995, p. 03E; March 8, 1998, p. D8; March 13, 1998, p. E4
Washington Times, August 26, 1999, p. C16.

—Laura Hightower

Jonny Lang

Guitar, singer

David Atlas. Reproduced by permission. ©

Those who subscribe to the notion that only age and a lifetime of hardships can produce a blues musician have probably never heard Jonny Lang play guitar. Just ask legendary bluesman Buddy Guy, who toured with Lang in the summer of 1998: "That kid has just got what it takes, man," Guy said to Sean McDevitt of *Guitar* magazine. "Someone told me once that blues is like whiskey. They keep whiskey in the barrel for so many years, and then they talk about how well it's aged. But I don't think that goes for him. I think this young man has just stepped in there sayin', 'I'm gonna prove you all wrong.' I think he's like a watermelon, man. He's ripe." Blues godfather B.B. King felt the same way, according to A&M Records, adding, "When I was young, I didn't play like I do today. So these kids are starting at the height that I've reached. Think what they might do over time."

The teenage Lang intends to dispel beliefs that he is just another child novelty and to gain an audience beyond the typical curiosity seekers. As he told Ray Rogers of *Interview,* "If you do anything that's unusual when you're young, people love to accentuate the novelty, and the press loves to exploit it. But I've always told myself I'm going to be rated as a musician, not by how old I am. I said, 'I'm not going to be good for my age; I want to be good period.'" Rogers added that in addition to his skill at playing blues guitar in a way that makes the music sing through with a voice of experience, "Lang also has the grace of someone untainted by the world, a free spirit whose music and very person refuse to be bound by class, race, age, or any other expectation."

In 1997, after the release of Lang's major-label debut *Lie to Me, Guitar* magazine readers voted the 16-year-old "Best New Guitarist" in the publication's annual readers poll, and the editors of *Newsweek* placed Lang's name on their prestigious Century Club list, a roster of 100 Americans expected to influence society and culture in the next millennium. Rock guitarist Jeff Beck realized Lang's talent as well and asked the young musician to appear with him at a ceremony for the Rock and Roll Hall of Fame. Two years later, Lang shook the blues scene again, releasing *Wander This World,* an album that incorporated elements of soul, rhythm and blues, funk, and hard rock in addition to blues standards and originals.

Jonny Lang was born and raised outside Fargo, North Dakota. The third child and only boy in a family of four children, Lang enjoyed a pleasant upbringing. His father played drums, and his mother revered roots music and the soul of the Motown era, so the Lang household was always filled with inspirational grooves. Growing up, Lang had fond memories of singing Motown tunes with

For the Record . . .

Born January 29, 1981, near Fargo, ND; son of a drummer; three sisters.

Took up saxophone at age 11; started to learn blues guitar at age 13; began performing in clubs around Fargo; recorded the independent release *Smokin'*, relocated to Minneapolis, MN, c. 1996; released major-label debut for A&M Records with producer David Z entitled *Lie to Me*, 1997; toured with Aerosmith, Rolling Stones, Buddy Guy, B.B. King, and landed cameo role in the film *Blues Brothers 2000;* released *Wander This World*, 1998.

Awards: "Best New Guitarist," *Guitar* magazine's annual reader's poll, 1997.

Addresses: *Home*—Minneapolis, MN. *Record company*—A&M Records, 1416 N. La Brea Ave., Hollywood, CA 90028, (213) 856-2695, fax (213) 856-2645.

his three sisters and mother. "It was pretty easy for me to identify with blues music after that because blues and soul are pretty close in a lot of ways. I could just hear it and mentally decipher it," Lang told Rogers. Despite his exposure to soul at home, Lang never felt out of sorts with the music his peers listened to. As he told Rogers, "I was into Nirvana like crazy, and Stone Temple Pilots and Pearl Jam, too. But for me, it was more real to play roots music."

During his time in school, Lang's father wanted his tall, lanky son to play basketball in additionto learning music. But Lang only lasted two games, admitting to Rogers, "I liked it all right, but I'd have rather sat at home and practiced saxophone." Starting out with saxophone at the age of eleven, Lang (at the time a huge fan of saxophonist Grover Washington, Jr.) concentrated on that instrument for a year before turning his attention to blues guitar. Guitarist Ted Larsen, a friend of Lang's father and former member of Lang's band, obliged to teach the anxious youngster how to play guitar if Lang agreed to learn only by playing the blues. Thus, "I was a blues snob at 13 years old. ... My teacher fed me records and I started learning early stuff," Lang conceded to *Guitar* magazine's Bob Gulla. Practicing as many as six hours every day, Lang delved deep into the blues tradition developed by some of the most celebrated guitarists in blues history. "The blues was such a great place for me to start," noted Lang, according to his record company, "with Robert Johnson, Albert Collins, B.B. King, Freddie King and all those guys. It's where it all started which makes it a really good well that you can always draw from."

Before long, Lang progressed enough to begin paying his dues in clubs in North Dakota with an outfit called Jonny Lang and The Big Bang. Soon thereafter, club goers spread the word about the young teenager with a remarkable talent, and Lang and his band recorded an independent-label album entitled *Smokin'*, a release that sold an estimated 25,000 copies. However, Lang felt that he had outgrown the confines of North Dakota and relocated to Minneapolis, a move he defined as "a very humbling musical experience." Full of ego as a consequence of his success in his native state, Lang immediately realized he still needed practice. "It didn't take long to see that there were a whole lot of bands that kicked our asses," he admitted to Gulla.

Motivated by the competition, Lang jumped into the Minneapolis club circuit with his band. One group that greatly inspired him to improve his technique was Doctor Mambo's Combo, a group that would frequently invite Lang on stage with them during their sets and force the teenage guitarist to improvise with them. He also made connections in Minneapolis with a number of former Prince cohorts, namely producer David Z, who offered to help Lang record a demo tape. Based on the demo with David Z, Lang received a contract offer from A&M Records.

Following his signing, Lang recorded his first major-label album, the platinum-selling *Lie to Me*, also produced, engineered, and mixed by David Z. The album debuted at number one on the *Billboard* New Artist chart, and critics marveled at the maturity and poise that Lang displayed considering his young age. Released on January 28, 1997 (one day before Lang's 16th birthday), *Lie to Me* spawned the record's title track hit. Shortly thereafter, Lang's zealous technique, aided by his boyish, movie star good looks, led him to land an hour-long television special with Disney, in addition to a cameo role in the film *Blues Brothers 2000* playing with rhythm and blues legend Steve Cropper. In tour dates that followed, Lang, not yet 17 years of age, performed with some of the most celebrated artists in both the blues and rock and roll, including Aerosmith, the Rolling Stones, Blues Traveler, B.B. King, Buddy Guy, and others. Lang also toured on his own, headlining concerts around the world.

Playing with some of the greatest blues legends in history, though, came to represent some of Lang's most memorable experiences. "Playing with B.B. has probably been the biggest thrill of my life," Lang admitted to Gulla. "Talk about humbling. I'm sitting next to God here. I justwanted to sit next to him and listen, not play at all. But he let me play, so I just... actually, I didn't know what I was doing. You don't wanna go 'diddly diddly diddly dee,' and play all these notes, 'cause B.B. will shut your ass up with one little 'biiinnggg,' and everybody will go wild. You can't be more tasteful than B.B. It's impossible."

Despite his admiration for the forbearers of blues, Lang also considered taking alternate musical directions, a contemplation resulting largely from his move to Minneapolis, a city where he could not ignore the music being created in other areas of music all around him. He admitted that when he first started playing blues, he was strictly a purist and refused to try anything else. Thus, after opening his eyes to other styles and using blues as a solid foundation, Lang released his follow-up album, *Wander This World*, in the fall of 1998. While *Wander This World* continued down the path of traditional blues, the album also incorporated a variety of unexpected musical destinations such as soul, rhythm and blues, and funk. For example, on the textured, mid-tempo title-track (written by band members Paul Diethelm and Bruce McCabe), Lang's seemingly aged vocal passion and finger picked guitar takes root amid Diethelm's accompanying Dobro. And the song "I Am," written by David Z (who produced the album as well) and Prince, featured a soulful funk sound, a thumping bass line, and a jazz saxophone.

"Playing funk on guitar is a different mind-set," Lang concluded to Gulla. "Junior Wells' stuff, or Buddy Guy's stuff like 'Good Morning Little School Girl' is so funky, you just have to listen to it. Funk is my favorite thing to play. I love funk more than anything. I could play rhythm guitar all day and be happy." One of Lang's friends from *Blues Brothers 2000,* Cropper, who Lang felt was one of the best funk guitarists, also came on board for the project. "Steve is so inspiring. He added the soul vibe to the whole album, so it's like listening to a Stax recording." Cropper's subtle technique sounded especially evident on the gospel-tinged "Leaving to Stay."

Lang's own heartfelt ballad "Breakin' Me" and the acoustic lament "The Levee" also forced critics to realize that the young star's career was only just beginning. He silenced those who labeled him as a fleeting child prodigy, demonstrating that not only could he draw from the rich blues tradition, but he could also learn to spread his creative wings in new directions with a sense of self-awareness rare in adults, let alone teenagers. The distinguished blues guitarist Luther Allison said of Lang before his death in 1997, as quoted by A&M Records, "Jonny Lang has the power to move the music into the next millennium by reaching the ears of a new generation. The great musicians have the power to break all of the 'isms'—race, age, sex, et cetera. Jonny Lang is one of those musicians."

Selected discography

Lie to Me, A&M, 1997.
Wander This World, A&M, 1998.

Sources

Books

Swenson, John, editor, *Rolling Stone Jazz and Blues Album Guide,* Random House, 1999.

Periodicals

Billboard, September 19, 1998, p. 12.
Blues Today: A Rolling Stone Special, 1998, pp. 2-3.
Guitar, November 1998, pp. 43-46, 108-113.
Guitar World, November 1998, pp. 40-42.
Interview, February 1999, pp. 114-118.
Request, May 1999, pp. 25-29.

Additional information provided courtesy of A&M Records, Inc., Press Department.

—*Laura Hightower*

Limp Bizkit

Rock band

Photograph by Joe Giron. Corbis. Reproduced by permission. ©

In the late 1990s, Limp Bizkit changed the belief that hard-edged rock was dead by developing a hybrid of rap and rock music. Formed in 1994, the group perfected their outrageous stage shows and released their 1997 debut release entitled *Three Dollar Bill, Y'All$,* which included the stereo-infused cover of George Michael's pop hit "Faith." Throughout 1998, Limp Bizkit performed with both the Warped and Ozzfest tours, as well as with the inaugural Family Values tours headlined by the rock band Korn. For their Ozzfest sets, Limp Bizkit shocked audiences by emerging from a gigantic toilet, and performances with Family Values came complete with a troupe of break dancers and a science fiction-themed stage. In order to gain female fans, Limp Bizkit also traveled on their own for two months to put on "Ladies Night in Cambodia," for which the first 200 women to attend each night received free admission.

By the end of 1999, *Three Dollar Bill, Y'All$* had gone double platinum. Their subsequent album, 1999's *Significant Other,* proved an even greater success and debuted at number one on the *Billboard* album chart, selling 635,000 copies in its first week alone. After another round with the Family Values tour, an appearance at Woodstock 1999, and a headlining tour of their own, Limp Bizkit secured their rock star status.

Although guitarist Wes Borland, bassist Sam Rivers, drummer John Otto, and turntable man DJ Lethal simply enjoyed performing and reaping the rewards of their newfound wealth, rapper Fred Durst had dreamed of the fame and attention for some time. A self described workaholic who moved to Los Angeles to live closer to the heart of the entertainment industry (his band mates stayed in Jacksonville), Durst wants to do it all. In addition to fronting Limp Bizkit, Durst directed two of the group's videos for the songs "Faith" and "Nookie," helped design his band's outlandish stages, worked as a representative for Flip/Interscope Records, and performed on records with other artists such as Korn, Videodrome, and Soulfly. In July of 1999, Interscope appointed Durst senior vice president and gave him his own imprint. In the midst of all this, he also started writing a screenplay, hoping to one day direct and produce movies.

Durst, born in Jacksonville, Florida, spent most of his childhood in the small, southeastern town of Gastonia, North Carolina, where he lived until he graduated from high school in a middle-class neighborhood. His father worked for the Gaston County police department, and at the time of his retirement, he served as chief of undercover narcotics. Durst's mother worked in a mental health facility as a social worker. While Durst's parents did not quite understand their son's interest in rap, punk music, and wearing wild clothes and earrings, they

For the Record . . .

Members include **Wes Borland** (born 1975), guitar; **Fred Durst** (born 1971 in Jacksonville, FL; son of a retired narcotics officer who became a landscaping business owner and a former social worker who later worked as an administrator for a Lutheran church; children: daughter Adriana, born 1990), rapper, vocals; **DJ Lethal** (born Leor DiMant in 1970; son of Jewish Latvian immigrants; former member of House of Pain; joined band 1995), turntables; **John Otto** (born 1978), drums; **Sam Rivers** (born 1977), bass.

Formed band, started traveling on a grass-roots tour, 1994; signed with Interscope and released debut album *Three Dollar Bill, Y'All$,* 1997; released follow-up album *Significant Other,* performed at Woodstock concert, 1999.

Addresses: *Home*—Jacksonville, FL (Durst lives in Los Angeles, CA); *Record company*—Interscope Records, 10900 Wilshire Blvd., Ste. 1230, Los Angeles, CA 90024, (310) 208-6574. *Website*—Limp Bizkit Official Website, http://www.limpbizkit.com.

nevertheless supported his taste in musical and popular culture. When Durst discovered break dancing, for example, his father built a studio in the family's garage, and his mother sewed uniforms for his break dancing group called the Dynamic 3.

Felt Like an Outsider

Living in a home with a police officer father made an impact on Durst and helped keep him out of trouble, as he explained to Jon Wiederhorn in an interview for *Allmusic Zine.* "I've seen him come home shot when I was real young, and I've seen the people he had to deal with because of drugs and stuff, and that kept me out of it. He's been shot a couple of times, and he'd come home from the hospital, and you're just like, 'Holy shit!' There were crazy raids and shit. The drug dealers attacked him.... I remember when pot came into my life, but I never did anything else. I was too scared to. I had horror stories straight from the mouth."

Durst attended racially mixed schools and made a lot of African American friends growing up who introduced him to the emerging hip-hop music by New York-based groups in the 1980s. He especially liked records by the Sugarhill Gang. He was known as one of the few white boys in Gastonia that lived for break dancing and old school hip-hop music, though he enjoyed skate boarding and listening to punk, ska, metal, and rock as well. Durst sometimes felt like an outsider at his school where blacks and whites seldom hung out together. "Gastonia's got this small-town attitude," Durst explained to Zev Borow in *Spin* magazine.

Even though Durst had his share of run-ins with other white kids because of his choice of friends, he nonetheless described life in Gastonia as "awesome" and "just as up-to-date as anywhere else." The future rock/rap star, who started break dancing around 1982, entering local dance contests around 1984, rapping in 1984, and deejaying in 1985, said to Wiederhorn, "I had a couple friends who were into what I was into: breakdancing, rapping, deejaying, skate boarding.... I was definitely the outcast of the city, but I still had those couple of friends who lived in their own little world." However, Durst liked other types of music in addition to rap and hip-hop. Some of his early influences included the rock band Ratt, as well as alternative rock acts such as Nirvana, Soundgarden, Pearl Jam, and Rage Against the Machine.

Went to Boot Camp

A good student throughout grade school and high school, after graduation Durst admitted that dreams of rapping, skate boarding, forming a metal-rap group, and achieving fame started to cloud his academic intentions. He decided to enroll at Gaston College to study art, but dropped his classes only four days later. As time passed, Durst ran out of money and resorted to sleeping on friends' couches. Feeling like a "loser," as he admitted to Steven Daly of *Rolling Stone,* and wanting to please his parents, Durst chose to enlist in the United States Navy. After serving 18 "soul-destroying" months at boot camp in San Francisco, California, Durst injured his wrist skate boarding and received a medical discharge. Returning to North Carolina, Durst worked at a skate park in the city of Charlotte, then moved to Jacksonville with his parents when his father retired from the police force. Within this time Durst also married, divorced, and had a daughter with his former wife named Adriana (born 1990), who lives with her mother in Florida.

In Jacksonville, Durst's father opened a landscaping business, and Durst worked for him as a foreman for a time, while his mother took a job performing administrative duties at a Lutheran church. Durst also started working part-time at a surf shop and learned how to tattoo. At first, he tattooed people just for fun and admits to making some mistakes on people in the beginning. Still, he harbored the idea of forming his own band, and in 1994, after seeing Rivers play with a local metal group at a club, Durst persuaded the bass guitarist to try something new. Rivers's cousin Otto, at the time studying jazz at a performing arts high school, joined the group on drums, and Borland offered his services on guitar after seeing Durst perform his rap onstage. "I'd never really seen someone sing-rap like that," Borland recalled to Borow. Although Borland was already fronting another band, he quit in order to join Limp Bizkit. Before the band was signed, though, Durst had kicked Borland out of the band because he felt that his musical tastes were too different, replacing him twice with other guitarists. DJ Lethal came on board the following year. Limp Bizkit met the former member of House of Pain when they opened for one of the group's final shows. Limp Bizkit spent two years of relentless grassroots touring before getting their big break, spending time on the Warped and Family Values tours and playing at numerous small clubs.

Near Death Experience

However, Durst soon discovered that there "wasn't anyone as good as him [Borland] who I liked as much," he told Borow. Also aiding his decision to ask Borland back involved living through a near-death experience. The band was on their way to Los Angeles to make their first record, driving through Texas near the town of Van Horn, when the driver of Limp Bizkit's van fell asleep at the wheel. He awoke in a panic and flipped the vehicle over several times. Fortunately, no one suffered serious injuries from the crash, although Durst crawled away from the wreckage with two broken feet. After the accident, Durst realized that recording without Borland didn't feel right. "It was kinda like God flipping the van," he said to Daly. "We took it as a sign to get Wes back and start all over again."

Prior to the eventful night, Durst continued to work as a tattoo artist in his spare time. By chance, he met the successful rock group Korn when the band toured in Florida and gave all the members tattoos. "Fred told us he'd been tattooing for years," Korn's front man Jonathan Davis told Daly. "But it turned out it was, like, his third tattoo! He did a KORN tattoo on [guitarist] Head's back—and it looked like HORN." Despite the mishap, Korn held no hard feelings and started spreading the word about Limp Bizkit after Durst sent Korn bassist Fieldy a demo tape. Before long, several record labels started calling to offer Limp Bizkit a contract. They were originally set to sign with MCA but backed out at the last minute. Instead, Limp Bizkit went with the Flip/Interscope label, a record company that helped artists such as Nine Inch Nails, Marilyn Manson, and Eminem gain a mass audience. Working with Korn producer Ross Robinson, Limp Bizkit released their 1997 debut album, *Three Dollar Bill, Y'All$,* and started touring with Korn.

However, before most people even heard Limp Bizkit's music on the radio, the band woke up one morning at the center of a controversy. It seemed that Interscope, known to promote groups by any means necessary, had paid a Portland, Oregon, radio station to play the "Counterfeit" single 50 times. Although the deal was technically legal because it was considered buying advertising time, many music industry insiders reacted with outrage, and the story appeared on the front page of the *New York Times.* Despite the commotion, Limp Bizkit remained calm and allowed the news to blow over, believing that in the end the event would not harm the group's credibility. "It wasn't like we were getting tons of radio play anyway," Durst said to Borow regarding incident.

Took Over MTV

The song "Faith," a pounding metal remake of George Michael's 1980s pop hit, did hit the airwaves, and the video took over MTV (Durst himself directed the video). Nonetheless, the album as a whole went largely overlooked at first, and many critics deemed it one dimensional. In addition, one of the tracks called "Stuck," full of misogynistic references, angered many female rock fans. Durst explained to Daly that his not so politically correct choice of lyrics resulted from a painful breakup with a former girlfriend. "If you heard what she called me... I understand that two wrongs don't make a right. I was reacting; I didn't think of the consequences. I've learned my lesson. Now I soak everything in and *then* I respond. And when someone criticizes my lyrics, it makes me think twice. Was I a dick? A homophobe? A chauvinist? No, but I go back to make sure." Limp Bizkit also tried to make up for Durst's lyrical mistake byputting on the two-month traveling show called "Ladies Night in Cambodia." And to promote the album, constant touring—again with pals Korn as well as turntable stylists the Deftones—helped put Limp Bizkit back in line for greater things.

In the summer of 1999, Limp Bizkit released their sophomore effort, the more creative *Significant Other.* The album debuted at number one on the *Billboard* album chart, knocking out the Backstreet Boys' *Millennium* for the top spot and becoming the 15th highest debut in *SoundScan* history. This time around, Limp Bizkit hired Terry Date (who produced albums for Helmet and Pantera) to produce the album. Date, who Borland described as more of an engineer than a producer, enabled the band to become more involved in the recording process. "We really feel like we produced a lot of this ourselves," the guitarist commented to Borow. Likewise, DJ Lethal's hip-hop sensibility sounded more apparent on *Significant Other.* "I choose songs to dig into," reported the turntablist. "If a track doesn't need DJing, I'm not going to force it. But even the straight-rock shit, almost all the drums are breakbeat hip-hop." Durst again directed a video to support the album, this time for Limp Bizkit's hit single "Nookie."

As before, Limp Bizkit set out on another round of touring. In addition to joining the Family Values crew, the group also took the stage at Woodstock 1999 and headlined their own tour later that fall. In July of the same year, Interscope named Durst senior vice president and gave the rapper his own imprint. His duties for the company included producing, remixing, shooting videos, and signing new acts. While so many activities may overwhelm most people, the ambitious, hard-working Durst insists that he can handle it all and more.

Selected discography

Three Dollar Bill, Y'All$, Interscope, 1997.
Significant Other, Flip/Interscope, 1999.

Sources

Periodicals

Rolling Stone, July 8-22, 1999; August 5, 1999; August 19, 1999.
Spin, August 1999.

Online

Limp Bizkit Official Website, http:// www.limpbizkit.com (October 11, 1999).
"Limp Bizkit's Fred Durst Lonely at the Top," *Allmusic Zine,* http://www.allmusic.com/zine/limp_interview.html (September 26, 1999).
Rolling Stone.com, http://www.rollingstone.tunes.com (October 11, 1999).

—*Laura Hightower*

Lit

Rock band

David Atlas. Reproduced by permission. ©

The Southern California alternative rock group Lit set fire to the modern rock scene in early 1999; *A Place in the Sun,* the quartet's major-label debut, went certified platinum, giving rise to two hit singles, "My Own Worst Enemy" and "Zip Lock." Likewise, the band's third single off the album, "Miserable," was expected to climb modern rock charts as well. As part of the same Orange County music scene that helped launch the careers of groups like Korn and No Doubt, Lit worked hard for their mainstream recognition, spending nearly ten years together earning their "overnight" success. And although the band welcomed their fame and prosperity, they admitted that the idea of radio and MTV (Music Television) stardom seemed somewhat strange. "We're driving through the middle of nowhere in Kansas at three in the morning, and we hear our song come on right after Def Leppard," guitarist Jeremy Popoff told *Rolling Stone* writer Noah Tarnow. "It's just a little surreal."

The members of Lit, brothers A. Jay Popoff, lead vocalist and songwriter and Jeremy Popoff, guitarist and songwriter; Kevin Baldes, bass guitarist; and drummer, Allen Shellenberger, met while students at the same Anaheim, California, high school. Brought up on large doses of Metallica and Iron Maiden, the foursome started out as a heavy metal band called Razzle—later renamed Stain—and found a loyal following in nearby Los Angeles, selling out shows at famous clubs like the Whiskey, Troubadour, and the Roxy. Around 1990, the foursome officially became Lit and transformed their musical image. Previously a solid rock and roll band, Lit now introduced alternative rock into their music and claimed singers such as Frank Sinatra, in addition to the Foo Fighters and Metallica, as inspirations. "I'd say that the way we like to live is more the Rat Pack [led by Frank Sinatra, Sammy Davis, Jr., and Dean Martin] way of life than the Motley Crüe way of life," Jeremy Popoff told David Derby in an interview for Rolling Stone.com.

However, Lit refused to follow the trend of other Orange County-based modern rock groups to revive ska and swing. Instead, the foursome adhered to a blend of rock-driven punk/pop music. "We've just always been a straight rock band," A.J. Popoff mused to Derby, "and I guess that's not always the cool thing to be."

In addition to not fitting into the Southern California scene as well as other bands, Lit also had to compensate for a lack of venues in Orange County. "What's cool is that there's so many kinds of bands from Orange County: Social Distortion, the Offspring, Korn, No Doubt," commented A. Jay Popoff to Launch.com's David Weiss, describing the area surrounding Lit's hometown. "A lot of bands that have been around for the last nine or 10 years are surfacing now. It seems like there's a huge Orange

For the Record . . .

Members include **Kevin Baldes**, bass; **A. Jay Popoff** (born c. 1974), vocals; **Jeremy Popoff**, guitar; **Allen Shellenberger,** drums.

The Popoff brothers, Baldes, and Shellenberger met during high school in Anaheim, CA; played together as Razzle, then as Stain; formed Lit, 1990; signed with Malicious Vinyl, 1996; released EP *Five Smokin' Tracks From... Lit*, 1996; released first album, *Tripping the Light Fantastic*, on Malicious Vinyl, 1997; signed with RCA Records, 1998; released platinum-selling, major-label debut, *A Place in the Sun*, 1999.

Addresses: *Record company—RCA* Records, 8750 Wilshire Blvd., Beverly Hills, CA 90211, (310) 358-4000. *Website*—Lit at RCA Records: www.bugjuice.com/lit; Lit

County scene, but there's not really a lot of clubs to play. There's not a huge nightlife." Consequently, the group focused on their live shows in order to draw in fans and frequently sold out dates at a Fullerton, California, night spot called Club 369.

In 1996, after finally signing with the independent label Malicious Vinyl, the band released an EP entitled *Five Smokin' Tracks From... Lit.* The following year, Malicious Vinyl issued Lit'sdebut album, 1997's *Tripping the Light Fantastic,* which failed to impress critics. Nonetheless, the album, aided by Lit's onstage enthusiasm and unpretentious approach, made a connection with rock fans, and both releases found underground acceptance. "I think our songs for the most part are pretty down to earth," A. Jay Popoff told Derby. "A lot of people can relate to our lyrics... we're not too political, we're not really poetic, we're really pretty cut and dry."

As Lit's popularity spread throughout Southern California, major label RCA Records offered the band a record deal. Subsequently, Lit signed with RCA in late 1998. The band entered the recording studio and returned in February of 1999 with their second album, *A Place in the Sun.* The major-label debut eventually earned platinum status (selling over one million copies) and gave rise to two hit singles, "My Own Worst Enemy" and "Zip Lock," the first of which peaked at number one on *Billboard* magazine's Modern Rock Tracks chart. Despite struggling for years to obtain mainstream recognition, Lit was nevertheless stunned by the album's sudden success. "It definitely happened a lot quicker than expected," admitted A. Jay Popoff in on Launch.com. "We're getting worked pretty hard, playing almost every night and not sleeping a lot. But we're definitely *not* complaining."

"My Own Worst Enemy," a power-pop tune that discussed morning-after regrets, became a modern rock radio anthem. About the song, A. Jay Popoff told Midnight Jones for Launch.com, "It isn't based on any one of our particular personal experiences. It's just a jumble of times where someone went out and had too much to drink. You say things you shouldn't say and do things you shouldn't do and then the next day you realize how bad you f**ked up. A lot of people comment on the lyrics, but the hooky guitar riff doesn't hurt either."

Although the Popoff brothers write the foundation for the group's songs, the whole band participates in arranging music and picking tracks for albums. Thus, Lit developed "My Own Worst Enemy" with the same approach they use for all of their songs. "Our jam sessions go through the 'Lit machine' and everyone puts in their two cents," A. Jay explained. "Within two minutes, we know if it's going to be a song. If everyone's not into it right away, we get rid of it. We're not one of those bands that writes 30 songs for a 12-song album."

Despite Lit's mainstream success, the group continued to give concerts top priority. "Having a song on the radio is something we've always dreamed of, but we're a total live band so validation to us is packing clubs, meeting the kids, and seeing how music affects them," A. Jay Popoff asserted, as quoted by Jones. "We are all about the whole showbiz thing. We like bands who are flashy, not ones where it's like you are watching a bunch of roadies on stage." Holding true to their word and upholding their flashy, Las Vegas-style attitude, Lit spent most of 1999 on tour, opening for groups such as Silverchair and Eve 6 and joining the Vans Warped Tour.

Considering the group's favorite recreational activities—collecting vintage Cadillacs, traveling to Las Vegas, playing poker, admiring the Rat Pack—it comes as no surprise that Lit never wanted to be a typical rock band. "Our sound is of today, but our vibe is classic," A. Jay Popoff told Jones. These interests came into play for video for "My Own Worst Enemy." Shot in a Las Vegas bowling alley by director Gavin Bowden (who also directed videos for the Red Hot Chili Peppers' "Aeroplane" and Matchbox 20's "3 a.m."), the video aptly projected the intended Litimage. "It's [the film] *Kingpin* meets a gangster flick that takes place in the '50s." revealed A. Jay to Jones. "We are the bowlers and the band playing inside the lounge. I think we can handle the stage, but we might need a few body doubles to roll some strikes."

Selected discography

Five Smokin' Tracks from... Lit, (EP), Malicious Vinyl, 1996.
Tripping the Light Fantastic, Malicious Vinyl, 1997.
A Place in the Sun, RCA, 1999.

Sources

Periodicals

Rolling Stone, May 27, 1999, p. 29; August 19, 1999, p. 104.

Online

Launch: Discover New Music, http://www.launch.com (December 4, 1999).
"Lit: Own Worst Enemy," http://www.angelfire.com/ab/lit (December 4, 1999).
Rolling Stone.com, http://www.rollingstone.tunes.com (November 19, 1999).

—*Laura Hightower*

Lo Fidelity All Stars

Rock band

Part rock and roll, part punk-pop, and mixed with hip-hop and dance beats, the Lo Fidelity All Stars' sound included elements from a variety of different musical genres. After the release of the group's first single, 1997's 'Kool Rok Bass,' the All Stars became an overnight sensation in their home base of London, England, and throughout the United Kingdom. The group was regularly featured in two of the nation's well-established music magazines, *Melody Maker* and *New Musical Express* (*NME*). The latter publication also presented the band with the Philip Hall On Award for Most Promising New Band at the annual *NME* Brat Awards in 1998. Several singles later and following the release of their full-length debut album in 1998 (released in the United States in 1999), the All Stars seemed well on their way to worldwide stardom. However, by the end of 1999, the All Stars' future appeared uncertain, largely resulting from major line-up changes and canceled tour dates.

The Lo Fidelity All Stars formed early in 1996. At the time, The Albino Priest (real name Phil) was working at a Tower Records store in London's Piccadilly area and

SIN/Martyn Goodacre/Corbis. Reproduced by permission.©

For the Record . . .

Members include **Albino Priest** (Phil; born in Leeds, England), decks, samples; **The Many Tentacles** (Martin; born in Leicester, England; joined band in 1998), keyboards; **A One Man Crowd Called Gentile** (Andy; born in Leeds, England), bass; **Sheriff Jon Stone** (Matt; born in Sussex, England; left band in 1998), keyboards; **The Slammer** (Jonny; born in Leicester, England), drums, percussion; **The Wrekked Train** (Dave; born in Sussex, England; left band in 1998), vocals, lyrics, artwork.

Formed band in London, England, and signed with Skint Records, 1996; released first single, "Disco Machine Gun" (single withdrawn after three days); released "Kool Rok Bass," Skint, 1997; released debut album, *How to Operate With a Blown Mind*, Skint, 1998.

Awards: Received Philip Hall ON Award for Most Promising New Band, *NME*, February, 1998.

Addresses: *Record company*—Sony Music, 550 Madison Ave., New York City, NY 10022-3211, (212)

writing instrumental music and working with samples in his spare time. The unusually pale, thin turntablist (hence the alias "Albino") had been mixing records for some time; during his childhood, Priest would earn extra spending money selling mix tapes to his friends. The decision to form a band arose after a beer-fueled night of recording with friend and vocalist/lyricist The Wrekked Train (real name Dave). "I left Dave alone in a room with one of our backing tracks and loads of beer and let him do whatever he wanted," remembered Priest, as quoted by the All Stars' unofficial website. "He just got pissed [drunk] and rambled through an echo unit, but it really seemed to fit. After that, we started letting loose on all our tracks." Train's vocals would become one of the trademarks of the All Stars' sound. In the May 31, 1997, issue of *Melody Maker,* in which the publication named the All Stars' debut single "Pick of the Week," columnist Sharon O'Connell called attention to the vocalist's "impressively deadpan delivery."

Joined by keyboardist Sheriff Jon Stone (real name Matt), drummer/percussionist The Slammer (real name Jonny), and bassist A One Man Crowd Called Gentile (real name Andy), Train and Priest started playing low-key shows around London. Priest explained to Joshua Ostroff in *SUNday* why the All Stars used nicknames rather than their true identities. "They're all nicknames that the band have had," he said. "Also we're all massive Funkadelic fans, so it's a tribute to them really. It's nothing too contrived. It's just names we had for years and it's a nod to those bands that have inspired us."

The band found inspiration in other soul and funk musicians as well, including Marvin Gaye, Isaac Hayes, and James Brown. They also praised the hip-hop genre, giving high nods to artists like Rakim and KRS-1. In contrast, the All Stars also cited punk and pop acts like the Sex Pistols, Oasis, the Verve, the Mondays, and the Stone Roses as major influences. Intending to incorporate elements of all the above mentioned musical styles into their overall sound, the All Stars thus refused to be fenced in or labeled. However, they often referred to their music as punk-based.

After seeing one of the All Stars' shows, the Skint Records (a hip Brighton imprint) label managing director, Damian Harris, signed the band to record two singles (the offer was later extended). "I was sent a tape of theirs about 10 months ago, the main track was 'One Man's Fear,' which is now the B-side of the first single," Harris said, according to the group's unofficial website. "It was so distinctive, mainly because of the singing, or rather ranting, on it. I went to see them play in a pub in Camden soon after that. It was one of their first gigs and a bit of a mess because they hadn't quite sorted out their live sound, but they obviously had potential. The show was exciting. They looked like they were going to fall apart any minute. That made them seem like a proper band, like a rock 'n' roll band that just happened to be making dance music."

Before entering the studio, the All Stars opened for more established acts in the hopes of gaining a wider audience and building anticipation for their first record. One set of dates included the band's first tour of the United Kingdom, for which they opened for the group 18 Wheeler. In addition, the All Stars put their sampling skills to work; they remixed a track for the band Cast, remixed a Pigeonhead single entitled "Battle Flag," and accepted an offer to do remix work for the band Supergrass. After only one year together and with no recorded work to their credit, the All Stars had already begun to establish a reputation. Nonetheless, Priest was quick to point out that the All Stars weren't DJs, but rather an up-and-coming act whose focus was to create their own music. As Priest expressed to O'Connell, "I want our tunes to be played at Cream as well as the Heavenly Social [two well-known London night spots]; I want Jeremy Healey to play us at the peak of his party set in the main room, as well as the Chemicals [Chemical Brothers] at the peak of their set in the back room."

The All Stars finally released their first single, "Kool Rok Bass," in the late spring of 1997. The sample-led song filled with sexual undertones led critics and radio stations to brand them "the Stooges of dance music" or "the dance Stone Roses," according to Priest, as quoted by O'Connell. Moreover, "Kool Rok Bass" earned the band critical acclaim; the song was named "Single of the Week" by *NME* and featured as *Melody Maker*'s "Pick of the Week."

Alternative rock enthusiasts took to the single and the All Stars as well. "We haven't got our heads shaved; we know we look like an indie band," Priest told O'Connell, "but we like that. We're massively into hip hop and we like the fact that there's all these new hip hop fans who look at us and think 'what the f**k do *they* know about all this?' We supported loads of indie bands when we started out and they used to think because we had a turntable we were going to sound like PWEI. Then we started up and they couldn't believe it. We like that." Train further explained, "We're electricity personified. You know those big cables under the road when they cut them off and they're flapping around? That's what the album's going to sound like—so many volts you wouldn't believe it." Shortly thereafter, the band released a second single entitled "Disco Machine Gun," which was taken off the market after only three days because of problems with clearance of a sample taken from the Breeders' "Cannonball." However, approximately 8,000 copies were sold to the public, and the single (now a highly collectible item) made the top 40 in the United Kingdom.

In February of 1998, the All Stars were presented with the Philip Hall On Award for Most Promising New Band from *NME.* They edged out such groups as the Beta Band and CampaqVelocet. Two months later, in April, the group released a third single, "Vision Incision," which included snippets from a night when Train took a dictaphone on a journey through the streets of London.

May 25, 1998, saw the release of the All Stars' highly anticipated debut album in the United Kingdom, *How to Operate With a Blown Mind* entered the British album chart at number 15, received critical accolades, and sold over 60,000 units in Britain alone. That same year, the band performed numerous live shows, including three tours the United Kingdom, various dates throughout Europe, and a headlining slot at the Glastonbury festival in 1998.

Despite the band's stunning rise, Train, one of the band's founding members, left the All Stars in December of 1998, citing musical and personal differences. Soon after Train's departure, keyboardist Sheriff Jon Stone left the group as well. Although The Many Tentacles (real name Martin) replaced Stone on keyboards, the group's future seemed uncertain.

Selected discography

"Disco Machine Gun," (U.K. single; withdrawn after three days on the market), Skint, 1997.
"Kool Rok Bass," (U.K. single), Skint, 1997.
How to Operate With a Blown Mind, Skint/Sony Music, 1998.
(with others) On the Floor at the Boutique, (mixed by Lo Fidelity All Stars), 1998.
"Vision Incision," Skint, 1998.

Sources

Periodicals

Independent on Sunday, January 25, 1998, p. 7.
Melody Maker, May 31, 1997, p. 14.
New Musical Express (NME), April 4, 1998.
SUNday, February 14, 1999.

Online

"Lo-Fidelity Allstars, How to Operate with a Blown Mind," *MTV Online*, http://www.mtv.com (December 1999).
"Old Allstars," *Unofficial Lo Fidelity All Stars Website*, http://www.underworl.net/lofi/index.html (December 1998).

—*Laura Hightower*

Jack Logan

Singer, songwriter

The prolific songwriter and singer Jack Logan, aided by his makeshift band called the Liquor Cabinet, made an impression on music industry critics in 1994 with his garage-style, low-fidelity debut entitled *Bulk*, a 42-track collection of country, pop, rock, blues, and folk songs written and recorded in his rural Georgia home in a town called Winder, located some 40 miles northeast of Atlanta. Logan and his drinking buddies spent more than a decade writing songs and recording them in various garages, barns, and the kitchens and living room of Logan's house. They worked during the evenings and weekends, mainly for their own amusement, never trying to land a record contract. Logan and friends all maintained day jobs (Logan repaired swimming pool pumps, while best friend Kelly Keneipp refurbished old refrigerators), and their only connection to the public consisted of performances every now and then at local hangouts. Then in the early 1990s, after amassing more than 600 recorded songs, Logan sent them to a producer, Peter Jesperson, just to see what would happen. When Jesperson, Logan's later manager and producer, received the demo, he listened with amazement. "He's one of the best songwriters anywhere on the planet—period," Jesperson assured Jon Bream in the *Minneapolis Star Tribune.* After a portion of the songs, consisting of everything from country ballads and upbeat rock tunes to long narratives about life and death, found their way onto *Bulk,* Logan and his friends were thrust into the media spotlight.

To Logan's amazement, the release scored a four-star review in *Rolling Stone,* as well as a rare page-one feature in *Billboard.* With Logan now a favorite among college radio stations, he was subsequently invited to appear with his band in January of 1995 on the television show *Late Night with Conan O'Brien.* Despite *Bulk*'s overwhelming critical reception, the work failed to catch on in terms of record sales, and Logan only attracted a cult following of listeners. Nonetheless, Logan would continue to stick with his favorite pastime, and by late 1994, Logan and friends had already recorded over 100 new songs. "We're going to keep doing it just like we always have. Record it listen to it—which is the kick—and add it to the shelf with the rest of our stuff," he told *People* magazine in January of 1995. Logan and his Liquor Cabinet followed *Bulk* with two more albums, *Mood Elevator* in 1996 and *Buzz Me In* in 1999; both records again were deemed critical favorites. Logan, although originally from the Midwest state of Illinois, evolved into an accomplished and witty storyteller in the southern style since relocating to the South in the mid-1980s. "His characters wear their humanity proudly," stated the *Trouser Press Guide to '90s Rock,* "and their circumstances update the southern gothic morality of [novelist] Flannery O'Connor to include the current society of the trailer park and the long-haul trucker."

Logan, born around 1959, spent his childhood in Lawrenceville, Illinois, a small rural town in the southern part of the state. In school, he met his best friend and future collaborator Kelly Keneipp. Upon graduating from high school, Logan studied art (he originally wanted to work as a cartoonist) at Illinois State University in Normal, Illinois, located near his hometown, while his childhood pal Keneipp attended the University of Illinois in nearby Champagne-Urbana. Together, the two friends made music throughout college, inspired by punk rock's do-it-yourself attitude, the idea of performing and recording without the use of high-tech equipment. Aftercollege in 1985, Logan and Keneipp moved to Winder, Georgia, a town located 40 miles northeast of Atlanta. With no plans of ever finding careers as musicians, both men accepted jobs with an electric shop in Atlanta repairing swimming pool pumps (Keneipp also refurbished old refrigeration units). However, both men still enjoyed writing and playing music. Consequently, Logan, Keneipp (who played second guitar and keyboards), and other drinking buddies, collectively known as the Liquor Cabinet, started making tapes and playing in local bars and at small venues in Atlanta and Athens, Georgia, just for fun. "This is something we do on weekends, the way other people play golf," Logan explained to *People.*

For the Record . . .

Born c. 1959 in Lawrenceville, IL. *Education:* Studied art at Illinois State University.

Moved to Winder, GA, with best friend Kelly Keneipp, 1985; started writing music, recording, and performing in local bars with group of friends called the Liquor Cabinet; released 42-track debut album *Bulk,* on Medium Cool/Twin/Tone, 1994; appeared on *Late Night with Conan O'Brien,* 1995; released *Out of Whack EP*, Guilt Ridden Pop, 1995, followed by second album *Mood Elevator*, Medium Cool/Restless, 1996; recorded music for third album *Buzz Me In,* 1997; released *Buzz Me In* after signing with Capricorn Records, 1999.

Addresses: *Home*—Winder, GA. *Record company*—Capricorn Records, 1100 Spring St. NW, Ste. 103, Atlanta, GA 30309. *Website*—http://www.capricorn.com

Before long, Logan and his crew had written and taped an amazing amount of work, over 600 detailed and poetic, yet simple, songs, some of which would appear on the debut album. "Kelly goes into the kitchen and comes up with the verse-chorus structure; then I write the lyrics on the spot," Logan revealed about his casual style of songwriting to *People.* "We do six or seven songs in a couple of hours." However, as he told Neal Justin in the *Minneapolis Star Tribune* in his self-depreciating and neighborly manner, "Trust me, they aren't all great, but usually there's one or two that has some sort of potential.... I can go in with the musicians, have no idea what I'm doing at all, and kind of force myself to come up with something."

Around the same time, Logan and his act caught the attention of R.E.M. guitarist Peter Buck and musician Vic Chesnutt, who both lived in Athens. The two musicians then spread the word about Logan to influential manager/producer Peter Jesperson from Minneapolis, known for discovering the successful pop group The Replacements and cofounding the Twin/Tone record label. He would eventually manage Logan and produce two albums for the ensemble on his Medium Cool Records label. It took Jesperson more than a year, though, to persuade Logan to mail him some demo tapes. When Logan finally obliged, Jesperson offered him a record deal right away. Jesperson then sorted through the diffuse collection of work, picking out the songs that would appear on Logan's debut release.

All of the songs included in *Bulk,* a 42-track double CD, were recorded in Logan's kitchen, living room, and other home studio settings. Listening to the eclectic album was considered a truly humbling experience for any person who had ever attempted to write music, especially considering the fact that reviewers found it impossible to select highlight tracks from the recording. Examples of the rock-oriented anthems include the reverent "Female Jesus" and a tale of a tragic end called "Floating Cowboy." The musician also extends his wit and attention to rural life in country songs like the self-explanatory "New Used Car and a Plate of Bar-B-Que." Logan's understated ballads move beyond the traditional, questioning the timeless concept of love in new ways. In the song "Would I Be Happy Then?," the singer wonders if acquiring the car, house, and woman he had always longed for will bring him true happiness. While the debut record proved a success in terms of critical response, the album lacked support in sales.

Thus, the Liquor Cabinet continued with their day jobs, performed locally and made more music in their spare time. "*Bulk* didn't tear up the charts or nothing, so our lives have remained the same," Logan remarked to Chris Dickinson of the *St. Louis Post-Dispatch.* "We still work every day. We haven't run into too many creeps or golddiggers." However, Logan did meet one fan, as he recalled to Dickinson. "We had a 12-year-old girl show up at the shop and ask for autographs. I'm old enough to be her grandfather! But she was really cool. She said 'I just want to shake your hand.' We were stunned." While Logan continued to work and develop new songs, his record company released *Bulk 101,* an 11-song sampler derived from *Bulk,* followed by *Out of Whack,* a four-song EP.

For Logan's next album, *Mood Elevator*—released in1996—the band recorded the songs in a barn in Indiana. After a week, Logan and the Liquor Cabinet had completed 30 songs, 17 of which ended up on the finished record. Unlike Logan's debut, which included a variety of musical genres, *Mood Elevator* centered on conventional rock songs and lacked the raw humor and ambition of *Bulk.* Nevertheless, Logan's novelistic imagery, use of simple language, focus on working-class and small-town concerns, and attention to detail remained present. In the song "Just Babies," for example, Logan tells the story of a father who misses his children, yet he stays away from them because of his alcoholism. The somber "My New Town" collects the thoughts of a man who feels alienated in his new environment. Although Logan attempted to make a more commercially appealing record this time, sales again were low. In addition, MTV rejected his video, and the Liquor Cabinet's shows continued to draw only modest crowds.

In 1998, Logan made an album with another friend, Bob Kimbell of the overlooked band Weird Summer. For *Little Private Angel,* which sounded similar to Logan's work with the Liquor Cabinet, Logan wrote the lyrics and sang lead vocals, while Kimbell played guitar and sang harmonies. Like Logan's other projects, critics raved about the artist's songwriting ability. "As a writer, Logan is a miniaturist," wrote Phil Sheridan in *Magnet,* "creating whole worlds of emotion from such small moments as 'Dialing Your Number' or stepping up to the plate and hitting a 'Frozen Rope.'" For the ballad "Rained Like Hell" Logan wears the heart of a man recalling the wedding day of a lost love.

Logan united again with his band to release their next album *Buzz Me In,* originally recorded under Logan's old label back in 1997, then rescued by Capricorn Records in 1999. The musician took a new approach with this record, adopting a studio sound, aided by former Clash producer Kosmo Vinyl, as opposed to his previous low-tech method of recording and keeping the length down to 14 tracks. Nevertheless, he still managed to include songs that span his usual country, rock, and blues spectrum. And in spite of the album's more polished sound, Logan asserted to Steve Dollar of the *Atlanta Journal and Constitution,* "It'll always be guitars and beating on boxes for me." In addition, Logan added other instruments to compliment the guitar and drums of the Liquor Cabinet. "All Grown Up," for example, includes the trombone and vocals of Chesnutt and a cast of gospel backup singers, and for "Hit or Miss," Logan opted for a string section. As Logan again reaped praise for his more refined and intimate glimpse into the world of ordinary life, the music industry predicted greater commercial rewards for *Buzz Me In.*

Selected discography

Bulk, Medium Cool/Twin/Tone, 1994.
Bulk 101 (11-song promotional sampler from *Bulk*), Medium Cool/Twin/Tone, 1994.
Out of Whack EP, Guilt Ridden Pop, 1995.
Mood Elevator, Medium Cool/Restless, 1996.
(With Bob Kimbell) *Little Private Angel,* Parasol, 1998.
Buzz Me In, Capricorn, 1999.

Sources

Books

musicHound Rock: The Essential Album Guide, Visible Ink Press, 1999.
Robbins, Ira A., editor, *Trouser Press Guide to '90s Rock,* Fireside/Simon & Schuster, 1997.

Periodicals

Atlanta Journal and Constitution, May 14, 1999, p. P5; May 20, 1999, p. C5.
Magnet, November/December 1998, p. 69.
Minneapolis Star Tribune, May 5, 1995, p. 01E; February 16, 1996, p. 01E.
Newsday, June 10, 1999, p. C07.
People, January 16, 1995, p. 70.
Rolling Stone, June 10, 1999.
Spin, June 1999.
St. Louis Post-Dispatch, February 8, 1996, p. 7; February 16, 1996, p. 04E.
Washington Post, May 14, 1999, p. N17.

—*Laura Hightower*

Lonestar

Country group

Lonestar, a band whose members all boasted Texas origins and all shared songwriting responsibilities, created music that naturally contained hints of traditional country and dance-hall swing. However, the band also explored folk-rock music and incorporated easy ballads into their overall sound. Since the release of the band's 1995 self-titled debut that earned the group an Academy of Country Music award for best new vocal group or duo, Lonestar attained respect within the country music industry built upon strengths such as solid group harmonies, danceable up-tempo tunes, and expressive lyrics. The group's subsequent albums, *Crazy Nights* relesed in 1997,and *Lonely Grill* released in 1999, produced a string of country hits, many of which peaked at number one.

The members of Lonestar include Richie McDonald, Dean Sams, Keech Rainwater, and Michael Britt; vocalist John Rich, born and raised in Amarillo, Texas, left the group in 1997. McDonald, Lonestar's lead singer and rhythm guitarist, was born on February 6, 1962, in Lubbock, Texas. After graduating from high school in Lubbock, where he first started singing and writing songs, he moved to Dallas to pursue a career in music. There, he joined an award-winning local band called Showdown and also sang in national commercials. Eventually, his advertising work earned him enough money to relocate to Nashville, Tennessee, a city known as the heart and soul of country music and home to the Grand Ole Opry. In addition to writing songs for Lonestar, such as "When Cowboys Didn't Dance," and "Everything's Changed," McDonald also wrote successful tunes for other country singers, including "She's Always Right" for Clay Walker and "I Couldn't Dream a Love (Better Than This)" for John Michael Montgomery.

Sams, who played keyboards and harmonica and provided background vocals for the group, was born on August 3, 1966, in Garland, Texas, where he lived until the late 1980s. Then, while in his early twenties, he migrated to Nashville, also hoping to find work in the music industry. When he arrived, Sams secured a position at Opryland USA theme park singing in shows. In addition, Sams, also a recording engineer and producer, set up a studio where he created demos for himself and other musicians. Like McDonald, Sams wrote songs for other well-known country singers; Joe Diffie, for one, recorded Sams's song "Willing to Try" for his 1995 album *Life's So Funny.*

Britt, born June 15, 1966, in Fort Worth, Texas, and raised in his place of birth, played lead guitar and sang background vocals for the band. A self-taught guitarist who played by ear and never took music lessons, Britt performed with numerous groups throughout high school and college. After a few years of college, though, he decided to leave in order to devote his attention to music. In 1990, he started playing professionally in Texas forvarious groups such as Santa Fe and Canyon, a band nominated for an Academy of Country Music award in the early 1990s, before moving to Nashville in 1992. Britt's song credits for Lonestar include "Runnin' Away With My Heart" for the band's debut album. Lonestar's drummer and percussionist, Rainwater, was born on January 24, 1963, in Plano, Texas, and grew up in the small town located just outside of Dallas. Before joining Lonestar, Rainwater played with numerous other country groups, including Canyon with Britt.

Lonestar's origins date back to 1992 when Sams and McDonald met in Dallas at an audition for the Opryland USA theme park. After moving to Nashville, the two men continued to discuss forming a band and soon invited Rich and Britt to join them. Still needing a drummer, they later enlisted Rainwater, at Britt's recommendation, to fill the opening. And by late 1992, they were ready to start playing before an audience.

Determined to spread word about the band, Lonestar hit the road, performing more than 500 shows between 1993 and 1994. Traveling in a Jeep Cherokee that pulled their equipment trailer, the group played an amazing four to five sets every night in towns across the southern United States and promoted Lonestar with a six-song live compact disc.

For the Record . . .

Members include **Michael Britt** (born June 15, 1966, in Fort Worth, TX), guitar, vocals; **Richie McDonald** (born February 6, 1962, in Lubbock, TX; wife: Lorie; children: son Rhett; daughter Mollie Ann, born 1999), songwriter, vocals, rhythm guitar; **Keech Rainwater** (born January 24, 1963, in Plano, TX; children: daughter Dakota, born 1992), songwriter, drums, percussion; **John Rich** (born January 7, 1974, in Amarillo, TX; left band 1997), vocals; **Dean Sams** (born August 3, 1966, in Garland, TX; wife: Kim; children: daughter Britney Deann), songwriter, producer, keyboards, harmonica, background vocals.

Sams and McDonald formed Lonestar, recruiting Rich, Britt, and Rainwater, 1992; signed with BNA Records, released debut album, *Lonestar,* 1995; released *Crazy Nights,* (includes number-one hit "Come Cryin' To Me,") 1997; released, *Lonely Grill,* 1999.

Awards: Academy of Country Music award for 1995's best new vocal group or duo, 1996.

Addresses: *Home*—Nashville, TN. *Record company*—BNA Records, 1 Music Circle N., Nashville, TN 37203; phone: (615)780-4400; fax: (615)780-4464. *Fan club*—P.O. Box 128467, Nashville, TN 37212. *Email*—fanclub@lonestar-band.com. *Website*—Lonestar (official website), http://www.lonestar-band.com.

Before long, Lonestar accepted an offer to record for BNA Records and released their self-titled debut, *Lonestar,* in 1995. Featuring four original compositions written by various member of the band, the album also yielded Lonestar's debut single, "Tequila Talkin'," a song that reached number four on the country charts. The group's follow-up single, the infectious "No News," proved even more successful, holding the number one spot for three consecutive weeks in 1996, and "Runnin' Away With My Heart," cowritten by Britt, entered the Top Ten. As a result of the popular success of *Lonestar,* which also included the single "Heartbroke Every Day," the album achieved gold status just one year after its release. The accomplishment also helped Lonestar earn their first major award. In 1996, the Academy of Country Music named Lonestar as 1995's best new vocal group or duo. Likewise, publications including *Billboard, Music Row,* and *Country Weekly* gave year-end awards to the group.

After trading in their Jeep for a van and eventually a tour bus, Lonestar continued to travel and promote their music. By June of 1997, they released their sophomore effort, for BNA entitled *Crazy Nights.* The album rendered yet another number one hit with "Come Cryin' To Me" and "You Walked In," a single composed by songwriters Bryan Adams and Mutt Lange, appeared on country charts as well. While the record contained standard romantic ballads, Lonestar's second release took on country rockers like a cover of Pure Prairie League's 1975 song "Amie" and questioned the shifting direction of American culture in "Everything'sChanged," another number one hit cowritten by McDonald. In this song, noted Brian Mansfield in *USA Today,* "the band shows its maturation by surveying middle America's changing economic geography without letting things lapse into political posturing or mawkish nostalgia. The song's resigned, bittersweet tone makes it sound like something [country singer] Dan Seals once might have done." Eventually, *Crazy Nights* earned the band a second gold album to their name.

Although the record fared well with both critics and country music fans, Rich left the group shortly after the release of *Crazy Nights* to pursue other interests. Nevertheless, the four remaining members lost no time in writing and selecting new material for Lonestar's next album, *Lonely Grill,* released in June of 1999. In preparation for the group's third collection of songs, Lonestar spent approximately eight hours each day, five days a week listening to potential songs at BNA Records. Once the band reached the studio, they spent long hours working together to arrange guitar sounds, percussion touches, keyboards, and vocal harmonies for each recording. Previously, for the group's first two albums, record producers opted to use other Nashville session musicians to arrange music. But when Lonestar found Dan Huff to produce *Lonely Grill,* they were allowed more creative freedom. And while Lonestar had always shared writing and developing responsibilities for their prior work, they nonetheless believed the band collaborated even more closely during these sessions by arranging songs together.

Like Lonestar's earlier albums, *Lonely Grill* yielded major hits. One song, a straightforward ballad entitled "Amazed," topped the *Billboard* and *Radio and Records* country music charts in the summer of 1999. Setting a new record, the single sat at the number one spot on both charts for nine consecutive weeks. The last record was set back in 1966 with a Jack Greene hit entitled "There Goes My Everything" that occupied the number one spot for seven consecutive weeks. Furthermore, the single later that summer debuted on the *Billboard* adult contemporary chart at number twenty-six as the "Hot Shot

Debut." With such mainstream acceptance, the group hoped to gain more country listeners and Lonestar fans. Regarding the success of "Amazed," McDonald humbly told Leanne Carter of the *Ottawa Sun,* "What separates the good acts from the really successful ones is finding the right song."

Another heartfelt ballad, "Smile," climbed country music charts, while "Tell Her" proved that Lonestar could take a love song in a different direction through moody, unusual lyrics detailing the simpler facts of life. Despite the group's talent for writing, singing, and performing standard romantic songs, *Lonely Grill* maintained Lonestar's focus on other styles of music. For example, "Saturday Night" combined an electronic rumble with country-infused rap and "Don't Talk About Lisa," co-written by Benmont Tench of rock star from Tom Petty's Heartbreaker band,sounded reminiscent of a Jimmy Buffett rock tune. Another album highlight included an acoustic version of a previous hit, "Everything's Changed."

In less than one month, *Lonely Grill* shipped over 500,000 copies, earning the group still another gold record; during the first week after *Lonely Grill* hit record stores, the release sold over 47,000 copies. Overall, the album debuted at number four on the *Billboard* country album chart and reached number three, behind Shania Twain and the Dixie Chicks, retaining this position for two months.

On August 3, 1999, the Country Music Association nominated Lonestar in two categories for their annual awards show. The group received one nomination, along with Alabama, Diamond Rio, the Dixie Chicks, and the Wilkinsons, for group of the year, in addition to a nomination for single of the year for "Amazed." The other artist nominated in this category included George Jones for "Choices," Mark Wills for "Don't Laugh At Me," Tim McGraw for "Please Remember Me," and the Dixie Chicks for "Wide Open Spaces." Although the Dixie Chicks won awards in both categories during the awards ceremony at the Grand Ole Opry that aired on television on September 22, 1999, Lonestar still felt honored just to have received nominations. As of 1999, Lonestar, whose members love making and learning more about music, performing, and staying busy, held no plans for slowing down. Even with their tremendous success, the band continued to maintain an extensive touring schedule, booking about 150 concert dates each year.

Selected discography

Lonestar, BNA Records, 1995.
Crazy Nights, BNA Records, 1997.
Lonely Grill, BNA Records, 1999.

Sources

Books

Kingsbury, Paul, editor, *The Encyclopedia of Country Music,* Oxford University Press, 1998.

Periodicals

Arizona Republic, June 24, 1999, p. 36.
Dallas Morning News, June 11, 1999, p. 4.
Ottawa Sun, August 22, 1999, p. S5.
Reuters, April 24, 1996; August 3, 1999.
Tampa Tribune, July 23, 1999, p. 15.
Toronto Star, August 4, 1999.
USA Today, April 25, 1996, p. 01D: July 7, 1997, p. 05D; June 1, 1999, p. 12D; August 4, 1999, p. 01D; August 20, 1999, p. 01E.

Online

"Lonestar, *Lonely Grill,*" *Great American Country Lonestar* Home Page, http://www.countrystars.com/artists/lonestar/html, (September 15, 1999).
Lonestar, http://www.country.com/gen/music/artist/lonestar.html, (September 15, 1999).
Lonestar (official website), http://www.lonestar-band.com, (September 15, 1999).

—Laura Hightower

Jennifer Lopez

Singer, dancer, actress

Photograph by Deidre Davidson. Archive Photos. Reproduced by permission. ©

Jennifer Lopez appeared as an overnight sensation when she burst onto the entertainment scene in the mid-1990s. She was a talented, well-rounded modern woman, with pizzazz and good looks, plus singing, dancing, and acting accomplishments to her credit. A veteran of music videos, television, live stage shows, and commercial modeling, Lopez appeared in only a handful of minor film roles before she suddenly rocketed to stardom in the role of the murdered Tejano singing sensation Selena Quintanilla Perez. When *Selena* was released in theatres, Lopez emerged instantly as one of Hollywood's most popular leading ladies. She hailed from middle class roots in New York City's Bronx borough, entered show business in her mid-teens, and appeared in miscellaneous roles as a background dancer, actress, and model before turning her sights to Hollywood. After she traveled the globe in musical revues and drifted through video and commercial work, she settled into steady employment in television work before starting a career as a film actress. She appeared in six motion pictures between 1995 and 1998 and then took a one-year hiatus to re-address her musical career. When Lopez released her first CD in 1998, the album sold over two million copies by the year's end.

Jennifer Lopez was born on July 24, 1970, in the Bronx borough of New York City, New York. She was the second of three daughters born to David and Guadalupe Lopez, originally from Ponce, Puerto Rico. David Lopez worked as a data processing manager for an insurance company and his wife was a kindergarten teacher. Lopez and her sisters, Leslie (two years older) and Lynda (the youngest) attended Holy Family School. The Lopez household was filled with music, good food, and fun. Lopez was destined for stardom even as a youngster—she espoused Rita Moreno as her greatest heroine and took dancing lessons from the age of five. Over the years she studied ballet and jazz, flamenco, piano, and classical theater training. She also studied gymnastics, ran track, and played softball. Briefly while in high school, she entertained the possibility of becoming a professional beautician. Her parents meanwhile dreamed that their daughter might go to college and law school. Lopez succumbed instead to the lure of show business, despite her parents' disappointment when she announced that she would forego college to pursue a career in the theater. Before long, Lopez was on her own and living wherever she could afford the rent. For a time she stayed in a dance studio in Manhattan and later moved into an apartment in Hell's Kitchen.

Lopez made her first film appearance in the small role of Myra in *My Little Girl* in 1986. She secured her first steady acting role in 1988 when she embarked on a five-month European tour of a live stage production called

For the Record . . .

Born July 24, 1970, in New York, NY; daughter of David and Guadalupe Lopez; married Ojani Noa, 1997; divorced, 1998.

Performed in musical shows on international tour; film actress, 1986—; television work, dancing and acting, 1990-1993; films include *My Family/Mi Familia,* 1995; *The Money Train,* 1995; *Jack,* 1996; *Blood and Wine,* 1997; *Anaconda,* 1997; *U-Turn,* 1997; *Selena,* 1997; *Out of Sight,* 1998; *Antz* (voice of Azteca), 1998; signed with Sony Records, 1998; debut release, *On the 6,* 1998.

Awards: American Latino Media Arts Award (ALMA) for Best Actress, 1998; ALMA Lasting Image Award, 1998; Lone Star Film & Television Award for Best Actress, 1998.

Addresses: *Management*—c/o United Talent Agency, 9560 Wilshire Blvd., 5th Floor, Beverly Hills, CA 90212. *Record company*—Sony, 550 Madison Ave., New York, NY 10022-3211, (212) 833-8000.

Golden Musicals of Broadway. She then toured Japan in a production of *Synchronicity.* Upon her return to the United States, she worked at dancing and modeling jobs, including appearances in music videos and commercials. Her dancing proficiency landed her a steady job in 1990 as a "fly girl" on the Fox television comedy show, *In Living Color,* with producer Keenan Ivory Wayans and choreographer Rosie Perez. Lopez quit *In Living Color* in 1991 to accept a role in a television pilot for a short-lived series called *South Central.* With the demise of that show, she moved into the role of Melinda Lopez on a CBS series called *Second Chances* starring Connie Selleca. The show lasted one season, and the writers carriedLopez's Melinda role into a spin-off series called *Malibu Road.* Following the *Malibu Road* series Lopez appeared as a nurse in a made-for-television movie called *Nurses on the Line: The Crash of Flight 7.* During the winter holidays in 1991-92 and 1992-93, she performed in the live-stage production of Charles Dickens's *A Christmas Carol* at McCarter Theatre in Princeton, New Jersey.

By 1993 her stage and television careers were a matter of history. As an up-and-coming young dancer that year she performed in music videos, including "That's the Way Love Goes" with Janet Jackson. Lopez was also seen in Puff Daddy (Sean Combs) & The Family's "Been Around the World." By 1995 she had moved to Los Angeles with her boyfriend of nine years. She landed two feature film roles that year: as Maria in Gregory Nava's *My Family/Mi Familia,* followed by the part of Grace Santiago in Joseph Ruben's, *Money Train* with Wesley Snipes and Woody Harrelson. Lopez received a nomination for the Independent Spirit Award for her role as Maria the Mexican immigrant in *My Family/Mi Familia.* The pace of Lopez's career accelerated rapidly with the acknowledgment. She appeared with Robin Williams in the 1996 release of Francis Ford Coppola's *Jack,* and the following year she appeared in the female romantic lead opposite Jack Nicholson in *Blood & Wine.* That same year moviegoers saw her as Terri Flores in the action/disaster feature, *Anaconda,* starring Jon Voight, and in 1997 she starred with Sean Penn in *U-Turn.*

A final film release in 1997 catapulted Lopez to stardom in what became her signature role as Selena Quintanilla Perez, the murdered Tejano singer in director Gregory Nava's production of *Selena.* Amid concerns from backstage critics that Lopez didn't physically resemble the real Selena, Lopez set out to recreate the aura of the legendary singer. Lopez learned all that she could about her subject and then summoned her own gifts for dancing and singing. She danced and acted her way through the scenes of *Selena,* recreating the spirit and actions of the slain Latina superstar. Although Lopez lip-synched her way through the vocal score, she performed from the heart with a zest and fire that effectively depicted the life and times of the real Selena. For her work in *Selena,* Lopez received a Golden Globe nomination in 1998 for the best performance by an actress in a motion picture.

On the heels of the success of *Selena,* Lopez appeared in 1998 as a romantic interest with George Clooney in *Out of Sight.* Also that year she dubbed in the voice of Azteca, the worker ant in an animated cartoon feature film from DreamWorks, called Antz.

Lopez felt inspired, in part by her starring role in *Selena,* to respite from her whirlwind film career for one year, in order to tape a debut vocal album. She spent much of 1998 in the production of her CD, *On the 6,* and thus the multi-faceted performer added singing and songwriting to her already impressive acting and dancing credits. The CD, released by SonyRecords, evoked a variety of musical styles, including pop and rhythm and blues. According to Lopez, every song she does bears a Latino undertone. Lopez was apprehensive at first when the producers approached her to write a song for the album; she expressed concerns against expanding her professional ventures too rapidly. But Lopez relented and co-wrote he album's "Should Have Never." Lopez developed the CD title, *On the 6,* by recalling the number of the subway train that she rode into Manhattan as a young girl. Lopez's platinum hit single, "If You Had My Love," is heard on the album—the song spent five weeks at number one on the music charts. The album itself sold over two million copies before the end of the first year of its release on Sony's Work Group/Columbia label. Lopez's frequent companion, Puff Daddy (Sean Combs) also contributed an original composition to one of the album's tracks. Also heard on the album is a duet between Marc Anthony and Lopez entitled, "No me ames (You Don't Love Me)," for which Lopez appeared in the music video in August of 1998.

Talent aside, Lopez established herself as a bona fide sex symbol very early in her career. It was a flattering concept, but she nonetheless had a difficult time escaping persistent remarks in the press regarding her "trademark" feature, a voluptuous backside. She was listed among the "50 Most Beautiful People in the World" in 1997 and again in 1999 by *People.* Her conscientious commitment to rigorous physical fitness training is common knowledge around New York and Los Angeles, both cities she considers to be home. Additionally, she aspires to a dream of settling in Miami, Florida to raise a family.

Lopez was married very briefly to Ojani Noa, whom she met at Gloria Estefan's restaurant, Larios on the Beach. Noa worked at the restaurant at the time while Lopez filmed her feature movie, *Blood and Wine,* on location in Florida. Their brief, but romantic courtship lasted approximately one year, into the filming of Lopez's next film, *Selena.* When the filming was over Noa proposed to Lopez in front of the entire cast and crew of *Selena.* They married on February 22, 1997, but separated less than one year later and divorced in 1998. In retrospect Lopez regarded the marriage philosophically and acknowledged that her career contributed significantly to the break-up. Regardless, she intends to raise a family and will not sacrifice her career in the process. After the separation between Lopez and Noa, rumors persisted concerning Lopez's romantic inclinations. Media reports linked her with an endless string of eligible suitors, including her perennial collaborator, Sean Combs. After much speculation about the nature of their relationship, Lopez and Combs confirmed their romantic involvement by appearing hand-in-hand at the MTV Music Video Awards in September 1999. The two made headlines when they left Club New York on December 27, 1999, after a member of Combs' entourage allegedly shot at three bystanders. Combs and two others were charged with criminal possession of a 9 mm handgun. One of the guns was found in the sport utility vehicle Combs and Lopez were riding in, but Combs denied the charges against him as "100 percent false." Lopez was not charged in the incident, but was questioned at length by police.

In 1998 Lopez received the American Latino Media Arts (ALMA) Lasting Image Award and the ALMA for best actress in *Selena.* Also for her portrayal of Selena, Lopez received the Lone Star Film & Television Award for Best Actress. In the midst of soaring stardom she came into popular demand as a media personality. In 1994 she hosted *Coming Up Roses,* and in 1995 she hosted the NCLR Bravo Awards. Additionally in 1995, she was a presenter for the VIDA Awards, and she was a presenter, along with Combs, at the MTV Video Music Awards in 1999. Biographer Patricia J. Duncan said of Lopez, "Her unique blend of beauty, talent, drive, and confidence have made her the hottest commodity in the film industry, and that will soon be true in the music industry as well."

Selected discography

On the 6 (includes "If You Had My Love"), Work Group/Columbia, 1999.

Sources

Books

Contemporary Theatre, Film and Television, Gale Research, Inc., 1998.

Duncan, Patricia J., *Jennifer Lopez,* St. Martin's Paperbacks, New York, 1999.

Periodicals

Cosmopolitan, April 1997; March 1999.

Entertainment Weekly, December 1, 1995; October 9, 1998.

In Style, June 1, 1999.

Interview, April 1997.

People, May 12, 1997; May 10, 1999; September 13, 1999.

Online

"Mr. Showbiz Celebrities: Jennifer Lopez Biography," http://mrshowbiz.go.com/people/jenniferlopez/content/bio.html (November 24, 1999).

—Gloria Cooksey

Luscious Jackson

Rock band

During the late1960s, when Luscious Jackson's name sake—Lucius Jackson—played for the Philadelphia 76ers in the National Basketball League, members of the all-female band were just coming into the world. Although they were born too late to notice the basketball star's greatness on the court then, they were impressed later when viewing memorable footage of his moves on the court, especially taking delight in an announcer's mispronunciation of Lucius's name as "luscious." As basketball fans—loyal season-ticket holders for the WNBA's New York Liberty—born during Jackson's time of greatness, the women thought it appropriate to call themselves "Luscious Jackson" when it came time to think of a name for the band they put together in the early 1990s. The funk-pop music group blends many different influences and elements into its sound, from 1970s disco and bossa nova to 1980s punk and rap. Sara Sherr of the *Village Voice* described their generation and brand of song this way: "Too young to wear a Disco Sucks button or sequined tube top, they'd come of age as cool club kids or wide-eyed suburban new wavers who understand the Jammin' Gold segue from 'Good Times to

SIN/Martyn Goodacre/Corbis. Reproduced by permission.©

For the Record . . .

Members include **Jill Cunniff**, bass, vocals, song writer; **Gabby Glaser,** guitar, vocals, songwriter; **Kate Schellenbach**, drums; and *Vivien Trimble* (left band in 1998), keyboards.

Group formed in New York City in 1991; signed with Grand Royal 1992; released debut album *In Search of Manny,* on Grand Royal, 1992; contributed to *Clueless* soundtrack with "Here," 1995; appeared on *Saturday Night Live,* 1995; hit the mainstream music charts with "Naked Eye," 1997; earned rave reviews for *Electric Honey* EP, 1999.

Awards: Best EP award in the *Village Voice* "Pazz & Jop" poll for *In the Search of Manny,* 1992.

Addresses: *Record company*—Grand Royal Records, P.O. Box 26689, Los Angeles, CA 90039, (213) 663-3000, fax (213) 663-5726. *Website*—Official Luscious Jackson website, http://www.lusciousjackson.com; Grand Royal website, http://www.grandroyal.com.

'Heart of Glass....' Luscious Jackson [lives] inside that segue too, making grown-up records for the kids who grew up eating to the beat indiscriminately." They've developed their image in their own way, even stamping to-become a prescription for hipness as they've come of age in their music. Billy Altman, in *Stereo Review's Sound & Vision,* applauded the band for its uniqueness in style, commenting, "From riot to Spice, girls with guitars who make it big in rock and pop tend to do so primarily by flaunting image and attitude. Luscious Jackson, like the old NBA hoopster the band is named after, has always approached its game stylishly but straight, choosing to chuck the tired —and ultimately regressive— gender issue in order to simply get to the heart of the matter—namely, making good music."

The band members, Kate Schellenbach, drums; Jill Cunniff, bass, vocals, songwriter; and Gabby Glaser, guitar, vocals, songwriter, met in their teens while frequenting Manhattan's punk clubs, including CBGB, where Glaser reportedly spent her thirteenth birthday, Hurrah, Tier 3, and Max's Kansas City. They bonded over their affinity for the acts at those venues, such as the Funky Four Plus One More, Grandmaster Flash and the Furious Five, Slits, ESG, and Bad Brains. Moreover, they shared tremendous adoration and respect for the punk diva of the early 1980s, Blondie's Deborah Harry, as was common among American women of that generation. Meanwhile, Glaser bought her first guitar and began teaching some covers and Schellenbach started playing drums for a popular local band, the then-hardcore Beastie Boys, whom she dubbed years later as "the Daytona Spring Break Sideshow," as well as the Lunachicks and Wench. Glaser, who was known to be a chum of the Clash's Joe Strumer , reminisced on those teen years at the clubs in a 1999 *Spin* article, stating, "We really packed a lot into those years. We were exposed to so much stimuli that by the time we were 17, we were jaded."

When the trio reconvened in Manhattan after finishing their college studies, they pulled together money to put out a demo tape, which landed them opening gigs for the Beastie Boys and Cypress Hill in 1991. Vivien Trimble, who had worked with dance companies in the New York City music scene, joined the band as a keyboardist. When the Beastie Boys launched their recordlabel, Grand Royal, they invited Luscious Jackson to be their first client. In 1992 the band released its debut album, *In Search of Manny,* on Grand Royal, which included three tracks from the band's original demo and won the Best EP award in the *Village Voice* "Pazz & Jop" poll. They promoted their album by touring as the opening act for bands like Urge Overkill and the Breeders in 1992-93 and by playing second stage in 1994's Lollapalooza.

In late 1994, Luscious Jackson released its sophomore EP, *Natural Ingredients,* which was co-produced by the band members and Tony Magurian. Cunniff recalled in a 1999 *Spin* article that the album sounded "fun but sloppy," which she blamed on the band not relinquishing enough control of production over to the label's production experts. They then promoted the album with its own headlining tour in the United States and abroad. The track "Here" was marketed as a single and chosen for a video release and to be included on the soundtrack for *Clueless.* In 1995, Lucious Jackson appeared on *Saturday Night Live* and toured as the opening act for R.E.M. and Live.

In 1996 Luscious Jackson recorded and released *Fever In Fever Out,* produced by Daniel Lanois, who had done work for U2 and Bob Dylan. Written by Cunniff during a rocky period in her relationship with her boyfriend, Scott, "Naked Eye" was the take-off release for that album and became a hit in early 1997. The single put Luscious Jackson's name on the relatively more mainstream music charts. Accompanied by a smooth, even, funky harmony, the song's lyrics tell of the benefits and healing power of bold and clear communication with the people in your life. *Billboard*'s Bradley Bambarger quoted Cunniff as describing the song as an expression of the "sense of relief" that comes from "emotional nudity—the feeling of not wearing all these layers...." She expressed further, "Even though it takes a lot of courage to be open. It's much easier to hide behind fences and wish the world understood." Luscious Jackson having yielded production control on *Fever In Fever Out;* Mike Kates, the new Grand Royal president, was disappointed with the album, because he felt that "it was more Daniel Lanois than [Luscious Jackson]," according to the same *Spin* article. By mid-1997 *Fever In Fever Out* achieved gold status. A fixture in American pop culture now, Luscious Jackson was featured in a colorful commercial for the GAP in late 1997, which gained distinction as *TV Guide's* Most Popular Ad that year.

Ready to get off the road and eager to pursue other musical projects, Trimble retired from the band, leaving the original trio. Glaser and Cunniff worked on developing their voices through voice lessons, studying in Miami and New York, respectively. Cunniff also spent time writing new songs. The band began recording it next release in 1998, which was released as *Electric Honey* in June of 1999. *Spin* applauded the release as Luscious Jackson's best, calling it "the most seamless fusion yet of the group's influences—punk, pop, New Wave, and funk ... more personal, less obsessed with unapologetic lust than it is with the benefits of hard-won maturity." The band members themselves called the album their first "top-to-bottom great record." They worked with four producers, including Tony Visconti, known for his work with David Bowie, and Mickey Petralia, who has worked with Beck, and accepted the advice of Kates and Mike D. The album features guest contributions by celebrities. Emmylou Harris, who also sang on *Fever In Fever Out,* sings on *Electric Honey's* first single release, "Ladyfingers." Ex-Brand New Heavies N'Dea Davenport contributes to "Christine." Kym Hampton of the New York Libertys-ings backup on "Friends." Deborah Harry sings on "Fantastic Fabulous." Ex-Breeder Josephine Wiggs contributes cello and Petra Haden violin to the track "Space Diva."

Harry, a fan of the band's, has been deeply admired by the women of Luscious Jackson since they were girls. Harry invited Schellenbach to replace drummer Clem Burke for a short time during a Blondie reunion tour in 1998, which was a dream come true for the longtime Blondie fan, who was even a member of the Blondie fanclub as a child. In an interview with the *San Francisco Gate,* Schellenbach called Harry "a sweet, generous, badass woman with an incredible voice." Schellenbach also had the opportunity to play drums for the Indigo Girls' latest EP release and tour in 1999.

The success of *Electric Honey,* however, frightened Luscious Jackson. Perhaps wide acceptance in the industry is a sign that they have lost their status of setting trends in the music industry from the fringe. Achieving biographical coverage in the popular media could mean that they have outgrown their celebrity in the NYC indie music science as music industry mavericks who are always way before their time. It is too soon to survey whether audiences have hastened towards their style or whether their style has slowed down to keep pace with the mainstream. Cunniff even expressed concern that her happiness in her marriage and in domestic life could put her in danger of not being able to write the great songs that can only be born of sadness. However, she admitted to *Spin* that the success of *Electric Honey* is likely a product of her being "better at life."

In 1999, Luscious Jackson's members, well into their thirties, confessed in *Spin* to a softening, maturing, and slowing down in setting the latest trends in popular American youth culture. Schellenbach noted that her "record collection peaks at '83." Cunniff admitted to preferring a score on a good bargain on slipcovers than to hitting the latest club. The band, however, set the tone for immensely popular genre-blending artists in the late 1990s like Beck and the up-and-coming Cibo Matto. Beastie Boys' Mike D surveyed in the same *Spin* article that had *In Search of Manny* come out pre-Beck, or, in other words, during the hightime of genre fusing rock with surreal or goofy lyrics, it would have been their biggest selling album. Schellenbach remarked regarding the Beastie Boys' confidence in Luscious Jackson's style and art when they were just starting out, "I don't think anyone else could have understood what Jill and Gabby were doing back then."

Selected discography

Daughters of the Kaos (demo), Grand Royal, 1992; released on Capitol, 1993.
In Search of Manny, Grand Royal, 1992; released on Capitol, 1993.
Citysong, Grand Royal/Capitol, 1994.
Natural Ingredients, Grand Royal/Capitol, 1994.
Deep Shag, Grand Royal/Capitol 1994.
Here, Grand Royal/Capitol, 1995.
Naked Eye, Grand Royal, 1996.
Fever In Fever Out, Grand Royal/Capitol, 1996.
Electric Honey, Grand Royal/Capitol, 1999.

Sources

Periodicals

Billboard, February 15, 1997; July 17,1999.
Esquire, June 1999.

Rolling Stone, July 8, 1999.
San Francisco Gate, July 14, 1999.
Spin, June 8, 1999.
Stereo Review's Sound & Vision, July/August 1999.
Vibe, June/July 1999.
Village Voice, August 24, 1999.

Online

Billboard website, http://www.billboard.com/daily/feature/luscious.html (November 18, 1999).
Grand Royal website, http://www.grandroyal.com, (November 27, 1999).
"The Luscious Jackson Source," http://www.homepages.go.com/~luscious77/ (November 27, 1999).
"The Official Luscious Jackson Website," http://www.lusciousjackson.com (November 27, 1999).
Rolling Stone website, http://www.rollingstone.com (November 18, 1999).

—Melissa Walsh Doig

M People

Dance music group

In 1992, M People released their first album, *Northern Soul,* in the United Kingdom. Since that time, the group from Manchester, England, consistently won critical praise for their unique ability to include elements of old-school funk and rhythm and blues into the youth-driven house or dance music genre. As Nilou Panahpour of *Rolling Stone* noted, "M People make the kind of dance music that could inspire even a banker to put on a platinum wig and try John Travolta moves in front of the mirror naked." From the onset, vocalist Heather Small, keyboardist Mike Pickering, bass guitarist Paul Heard, and drummer/percussionist Shovell sought not only to create modern club grooves that inspire listeners to dance, but also to pay tribute to the music of the past. "Paying respect to the original soul players has always been of the utmost importance to us," asserted Pickering, as quoted by the band's record label. "The bottom line is that without them, we couldn't be here."

The group's 1999 release, *Testify,* further explored a funk/dance music tradition. However, a few songs on the album showed M People taking a slight detour by

Capital Pictures/Corbis. Reproduced by permission. ©

For the Record . . .

Members include **Paul Heard**, bass guitar; **Mike Pickering**, keyboards; **Shovell**, drums, percussion; **Heather Small**, vocals.

Formed band, 1991; released debut in the U.K., *Northern Soul,* 1992; released *Elegant Slumming* in the U.K., 1993; released U.S. version of *Elegant Slumming,* 1994; released *Bizarre Fruit* in the U.S., top ten British singles totaled nine, 1995; released compilation and remix album *Testify* in the U.S., 1999.

Awards: Brit Award for best dance act of 1992-94; Brit Awards for album of the year for *Elegant Slumming,* 1993; Mercury Music Prize for 1993; best album of the year from the U.K. and Ireland for *Elegant Slumming,* 1994; Silver Clef Award, 1999.

Addresses: *Home*—London, England. *Record company*—Epic Records, 550 Madison Ave., New York City, NY 10022-3211, (212) 833-7442, fax (212) 833-5719; 2100 Colorado Ave., Santa Monica, CA 90404, (310) 449-2870, fax (310) 449-2559.

traveling down a more overtly rhythm and blues road. For singer Small, known for her soulful alto vocal range, the diversion was a welcomed change. "I've always enjoyed performing softer, more introspective songs," she professed. "It allows me to use my voice in ways that a dance beat doesn't allow—not that I don't love to cut loose on an uptempo dance track, because it's great fun. I'm just so pleased to have the opportunity to explore every color on the palette, if you will."

M People's roots can be traced back to the city of Manchester, England, Mike Pickering's hometown and the birthplace of other notable acts such as Simply Red and Joy Division, one of Pickering's favorite groups. In fact, before forming M People, Pickering used to work as a Joy Division roadie. After this, he worked as a chef, then a roadie again for the group Kraftwerk and singer Julio Iglesias, among others, and finally as a window washer.

Obviously unsatisfied with his former jobs, Pickering longed to create music himself rather than work behind the scenes. Eventually, he started working the turntable decks at a legendary Manchester nightclub, The Hacienda. Soon after this, Pickering joined his first band, Factory Record's Quano Quango. He honed his musical skills playing saxophone for the group. During the same time, he also played saxophone with one of the first house music bands in Britain, T-Coy. In addition to playing music, Pickering worked as a Factory Records recruiter, signing two groups that later witnessed popular success, both Happy Mondays and James.

Dance Beats Met Motown

By 1991, as dance music was taking over Manchester's club scene, Pickering realized his true musical mission. His goal, according to M People's record company, was "to bring dance music back to the song, like Motown, Stax or the Philly International era. A classic song is the foundation of any kind of music." In order to fulfill the idea of uniting dance and soul/funkmusic, Pickering first enlisted the aid of Paul Heard, a bass guitarist. Prior to meeting Pickering, Heard, a professionally trained musician, had played bass for various British groups, including Working Week, Strawberry Switchblade, and Orange Juice. The two composed a number of songs together; one such composition was written with a particular singer in mind, vocalist Heather Small, a petite but passionate performer of West Indian descent from a well-established, London-based soul band called Hot! House.

Pickering, along with Heard and Small, entered the studio to record songs together. Although the trio's initial plans were to simply put down some tunes, the aforementioned sessions eventually led to the makings of a first album. At first, Pickering held to his plan of using a variety of vocalists in addition to Small. But after playing together, Pickering realized that Small's vocals contributed a unique quality to the music unmatched by any other singer. "It was obvious as we were recording that what we had musically was much more than just a one off thing," Pickering realized, according to Epic Records. "It had turned into something really coherent. We never went back to rotating vocalists." Defining her singing style, Ron Givens of *Stereo Review* remarked, "The sound that erupts from her throat is deep and throbbing, edged with raw passions or tender mercies."

From Studio to Stage

With Small as lead vocalist, M People released their debut album, *Northern Soul,* issued in 1992 in Britain on deConstruction/RCA Records. An instant success, the record featured the top ten British singles "Colour My Life" and "How Can I Love You More." Consequently, the group evolved into one of Europe's most popular live acts within no time, and their shows regularly sold out stadiums and arenas. In the meantime, Pickering realized that the group had grown beyond the studio and assimilated a full band (usually a ten-piece unit) for touring. While many dance bands refrain from performing live and limit playing to the studio, M People flourished before an audience. "People say, 'Isn't it strange for a dance band to play live?'" remarked Pickering, as quoted by Epic. "Don't they remember? That's the way it always was." Around the same time, the trio also enlisted Shovell as the group's full time drummer and percussionist.

In October of 1993, M People released their second album in the United Kingdom, *Elegant Slumming,* later issued in the United States in May of 1994 by Epic Records. Surpassing the success of their debut, *Elegant Slumming* reached number two on the United Kingdom album chart and spurred three additional British top ten singles, including "Moving On Up," "One Night In Heaven," and a cover of a Dennis Edwards classic entitled "Don't Look Any Further." By September of that year, the album had sold 1.7 million copies worldwide (excluding the United States) and over 600,000 units in the United Kingdom alone. For the 1993 Brit Awards (the British equivalent to the Grammy Awards) held in February of 1994, the release was named album of the year, and the group was voted best British dance act for the second year in a row.

The best singles from both *Elegant Slumming* and *Northern Soul* were later released in the United States by Epic in June of 1994 under the title *Elegant Slumming.* While M People had yet to receive significant recognition in the States, the British hit "One Night In Heaven" peaked at the number one spot on *Billboard* magazine's Hot Dance Music/Club Play chart in September. In addition, the album reached number 12 on the Heatseekers album chart and had sold approximately 36,000 copies in the United States, according to *SoundScan.*

Acclaim Beyond the Dance Genre

After issuing an American version of their first two efforts, M People became the subjects of further acclaim. On September 13, 1994, the group won the third annual Mercury Music Prize for 1993's best album of the year from Britain and Ireland for *Elegant Slumming,* edging out the internationally famous Blur and eight other nominees. "From a musician's point of view, it's very gratifying to win this award cause it reaches beyond the categories of dance, or indie, or rock, or whatever," Pickering told *Billboard,* according to reporter Thom Duffy, after he and his band mates accepted the honor at London's Savoy Hotel. Rather than dividing the sum among themselves, the group announced they would donate the 25,000 pound—about $38,000—prize money to charity.

By the spring of 1995, M People boasted a total of nine British top ten singles, and further successes were yet to come. *Bizarre Fruit,* released on November 14, 1994, in Britain on deConstruction, and in mid-1995 in the United States on Epic, saw favorable reviews as well. As Panahpour concluded, *Bizarre Fruit* "continues the hook-laden disco-soul gallivanting of *Elegant Slumming.* This self-produced album is not one long throbbing dance marathon; the group's unifying vision of emotive pop music pulls together a collection of actual songs." The *Rolling Stone* critic also praised the group's skill of making "corny" lyrics work: "Anywhere else, lyrics like "Search for the hero inside yourself" would sound silly; here they contribute to the pure emotionality and sing-along beauty that only the best dance music evokes."

And although Givens argued that the lyrics of some of the tracks were for the most part dismissible, the reviewer nonetheless described the music, notwithstanding Small's singing ability, as "ravishing." Moreover, wrote Givens, "while relying heavily on synthesizers for melody and rhythm, the tracks also employ what [rock musician] Graham Parker describes as 'basically organic keyboards.' Many of the riffs and solos that may have been played on amplified programmed instruments actually sound natural. And the judicious use of such non-electronic gadgets as saxophones ant strings, as well as a couple of guitars, help to leaven the technological accomplishments of the band."

Hinting at the Motown era, M People's melodies and lofty vocals added a sense of euphoria to songs like "Sugar Town," a rhythm and blues inspired track with elements of both reggae and gospel, and "Sight For Sore Eyes," a choir-like tune featuring a rolling piano and traces of salsa music. Other standout tracks included "Search For The Hero" and "Open Your Heart."

Following the success of *Bizarre Fruit,* M People released the rhythm and blues-inspired *Fresco* in 1997 and *The Best of the M People,* both issued only in the United Kingdom. *Fresco* bore another string of British hits, including "Sight For Sore Eyes," "Search For The Hero," and "Just For You," all of which appeared on *Testify,* primarily a compilation of tracks from the abovementioned albums issued in the United States in May of 1999. However, *Testify* offered more than a packaging of "greatest hits." While the release comprised several choice tracks from *Fresco* and *The Best of M People,* the American issue also contained four previously unavailable remixes of classic M People recordings: "Sight For Sore Eyes" (M People

Master mix), "Colour My Life" (Joey Negro's Agoura mix), "Moving On Up" (Mark Picchiotti's Millennium Vocal remix), and "How Can I Love You More" (Jimmy Gomez's 6am mix). Moreover, *Testify's* title-track and first single pays homage to the roots of soul—"a lovely down tempo jam that is steeped in soulful rhythms and vocals," noted *Billboard* magazine.

On June 25, 1999, the British soul outfit received another important honor. This time, the band took the Silver Clef Award during a luncheon ceremony in London. The annual event, at that time in its twenty-fourth year, raises money for the Nordoff-Robbins Music Therapy Charity, which uses music to help children overcome language difficulties. Accepting the honor on behalf of the band, *Billboard* reported, Small told the audience, "We're all about making music. That music is our reward."

Selected discography

Northern Soul, (U.K.), deConstruction/RCA, 1992.
Elegant Slumming, (U.K.), deConstruction/RCA, 1993.
Elegant Slumming, (includes tracks from U.K. releases *Northern Soul* and *Elegant Slumming*), Epic, 1994.
Bizarre Fruit, (U.K.), deConstruction/RCA, 1994, Epic, 1995.
Fresco, (U.K.), deConstruction/RCA, 1997.
The Best of M People, (U.K.), deConstruction/RCA.
Testify, (includes remixes and tracks from U.K. releases *Fresco* and *The Best of M People*), Epic, 1999.

Sources

Billboard, September 24, 1994, p. 1; October 8, 1994, p. 33; November 19, 1994, p. 33; June 24, 1995, p. 1; October 11, 1997, p. 33; February 13, 1999, p. 50; May 22, 1999, p. 33.
People, May 22, 1995, p. 20.
Rolling Stone, August 10, 1995, p. 58.
Stereo Review, November 1995, p. 116.
Village Voice, June 27, 1995, p. 74.

Additional information was provided courtesy of Epic Records.

—Laura Hightower

Madness

Ska group

Madness stood at the forefront of the ska revival that moved through the British pop music scene in the late 1970s and early 1980s. Incorporating the rhythms and horn arrangements of the sound that later spawned reggae, Madness paid tribute to the music they had listened to while growing up in London. The group didn't just copy what had gone before, though. The distinctive, jerky, and enthusiastic dancing styles of horn player and emcee Chas Smith and lead singer Suggs marked a Madness concert. Adding touches such as Smith's shouting, "Hey, you! Don't watch that, watch this!" at the beginning of their song "One Step Beyond," the group created what they themselves called a "nutty sound." For all the fun in their performances, their lyrics often made thoughtful observations on everyday concerns of working-class London.

This combination of silly and serious helped make Madness one of the most popular music acts in the United Kingdom and Europe, although they remained mostly unknown in the United States. As the members' lives began to change, so did the band's fortunes, and in

Photograph by Andy Sin/Wilsher. Corbis. Reproduced by permission.

For the Record . . .

Members include **Mike Barson** (born April 21, 1958, in London, England), keyboards; **Mark Bedford** (born August 24, 1961 in London), bass; **Chris Foreman** (born August 8, 1958, in London), guitar; **Graham "Suggs" McPherson** (born January 13, 1961, in Hastings, England), vocals; **Chas Smash** (born Cathal Smythe, January 14, 1959), emcee and trumpet; **Lee Thompson** (born October 5, 1957, in London); **Dan Woodgate** (born October 19, 1960, in London), drums.

Band formed as Morris and the Minors, 1978; changed name to Madness and released first single, "The Prince," 1979; released first album, *One Step Beyond,* 1980; scored first American hit with single "Our House," 1982; Barson left band, 1983; formed own label, Zarjazz, 1984; released *Utter Madness*, Zarjazz, 1985; group disbanded, 1986; group reunited for first of four annual Madstock concerts, 1992; went on first tour since disbanding, 1998; released first studio album in thirteen years, *Wonderful,* 1999.

Awards: *New Musical Express* Singles Act of the Year, 1980.

Addresses: *Record company*—Virgin Records Ltd., 553-579 Harrow Road, London, W10 4RH, UK. *Web site*—http://www.madness.co.uk.

1986 they disbanded. But they never totally stayed apart, reuniting occasionally for live performances. In the meantime, another ska revival occurred, and the bands that led it—No Doubt, Sublime, and Mighty Mighty Bosstones—acknowledged Madness as a major influence. Unwilling to be merely legends, Madness got together again, releasing not only a live album, but also, in 1999, their first studio album of new material in thirteen years.

Madness began to take shape in London, England in 1976 with a band called the Invaders. The included such future members of Madness as keyboard player Mike Barson, saxophonist and vocalist Lee "Kix" Thompson, guitarist Chris "Chrissie Boy" Foreman, and Smith. These four hooked up with Suggs, bass player Mark Bedford, and drummer Dan "Woody" Woodgate to form Morris and the Minors in 1978. Smith had been playing bass, but he traded it for horns and the emcee's role. Meanwhile, with his distinctive vocal style, Suggs became the group's front man. The band became Madness the next year, taking the name from a song by legendary 1960s ska performer Prince Buster. Their first single, titled "The Prince," continued their tribute to their idol. It also became the first of their 21 singles to make the Top 20 on the British charts.

The success of "The Prince" earned Madness a contract with one of the most prominent labels of the British New Wave, Stiff Records. Their first single for their new label, "One Step Beyond," reached the British Top Ten, and the album of the same name remained on the charts for a year. Their follow-up album *Absolutely* repeated the success in 1980. The hit songs from their second album included "Embarrassment", "Baggy Trousers," and "The Return of the Los Palmas Seven." All in all, there was a Madness song on the British charts for 46 weeks out of that year, earning them *New Musical Express* magazine's Singles Artist of the Year award. Still, their popularity remained confined to their side of the Atlantic. Although Sire Records had released the first two albums in the United States, neither had cracked the Top 100 lists, a weak performance that cost Madness their access to the American record market.

Madness was not the only popular ska group in England at the time. Acts such as the Specials, Selecter and the Beat (known as the English Beat in the United States) also thrived on reviving the popular dance music that came out of London youth clubs in the 1960s. Madness, though rooted in ska, also drew on other music that they heard while growing up in racially mixed, working-class neighborhoods. This meant that the traditional styles of English music halls also came into Madness's sounds. Combining the music of their childhood with songs about the lives that they saw around them, the group earned comparisons with the Kinks as keen observers of British society.

Madness's popularity continued to grow in England and throughout Europe with an almost universal appeal. They found themselves playing in front of audiences that included children and senior citizens. In order to accommodate all their fans, the band even started performing matinee concerts so children under sixteen could attend. Still, they found their appeal a bit too broad. Young skinheads associated with the racist National Front movement flocked to Madness shows, evidently drawn in by this all-white band playing black music about working-class life. In an effort to end this unwanted appeal, the group included an explicit attack on the National Front on their EP *Work Rest and Play*. Madness also continued to write surprisingly controversial lyrics for such a popular group. Their 1982 single "Cardiac Arrest" failed to make the British Top Ten because of radio programmers squeamish about its graphic anti-stress message.

"Cardiac Arrest" from the album *The Rise and Fall*, showed Madness's increasing musical maturity. Incorporating more pop styles into their compositions, their songs became more serious while retaining the band's trademark wit. According to the *Encyclopedia of Popular Music*, songs such as "Grey Day" and "Our House" displayed an "ability to write about working-class family life in a fashion that was piercingly accurate, yet never patronizing." The latter song became their first hit in the United States, appearing on their first American record in three years, a compilation album called *Madness.* Not that the band had been completely invisible in the States (their creatively whimsical videos had appeared on MTV), but there had never been any records available to go with the television presence. The situation changed with "Our House," and with heavy video and radio play, the song finally put Madness in the American Top Ten.

The band's fortunes took a downward turn at the end of 1983 when Barson left. One of their most important songwriters, he became tired of the pop star life and moved with his family to Holland. Madness carried on, with their first single after Barson's departure, "Michael Cane." The song and the album *Keep Moving* did well on the British charts. The group also formed their own label, Zarjazz, which soon ran into financial difficulty. Their first album on Zarjazz, *Mad Not Mad,* did not make the Top Ten, nor did any of the singles from it. At the end of 1986, the band announced that they were calling it quits. Their final single, "Waiting for the Ghost Train," peaked at number eighteen on the charts two months later.

Madness did not stay gone for long. In 1988, Suggs, Smith, Foreman, and Thompson joined with keyboardist Jerry Dammers from the Specials, along with keyboardist Steve Nieve and bassist Bruce Thomas from the Attractions. They called this band the Madness and released an album of the same name. It came nowhere near the success of the group's earlier incarnation, though, and they disbanded once again. The members of the band went their various ways, forming orworking with other bands, with some even taking on other roles in the music industry. In the summer of 1992, the original lineup came together again in London for a pair of outdoor concerts. They dubbed the show "Madstock." The shows proved to be such a success that they held one each summer for the next four years, until announcing once again that they would not reunite for any future shows. In the meantime, Suggs had released his first solo album, *The Lone Ranger,* in 1995 with some modest success.

However, the appeal of performing on-stage and the popularity of their shows proved too much for Madness to stay separated. In 1998 they went on tour, including stops in the United States. They recorded a show in Los Angeles, which they released as the album *Universal Madness* in 1999. This reappearance of Madness in the midst of another ska revival prompted an assessment of the band's legacy and how well they were holding up. *Washington Post* reviewer Mark Jenkins was especially impressed by the performance of "Our House" on the live album and wrote, "If the band can write some new songs as playfully indelible as this one, Madness will be as much competition as inspiration to its contemporary American disciples."

Evidently, the band had the same idea, and in 1999 they went back into the studio, with Barson participating. They also turned to their original producers, Clive Langley and Alan Winstanley. The sessions resulted in their first album since 1986, *Wonderful,* released in England in November of that year. Musically they picked up right where they left off. Dele Fadele wrote in *New Musical Express*, "A fine balance is kept between kitchen-sink miserabilist tendencies and jolly grown-up japes." Their ability to counterpoint their musical exuberance and, at times, their downright silliness with mature themes in some of their lyrics had always been a Madness hallmark. By returning with new material in the same vein, they created an opportunity for an audience familiar with ska through Madness's pupils to learn from the masters themselves.

Selected discography

One Step Beyond (includes "One Step Beyond"), Sire, 1979.
Work Rest & Play (EP), Stiff, 1980.
Absolutely, Sire, 1980.
Seven, Stiff, 1981.
Rise and Fall (includes "Our House"), Stiff, 1982.
Madness, Geffen, 1983.
Keep Moving, Geffen, 1984.
Mad Not Mad, Geffen, 1985.
Utter Madness, Zarjazz, 1986.
Total Madness: The Very Best of Madness, Geffen, 1997.
Universal Madness, Golden Voice, 1999.
Wonderful, Virgin, 1999.

Sources

Books

Buckley, Jonathan and Mark Ellingham, editors, *Rock: The Rough Guide,* Penguin, 1996.

Larkin, Colin, editor, *The Encyclopedia of Popular Music,* volume 5, Muze, 1998.
Robbins, Ira, editor, *The Trouser Press Record Guide,* fourth edition, Collier, 1991.

Periodicals

Washington Post, April 30, 1999, p. N16.

Online

"Madness," *All Music Guide,* http://www.allmusic.com.
"Madness," *Rolling Stone,* http://www.rollingstone.tunes.com.
"Madness Wonderful," *New Musical Express,* http:www.//nme.com, November 11, 1999.

—Lloyd Hemingway

Russell Malone

Singer, guitar

Jazz guitarist Russell Malone provided an interesting analogy to describe his approach to music. As he told *Billboard* magazine's Steve Graybow, "One of the things that made Franklin Roosevelt such a good president was that while he was educated—an aristocrat—he still knew how to talk to the common man. That principle should apply to music. Every song doesn't have to be a lesson in theory and harmony. A lot of guys feel a need to educate the audience; I'd rather reach people."

Born in Albany, Georgia, in 1963, Malone grew up within a deeply spiritual church environment that influenced his early interest in music. He received his first instrument, "a green plastic four-string" according to Malone, at the age of four. However, after watching legendary blues guitarist B.B. King play "How Blue Can You Get" during an episode of the popular 1970s sitcom *Sanford and Son,* Malone started gravitating to various other musical forms besides gospel. And as the young guitarist discovered the blues, country, and jazz, he began to marvel at the musicianship of both country singers/guitarists such as Chet Atkins and Johnny Cash, as well as jazz guitarists like Wes Montgomery and George Benson.

Listening to the songs of the aforementioned performers and others, Malone taught himself how to play guitar. By the time he reached 25 years of age, he accepted his first gig playing with master organist Jimmy Smith. During his first performance with Smith, Malone recalled, "It made me realize that I wasn't as good as I thought I was," according to the Verve Music Group. Two years later, Malone joined singer/pianist Harry Connick, Jr.'s orchestra, holding this position from 1991 through 1994. In the meantime, Malone also worked with a diverse variety of other musicians, including Clarence Carter, Little Anthony, Peabo Bryson, Mulgrew Miller, The Winans, Eddie "Cleanhead" Vinson, Bucky Pizzarelli, and Jack McDuff.

Malone recorded his first solo album from August of 1991 until March of 1992. Released by Columbia Records in 1992, the self-titled debut provided an opportunity for Malone to display his classic, though modernized, technique. Covering most of the jazz spectrum and utilizing both electric and acoustic guitar, the album featured uplifting songs such as "When I Take My Sugar to Tea" and "I Can't Believe That You're in Love With Me" (a duet with friend Connick), in addition to more relaxed compositions like "Moonlight Serenade" and "London By Night." Pianist Donald Brown, bassists Milt Hinton and Robert Hurst, and drummers Yoron Israel and Shannon Powell also joined Malone for recording sessions. The following year, Malone returned with a second solo effort entitled *Black Butterfly,* recorded March through April of 1993 and again issued by Columbia. His accompanying lineup included Gary Motley on piano, Steve Nelson on vibraphone, Paul Keller on bass, and Peter Siers on drums. Similar to his previous release, Malone's follow-up effort, a collection of both original and cover tunes, was marked by his ability to combine the rich jazz tradition of master guitarists with clever melodies and youthful arrangement. Yet at the same time, Malone played more tightly with his backing musicians.

Up to this point in his career, the young singer/guitarist remained virtually overlooked by the mainstream jazz audience. But with *Black Butterfly,* critics and jazz enthusiasts began to take notice. Reviewer Michael Wright surmised in *Audio*: "Malone takes command immediately with an aggressive tribute to Wes Montgomery highlighted by nimble, hellbent lines; next comes a salute to Kenny Burrell, loaded with surprising and delightful intervalic skips that wind up the tension and get you in the mood for more electric improvisations. Whether it's bluesy bends and rapid jumping between fast, angular scales and glissando chords or the gentle, rippling arpeggios of a lullaby, Malone is remarkably precise and expressive."

Despite his accomplishments as a bandleader, Malone opted to place his solo aspirations aside for the time being. Rather than focus his attentions on a third album right away, the musician instead returned to joining other solo artists. In addition to continuing to record with

For the Record . . .

Born 1963 in Albany, GA.

Started playing guitar at the age of four; joined organist Jimmy Smith's band at age 25; played with Harry Connick, Jr.'s ensemble, 1991-1994; released two solo albums on Columbia Records, *Russell Malone*, 1992; and *Black Butterfly*, 1993; member of Diana Krall's live and studio band, c. 1995-; released third solo effort, *Sweet Georgia Peach,* on the Impulse!/GRP label, 1998.

Awards: *Down Beat* magazine critics poll award for best jazz guitarist, 1998.

Addresses: *Record company*—Verve Music Group, 555 W. 57th St., New York, NY 10019, (212) 424-1000, fax (212) 424-1007.

Connick and landing a small role as a guitarist in Robert Altman's 1996 film *Kansas City,* Malone also appeared on Stephen Scott's 1997 release *The Beautiful Thing* and on Benny Green's 1997 album *Kaleidoscope.* Other recordings included sessions with Roy Hargrove and Gary Bartz.

Around 1995, Malone joined Diana Krall's studio and live band. From the onset, according to Malone, he and the singer/pianist developed a near telepathic relationship. "It's good working with a singer who can sing," the guitarist told Willard Jenkins in *Down Beat,* "and Diana is a musician, so it makes it easy; singing good songs and trusting in each other. My favorite part of the show is when we do duets, just voice and guitar." Considered his most precipitous hook-up, Malone's work with Krall included appearing on the singer's two Grammy-nominated albums, *All For You* in 1996 and *Love Scenes* in 1997, in addition to touring and performing with Krall's band throughout the world.

Although Malone's career was anything but inactive in the years following *Black Butterfly,* many jazz enthusiasts wondered what had become of the guitarist's acclaimed solo work. Finally in October of 1998, Malone eased the minds of fans and critics alike with the release of the highly praised *Sweet Georgia Peach,* his Impulse!/GRP (an imprint of the Verve Music Group) label debut. For his third solo effort, Malone assimilated a cast of jazz music's most noted players: bassist Ron Carter, pianist Kenny Barron, and drummer Lewis Nash. "I've been listening to Ron Carter since I was 8 or 9 years old," the guitarist told Graybow. "When I put the headphones on and I heard that sound coming through, well, it took maybe two hours for me to get my composure back. People talk about the late-1960s Miles Davis Quintet, and how much the sound revolved around Tony Williams. That may have been true to some extent, but I don't think it would have sounded the way it did without Ron Carter." And Malone gave similar adulations to his other backing musicians. "Lewis Nash has the ability to fit into any situation. But at the same time he manages to stand out and do something unique," remarked Malone. Describing Barron, the guitarist noted, "there are a lot of piano players who may play slicker or faster, but you'd be hard pressed to find a better piano player than Kenny Barron."

GRP President Tommy LiPuma, who produced the album, also inspired Malone's ensemble, sitting beside the musicians rather than behind the console during recording sessions. "He loves melody and honesty and honesty and beauty, and I think that came out here. I will never forget one of my earlier conversations with the powers that be—they told me 'you have a lot oftechnique and chops and we want to showcase that.' Basically, they wanted me to play fast. But working with Tommy was a musician's dream," said Malone, as quoted by his record label.

Sweet Georgia Peach consisted of both original and cover tunes, including a version of Herb Albert's radio pop song "Rise," Thelonious Monk's "Bright Mississippi," and a rendition of "Swing Low, Sweet Chariot," a tribute to the African American church tradition of Malone's childhood. Of all the songs on the album, though, Malone was most proud of his own "Song For Darius," written for and dedicated to the musicians then ten-year-old son. Holding to his belief in placing melody above technique, Malone declined the inclusion of "complexity for complexity's sake," the musician told Verve. "I was down in Georgia visiting my mother; she doesn't know anything about the technical aspects of music. And when I played the album for her, she liked it. A lot of people write songs that are understandable only to them and other musicians, but I like to write things that the average person can get into. And when you see your kids running around dancing to what you're playing, that is a good indication that you've got it."

Likewise, critics agreed that Malone succeeded in making a comprehensible record without compromising musical style and craftsmanship. "It isn't just the uncluttered flow of Malone's phrasing or the deft assurance of his touch that makes this disc such a... well, a peach," concluded Gene Seymour of *Newsday.* "There's also an easygoing ingenuity in both his original compositions (such as the hard-driving 'Mugshot' and the frisky title tune) and his arrangements of such boilerplate pop as 'With You, I'm Born Again' (seamlessly melded with his original ballad, 'Strange Little Smile')." And although the guitarist's collection featured such an adept backing rhythm section, "Malone brings enough control, vitality and intelligence to his material to make him more than worthy of such auspicious company."

During the summer of 1999, Malone took a break from Krall's live group to play dates with a trio that also consisted of bassist Christian McBride and pianist Benny Green. He also toured with his latest working group, which included Richie Goods on bass, Byron Landham on drums, and Anthony Wonsey on piano. These musicians also worked with Malone for the guitarist's forthcoming album, expected to be issued in the year 2000 by the Verve label. Regarding the follow-up release to *Sweet Georgia Peach,* Malone revealed to Jenkins, "I wrote some new material, and I did some arrangements of some popular tunes that are a bit left of center. I did the theme from *The Odd Couple* and I did a Stevie Wonder tune called 'You Will Know.'" Also in 1999, Malone received *Down Beat* magazine's critics poll award for best jazz guitarist of 1998.

Selected discography

Russell Malone, Columbia, 1992.
Black Butterfly, Columbia, 1993.
Sweet Georgia Peach, Impulse!/GRP, 1998.

Sources

Books

Cook, Richard and Brian Morton, editors, *The Penguin Guide to Jazz on Compact Disc,* Penguin Books, 1998.

Periodicals

Audio, January 1994, p. 128.
Billboard, March 14, 1998, p. 46.
Down Beat, August 1999, p. 50.
Newsday, August 30, 1998, p. D26.
Newsweek, November 9, 1998, p. 76.
Record (Bergen County, NJ), February 2, 1993, p. b05; October 2, 1998, p. 013.

Additional information provided by the Verve Music Group.

—*Laura Hightower*

Manic Street Preachers

Rock group

Manic Street Preachers created controversy almost from the moment they started playing together, but by the end of the 1990s they had become one of the most popular bands in Britain. Influenced by musical trends from the 1970s—punk and heavy metal in their attitude and sound, and glam rock in their stage appearance—the foursome seemed never to hold back their strong opinions when it came to discussing the state of pop music or the world in general. While their early declaration that a group should release one big album and then disband earned them derision from the press, fans did not hold it against them for staying together. The band came to be familiarly known as the Manics, and elements of their offstage life seemed to live up to the term, especially for rhythm guitarist Richey James. His disappearance and possible suicide in 1995 deprived the other three members of a close friend, and was also one of a series of ill-timed setbacks that prevented the Manics from touring and promoting themselves in the United States. But James Dean Bradfield, Nicky Wire, and Sean Moore carried on the band's name as a trio and continued to attract a larger audience and respect in England.

Capital Pictures/Corbis. Reproduced by permission. ©

For the Record . . .

Members have included **James Dean Bradfield** (born February 21, 1969 in Blackwood, Gwent, Wales), vocals and guitar; **Richey James** (born Richey James Edwards on December 22, 1966, in Blackwood, disappeared in 1995), rhythm guitar; **Sean Moore** (born July 30, 1971, in Blackwood), drums; **Nicky Wire** (born Nick Jones on January 20, 1969, in Blackwood), bass.

Group formed at the University of Wales, Swansea, 1986; released *New Art Riot* EP, 1990; James created stir with self-mutilation, 1991; released debut album, *Generation Terrorists,* Columbia, 1992; released *Gold Against the Soul*, Columbia, 1993; released *Holy Bible*, Epic, 1994; scheduled for first American tour when James disappeared, presumed dead, 1995; tour canceled; released first album without James, *Everything Must Go,* 1996; released *This Is My Truth Tell Me Yours,* 1998.

Awards: *Melody Make's* album of the year for *Everything Must Go,* 1996; band of the year, best single of the year for "If You Tolerate This Your Children Will Be Next," and best album of the year for *This Is My Truth Tell Me Yours* in *New Musical Express* readers poll, 1998.

Addresses: *Record company*—Virgin Records, 338 N. Foothills Road, Beverly Hills, CA 90210. *Web site*—http://www.manics.co.uk.

Although they formed the band while at the University of Wales, Swansea, the Manics had grown up together in the working-class Welsh community of Blackwood. The band had their genesis in a foursome called Betty Blue, which had the Manics line-up, with the exception of a man known as Flicker playing rhythm guitar instead of James. This group formed in 1986 to commemorate the tenth anniversary of a band they idolized—the Sex Pistols. By the time they released the self-financed, limited release single "Suicide Alley" in 1989, they had become the Manic Street Preachers. That same year Flicker left the band, and James joined his old friends. He would prove to be a figure who would help bring the Manics a wide notoriety, often at the expense of his own physical well-being.

At the outset the Manics' attitude, sound, and appearance owed much to three of their major influences: outspoken rap group Public Enemy, the punk sound of the Clash, and the heavy metal of Guns N' Roses. They attracted controversy, sometimes purposefully. Bradfield told Johnny Walker (Black) for the web magazine *Addicted to Noise,* "From the beginning we've set ourselves up to be judged, so it's obvious we've always liked to be judged anyway." Their early stance that a band should break up after releasing one huge album certainly brought judgment from the British music press. The notoriety helped bring attention to their 1990 EP *New Art Riot* and their 1991 singles "Motown Junk" and "You Love Us." These two songs exemplified the band's attitude toward the music that was popular in England at the time. The first one trashed a revered pop music sound of the 1960s, while the second mocked the self-serving acceptance speeches of music awards ceremonies.

The confrontational lyrics of the Manics' songs came from James and Wire. After they had written their words, Bradfield and Moor would put them to music. While both lyricists expressedthe same kind of working-class anger at popular culture and social structures, James' tended to be more personal than Wire's. Bradfield described the difference between the two to Walker (Black): "Nick's quote was 'Richey always wanted to be understood, but [I] never wanted to be understood.' The ironic thing is ... Nick would write lyrics that more people understood, while Richey's lyrics nobody understood." Bradfield wrote music to their lyrics from the time they first started writing, finding the inspiration for his melodies and arrangements in their words. He told Lili Moayeri of *Launch,* "I spend ages reading the lyrics before I write any music to it ... I've always found that I connect to the music first, but within the lyrics is the sole reason the music's connected with me."

But the Manics' notoriety continued to grow for reasons other than their lyrics and music. James propelled them into the limelight during a 1991 interview with *New Musical Express.* When a reporter questioned the sincerity of the Manics' proclamations about music and themselves, James stunned the interviewer by grabbing a razor blade and carving "4 Real" in his own arm. The incident solidified the Manics' place as the inheritors of the punk legacy and attracted a lot of attention from the press, fans, and major record labels. Shortly thereafter they signed with Sony records and released their first single to reach the British Top 40, "Stay Beautiful."

Starting to make a name for themselves, the Manics made huge claims for their debut album, 1992's *Generation Terrorists.* They boasted that it would outsell the biggest album by one of their rock and roll idols, Guns N' Roses' *Appetite for Destruction.* While the album didn't quite live up to the commercial hype, the individual songs continued to showcase the Manics' attitudes toward contemporary culture. Songs such as "Slash n' Burn," "Stay Beautiful," and "Another Invented Disease," tackled consumerism, youth culture, and drugs, respectively, with the group's usual bite. They then proceeded to put to rest the question of whether or not they would actually break up by releasing the single "Suicide is Painless," a cover of the theme song from the movie *MASH.*

Their second album, *Gold Against the Soul,* brought a change in the Manics' sound. Drawing more on Guns N' Roses as an influence than on their punk roots, the album sounded more polished than their previous work. In retrospect Bradfield told Walker (Black) that he "absolutely despised" the album. Even if the music sounded more mainstream than their previous work, the band had not become conformists, creating controversy with their public statements and behavior. Wire drew criticism for an on-stage remark that R.E.M.'s lead singer Michael Stipe resembled a dying AIDS patient. The more colorful figure who continued to draw attention for his behavior was James. Plagued with repeated bouts of depression, drinking, and anorexia, James took his penchant for self-mutilation to new depths by appearing on stage in Thailand with knife-slashes across his chest.

In the midst of all this personal turmoil, James took on most of the lyric writing responsibilities for the Manics' next album, *The Holy Bible.* Released in 1994, the album returned punk sounds to their repertoire, while retaining some of with the glam and metal sound that had dominated *Gold Against the Soul.* The lyrics, though, especially distinguished *The Holy Bible. The Trouser Press Record Guide* characterized them as "some of the most articulate, upsetting and brutally decadent in pop memory." Again they tackled social ills from personal, political, and philosophical perspectives. "4st. 7lb." gave a first-person account of anorexia, while "IfWhiteAmericaToldTheTruthForOneDayItsWorldWouldFallApart" expressed a blunt social outrage, and "Archives of Pain" directly acknowledged the work of French philosopher Michel Foucault.

This personal writing evidently failed to exorcise James' demons, though, and he entered a mental hospital for a short stay. When he returned the Manics were on the verge of an American tour. While a previous trip had failed to draw much attention across the Atlantic, the strength of their latest work gave hope that this time they would break through. Before they could go, though, James disappeared. His car was discovered near a bridge notorious for suicides, but no body was ever found. Eventually, police called off the search, even though reported sightings of James, alive and well, persisted for years. Under the circumstances the remaining Manics' understandably canceled the American tour. Without the tour, their record company decided not to release *The Holy Bible* in the United States.

Bradfield, Wire, and Moore decided to keep the Manics going as trio. In 1996, they released *Everything Must Go,* which included lyrics that James had written before vanishing. This new version of the group received high praise for their first album, which was named the number one album of the year by *Melody Maker* magazine and ranked number two in the *New Musical Express* critics' poll for the year. The web site *Excite* noted a change for the better for the band: "Perhaps most striking was their new sober image—the make-up, military garb and much of the bravado were gone—and their characteristic disaffection seemed more pertinent and controlled. Despite losing a member, the band had discovered a new voice, delivering a collection of powerful and socially aware songs." On the heels of this strong performance, the Manics again made plans for an American tour, this time opening for the immensely popular band Oasis. Unfortunately for the Manics, Oasis' Gallagher brothers had one of their infamous feuds, and the tour was canceled.

Even though they couldn't seem to make it across the Atlantic, their popularity and stature continued to grow at home. In 1998, they scored their first number one single with "If You Tolerate This Your Children Will Be Next." The song, along with its album, *This Is My Truth Tell Me Yours,* continued to rack up honors for the Manics. They swept the major categories for the *New Musical Express'* annual awards, earning honors for best album and single of the year, along with being named band of the year. In spite of this success, the Manics had to wait almost a year for the album to be released in the United States. Bradfield insisted that making it big in American no longer mattered as much as it once did, telling Moayeri, "With America, you either got to be mentally in love with conquering it or you just go and not care. I think we're like that."

This Is My Truth Tell Me Yours showed the Manics continuing to evolve musically while stilltackling social injustice. The range of Bradfield's guitar on the album prompted Michael Molenda of *GuitarPlayer* to describe it as "a brilliant tutorial for guitarists wishing to develop a facility for evocative textures." Lyrically, though, the familiar anger remained. The Manics stirred some controversy with "S.Y.M.M." (South Yorkshire Mass Murderer), an attack on how police handled a deadly soccer riot. This unflinching commitment to what they believe in has remained a constant throughout the band's somewhat star-crossed career. Their fans appreciate the Manics' integrity so much that they voted for Wire as their top choice for Prime Minister in a poll conducted by *New*

Musical Express. Perhaps nothing else sums up so well the status and respect that the band has achieved.

Selected discography

Stay Beautiful (EP), Columbia, 1991.
Generation Terrorists, Columbia, 1992.
Gold Against the Soul, Columbia, 1993.
The Holy Bible, Epic, 1994.
Everything Must Go, Epic, 1996.
This Is My Truth Tell Me Yours, Virgin, 1998.

Sources

Books

Buckley, Jonathan and Mark Ellingham, editors, *Rock: The Rough Guide,* Penguin, 1996.
Larkin, Colin, editor, *The Encyclopedia of Popular Music,* volume 5, Muze, 1998.
Robbins, Ira, editor, *The Trouser Press Guide to '90s Rock,* Fireside, 1997.

Periodicals

Guitar Player, September 1999, p. 84.

Online

"Everything Must Go," *Excite, http://music.excite.com.*
"Manics Landslide Victory at Polls," *New Musical Express,* http://www.nme.com, (January 26, 1999).
"Manic Street Preachers," *Excite,* http://music.excite.com, (November 26, 1999).
"Manic Street Preachers," *Launch,* http://www.launch.com(November 26, 1999).
"Manic Street Preachers," *All Music Guide,* http://allmusic.com, (November 26, 1999).
"The Manic Street Preachers: (Do) You Love Us," *Addicted to Noise,* http://www.addict.com, (November 15, 1999).
"Manic Street Preachers: The Whole Truth," *Launch,* http://www.launch.com, (May 17, 1999).

—*Lloyd Hemingway*

Amanda Marshall

Singer, songwriter

Photograph by Marko Shark. Corbis. Reproduced by permission.

Blues-styled Canadian pop singer Amanda Marshall gathered fans from around the globe after the release of her self-titled debut in 1996, an album that sold an estimated 2.2 million copies worldwide and went platinum eight times in her native Canada. However, Marshall's ascent to the top of the pop charts didn't happen overnight. It was instead a lifelong pursuit. She began playing piano and singing at the age of three, performed in clubs and theaters since her teens, toured with big name acts such as the Jeff Healey Band, and was dropped by another record company before releasing *Amanda Marshall* with Sony Canada (released by Epic in the rest of the world). Her bluesy, somewhat husky vocals led one critic to describe her as "the love child of Joe Cocker and Janis Joplin," as quoted by Nicholas Jennings of *Maclean's.*

But despite the success of her first record, Marshall realized she was capable of more. For *Amanda Marshall,* the young singer had only written one song and co-written two others. Believing that she could compose songs as well as sing them, Marshall either fully composed or collaborated with other songwriters on all but one track of her follow-up effort, 1999's *Tuesday's Child,* a record that Marshall considered a debut in its own right. "I'd really gotten my legs as a live performer when I made the first record," said Marshall, as quoted by the singer's record company, "but I only wrote one song on it, and I thought of that as a complete fluke. I didn't realize at the time that it was the beginning of a world of possibility." During her career, Marshall's records yielded seven Canadian top ten singles, including "Let It Rain," "Birmingham," "Fall From Grace," "Beautiful Goodbye,"" Dark Horse," "Sitting On Top of the World," and "Believe In You."

Born on August 29, 1972, in Toronto, Canada, Marshall displayed a love for music as far back as she could remember. "I was a very musical kid," said Marshall, according to the singer's record company, "and a kid who loved to write. I wasn't a songwriter—well, I dabbled—but I loved creative writing and storytelling. And I was a really outgoing, gregarious kid who desperately wanted to sing. There isn't a time in my life I can remember not being consumed with the idea of music and performing." Her passion for music started to blossom when Marshall was just a toddler, and at the tender age of three, her parents decided to encourage their daughter by enrolling her in classical training for piano. "Fortunately, my parents were infinitely supportive," Marshall added. "They were always shuffling me back and forth to some lesson, sitting in the car and waiting for me to come out." As a result of her parents' enduring support, Marshall was playing piano and singing in public by the time she reached kindergarten.

For the Record . . .

Born August 29, 1972, in Toronto, Canada; daughter of a Trinidadian mother and white Canadian father; *Education*: Studied piano at Toronto's Royal Academy of Music.

Met musician Jeff Healey, 1990; signed with Columbia Records, 1991, but was released from contract; accepted recording offer from Sony Canada, 1994; released self-titled debut in Canada, 1995; released worldwide by Epic Records, 1996; nominated for one Juno award, 1996; nominated for three Juno awards, 1997; released second effort, *Tuesday's Child,* 1999.

Addresses: *Home*—Toronto, Canada. *Record company*—Epic Records, 550 Madison Ave., New York, NY 10022-3211, (212) 833-7442, fax (212) 833-5719; 2100 Colorado Ave., Santa Monica, CA 90404, (310) 449-2870, fax (310) 449-2559.

Her Trinidadian mother and white Canadian father (a lineage she later explored in the song "Shades of Gray" from *Tuesday's Child*) encouraged her musical aspirations in other ways as well. Listening to her mother's calypso and jazz records, not to mention her father's collection of rock and roll albums, further sparked her imagination. She grew up listening to their Tina Turner, Stevie Nicks, Otis Redding, and Ray Charles records in addition to various folk artists. Consequently, Marshall's sound would later become a combination of Southern rhythm and blues and folk that she picked up from her parents over the years. From the ages of nine to 17, Marshallattended Toronto's Royal Conservatory of Music, continuing to study piano but never pursuing formal vocal training.

After graduating from high school, Marshall worked as a switchboard operator for a musicians' answering service, harboring the dream to one day work as a professional herself. Then in 1990, her hopes turned into reality after a chance meeting with Toronto guitarist and singer Jeff Healey, who encouraged her to sing onstage at a local club on open-mic night. "A group of us went to a jam at [the Toronto tavern] Victoria and Albert," Healey recalled to *Billboard* magazine's Larry LeBlanc. "I remember that her performance was many notches above what you see at the average jam." Obviously impressed by Marshall's soulful voice, Healey realized that the young singer possessed the talent to make it in the music industry and wanted to help promote her career. Shortly after Healey discovered Marshall, she signed with Forte Records and Productions, a Toronto-based production and management company that Healey ran with his bandmates Tom Stephen and Joe Rockwan. Next, Marshall formed her own band and started performing a combination of original songs and covers in local clubs. Although she quickly earned a reputation around Toronto because of her deep voice as a Janis Joplin-styled vocalist, Marshall insisted that she never intended to draw such a comparison or imitate the legendary singer. "I actually made a point of staying away from Joplin covers because of the comparison," Marshall told LeBlanc. "I don't even think I was a blues singer. I was a very rootsy singer, which with my connection to Jeff, people drew upon [the Joplin comparison] for a descriptive term."

Marshall spent the next seven months honing her stage presence, performing solo around Toronto and touring North America with the Jeff Healey Band. Then in 1991, Stephen secured her a record deal with Columbia Records, a label based in the United States. Despite her stage experience and musical training, Marshall remained unprepared when the opportunity arose. She held few ideas regarding the style of music she should pursue, and when Columbia executives suggested she try grunge rock, Marshall met the label's proposal with a flat denial. After a frustrating year in the studio trying to develop tracks for a debut album, Marshall and record producers made little headway. Consequently, Columbia released the hopeful performer from her contract.

Despite Marshall's regrettable experience with Columbia, her management refused to give up on the promising singer. Thus, Stephen proceeded to contact Richard Zuckerman, a marketing executive with Sony Canada, to inquire about a Canadian-based recording contract. Following a period of negotiations, Marshall accepted an offer from the label in 1994 and started to record demo tapes. But again, the singer's inability to focus on a musical direction persisted. Rather than focus on a single style, Marshall sought to combine all of her past influences into a cohesive body of work. In order to remedy the situation, another Sony executive, Michael Reth, suggested adding Los Angeles-based songwriter/producer David Tyson to the project as a songwriting collaborator. After accepting Sony's proposal, Tyson listened to Marshall's demo and was instantly floored by her voice. "I really liked the voice and her phrasing," the songwriter noted to LeBlanc. "There were some decent songs on the tape, but there wasn't enough happening to imply a [musical] direction." In fact, only two of the songs from Marshall's tape appeared on her debut release: the singer's rendition of Marc Jordan and John Capek's "Promises" and her own composition "Sitting On Top of the World," a Canadian top ten hit later covered by countrysinger LeAnn Rimes. She also helped write two other tracks that appeared on her debut, including another Canadian top ten single, "Dark Horse."

Under Tyson's guidance, Marshall learned to trust herself and also shed the burden of inexperience and youth. As she commented to LeBlanc, "Making the record was a real life-changing experience. I was in a strange city by myself and I was on my own in this apartment, writing songs and getting around without a car. I was taking cabs and buses. It was really exciting." Working together from February until August of 1995, Marshall's self-titled debut was produced mostly at Tyson's home studio in Beachwood Canyon in the Los Angeles area. *Amanda Marshall* was released in Canada by Sony Music Entertainment (Canada) on October 17, 1995, and released worldwide on Epic Records in January of 1996. Marshall's collaboration with Tyson proved monumental, as sales of her debut soared. The singer's blend of folk, jazz, and rhythm and blues, brought to life by her husky, soulful voice, propelled her into a global audience. By 1999, *Amanda Marshall* had hit the platinum mark eight times in the artist's native Canada, remained in that country's list of top 200 albums since its release three years prior, and sold an estimated 2.2 million units worldwide. In 1997, Marshall went on to receive three Canadian Juno Music award nominations to add to her single nomination she earned in 1996.

The singer saw an overwhelming success in the international market, particularly in Scandinavian countries and most notably in Norway. As of 1999, *Amanda Marshall* was certified gold in Germany, Norway, Holland, and Australia. Likewise, Americans applauded Marshall's efforts, and after an appearance on the *Rosie O'Donnell Show* in 1997, pop sensation Elton John lauded Marshall as the world's brightest rising star. By 1999, Marshall's debut had sold over 300,000 units in the United States. Her profile in the United States was further enhanced by the inclusion of one of her songs, "This Could Take All Night," on the soundtrack for the Kevin Costner film *Tin Cup.*

In addition to touring with her own band and with Healey's group to support her debut, Marshall also performed with Joe Cochrane during his "Life Is a Highway Tour" and with the pop group Tears for Fears in 1996. Her travels continued throughout 1997, again singing with her own ensemble and opening for rock musician John Mellencamp. While such an intense touring schedule may seem tiring for many, Marshall said she thrived on singing before a live audience. "I am really comfortable being a performing artist," she revealed to Debbie Hodges of the *Christian Science Monitor,* "and to me that is why I make records—to get out and tour." That year, Marshall toured 15 countries in 14 months, including Norway, where her debut topped the charts. "People abroad keep asking me what's in the water in Canada, because of all the women singers," Marshall told Diane Turbide in an interview for *Maclean's,* in reference to the success of other successful Canadian women who achieved an international following during the 1990s such as Shania Twain, Sarah McLachlan, Alanis Morrissette, and Celine Dion. However, Marshall refused to lump herself in a category with other female pop stars, Canadian or otherwise. "I really don't know any of them," she remarked to Jennings, adding, "it's ridiculous to think that I would feel connected to Sheryl Crow by virtue of the fact that we're both female and have curly hair. We're all pop singers. We have that much in common. But it diminishes the value of what we do individually to think that we all feel the same way or share any kind of sisterhood."

During the two demanding yet rewarding years following the release of her debut, Marshall gathered much of the material brought to life in the songs of her second album, *Tuesday's Child,* released in May of 1999. Throughout her time on the road, Marshall, who had enjoyed writing stories since her childhood, kept notebooks to capture her ideas and feelings. "It [touring} allowed me to get out in the world and live a little bit," the singer reflected, as quoted by Epic. "But your life becomes a series of extremes. Your day is great, or there's a horrible crisis. You're always meeting people but rarely getting to know them." In order to organize her thoughts into songs, Marshall sought the help of songwriter/producer Eric Bazilian, who also wrote songs for Joan Osborne and the Hooters. The two songwriters clicked right away and arranged to write together at Bazilian's home in Philadelphia.

Tuesday's Child, largely produced by Don Was (producer for well-known musicians such as the Rolling Stones and Bonnie Raitt), featured a host of famous recording artists such as Richie Sambora of Bon Jovi and Benmont Tench of Tom Petty's group the Heartbreakers, in addition to notable session musicians like Steve Jordan, Waddy Wachtel, and Kenny Arnoff. Songwriters Carole King and Desmond King also collaborated with Marshall, although Bazilian helped pen ten of the record's 13 tracks. In all, Marshall wrote or cowrote all but one of the bluesy ballads and radio-friendly rockers for *Tuesday's Child.* One of her own original singles, "Believe In You," also appeared on the platinum-selling soundtrack for the television show *Touched By An Angel.*

Although some critics believed that Marshall wasted her unique vocals on safe and radio-ready pop songs, the artist herself saw *Tuesday's Child* as an unqualified success given her songwriting involvement. "This album is not a huge musical left turn, but it's closer to me musically," Marshall explained to LeBlanc. Following the release of her second album, the singer toured for a short time around Europe, returned to perform in Canada in June, and began touring the United States in July. Marshall prefers to keep some secrecy about her personal life. Her boyfriend of several years is also a member of her performing band.

Selected discography

Amanda Marshall, Epic, 1996.
Tuesday's Child, Epic, 1999.

Sources

Billboard, November 11, 1995, p. 68; May 22, 1999, p. 18.
Calgary Sun, May 21, 1999, p. G8.
Christian Science Monitor, April 7, 1997, p. 14.
Edmonton Sun, May 23, 1999, p. SE4; July 5, 1999, p. 29.
London Free Press, June 18, 1999, p. C6.
Maclean's, March 24, 1997, p. 52; May 24, 1999, p. 52.
Ottawa Sun, June 12, 1999, p. 25.
Toronto Star, May 26, 1999.

Additional information provided courtesy of Epic Records.

—*Laura Hightower*

Mary Martin

Singer, actress

The Library of Congress ©

Mary Martin was one of the brightest stars of Broadway and the musical theater. Although she was never regarded as a popular singer, her musical contributions thrilled millions. Mary Virginia Martin was born December 1, 1913 in Weatherford, Texas to Preston Martin, an attorney and Juanita Presley Martin a violin teacher at Weatherford College. Her mother became a violin teacher when she was only seventeen.

From an early age Mary was prone to neck breaking stunts and singing. When she was eight, she climbed on a garage roof and jumped off believing she could fly. She ended up with a broken collar bone. Her home had a small orchard and Martin eventually climbed every single tree but it would be nearly three decades before she learned to fly with the help of a beautiful idea and a very strong wire. When she was 16, her parents sent her to Ward Belmont, a young ladies finishing school in Nashville, Tennessee. Less than months later, her mother consented to let her marry Ben Hagman. The two were married in Hopkinsville, Kentucky on November 3, 1930. Ten months later, on September 21, 1931, their son Larry Martin Hagman was born. Years later he would star in the television series *I Dream of Jeannie* and *Dallas*.

Bored with her marriage and her new husband living in Austin studying law, she opened a dance studio in Weatherford in her Uncle Luke's grain storage loft. With the help of her sister, Geraldine, who had taken a few dance lessons while studying physical education at Columbia University in New York, and by watching the dance routines of actresses Ruby Keeler and Eleanor Powell, Martin received some dance training. In addition, Martin had been a member of a dance gang in Ft. Worth, Texas, because she could Charleston so well. Ginger Rogers was also a member. Her business quickly grew and to augment her existing dance knowledge, she enrolled in the Fanchon and Marco School of Theater in Hollywood, California. At Fanchon & Marco, Martin was tutored by Nico Charissse, the splendid modern and Spanish dancing instructor and one time husband of dancer Cyd Charisse. After she returned to Texas, she opened two more dance studios.

Audition Mary

While in Weatherford, she learned of an audition by the great showman Billy Rose. It would be held in Fort Worth for a super colossal extravaganza at the Casa Manana and a local chorus was needed. Not only did Rose turn her down, but hed advised her to stay out of the entertainment industry altogether. His advice helped crystallize her desire to go into the entertainment indus-

For the Record . . .

Born Mary Virginia Martin, December 1, 1913 in Weatherford, TX, (died November 4, 1990 Rancho Mirage, CA of cancer); daughter of Preston, (an attorney) and Juanita Martin, (a violin teacher at Weatherford College); married Benjamin J. Hagman, November 3, 1930, (divorced 1935); married Richard Halliday, May 5, 1940 (died 1973); children: Larry (from first marriage) born September 21, 1931; Mary Heller (from second marriage) born .c. 1942; *Education:* Attended the University of Texas, Fanchon and Marco School of the Theater, Hollywood, CA.

Made her broadway debut in *Leave it to Me*, 1938; starred in *South Pacific*, 1949; *Peter Pan*, 1954; *The Sound of Music*, 1959; *I Do I Do*, 1969; also starred in ABC's 1969 production of *Valentine* with Jack Albertson.;1986; appeared on stage in *Legends* with Carol Channing; appeared in over 11 Hollywood films.

Awards: Emmy Award, 1955 for *Peter Pan*; Kennedy Center Performing Arts Achievement Award, 1989.

try and triggered her leaving for Hollywood. Back in Hollywood, she again entered the Fanchon and Marco School and spent two long years of trying to crack open the door of show business. Folks in Hollywood nicknamed her audition Mary because of her frequent attempts to obtain work. She finally landed a job on a national network radio program *Gateway to Hollywood* but receivedno pay. She later worked for NBC radio for no pay as well.

Her first real break came when she was still an unknown and performing at a talent show at the Trocadero nightclub. Her opening number was a tune called "The Weekend of a Private Secretary" and it was followed by "Il Bacio" sung in a jazz fashion. The house came down and the crowd shouted, whistled, echoed calls of bravo while they stood on tables and chairs. In the audience was Lawrence Schwab, one of Broadway's most important and respected producers. Schwab offered her a part in an upcoming Broadway musical *Ring Out The News* and paid her way to New York. Martin later said it was the most important ten minutes of her life. Although she went to New York to perform in *Ring Out the News*, the show received such unfavorable reviews that Schwab canceled the production entirely.

In 1938, her next audition was for *Leave it to Me*, a Broadway musical remake of Sam and Bella's Spewack's *Clear All Wires*. Martin auditioned for the Spewack's and Cole Porter and won the part by performing Porter's famous "My Heart Belongs to Daddy." The audition opened many doors for Martin and while the production, which included a young Gene Kelly was still going strong on Broadway, Hollywood's Paramount Pictures offered her a contract to appear in films. In 1939, Martin appeared in the motion picture *The Great Victor Herbert* opposite singing star Allan Jones, followed by *Rhythm on the River* with Bing Crosby in 1940. While Crosby and Martin were making films together, they also appeared on radio's Kraft Music Hall. These films were followed by *Love Thy Neighbor* with Jack Benny and Fred Allen in 1940, *Kiss the Boys Good-Bye* in 1941 with Don Ameche and Oscar Levant, *New York Town* with Fred MacMurray and Robert Preston in 1941 and *Happy Go Lucky* with Rudy Vallee and Dick Powell in 1942.

In 1939, she became engaged to Frederick Drake, publisher of Harper's Bazaar. At about the same time she met Richard Halliday, a story editor. Martin and Halliday quickly fell in love and he soon became her second husband in 1940 before she could talk with Drake and break off their engagement. The two were married thirty three years until Halliday's death in 1973.

Catapulted to Superstardom

Longing for the stage, Martin returned to Broadway October 7, 1943 in Kurt Weill's and Ogden Nash's *One Touch of Venus*, which had been written for Marlene Dietrich, who had turned it down. Martin was apprehensive of playing the role of Venus since she could not picture herself as Venus. Her husband came up with a creative idea and took her to the Metropolitan Museum in New York where over fifty varieties of Venus statues were displayed. These ranged form short to tall, fat to thin. This convinced her and Martin remained in the lead role for 567 performances before taking it on the road.

Martin's career zoomed when she took the role of Annie Oakley on stage in the touring production of *Annie Get Your Gun*, a role created on Broadway by Ethel Merman. She toured with the National Company opening in Dallas and winding down eleven months later in San Francisco. The role of Annie catapulted Martin to stardom.

As *Annie Get Your Gun* was winding down, Martin was approached to play the role of army nurse Nellie Forbush in a new Broadway play entitled *South Pacific* opposite opera singe Ezio Pinza. The play was based on two books by James Michener, *Tales of the South Pacific* and was set against a World War II backdrop. Martin was apprehensive about working with Pinza because of his reputation as one of the premier operatic singers and because of her dislike of hospitals. She almost turned down the part. She introduced "A Cockeyed Optimist," "I'm Gonna Wash That Man Right Outa My Hair," and "A Wonderful Guy." *South Pacific* was an enormous success and ran from April of 1949 until June of 1951 for a total of 1,925 performances when Martin and Pinza traveled to London where the play opened in November.

Over the years Martin turned down the lead roles in *Kiss Me Kate*, *My Fair Lady*, and *Mame*. After a lack luster venture into her first non-musical play, *Kind Sir*, opposite Charles Boyer, she was offered the role of Peter in an entirely new musical version of *Peter Pan*. Martin felt it was the most important thing she had ever wanted to do in the theater and in her autobiography said, "When I was a child I was sure I could fly. In my dreams I often did, and it was always the same; I ran, raised my arms like a great bird, soared into the sky, flew." Martin and her husband were given their choice of composer, director and choreographer. She hired an Englishman named Peter Foy, who had learned his trade from his family who had flown across the stage for fifty years. Equipped with wires, ropes, pulleys, and machines, he used his trade to establish a flying ballet which covered an area of more than sixty feet across the stage as well as in and out of windows. It was a tremendous hit in San Francisco and Los Angeles in 1954 and opened on Broadway later that year. Her talents were recorded for future generations in the 1995 and 1956 television version of *Peter Pan*, which one her an Emmy Award the year. But it was the Broadway version of *Peter Pan* that she is most identified with.

Another successful collaboration between Martin and Rodgers and Hammerstein was the role of Maria in *The Sound of Music*. Based on a book by Maria Baroness Von Trapp about her experiences as a lively young Catholic postulant in Austria, who was sent to be a governess to the seven children of a widowed naval officer. In 1956, a German motion picture had been an enormous hit in Europe and South America. To prepare for the part, Martin enlisted the help of Maria Von Trapp, who taught her how to kneel properly, make the sign of the cross, and how to play guitar. Martin reciprocated by teaching Von Trapp how to yodel. Her performances were well received and she won the coveted Tony Award and the New York Drama Critics Award for her performance as Maria in 1959. *The Sound of Music* was another major success and ran for 1,443 performances. It was also the last collaboration of Rodgers and Hammerstien and the second longest running musical of the fifties.

Semi-retirement

Two other roles which Martin played to great acclaim were Dolly Levi in *Hello Dolly*, and Agnes in *I Do! I Do!* with co-star Robert Preston. *I Do! I Do!* was based on a play, *The Fourposter*, about the lives of a couple from their wedding day until their golden anniversary. Martin felt that the subject matter of this play—marriage—would represent the essence of her life. It was the last musical Martin appeared in before her semi-retirement. Although her stage career was the mostprominent piece of her career, she also appeared in many television specials and as a featured guest in many network shows.

In 1969, Martin and her husband moved to Brazil and bought a farm. For several years she operated a boutique featuring her fashion designs and her needlepoint, about which she and her husband published a book in 1969. While in Brazil she was also the subject of the television show *This Is Your Life*. Martin returned to the United States after the death of her husband where she co-hosted the PBS television show *Over Easy*, which focused on issues of the elderly.

Martin died on November 3, 1990, at the age of 76 of liver cancer. Her long-time friend, Carol Channing, was at her bedside at Martin's Rancho Mirage, California home, less than an hour before her death. "She was heaven," said Channing.

Selected discography

Mary Martin Sings, Richard Rodgers Plays, RCA, 1990.
16 Most Requested Songs, Columbia, 1993.
On Broadway, Encore.
Mary Sings and Swings, Buena Vista.
Sound of Music (soundtrack), Columbia.
South Pacific (soundtrack), Columbia.
Musical World of Richard Rodgers, Columbia.
One Touch of Venus/Lute Song, MC.
Best of Broadway, Rhino.
Decca Years, Koch.
Rodgers & Hart, Smithsonian Collection.

Sources

Books

Claghorn, Charles Eugene, *Biographical Dictionary of American Music*, Parker Publishing Co. 1973.
Clarke, Donald, *Penguin Encyclopedia of Popular Music*, Penguin Books Ltd. 1989.

Frommer, Myrna Katz and Harvey Frommer, *It Happened on Broadway*, Harcourt Brace & Co., 1998.
Gammond, Peter, *The Oxford Companion to Popular Music*, Oxford University Press, 1993.
Larkin, Colin, *Guinness Encyclopedia of Popular Music,-Volume 5*, Guinness Publishing Ltd., 1995.
Lax, Roger and Frederick Smith, *The Great Song Thesaurus*, Oxford University Press, 1989.
Osborne, Jerry, *Rockin Records*, Osborne Publications, 1999.
Stambler, Irwin, *Encyclopedia of Popular Music*, 1966.

Periodicals

Los Angeles Times, November 5, 1990.
New York Times, November 5, 1990.

Online

"Hoagy Carmichael," *A&E Biography*, www.biography.com (August 1999).

Additional information provided by Didier C. Deutsch, *Mary Martin 16 Most Requested Songs*, Liner Notes.

—*Francis D. McKinley*

Mase

Rap artist

Within months after the release of his debut solo project, Mason Betha, Jr., better known as Mase to the hip-hop world, found himself at the top of rap music. Despite his almost overnight prosperity and release of a well-received second solo album, Mase shocked fans and those within the music industry when he announced his retirement from rap on April 20, 1999, for religious reasons. A young protegé of Sean "Puffy" Combs, also known as Puff Daddy, Mase was recognized for his simplistic, yet profound lyrics that transcended musical barriers by achieving success on the hip-hop, rhythm and blues, pop, and *Billboard* charts as his debut solo album ascended to the number one spot. During his music career, he appeared on hits and worked with other stars such as Mariah Carey, Brian McKnight, the Notorious B.I.G., and Brandy. Although Mase, a devout Christian, was drawn to hip-hop music and displayed an obvious talent for writing rhymes, he stayed away from the gangster lifestyle and image that surrounds so many rap artists. Instead, Mase was a dimpled-faced, smiling "let's-just-have-fun type" with an "infectious grin," wrote Smokey D. Fontaine of the *Source* magazine, who devoted much of his time and money to help improve the lives of children in his old Harlem neighborhood. Even after he acquired the wealth, fame, and expensive accessories that accompany super stardom, he regularly wore a dingy rubber band around his wrist to remind him of his humble beginnings in the inner-city of New York.

Mase was born Mason Betha, Jr., in Jacksonville, Florida, on August 27, 1978, along with his twin sister, Stase, who arrived five minutes after him. Shortly after his birth, Mase's father, Mason "Father Lucky" Betha, left his mother, "P.K.," alone to care for the couple's six children, which included three boys and three girls. At around age five, Mase and his remaining family relocated to Harlem, a section of New York City in Manhattan. Like so many of his peers, young Mase was left without a father figure, and to make matters worse, he had watched his mother suffer from cancer. However, Mase's mother felt determined to support her children to the best of her ability, and she wanted to keep her son away from the violence that pervaded the inner city neighborhood. As Mase told Fontaine, "I grew up on a block with ten guys. Now eight of them have been killed, and the other two are still in jail . ... It's like if half of the people in the world knew my real story, they would be like, 'How could he smile everyday?'" Some of these negative childhood experiences include carrying a friend to the hospital, but not reaching the emergency room in time to save his life, as well as living in a home that at times had no heat during the cold winter months. When the atmosphere of Harlem started to draw Mase into trouble and life-threatening situations when he reached his early teens, his mother decided to send him back to the South for awhile to live with relatives.

While living in his new neighborhood, Mase started attending church services on a regular basis. "Down there, I started going to church because I had to," Mase related to Kris Ex in an interview for *XXL* magazine. "You know, down South, you have to go to church. I don't care how hard you think you are, but any down South parents or guardians are like, 'You going to church.' When I came back [to Harlem], I was like a different person and I guess all my good deeds, they finally coming back to play. I'm just finally reaping what I sow." Even after young Mase returned to hismother and siblings back in Harlem, the lessons he learned about religion continued to stay with him and ultimately altered his career in rap music.

Despite his talent for rhyming with friends and schoolmates in Harlem, Mase did not always aspire to climb to the top of the hip-hop scene and music charts. During his high school and college days, Mase dreamed of one day playing for the National Basketball Association (NBA) and looked up to basketball superstar Michael Jordan, rather than to Puff Daddy. At Manhattan Central, his East Harlem high school, Mase stood out as his team's leading point guard. "I was rapping on the bus going to basketball games, playing around," Mase related to Ex. "I was more or less thinking, 'I'ma go to the NBA: I'ma buy my mom that big house, that big car' I used rap as 'Plan B.'"His chances of playing professional basketball

For the Record . . .

Born Mason Betha, Jr., August 27, 1978, in Jacksonville, FL; son of Mason "Father Lucky" and P.K. Betha; divorced c. 1978; siblings: two brothers and three sisters. *Education:* Attended SUNY Purchase on basketball scholarship.

Signed record deal with Sean "Puffy" Combs of Bad Boy Entertainment, 1997; released debut solo album, *Harlem World,* 1997; formed All Out Records and group Harlem World, hired Earvin "Magic" Johnson as new manager, released *Mase Presents Harlem World: The Movement,* 1999; announced retirement from rap, April 1999; released second solo album on Bad Boy, *Double Up,* June 1999.

Addresses: *Home*—Atlanta, GA. *Agent*—Magic Johnson Entertainment. *Record company*—Bad Boy Entertainment, 8-10 W. 19th St. 9th Floor, New York, NY 10011. *Website*—http://www.badboy-ent.com.

grew dimmer when he failed to make the cut for a Division I college because of his low SAT scores, and Mase found himself attending SUNY Purchase on a basketball scholarship.

Gradually realizing his slim chances of landing a spot on an NBA team, Mase spent more and more of his spare time making amateur demo tapes and performing in clubs with other rap hopefuls around his neighborhood. Some of his early rhyming partners included Lox, DMX, McGruff, Big L (now deceased), and a group called Children of the Corn, whose members included Mase (then known as "Murder" to the rap scene of Harlem), Killa "Cam'ron" Cam, and Bloodshed (also deceased). "I remember for years I used to invite my friends over to listen to his demos," sister Stase told Fontaine. "They used to always think he was hot and wonder why this song or that song wasn't on the radio." Subsequently Mase, driven by the compliments of his fellow rappers and his family, decided to concentrate on a career in music. He hired a manager named Country, who encouraged the young hopeful to tone down his rhetoric, and produced a new demo tape that he hoped would catch the attention of a record company.

Confident about his new sound and direction, Mase traveled to Atlanta, Georgia, to attend a music convention. Upon his arrival, he hoped to meet and impress producer and rap artist Jermaine Dupri of So So Def Records with his talent. However, Mase instead caught the eye of another famous record producer, Sean "Puffy" Combs, or Puff Daddy, who requested an impromptu performance from Mase. Combs had heard about Mase through rappers such as Lox, at that time a newly signed act for Puffy's Bad Boy Entertainment label, and he offered Mase a record deal after hearing only 16 bars of the rapper's music. Soon thereafter, Mase helped write and rap for two multi-platinum singles that brought his name, face, and voice into millions of American homes: Puffy's "Can't Nobody Hold Me Down" and the Notorious B.I.G.'s "Mo Money, Mo Problems," both released in 1997. Consequently, the immediate success of these crossover hits set the stage for Mase to release his first solo album, 1997's *Harlem World,* which eventually went double-platinum and sold more than three million copies. That same year, Mase also appeared with Puff Daddy for two more collaborations, including Puffy's album *No Way Out,* in addition to the single "I'll be Missing You," an anthem in memory of two fellow rappers (Tupac Shakur and the Notorious B.I.G) who had died of gunshot wounds.

With his solo career in full swing, Mase then formed his own record company, All Out Records, through Dupri's So So Def label, and signed his first new group called Harlem World. Although Mase still enjoyed working under the guidance of Puffy and Bad Boy Entertainment, he felt thatother rap and hip-hop artists, including his sister, also a member of Harlem World, desired more creative control. Mase commented in an interview with *Vibe* magazine regarding his decision to make a deal with Dupri rather than Combs, "When I did *All Out,* I knew I could deal with Puff, but I wasn't sure if my sister could deal with Puff. He's a perfectionist. He stays on top of you, and everybody can't take that. Once you put all of that in the same basket, then you're forced to make the decision of money and family. And guess what? I'ma be with family." Mase's new group, which included loyal friends from Harlem in addition to sister Stase, released their first album entitled *Mase Presents Harlem World: The Movement* in 1999. Critics gave the release overall praise, and *Vibe* stated that *Harlem World* "is a well-produced posse album that bounces the sounds of the world's most famous neighborhood off of seven young, energetic, and strikingly different MCs."

In the meantime, Mase hired a new manager, basketball legend Earvin "Magic" Johnson, owner of Magic Johnson Music, and was already working on his second solo release for Bad Boy Entertainment. *Double Up,* also released in 1999, marked a creative shift for the rap artist. "My first album I gave the people what they wanted, but this time, it's gonna be a whole different Mase," he told Fontaine. "When I wrote *Harlem World,* I was on the road with Puff every day, and there wasn't too much hardcore music I could make out of that scenario. But this album I was in the 'hood, and it's going to be 100% me. No glitter, no nothing." Despite his enthusiasm, though, several critics did not find his second album as promising as his solo debut. As Ex wrote in a review for *Rolling Stone* magazine, "In trying to distance himself from Puff Daddy, Mase has fallen well short of his former Svengali's slick standards." Nevertheless, many critics and fans found his tone and lyrics more reflective and honest.

However, before the album even hit record store shelves in June of 1999, Mase shocked the music industry as well as his faithful fans when he announced his retirement from rap on April 20, 1999. The official press announcement came from Magic Johnson Entertainment, stating "as of today Bad Boy multi-platinum artist Mase declares that he will be retiring from music to follow God, effective immediately," as quoted by the MTV (Music Television) website. Disillusioned with the music industry, Mase himself declared to *Newsweek*, "It's time for me to serve God in his way. I've always known that there was something else out there for me to do. Not just this stuff because, like I said before, this isn't real and I gotta deal with reality. There's no other way to stay true to the game—the real game of life." Many observers speculated that the rapper would one day make a return to music, but Mase insisted that his decision was final. And while Mase knew that he would miss making his music, he said in an MTV interview, "it's almost like you become unhappy with something regardless of what it pays you. I'm just a man of more morals." In support of his new album, Mase planned to make appearances to sign autographs, but not actually perform.

As for Mase's future, the retired rap star wanted to continue to give back to his community through basketball programs, helping children go to college, donating scholarship money, and sponsoring charity events. He told MTV, "I've been blessed with a lot and I'm just trying to make sure I give back the way I should." Mase, who enjoys working with children, also contemplated returning to college to earn a psychology degree in order to counsel less fortunate youth. In addition to helping children within his old Harlem neighborhood, Mase appeared, along withother musicians such as rhythm and blues singers Deborah Cox and Kelly Price and rap artist Warren G, as a spokesperson for the National Breast Cancer Awareness Initiative, a campaign sponsored by the Magic Johnson Foundation.

Selected discography

Singles

"Lookin' At Me," Bad Boy/Arista, 1998.

Albums

Harlem World, Bad Boy/Arista, 1997.
(With others) Money Talks (soundtrack), BMG/Arista, 1997.
(With Others) *Chef Aid: The South Park Album (Television Compilation),* Sony/Columbia, 1998.
(With others) *Bad Boy's Greatest Hits Vol. 1,* Bad Boy/Arista, 1999.
Double Up, Bad Boy/Arista, 1999.
(With others) *Grammy Rap Nominees 1999,* WEA/Elektra Entertainment, 1999.
Mase Presents Harlem World: The Movement, All Out Records/So So Def, 1999.

Sources

Periodicals

Business Wire, July 19, 1998.
Newsday, March 11, 1997; November 13, 1997; January 14, 1999.
Newsweek, June 21, 1999.
Rolling Stone, July 8-22, 1999.
Source, March, 1999.
USA Today, November 7, 1997.
Vibe, June/July, 1999.

Online

CDNow website, http://www.cdnow.com (August 15, 1999).
MTV News Gallery, http://www.mtv.com (August 13, 1999).
RollingStone.com, http://www.rollingstone.tunes.com (August 13, 1999).
XXL magazine interview, http://tmoney.simplenet.com/puffy (August 13, 1999).

—Laura Hightower

Matchbox 20

Rock band

Florida-based Matchbox 20 delivered enough hit tracks from its quadruple-platinum debut, *Yourself or Someone Like You,* to ride the wave of music stardom on that release alone for three years. First appearing in the alternative rock market and then crossing genres into pop and easy listening, the band has built a large and diverse fan base. Band members claim to have enough songs tucked away to keep them recording new albums for years to come, and the group is working hard to continue in the harmonious, solid, fraternal momentum that drives them to perform continuously on the road. They consistently report in interviews, chat groups, and responses to fans on their website that they are aware of what brought them success and that they will strive to keep those factors alive. Hard work, camaraderie among band members, and interaction with fans keep them grounded and focused on being creative.

Lead vocalist and songwriter Rob Thomas, bassist Brian Yale, and drummer Paul Doucette formed the band in the mid-1990s after quitting the band Tabitha's Secret. The name "Matchbox 20" was inspired by a patron of a

David Atlas. Reproduced by permission.©

For the Record . . .

Members include **David Kyle Cook** (born August 29, 1975), lead guitar, background vocals; **Paul John Doucette** (born August 22, 1972), drums; **Adam Gaynor** (born November 26, 1963), rhythm guitar, background vocals; **Rob Thomas** (born February 14, 1972), lead vocals, songwriter; **Brian Yale** (born November 14, 1970), bass.

Group formed in the mid-1990s in Orlando, FL; released debut album *Yourself or Someone Like You* on Lava/Atlantic label, 1996; contributed to *Legacy: A Tribute to Fleetwood Mac's Rumours,* Lava/Atlantic, 1998. Thomas contributed to Santana's 1999 hit single "Smooth."

Awards: Best New Band *Rolling Stone* Readers' Poll, 1997; Best New Rock Act *Performance Magazine* Readers' Poll, 1997; *Billboard* Album Artists Duo/Group, 1997; NARM Convention Best Selling Recording by a New Artist, 1998; Diamond Award by the Recording Industry Association of America (RIAA) for selling over ten million albums in the United States, 1999; Thomas was recognized as one of BMI's Songwriters of the Year, 1999.

Addresses: *Record company*—Atlantic Records, 9229 W. Sunset Blvd. #900, Los Angeles, CA 90069, (310) 205-7450. *Website*—Official Matchbox 20 Web Site: http://www.matchbox20.com.

restaurant Thomas and Doucette were waiting tables at. The man was wearing a jersey marked with the number 20 that was covered with patches. The only word Doucette could make out on the shirt was "matchbox." Influenced by legendary artists like Van Morrison, R.E.M., Neil Diamond, Elvis Costello, Ani DiFranco, and Elton John, Thomas tapped into his adventurous and troubled experiences as a youth to pour out soulful, autobiographical lyrics and stirring tunes that grabbed audiences with a punch of acoustic sparring like other contemporary post-grunge bands, such as Collective Soul and Live. Lead guitarist (David) Kyle Cook, rhythm guitarist and background vocalist Adam Gaynor, and producer and keyboardist Matt Serletic joined the trio to form Matchbox 20. Serletic, who also produced two albums for Collective Soul, was instrumental in leading the band into making quality demos and getting them on the road to perform in gigs around the United States. He felt that this would help the group secure a grassroots following and a name in the industry. They opened for bands like the Lemonheads, Offspring, and Jackopierce.

The band signed with Lava Records in 1996 and recorded *Yourself or Someone Like You,* which was released the same day it was announced that Atlantic Records acquired Lava. This was a big break for the band in the way of publicity and marketing for the new album; a huge label like Atlantic had superior resources for promoting its bands. "Long Day," the first track released to alternative rock radio stations, received a promising response and remained on the *Billboard* Mainstream Rock Tracks chart for 22 weeks. The sophomore release, "Push," pushed the band to the number one spot on six of the modern rock, alternative, and pop charts during the summer of 1997 and put them in the music news headlines as well. The cut's lyrics—" I wanna push you around, I will, I will"—raised the ire of women's advocacy groups who interpreted the song as condoning violence towards women. Thomas, who wrote the song, dismissed the allegations because he felt they had come from simple-minded people who obviously did not listen to and understand the lyrics. The song was inspired by an unhealthy romantic relationship Thomas experienced, one in which he was the receiving party of emotional abuse and manipulation.

Matchbox 20's next release, "3 AM," hit number one on the alternative and adult contemporary charts and put the band in the news again. Former Tabitha's Secret bandmates filed a lawsuit against Thomas, Doucette, Yale, and Serlectic in 1998 for a cut of the profits from the hit single. The conflict essentially centered on determining on what terms the three Matchbox 20 members left Tabitha's Secret, which still existed and was even about to release a CD entitled *Don't Play with Matches.* Thomas wrote and performed the song "3 AM" in the early 1990s as a member of Tabitha's Secret. The song is about a tumultuous period in his life when he had to contend with his mother's battle with cancer and her efforts to overcome a drinking problem. During 1998, Matchbox 20's fourth single, "Real World," brought them more praise among their staple fan base—young modern rock listeners—as well as increased notoriety across genres as the single worked its way up the pop and adult contemporary charts. In early 1999, Matchbox 20's fifth single, "Bad 2 Good," got huge radio play and its video was a favorite on the MTV and VH-1 cable television networks.

Thomas and other band members have a wealth of songs already composed and the ideas and inspiration to write many more. In an interview with "The Dude on the Right" on the Internet's *Entertainment Avenue,* Thomas explained why the band is not in danger of going down in music history as a one hit wonder: "For a lot of people's first record they have their whole life to write that record. They've been working on it since they were ten, culminating it into a record, and then the next record they have a year to put together twelve songs. Now you've got the pressures while you're writing, worrying if people are going to like this." Apparently Thomas is a natural at expressing himself in song and is not bothered by writer's block. He even writes for other artists. However, the band recognizes that the industry can be at fault for the ill sales of an artist's second release as it is always looking to promote new names. Sometimes the success of a next release may be luck in trends and timing and in how it is distributed to and received by audiences. In the fall of 1998, Matchbox 20 joined the ranks of bigtime bands like Pearl Jam and Foo Fighters as an opening act for the Rolling Stones' Bridges to Babylon tour in Texas.

Despite the charisma and genuine star quality of the band, Matchbox 20 focuses on being true to the music and to the fans. Chuck Taylor of *Billboard* observed, "Like any group of guys who suddenly find themselves living in the rock star dream instead of pursuing it over a bowl of rubbery macaroni, Matchbox 20 is conscious of remaining grounded and keeping the focus on the music." Frank Tortorici, in his report on MTV's "Live at the 10 Spot" segment that featured Matchbox 20 in early 1999, hailed the band's performance in its first nationally televised concert. He described the band as playing "like a group of college kids looking for a record deal. The idea was to show that its mega-platinum debut album is no studio-manufactured fluke and that there is a real rock 'n' roll band behind the flashy videos and radio-friendly singles." In concert Matchbox 20 enjoys playing some of its favorite covers, such as Marvin Gaye's "Mercy Mercy Me," Cyndi Lauper's "Time after Time," and "Always and Forever," which is always an opening number as a good luck measure for the show. In preparation of its second release in 2000, the band played tracks from the CD at its concerts in 1998 and 1999. After shows, band members stuck around to meet fans and sign autographs for as long as their schedule would permit.

In 1998, Matchbox 20 joined artists such as Jewel, Elton John, and Shawn Colvin in recording a tribute album of Fleetwood Mac's *Rumours,* performing "Never Going Back Again." In thesummer of 1999, Thomas released a single with Santana, "Smooth," which enjoyed overwhelming success among music critics and fans, going triple-platinum by the fall of 1999. The single also earned Thomas an excellent reputation across a wide fan base and respect as an artist who could be flexible in creating music across genres. In August of 1999, Matchbox 20 recorded its second album, scheduled to be released in 2000.

In 1997 *Rolling Stone* and *Performance* magazines named Matchbox 20 Best New Band, based on readers' polls. The band was nominated for a Best Rock Performance Grammy and the Favorite New Artist/Pop Rock and Favorite Album/Pop Rock American Music awards in 1998. In October of 1999, the group was awarded a Diamond Award by the Recording Industry Association of America (RIAA) for selling over ten million albums in the United States. Only 62 other artists, such as Pink Floyd and The Beatles, have had sales to qualify for this distinction in music history. Also in 1999, Thomas was recognized as one of BMI's Songwriters of the Year, praised specifically for his band's hits, "Push," "Long Day," "3 AM," and "Real World," all included on *Yourself or Someone Like You.* Pleased with being prestigiously recognized by his peers in this way, Thomas commented, according to an article found on SonicNet, "I think it means more than any other [award]. At the end of the day, you'd much rather be noticed as a songwriter than a pop star. That's what I want to do—write great songs."

Keeping in touch with their fan base is important to band members. Despite their hectic touring schedule, they respond to most of the mail that comes into their website, www.matchbox20.com. Gaynor, who has been playing guitar since the age of 12, responded to a fan's question on the website regarding advice for start-up bands this way: "The main thing is you play because you love it. ...You should do it because you HAVE to play. It's in your heart. ... Music is a very special place to visit. Sometimes I never want to leave." Band members express a sincere desire to communicate the meaning and motivation for their songs to fans. They feel performing for live audiences is crucial to retaining a fan base and continuing to get their music airplay and sales. As a hardworking band, they believe that toughing it out on the road, hitting as many towns and cities as they can, is the way to stay creative and stay on top. Thomas emphasized on *Entertainment Avenue,* "All we can do is play and play and play and do the best we possibly can."

Selected discography

Yourself or Someone Like You (includes "Push," "3 AM," and "Back 2 Good"), Lava/Atlantic, 1996.

(Contributor) *Legacy: A Tribute to Fleetwood Mac's Rumours,* Lava/Atlantic, 1998.

Sources

Periodicals

Billboard, May 17, 1997; June 21, 1997; May 9, 1998

People, May 11, 1998.

Online

Atlantic Records, http://www.atlantic-records.com (November 27, 1999).

Entertainment Avenue, http://www.e-ave.com (November 18, 1999).

MTV's Website, http://www.mtv.com (October 28, 1999).

"The Official Matchbox 20 Website," http://www.matchbox20.com (November 18, 1999).

"The Original Unofficial Matchbox20 Page," http://www.surf.to/mb20 (November 18, 1999).

Rolling Stone Online, http://www.rollingstone.com (November 18, 1999).

SonicNet Music News Service, http://www.sonicnet.com (November 18, 1999).

—Melissa Walsh Doig

MC Eiht

Rap artist

One of the original "gangsta" rap artists from the West Coast, MC Eiht helped make the city of Compton, located near Los Angeles, a well-known center for rap and hip-hop culture. Fellow Compton rapper Ice Cube called the gangsta genre "reality rap" for the style's descriptions of brutal street life, urban alienation, autobiographical rage, and action-movie fantasies. After Ice Cube and his group N.W.A. (Niggaz With Attitude) brought Compton street life to mainstream America, Eiht followed suit with his act, Comptons Most Wanted (CMW). He recorded three albums as Comptons Most Wanted, then earned top billing for his subsequent four records. *We Come Strapped* marked Eiht's major breakthrough. The 1994 album went gold album, selling about 621,000 copies in all. Moreover, the record entered the *Billboard* R&B album chart at number one, holding the spot for five weeks, and the pop album chart at number five. After the release of two not so well-received albums, Eiht signed with a new label, Hoo Bangin', and returned with *Section 8,* redeeming his reputation as a rap star.

In addition to recording as Comptons Most Wanted and MC Eiht, the rap artist has appeared on several best-selling movie soundtracks, including *Boyz N The Hood, Menace II Society, Tales From The Hood, New Jersey Drive,* and *The Show.* Lending his face to the silver screen as well, Eiht played a cameo role in John Singleton's Academy Award-nominated *Boyz N The Hood* and played the part of A-Wax in the critically-acclaimed Hughes Brothers film *Menace II Society.* For the role, Eiht received an award at the First Annual *Source* Magazine Awards for best acting performance in a film or for television.

MC Eiht, born Aaron Tyler in 1970 to hardworking parents, watched his mother and father separate at an early age. After the breakup, Eiht's father left the family and moved to Oklahoma, while his mother settled in Compton, California, near Los Angeles. Spending most of his childhood in the low-income neighborhoods of Compton, Eiht first attended a Catholic school before being expelled. As a result of the expulsion, Eiht was forced to go to school within the Compton public school system, considered one of the worst school districts in the state. In fact, the California state legislature later ended up taking over the district in 1996 to try and make improvements.

Like many urban rap artists, Eiht first experienced street life by joining a gang and dealing drugs in his teens, although he admitted that he never excelled as a criminal. "I wanted to be on the streets so much that I started gangbanging and selling crack just because everybody else was doing it," remembered Eiht, as quoted by Solomon Moore in a feature for *Blaze* magazine. "If youwas from the hood, that's what you did." But after siring a son and not selling enough crack to feed his baby, Eiht came to the realization that he needed to find a new direction in life. "I was gettin' high one night... and the shit just came to me. I started rappin'. It was just like a wake-up call."

Around this time, a group called N.W.A. had just succeeded in taking the gangsta genre, or reality rap, to the mainstream. Also formed in Compton, N.W.A. included several rap artists who later achieved success as solo acts, namely Ice Cube, Dr. Dre, the late Eazy-E, and MC Ren. These rap stars would put their city and their West Coast sound on the map, sell millions of records, and raise political and social concerns over the gangsta genre's use of rhymes that describe violence, misogyny, and sociopathic behavior.

Taking cue from N.W.A, Eiht formed a rap group with some of his neighborhood pals, including Unknown DJ, DJ Mike T, DJ Slip, and the Chill MC, called Comptons Most Wanted. They made their initial mark in 1989 with the release of two singles: "Rhymes Too Funky" and "This is Compton." For their first album in 1990, *It's a Compton Thang!,* only three of the original members participated, one of which was Eiht. Though not an especially hardcore rap album, the record gave the group some street credibility with the track "One Time Gaffled

For the Record . . .

Born Aaron Tyler in 1970; one son.

Moved to Compton, CA; formed Comptons Most Wanted, c. 1989; released first album, *It's a Compton Thang!*, 1990; released hit album *We Come Strapped,* 1994; signed with Hoo Bangin' label c. 1998; released *Section 8,* 1999.

Addresses: *Record company*—Hoo Bangin'/Priority Records, 6430 Sunset Blvd., Ste. 900, Hollywood, CA

Em Up," and the single "Growin' Up in the Hood" captured the hopeless desperation of street life and was commissioned for the movie *Boyz N The Hood.* Eiht also made a cameo appearance in the film.

Comptons Most Wanted released *Straight Checkn 'Em* the following year. This time around, DJ Slip and Unknown DJ joined Eiht on the album (Chill MC went to serve jail time half way through the recording process). On the largely overlooked gangsta classic, Eiht began to find his cool yet deadly voice on tracks such as "Compton's Lynchin" and "Def Wish," the rap that started a supposed rivalry between Eiht and another Compton rap artist named DJ Quik. As years passed, the tension eventually subsided. "The whole DJ Quick situation is some he said/she said shit, strictly negative," Eiht explained to John Rhodes in a 1999 interview for the Launch: Discover New Music website. "I'm at the point in my career where I'm just trying to stack some chips, maintain my hustle, and just kick it. I stay away from all the drama." The group released *Music to Driveby* in 1992, which, in truth, lacked the provocative nature implied by the album's title. In some of the songs, Eiht lacked the lyrical quality of the group's previous release. For example, he led an attack on women in "Hoodrat" and made an unconvincing attempt with the blues-styled track "Niggaz Strugglin." Nonetheless, Eiht proved his skill at storytelling with "Hood Took Me Under," a song thatcontinued the hopelessness of "Growin' Up in the Hood."

Eiht received his first major break in 1993 when played the role of A-Wax in the acclaimed Hughes Brothers film *Menace II Society.* For the platinum-selling movie soundtrack, Eiht contributed a stunning single entitled "Streiht Up Menace." Both the role and the song strengthened his profile. In April of 1994, Eiht received the award in the category of best acting performance at the First Annual *Source* Magazine Awards. Until this point, Eiht had only earned an underground following for his eerie-sounding rhythmic style and undaunted tales of street realism.

Like his heightened public image, Eiht's music improved as well. He received top billing for the next album, *We Come Strapped,* released in 1994. As Comptons Most Wanted was reduced to a duo consisting of Eiht and DJ Slip, the record was released under the name MC Eiht Featuring CMW. Eiht's greatest success until that time, the gold album that sold about 621,000 copies entered the *Billboard* R&B album chart at number one, holding the spot for five weeks, and the pop album chart at number five. "People said Jay-Z was the first rapper to hold the number one spot for five weeks, but it's not true," Eiht said to Moore, setting the record straight. "I held the spot for five weeks back in 1994, back when Boyz II Men was on the charts.... So Jay-Z's the second rapper."

Critics attributed much of *We Come Strapped*'s success to the fact that both Eiht and DJ Slip took a dramatic new direction in style to create a record that sounded unique from their past efforts. DJ Slip, for one, experimented with more spacious, largely sample-free music dominated by synthesizers and a loud bass, while Eiht slowed his delivery and increased his lyrical dramatics. The most noted tracks included "Take 2 With Me," "Compton Cyco," and "All for the Money." With *We Come Strapped,* the duo "achieved a nearly cinematic scope, an apex of reality in music," concluded the *Trouser Press Guide to '90s Rock.* But despite the album's achievements, Eiht claimed that his label, Epic Street, offered him little support. Although he believed that *We Come Strapped* could go platinum, Epic stopped promoting the album early and shuffled Eiht off to the recording studio. The label offered him a $1.125 million contract for four additional albums, as well as two releases he owed Epic under his prior contract. After slashing his budget in half, Epic's attorneys started calling Eiht to persuade him to sign the deal. Eiht finally obliged, although with hesitation. "As far as sales and royalties, they [Epic] made sure that I didn't get a dime. So basically, I just started giving them mediocre shit," he told Moore.

Consequently, Eiht claimed that he never intended for his next two albums to reach the level of *We Come Strapped* and simply setout to fulfill his obligation to Epic. Although 1996's *Death Threatz* yielded some noteworthy tracks, such as the potent and hostile "Run 4 Your Life" and the toned down "Late Nite Hype Part 2," a seductive expression of violence, the album and its 1997 follow-up, *Last Man Standing,* failed to impress rap enthusiasts. Eiht himself confessed that overall, the songs on those two albums seemed mediocre as compared to his previous hit record. "The lyrics were boring, the beats plodding, the inspiration lacking," wrote Moore in agreement.

Desperate to find another record company, around 1998 Eiht signed with Time Warner. However, the United States legislature and the news media had just come down hard on gangsta rap, and Eiht's new label wanted the rap artist to tone down his lyrics and take a new direction with his music. But Eiht would have no part of such a suggestion. "MC Eiht's direction is the street. Period," the committed rapper told Moore. "That's like trying to tell Cube how to make records. You can't tell no vet how to make a record! We know how to make records for the fans who buy our music." As a result, Eiht never released a record for Time Warner, and the label eventually cut ties with the rap artist. "As everybody knows, Atlantic/Time Warner can't put out gangsta shit. They let Ice-T go; they let the who Death Row deal go. If they ain't gonna put out Tupac, they sure ain't gonna put me out."

Left without record company backing, Eiht spent the year making appearances on other artist's albums from Cypress Hill, an interracial rap trio from a Latin Los Angeles neighborhood, to New York R&B/hip-hop artist Pete Rock's *Soul Survivor* album. Then, after declining an offer to sign with No Limit Records, home to rapper Snoop Dog, Eiht accepted a record deal with Mack 10 and his new Hoo Bangin' label. As Mack 10 told Moore, "We had this new label ... and I thought I needed somebody who's been around but who still got legs. Eiht ain't no rookie. You can't just tell 'em anything."

With Hoo Bangin' and a restored sense of creative freedom, Eiht returned in 1999 with *Section 8,* considered his strongest work since *We Come Strapped.* For the effort, Eiht assembled a cast of well-known producers and rap artists to contribute, including Mack 10, Ice Cube, members of Comptons Most Wanted, Ant Banks, Young Tree, and Binky Mac. "This album provides the same style as always, but much tighter delivery and tracks," Eiht told Rhodes. "I wanted to give everybody nationwide something to feel. Hooking up with Mack 10 was a blessing. He understood my vision from the start, and we just clicked." Also providing insight into Eiht's personal experiences growing up on the streets of Compton, the album boasted such performances as "Living N' tha Streetz," "My Life," and "Days of '89."

Selected discography

with Comptons Most Wanted

It's a Compton Thang!, Orpheus, 1990.
Straight Checkn 'Em, Orpheus/Epic, 1991.
Music to Driveby, Orpheus/Epic, 1992.

with MC Eiht Featuring CMW

We Come Strapped, Epic Street, 1994.
Death Threatz, Epic Street, 1996.
Last Man Standing, Epic Street, 1997.
Section 8, Hoo Bangin', 1999.

Compilations

Menace II Society, (soundtrack), Jive Records, 1993.
Tales From The Hood, (soundtrack), 40 Acres And A Mule, 1995.
New Jersey Drive Vol. 1, (soundtrack), Tommy Boy, 1995.
Rhyme & Reason, Priority Records, 1997.
Master P Presents: West Coast Bad Boyz II, No Limit Records, 1997.
N.W.A. Straight Outta Compton 10th Anniversary Tribute, Priority Records, 1998.

Sources

Books

Robbins, Ira A., editor, *Trouser Press Guide to '90s Rock,* Fireside/Simon and Schuster, 1997.

Periodicals

Blaze, August 1999, pp. 80-82.
Dallas Morning News, November 8, 1998, p. 10C.
Entertainment Weekly, August 12, 1994, p. 56.
Newsday, April 26, 1994, p. A08.
Tampa Tribune, August 20, 1999, p. 15.

Online

Launch.com: Discover New Music, http://www,launch.com (June 18, 1999).
iMusic Urban Showcase—MC Eiht, http://www.imusic.com/showcase/urban/mceiht.html (October 11,1999).
MC Eiht at Epic Records, http://www,epiccenter.com (October 15, 1999).

—Laura Hightower

Susannah McCorkle

Singer, writer

Though not a household name in America, jazz-pop vocalist Susannah McCorkle has released 17 albums during her 20-year career which have earned international critical acclaim. McCorkle's repertoire of over 3,000 songs has helped keep the music of such songwriters/composers as George Gershwin, Antonio Carlos Jobim, and Johnny Mercer alive in cabarets and on concert stages around the world. For a person whose original intention was to be a simultaneous language interpreter for the Common Market in Brussels, utilizing her skills in German, Spanish, French, and Italian, McCorkle instead decided to begin a singing career and move to London. McCorkle discovered jazz for the first time after moving to Europe in 1970. The American singer, Billie Holiday, made a particularly strong impact on McCorkle. When she heard the recordings of the blues and jazz giant, McCorkle was inspired enough to follow her own dream of singing. McCorkle grew up on top 40 hits and Broadway show tunes, but it would be the American jazz standards that would eventually take her to the top of the charts.

Susannah McCorkle was born in Berkeley, California, in 1946. She received a Bachelor's degree in Italian literature and studied language in Mexico, France, Italy, and Germany. When she decided to head to London to try a career in music, McCorkle was also well on her way to becoming a prolific writer. Her fiction has been published in *Mademoiselle*, *Cosmopolitan*, and the *O. Henry Book of Prize Short Stories*. Her non-fiction includes articles published in the *New York Times Magazine*, and *American Heritage.* Some of those articles include 10,000 word pieces on such people as singer and actress Ethel Waters, legendary American blues singer Bessie Smith, and composer Irving Berlin. McCorkle also wrote English translation versions of countless Brazilian, French, and Italian songs, including those of Brazilian musician Antonio Carlos Jobim. In addition, McCorkle writes all of her own shows, including her own anecdotes about the songwriters and songs she performed.

In a review of her cabaret show in New York in June of 1998, Stephen Holden of the *New York Times* made the observation that her, "sweet, smoky voice and insinuating delivery suggest Billie Holiday filtered through Julie London by way of Lee Wiley, finds a common strain of erotic longing in both songwriters." Her interpretation of such composers as Gershwin and Jobim, Holden noted, "belonged to different nationalities and generations," were celebrated with "her crisply informative biographical asides," he said, calling attention to her studied performance, both in song and as a writer.

McCorkle does not deny her appeal to the "over 40" crowd, especially with one of Jobim's songs, "Caminhos Cruzados." "I call it the best love song ever written for people over 40," McCorkle said in comments included at the Concord Records website. "The character who's singing is generalizing. You realize only gradually during the course of the song that she is in love with the person she is singing to but afraid to say it, trying to hint at it, hoping he will get the hint. And we the listeners are in on the secret, so by the end of the song we're hoping too that he'll understand what she wants to say but can't. I love it!... I was once called by *People* magazine a 'bruised romantic.' It's a great description of me."

One of McCorkle's "quirks" is that she must record live in the studio, with all the musicians present and playing together, according to her Concord Records biography. "I don't come in later and overdub, because I want that spontaneity that I first experienced on Billie Holiday record," she said. "I just love it when you feel people in a room making music together and responding to each other right in the moment." In discussing her tastes in music, McCorkle said that she was as "comfortable" delivering the song, "I Ain't Gonna Play No Second Fiddle," a Bessie Smith wild and rowdy "protofeminist" blues tune, as she is singing a song she found on a Ray Charles record titled, "Losing Hand." She related that she "recorded 'I Ain't Gonna Play...' because Nick Phillips heard me do it at the San Jose Jazz Festival and people just roared." McCorkle added, "I think people think it's funny since I don't usually belt a song, and yet they can

For the Record . . .

Born in1946, in Berkeley, CA. *Education*: Bachelor's degree in Italian literature from University of California, Berkeley.

Jazz singer and writer; began singing career in Europe, 1970; released first album (in the U.K.), *The Songs of Harry Warren,* 1976; has released 16 subsequent albums including *The Songs of Johnny Mercer,* 1977; *Thanks for the Memory: The Songs of Leo Robin,* 1985; *Sabia,* 1990; *From Broadway to Bebop,* 1994; *Let's Face the Music and Dance: The Songs of Irving Berlin,* 1997; and *From Broken Hearts to Blue Skies*, 1999; has had works of fiction and non-fiction published in major magazines.

Awards: Three-time winner, Album of the Year, *Stereo Review*; Singer of the Year, *Los Angeles Times*.

Addresses: *Record company*—Concord Records, Inc., P.O. Box 845, Concord, CA 94522, (925) 682-6770, fax (925) 682-3508. *Bookings*—c/o Anne Jeffreys or Andrew Lipman, Susannah McCorkle Music, 41 W. 86th Street, #16C, New York, NY 10024, (212) 877-5918. *Website*—http://susannahmccorkle.home.mindspring.com. *Email*—smccoffice@aol.com.

tell I've really listed to Bessie's phrasing and timing." Regarding the Ray Charles song, McCorkle said, "all the way through he got a down, sad feel as if he were singing it just to himself. I have a lot of blues in my soul too, and I wanted to pay tribute to him."

McCorkle never stops looking for songs to sing. She is always hunting out the new and the old, and anything to which she could add her own soulful interpretation. "I need to feel a personal connection to a lyric. It needs to be something I've gone through in my life or something that I find wonderfully amusing or deeply moving. I have to have something to say with a song," McCorkle was quoted in her Concord Records biography.

In his June 1998 review of her latest cabaret show, Holden said that, "grounding her interpretations is a sexiness that veils everything in a light mist." For Holden, the high point of the show was her rendition of "I Loves You Porgy," from the Gershwin musical, *Porgy and Bess.* "Her blend of scholarship and musicality," suggested Holden, "has never appeared more seamless." In quotes included at McCorkle's website, *Time Out New York* noted in 1997 that "McCorkle may make her living on the cabaret circuit, but you'd have to look pretty hard to find a jazz singer with her precision, articulation, and timing." That same year, a notice in the *Chicago Tribune* said that McCorkle was, "as much stage actor as vocal stylist," and that, "she persuades the listener to hang onto her every syllable, as if one hadn't heard these tunes so many times before."

McCorkle's website offers insight into her diversity. She is as comfortable performing at Carnegie Hall with renowned Pops conductor Skitch Henderson, as she is in the quiet confines of the famed Algonquin Hotel in New York City. Her website lists her workshops for children, as well as her availability for private parties.

Selected discography

on Concord Jazz

No More Blues, 1989.
Sabia, 1990.
I'll Take Romance, 1992.
From Bessie to Brazil, 1993.
From Broadway to Bebop, 1994.
Easy to Love: The Songs of Cole Porter, 1996.
Let's Face the Music and Dance: The Songs of Irving Berlin, 1997.
Someone to Watch Over Me: The Songs of George Gershwin, 1998.
From Broken Hearts to Blue Skies, 1999.

on EMI

The Songs of Harry Warren, (LP), 1976.

on Jazz Alliance

The Songs of Johnny Mercer, 1977.
Over the Rainbow: The Songs of E. Y. "Yip" Harburg, 1981.
The People that You Never Get to Love, 1982.
Thanks for the Memory: The Songs of Leo Robin, 1985.

Sources

Books

George-Warren, Holly, editor, *The Rolling Stone Jazz Record Guide,* Random House, 1999.

Periodicals

New York Times, June 10, 1996; May 15, 1997; November 28, 1997; June 4, 1998; June 5, 1998.

Online

"Susannah McCorkle Biography," *Concord Records website*, http://www.aent.com/concord.

Susannah McCorkle Website, http://susannahmccorkle.home.mindspring.com/.

—Jane Spear

The McGuire Sisters

Singing group

Photograph by R. Corkery. Corbis. Reproduced by permission. ©

The most popular female singing group of the 1950s and well into the 1960s was the McGuire Sisters. They earned the crown by easily edging out the Chordettes and the Fontane Sisters. Through their exceptional talent in harmony, they became America's favorites as well as around the world. Asa McGuire, a veteran steelworker with Armco Steel, who played guitar and Lillie, an ordained minister and pastor of the Miamisburg, Ohio First Church of God were the parents of the talented trio that included, Christine, born July 30, 1928, Dorothy, born February 13, 1930 and Phyllis, born February 14, 1931 in Middleton, Ohio to Asa, a steelworker who played guitar, and Lillie McGuire, an ordanined minister and pastor.

In 1935 when Phyllis was only four they began to sing in the choir and soon realized their uncanny knack for close harmony. Their foundation was Gospel, and throughout high school, they performed at church events, weddings, funerals, Sunday school picnics as well in senior citizen's homes. They also sang at revival meetings, where they would gather "love offerings" after the service to pay their expenses. Times were hard and they often didn't collect enough to pay gasoline expenses. But they always got a handshake, heard some wish "May the Good Lord Richly Bless You" and gained plenty of experience. Their voices blended so uniformly, their parents could not tell them apart over the telephone.

The sisters were forbidden by their parents to listen to secular music, forcing them to sneak and listen to their favorites like the Andrews Sisters and the Dinning Sisters over the radio. In 1949, they switched from hymns to popular music and began singing at military and veterans hospitals touring for nine months with the USO. Sunday mornings were spent singing in Baptist and Methodist churches and when they returned to Ohio they began a religious radio program that was broadcast daily on Dayton Radio Station WLW from their mother's church in Miamisburg.

They were singing on the radio when agent Karl Taylor and his wife, Inez heard their performance in their car. He drove to the church and offered to help them by booking them in a Dayton Hotel. One month later they were singing with Taylor's band at the Van Cleef Hotel in Dayton, Ohio. They soon began appearing regularly in supper clubs and performing on local television stations.

While modeling, and holding down multiple jobs, they decided to go to New York and audition for Arthur Godfrey's Show. They took their savings, borrowed some additional money, and went to New York where they learned Godfrey was on vacation. Still, they landed an eight week stint in 1952 on Kate Smith's radio show.

For the Record . . .

Members include **Christine McGuire**, born July 30, 1928, in Middleton, OH, vocals; **Dorothy McGuire** born February 13, 1930, in Middleton, OH, married Lowell Williamson, vocals; **Phyllis McGuire** born February 14, 1931 in Middleton, OH, vocals; all daughters of Asa , (a steelworker) and Lillie McGuire, (an ordained minister and pastor of the First Church of God in Miamisburg, OH). *Education:* All studied with vocal Instructor Mrs. Helen Ramsdell.

The most popular female singing group in the United States during the fifties and sixties; placed eight songs in the top twenty in the United States ; debuted on the *Arthur Godfrey Talent Scouts*, 1952; replaced the Chordettes;.charted more hits than any other female singing group from December 1952 until September 1961; Phyllis appeared in the 1964 film *Come Blow Your Horn* with Frank Sinatra; the group appeared before Presidents Richard Nixon, Jimmy Carter, Gerald Ford, Ronald Reagan and at George Bush's 1989 inauguration and a command performance for the Queen of England; ended their careers, 1968 during the peak of their popularity; Phyllis began performing as a comedienne and singing for Reprise Records; performed at family functions only for the next seventeen years; banded together and for six months in 1985 continued to perform all over the world in venues from Las Vegas to Chicago's Drury Lane Theater to London.

Awards: Broadcasters Hall of Fame; Las Vegas Casino Entertainers Hall of Fame; Middletown High School Hall of Fame, Middletown, OH.

Addresses: *Home*— Phyliss McGuire 100 Rancho Circle, Las Vegas, Nevada 89107.

Afterward they returned to Ohio and later returned to New York. By December 1st, they had won the talent competition on *Arthur Godfrey's Talent Scouts* television program having auditioned with the Academy Award winning song"Mona Lisa" and "Pretty Eyed Baby." They were signed to Godfrey's morning show and replaced the Chordettes,. They remained on Godfrey's show for six years.

In 1952, they were also signed to perform under the Coral Records label supervised by Gordon Jenkins. After Jenkins left Coral and went to Capitol, Bob Thiele was hired to replace him andbrought in top flight musicians to complement the McGuires. From July 1954 until January 1958, they placed the following singles in the top 20: "Goodnight, Sweetheart Goodnight" in 1954; "Muskrat Ramble" in 1954; "No More" in 1955; "He" in 1955; "Picnic" in 1956; "Sincerely" in 1955— number one for ten weeks—"Something's Gotta Give" in 1955; "Sugartime" in 1958; "May You Always" in 1958; and "Just for Old Time's Sake" in 1961.

Cosmopolitan's November 1953 issue called them "Godfrey's Merry McGuires." In 1955 they recorded Johnny Mercer's "Something's Gotta Give" from the Fred Astaire musical *Daddy Long Legs* and both Mercer and Astaire were present at the recording. It rose to number five on the charts and was the first of several hits that were included in motion pictures. They also made their rendition of "Heart" from the Broadway show, *Damn Yankees* and in the version, their arranger Murray Kane actually joined in the harmony.

In 1956 Thiele asked entertainer Steve Allen, a former high school classmate of singer Mel Torme, to write a lyric for the popular theme to the blockbuster motion picture *Picnic* that had starred William Holden, Kim Novak and marked the debut of Cliff Robertson. The McGuire Sister's recording rose to number 13 and was followed by "Delilah Jones" at number 37 from the film *The Man With the Golden Arm* that starred Frank Sinatra and Kim Novak. They also recorded "Weary Blues" with Lawrence Welk that rose to Number 32.

In 1957 they recorded "Sugartime" with Steve Allen at the piano and it became their signature song. The word "sugar" appears twenty eight times in the song's two and one half minutes. The March issue of *Life Magazine* featured the McGuires on the cover and reported they were the best selling vocal group of the time. That same year Coral Records decided they should record their version of "Around the World in 80 Days" the theme from Mike Todd's film that starred David Niven. The McGuires were flown from Nevada to San Francisco by sea plane, cut the recording and returned for an evening show in Las Vegas.

.In 1968 one of their last performances was on *The Ed Sullivan Show*, which broadcast from Las Vegas's Caesar's Palace. At the peak of their popularity in 1968, the McGuire Sisters decided to end their careers with Christine and Dorothy devoting their time to their families. Phyllis, an excellent entertainer and skilled comedienne went solo and performed with many singers and other personalities including Sammy Davis Jr., Johnny Carson. She also appeared in the film *Come Blow Your Horn* with Frank Sinatra, Lee J. Cobb, Barbara Rush and Jill St. John.

For the next seventeen years the only time the McGuire Sisters performed was when they were together at family gatherings. But in 1985 they decided to make a comeback and for six rigorous months they rehearsed at Phyllis's home in Las Vegas. They opened at Harrah's in Reno, Nevada and were met with enthusiastic fans and they have sustained that warm acceptance through the years.

They have performed before Presidents Richard Nixon, Jimmy Carter, Gerald Ford, Ronald Reagan and George Bush at his inaugural ball in Washington as well as in front of Queen Elizabeth. They have continued to do the Las Vegas/Reno circuit into the 1990's as well as appearing all across the United States.
All three sisters are active in their communities giving endless hours of time to humanitarian causes and other philanthropic work including a performance on the Labor Day Muscular Dystrophy Telethon in 1991. Phyllis is known as Las Vegas's leading hostess and its unofficial ambassador entertaining royalty, social and the business elite in her 50,00 square foot French Provincial estate home. It is filled with expensive artwork and priceless memorabilia that span over four decades of her work in the world of entertainment. Today, Christine enjoys an active social life in Las Vegas and is an avid golfer. Dorothy and her husband of forty years, Lowell Williamson, live in Scottsdale, Arizona, where they are also active in community affairs and philanthropic activities.

Selected discography

By Request, Coral.
Children's Holiday, Coral.
Do You Remember When?, Coral.
Dottie, Chris, Phyllis, Coral.
Greetings from the McGuire Sisters, Coral.
In Harmony With Him, Coral.
Just For Old Time's Sake, Coral.
May You Always, Coral.
McGuire Sisters Sing Songs Everybody Knows, Coral.
Musical Magic, Coral.
Showcase, Coral.
Sugartime, Coral.
Teenage Dance Party, Coral.
While the Lights Are Low, Coral.
McGuire Sisters, The Anthology, MCA.
McGuire Sisters, 36 All-Time Greatest Hits, MCA.
McGuire Sisters, Greatest Hits, UNI-MCA.
Do You Remember When/While the Lights Are Low, Jasmine (UK).

Sources

Books

Lax, Roger& Frederick Smith, *The Great Song Thesaurus,* Oxford Univ. Press 1989
Maltin, Leonard, *Movie and Video Guide 1995,* Penguin Books Ltd., 1994
McAleer, Dave, *The All Music Book of Hit Singles*, Miller Freeman Books, 1994
Osborne, Jerry, *Rockin Records,* Osborne Publications 1999
Warner, Jay, *The Billboard Book of American Singing Groups, A History 1940-1990*, Billboard Books 1992

Periodicals

Life Magazine, March 17, 1958.

Online

"McGuire Sisters," *The Wire: News from the Associated Press*, www.Enquirer.com/editions/1998/05/09/midhall.html, (September 1999).
"King Curtis," www.crl.com/~tsimon/curtis.htm, (September 1999).
The Middletown Journal News, www.middletown.com/feature/ramsdell.htm, (September, 1999).

Additional information was obtained through an interview with Phyllis McGuire on September 2, 1999; and from the liner notes of, *The McGuire Sisters, The Anthology* by Joseph Laredo.

—Francis D. McKinley

Brad Mehldau

Piano

By the end of the 1990s, jazz pianist Brad Mehldau had slowly worked his way into the musical world as a dynamic force who pulled his inspiration from influences that included rock, jazz and classical. According to Ed Enright in *Down Beat* magazine in June of 1999, Mehldau wanted to "jar you back to consciousness. Not in some head-banger sense.... Mehldau would rather rock your *inner* world with something much more powerful and pure: thoughtful, expressive pianism."

From the time his first album, *Introducing Brad Mehldau*, was released in 1995, Mehldau became a familiar name among the most ardent jazz critics. In comments included at the Jazz Online website, a review in the *Chicago Tribune* said that the album was "a recording that achieves its most vivid moments when Mehldau is playing original compositions. The elliptical lines, volatile rhythmic figures and unexpected bursts of color and dissonance ... prove that Mehldau writes as cleverly as he plays. The originality of these compositions is startling to behold." By 1997, when he debuted at the Village Vanguard in New York City, the long-held bastion of premiere jazz clubs, he caught the attention of the inner circle of jazz critics then, too. In his review of Brad Mehldau and his trio for the *New York Times,* Peter Watrous said that "Mr. Mehldau's obsessions make his music tense." He added that, "where jazz musicians traditionally are adept at doubling or halving tempos, Mr. Mehldau and the band were working every angle of time."

With his roots in classical music, and a repertoire that included an array of standards, Mehldau had proven from the beginning that his music represented a deeper commitment to more than commercial popularity. He told Enright, "I know that audiences are very savvy and hip to whatever spin the media or record company marketing department puts on an artist, and they're sick of it."

Brad Mehldau was born in Jacksonville, Florida, and spent the first ten years of his life moving between Georgia, New York, and New Hampshire, before his father settled his medical practice as in Hartford, Connecticut. Mehldau began studying piano at age six and continued until he was 14. At that time, as a student at Hartford's Hall High School, he joined the school's accomplished jazz band. Through his performances with that band, he won the prestigious Berklee School of Music (Boston, Massachusetts) high school competition as Best All-Around Musician. As a student at the New School for Social Research in Manhattan, he was enrolled as part of that school's well-known jazz and contemporary music program, studying with Junior Mance, Kenny Werner, and Fred Hersch. Another instructor, long-time drummer Jimmy Cobb, brought Mehldau into his quartet.

While still a student, Mehldau began touring the United States and Europe with various groups. European jazz festivals particularly brought attention to his rising fame. It was when he joined Joshua Redman's quartet that he began to gain recognition that only heightened with the release of his first album. In 1997, Mehldau moved to Los Angeles while continuing to tour worldwide and record. He told Enright that what he liked about Los Angeles was the fact that there was "no geographical scene like you have in New York, with the West Village and the East Village and Lincoln Center Uptown." In Los Angeles he noted, the scene was "all spread out," and "you can go to a club in West Hollywood where on any given night they'll have anything from brash metal to a big band with a torch singer. It's almost like nothing is sacred."

The intensity of Mehldau's music has been compared to musicians that preceded him long before. In billing for the North Sea Jazz Festival in The Hague, Netherlands, in 1997, Mehldau's piano style was described in comments at the North Sea Jazz Festival website as having, "the power and energy of Beethoven, the improvisational richness of [legendary jazz saxophonist] John Coltrane and Miles Davis and the emotional approach of Bill Evans." Much of his style was born of his own love and inspiration from jazz piano greats such as Oscar Peterson, Wynton Kelly, McCoy Tyner, and Keith Jarrett. In his review of Mehldau's June 1999 appearance at Sym-

For the Record . . .

Born in 1970 in Jacksonville, FL. *Education*: Studied at The New School for Social Research, New York City.

Began playing piano at age six; studied at The New School for Social Research with Junior Manse, Kenny Werner, Fred Hersch, and Jimmy Cobb; joined Joshua Redman's quartet, released debut solo album, *Introducing Brad Mehldau*, 1997.

Awards: #1 Talent Deserving Wider Recognition, *Down Beat* Critics Poll, 1997.

Addresses: *Record company*—Warner Brothers Records, 3300 Warner Blvd., Burbank, CA 91505-4694, (818) 846-9090. *Management*—Hopper Management, Munich, Germany.

phony Space in Manhattan and Mehldau's creation, "Elegiac Cycle," Adam Shatz wrote in the *New York Times* that the comparison of Mehldau to the legendary Bill Evans, considered one of the greatest white jazz pianists was a bit misleading, at best. "The real reason behind the Evans analogies, one suspects," wrote Shatz, had "less to do with music than with race." Yet Shatz agreed that his "eccentric sensibility" was reminiscent of Evans. "Like Evans, he is profoundly drawn to classical music, but where Evans invoked early French modernists like Debussy and Ravel, Mr. Mehldau demonstrates affinities with 19th-century German Romantics like Schubert and Brahms." Mehldau's particular fascination with German musicians and literature brought a reflection from a recent interview Shatz quoted. Mehldau said that "if there's any German ethos that attracts me, it has to do with the incredible amount of welled-up emotion that's being conveyed. There's a kind of longing that you feel in the literature and in the music of Schubert and Schumann."

In the years following his studies at the New School, Mehldau returned to his classical roots. Around the same time, he discovered German writer, Thomas Mann and his book, *Doctor Faustus,* an allegory about Germany's embrace of fascism under the influence of Hitler. A trip to Germany in the summer of 1998 led him to Berlin and the celebration the 50th anniversary of Mann's novel. It was there that Mehldau conceived his "Elegiac Cycle," which he says came from the song cycles of the German lieder [often songs about simple folk heroes] tradition of Schubert's "Winterreise." Shatz noted that Mehldau wrote about it in his album liner notes saying, "The process of improvisation is a kind of affirmation of mortality. Even in the moment you're creating something, it's already gone forever, and that's precisely its strength. Improvisation would seem to solve the problem of death by constantly dying as it's being born. It scoffs at loss, and revels in its own transience."

"I'm not too goal-oriented," Mehldau revealed in his discussion with Enright. "That's probably my one spiritual mantra. It's something vaguely Eastern that has to do with being right here right now, and I've probably had to reaffirm that even more because it's such a zany time we live in now," he went on to say. "I like things with permanence. They make you feel comfortable."

Selected discography

New York Barcelona Crossing, (with Perico Sambeat), Fresh Sound, 1993.
The Art of the Trio, Volume One, Warner Records, 1997.
Introducing Brad Mehldau, Warner Records, 1997.
The Art of the Trio, Volume Three, Warner Records, 1998.
Elegiac Cycle, Warner Records, 1998.
Live At the Village Vanguard: The Art of the Trio, Volume Two; Warner Records, 1998.
Art of the Trio 4: Back at the Vanguard, Warner Records, 1999.
"Blame It on my Youth," (written by Oscar Levant and Edward Heyman soundtrack *Eyes Wide Shut* motion picture), Warner Sunset, 1999.
Jazz Bakery Sessions, (with Lee Konitz and Charlie Haden), Blue Note, 1999.

Sources

Books

Cook, Richard and Brian Morton, *The Penguin Guide to Jazz on Compact Disc,* Penguin Books, 4th edition, 1998.
George-Warren, Holly, editor, *The Rolling Stone Jazz Guide,* Random House, 1999.

Periodicals

Down Beat, June 1999.
New York Times, February 1, 1997; September 28, 1998; July 25, 1999.
Washington Post, January 9, 1999; June 18, 1999.

Online

"Brad Mehldau," *Jazz Online,* http://www.jazzonline.com.
"Brad Mehldau," *Jazz Radio,* http://jazzradio.org/brad/.htm.
"Brad Mehldau," *North Sea Jazz Festival,* http://www.northseajazz.nl/northsea/97/visw/bmehldaue.html.

–Jane Spear

Ethel Merman

Singer, actress

AP/Wide World Photos. Reproduced by permission. ©

On October 13, 1930 an 18-year-old singer named Ethel Agnes Zimmermann came on the stage at Broadway's Alvin Theater and introduced "I've Got Rhythm" in George Gershwin's new musical, *Girl Crazy* and changed Broadway forever. A few minutes before she had entertained the crowd with her version of "Sam and Delilah," which had attracted attention, but when she began to sing "I've Got Rhythm" near the end of the first act using her voice to transmit a single note for an entire 16-bar chorus, the audience was certain that a new star had been born. She was later characterized as being able to hold a note longer than the Chase Manhattan Bank.

Born Ethel Agnes Zimmermann on January 16, 1909 in Astoria Long Island, New York, Ethel Merman made her debut as a five year old at the Astoria, Long Island Republican Club. Accompanied by her father, she was billed as Little Ethel Zimmermann. Before long she was appearing for civic, fraternal and philanthropic organizations such as the Knights of Columbus, the Masons, and the Long Island Society for the Prevention and Relief of Tuberculosis. She also appeared at Camp Yaphank on Long Island during a period when Irving Berlin was also helping to cheer World War I soldiers. Although she never had any formal voice training, she sang in the choir of the Dutch Reformed Church and her father taught her to read music and play the piano.

Merman took a four year business course at William Cullen Bryant High School and became proficient in typing, shorthand, and bookkeeping. Upon graduation she obtained a $23 a week job as a stenographer at an automobile anti-freeze business and later was hired as a secretary to Caleeb Bragg, President of the Bragg Kliesrath Corporation, a manufacturer of early vacuum brakes. She continued to sing at social events and company outings, which soon led to singing in local clubs. Her boss got her an opportunity to sing on Broadway with George White, the famed producer, but when she was offered work in the chorus only, she declined the offer indicating she only wanted a singing job.

She continued to perform at local clubs including Jimmy Durante's Les Ambassadeurs Club on Broadway, where the two became life long friends. In addition, Merman performed at the Ritz Theater in Elizabeth, New Jersey on weekends and during the week at the Paramount Theater in Brooklyn. She was noticed at the Paramount by Vinton Freedley, who obtained an audition for her with George Gershwin in his penthouse apartment. The audition led to her Broadway debut in the 1930 Gershwin Broadway musical *Girl Crazy*, where she stopped the show. Ginger Rogers singled her out for the part when

For the Record . . .

Born Ethel Agnes Zimmermann on January 16, 1909, in Astoria Long Island, NY, (died February 15, 1984, New York, NY); daughter of Edward (an accountant) and Agnes Gardner Merman, (homemaker and choir singer); married William B. Smith (a theatrical agent) November 15, 1940, (divorced 1941); married Robert D. Levitt (newspaper executive) 1941, (divorced June 7, 1952); married Robert F. Six (airline executive) 1953, (divorced 1960); married Ernest Borgnine (actor) June 26, 1964, (divorced November 1965); children (with second husband): Ethel born July 20, 1942 (died 1967) and Robert Daniels Jr. born August 11, 1945.

Made Broadway debut in *Girl Crazy*, 1930; also starred in other Broadway performances including *Annie Get Your Gun*, 1946; *Call Me Madam*, 1950; and *Gypsy*, 1959; performed on KNK radio with her two sisters calling themselves the Stafford Sisters, 1935; formed the Pied Pipers 1938; performed with Tommy Dorsey and his orchestra, 1939; joined the *Johnny Mercer Show*, 1944; signed with Capitol Records 1944; had a series of radio shows 1944-1949; broadcast for Radio Luxembourg (Europe) and Voice of America 1950; *Jo Stafford Show*-CBS-TV 1954;

Awards: Special Tony Award, 1974; New York Drama Critics Awards for *Something for the Boys*; *Annie Get Your Gun;* and *Gypsy*; Tony Award for *Call Me Madam*, Drama Desk Award for *Hello Dolly*; Donaldson Award for *Annie Get Your Gun*.

she saw Merman's act in a night club in White Plains, New York.

After *Girl Crazy*, Merman appeared in George White's *Scandals* with Rudy Vallee, Alice Faye and Ray Bolger. *Scandals* closed after seven months and 202 performances, and the show introduced such notable songs such as "Life is Just a Bowl of Cherries" and "The Thrill is Gone." After *Scandals* Merman became a vaudeville head liner until she returned to Broadway in November of 1932 in the show *Take a Chance.*

Over the span of her career Merman appeared in five of Cole Porter's legendary shows including *Anything Goes* with Victor Moore in November of 1934, *Red Hot and Blue* in October of 1936 with Jimmy Durante and Bob Hope, and *DuBarry was a Lady* in 1939. She also performed in *Panama Hattie* in October of 1940 and referred to herself as "Iron Lungs Merman" and *Something for the Boys* in 1943. Porter once described her as a "brass band going by" and she became dubbed as "The Queen of Broadway." In fact, one of the most uncomfortable times in Porter's life came when he and producers were trying to recruit Merman for one of his new productions. Merman refused to sign a contract until Porter came to her mother's apartment and played and sang his songs for the entire Zimmermann family. He came and eventually performed many of his songs including "You're the Top," "All Through the Night," "Anything Goes," and "I Get a Kick out of You." Afterwards, she signed the contract.

Merman was a kid at heart and in her apartment she collected Raggedy Ann and Andy dolls, which sat in a rocking chair; she even had Raggedy Ann stationery. She also kept a small Christmas tree in the foyer in her home in Queens, and every night she lit its lights because she felt it kept the wonderful spirit of Christmas throughout the year. Merman also volunteered her time every Wednesday at the Roosevelt Hospital in New York because she was very pleased with the care her parents had received there. She worked in the hospital's gift department.

Irving Berlin wrote two of Merman's most memorable plays, *Annie Get Your Gun* and *Call Me Madam. Annie Get Your Gun* opened on Broadway in May of 1946 and ran for 1, 147 performances. The show co-starred Ray Middleton. It was the biggest hit of both Berlin and Merman and received rave reviews by *New York Times* critic Brooks Atkinson citing "her brass band voice, infectious sense of rhythm and her razzle dazzle performance gave her songs a remarkable beat and relish." Berlin had replaced Jerome Kern who had died of a heart attack when he was about to begin work on the play. The play was a huge success and Berlin and his wife, Ellin, celebrated their twentieth anniversary by going on a cruise after receiving a telegram from Merman after the show. It read "Thanks". In 1966, she returned for a brief revival of *Annie Get Your Gun* and although her voice was still powerful and pleasing, critics questioned a 59 year old woman playing a love struck girl.

The second major collaboration between Merman and Berlin was the introduction of his Broadway musical comedy *Call Me Madam*, that opened in October of 1950 and ran for 644 performances. It was a satire based on former United States President Harry S. Truman appointing Washingtonian party giver Perle Mesta to the Ambassadorship to Luxembourg and co-starred Paul Lukas and Russell Nype. Merman let everyone know that she would not accept any changes in her songs less than a week before opening. When Berlin came to her with some changes in one song's lyrics she bluntly turned him down saying "Call me Miss Birds Eye. It's frozen." During the preparation of *Call Me Madam*, Berlin struggled with the second act and overnight he wrote a new song "You're Just in Love" which revitalized the act and became a popular standard. It marked the first time in 36 years that Berlin had introduced a two part number, and at age 62, he was very delighted to have another major hit production.

Her favorite role and perhaps her most important contribution to Broadway musical theater was her role as the ruthless mother of stripper Gypsy Rose, Lee, in *Gypsy*. It opened in May of 1959 and brought Merman out of semi-retirement. *Gypsy* ran for 702 performances and co-starred Jack Klugman with music by Jule Styne and lyrics by Stephen Sondheim. Jerome Robbins the director of *Gypsy* wanted Sondheim to write the music but Merman, who exercised considerable control over the show, felt he was too inexperienced and insisted on Styne instead. She later agreed to let Sondheim write the lyrics. Merman's role as Mama Rose was the last she created and the first she took on tour. The tour lasted from March through December of 1961.

In July 1965, Merman revived *Call Me Madam* in Los Angeles at the Valley Theater, and in 1966, she revived *Annie Get Your Gun* at the New York State Theater, and later brought it back to Broadway. In 1968, she appeared in *Call Me Madam* at the Coconut Grove Playhouse in Miami and, in March of 1970, she took over the lead role of Dolly Levi Gallagher in *Hello Dolly*.

Merman also appeared in fourteen musical films. Her major film credits include *It's a Mad Mad Mad Mad World* in 1963 with Spencer Tracy, Edie Adams and Milton Berle, *The Art of Love* in 1965, *Airplane* in 1980 with Robert Stack and Lloyd Bridges, *We're Not Dressing* and *Kid Millions* in 1934, *Strike Me Pink, Alexander's Ragtime Band* in 1938, *There's No Business Like Show Business* in 1954, *Anything Goes* in 1936 with Bing Crosby, *Call Me Madam* in 1953 with Vera Ellen, Donald O'Connor and George Sanders. "The Best Thing for You," which was performed in *Call Me Madam*, also served as the theme song for Dwight D. Eisenhower's Presidential campaign helping to elect him to the White House. She also appeared in many television productions including a special in 1953 with Broadway star, Mary Martin. In addition she had a regular weekly radio program in New York on Radio Station WABC.

Merman was married and divorced four times including her third marriage to Robert Six, the President of Continental Airlines and her fourth marriage to Academy Award winning actor, Ernest Borgnine, which lasted only thirty eight days. Her first marriage to William Smith lasted three days only, but it was over a year before their Mexican divorce was finalized. She had two children Ethel and Robert Jr. with her second husband Robert D. Levitt.

Merman amassed over 6,000 performances in fourteen Broadway hit shows and Lloyds of London once said she had the highest rating for health and dependability of any actress in the American theater. In her role in *Call me Madam*, which spanned over six years, she never missed a performance. After a career of over fifty years, her final performance was at a Carnegie Hall Benefit Concert in 1982. She died of a heart attack in 1984 in Manhattan ten months after undergoing brain surgery at Roosevelt Hospital; the same facility she had regularly worked as a volunteer. On May 5, 1989, William Cullen Bryant High School renamed its auditorium in honor of its famous alumna and in attendance was her son, Bob. A performance of *Gypsy* followed the ceremony.

Selected discography

The Ethel Merman Collection, Universal.
Victory Collection-The Smithsonian Remembers When America Went to War, RCA.
I Get a Kick Out of You, PAL.
American Legends Series- You're the Top, PRT.
Ethel Merman Collection, RZT.
There's No Business Like Show Business: Ethel Merman Collection, RZT.
Autobiography, Decca.
Songs She Made Famous, Decca.
Memories, Decca.
On Stage, VIK.
Gypsy, Columbia.
Call Me Madam, MCA.
Annie Get Your Gun, Decca.

Sources

Books

Barrett, Mary Ellin, *Irving Berlin, A Daughters' Memoir*, Simon & Schuster 1994.
Bering, Rudiger, *Musicals*, Barron's Educational Series Inc., 1998.
Frommer, Myrna Katz and Harvey Frommer, *It Happened on Broadway,* Harcourt Brace & Co., 1998.
Gammond, Peter, *The Oxford Companion to Popular* Music, Oxford Univ. Press 1993.

Green, Stanley, *Broadway Musicals, Show by Show*, Hal Leonard Corp., 1996.

Maltin, Leonard, *Movie and Video Guide 1995,* Penguin Books Ltd., 1994.

Merman, Ethel, *Merman An Autobiography*, Simon and Schuster 1978.

Morley, Sheridan, *The Great Stage Stars*, Facts File Publications 1986.

Osborne, Jerry, *Rockin Records,* Osborne Publications 1999.

Stambler, Irwin, *Encyclopedia of Popular Music*, St. Martin's Press, 1966.

Young, William C., *Famous Actors and Actresses of the American Stage*-R. R. Bowker Co. New York and London, 1978.

Periodicals

Los Angeles Times, February 16, 1984

New York Times, November 22, 1934; February 16, 1984

Online

"Ethel Merman," *A&E Biography*, www.biography.com, (August 1999).

Additional information provided by Will Friedwald in the liner notes of *The Ethel Merman Collection* and a Jo Stafford interview in November of 1998.

—Francis D. McKinley

Moby

Musician, performer, producer

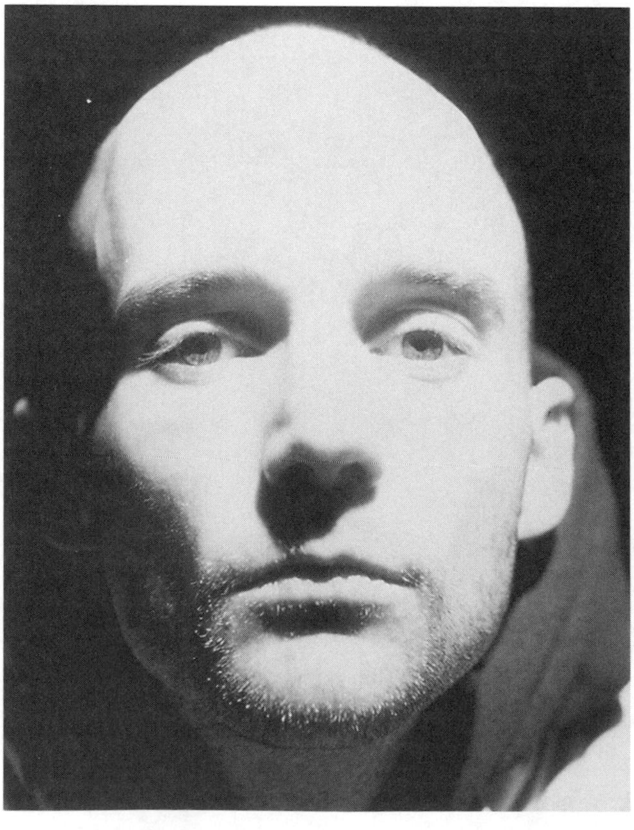

Photograph by Tibor Bozi. Corbis-Bettmann. Reproduced by permission. ©

Moby is perhaps the most well-known name in the subculture of music and style known as techno. This fast-paced electronic dance music is mainly heard at nightclubs, parties, and especially "raves," generally described as giant, marathon dance parties. While raves are notorious for rampant drug use, Moby is substance-free and Christian, although he admits a weakness for chasing members of the opposite sex. He steers clear of alcohol, drugs, and tobacco, and is also a vegan, someone who does not consume any meat or animal products, including dairy or eggs. Despite the contradictions inherent between this lifestyle and that of hedonistic ravers, Moby is arguably the leader of the techno genre, though he did take a detour in 1997 with a heavy metal album, *Animal Rights.* But in 1999 he went back to his roots with *Play,* which once again showcased techno, though it was an eclectic melange that reached beyond sheer dance music.

Moby was born Richard Melville Hall on September 11, 1965, in New York City and raised in the suburb of Darien, Connecticut. His singular nickname, which he has had since he was a baby, is based on the novel *Moby Dick,* written by his great-great-great uncle, Herman Melville. Moby's father, chemistry professor James Melville, died in a car accident after driving drunk when his son was two. His mother, Elizabeth, who became a doctor's aide, then worked as a secretary by day and played keyboards in a band at night. Moby lived during the week at the spacious home of his well-to-do grandparents, who belonged to the country club and played golf, but spent weekends with his unconventional mother at her apartment. His grandparents also taught Sunday school, but Moby's childhood was not particularly religious. He told Chris Norris in *New York* that he was raised "sort of Presbyterian."

Discovering music and drugs at a young age, Moby played the guitar in elementary school and was smoking pot and listening to Led Zeppelin at around age ten. His tastes switched to the Clash and Sex Pistols by age 14, and at that stage, he quit using drugs and alcohol and began a "straight-edged" hardcore punk band, so called because the members were devoted to staying straight, or sober. The Vatican Commandos, as they were called, performed at high-profile Manhattan punk clubs like CBGBs and Great Gildersleeves. However, when he went off to the University of Connecticut, he fell into drinking again, attending parties and playing in bands in addition to studying religion and philosophy. Some of his other musical collaborations included the Pork Guys, Shopwell, and Peanuts.

In college, Moby began spinning records at the campus radio station, most of it "New Wave alternative stuff of

For the Record . . .

Born Richard Melville Hall, September 11, 1965, in New York, NY. *Education:* Attended University of Connecticut.

Club deejay, c. late 1980s-early 1990s; began releasing singles on Instinct, 1989; signed with Elektra Records and released EP, *Move,* 1993; released debut album, *Everything Is Wrong,* 1995. Also creator of music for film soundtracks. Has done remixes for artists such as Aerosmith, Brian Eno, Michael Jackson, Metallica, Red Hot Chili Peppers, Smashing Pumpkins, and Soundgarden; has produced for Ozzy Osbourne. Toured with Lollapalooza festival, 1993.

Addresses: *Home*—New York City. *Office*—c/o Elektra Records, 75 Rockefeller Plaza, New York, NY 10019; 345 North Maple Dr., Ste. 123, Beverly Hills, CA 90210.

early '80s—New Order, Big Country and the Clash," he told Roger Catlin of the Minneapolis *Star Tribune.* He dropped out after just eight months and began hanging out in clubs in New York City, where he learned to love dance music. "I just realized how powerful and celebratory dance music was," he recalled to Norris. "I love that real anthemic quality. Just big piano breaks, screaming diva vocals, and real high energy." He began working as a DJ for a club in Port Chester, New York, and then moved to venues in New York City, including the club Mars. By 1987, under a variety of stage names like Voodoo Child, Barracuda, and Mindstorm,Moby was spinning for big names like Cher, Run-D.M.C., and Big Daddy Kane and started recording his own club mixes on the Instinct label in 1989.

In the meantime, just about the time Moby left college, he became a born-again Christian. Though he does not belong to any specific church and has been known to sharply criticize religious conservatives, he is open about the fact that he lives his life trying to live by the principles taught by Jesus Christ. He does admit that he has trouble at times, especially when it comes to resisting sex, as well as in his efforts to be humble, unselfish, and nonjudgmental, but says that he puts in a sincere effort. "I try to live up to his teachings but fail all the time," he told Lorraine Ali in *Rolling Stone.* In addition to living according to Christian principles, which includes reciting the Lord's Prayer daily, Moby is a vegan, meaning he consumes no animal products, and he does not drink alcohol, smoke cigarettes, or bleach his clothes (citing that bleach harms the water supply).

When Moby remixed the theme song from the popular David Lynch television series *Twin Peaks* with a thumping beat to create the track "Go," he became a major name not only among the ranks of deejays but also on the charts. The song reached the top ten in Britain in 1991, and Moby continued to churn out club singles for Instinct, like subsequent hits "Next Is the E" and "Thousand." He also compiled a number of singles on *Moby,* 1992, and experimented with a minimalist sound on *Ambient,* 1993. Also in 1993, Moby signed a five-record deal with Elektra and released the EP *Move,* appealing to many fans who were not previously fond of dance music.

Right after the release of *Move,* Moby toured with the Lollapalooza festival concert headlined by the Red Hot Chili Peppers. He fit in with the rollicking tour, because unlike some deejays who somberly stand at the turntables, Moby's stage antics are bombastic. This exposure helped reveal Moby to a much more mainstream audience and made him virtually the only techno deejay at the time known outside the clubs to a widespread audience. The next year, 1994, Neil Strauss wrote in *Rolling Stone,* "A year ago, the name Moby and the word *techno* were practically synonymous." However, Strauss went on to say that some techno fans began to think of Moby as a "traitor," due to his lifestyle, not to mention the fact that he had worked on a remix for pop star Michael Jackson.

In 1995, Moby released his debut album, *Everything Is Wrong,* deriving the title from his philosophy of the world. "I think 500 years from now, people are going to wonder what was going on now," Moby related to Strauss. "They'll see this race of people that smoked cigarettes and drove cars and fought wars and persecuted people for their beliefs and sexual orientation, and none of it accomplished anything.... Everything is absolutely 100 percent wrong, and how do we change it is the question." For the album's liner notes, Moby wrote two essays about what he believes is wrong with the world and ticked off 67 statistics concerning topics such as the plight of the rain forests and the destruction of trees to make disposable diapers.

Everything Is Wrong cut across several musical genres, from jazz to classical piano to hard rock to disco grooves, but as Ali noted in *Rolling Stone,* "Amazingly, these transitions aren't jerky or abrupt; rather, the music evolves naturally from one style to the next." The album soon became a critical favorite but some techno purists rejected it as a "sell-out." He explained that the changecame because he moved in a different direction from the rest of the dance community. "Lately I've been bored to death with techno," he remarked to Ali. "It all sounds the same to me." He also noted to Catlin in the *Star Tribune,* "In the rave community,... the enthusiasm is more for the drugs and the clothes than for the celebratory aspects of it. It just seems very unhealthy."

Moby's discontent with dance music came to a head with *Animal Rights,* 1997, in which he gave up his synth sound in favor of a hard rock style. Much of the content revealed his early punk influences and featured his screaming voice and wailing guitar riffs. This effort was not warmly received, but did not slow down his career. In the meantime, Moby was busy working on other artists' projects, remixing "1979" for Smashing Pumpkins, "Falling in Love (Is Hard on the Knees)" for Aerosmith, "Until It Sleeps" for Metallica, and "Dusty" for Soundgarden; he also produced "Walk on Water" for Ozzy Osbourne. In addressing the fact that his religious beliefs seem to run counter to the kind of company he keeps, Moby explained in a *New York* interview, "Well, if *I* were Satan, I wouldn't spend my time with guys who wear black leather and listen to metal. I would spend my time with *CEOs!"*

Subsequently, Moby began getting calls to mix music for film soundtracks. In 1997, he came out with the album *I Like to Score,* a collection of 12 pieces that he originally created for movies and television (thus the title, a pun on the word "score," which refers to making music for such media). It included an energetic re-mix of the "James Bond Theme," as well as his early hit "Go" in addition to "First Cool Hive" from the horror flick *Scream* and a cover of Joy Division's "New Dawn Fades" from the film *Heat.* After this, he began to indicate that he was regaining his enthusiasm for techno. "Overall, the scene feels healthier to me, and I certainly like the music more than I did two or three years ago," Moby noted to Michael Mehle in the *Rocky Mountain News.*

In the summer of 1999, Moby issued *Play,* an effort that harkened back to his techno roots while displaying an even more fervent eclecticism that intrigued and delighted many critics. In addition to the drum machines and hip-hop beats, much of the structure is developed from old blues and gospel music. Moby sampled, or excerpted, a 1943 version of the gospel classic "Run On for a Long Time," featuring slide guitar and a haunting piano. He also used samples from Alan Lomax's field recordings of African American folk music from the early twentieth century, not to mention the Bessie Jones blues tune "Honey."

Play seemed to indicate a shift from Moby's earlier works in that it did not contain any overt references to his thoughts on subjects like the environment, politics, veganism, and the like. He commented to David Proffitt in the *Arizona Republic,* "With *Play,* I wanted to make a record that was very personal but also that people could bring into their lives and fall in love with." He also remarked to Vickie Gilmer of the Minneapolis *Star Tribune,* "The songs I used are human and there's this quality of striving to them. They're beautiful songs, and the lyrics are interesting. But it's me singing, too." He noted that it was a pet peeve of his that people think his electronic music consists solely of samples.

Moby, who is five feet, eight inches tall and sports a shaved head, lives in Manhattan's East Village where he keeps a stash of equipment including keyboards, mixers, samplers, recordingequipment, and more. Keeping with his conviction about not harming living creatures, Moby refuses to even kill cockroaches or mosquitoes, living with a bevy of bugs in his studio.

Selected discography

"Mobility," Instinct, 1990.
"Go," Instinct, 1991.
"Voodoo Child," Instinct, 1991.
(Contributor) *Instinct Dance: A Collection of Dance Music from Instinct Records,* 1991.
Moby, Instinct, 1992.
The Story So Far, 1993.
Ambient, Instinct, 1993.
Early Underground, Instinct, 1993.
Move (EP), Elektra, 1994.
Everything Is Wrong, Elektra, 1994.
Rare: The Collected B-Sides 1989-1993, Instinct, 1996.
Animal Rights, Elektra, 1997.
I Like to Score, Elektra, 1997.
Play, Elektra, 1999.

Sources

Books

Contemporary Musicians, volume 17, Gale Research, 1996.

Periodicals

Arizona Republic, August 12, 1999, p. 32.
Entertainment Weekly, February 21, 1997, p. 125.
Interview, March 1996, p. 92.
Newsday, May 25, 1995, p. B9.
Newsweek, June 14, 1999, p. 69.
New York, March 27, 1995, p. 48; March 17, 1997, p. 48.
New York Times, July 31, 1999, p. B17.

People, November 1, 1993, p. 82; March 10, 1997, p. 24; August 23, 1999, p. 45.

Rocky Mountain News, November 23, 1997, p. 18D.

Rolling Stone, November 17, 1994, p. 102; March 23, 1995, p. 125; May 4, 1995, p. 58; October 30, 1997, p. 68; June 24, 1999, p. 64.

St. Louis Post-Dispatch, September 6, 1999, p. E2.

Star Tribune (Minneapolis, MN), June 4, 1995, p. 3F; August 20, 1999, p. 3E.

Time, August 17, 1992, p. 60.

Online

Moby web page, Elektra Records web site, http://www.elektra.com/ambient_club/moby (October 19, 1999).

"Moby," *Rolling Stone* web site, http://rollingstone.tunes.com (October 24, 1999).

—Geri Speace

Mogwai

Instrumental rock band

For a band with a repertoire of songs largely without words, Mogwai has never found difficulty expressing a profound musical statement. Formed in the outskirts of Glasgow, Scotland, by a group of friends barely in their twenties, Mogwai quickly became one of the most inspiring bands on the independent music scene. As Steve Malkmus of the successful band Pavement predicted in a 1997 interview for *Melody Maker,* "Mogwai—they're gonna rock the world! Creedence were the best band of the Sixties, The Groundhogs the best band of the Seventies, Butthole Surfers the best of the Eighties, The Incredible String Band the best over the three decades. Mogwai will be the best band of the 21st century."

Mogwai formed when guitarist, keyboardist, and percussionist Stuart Braithwaite, bassist and guitarist Dominic Aitchison, and drummer Martin Bulloch met through common friends and quit their various bands on the fringes of the Glasgow indie rock scene. All hailing from various satellite towns around Glasgow and raised on a range of music from the Cure, Joy Division, and Jesus and Mary Chain to the Pixies, Slint, Celtic FC, and My Bloody Valentine, the young men initially set out to attend college, but found learning chord changes preferable to studying. "I first met Stuart at a Ned's Atomic Dustbin gig," recalled Aitchison to Fred Mills of *Magnet,* "and my best pal was there with Stuart's pal, who came up to me and said, 'All right, you're a bass player, meet Stuart, he's a great guitarist.' So one night both our bands were playing the same venue and we just hit it off. One day, we decided to form a band."

Following in the paths of other successful independent Scottish bands—such as Urusei Yatsura, Bis, Delgados, Belle and Sebastian, and Arab Strap—Mogwai arrived just in time to capitalize on the excitement. By mid-1995, Mogwai started rehearsing and landed their first gig in the fall of that year. Desiring to craft serious guitar music, the group recruited a second guitarist, John Cummings, who helped Mogwai fulfill their purpose. The resulting Mogwai sound, according to Mills, revealed itself as "a shotgun wedding of My Bloody Valentine vertigo, Sonic Youth overdrive and Spacemen 3 drone."

In 1996, the band scraped together enough money to record their first single, "Tuner," which caught the attention of a host of independent labels. Over the next 18 months, Mogwai released a succession of original songs on some of the most hip indie labels around at the time, including Wurlitzer Jukebox, Love Train and Ché. The New York-based Jetset label later released the singles in the United States on a collective LP entitled *Ten Rapid* in April of 1997.

Gained Esteem

Subsequently, the British press showered the group with accolades, repeatedly naming each succeeding new song "single of the week." Along with such critical acclaim came an increasing tendency for excess. At the London nightclub Garage in May of 1997, for example, Mogwai—driven by alcohol and the opening performance of Arab Strap (one of Braithwaite'sfavorite bands)invited the audience to dismantle their equipment. Despite the—group's propensity for overrunning a stage, Mogwai were also known to care deeply about their music, as well as for their good humor, intelligence, and despair at the average grade of music pushed by the music industry during the mid to late 1990s. Adopting a "we've-been-lucky" attitude in regards to the favorable media coverage, Mogwai also realized that the press could turn on them at any given moment. "One reviewer of a live gig said we were just going 'wank, wank, wank' and that we should all be tortured horribly and deserved to die in a really painful manner," Aitchison noted to Mills. "Another one recently said that we were 'soulless.' And we get the term 'heavy metal' a lot, too. When we play live, we play loud—and we've toned down a lot lately, anyway—but we could never be metal if we tried."

Nonetheless, most reviewers and underground music fans felt otherwise. And while Mogwai's reputation continued to spread throughout the U.K., the group gained an

For the Record . . .

Members include **Dominic Aitchison** (born near Glasgow, Scotland), bass, guitar; **Stuart Braithwaite** (born near Glasgow, Scotland), guitars, keyboards, percussion; **Martin Bulloch** (born near Glasgow, Scotland), drums; **Barry Burns** (born near Glasgow, Scotland; joined band late 1998; former music teacher), flute, oboe, guitar, keyboards; **John Cummings** (born c. 1979 near Glasgow, Scotland), guitars, piano; **Brendan O'Hare** (born c. 1970; joined band in May of 1997; left band fall of 1997), drums.

Formed band, landed first gig, 1995; released first single, "Tuner," 1996; released collective EP, *Ten Rapid,* followed by full-length debut, *Mogwai Young Team,* and performed in U.S. for first time, 1997; toured extensively throughout Europe, U.K., and U.S. East Coast, 1998; released second album, *Come On Die Young,* 1999.

Addresses: *Home*—Glasgow, Scotland. *Record company*—Matador Records, 625 Broadway, New York, NY 10012, (212) 995-5882, fax (212)995-5883. *Website*—Matador Records, http://www.matador.recs.com.

audience in the U.S. as well, thanks to college radio airplay and steady sales of *Ten Rapid.* In the summer of 1997, Mogwai performed before American audiences for the first time as the opening act for the high-profile band Pavement. Soon thereafter, the group signed with the influential, Glasgow-based Chemikal Underground label, and then with Jetset in the U.S. With the record deals complete, the group started work on their debut album, *Mogwai Young Team.*

In the meantime, Mogwai enlisted a fifth member and second drummer, Brendan O'Hare (former member of Teenage Fanclub and Telstar Ponies), whom they met when his group Macrocosmica opened for a Mogwai show. The group also adopted pseudonyms for their upcoming release; Cummings took the nickname Captain Meat after his obsession for eating chops, Bulloch adopted the alias Bionic because of his artificial pacemaker, Aitchison chose the name Demonic after his childhood nightmares about Lucifer (Satan), Braithwaite was dubbed Plasmatron, and O'Hare, the oldest of the bunch, became The Relic.

By the time *Mogwai Young Team* was released in October of 1997, the group had booted O'Hare from the lineup, allegedly for not keeping quiet during an Arab Strap performance. Although Mogwai repeatedly refused to go into further detail regarding O'Hare's departure, Aitchison later reported, according to *Select* magazine, "Recording that album, there were a lot of sketches [arguments] going on." Critics hypothesized that O'Hare's age—he was around 27 at the time, while the other members were just above or below 21—and his outside pursuits with Macrocosmica and his solo project Fiend, made him unable to fit in and feel totally committed to Mogwai.

Debut Album Solidified Reputation

The remaining members witnessed the enormous success of *Mogwai Young Team,* and reviewers praised the effort as evidence of the group's rapid maturity. Sharon O'Connell of *Melody Maker* wrote, "*Mogwai Young Team* is blessedly audacious—a mad risk taken by reckless noise-monsters, a fleet-footed, sure-handed miracle in an age that's become too safe by half. Buckle in and prepare for bliss." And John Mulvey of *New Musical Express* agreed, declaring *Mogwai Young Team* "a phenomenal piece of work." The reviewer further added, "It is shamelessly avant-garde, but shows the avant-garde can match 'straight' music for both heart-stopping melodies and adrenalised rock 'n' roll ferocity. It is largely instrumental, but proves—as if it really needed proving—that instrumental music can express a generous sweep of emotions every bit as eloquently as lyrics."

The album included tracks that held to Mogwai's signature soft-to-loud musical scheme, exemplified in songs such as "Like Herod" (originally titled "Slint"). But Mogwai also desired to show they were willing to try new dynamics, and as a result, the group projected a sense of tranquility and expanded instrumentation (including the glockenspiel and string section) into the arrangement. One noteworthy track, the graceful "R U Still In 2 It," illustrated such expansiveness and featured Arab Strap's Aiden Moffat as guest vocalist. As of late 1999, *Mogwai Young Team* sold over 35,000 units in the group's native U.K. and reached number two on American college charts.

In 1998, Mogwai toured extensively for six months throughout Europe and the U.K. before landing in the U.S. for an East Coast excursion with the Manic Street Preachers. With little time to work on a new full-length album, Mogwai opted to focus on remixes of prior work. First, the group recorded a version of David Holmes's "Don't Die Just Yet." Holmes reportedly liked Mogwai's harder approach to the song so well that he christened his new Belfast, Ireland, bar "Mogwai." Next, the band turned to reworking their own songs with the LP *Kicking A Dead Pig* and an EP entitled *Mogwai Fear Satan Remixes,* both released in 1998 on Eye-Q, a dance-oriented label, and Jetset respectively. For these projects, Mogwai assembled a cast of well known producers/ engineers that included Kevin Shields, Third Eye Foundation, DJ Q, Arab Strap, Atari Teenage Riot's Alec Empire, and u-ziq.

Eventually, Jetset issued the two works together as *Kicking A Dead Pig + Mogwai Fear Satan Remixes.* "Per usual, Mogwai's two-CD set pits understated guitar figures against peals of noise," concluded Will Hermes in *Entertainment Weekly,* giving the release a grade of A- overall. "u-ziq and Alex [spelled Alec] Empire get beat crazy, but the idea is rock mutation, not murder. When it works, it's visionary stuff." Likewise, Braithwaite himself approved of the final product, concluding that the remixes "worked really well," as he stated to Mills. "A lot of the stuff is totally different to the original, and that's what we wanted to do. We didn't want to just add hip-hop beats or something."

1998 also witnessed Mogwai putting their musical influence to political use. When the Glasgow City Council implemented a nightfall curfew for school-aged children, Mogwai lashed out against the legislation by joining forces with the Scottish Human Rights Project, printing and distributing thousands of "Fuck The Curfew" stickers, and releasing the *No Education = No Future (F--- The Curfew)* EP. Upholding the campaign of the Human Rights Project, Mogwai believed improving education and providing amenities for children were the true solutions to curbing the rising crime rate among the youth of Glasgow.

Geared Up for Follow-up Release

Returning to more artistic pursuits toward the end of 1998, Mogwai decided to expand their instrumentation by hiring another musician, Barry Burns, a talented flutist, guitarist, and keyboardist. The band also signed with a more established record company in the U.S., Matador Records, a label that also supported the likes of Arab Strap and Belle and Sebastian. Although Mogwai remained with Chemikal Underground in the U.K., Matador and the group planned to record a second full-length album on American soil with producer David Fridmann, a former member of Mercury Rev who also produced albums with the Flaming Lips.

For previous Mogwai singles, EPs, and the first album, the group recorded at MCM studios with Chemikal Underground producer Paul Savage. "We knew all the people there and it was really handy, but we didn't want to stay in Glasgow this time," Bulloch explained to Mills. "We wanted to go to the country and take up residence someplace where we could be there all the time with no distractions. The Delgados suggested Fridmann, and Chemikal Underground arranged it all."

The quintet packed their gear and retreated to Fridmann's backwoods Tarbox Road Studios, located in Cassadaga, New York, about 50 miles from Buffalo and 500 miles from New York City. They spent three weeks during the winter in the remote town populated mostly by deer, trees, and over-zealous hunters. "I was out shopping and I saw this red light pin-pointed on my head," recalled Bulloch for an interview with *Select.* "It was a viewfinder from a gun. The hunter came up and said, 'Sorry son, I thought you were a deer.' Jesus Christ."

Despite such obstacles and close calls, Mogwai emerged from the forest with a second astonishing album, *Come On Die Young,* released in April of 1999 by Matador in the U.S. Substituting loudness for further depth and composition, Mogwai's follow-up release contained tracks such as "Christmas Steps," revealing just one guitar/bass overture, as well as "Ex-Cowboy," ending with a single orchestral swell. Expected to further enhance the band's reputation, *Come On Die Young* earned eminent critical attention. "The album is as elegant and expansive as any concept piece from 25 years prior, but it's forward-looking enough to signify the arrival of a major, unique player," wrote Mills. "At times it sounds resolute, if slightly lachrymose (the yearning ballad 'Cody'), stately and dignified ('Helps both ways' is a slow ballet marked by newcomer Burns' oboe), and even enticingly ambient (the minimalist piano and deep mix effects swirling throughout 'Chocky')."

Selected discography

Singles

"Tuner," Rock Action, 1996.
"Summer," Love Train, 1996.

EPs

4 Satan, Jetset, 1998.
Mogwai Fear Satan Remixes, Eye-Q, 1998.
No Education = No Future (F--- The Curfew), Chemikal Underground, 1998.

Albums

*New Paths to Helicon,*Wurlitzer Jukebox, 1997.
Mogwai Young Team, Jetset, 1997.

Ten Rapid (Collected Recordings 1996-1997), Jetset, 1997.
Fear Satan Remixes, 1998.
Kicking A Dead Pig, Eye-Q, 1998.
Kicking A Dead Pig + Mogwai Fear Satan Remixes, Jetset, 1998.
Come On Die Young, Matador, 1999.

Sources

Periodicals

Alternative Press, January 1998; October 1998.
Entertainment Weekly, July 10, 1998.
Guardian, October 31, 1997.
Magnet, June/July 1999, pp. 45-47, 92.
Melody Maker, May 17, 1997; November 1, 1997
New Musical Express, October 25, 1997; June 20, 1998; February 6, 1999.
New York Press, March 10-16, 1999.
Q, December 1997.
Rolling Stone, September 3, 1998.
Select, December 1997; April, 1998; March 1999.
Times (London), October 25-31, 1997.

Online

Mogwai discography, http://www.chemikal.demon.co.uk/bands/mogwai_discography.html (November 4, 1999).

Additional information provided by Matador Records.

—Laura Hightower

Randy Newman

Singer, songwriter, piano

Henry Diltz/Corbis. Reproduced by permission. ©

Grammy award-winning musician Randy Newman attained prominence by using humor, irony, and cynicism to draw attention to society's ills, such as prejudice, materialism, and racism, in addition to the absurdities and ironies of life. For example, he took on the personae of apartheid-supporting South Africans with "Christmas in Capetown," insecure homophobics in "Half a Man," and Southern bigots in "Rednecks." Newman, who thrives on misinterpretation, set his sometimes misunderstood lyrics to music ranging from rock and roll, folk, pop, ragtime, blues, and soul to lounge piano, orchestra, and big band. Most people remember him for his sole top 40 hit in 1977, "Short People," a song which also angered many small listeners who did not realize his aim was to attack prejudice in general. As he stated in an interview with Scott Benarde in the *Baltimore Jewish Times,* "If I died tomorrow, my tombstone would say, 'Composer of "Short People" and others.' That's the way it is.... 'Short People' was the worst hit I could have. I had the worst tour when it was out. No one came—and I got death threats." Other recognized songs brought to life by Newman include "I Love L.A.," "I Love to See You Smile," "You Can Leave Your Hat On" (a song that angered many women's groups), and Three Dog Night's hit single "Mama Told Me Not to Come." And recording artists like Barbra Streisand, Peggy Lee, Dusty Springfield, Manfred Mann, Eric Burden, and Ringo Starr all called upon Newman for material.

However, Newman's accomplishments extend beyond his own recordings of sarcastic, witty songs and his compositions for legendary musicians. He also composed numerous songs for movie soundtracks, including *Awakenings, Forrest Gump,* and the animated film *Toy Story,* and wrote a musical called *Faust* in 1995. In all, Newman has earned 12 Academy Award nominations, but he has never taken home the prize. Although he focused much of his energy on composing music for Hollywood films during the 1980s until the mid-1990s, Newman returned to his solo work in 1999, releasing his first album of new songs since 1988's *Land of Dreams.* In addition to the release of his most recent record, *Bad Love* in 1999, Newman also received an astonishing three nominations for composing film scores for *Babe: Pig in the City, A Bug's Life,* and *Pleasantville* (all released in 1998), but again went home empty handed.

Newman was born in New Orleans, Louisiana, on November 28, 1943. His father, Irving, was a physician who practiced internal medicine and a veteran of World War II, while his mother, Adele, stayed at home to care for Newman and his younger brother Alan, who also pursued a career in medicine. Newman's interest in music formed at an early age, and several members of his family were already respected professionals within the recording

For the Record . . .

Born November 28, 1943, in New Orleans, LA; son of Irving Newman (a physician) and Adele Newman (a homemaker); younger brother, Alan, a physician; married first wife, Roswitha, 1966; (divorced 1989); married second wife, Gretchen, c. 1992; children (from first marriage): Amos, born 1968; Eric, born 1971; John, born 1978. *Education*: Studied music composition at University of California at Los Angeles (UCLA).

Worked in music publishing and wrote own music; released debut album *Randy Newman*, 1968; continued to release solo recordings throughout the 1970s, including *Sail Away*, 1972; *Good Old Boys*, 1974; *Little Criminals*, 1977; and *Born Again*, 1979; focused on movie soundtracks for much of the 1980s with scores such as *The Natural*, 1984, and *Parenthood*, 1989; released acclaimed solo album *Land of Dreams*, 1988; nominated for three Academy Awards at the same time for film scores for *Babe: Pig in the City, A Bug's Life*, and *Pleasantville*, 1998; released first solo project since *Land of Dreams* entitled *Bad Love*, 1999.

Addresses: *Home*—Pacific Palisades, CA. *Record company*—DreamWorks, 9268 W. Third St., Beverly Hills, CA 90210.

business and Hollywood film industry. Alfred Newman, one of his uncles, received 45 Academy Award nominations and won nine during his career, scoring such films as *How Green Was My Valley, The Robe,* and *The Grapes of Wrath,* in addition to heading the music department at 20th Century Fox. When Alfred retired from his post at the film studio, Newman's other uncle (Alfred's brother), Lionel, succeeded him. Another uncle and brother to Alfred and Lionel, Emil, penned music for dozens of films during his lifetime as well. Later, two of Newman's cousins found success writing in Hollywood; David scored *The War of the Roses* and *I Love Trouble,* while Thomas worked onthe films *Desperately Seeking Susan* and *The Shawshank Redemption.* "I was about four or five when I had my first memories of my uncles. Uncle Alfred did *All About Eve* in 1951, and I remember that. I remember *The Gunfighter, Yellow Sky* and I was on stage for *The Robe* when I was a little boy," Newman recalled to Brett Anwar in the *Sunday Telegraph.* "I can remember having to be very quiet while he conducted the big orchestra on the soundstage. I realized it was something to do with what I wanted to do, and I was lucky because it was such a great orchestra, and I had the sound in my ear very early. Live, it's a very impressive thing to hear."

Although Newman considered himself fortunate to have been exposed to such experiences as a child, his early life included it's share of difficulties as well. During the time his family lived in Louisiana, he often felt isolated by his Jewish heritage, although his parents never actively practiced the spiritual aspect of the religion (his father, as well as Newman himself, defined themselves as atheists). Moreover, Newman suffered problems with his eyes and vision from the time of his birth. "It was tough for him having the problem with bad eyes," longtime friend and frequent producer Lenny Waronker told Susan Toepfer in *People.* "It wasn't just that he had to wear glasses, he also had to have surgery." Beginning at age five, Newman underwent four operations to correct his severely crossed eyes. Newman, who felt shunned by other children and frequently endured teasing by peers, recalled to Toepfer, "School was painful. It was not the best time of my life, like they said it was going to be. ... I've had a low opinion of myself since childhood. I'm hard on myself." Later, Newman, ordinarily contemptuous of personal revelation in music, would document these emotional hardships on his 1988 release *Land of Dreams* in songs like "Dixie Flyer," "New Orleans Wins the War," and "Four Eyes."

Around 1948, when Newman was about five years old, his father returned to New Orleans after serving in World War II and moved the family to Los Angeles, California, where Newman spent the remainder of his childhood. After studying music composition at the University of California at Los Angeles (UCLA), he worked in music publishing for awhile before turning to writing his own lyrics and composing at the piano. In 1968, he released his self-titled debut album. Though critics in general complained about Newman's overworked orchestrations, the record contained the notable songs "Davy the Fat Boy" and "I Think It's Going to Rain Today."

Throughout the 1970s, Newman enjoyed a prolific and critically successful solo career, releasing acclaimed records such as the sardonic *Sail Away,* where Newman plays a huckster enticing slaves to America in the album's title track and advocates dropping the atomic bomb in "Political Science;" as well as *Good Old Boys,* a concept album about the South that celebrates redneck ignorance. During the 1980s, at the same time he started focusing more on film scores, Newman managed to record two more noteworthy albums.

In 1995, Newman took another direction in his career by writing his first musical called *Faust,* a twisted adaptation of Wolfgang von Goethe's classic epic drama set in South Bend, Indiana. In Newman's adaptation, God, a corporate CEO who carries a PowerBook, and Lucifer, a cynic, battle for the soul of Henry Faust, a college student in his third year as a freshman at Notre Dame. "I wanted to try one [a musical], just to see if I could do it," he told Michelle Green and Lorenzo Benet in an interview with *People* magazine. "I did a couple of songs and an embryonic version of the book and put it aside until 1993 to earn a living." Audiences and critics alikeagreed that Newman could indeed write a musical. The companion album to the work featured a cast of well-known musicians, including James Taylor and Elton John.

After this, Newman went back to scoring for Hollywood and also wrote material for a new album. In the meantime, the songwriter released *Guilty: 30 Years of Randy Newman,* an album which spans his entire career and includes hits he wrote for other musicians, such as "Mama Told Me Not to Come" and "You Can Leave Your Hat On," as well as music he previously recorded himself, such as "Short People" and "I Love L.A." With his next solo release, 1999's *Bad Love,* Newman explored the peculiarities of living in the 1990s with his trademark New Orleans piano sound and included both love tunes and biting commentaries. "On the magnificently dispiriting *Bad Love,*" wrote Rob Tannenbaum in *Rolling Stone,* "the fifty-five-year-old pianist reprises his blend of rock bluster, blues shuffles and classic dissonance, and introduces a vivid new batch of fools: rich older men who beg for younger girls' notice or nap blankly in the shade of a big-screen TV; chronic liars; hurtful exes; uncomprehending couples; and, in 'I'm Dead (But I Don't Know It),' rock stars who tour long past their expiration date." The record, concluded critics, was sure to become another Newman classic.

Newman lived with his parents until he married at age 23, to a German-born woman, Roswitha. They had three sons together: Amos, born in 1968, Eric, born in 1971, and John, born in 1978. The couple separated in 1985 and divorced in 1989. The news that the marriage ended surprised many, because Newman always credited his first wife with keeping him on the right creative path throughout his productive career. Nevertheless, Newman and Roswitha remained close friends. Roswitha remarried in 1992, and Newman later married a second time to Gretchen.

Newman's father died of cancer in 1990, just 18 months after his mother passed away. Throughout his life, Newman always struggled for his father's approval. "We were close, but there was a contentiousness in our relationship," he confided to Green and Benet. Sometime in 1985, doctors diagnosed Newman with an illness known as Epstein-Barr, a virus that leaves victims depressed and fatigued. But with changes in his diet and rest, the musician gradually gained control of his condition. Following the release of *Bad Love* and a 14-date tour in the fall of 1999, Newman planned to work on the soundtrack for the sequel to *Toy Story.* "I love an orchestra," Newman explained to Marc Shulgood of the *Denver Rocky Mountain News.* "That's the reason I got into film scores. Plus, I respond well to specific assignments, to solving technical problems that come up all the time." Nonetheless, Newman regards himself as a songwriter first and foremost and intended not to let so much time pass before producing another solo record. "I hope never to go very long again [between albums]," Newman said to Jane Stevenson of the *Toronto Sun.* "Unless I think I'm really not as good and then I'll quit, which is possible."

Selected discography

Albums

Randy Newman, Reprise, 1968.
12 Songs, Reprise, 1970.
Randy Newman Live, Reprise, 1971.
Sail Away, Reprise, 1972.
Good Old Boys, Reprise, 1974.
Little Criminals, Warner Brothers, 1977.
Born Again, Warner Brothers, 1979.
Trouble in Paradise, Warner Brothers, 1983.
Lonely at the Top, WEA International, 1987.
Land of Dreams, Reprise, 1988.
Faust, Reprise, 1995.
Guilty: 30 Years of Randy Newman, Warner Brothers, 1998.
Bad Love, DreamWorks, 1999.

Soundtracks

The Natural, Warner Brothers, 1984.
Down and Out in Beverly Hills, MCA, 1986.
Major League, Curb, 1989.
Parenthood, Reprise, 1989.
Avalon, Reprise, 1990.
Awakenings, Reprise, 1990.
Blaze, A&M, 1990.
Forrest Gump, Epic, 1994.
Maverick, Atlantic, 1994.
Walt Disney's Toy Story, Disney, 1995.
Walt Disney Pictures Presents James and the Giant Peach, Disney, 1996.
Babe: Pig in the City, 1998.
A Bug's Life, Disney, 1998.
Pleasantville, 1998.

Sources

Books

musicHound Rock: The Essential Album Guide, Visible Ink Press, 1999.

Periodicals

Atlanta Constitution, May 5, 1999, p. F9.
Baltimore Jewish Times, November 13, 1998, p. 51.
Denver Rocky Mountain News, September 12, 1997, p. 20D.
People, December 5, 1988, p. 71; October 30, 1995, p.79.
Rolling Stone, July 8-22, 1999; August 19, 1999.
Sunday Telegraph, February 7, 1999, p. 10.
Time, October 2, 1995, p. 81.
Toronto Sun, June 4, 1999, p. 71.

Online

Rollingstone.com, http://www.rollingstone.com (August 31, 1999).

—Laura Hightower

Orgy

Rock band

The Los Angeles-based rock band Orgy chose their namesake not so much for the sexual reference as for "a description of their various influences—drum-and bass, hair metal, funk grooves and Eighties synth bands—all getting it on together," according to Gavin Edwards of *Rolling Stone.* "Anything you can imagine is what we use to make a record," agreed Orgy's guitar synth player Amir Derakh on the group's official website. "From old-school to state-of-the-art and everything in between." Following their 1998 debut release entitled *Candyass,* Orgy went straight to the top with a spot on the major Family Values Tour and a hit single, "Blue Monday."

The members of Orgy, at the time of their success either approaching or in their thirties despite their youthful glam-rock image, found themselves cast into the limelight in 1998 and throughout 1999. They had all been in the music industry, albeit on the fringes, for some time. Lead vocalist Jay Gordon spent his entire life around the music world. His father, Lou Gordon, managed musicians from the (San Francisco) Bay area, working with

Corbis/Mitch Gerber. Reproduced by permission.©

For the Record . . .

Members include **Amir Derakh** (born 1963; former member of Rough Cutt), synth guitar; **Jay Gordon** (born and raised in San Francisco, CA), vocals; **Paige Haley**, bass; **Bobby Hewitt**, drums; **Ryan Shuck** (born 1973 in Taft, CA), guitar.

Signed with Korn's Elementree Records, 1997; released debut album *Candyass*, joined Family Values Tour, 1998; toured with Love and Rockets, 1999.

Addresses: *Home*—Los Angeles, CA. *Record company*—Reprise Records, 3300 Warner Blvd., Burbank, CA 91505-4694, (818) 846-9090; Fax— (818)953-3211. *Website*—Official Orgy Home Page, http://www.orgymusic.com.

acclaimed bands such as Tower of Power and Sly and the Family Stone. Sly Stone even became Gordon's godfather when he was born. "I was onstage with Sly and the Family Stone at age two, shaking a little tambourine," Gordon recalled to Edwards.

While Gordon spent a lot of time with his father during his early childhood, his parents divorced after his father was charged with possession of drugs. Afterwards, his mother continued raising her son alone in the Excelsior neighborhood of San Francisco. Periodically during his grade school years, possibly in response to his parents' breakup, Gordon ran away from home, but would always return when he felt hungry. Around the eighth grade, Gordon started playing sports. Larger than most of his peers (as an adult he grew to six feet, four inches tall), Gordon excelled at his favorite sport—football. On his team, he switched between positions, playing both quarterback and tight end.

Gordon began hanging around with the wrong crowd, and at age 13, he suffered a gunshot wound to the leg while walking home from school. Even though he did not provoke the assault, according to Gordon, the event made him reconsider the dangers of associating himself with criminal-minded people. Gordon next turned to heavy metal and glam-rock music, admitting to sneaking out of his house at night to attend Metallica (when the band was just starting out in the early 1980s) shows at a club in San Francisco called the Stone. Inspired by Metallica and other metal groups, Gordon sang in his own band for awhile until he damaged his voice as a result of screaming too much. After undergoing laser surgery at just 16 years of age to try and repair his throat, Gordon never thought he would be able to sing again. Consequently, into his adultcareer with Orgy, he continued to sing with a deep, growling voice.

After graduating from high school, Gordon moved to Los Angeles where he imitated his glam-rock, goth-rock, and heavy metal idols by dying his hair red and wearing pale make-up. Now a fan of groups like Ratt and Poison, Gordon never tried to join another band. Instead he kept his interest in music alive by going to school to study audio engineering and supporting himself as a DJ. Around this time, he also started promoting parties, producing for other hopeful acts, and introducing musicians to each other to form their own bands. One such group, Lit, prospered in the late 1990s after they bought the rights to their band's name from Gordon.

Ryan Shuck, Orgy's guitarist, grew up in the small California town of Taft, moving to nearby Bakersfield at age 18 to attend beauty school. Around this time, he met and befriended Jonathan Davis, who was working at a mortuary in Bakersfield. (Davis would later form his own group and become the lead singer of the successful rock group Korn.) "I used to cut his hair at beauty college—he was my guinea pig," said Shuck to Edwards. In 1992, the two friends played and wrote songs together in a short-lived band called Sex Art. One song written by Shuck and Davis included the Korn hit single "Blind." Shuck eventually sued Korn for songwriting credit, but Davis and Shuck settled the matter out of court. Thus, Shuck's name appeared on the album, and he received royalty checks from record sales.

Claiming that he only wanted his name attached to the song to help further his own music career and not realizing that money would be involved, Shuck later admitted to feeling embarrassed about the lawsuit. As he concluded to Edwards, "It's not cool to sue your friend." The legal matter did not harm Shuck and Davis's relationship, and Korn later helped to promote Orgy. After completing beauty college, Shuck moved to Los Angeles and styled hair for a living. In fact, he continued to cut hair for his fellow band mates and admitted that he would not mind working in a salon again if his music career fell through.

Before joining Orgy as synth-guitarist, Amir Derakh also held experience in the music business. In between jobs playing guitar for several Los Angeles bands, including the 1980s act Rough Cutt, Derakh developed an interest in producing and being a DJ. Orgy's drummer Bobby Hewitt, at the time supported by his adult film star wife Shane, played in another Los Angeles band called the

Electric Love Hogs, while bassist Paige Haley earned a living painting houses.

Orgy came together in 1997 when Gordon decided that despite his rough voice, he wanted to try singing again and contacted producer Josh Abraham to help him record some demo tapes. He then called several of his musician friends around Los Angeles, inviting them to join in the sessions. Before long, realizing howwell they worked together, the casual cast of musicians officially named themselves Orgy and spent the next six months writing and recording. Their collection of demos led to several record company contract offers, but Orgy decided to go with Davis's Elementree Records, Korn's new Reprise-distributed label.

To record their debut album as the first group to sign with Elementree, Orgy rented a house located on a snow-capped mountain in Lake Tahoe. The atmosphere, admitted the band, brought a definite influence to the song-writing process. "It was along the lines of [the Steven King horror film] 'The Shining,'" remarked Gordon on the band's official website. "Cabin-fever set in after about 15 minutes, right after the truck left back for Los Angeles." Shuck further added, "It's a raw record. It's all five-in-the-morning, pissed-off, fighting-with-each-other, kill-each-other kinda stuff. There's an innovative, futuristic feel to the music. Yeah, it's pretty cool." Paige contributed, "It's kind of like death pop. Our songs are all just slightly deranged, but I can definitely hear them on the radio."

After the album *Candyass* with its blend of metal, pop, and techno hit store shelves in August of 1998, Orgy found themselves thrust into the limelight, largely due to their hit single "Blue Monday," a cover of the classic New Order song. The idea to record their own version came about during Orgy's stay in Lake Tahoe when they saw a copy of New Order's *Substance* album in a record store. Although Orgy felt unsure about covering the single because of its past success, they nonetheless took the cassette home to help them record their own rendering. Faithfully following the original song, Orgy also added guitars to the chorus and an unintended, overall darker feel with Gordon's vocals.

Almost simultaneously, Orgy started performing for thousands of fans in large arenas, opening for Korn as part of the inaugural Family Values Tour. In the spring of 1999, Orgy hit the road again, this time opening for Love and Rockets. Eagerly anticipating their next tour, Gordon commented to MTV (Music Television) News's Robert Mancini, "It's gonna be a lot different because, I mean, it's smaller venues and whatnot ... And you know ... we know who Daniel Ash [of Love and Rockets] is, but he has no idea who we are."

Well into the fall of 1999, Orgy performed with Love and Rockets as well as on their own, with *Candyass* on the verge of going platinum. Also that year, Shuck and Gordon appeared in advertisements for Calvin Klein. The thirty-something Gordon, who refuses to discuss his age in order to maintain some sense of mystery about Orgy, confessed, according to the group's website, "We never know how people are going to react to our band. But they always react."

Selected discography

Candyass (contains "Blue Monday"), Elementree Records, 1998.

(With others) *I Still Know What You Did Last Summer,* (soundtrack), Warner Brothers Records, 1998.

Sources

Periodicals

Rolling Stone, September 16, 1999, pp. 53-56.

Online

Launch: Discover New Music, http://www.launch.com (October 2, 1999).

MTV Online, http://www.mtv.com (October 2, 1999).

Official Orgy Home Page, http://www.orgymusic.com (October 2, 1999).

RollingStone.com, http://www.rollingstone.tunes.com (October 2, 1999).

—*Laura Hightower*

Leon Parker

Jazz percussionist

Both Leon Parker and his music have been difficult to categorize, but Parker firmly believes in what his ongoing evolution must be. "My work is a personal statement in a society that discourages that which the true spirit of jazz is," Parker said during a telephone interview with *Contemporary Musicians* in November of 1999. Criticism for his departure from "mainstream" jazz and percussion echoed similar criticism hurled at another jazz pioneer. Sun Ra died in 1993 after evolving from piano sideman to conductor of his "Myth Science Arkestra," reaching further out into the sounds of soul and spirit, hearing the "percussion" of the universe and trying to reveal it to his audiences. For Parker, as with Sun Ra, the criticism did not deter him from continuing his exploration further into the soul of jazz.

According to Nicky Baxter in *Newsnet*, "there was a time when many of Leon Parker's contemporaries thought the man was several cents short of a dollar." A cursory glance at the jazz drummer's gear in the 1980s appeared to confirm Baxter's suspicion: Parker's drum kit consisted of a single cymbal. By 1999, Parker began to simplify his music more. When speaking to Herb Boyd of *Down Beat*, he was on his way to Boston for a performance. He told Boyd that he would "be doing a solo performance and playing my drums, but mainly I'll be doing my vocal/body/rhythm technique, including audience participation." As Boyd explained it, his body became a living drum. Yet for Parker in his innovative approach to his use of the "human" as instrument is as much indicative of his freedom of thought as it is his uncovering of a pure essence of jazz. As a teacher, as a musician, as an artist, Parker insists on holding to a standard unusual in the commercial world.

Leon Evans Parker, Jr., was born in White Plains, New York, on August 21, 1965, to Elaine Tucker and Leon Evan Parker, Sr. Parker's mother was a musician who did social work, and his father was a postal service employee. "I get my music from my mother, and my integrity from my father," Parker told *Contemporary Musicians.* When asked about his family, Parker indicated that it was a complicated, extended one with blacks, Native Americans, and whites. His interest in music began early, and he was "beating on things at the age of three," according to Whitney Balliet in the *New Yorker* in 1997. The music he heard as a child around the house included his parents' collection of such jazz greats as Miles Davis, Dave Brubeck, Count Basie, Thelonious Monk, and Tito Puente. They all contributed to his direction as a musician. As a teenager Parker started playing in a black band in Westchester County where he lived. The band travelled into nearby Connecticut as well, playing "every kind of music for weddings and dances and parties," Parker told Balliet. "We were there to make people happy. I loved it. It was where I got my foundation, the social connection." His later hit entitled "Don't Worry, Be Happy," was a testimony to what pleased him from his early days of performing for people.

Instead of attending Fordham University in New York City where he was offered a scholarship, Parker decided to stay with music. He spent time with alto saxophonist Arnie Lawrence, taught at New School, and was "jamming" at Augie's, a club on upper Broadway in New York, with alto saxophonist Jesse Davis, and pianist and organist Larry Goldings. Parker met his wife Lisa at Augie's. The couple had one daughter. Now divorced, Parker has made a permanent home in Westchester County. He believes that living there and raising his daughter is what keeps him balanced.

Parker began his career by paring down his drum set. He explains it on his website by saying that he trimmed down his drum kit to one lone cymbal because, "Why wouldn't it work? When you listen to Bill Higgins or Ben Riley, what do you hear? You hear a cymbal." He felt that by using just one cymbal, he was "forced to encompass the textual and dynamic possibilities of an entire drum set into one piece of equipment." For awhile, according to Balliet, Parker went back to the drums of the 1930s and 1940s that New Orleans drummer Baby Dodds used. As a percussionist more than a drummer, Dodds "thought of his drums in terms of colors," said Balliet,

For the Record . . .

Born Leon Evans Parker, Jr., on August 21, 1965, in White Plains, NY; son of Elaine Parker, a musician and social worker, and Leon Evans Parker, Sr., a postal service employee; wife: Lisa; one daughter, Evandrea. *Education*: Studied with Arnie Lawrence, alto saxophonist; Jesse Davis, alto saxophonist; Larry Goldings, pianist/organist.

Awards: "Percussion Talent Deserving Wider Recognition," *Down Beat* magazine, 47th Annual Critics Poll, 1998; *Belief*, Album of the Year, 1996; New York Jazz Critics' Circle, 1996.

Addresses: *Home*—P.O. Box 473, Mohegan Lake, NY. *Record company*—Sony, 550 Madison Ave., New York, NY 10022-3211, (212) 833-8000. *Email*—lpsolo@leonparker.com.. *Website*—www.leonparker.com.

"and how to mix them." Pianist Bill Charlap commented that Parker, like Dodds "gets many different colors, and he's got brilliant time. Many drummers just don't groove; they lack that intensity in their beat. But Leon's got real pop to this time. Wham! And his sense of intricate rhythms never gets in the way of his grooving," according to Balliet.

Parker's direction began to change further by 1999. Boyd noted that "mentioning his former record company [Sony/Columbia] makes this percussionist deserving wider recognition a little uncomfortable." Parker commented further to *Contemporary Musicians*, "Let's just say we made three beautiful artistic statements together that I'm very proud of, and I'm really happy with the way they distribute records. It was a great learning experience, but I'm happy where I am right now."

Parker focused on solo work in 1999. In New York City during that summer he conducted Vocal Body Rhythm Workshops under the sponsorship of the Central Park Summerstage Commission. He told Boyd he was "very busy developing this vocal/body/rhythm technique and my ensemble." His art was expanding into the world of Dance, a natural next step, according to Parker. In his management, as well, Parker was going solo. A big part of that included the establishment of his website. "Having a Website means I don't have to rely on a big corporation to present me to the world," he told Boyd. "I want to define my image, to control the rate of my own growth and exposure, and a Web site is a good way of advertising and promoting what you do."

As Parker put it, "things come to me." He used his own contacts to pick and choose where he would go next with a performance. Cyberspace brought him to an audience eager to witness his next move. Whether he is updating his website, composing, or in his studio, Parker is clearly a person in control of his destiny, not content to simply emulate someone else's style or even his own of a few years ago. If critics have judged Parker harshly because of his exploration into the other forms of his art as a purveyor of jazz for himself, and for others, he is not concerned. The tension in Parker's voice during his phone interview with *Contemporary Musicians* was one that spoke to the happy struggle an artist meets daily in understanding his role in the universe, and how his work could reach new heights. He is content that his way is necessary in leading him to a deeper dimension, forever grounded in the same county that gave him the roots he needed to travel freely.

Selected discography

Above and Below, Sony/Columbia, 1994.
Belief, Sony/Columbia, 1996.
Awakening, Sony/Columbia, 1998.
Duo,(with Charlie Hunter), 1999.

Sources

Books

George-Warren, Holly, editor, *The Rolling Stone Jazz Record Guide,* Random House, 1999.

Periodicals

Down Beat, August 1999.
New Yorker, January 13, 1997.
New York Times, March 16, 1996; June 13, 1997; January 10, 1998; August 2, 1998; January 11, 1999; June 29, 1999.

Online

Leon Parker Website, http://www.leonparker.com, (November 1999).
"Spiritual Rhythms," *Newsnet (*Santa Rosa, California), http://www.santarosa.net/paper/metro/12.03.98/park, (November 1999).

Additonal information was obtained through a phone interview with Leon Parker on November 23, 1999.

—*Jane Spear*

Nicholas Payton

Jazz musician, trumpet

Prominent among the "young lions" of jazz, trumpeter Nicholas Payton was born and raised in New Orleans, a city where jazz resounded regularly from the streets and clubs. He was a hard bop prodigy from early adolescence, and from his earliest years he fit squarely into the proverbial mold from which jazz legends were formed. At age five he was heard (very) briefly on a live recording from Snug Harbor, with Ellis Marsalis and Art Blakey, and Payton performed professionally for the first time at age eight. As the young trumpeter matured, his musical charisma blossomed, and he developed the ability to temper his loud, hard bop musical style with renditions of soft and slow ballads. To complete the aura of Nicholas Payton, observers noted often that he bore a striking physical resemblance to the late jazz trumpeter, Louis "Satchmo" Armstrong.

Nicholas Payton was born in the Broodmoor District of New Orleans on September 26, 1973. He was raised in Treme, a district of New Orleans near Armstrong Park known to be a traditional haven for brass jazz band activity. His father, bassist Walter Payton, was a professional jazzman who nurtured the seed of talent in his young son. Walter Payton presented the boy with a trumpet as a Christmas present when the boy was only four years old and taught him to read music in the third grade. Payton's mother, Maria, was a singer and pianist who provided her son with classical instruction on the piano. As a result, the Payton home was generally filled with music, and Payton was very young when he first developed instincts about musical instruments and their idiosyncratic sounds. As a youngster Payton also grew accustomed to his father's band rehearsals and developed a personal familiarity with the professional musicians that frequented the household. By the age of ten, Payton was acquainted with such improvisational trumpeters as Wendell Brunious, Leroy Jones, Clyde Kerr, Jr., and saxophonist Earl Turbinton. It was in those boyhood friendships with the grown men of jazz that young Payton focused his early admiration.

According to those who knew Payton well, he possessed a special confidence about his music even as a youngster when he performed with a group called the Young Tuxedo Brass Band. At age 12 he joined a youth group called the All-Star Jazz Band that played not only around town and at jazz festivals, but also traveled to Europe. It was just around that time, at age 12 or 13, that Payton took the initiative to play an impromptu audition—through the telephone wires—for Wynton Marsalis. The anecdote was widely related of how the adolescent Payton played his horn in the background one day, while his father spoke with Marsalis over the phone. Marsalis was duly impressed and from that day forward never ceased to recommend the young Payton to bandleaders. On the recommendation of Marsalis, Payton went to New York City at age 16, where sat in at the Bottom Line with bass player Marcus Roberts.

Payton attended the New Orleans Center for Creative Arts, and there he studied under Clyde Kerr, Jr. Payton also worked at jazz clubs around New Orleans while he was in high school. After graduation he enrolled briefly at the University of New Orleans. Although he attended college for only one year, he worked with such jazz legends as Harold Battiste, Ellis Marsalis, and Victor Goines. Among Payton's most memorable experiences in college were thesemi-weekly jam sessions hosted by the music department. Participants at the university jams included Peter Martin on piano, Chris Thomas on bass, and Brian Blade on drums. Payton was particularly gratified at the opportunity to bring his own musical compositions and hear the music performed on an assortment of instruments simultaneously. Unlike his own hard-bop style of trumpet playing in those days, Payton's musical compositions were less harsh and more melodic overall. He was quoted by Bill Milkowski in *Down Beat*, "My whole thing when I write is to come up with a singable melody that would be easily discernible to listeners and that would stick with them."

Payton admitted freely that as a youth he was much more inclined to wail and blare when he played his trumpet, and to improvise with extra notes. In order to

For the Record . . .

Born September 26, 1973, in New Orleans, LA; son of Walter and Maria Payton. *Education*: University of New Orleans; also studied under E. Diane Lyle, Connie Breaux, Dr. Bert Braud, Clyde Kerr, Ronald Benko, Ellis Marsalis, and Harold Battiste.

Performed with Carl Allen's Manhattan Projects, Elvin Jones' Jazz Machine, Doc Cheatham, Lincoln Center Jazz Orchestra, Carnegie Hall Jazz Band, and George Wein's Newport Jazz Festival All-Stars; signed with Verve Records as a bandleader and released debut solo album *From This Moment*, 1995; released *Gumbo Nouveau*, 1995; released Grammy Award-winning *Doc Cheatham and Nicholas Payton*, 1997; released *Payton's Place*, 1998; released *Nick@Night*, 1999.

Awards: Grammy Award, Best Solo Jazz Performance, National Academy of Recording Arts and Sciences, 1997.

Addresses: *Record company*—Verve Records/Verve Music Group, 555 W. 57th St., New York, NY 10019, (212) 333-8000, fax (212) 603-7919.

perform his own compositions, however, Payton developed excellent control of his instrument. He attributed that control to a combination of maturity and experience and noted that slow smooth sounds are particularly difficult for trumpeters to reproduce. In 1997 it was just such mature and refined musical interpretation that won Payton his first Grammy award.

By the time Payton left college, he was a seasoned performer. In September of 1991 he joined Teresa Brewer in an all-star tribute to Louis Armstrong. The show featured trumpeters Clark Terry, Red Rodney, Dizzy Gillespie, Terence Blanchard, Ruby Braff, Harry "Sweets" Edison, and Freddie Hubbard. In 1992 Payton toured once again with his former colleague, Marcus Roberts. Payton also worked with Elvin Jones' Jazz Machine that year. In addition to playing the trumpet, Payton served as the musical director for the Jazz Machine. It was a rewarding experience that gave him primary responsibility for putting the musical sets in order and overseeing the rehearsals, while Jones personally retained responsibility for selection of the musical content. Payton played with the Jazz Machine at the Blue Note in New York City, among other performances, and remained with the Jones band for two years. Additionally Payton was heard on recordings with Jones. By Payton's admission he learned much from working with the popular drummer, including how to "pace" a set of songs, and most importantly how to blast his music loud and clear over the uncanny loudness of Jones's drumming. As Payton matured, critics noted the ease with which he played. According to the consensus of commentary he displayed an unusual "restraint" and an easy stance that belied his youth as he performed on his trumpet, an instrument regarded by many observers as the most difficult to play of all jazz instruments.

Also in 1992 Payton toured with Jazz Futures, a group of young jazz musicians, and again in 1994 he toured through Europe with Jazz Futures II. Payton was heard on *New Orleans Collective* in 1993 and later on *Evidence* in 1995. He secured his own recording contract with Verve Records as a bandleader, and released his first album, *From This Moment,* in 1995. Among Payton's assembled band members, he habitually worked with Jesse Davis on alto saxophone, Tim Warfield on tenor saxophone, Anthony Wonsey and Mulgrew Miller on piano, Reuben Rogers on bass, and Adonis Rose on drums. Payton often played with the Lincoln Center Jazz Orchestra and became an active participant in the many youth programs of Lincoln Center Jazz. He also performed with Carl Allen's Manhattan Projects, with the Carnegie Hall Jazz Band, and with George Wein's Newport Jazz Festival All-Stars. In 1996 Payton appeared in the role of Oran Page in the Robert Altman movie, *Kansas City*, and in July of 1997 Payton performed atthe *Donostiako Jazzaldia* (San Sebastiain Jazz Festival) in the Basque country of Spain.

Payton's musical style, as well his looks, conjure memories of Louis Armstrong, according to Tom Turco of Gannett New Service. Payton "can sear a room with the white-hot intensity of his horn, which he wields with laser-like precision.... Like the legendary Satchmo, Payton commands attention with his innovative phrasings, flawless technique and passionate sound. He makes his trumpet growl, croon and swoop...." Turco said. The late jazzman Doc Cheatham, a mentor of sorts to Payton, was also one of Payton's biggest fans. The two recorded an album together in 1997 and won a Grammy award for their instrumental rendition of "Stardust." Cheatham, who never presumed to play solo until the age of 70, publicly applauded Payton's own humility and never ran out of kind words for Payton. Ira Gitler dubbed Payton a "trumpeter for the millennium," in *Down Beat.*

Selected discography

New Orleans Collective, 1993.
Evidence, 1995.
From This Moment, Verve, 1995.
Gumbo Nouveau, Verve, 1995.
Doc Cheatham and Nicholas Payton, Verve, 1997.
Payton's Place, Verve, 1998.
Nick@Night, Verve, 1999.

Sources

Books

Cook, Richard and Brian Morton, *The Penguin Guide to Jazz on Compact Disc,* Penguin Group, 1992.

Erlewine, Michael, editor, *All Music Guide to Jazz,* Miller Freeman, San Francisco, 1996.

George-Warren, Holly, editor, *The Rolling Stone Jazz Blues Album Guide,* Rolling Stone Press, 1999.

Periodicals

American Visions, October-November 1996.
Down Beat, March 1995; November 1997; July 1998.
Fortune, July 20, 1998.
Gannett News Service, July 26, 1996.

Online

AMG All Music Guide, http://www.allmusic.com (November 26, 1999).

"Nicholas Payton," http://www.riverwalk.org (November 28, 1999).

—Gloria Cooksey

Pennywise

Punk band

Combining powerful guitar riffs with optimistic lyrics—a form of skate-punk popular in the Southern California hardcore punk scene of the late 1980s—Pennywise embraced the same calculated sound to become one of the most well-known punk acts of the 1990s. Often compared to bands such as Bad Religion, NOFX, and the Gorilla Biscuits, all of which served as influences, Pennywise has also earned a reputation for their energetic live performances.

Pennywise formed in 1988 when former high school classmates and surfing enthusiasts Jim Lindberg on vocals, Fletcher Dragge on guitar, Jason Thirsk on bass, and Bryon McMackin on drums decided to quit their various fledging punk bands in their hometown of Hermosa Beach, California, in order to create punk music together. In 1989, Pennywise released an EP on the local label Theologian Records entitled *A Word From the Wise.* Shortly after the group released the EP, Lindberg left the band to settle down and marry. To compensate for the loss, Thirsk moved to vocals, and new member Ray Bradbury substituted on bass.

Photograph by Tibor Bozi. Corbis. Reproduced by permission.

For the Record . . .

Members include **Randy Bradbury** (bandmember from c. 1990-1992; rejoined in 1996 to replace Thirsk), bass; **Fletcher Dragge**, guitar; **Jim Lindberg** (left group 1989; rejoined in 1992), vocals; **Bryon McMackin,** drums; **Jason Thirsk** (d. 1996 from a self-inflicted gunshot wound), bass.

Formed band in Hermosa Beach, CA, 1988; signed with Epitaph Records; released debut *Pennywise*, 1991; released *Unknown Road*, 1992; joined Vans Warped Tour for first time, 1994-1995; released *About Time*, 1995; released the self-examining *Full Circle* following Thirsk's death, 1997; released *Straight Ahead*, which contained "Alien," a song written about Thirsk, 1999.

Addresses: *Record company*—Epitaph Records, 2798 Sunset Blvd., Los Angeles, CA 90026, (323) 413-7353, fax (323) 413-9678.

Although *A Word From the Wise* received some unfavorable reviews, the EP managed to make an impression on Brett Gurewitz of the punk band Bad Religion. Subsequently, Pennywise signed with Bad Religion's label, Epitaph, and the reformed group recorded their first full-length, self-titled album in 1991. This time around, critics applauded the band's effort. Most tracks on *Pennywise* focused on advice for surviving high school; "Rules," "Living for Today," and "The Secret" tackled ways to repel peer pressure and defy conformity, while "Come Out Fighting" and "Side One" took a different stance by calling for punk-scene unity. However, one song, "Homeless," called attention to more grown-up issues through lyrics that urged government to aid the less fortunate before spending dollars overseas.

The following year, Thirsk, McMackin, Bradbury, and Dragge persuaded pal Lindberg to rejoin the band. With the original lineup intact, except for Bradbury's substitution for Thirsk on all but two tracks, Pennywise returned to release *Unknown Road* in 1992. Like *Pennywise,* the group's follow-up album bore similarities to Bad Religion, exemplified most notably in the title track and the song "Homesick." Yet *Unknown Road* also saw Pennywise developing an identity of their own. First, Thirsk and Bradbury, alternately joining drummer McMackin, added a throbbing foundation to the group's machine-gun tempos. Second, Pennywise experimented with feedback and other electronic effects. Third, Dragge, showing a more skillful playing technique, provided a wider range of guitar riffs. And finally, although most songs again aimed at adolescent concerns, Pennywise nonetheless exhibited an obvious maturity with fuller and more poetic lyrics. For example, "City Is Burning," a song about race riots that plagued inner-city Los Angeles, directed anger not at the rioters, but at complacent suburbanites who hide themselves away in comfortable homes from such problems. *Unknown Road* also marked the band's first commercial success, selling over 200,000 copies, a substantial number for an independent-label release.

Pennywise's growing popularity was driven largely by constant touring and appearances inskateboarding videos. Moreover, the band joined the first installment of the Vans Warped Tour in 1994-1995. The Warped Tour featured bands playing a range of music from metal and punk to progressive hip-hop and swing. Considered a catalyst for propelling bands to greater fame, the Warped Tour boasted future well-known outfits such as No Doubt, Sublime, Limp Bizkit, and the Mighty Mighty Bosstones. In addition to music, festivities at the concerts included skateboarding, BMX bike racing contests, and famous snowboarders. Introducing the extreme sport lifestyle and music to countries abroad as well, the tour regularly traveled to Europe, Asia, and Australia. Over the years, Pennywise has never lost their touch at the festival. As Charles R. Cross of *Rolling Stone* noted, "Warped '99 belonged to four-time tour vets Pennywise, who drew the biggest crowd.... This was punk undiluted by the past decade: furious drums, rage-driven guitar riffs and unintelligible vocals."

Around 1994, Green Day, closely followed by the Offspring, led punk music back into the mainstream. Thus, several major labels started inquiring about signing Pennywise. However, Pennywise opted to stay with Epitaph to release their next album, 1995's *About Time.* In the wake of Green Day's success, the album revealed a more confident, radio-friendly side of Pennywise. Produced by Epitaph executive Brett Gurewitz, *About Time* included songs with a driving, metal rock-sounding guitar and bass, while Lindberg's vocals completed each track with a pop-metal swagger. Though the album continued to preach positive thinking to teens, Pennywise also found new ideas to sing about. On "Freebase," for example, the band recites a cautionary drug story from the point of view of a drug dealer, and the self-depreciating "Perfect People" showed Pennywise displaying an uncommon sense of humor.

In the summer of 1996, Pennywise started work on their next album. In July of that year though, devastating news took the band by surprise; Thirsk, who had taken a leave of absence to deal with an alcohol problem, killed himself with a shotgun. Although his death was first reported as an accident, authorities later ruled Thirsk's death as a suicide. Despite the tragedy, the remaining members of Pennywise, with Bradbury filling in on bass, held on to complete *Full Circle,* issued in the spring of 1997. Forced to re-evaluate their priorities following Thirsk's suicide, the once reckless, carefree punk act spent nearly a year of self-examination to finish songs for the album. On the track "Date With Destiny," Pennywise summed up their new philosophy, asking "What would you do with just one more hour?/Live that hour out every day/Like it was your last, you'll live much better that way." Overall, the album received favorable criticism and again drew comparisons to Bad Religion, Pennywise's longtime mentors. "A full-throttle metallic punk album that revolves around themes of mortality and rebellion, *Full Circle* attacks with the ferocity and survival instinct of a wounded Doberman," concluded Jon Wiederhorn in *Rolling Stone.* "But no matter how frenzied the guitars or frenetic the drumbeats, the band's melodic vocals keep the tunes from becoming a meaningless blur."

In the summer of 1999, Pennywise released *Straight Ahead,* the band's fifth album and the second since the death of Thirsk. However, *Straight Ahead* made little impression on music critics. For example, *Rolling Stone*'s Neva Chonin wrote, "To their credit, Pennywise infuse their lyrics with a sense of hope rare in Southern Cali punk.... But too often messages are lost in a dense dogma pudding. Pennywise may still rock hard and fast, but their ham-fisted rhetoric is beginning to drag them down." Nonetheless, the single "Alien" stood apart. Unlike *StraightAhead*'s other tracks, the song displayed more experimentation than Pennywise's usual fast and vicious punk anthems. "We are getting older, and it is important as a creative person to move forward and experiment. Not that this is too much of a stretch for us. It is still punk," Lindberg told Carrie Bell in *Billboard* magazine. "Most of our songs go 100 miles an hour, and this one clocks in at about 50. Every song can't be angry or extremely fast. That wouldn't convey all the emotions a person feels."

In fact, Lindberg wrote the song, sitting alone in his garage, to explain the emotions he dealt with during the months following best friend Thirsk's death. "I didn't even mean for it to be included on a Pennywise album. It was written a year an a half ago, when I was still dealing with what went on with Jason," said Lindberg, as quoted by Bell. "I certainly never pictured it being on the radio. It's very strange for me to hear it, because it is so dark and serious and personal." But when the other members of the band heard Lindberg play an early version of the song, they insisted on including the piece on *Straight Ahead.* "I think the message really hit them," explained Lindberg. "When your best friend, who always had a love for life, kills himself, things get blown apart. Your reality is shaken up. It's a cruel world, but you have to maintain a sense of hope. Hopefully pointing it out will help people realize they need to make changes."

Selected discography

A Word From the Wise, (EP), Theologian, 1989.
Pennywise, Epitaph, 1991.
Wildcard, (EP), Theologian, 1992.
Wildcard/A Word From the Wise, Theologian, 1992.
Unknown Road, Epitaph, 1993.
About Time, Epitaph, 1995.
Full Circle, Epitaph, 1997.
Straight Ahead, Epitaph, 1999.

Sources

Books

Robbins, Ira A., editor, *Trouser Press Guide to '90s Rock,* Fireside/Simon and Schuster, 1997.

Periodicals

Billboard, August 28, 1999.
Boston Globe, July 25, 1997; July 31, 1997.
Los Angeles Times, October 17, 1997; August 23, 1999.
Rolling Stone, May 29, 1997; September 4, 1997; July 8, 1999, p. 155; August 19, 1999, p. 38.

Online

Rolling Stone.com, http://www.rollingstone.tunes.com (December 5, 1999).

—*Laura Hightower*

Bernadette Peters

Singer, actress, dancer

Photograph by Karl Feile. Archive Photos, Inc. Reproduced by permission. ©

With her cherubic face, saucer-like eyes, full, pouty lips, and springy mass of curly red hair, Bernadette Peters is one of the most recognizable actors on stage and screen. Her energetic performances add zest and vitality to virtually all of the projects in which she appears, from children's shows to zany movies to her best-known vehicles, Broadway musicals. Peters got her start as a child actor on television shows and in plays, and by the late 1960s, had begun raking in theater awards and nominations for several productions. In the 1970s, she ventured into television and film, earning accolades for her work on *The Muppet Show* and standing out as a comic force in films like *Silent Movie* and *The Jerk.* Returning to the stage in the early 1980s, she became a standard in Stephen Sondheim musicals, but earned her first Tony for the Andrew Lloyd Weber production *Song and Dance.* In 1999, she was the darling of Broadway when she amassed three important awards, including another Tony, for her work in the musical *Annie Get Your Gun.*

Peters was born Bernadette Lazzara on February 28, 1948, in the Queens borough of New York City and grew up in the Ozone Park area. She was the youngest child of Peter and Marguerite Lazzara. Her father, Peter, drove a bread truck, and her mother was a homemaker, but had a keen interest in show business and urged her daughter to perform. By age three-and-a-half, Peters was taking singing and tap dancing lessons, and soon began making appearances on television. She started out on *The Horn & Hardart Children's Hour* and also appeared on *The Juvenile Jury* and *Name That Tune.* At age ten, her Italian American surname was changed to prevent her from being typecast; her father's first name became the source of her stage name.

Even before she was in her teens, Peters was landing roles in stage productions such as *This is Google,* directed by the legendary Otto Preminger, as well as *The Most Happy Fella* and *The Penny Friend.* At age 13, she was cast as Baby June in a touring company of *Gypsy.* During her high school years, she backed off from her career temporarily and attended private school, Quintano's School for Young Professionals in Manhattan, graduating in 1966. In the meantime, she studied acting with David Le Grant, tap dancing with Oliver McCool III, and singing with Jim Gregory.

Broadway Darling

After graduation, Peters performed in some off-Broadway shows, then landed her Broadway debut in 1967 in *Johnny No-Trump.* The following year, she garnered acclaim when she starred with Joel Gray in the musical

For the Record . . .

Born Bernadette Lazzara, February 28, 1948, in Queens, NY; daughter of Peter (a truck driver) and Marguerite (a homemaker; maiden name, Maltese) Lazzara; married Michael Wittenberg (an investment adviser), July 20, 1996. *Education:* Attended Quintano's School for Young Professionals, New York City; studied acting with David Le Grant, tap dancing with Oliver McCool III, and singing with Jim Gregory.

Actor, singer, and dancer. Stage appearances include *The Most Happy Fella,* 1959; *The Penny Friend,* 1966-67; *Johnny No-Trump,* 1967; *Curley McDimple,* 1967-68; *George M!,* 1968; *Dames at Sea,* 1968-69; *On the Town,* 1971-72; *Mack and Mabel,* 1974; *Sunday in the Park with George,* 1983, 1984-85; *Song and Dance,* 1985-86; *Into the Woods,* 1987-89; *Goodbye Girl,* 1993; and *Annie Get Your Gun,* 1999. Also toured with *Gypsy,* 1961-62, and *W.C.,* 1971, and appeared in *This Is Google,* 1962; and *Riverwind,* 1966.Television appearances include episodes of *Maude,* 1972, 1975; *All in the Family,* 1971, 1975, *Love, American Style,* 1973; *McCoy,* 1976; and *The Closer,* 1998; series *The Carol Burnett Show,* 1970s and 1991; miniseries *The Martian Chronicles,* 1980; and *The Odyssey,* 1997; and movies *Paradise Lost,* 1974; *An American Portrait,* 1984; *The Last Best Year,* 1990; *The Last Mile,* 1992; and *Holiday in your Heart,* 1997. Film appearances include *The Longest Yard,* 1974; *Silent Movie,* 1976; *W.C. Fields and Me,* 1976; *The Jerk,* 1979; *Heartbeeps,* 1981; *Pennies from Heaven,* 1981; *Annie,* 1982; *Slaves of New York,* 1989; *Pink Cadillac,* 1989; *Alice,* 1990; *Impromptu,* 1991; and *Snow Days,* 1999.

Awards: Golden Globe Award for best film actress in a musical/comedy, 1981, for *Pennies from Heaven;* Antoinette Perry ("Tony") Award for best actress in a musical, 1986, for *Song and Dance;* Distinguished Performance Award, Drama League of New York, 1986; Outer Critics Circle Award for outstanding actress in a musical, and Tony Award for best actress in a musical, all 1999, for *Annie Get Your Gun;* Sarah Siddons Actress of the Year Award; youngest person inducted into the Theatre Hall of Fame.

Addresses: *Home*—New York City. *Agent*—Jeff Hunter, William Morris Agency, 1325 Avenue of the Americas, New York, NY 10019.

George M! For the role of Josie Cohan, she earned a Theatre World Award. Also in 1968, she brought in a Drama Desk Award for the humorous off-Broadway *hit Dames at Sea,* in which she played Ruby. Some subsequent plays, including an adaptation of Federico Fellini's *La Strada,* were not well-reviewed, but Peters was often singled out for praise. For example, reception was mixed regarding a 1971 revival of *On the Town* and 1974's *Mack and Mabel,* but Peters was nominated for Tony Awards for both.

By the early 1970s, Peters began trying her hand in Hollywood, but although she was a star on the stage, she was relegated mainly to supporting parts in film. Her screen debut came in theobscure 1973 movie *Ace Eli and Rodger of the Skies,* then she played a secretary in the football film *The Longest Yard,* 1974, starring Burt Reynolds. Later, she demonstrated her comedic talent in the Mel Brooks slapstick spoof *Silent Movie,* 1976, and the romp *The Jerk,* 1979, written by and starring Steve Martin. Although *The Jerk* was widely panned by critics for its lowbrow humor, Peters received kinder notices for her role as the cosmetologist girlfriend of Navin Johnson (Martin), a goofball who becomes wealthy off of a simple invention. Martin was romantically involved with Peters off-screen during this time as well and had written the part specifically for her.

Peters and Martin teamed up again in 1981's *Pennies from Heaven,* an unusual musical about a schoolteacher during the Depression who is seduced, then dumped, by an out-of-work salesman (Martin); she subsequently has an abortion and becomes a prostitute. Attempting to deal with her bleak situation, she imagines herself in a series of fanciful musical numbers. Based on a successful British television miniseries, *Pennies from Heaven* received mixed reviews, but Peters was hailed for her role as the teacher and won a 1981 Golden Globe. She also starred that year in the dismal *Heartbeeps,* about a lovestruck robot who falls for another android (played by Andy Kaufman). Afterward, in 1982 she worked with Carol Burnett in a film version of *Annie.* She was also cast as the lead character in the movie version of the Tama Janowitz novel *Slaves of New York,* as a New York bohemian who develops self-confidence upon finding success at making and selling quirky hats. In 1990, Peters played the Muse in the Woody Allen film *Alice,* starring Mia Farrow, and the next year, worked with Hugh Grant, Judy Davis, and Mandy Patinkin in *Impromptu,* a romantic comedy about composer Frederic Chopin.

In addition to making films, Peters was busy during the 1970s with television appearances. She was nominated for an Emmy Award for her work on the lovable children's variety program *The Muppet Show,* and was also a regular on *The Carol Burnett Show.* In 1976 she took a part in the series *All's Fair,* about a liberal photographer in love with a conservative journalist; though the series was critically liked, it did not catch on with audiences and was canceled after one season. Peters has also made a number of television movies, including *David,* 1988, and *The Last Best Year,* 1990, with Mary Tyler Moore. In addition Peters provides the voice of Rita the Cat on Steven Spielberg's popular cartoon program *The Animaniacs.* She also starred in Terrence McNally's *The Last Mile,* 1992, for the *Great Performances* series on PBS, and played the stepmother in *Cinderella,* 1997, one of the highest-rated television movies of that year.

Returned to Broadway

After being away from the theater for nearly ten years, Peters returned to Broadway in 1982. Moving completely into new territory, she portrayed a frumpy homemaker from South Dakota in *Sally and Marsha,* and critics applauded her performance for showing a new depth. She carried this over to the Stephen Sondheim production *Sunday in the Park with George* (which won a Pulitzer Prize), playing the mistress and model of pointillist painter George Seurat. This brought her a third Tony Award nomination. Peters was also nominated for a Drama Desk award for her role as the Witch in Sondheim's *Into the Woods,* 1987. Finally in 1986, Peters nabbed her first Tony Award, as well as her second Drama Desk Award, for her sparkling performance in Andrew Lloyd Webber's hit musical *Song and Dance.* Also in 1986, she was honored with the Drama League of New York's Distinguished Performance Award. Peters also received the Hasty Pudding Woman of the Year Award in 1987 and has a star on the Hollywood Walk of Fame. Shewas also the youngest person to be inducted into the Theater Hall of Fame.

In the early 1990s, Peters took a hiatus from Broadway for a few years to concentrate on recording albums and giving concerts. Her first self-titled solo release came out in 1980 and featured a conglomeration of cover tunes by a range of artists such as Elvis Presley, Marvin Hamlisch, and Fats Waller. The next year, she released another disc, *Now Playing.* In 1996, Peters was nominated for a Grammy Award for the best-selling *I'll Be Your Baby Tonight,* which is a cornucopia of popular songs from composers including John Lennon, Paul McCartney, Lyle Lovett, Hank William, Sam Cooke, and Billy Joel. Of course, it also contains many Broadway classics by Leonard Bernstein, Rogers and Hammerstein, and others.

When Peters puts an album together, she chooses a surprising mix of material based on whether she feels a connection to the songs. As she noted to Jon Bream in the *Minneapolis Star Tribune,* "The connection can be from anywhere. It can be from something spiritual or something uplifting or something dramatic, funny, just a witty song." In April of 1996, Peters performed at the White House for President Bill Clinton, and also sang and provided a voice-over for the animated film *Anastasia,* 1997. Her fourth solo work, *Live at Carnegie Hall,* came out in 1999. Peters's voice can also be heard on cast recordings of various musicals, including *Dames at Sea, Mack and Mabel,* and *Sunday in the Park with George.*

Revived *Annie Get Your Gun*

In 1999, Peters had a blowout year starring in a revival of the 1946 Irving Berlin hit *Annie Get Your Gun,* which first opened for a pre-Broadway run on December 29, 1998, at the Kennedy Center in Washington, D.C. In a role made famous by the big-boned, booming-voiced Ethel Merman as the bawdy Wild West sharpshooter Annie Oakley, many were skeptical that the petite, squeaky-voiced Peters could pull it off. After all, the number "There's No Business like Show Business" was a signature Merman tune throughout her career. Peters, in fact, had doubts as well. Not only was she reluctant to do a revival, she was also initially concerned about some of the politically incorrect references to women and American Indians. However, her fears were put to rest when she discovered that the writor was committed to doing a revision of the original.

As a result of the script changes, the character of Annie is more self-directed, and her lover, Frank Butler (played by former *Dukes of Hazzard* star Tom Wopat), is more sensitive. Though she still purposely misses her shots to make her man feel better, it is Annie's own choice, and Frank's response helps even the balance of power in the relationship. As Pacheco observed in *Newsday,* "Loving compromise, not female sacrifice, is what finally unites the two." This updated text was imbued with irony to make it more palatable, and in the eyes of most fans and critics, it worked. Though some reviewers found fault with nuances, such as the stereotypical Indian dialogue or the contradictions in Annie's pseudo-feminist character, most considered the show a success and were especially please with Peters's talent. For *Annie Get Your Gun,* she won a Drama Desk Award and Outer Critics Circle Award as well as her second Tony for best actress in a musical, and the play itself earned a 1999 Tony Award for best revival of a musical.

On July 20, 1996, Peters married for the first time, to investment advisor Michael Wittenberg. The ceremony was performed at the home of Mary Tyler Moore in Millbrook, New York. They met serendipitously, as she recalled to David Patrick Stearns in *USA Today:* "I was just standing in front of my (apartment) building waiting for somebody and he walked by. He was wearing a tuxedo and I was all dressed up and he said, `Well, are you ready to go?'" The two reside in New York City. Peters considers herself a "late bloomer" in both her love life and her career, as she remarked to Patrick Pacheco in *Newsday,* adding, "I guess I've been blooming all along, but I think I'm really just beginning to get it right. When I'm considering a role I'm looking for what I may learn from it, and I've still got a lot to learn."

Selected discography

(with others) *Dames at Sea,* Sony, 1968.
George M!, Columbia, 1969.
Mack and Mabel, Columbia, 1974.
Bernadette Peters, MCA, 1980
Now Playing, MCA, 1981.
Annie, Columbia, 1982.
(with others) *Sunday in the Park with George*, RCA, 1984.
Song and Dance, RCA, 1986.
Into the Woods, RCA, 1988.
Sondheim: A Celebration at Carnegie Hall, RCA, 1984.
The Goodbye Girl, Columbia, 1993.
I'll Be Your Baby Tonight, Angel/EMI, 1996.
Sondheim, Etc., Angel/EMI, 1997.
Annie Get Your Gun, Angel, 1999.

Sources

Books

Contemporary Musicians, volume 7, Gale Research, 1992.
Contemporary Theatre, Film and Television, volume 10, Gale Research, 1993.

Periodicals

Atlanta Journal and Constitution, October 16, 1998, p. 1; March 5, 1999, p. F2.
Columbian, July 2, 1999.
Dallas Morning News, March 6, 1999, p. 41A.
Entertainment Weekly, August 9, 1996, p. 12.
In Style, June 1999, p. 218.
Newsday, February 28, 1999, p. D10; March 5, 1999, p. B2.
People, March 29, 1982, p. 70.
St. Louis Post-Dispatch, July 2, 1998, p. 21.
Star Tribune (Minneapolis, MN), June 22, 1996, p. 1E.
Time, March 15, 1999, p. 86.
USA Today, January 28, 1999, p. 3D.
USA Today Magazine, May 1999, p. 81.
Variety, March 8, 1999, p. 72.

Online

Bernadette Peters Official Web site, http://www.bernadettepeters.com (October 14, 1999).
"Bernadette Peters," *Internet Movie Database web site*, http://us.imdb.com (October 13, 1999).

—*Geri Speace*

Placebo

Punk rock band

Photograph by Tibor Bozi. Cobris. Reproduced by permission ©

The London-based trio known as Placebo takes pride in creating provocative music. "We like to provoke strong reaction in people," bassist Stefan Olsdal admitted in an interview with the iMusic.com website. "Indifference is something we try to avoid. Sometimes that leads to confusion, or anger, or interest—but you can never really predict the outcome." And for those who follow up-and-coming pop-rock bands, figuring out Placebo did prove challenging at first.

Based on appearances alone—frontman Brian Molko favored an androgynous look with heavy dark makeup—reviewers most often dubbed Placebo a goth-rock ensemble. But after the release of the band's eponymous debut in 1996, followed by 1998's *Without You I'm Nothing,* pop enthusiasts discovered that there was more to Placebo than meets the eye. *Rolling Stone* writer Chuck Eddy, for instance, asserted, "Placebo are the latest—and toughest—in the recent line of English pretty-boy guitar-glam bands ([London] Suede, Supergrass, Mansum, Rialto, Elcka)." Soon, the band earned a reputation for their eclectic songcraft, as well as for their ambiguity and uncertainty, and also gained admiration from such accomplished musicians as R.E.M.'s Michael Stipe, U2's Bono, David Bowie, and Marilyn Manson, all of whom Placebo claimed as friends.

Gender-bending lead singer Brian Molko first met Swedish-born bassist/guitarist/keyboardist Stefan Olsdal while attending school in Luxembourg. However, even though both students shared the common interest of music, the pair didn't become fast friends. Olsdal was a jock and played sports, on the one hand, while on the other hand, Molko was a self-described loser. Although they never hung out together much during their school days, the two did meet up again by chance years later in London and decided to form a band. Together, along with drummer Robert Schultzberg, Molko and Olsdal formed a group called Ashtray Heart. By around 1995, Ashtray Heart transformed into Placebo.

For Placebo's first release, the band enlisted the technical skills of Chicago-based producer Brad Wood, who also worked with Liz Phair, Sunny Day Real Estate, and Jesus Lizard. On the surface, *Placebo*, issued by Caroline Records in the United States, contained some more traditional rock and roll ingredients, like heavy-metal guitar riffs and lyrics that celebrated sex and drugs. However, as Mark Jenkins concluded in a review for the *Washington Post*, "the effect of the band's self-titled album is not exactly routine. Indeed, such ironically titled songs as 'Teenage Angst' and 'Hang on to Your IQ' are engagingly askew.... Molko's vocals are so ambiguously high-pitched, on 'I Know,' he scales heights reminiscent of the Undertones' Feargal Sharkey." Placebo's

For the Record . . .

Members include **Steve Hewitt** (born c. 1971 in the U.K.; joined band c. 1997), drums; **Brian Molko** (born c. 1973; son of Scottish and American parents), vocals; **Stefan Olsdal** (born c. 1974 in Sweden), bass, guitar, keyboards; **Robert Schulzberg** (left group c. 1997), drums.

Formed in London around 1995; released self-titled debut on Caroline Records, 1996; toured with the Sex Pistols, U2, and Weezer, 1996-1997; released *Without You I'm Nothing* on Virgin Records, played cameo role in *Velvet Goldmine* and appeared on the film soundtrack, 1998.

Addresses: *Home*—London, England. *Record company*—Virgin Records, 338 N. Foothill Rd., Beverly Hills, CA 90210. *Management*—Riverman Management. *Booking*—Creative Artists Agency (U.K.).

debut also spawned the band's first hit single, "Nancy Boy," which peaked at number four on the British charts.

Soon after releasing their highly-anticipated, self-titled debut album, the group seemed well on their way to establishing a name for themselves, appearing on the covers of both *New Musical Express* and *Melody Maker,* two well-known British publications. Moreover, they opened for the legendary punk group the Sex Pistols, David Bowie, and U2 in Europe, as well as for the pop band Weezer during that band's American tour. "A lot of people were there just to hear [Weezer play] 'Buddy Holly,'" Olsdal recalled of Placebo's lukewarm welcome from Americanaudiences, as quoted by Doug Reece in *Billboard.* "We were getting coined [having coins thrown at them by the audience], so we just punked it up and ended up winning over a lot of crowds." Spending most of 1996 through 1997 touring in Europe and abroad, Placebo was also invited to perform for Bowie's fiftieth birthday celebration held at New York's Madison Square Garden. By the end of 1997, Placebo had gained a respectable audience in Europe, and their fan base continued to grow in the United States.

Before starting work on their follow-up and debut major-label release for Virgin Records, Placebo replaced Schultzberg with a new drummer, Steve Hewitt, and also enlisted producer Steve Osborne. The addition of Hewitt and Osborne to the team, Olsdal believed, helped the band achieve a new direction for *Without You I'm Nothing,* released in November of 1998. Comparing the band's first album to *Without You I'm Nothing,* Olsdal described the latter as "more schizophrenic," according to Reece. "The first album was a very sexual record," Molko further explained, "packed full of youthful vigor and lust. The new album is introverted, more of a post-coital depression: the comedown. It deals with an ever-pervading heartbreak and loneliness that seems to be in the air. The morning after is usually more analytical than the night before, and it's often more painful," as quoted iMusic.com. "On this album, we wanted to go away from that classic rock sound toward a more modern sound," Olsdal added, as quoted by Reece. "It's more textured with expensive toys. On the first album, we were using toy instruments."

The time between *Placebo* and the debut's follow-up allowed the band to explore other musical pursuits and renewed their focus and energy. "There's two years between the two albums, and there's been a hell of a lot of living going on during that time," admitted Molko to iMusic.com. "In many ways it feels like a different band. This is our first album with Steve on drums, and the band dynamic has changed. It can seem a bit schizophrenic, but we're just trying to take it as far as possible in each direction: stretch it, and aim for a wider scope." And although Molko wrote most of the lyrics for the tracks on *Without You I'm Nothing,* all of the band members contributed to the music's sonic flow. "The first album was pretty much written by Brian in his bedroom. This album has been a three-way collaboration," revealed Olsdal.

The album's first single, "Pure Morning," introduced *Without You I'm Nothing* in a big way, debuting on the British singles charts at number four. A song that sounded somewhat reminiscent of the Butthole Surfers' hit "Pepper," "Pure Morning" immediately took hold of modern rock radio in the United States as well. "I personally feel this is one of the most compelling-sounding albums to come out of England since Radiohead," a Los Angeles radio station executive, KROQ's Gene Sandbloom, commented to Reece. "['Pure Morning'] is very unique, very alternative, and just something that immediately stands out on the air." Likewise, the expansive concept video for the single earned positive feedback on cable television network MTV.

In addition to giving a nod of approval to "Pure Morning," music critics such as Eddy provided favorable references to the album's other songs as well. "Tracks like 'Every You Every Me' and 'Scared of Girls' gallop with exhilaration; 'The Crawl' and 'My Sweet Prince' prance into preening spaces of piano gloom," wrote Eddy. "The disc winds down to the triumphantly downtrodden 'Burger Queen' (which swipes its sad tune from Altered Images' 1981 New Waveclassic, 'I Could Be Happy').... Molko's hissy-fit voice cracks toward transcendence whenever he hitches its pitch up another fruity notch."

By coincidence, the release of *Without You I'm Nothing* corresponded with the November/December release of the glam-rock-era, Mirimax film *Velvet Goldmine,* produced by Michael Stipe. The movie includes a cameo appearance by Placebo, for which the band performed a cover of Marc Bolan's [formerly of the now disbanded T. Rex] "20th Century Boy." Placebo's version of the song also appeared for the soundtrack. "In the great tradition of T. Rex—whose '20th Century Boy' they actually improved for the *Velvet Goldmine* soundtrack—Placebo's hooks are no less muscular for their androgyny," commented Eddy. About Placebo's role in *Velvet Goldmine,* Olsdal recalled to Reece, "We got dressed up in these ridiculous glam clothes and a lot of makeup and strut around onstage. It was a bit like being on a video shoot."

Selected discography

Placebo, Caroline, 1996.
(With others) *Velvet Goldmine,* (soundtrack), 1998.
Without You I'm Nothing, Virgin, 1998.

Sources

Periodicals

Alternative Press, August 1999, p. 42.
Billboard, October 10, 1998, pp. 14, 20.
Melody Maker, July 24, 1999, p. 4.
Rolling Stone, February 4, 1999, p. 61.
Washington Post, September 20, 1996.

Online

iMusic.com, http://www.imusic.com/showcase/modern/placebo.html (November 29, 1999).
Rolling Stone.com, http://www.rollingstone.tunes.com (December 7, 1999).

—*Laura Hightower*

The Roots

Hip-hop group

Peter Williams/Corbis. Reproduced by permission.©

Since the release of their 1995 major-label debut *Do You Want More?!!!??!*—considered one of the most groundbreaking works to emerge from the jazz/hip-hop subgenre—the Roots have become one of the few rap acts to cross over into college and alternative radio while maintaining a solid following among hip-hop enthusiasts. The Roots and their unique musical style led *Billboard* magazine in 1999 to contend, "The Roots are arguably the best hip-hop outfit out there: a live band with jazz chops, an inhuman beat box, and a lead MC, Black Thought, with plenty to say and a quicksilver flow." Relying on innovative rhyming, jazz-inspired instrumentals, and an actual human beat machine rather than on a deejay or samples, the Roots developed a truly organic sound. They approached their craft much like jazz ensembles do, allowing the music to change and breath amid the interplay between musicians.

The Roots originally formed in 1987 at a Philadelphia, Pennsylvania, performing arts high school and called themselves the Square Roots. Education in music and specialized talent have helped the group mesh both popular and traditional sounds. "We're all classically trained musicians," Malik B. told *Billboard*'s Brett Atwood in 1994. "Each member has a solid history with music. It's all second nature to us. For example, I've been rapping since I was 11 years old. Each of us plays the styles that we grew up with, and collectively, it all fits." Initially a duo, the Square Roots built a reputation playing in local talent shows and on street corners in Philadelphia's South Street shopping district. Before long, the outfit, whose members include drummer ?uestlove (also known as B.R.O. the R. ?, Khalid, and Ahmir-Kalib Thompson), vocalist and lyricist Black Thought (also known as Tariq Luqmaan Trotter), bassist Hub (also known as Leonard Nelson Hubbard), vocalist and lyricist Malik B. (also known as Malik-Abdul Basit), and human beat box Rahzel (also known as Raazel), had proven it possible to unite elements of jazz and rap without turning hip-hop into a variety show or trivializing an essential art form. In 1993, the Roots received an invitation to play at a festival in Germany. After recording a limited-edition album entitled *Organix* (issued in Germany on the Remedy label and in the United States on Cargo) to sell while touring, the group headed to Europe. During the group's travels abroad, the Roots mesmerized European audiences with their live performances.

Upon the Roots' return to Philadelphia, word spread around the United States about the groundbreaking rap act. Soon after, the Roots signed a record deal with DGC/Geffen Records and released their first major-label album, *Do You Want More?!!!??!,* in early 1995. Listeners were amazed to find that the supposed samples throughout the record were in fact played live by band

For the Record . . .

Members include **?uestlove** (also known as B.R.O. the R. ?, Khalid, and Ahmir-Kalib Thompson), drums; **Black Thought** (also known as Tariq Luqmaan Trotter), vocals, lyrics; **Hub** (also known as Leonard Nelson Hubbard), bass; **Malik B.** (also known as Malik-Abdul Basit), vocals, lyrics; **Rahzel** (also known as Raazel), human beat box.

Formed band in Philadelphia, PA, at a performing arts high school, 1987; released *Organix* and played at a European music festival in Germany, 1993; released major-label debut for DGC/Geffen, *Do You Want More?!!!??!*, toured with Lollapalooza concert series, 1995; released *Illadelph Halflife*, 1996. signed with MCA, c. 1998; released *Things Fall Apart* and *The Roots Come Alive*, 1999.

Addresses: *Home*—Philadelphia, PA. *Record company*—MCA Records, 70 Universal City Plaza, Universal City, CA 91608, (818) 777-4000, fax (818) 733-1407.

members. "All the sample credits in the liner notes are a joke. They are 100% false," ?uestlove said. "It's sort of an inside joke, because we do all the samples live. I will play the drums as if I were playing a sample. I drum the barest, most minimal kind of beat I can find."

The Roots departed from mainstream rap artists in other areas as well. For example, whereas many rappers use offensive lyrics when referring to women, the Roots opted to turn the tables by featuring a female rap by Ursula Rucker ("The Unlocking") intended to shock hip-hop traditionalists. "We were hoping to spark some conversation about misogyny with that song,"?uestlove said to Atwood. "Right now, there seems to be an atmosphere that it is cool to say whatever you want on a record. Everyone is getting numb. We thought about reversing things. What would happen if a female came on with these strong words? We just wanted to hold the mirror up without being judgmental." Although *Do You Want More?!!!??!* was largely ignored by rap fans, the album caught on with alternative rock listeners. The Roots also toured in the summer of 1995 with the Lollapalooza concert tour, which drew a mainly modern rock and college radio crowd.

The following year, which brought the release of *Illadelph Halflife,* saw the Roots giving in somewhat to commercial pressures levied by the act's record label. Some of the tracks contained actual samples, and the Roots allowed a censored version of the album to fill the shelves of chain stores. Nonetheless, group members stood by their decision, claiming that they didn't want to be pigeonholed or limited to playing only one style of music. Regardless of whether or not the Roots had "sold out" or merely explored new territory, the artistic compromise proved beneficial in terms of record sales and mainstream recognition. Winning over rap fans as well as holding on to alternative rockers, *Illadelph Halflife* outsold the Roots' previous album. The release also produced the group's first hit single, "Keep It Real." Another track, "What They Do," found the Roots expressing "displeasure over everything from the condition of urban America to the growing population of platinum-selling cartoonish rapper-thugs," stated Tom Moon in *Rolling Stone.* The corresponding video parodied such rap clichés, such as flaunting materialistic items and degrading women. "The R&B scene is flooded with this whole materialistic, living-in-wealth thing," video director Charles Stone III told Jill Hamilton of *Rolling Stone.* "Including women as just another car in the garage. I'm sick of it. That shit is tired."

In 1997, the Roots traveled with other popular "college rap" acts, including Pharcyde and Cypress Hill for the Smokin' Grooves package tour. After signing with a new label, MCA Records, the Roots released *Things Fall Apart* in early 1999. Again winning critical approval, *Things Fall Apart* "fulfills the Roots' vision of hip hop as both art and culture," insisted *Billboard* magazine. "Shifting acoustics and energies from track to track give the album an extraordinary sense of immediacy, bringing to life scenes from hip-hop's present and past.... Love song and lead single 'You Got Me,' featuring Erykah Badu, is the most obviously commercial track, but it's no sellout. Rather, it's a paradigm of hip-hop aural love and the inspiration for a heart-stopping tour de force of a video." Other notable songs included "100% Dundee," a tribute to hip-hop duo Double Trouble, and "Act Won," a portrait of a world falling apart that also conveys a sense of change and hope.

In late 1999, the Roots released a live album entitled *The Roots Come Alive*, containing songs recorded during performances throughout the same year in Europe and New York City. One highlight included a ten-minute version of "You Got Me" that captivated the audience throughout.

Selected discography

Organix, Cargo, 1993.
Do You Want More?!!!??!, DGC, 1995.

Illadelph Halflife, DGC, 1996.
The Roots Come Alive, MCA, 1999.
Things Fall Apart, MCA, 1999.

Sources

Books

Robbins, Ira A., editor, *Trouser Press Guide to '90s Rock*, Fireside/Simon and Schuster, 1997.

Periodicals

Billboard, September 3, 1994, pp. 38-39; February 13, 1999, p. 40.
Rolling Stone, November 28, 1996, p. 44; February 6, 1997, p. 18.
Source, March 1999, pp. 146-154.
Vibe, December 1999.

Online

Rolling Stone.com, http://www.rollingstone.tunes.com (December 8, 1999).

—Laura Hightower

Sawyer Brown

Country band

Sawyer Brown is one of the few bands in country music history to be thrown into the spotlight early in their career as winners of a national award, then forced for the next decade to try and live it down. However, such obstacles didn't stop the group's energetic members from giving their all to their music. While the Nashville-based country music industry proved to be a tough to break into, the band's high-energy compositions have won them legions of fans along the road to Music City acceptance.

The band got its start when Ohio-born singer/songwriter Mark Miller hooked up with Gregg "Hobie" Hubbard while both men were studying at the University of Central Florida in the late 1970s. After moving to Nashville in 1981, Miller and Hubbard formed the band Savannah along with bassist Jim Scholten, guitarist Bobby Randall, and drummer Joe Smyth. The group soon decided that they needed a more original name; they changed their name to the Nashville street where they went to rehearse—Sawyer Brown. Miller's rough-edged vocals provided a perfect instrument for the up-tempo songs about cars and girls that made up much of the group's early material. Their music was a reflection of the band members' own youth and exuberance. And while the group was full of confidence after winning the music competition on the syndicated television program *Star Search* in 1984, their award was an honor that didn't mean much to the Nashville music industry.

After winning the $100,000 first prize on *Star Search*, the band signed with Curb Records in Nashville. By the end of 1985, they scored three straight top ten hits. Sawyer Brown's first number one hit, "Step That Step," stayed on the *Billboard* country charts for 21 weeks and earned the band the Country Music Association's Horizon Award for new talent. Unfortunately, gaining a position on the charts turned out to be the exception for Sawyer Brown, rather than the rule. The group only managed two more top ten records through the end of the decade: "This Missin' You Heart of Mine" and "The Race Is On."

Some critics believe the *Star Search* win brought a stereotype along with it that was hard for the band to overcome. In 1999, Richard Quinn stated in *Country Music*, "It's hard to get respect when your big break came in winning the Ed McMahon-hosted shlockfest *Star Search*." The members of the band are bothered by the criticism they have received regarding *Star Search*. "The way people put that whole *Star Search* thing down really bothers us," said Jim Scholten who plays lead bass for the group. "When *Star Search* came along, we were an aspiring band playing clubs and beating our heads against the wall. When somebody says 'You have a chance to go do a TV show and play in front of millions of people,' what kind of idiots would be too cool to do it?" Hubbard felt that the lack of success was because the band wasn't "country" enough for Nashville. He echoed the criticism while talking to Quinn, "Too energetic, stand still, wear cowboy boots, somebody needs to have a cowboy hat, you're not country, you don't sound like everyone else in Nashville..."

Despite the lack of radio play, Sawyer Brown was determined to move forward. With a rigoroustouring schedule of over 220 shows per year, they built a base of loyal fans throughout the United States. Sawyer Brown's energetic performance on stage was one of the reasons their concerts continued to draw large audiences; the group's musicianship and song writing abilities boosted record sales among their growing following and accounted for their longevity despite lack of mainstream success during the 1980s.

1990 marked a turning point for the band. Sawyer Brown welcomed guitarist/songwriter Duncan Cameron to the group as Randall departed—the only change within the band since its start. The group's 1991 album *The Dirt Road*, featuring "The Walk," a single written by Miller, as well as *Café on the Corner*, released the following year, each received favorable critical reviews and went on to become gold records. Sawyer Brown had claimed their position as one of Nashville's top country bands, and the popularity of "The Walk" helped solidify their spot among country music's most respected acts. A poignant look at

For the Record . . .

Members include **Duncan Cameron** (born July 27, 1956; joined band, 1990), lead guitar, dobro, mandolin, steel guitar, background vocals; **Gregg "Hobie" Hubbard** (born October 4, 1960), keyboards, background vocals; **Mark Miller** (born October 25, 1958), guitar, vocals, songwriter; **Bobby Randall** (born September 16, 1952; band member, 1981-90), lead guitar; **Jim Scholten** (born April 18, 1952), bass; **Joe Smyth** (born September 6, 1957), drums.

Group formed as Savannah, c. 1981; changed name to Sawyer Brown and worked the club circuit in Nashville, TN; won grand prize on *Star Search*, 1984; signed with Capitol Records, 1985; released first number one single "Step That Step," 1985; signed with Curb Records, 1993; October 25, 1998, marked the band's 3,000th show.

Awards: Winners of *Star Search* competition, 1984; Horizon Award, Country Music Association, 1985; named TNN/*Music City News* vocal band of the year, 1993; Video Group of the Year Award, Country Music Television (CMT), 1993.

Addresses: *Record company*—Curb Records, 47 Music Sq. E., Nashville, TN 37203.

the growth of a relationship between a father and son, the song garnered several media top ten honors and held chart-topping positions for weeks on end. In 1999, Miller still felt like Sawyer Brown had more ground to walk. He stated in *Country Music*, "We're still not widely accepted by the industry, and I think that keeps an edge on us. That keeps us hungry. We're not, never have been and are never going to be the darlings of the month. So that keeps us fighting."

The 1991 hit album *The Dirt Road* was not the only "dirt road" for lead singer Mark Miller. During off-stage hours, Miller, along with brother, Frank, developed a strong herd of Polled Hereford cattle at his Tennessee farm familiarly named Dirt Road Farms. Miller commented in *Successful Farming*, "When my brother and I attended our first sale, we didn't even have a farm name. I bought a cow and had to think of a name on the spot." Miller continued, "I blurted out the name 'Dirt Road Farms' and it stuck."

Farming is not the only extracurricular activity for Miller. At 39 years of age, Miller became the only multimillion-selling recording artist ever to sign a pro sports contract. Miller played backup point guard for the Continental Basketball Association's Fort Wayne Fury in Indiana. In a Billboard review of *Drive Me Wild*, Chuck Taylor stated, "Mark Miller always puts an abundance of energy and personality into everything he does, whether it's singing, dancing, or, for that matter, playing basketball." (Miller has had five knee surgeries to prove it.) Miller started with the team tryouts in October 1996 and played with the team for two years. Although he did not "dress out for the 1998-99 season," Miller remained part of the team. Because of Miller's involvement with the team, and the group's desire to be more selective in concert dates, Sawyer Brown went from an average of 220 concerts a year to a little over 100.

Sawyer Brown's wealth of original material, most of it penned by Miller, was supplemented when songwriter Mac McAnally hooked up with the group on their 1992 release, *Café on the Corner*. The successful songwriting partnership of Miller and McAnally found its way into the recording studio when McAnally signed on as co-producer of both *Café on the Corner* and 1993's *Outskirts of Town*. McAnally continued to be influential in the 1999's release *Drive Me Wild*, Sawyer Brown's sixteenth album which he co-produced with Miller. Miller knows that McAnally has been an important influence on the band. He told *Country Music*, "Mac came up with this philosophy a few years ago ... before *Café on the Corner* ... he said, 'You guys shouldjust figure out what it is you want to say, and we'll make records about it.' And that's been the philosophy."

In 1999 Sawyer Brown observed its eighteenth year in Nashville. What has led to the group's success in a business that has the odds stacked against them? Miller says simply that the band isn't done yet. He stated in a Curb Record press release, "It's been a case of looking at ourselves and saying, 'We can do more. We can be better. We still have things to say, and we want you to hear it.'" Miller also observed that there is nothing to complain about. He said in *Country Music*, "At this stage in our career how could we get upset about anything?" Miller continues with a shrug, "We're still here! ... Ultimately God has his hand in everything. There's a reason why we're still here. I don't think any of us could pinpoint it and tell you why. It's just one of those meant-to-be kind of things."

Selected discography

Out Goin' Cattin, Liberty, 1986.
Shakin', Liberty 1986.

Sawyer Brown, Liberty 1987.
Somewhere in the Night, Liberty, 1987.
Wide Open, Liberty, 1988.
The Boys Are Back, Liberty, 1989.
Buick, Liberty, 1991.
Café on the Corner, Capitol, 1992.
The Dirt Road, Liberty, 1992.
Outskirts of Town, Capitol/Curb, 1993.
Greatest Hits 1990-1995, Curb, 1995.
This Thing Called Wantin' and Havin' It All, Curb, 1995.
Treat Her Right/She's Getting There, (EP), Curb, 1996.
Hallelujah He Is Born, (Christmas album), Atlantic, 1997.
Six Days on the Road, Curb, 1997.
Drive Me Wild, Curb, 1999.

Sources

Books

Kingsbury, Paul, editor, *The Encyclopedia of Country Music*, Oxford University Press, 1998.

Periodicals

Amusement Business (New York), August 3, 1998, p. 5.
Atlanta Constitution, March 4, 1999, p. C7.
Billboard, December 5, 1998, p. 85; March 6, 1999, p. 25; May 29, 1999, p. 22.
Country Music, June/July 1999, p. 60.
People Weekly, December 15, 1997, p. 71.
Successful Farming (Des Moines), December 1998, p. B10.
USA Today, March 9, 1999, p. D3.
Washington Post, May 4, 1998, p. D5.

Online

"Sawyer Brown Discography," *Rolling Stone. com,* http://www.rollingstonc.tunes.com (December 3, 1999).
"Sawyer Brown," *Curb Records biography*, db.system-x.com/curb2/artists/artistbio_T1.cfm?1D=57 (November 22, 1999).

—Julie Sweet

Ron Sexsmith

Singer, songwriter, guitar

Photograph by Lynn Goldsmith. Corbis. Reproduced by permission. ©

Hailed as "one of the best songwriters alive" by *Washington Post* writer Eric Brace, Toronto-based singer, composer, and acoustic guitarist Ron Sexsmith has earned a slew of critical accolades throughout his recording career, yet has never seen the same success in album sales. Regardless of the unpredictable record-buying market, Sexsmith refused to give up on songwriting, penning hundreds of songs at a fluid pace. Referring to Sexsmith's undeniable musicianship, Billy Altman noted in *People* magazine, "Ron Sexsmith's voice hovers so gently around a melody that it's hard to believe his tough-minded lyrics could emanate from the same person." Although Sexsmith admitted that some of his pieces take years to complete, he nonetheless experiences trouble picking from his bag full of songs when it comes time to enter the recording studio. "With the first album there were 80 songs, and the last two have been like 30-something," Sexsmith told Rob O'Connor for a Launch.com interview. "We recorded 17 this time around [for Sexsmith's third album, 1999's *Whereabouts*]. I'm really inspired by Tom Waits, Elvis and his thing with Bacharach, Joni Mitchell's *Turbulent Indigo.* My thing is I'm afraid that it'll stop."

The Canadian singer, born in Ontario around 1964, started out working as a messenger in his hometown of Toronto before breaking into the music business. In 1991, he produced his first recorded work under the name Ron Sexsmith and the Uncool, a self-released cassette entitled *Grand Opera Lane.* Ira A. Robbins in the *Trouser Press Guide to '90s Rock* characterized the tape as "a concerted effort to gumbo up syncopated rhythms and spark up what could fairly be described as a small-scale northern John Hiatt vibe." Backed by an overly energetic drummer and bassist, as well as unnecessary horns and guitars, the singer's compassionate vocals appeared intruded upon by his band and producer Bob Wiseman. Nevertheless, Sexsmith's tape managed to provide evidence of what was to come, exemplified by the roomy, acoustic "Speaking With the Angel," the only fully-developed composition. "The similarly intimate 'Trains,' the joyous romantic declaration of 'Is This Love' and the country sweetness of 'Every Word of It' all shine with the raw ingredients *Ron Sexsmith* [the musician's major-label debut] burnished to such glowing power," concluded Robbins.

Before long, Sexsmith's songwriting and vocal gifts caught the attention of a host of record labels. Despite his knack for composing and singing classic songs, Sexsmith opted to sign with Interscope Records, a label dominated at the time by the likes of Nine Inch Nails, Marilyn Manson, Primus, Bush, and rap artist Snoop Doggy Dog. However, Interscope, with its focus on these and other harder rock acts and pop sensations, never

For the Record . . .

Born c. 1964 in Ontario, Canada; wife: Jocelyne; two children: born c. 1985 and c. 1990.

Signed with Interscope Records; released major-label debut, *Ron Sexsmith*, 1995; released *Other Songs*, 1997; toured with Elvis Costello, the Chieftans, the Cardigans, and Radiohead, 1996-97; released *Whereabouts*, 1999.

Addresses: *Record company*—Interscope Records, 10900 Wilshire Blvd., Los Angeles, CA 90024, (818) 777-1000. *Website*—Ron Sexsmith at Interscope Records, http://www.interscoperecords.com.

interfered with the inherent loveliness of Sexsmith's music. In fact, Sexsmith originally took a job with Interscope Music Publishing to write songs for other artists. But once Jimmy Iovine and Ted Field, two Interscope executives, heard Sexsmith's own recordings, they offered him a contract on the spot.

In 1995, Interscope issued Sexsmith's major-label, self-titled debut, an album that centered around "Sexsmith's limber, well-oiled tenor and inspired phrasing," remarked Bud Scoppa in *Rolling Stone.* "He just may be the most fluent balladeer to come along since Tim Hardin (whose-hushed, bittersweet soulfulness is strikingly evoked on the exquisite 'Several Miles')." In comparison to Sexsmith's tape, his new producer Mitchell Froom—former member of Crowded House who also worked with Los Lobos, Suzanne Vega, and his own Latin Playboys—added sparing instrumentation that avoided sentimentality. Rather than allowing the music to overpower Sexsmith's vocals and skillful acoustic guitar, Froom instead employed a subtle rhythm section and occasional keyboards and cello. "No matter how delicate the sentiment," wrote Scoppa, "Froom delights in setting it off with some element of ironic noise: compressed, tinny drums and spooky, B-movie keyboards." Sexsmith, aided by Froom, was able to stretch his creativity to accommodate several musical styles. Tracks like "Summer Blowin' Town" and "First Chance I Get" illustrated Sexsmith's rock and roll tendencies, "In Place of You" came to life with a hint of gumbo, and "Wastin' Time," a love song, swooned with classic pop stylings. Slower-tempo renditions included the lamentful "Secret Heart" and the lullaby "Speaking With the Angel," a song Sexsmith composed for his then infant son.

Sexsmith spent most of 1996 and 1997 promoting his music, touring with the likes of Elvis Costello, a fan himself who considered Sexsmith one of the decade's most talented songwriters, the Chieftains, the Cardigans, and Radiohead. Also in 1997, the singer released his second album, *Other Songs*, "a perfectly shaped 14-song gem without a false or stray note anywhere and it remains his peak achievement," according to Rob O'Connor in *Audio.* Joined again by Froom, Sexsmith managed to create songs that were romantic without sounding too sentimental. As *People*'s Altman noted, "as hard on himself ('It Never Fails,' 'Average Joe') as he is on a universe that never quite adds up ('Strawberry Blonde,' 'Pretty Little Cemetery'), Sexsmith presents a wise and witty worldview that makes him a somewhat wanly smiling optimist."

After another round of performances, Sexsmith returned in 1999 with his third album, *Whereabouts,* produced by Froom and Tchad Blake. The singer said that most of the songs arose from his own self-scrutiny during a difficult year in 1998; seven months of constant traveling and touring had strained his 15-year relationship with wife Jocelyne, his mind became overwhelmed with uncertainties about his musical career. He worried that Interscope, then in the midst of a corporate rearrangement, might not release his new songs. "I found myself depressed a lot of the time last year," Sexsmith told *Los Angeles Times* writer Mike Boehm. The singer further revealed that his wife "finds this record a kind of difficult album to listen to. I don't want my songs to get so personal it's like a diary, a claustrophobic sort of thing. I wasn't trying to write these little messages, although even she thinks that sometimes. She definitely had a lot of questions about certain songs."

However, Sexsmith need not have worried over how critics would receive his latest collection, described as "a marginally bolder record than 1997's lovely *Other Songs,*" by *Rolling Stone* reviewer Barney Hoskyns. Tracks such as "The Idiot Boy" and "Beautiful" view were commended for their resemblance to the Kinks and Harry Nilsson, while the ballad "Right About Now" sounded reminiscent of a tune that "Boz Scaggs might have sung back in 1976," concluded Hoskyns.

Despite all the praise, though, Sexsmith's third release failed to translate into record sales. He asserted that he doesn't need sympathy from others and cherishes the loyal fans that follow hismusic. "A lot of artists are struggling to get off the ground, and a lot of songwriters who sell more than me don't have the profile I have," Sexsmith told Boehm. "People who do like it are into it in a big way. They're not coming just to hear one [hit] song."

Selected discography

Ron Sexsmith, Interscope, 1995.
Other Songs, Interscope, 1997.
Wherabouts, Interscope, 1999.

Sources

Books

Robbins, Ira A., editor, *Trouser Press Guide to '90 Rock,* Fireside/Simon & Schuster, 1997.

Periodicals

Audio, September 1999, pp. 119-120.
Los Angeles Times, June 18, 1999.
People, July 21, 1997, p. 23.
Rolling Stone, September 7, 1995, p. 72; June 10, 1999.
Spin, August 1999.
Washington Post, June 4, 1999.

Online

"Sexsmith the Songsmith," *Launch.com: Discover New Music*, http://www.launch.com (December 3, 1999).
"Ron Sexsmith," *Rolling Stone.com*, http://www.rollingstone.tunes.com (December 3, 1999).

—Laura Hightower

Woody Shaw

Trumpet

AP/Wide World Photos. Reproduced by permission©

Jazz trumpeter and flügelhorn player Woody Shaw significantly influenced the direction of American jazz during the hard bop and post-bop eras. He released over two dozen solo recordings before his early death in 1989. In terms of jazz styles, he was a contemporary of Eric Dolphy and Charles Tolliver, with influences stemming from Dizzy Gillespie, Miles Davis, John Coltrane, and Clifford Brown. Highly syncopated rhythms contributed to the unique Woody Shaw sound, a distinctive combination of pentatonic scales and chorded tones. Shaw's influence was seen later in the styles of modern mainstream jazz players, and to a great extent on saxophonists such as Wayne Shorter than on trumpeters and coronet players. Later artists who were ranked among Shaw's successors included Terence Blanchard, Wynton Marsalis, Steve Turre, and Ingrid Jensen, many of whom were collectively categorized as the "young lions" of jazz of the late twentieth century. In addition to his own compositions Shaw typically performed songs and arrangements ranging from works by Thelonious Monk and Ramez Idriss, to Oscar Hammerstein II.

Shaw was born Woody Herman Shaw II on December 24, 1944, in Laurinburg, North Carolina, the son of Woody and Rosalie (Pegues) Shaw. The young Shaw spent most of his childhood in Newark, New Jersey, where his father was a member of the renowned Diamond Jubilee Singers gospel group. Shaw, according to his own recollection, was raised around jazz. He began his musical education playing the bugle and switched to the trumpet when he was eleven years old. He left home at age 18, toured with Rufus Jones, and later joined Willie Bobo's band for a time.

In 1963, saxophonist Eric Dolphy invited Shaw to contribute to the *Iron Man* album. Shaw accepted, and the following year Dolphy offered to pay Shaw's expenses to work with him in Paris. Shaw received his plane ticket, although Dolphy died before Shaw's departure. Shaw proceeded nonetheless with the plan to visit Paris, where he appeared with Bud Powell, Kenny Clarke, and Johnny Griffin.

Professional Career

During the French tour Shaw earned a reputation among his peers as a hard blowing trumpeter with exceptional fluency. Upon his return to the United States, he invested his efforts in forming his own band and in 1965 financed sessions wherein he performed with Joe Henderson, Ron Carter, and Herbie Hancock. Shaw's professional associations during the late 1960s kept him in the company of some of the most revered musicians of the era. He appeared with the Horace Silver Quintet from 1965-66

For the Record . . .

Born Woody Herman Shaw II on December 24, 1944, in Laurinburg, NC; died May 9, 1989, in New York, New York; son of Woody and Rosalie (Pegues) Shaw; married Maxine Gree; one son, Woody Louis Armstrong.

Post-bop and hard bop jazz trumpeter and coronet player with Horace Silver, 1965-66; played with Max Roach, 1968-69; played with Art Blakey and the Jazz Messengers, 1973; assembled bands including the Woody Shaw Concert Ensemble, Woody Shaw Quintet, and the Paris Reunion Band; added flügelhorn to his repertoire during the late 1970s and 1980s; recorded for Muse, Columbia, Elektra, Contemporary, Red, Enja, Timeless, and Blue Note; posthumous reissues available on 32 Jazz.

Awards: Grantee, National Endowment for the Arts, 1977; Number One Jazz Trumpeter, *Down Beat* Readers Poll, 1978; New York Jazz Award, 1979; Number One Jazz Album (*Rosewood*), *Down Beat* Readers Poll, 1978; inducted into *Down Beat* Jazz Hall of Fame.

and later joined the Max Roach Quintet from 1968-69. Art Blakey offered Shaw a seat with the Jazz Messengers in 1973, and Shaw was heard on several of Blakey's recordings. The three band leaders—Silver, Blakey, and Roach—were renowned as being among the best hard-bop bands worldwide. Also during the late 1960s Shaw recorded at various times with alto saxophonist Jackie McLean, pianist McCoy Tyner, and Andrew Hill. It was Shaw's overriding goal as a jazzman however to branch completely into his own territory asa bandleader.

In 1970 Shaw released an album entitled *Blackstone Legacy.* The disk, originally waxed as a double album for Contemporary Records, included two long keyboard sets by George Cables and featured bassists Ron Carter and Clint Houston, with Bennie Maupin on saxophone and drummer Lenny White. Shaw's own musical arrangements and several of his own compositions enhanced the album, and critics hailed the recording. It was Shaw's first solo effort, although in 1997, nearly ten years after Shaw's death, an earlier album was discovered and released by 32 Jazz under the title *Last of the Line.* Shaw's follow-up album to *Blackstone Legacy* was called *Song of Songs* and overall featured a less impressive medley of supporting musicians. Shaw's most notable contribution to jazz during those early years was embodied in a conscientious attempt to keep alive the jazz genre of hard bop. In time he collaborated with many of the greatest musicians of the post-bop era in the 1970s, and to a large extent his work bridged a stylistic gap that separated such post-bop musicians as Freddie Hubbard from the subsequent era of jazz players who became known as the "young lions," characterized by trumpeter Wynton Marsalis.

Leader of the Band

In the early 1970s, Shaw spent some time on the West Coast where he worked with Joe Henderson in Los Angeles and with Bobby Hutcherson in San Francisco. In New York City, Shaw teamed with drummer Louis Hayes even into the later part of the 1970s, and on occasion joined with the Junior Cook Quintet. Sometime around 1972 in San Francisco, Shaw met a young trombonist name Steve Turre. Shaw was impressed with Turre's talent and within two years assembled a quintet that featured Turre on trombone, with pianist Mulgrew Miller, drummer Tony Reedus, and bassist Stafford James. By 1974 Shaw's efforts of the previous 12 years realized fruition; his stature escalated with the release of *The Moontrane,* a Muse issue that featured Steve Turre on trombone and Victor Lewis on drums, with pianist Onaje Allan Gumbs.

In 1975, Shaw along with the Louis Hayes Quintet served as sidemen on tour with Dexter Gordon after the bandleader's return to North America from a self-imposed European exile. Shaw's subsequent collaborations with Dexter Gordon were also well received and Columbia Records awarded Shaw a recording contract to lead jazz bands. Shaw then collected Gumbs, Houston, Lewis, and Carter Jefferson on saxophone, and expanded his repertoire to include a mixture of bop and modal, with lots of "dialogues" between the band as opposed to improvisational solos that frequently took center stage. Shaw took up the flügelhorn and used it on many of the slower songs, but consistently favored the coronet for fast, loud, and piercing themes. The rapport between Shaw and Jefferson proved inventive and the two became highly adept in their collaborative efforts. Their first album for Columbia, a popular release called *Rosewood,* also featured Joe Henderson. A follow-up album, *Stepping Stones,* gained even greater popularity.

By 1976 Shaw worked almost exclusively on his own terms. That year he formed a septet with Fran Foster, trombonist Slide Hampton and four other colleagues. That group released one album together, called *Woody Shaw Concert Ensemble at the Berliner Jazztagge.* That recording servedto showcase the intensive horn harmonies characteristic of Shaw's personal style. Shaw's career approached a climax in 1979 with the release of *Woody III.* For that album Shaw collected a 12-piece ensemble; they performed an original Shaw compositions which constituted a three-part autobiographical suite. *Woody III* was perhaps Shaw's best work with respect to the presentation of hard horn rhythms. After that time he experimented with assorted styles, including Latin rhythms and string compliments, much of which was heard on *For Sure!*

In 1981, Shaw's appeal waned slightly. The overall "cohesiveness" of his instrumental assemblage was less pronounced on his 1981 album, *United;* although by 1982 the charisma resurfaced, once again revitalized with the release of *Lotus Flower.* During the late 1980s, Shaw teamed with drummer Louis Hayes and the Woody Shaw Quintet, yet much of their best collaboration remained unheard until TCB released *Lausanne 1977* in 1997, eight years after Shaw's death. *Bemsha Swing,* released in 1986, was among Shaw's final albums. Jon Andrews of *Down Beat* called Shaw's tones on that album, "clear and strong."

During the course of his career, Shaw performed in venues around the world, including Europe, Mexico, Canada, Latin America, Australia, and Japan. Among his last performances was a 1988 concert given in West Germany with a group called the Paris Reunion Band. That group, which featured Cannonball Adderly, Walter Bishop Jr., Idris Muhammad, Joe Henderson, and Curtis Fuller, convened in tribute to the American jazzmen who sought artistic freedom in Paris during the 1950s and '60s. A live video recording of the Berlin concert was released in 1989, within weeks of Shaw's death. The group also released an earlier album, *French Cooking,* in 1987. Many of Shaw's recordings appeared in re-issue after his death, including *Two More Pieces of the Puzzle,* the live track of the Woody Shaw Concert Ensemble performance at the Berliner Jazztagge in 1976.

Philosophy

In a 1983 interview with Linda Reitman of *Down Beat* Shaw said that "the trumpet is the prince of horns" and that "takes a strong constitution ... both mental and physical prowess to play this instrument." He reiterated to Reitman the unusual difficulties involved in playing the trumpet, contrasting the piano's elaborate 88-key design and the 22 keys on the saxophone against the simple three valves of the trumpet. In an effort to improve his concentration Shaw studied the ancient Oriental dance art of Tai Chi during the early 1980s and affirmed that the discipline was extremely helpful to him as a musician and especially as a trumpeter.

According to critic Ron Wynn, Shaw was, "on the verge of stardom" when he met with an untimely death from heart failure at age 44. He was a highly creative musician who struggled to maintain the purity of hard bop. The *Rolling Stone Jazz Record Guide* discussed Shaw's works as, "rewarding examples of the best postbop, analogous to the work of Dexter Gordon and McCoy Tyner during the same period," and unlike many of his peers Shaw adeptly created musical narratives rather than spotlighting the techniques of "jamming soloists." Shaw's music, in fact, required some rehearsal, atypical of many jazz artists before and afterward. He remained determined throughout his lifetime to never compromise his purist styles in return for commercialized adaptations of his music.

Shaw by 1989 was legally blind from retinitis pigmentosa. Early that year he lost an arm in a tragic fall from a subway platform in New York City. He died not long afterward, on May 9, 1989. Shaw made his home in New York City. He was married to Maxine Gree and had one son, Woody Louis Armstrong.

Tributes

After Shaw's death, much of his work was re-issued during the 1990s. He recordings involved a wide range of his contemporaries including other trumpeters such as Joe Henderson, as well as pianists Chick Corea, George Cables, and Mulgrew Miller, tenor saxophone player Bobby Hutcherson, bassist Cecil McBee, and drummer Joe Chambers. Additionally Shaw worked with Michael Cuscuna, Rudy Van Gelder, Cedar Walton, Tony Waters, Alfred Lion, James Spaulding, Horace Silver, and Carter Jefferson. Trumpeter Freddie Hubbard greatly influenced Shaw, although Shaw was more advanced harmonically according to Scott Yarrow of *All Music Guide.* The two collaborated on a number of recordings, including *Time Speaks* and *Double Take* in 1985, and *The Eternal Triangle,* which was re-released as part of an anthology by Blue Note in 1995.

Shaw is remembered most frequently as the "forgotten" hard bop trumpet player who failed to receive due homage during his lifetime. In 1994 jazz saxophonist Antonio Hart recorded a tribute album, *For Cannonball and Woody,* including such memorable Woody Shaw classics as "Woody I," "Rosewood," and "Organ Grinder," reworked with Hart's own arrangements. Woody Shaw's cohort, trombonist Steve Turre, contributed to the album.

When the *Down Beat* Jazz Hall of Fame opened at a permanent site on the Universal Studios CityWalk in Orlando, Florida, on February 5, 1999, Woody Shaw's trumpet appeared on permanent display with those of Lee Morgan, J. J. Johnson, Clifford Brown, and along with hundreds of other pieces of jazz memorabilia.

Selected discography

In the Beginning, Muse, 1965.
Cassandranite, Muse, 1965.
Blackstone Legacy, Contemporary, 1970.
Song of Songs, Contemporary, 1972.
The Moontrane, Muse, 1974.
Little Red's Fantasy, Muse, 1976.
The Woody Shaw Concert Ensemble at the Berliner Jazztagge, Muse, 1976.
Rosewood, CBS, 1977.
The Complete CBS Studio Recordings of Woody Shaw, Mosaic, 1977.
Stepping Stones: Live at the Village Vanguard, Columbia, 1978.
Woody III, Columbia, 1978.
United, Columbia, 1981.
Lotus Flower, Enja, 1982.
Time is Right, Red, 1983.
Woody Shaw with the Tone Jansa Quartet, Timeless, 1985.
Solid, Muse, 1986.
Bemsha Swing, Blue Note, 1986.
Imagination, Muse, 1987.
In My Own Sweet Way, In & Out, 1987.
Lausanne 1977 (with Louis Hayes/Woody Shaw Quintet), TCB, 1997.
Last of the Line, (Cassandranite/Love Dance) 32 Jazz (reissued), 1997.

with others

History of Jazz Messengers (with Art Blakey), 1954.
Conversations (with Eric Dolphy), 1963.
Iron Man (with Eric Dolphy), 1963.
Blue Note Years (with Joe Henderson), 1963.
Inner Space (with Chick Corea), 1966.
Sundance (with Chick Corea), 1969
Ichi-Ban (with Louis Hayes and Junior Cook), Muse, 1979.
Child's Dance (with Art Blakey), 1972.
Anthenagin (with Art Blakey), 1973.
Buhaina (with Art Blakey), 1973.
For Sure! Columbia, 1980.
Master of the Art (with Bobby Hutcherson), Elektra Musician, 1982.
Night Music (with Bobby Hutcherson), Electra Musician, 1983.
French Cooking (with the Paris Reunion Band), 1987.
The Freddie Hubbard and Woody Shaw Sessions (includes *The Eternal Triangle*), Blue Note (reissued), 1995.

Sources

Books

Cook, Richard and Brian Morton, *The Penguin Guide to Jazz on Compact Disc,* Penguin Group, 1992.
George-Warren, Holly, editor, *The Rolling Stone Jazz Blues Album Guide,* Rolling Stone Press, 1999.

Periodicals

Down Beat, March 1994; June 1995; December 1997; October 1998; July 1999.
People, July 3, 1989.
Serasota Herald Tribune, March 2, 1999.

Online

AMG All Music Guide, http://www.allmusic.com (November 22, 1999).
"CD Review: Blackstone Legacy," http://visionx.com/jazz/REVIEWS/R0699_111.HTM, (November 22, 1999).

—Gloria Cooksey

Sheep On Drugs

Techno rock band

Bands in the past typically included a lead singer, guitar player, bass player, keyboard player, and drummer, but Sheep On Drugs followed the lead of other techno bands that have replaced band members with more technically-advanced synthesized music. *Industrial Nation #9* called the band, "the prototype of a cyber-rock band ...[who] disregarding all the notions of purity so pervasive in rock today, [have] successfully infused beats and sounds from techno into what is otherwise rock and roll."

"Dead" Lee and "King" Duncan formed Sheep On Drugs in England in 1988. As Lee recalled in *Industrial Nation #9*, "Me and Duncan met in the gutter in New Cross ... in kind of a drugged haze." Lee and Duncan instantly bonded over Acid House music and because, as Lee recalled, "[Duncan is] someone who's got so much to say but isn't a musician." Lee and Duncan then began imagining the kind of '90s band they wanted to form. Because both liked Acid House, as Lee described in *Industrial Nation #9*, "a really excellent kind of weird new kind of music ... [with its] blips and bleeps and squeaks and drumbeats," Lee and Duncan decided that Acid House was the way to go. However, Lee and Duncan's ambition was to not be just any band, but, as quoted by *The Rough Guide to Rock*, "to be the last band ever." They wanted to "push it [in reference to music]," as Lee further told *Industrial Nation #9*, "change how music is heard."

In 1991, Sheep On Drugs began their quest to achieve their ambitions by releasing their first single, "Catch 22"/ "Drug Music." *The Rough Guide to Rock* described the two songs as "two sides of sardonic observation of the world of work and the rave scene." Next, Sheep On Drugs hit the road, and soon perfected a live show that MTV.com described as "filled with more theatrics, sexual intensity, and general mayhem than Marilyn Manson." These stage theatrics included, as *The Rough Guide to Rock* further stated, "buckets of fake blood, syringes and a pulpit from which Duncan could rant...." With their live shows drawing in fans, Sheep On Drugs released an EP of remixed singles including "Motorbike"/ "Mary Jane." This EP caught the attention of Island Records who signed the band in 1992. The release of the band's first major-label single, "Fifteen Minutes of Fame," allowed Duncan to rant about, as *Voltage* magazine writer Johnny Victory wrote, "a future of dreadful nothingness and torture, caste-system mentalities, letdowns and addiction." *Melody Maker* and *New Musical Express* named "Fifteen Minutes of Fame" their "Single of the Week." Lee and Duncan, not about to waste Sheep On Drugs' fifteen minutes of fame, released their first full-length album, *Greatest Hits,* in 1993.

Greatest Hits offered, as *CMJ New Music Report* stated, "more songs about sex, death and dance from a mocking perspective." The album's first track, "Uberman," shows just how mocking Sheep On Drugs could be. "Uberman" begins with "the all too familiar goosesteps off the Pistol's 'Holidays in the Sun' shot through with cheesy organ riffs which finally succumb to a blistering, rhythmic throb," as *Voltage*'s Victory reported, "leaving only this conclusion: Punk is mere fashion, fashion a consciousness-obliterating disease and the future a bright, bleak wasteland."

Sheep On Drugs followed up *Greatest Hits* with not only two EPs: *From A to H and Back* and *Let the Good Times Roll*, but also a full-length album, *On Drugs*. However, as *The Rough Guide to Rock* stated, *On Drugs* "failed to work as a coherent album; the attempted subtlety and seriousness of some of the tracks fell short of their [the band's] own previous stands." Thus, just two years after signing Sheep On Drugs, Island dropped the band. It seemed Sheep On Drugs' fifteen minutes had expired.

Not ones to pity their separation from Island Records, Sheep On Drugs formed their own label, Drug Squad, in 1995 and released two EPs: *Suck* and *Strapped for Cash*. *Suck* presented a different, balladic sound from the band. "We wanted a definite change to our music," Duncan told *Sonic Boom*, "to send a message to both our listeners and our former label that we had changed for the better." However, this sweeter sound only lasted until

For the Record . . .

Members include **Duncan X,** vocals, songwriting; **Lee Fraser**, guitar, keyboards, music programming.

Formed band, 1988; released first single, "Catch 22"/ "Drug Music," 1991; released debut album, *Greatest Hits,* 1993; released *On Drugs,* 1994; dropped by Island, formed own label, Drug Squad, in 1995; met Martin Atkins and signed to his label, Invisible, in 1996; released *Double Trouble,*1996; released *One For The Money,* 1997; released *Never Mind the Methadone*, remix album of previously released singles, 1997; released *Two For the Show*, 1998.

Addresses: *Record company*—Invisible Records, P.O. Box 16008, Chicago, IL 60616; *Website*— http://www.invisiblerecords.com.

track two—"X-lover." This mixing of mellow with metal caught the attention of Martin Atkins, the founder of Invisible Records. "Sensing their [Sheep On Drugs] lucrative potential," *Voltage*'s Victory stated, "he set about pulling Duncan and Lee under his wing, giving them the resources and avenues to get their product into the grasping claws of their zombie fans."

In 1996, "zombie fans" clutched *Double Trouble*, Sheep On Drugs' third full-length album. *Double Trouble* was an "overtly flashy wave of seemingly disposable electro-haze," as Victory reviewed, and "nowhere near as fulfilling as what has come to be expected." Thus, even with their new record company's resources, Sheep On Drugs' had seemingly failed. Yet, the group redeemed themselves on their next album, *One for the Money*, released in 1997. *One for the Money* returned to the group to its dark roots. *CMJ New Music Report* described the album as "dark and dirty as it comes, uniting speedy electro-percussion, growling guitar bites and layers of industrial noise under a blanket of digitally mangled vocals." *One for the Money* also earned Sheep On Drugs critical success. The website southwind.net called the album "the best disc yet from England's devilishly fun duo. *CMJ New Music Report* also praised Lee and Duncan's ability to "transform paranoia into an artform."

Sheep On Drugs released their fifth album, *Never Mind the Methadone* in 1997. This remix album, as Chris Best described on lollipop.com is "a veritable treasure trove of some of your [audience's] favorite ditties rendered totally unrecognizable by the miracle of modern technology." In 1998, Sheep On Drugs followed up this remix album with *Two for the Show*, an album of new songs. Yet, Sheep On Drugs found their live performances the most rewarding. "I really enjoy being told how much they [fans] love my music," Duncan told *Sonic Boom*. "A stroke on the ego is always good."

Thus, rejecting live musicians for technology and sending messages through their songs has not only made Sheep On Drugs a critical success, but also a fan favorite. But what exactly is Sheep On Drugs' message? "SOD is an anti-drug statement," Lee told *Industrial Nation #9*. "Not just chemicals, but like television or sex or anything else you can be addicted to. The audience, everybody are sheep on drugs.... We're about making people look at themselves and break out of this [addiction]."

Selected discography

EPs

From A to H and Back, Island, 1993.
Let the Good Times Roll, Island, 1994.
Suck, Drug Squad, 1995.
Strapped for Cash, Drug Squad, 1995.
Track X

Albums

Greatest Hits, Island, 1993.
Double Trouble, Invisible Records, 1996.
One For the Money, Invisible Records, 1997.
Never Mind the Methadone, Invisible Records, 1997.
Two for the Show, Invisible Records, 1998.

Sources

Periodicals

Industrial Nation #9, Summer 1994.
Sonic-Boom, May 1996.
Voltage, Issue 8, 1996.

Online

"Sheep On Drugs," *New Music Report*, http://www.cdnow.com (November 15, 1999).
"Out From Underground: Sheep On Drugs," *MTV Online*, http://mtv.com/mtv/music/underground/cdreviews/money.html (November 15, 1999).

"Sheep On Drugs," *The Rough Guide to Rock*, http://www-2.roughguides.com (November 15, 1999)

"Sheep On Drugs: Never Mind the Methadone," *Lollipop.com*, http://www.lollipop.com/issue43/43-4d-10.html (November 15, 1999).

"Sheep On Drugs: One for the Money," *Invisible Records*, http://www2.southwind.net/~markw/cdreviews/money.html (November 15, 1999).

—Ann Schwalboski

Skunk Anansie

Rock band

Formed in London, England, in February of 1994, Skunk Anansie—named after the black and white striped animal (two of the band members are black, while the other two are white) and a spider predominately featured in Jamaican folklore—became known as the perfect metal/punk outfit to represent the future of rock music. From the moment the group released their hit debut album, *Paranoid and Sunburnt,* the music industry and rock fans immediately recognized that Skunk Anansie, described as Grace Jones meets Rage Against the Machine, had an electrifying and unique sound unlike any rock band heard before. Even critics who disliked the music agreed that Skunk Anansie was truly different. The group's spectrum—which includes hints of R&B, pop, soul, and funk—mixes electronica-tinged heavy metal guitar with the energy of punk. Their diverse influences range from Sly Stone and Stevie Wonder to the Sex Pistols, the Clash, Public Enemy, Living Colour, Black Sabbath, and PJ Harvey. Skunk Anansie's live shows have been described as ferocious, dynamic, mad, and angry.

SIN/Martyn Goodacre/LGI Photo Agency/Corbis. Reproduced by permission. ©

For the Record . . .

Members include **Ace**, guitar; **Cass Lewis**, bass; **Mark Richardson**, drums; **Skin** (born Deborah Dyer at Brixton, London, England), vocals.

Formed in February of 1994; signed with One Little Indian Records, July 1994; released debut album, *Paranoid and Sunburnt,* 1995; signed with Epic Records and released *Stoosh,* 1997; released *Post Orgasmic Chill,* 1997.

Addresses: *Home*—London, England. *Record company*—Epic Records, 550 Madison Ave., New York City, NY 10022-3211.

The group's lead singer Skin (born Deborah Dyer) propelled Skunk Anansie's acclaim and notoriety with her dangerous, yet exhilarating persona. Most critics agreed that Skin was the most visually striking front person to come along since David Bowie's incarnation of Ziggy Stardust. *Melody Maker*, in comments included at the One Little Indian website, once said, "If, as Sly Stone once said, everybody is a star, Skin is a solar system...." The first black woman known to ever front a metal rock group in a scene still dominated by long-haired white men, Skin, a stunning six-foot-tall, openly bisexual woman, at times sang with the harshness of artists like Courtney Love (of the group Hole) or punk rocker Johnny Rotten, while maintaining the ability to shift to the vocal range and purity embraced by Irish singer Sinéad O'Connor.

Skin formed the London-based quartet after attending a furniture design course at Teesside Polytechnic in Middlesborough, England. From there, she moved back to London and started meeting local musicians. Although Skin shelved her first band, which she considered too rock-oriented, she retained the services of bass player Cass Louis, and started rehearsing as Skunk Anansie. Guitarist Ace and drummer Mark Richardson were also added to the lineup. By July of 1994, the group signed their first contract with the independent label One Little Indian after company executive Rick Lennox attended their second gig. Soon thereafter, the BBC (British Broadcasting Company) Radio One *Evening Session* program picked up on the band, and for the first time in British music history, the broadcasting company recorded Skunk Anansie's first single, the anti-racist "Little Baby Swastikkka." For a time, the song was exclusively aired on Radio One and used as a competition giveaway, then made available by mail order only. Two more singles followed: the controversial "Selling Jesus" and "I Can Dream," which appeared on the British top 40 list.

In the meantime, the group toured with the rock bands Therapy? and Senser and collaborated with singer Björk for her "Army of Me" single, before recording their debut album, 1995's *Paranoid and Sunburnt.* Produced by Sylvia Massey (who also records for musicians such as Tool and Prince) and Skunk Anansie, and mixed by Andy Wallace (who worked with Nirvana,Faith No More, Jeff Buckley, and Bad Religion), the 11-track collection ranged from heavy rock to emotional ballads delivered by Skin with style, grit, and conviction. The album, which eventually went multi-platinum, illustrated Skin's scalding voice in songs like "Intellectualize My Blackness," an attack on manipulative liberals, as well as her versatility on "100 Ways to Be a Good Girl," a tender meditation about emotional abuse, and the softer "Charity." Already a well-known group across Europe, the band then took their eclectic music and frenetic stage show to the United States.

In 1997 Skunk Anansie signed with a major label, Epic Records, and released their follow-up album, the harder-edged *Stoosh,* a West Indian term meaning crisp. "It's a complimentary term," bassist Lewis, also of African ancestry, told Kendall Morgan in the *Dallas Morning News* during the group's tour with punk rock god Henry Rollins that year. "Stoosh [the word] is almost like someone that appreciates the finer things in life, but they come from the streets. It's pretty dangerous. It's when you're just massive and large." Like the debut album, *Stoosh* continued to promote the group's social commentary, but Lewis was quick to point out that Skunk Anansie's stands are not as political as the messages of other rock bands. "Our politics are a natural stance. It's not that we've got to be political. It's social commentary, really. We're not political like Rage Against the Machine—no one's got a degree in political science. The things that Skin writes about are common views," he reassured Morgan.

Stoosh includes unrestrained metal rock tracks, both musically and lyrically, such as "Yes, It's (expletive) Political" and "We Love Your Apathy." Notwithstanding, Skin showed off her formidable vocals and the group's softer side with ballads like "She's My Heroine" and "Infidelity (Only You)," as well as with the pop-structured "Hedonism (Just Because You Feel Good)." Like their debut, Skunk Anansie's second album, produced by Garth Richardson, went multi-platinum. In addition, MTV (Music Television) nominated the group in September of 1997 for best rock act and for best live act, although the awards went to other artists. The same year, the British music magazine *Karrang!* named Skunk Anansie best British band and top live act.

Skunk Anansie returned in the spring of 1999 with the release of *Post Orgasmic Skill,* destined to earn accolades as well. "The demon diva's vocal performances on Skunk Anansie's third and finest album are utterly transfixing and not a little disquieting," noted David Veitch in the *Calgary Sun.* "Her bandmates, finely attuned to Skin's wild mood swings, make the transition from high-intensity guitar riffing and hammer-fisted drumming to shimmering, string-sweetened loveliness seem effortless and perfectly natural."

Continuing to branch out from mainstream music, the group further widened the space between pounding guitar electronica and soulful pop. Tracks such as the spleen-venting "On My Hotel TV" displayed the group's ability to hold their own against any heavy metal band, while "Tracy's Flaw" and "You'll Follow Me Down" exposed Skin's vulnerability. The group showed even more stylistic diversity on *Post Orgasmic Chill.* For example, the album's opening song entitled "Charlie Big Potato" was reminiscent of the Led Zeppelin classic "Kasmir." With three successful albums to their credit and a major label contract, Skunk Anansie appeared to have no plans of slowing, or quieting, down.

Selected discography

Paranoid and Sunburnt, One Little Indian/Epic, 1995.
Stoosh, Epic, 1997.
Post Orgasmic Chill, Epic, 1999.

Sources

Books

musicHound Rock: The Essential Album Guide, Visible Ink Press, 1999.

Periodicals

Business Wire, September 17, 1997.
Calgary Sun, August 22, 1999, p. 46.
Daily Telegraph, March 20, 1999.
Dallas Morning News, June 13, 1997, p. 35.
Independent, August 22, 1997, p. 2; March 20, 1999, p. 13.
Independent on Sunday, December 1, 1996, p. 16.
Jerusalem Post, August 5, 1997, p. 08; May 11, 1999, p. 11.
Minneapolis Star Tribune, November 5, 1995, p. 02F.
St. Louis Post-Dispatch, September 26, 1997, p. 04E; August 19, 1999, p. 26.
Time, October 16, 1995, p. 103.
Voice, April 7, 1997, p. 30.

Online

"Skunk Anansie," *One Little Indian website*, http://www.indian.co.uk (September 5, 1999).
"Skunk Anansie Discography - Biography," *Yahoo! Music*, http://www.musicfinder.yahoo.com (September 5, 1999).

—Laura Hightower

Slick Rick

Rap musician

Photograph by Mitch Gerber. Corbis. Reproduced by permission. ©

British-born rap artist Slick Rick epitomized the "pimpster" attitude, complete with rope gold chains, diamond rings, flashy suits, and Rick's own distinctive eye-patch, when he came into the rap/hip-hop scene during the 1980s. His 1989 debut album *The Great Adventures of Slick Rick* rose to platinum status, and his image of material excess, as well as his use of explicit lyrics, helped shape the direction of rap music for years to come. However, just as Rick's future seemed certain, in 1990 the young rapper was sentenced to a six-year prison sentence for attempted murder. Although he released two albums from behind bars, projects that Rick and many hip-hop fans would rather forget, neither matched the commercial success of his first release. He later admitted to *URB* magazine, "They were garbage. I didn't like them, I thought they were junk... It was a rushed job, it was terrible, it was horrible. It was a bad job." Then, following his release from jail in 1996, Rick emerged again in 1999 with a more substantial collection of hip-hop songs entitled *The Art of Storytelling.*

While some hip-hop fans viewed Rick as a rapper beyond his prime and not part of the new look of rap—which had traded the gold jewelry and bright-colored suits in for designer sportswear and Nike basketball shoes—most welcomed the return of his old school style and accented storytelling. Likewise Rick, who promised not to retire his suits and chains, agreed, reassuring *URB* that "I think it's what hip-hop needs.... I think it's always good to see a star. You don't want to always see somebody regularly dressed. Sometimes you want to see color, you want to see something that's pretty to look at."

Born Richard Walters to Jamaican parents in South Wimbledon, London, on January 14, 1965, Rick was blinded by a piece of broken glass as an infant. He took to wearing an eye patch from an early age, an accessory that would later serve as part of his image. In the late 1970s at age 14, he emigrated with his family to the Bronx in New York and attended the La Guardia High School of Music and Art. At school, he met and befriended another future rapper, Dana Dane, and the two boys formed the Kangol Crew and began performing at hip-hop parties around their neighborhood. During one performance in 1984, Rick met rap artist Doug E. Fresh, who asked him to play with his Get Fresh Crew (which also included Chill Will and Barry Bee). By 1985, Fresh saw one of the groups songs called "The Show" ascend to number four on the R&B charts, and the single "La-Di-Da-Di" would become a rap classic. Upon the success of their hit singles, MC Ricky D, as Rick was then known, left the Get Fresh Crew in 1987 to sign a solo contract with Def Jam Records, the biggest label in hip-hop at the time.

For the Record . . .

Born Richard (Ricky) Walters on January 14, 1965, in South Wimbledon, London, England, to Jamaican parents; family emigrated to the United States, settled in the Bronx, New York, in the late 1970s.

Met fellow rapper Dana Dane while attending La Guardia High School of Music and Art; Rick and Dane formed the Kangol Crew and performed at hip-hop clubs; met Doug E. Fresh in 1984 and joined his Get Fresh Crew as MC Ricky D; signed solo contract with Def Jam Records, 1987; reinvented himself as Slick Rick and released solo debut *The Great Adventures of Slick Rick,* which earned platinum status, 1988; convicted of attempted murder and sentenced to six years in jail, 1990; released two albums during prison sentence, *The Ruler's Back* ,1991, and *Behind Bars*, 1994; released from prison, 1996; released *The Art of Storytelling,* 1999.

Addresses: *Record company*—Def Jam Music Group, 160 Varick St., New York, NY 10013.

In 1988, Rick reinvented himself as Slick Rick and released his debut album entitled *The Great Adventures of Slick Rick,* which became an instant rap classic. As with the Get Fresh Crew, Rick continued to deliver his rhymes in his relaxed and signature British/Bronx drawl, but some of his songs were now loaded with shocking vulgarity and misogynistic lyrics. Although the single "Treat Her Like a Prostitute" became a street favorite, most R&B radio stations refused to play the degrading song. Instead, they pushed his duet with singer Al B. Sure! called "If I'm Not Your Lover," which climbed to number two in 1989. Also that year, the single "Children's Story," asong which ambiguously moralized criminal behavior and pioneered the hip-hop storytelling aesthetic, made it to the R&B top five list. Other tracks including "Mona Lisa," "Hey Young World," and "Teenage Love," in addition to "Children's Story," were deemed the rapper's best works.

While Rick had always shunned the "gangsta" aspect often associated with rap music in his private life, the criminality he sometimes alluded to in his debut album eventually came to depict his own reality. In early 1990, he was charged with and later convicted of attempted murder after he shot at his cousin, who Rick claimed had harassed his mother, and led police on a high-speed chase. While awaiting sentencing, Rick hastily recorded 21 songs for follow-up albums. Later that year, Rick headed to prison in upstate New York to begin a six-year jail term. In 1991, with Rick now locked in a jail cell, the rap artist released his second album entitled *The Ruler's Back,* named for a track on his debut. Despite his recent run-in with the law, critics felt he used surprisingly good judgment by not making use of his legal situation and in toning down his offensive lyrics. Rather, Rick opted to relate a tale of regret with "I Shouldn't Have Done It," an account of a drug deal in "Bond," and a romantic endeavor with "Venus." In addition, *The Ruler's Back* featured faster dance beats and loops of the hit "La-Di-Da-Di." Nonetheless, Rick's second effort failed to sell, even though his confessional "I Shouldn't Have Done It" single appeared on the R&B charts later that year.

In 1993, Rick was allowed to leave prison for a time on a work release program and recorded tracks for his 1994 *Behind Bars* album. Except for the opening title track, the rapper declined to elaborate on his experiences as a prisoner. The project also included leftover songs recorded in 1990, a cameo appearance by Fresh for the successful ballad "Sittin' in My Car" (a remake of Billy Stewart's "Sitting in the Park"), and remixes of Rick's previous work. However, his offensive rhetoric came to light again in songs such as "A Love That's True," which offers the fatherly advice "Son... you just don't trust no bitch." Like Rick's 1991 release, the obviously fragmented *Behind Bars* failed to attract rap and hip-hop record buyers and did little to further Rick's career.

After Rick completed his prison sentence in 1996, he started to stage a comeback by making guest appearances with other artists such as Dave Hollister, Kid Capri, and Montell Jordan. In the meantime, he started work on a new album. In the late spring of 1999, Def Jam released *The Art of Storytelling,* another example of Rick steering clear from the thug life. "To (glorify the gangsta life) would be to fall into a trap and glorify negativity," Rick explained to Errol Nazareth of the *Toronto Sun.* "The youth [younger rap artists] say a lot of crazy things. They promote selling drugs, gangsterism, robbing each other and all that stuff. It makes black people look real ignorant, you know what I mean? I can't get with that. I can't see myself, at 34 years old, promoting robbery or the sale of crack cocaine."

Instead, *The Art of Storytelling* resurrected the artist's cinematic tales of X-rated fantasies, as well as his humorous old-school rap technique. In the song "Who Rotten 'Em," Rick returns to ancient Egypt and imagines himself as a rapping slave. The more cohesive record, which also included tightly constructed songs like "2

Way Street," "I Sparkle," and "I Own America Part I" proved that Rick was well on his way to reassuming his former reputation as a talented rap artist. Whilecritics agreed that Rick performed at his best on the solo tracks, the album also featured appearances from fellow rappers and hip-hop artists such as Clark Kent, Large Professor, Q-Tip, Nas, Outkast, and Raekwon.

Selected discography

EPs

Children's Story/Teacher, Teacher, Def Jam, 1988.
Teenage Love/Treat Her Like a Prostitute, Def Jam, 1988.
Hey Young World/Mona Lisa, Def Jam, 1989.
It's a Boy/King, Def Jam, 1991.
Mistakes of a Woman in Love with Other Men/Venus, Def Jam, 1991.
Sittin' in My Car/Cuz It's Wrong, Def Jam, 1995.

Singles

"I Shouldn't Have Done It," Def Jam, 1991.
"Behind Bars," Def Jam, 1994.

Albums

The Great Adventures of Slick Rick, Def Jam, 1988.
The Ruler's Back, Def Jam, 1991.
Behind Bars, Def Jam, 1994.
The Art of Storytelling, Def Jam, 1999.

Sources

Books

Robbins, Ira A., editor, *Trouser Press Guide to '90s Rock,* Fireside/Simon & Schuster, 1997.

Periodicals

Business Wire, May 12, 1999.
Newsday, December 18, 1994, p. 21.
People, January 30, 1989, p. 18.
The Record (Bergen County, NJ), August 29, 1991, p.d12.
Toronto Sun, May 28, 1999, p. 79.
URB, August 1999, pp.60-61.
Vibe, June/July 1999.
Washington Post, May 26, 1999, p. C05.

Online

"Slick Rick," *All Music Guide website,* http://www.allmusic.com (September 3, 1999).
"SlickRick," *RollingStone.com*, http://www.rollingstone.tunes.com (September 4, 1999).

—Laura Hightower

Smash Mouth

Rock band

Photograph by Joe Giron. Corbis. Reproduced by permission. ©

When Smash Mouth released their 1999 sophomore effort, *Astro Lounge,* many doubted the group's ability to produce a more diverse collection of songs. The band's debut album, 1997's *Fush Yu Mang,* contained a steady dose of upbeat pop tunes and yielded the number one hit single "Walkin' on the Sun," a song that led several critics to label Smash Mouth a one hit wonder. Although lead vocalist Steve Harwell said the debut was a "fun record," he and his band mates believed they could take their music a step further. "The first one was almost like a speed high, and it kinda pissed me off because I felt that it didn't show even a third of what we were capable of," the singer told Neva Chonin in *Rolling Stone.* "With this one, I can just kick back and enjoy it. ... A lot of people said that we weren't talented enough to do that type of shit. Well, we did it, and I want them to eat their words. We got slagged so much by people who wanted us to fail."

Smash Mouth—named after football player/coach Mike Ditka's term "smash mouth football"— set out to prove the world wrong in 1994 in San Jose, California, when vocalist Steve Harwell and drummer Kevin Coleman, two childhood friends who at one time played in a garage band together, recruited guitarist Greg Camp from a local cover band. Camp, in turn, asked bassist Paul De Lisle, who he had played with in a previous band, to join the new group. After some persuading by Camp, De Lisle accepted the offer, completing the Smash Mouth lineup. The band opted not to hire a permanent keyboardist, but instead featured various guest keyboard players for their first two releases. Although Camp and De Lisle were veterans of the bar circuit and Harwell and Coleman lacked experience, the foursome felt an instant chemistry from day one. "The first time we played together, I knew we had it," recalled Camp, the band's primary songwriter, to Chonin. "It was like the innocents meeting the professionals." De Lisle revealed a similar premonition about the band, according to the group's record label. "These hot-shots I was playing with were like, 'Dude, those guys are stupid and they suck. You got to quit this Smash Mouth thing and play with us full time—it's us or them.' And I said, 'There's something going on with those guys that I can't describe, but I really like it.' What I said to myself, though, was, 'Oh my God, Greg Camp's the best songwriter in the Bay Area, and no one knows it."

While Harwell was regarded as a natural entertainer and beloved conversationalist, the group nonetheless struggled for the next two years performing at clubs in and around San Jose. Their first significant break came in April of 1996 after a local radio station, KOME, started playing one of the band's songs entitled "Nervous in the Alley." This unprecedented move by KOME marked the

For the Record . . .

Members include **Greg Camp** (born c. 1967), songwriter, guitar; **Kevin Coleman** (born c. 1966), drums; **Paul De Lisle** (born c. 1963), bass guitar; **Steve Harwell** (born c. 1967), vocals.

Formed band in San Diego, CA, 1994; San Diego radio station, KOME, started playing single "Nervous in the Alley" and invited Smash Mouth to appear with No Doubt, Beck, and 311 for the Kamp KOME music festival, 1996; released debut album *Fush Yu Mang,* single "Walkin' on the Sun" reached number one on *Billboard* Modern Rock chart, 1997; released follow-up album *Astro Lounge,* 1999.

Addresses: *Record company*—Interscope Records, 10900 Wilshire Blvd., Ste. 1230, Los Angeles, CA 90024, (310) 208-6547, fax (310) 208-7343.

first time an unsigned band received regular rotation on a radio station supported by the modern rock market. In addition to playing the band's single, the station also invited Smash Mouth to appear with such accomplished acts as No Doubt, Beck, and 311 for the Kamp KOME music festival. "We played Kamp KOME at Shoreline [an amphitheater south of San Francisco] and were on the cover of *BAM* [Bay Area Music] before we even got signed, and everyone freaked out," Camp told *Billboard*'s Doug Reece. "Other bands were like, 'Why are these guys getting all this attention? They haven't been in the trenches that long.' But the truth is that, individually, we had all been playing for a long time in different bands." In spite of the envy expressed by other musicians, Smash Mouth caught the attention of numerous record companies. Prior to forming Smash Mouth, Harwell once fronted a hip-hop group called F.O.S. (Freedom Of Speech), a group that also landed a record deal with Taboo Records after a radio station started supporting an F.O.S. song. This experience, as well as the Smash Mouth connection with KOME, sparked Harwell's interest in the business side of music. Thus, Harwell, unlike so many recording artists, played a prominent role in deciding among record deals and contemplated one day establishing his own label. "When our lawyer was setting up meetings with record labels, I would ask him if he could just let me go down and talk to people myself," the singer told Reece. "Even if they weren't into the music, it was cool to make friends and build relationships. Someone in radio once told me that you meet the same people on the way up that you do on the way down, so I've been trying to look at things that way and avoid burning bridges."

After weighing several offers, Harwell and Smash Mouth decided to sign with Interscope Records. Smash Mouth's 1997 debut, *Fush Yu Mang* (named for one of Al Pacino's drugged-out slurs in the film *Scarface*), soon followed. Deemed a collection of suburban party anthems that contained elements of soul, punk, and funk, the double platinum-selling record included one of the biggest his of 1997, "Walking on the Sun," and a cover of War's "Why Can't We Be Friends." To support the debut, Smash Mouth commenced on an extensive tour, which included dates with Sugar Ray, Blur, Third Eye Blind, and others. The group also contributed a version of the Mysterians' "Can't Get Enough of You Baby" to the soundtrack for *Can't Hardly Wait.* The song later appeared on Smash Mouth's follow-up album, *Astro Lounge.*

While Smash Mouth expressed gratitude for their rising popularity, they also felt overshadowed by the success of "Walkin' on the Sun," a single that hit number one on the *Billboard* Modern Rock chart. Consequently, the music press declared the group a one-hit wonder, and for the most part ignored other tracks on *Fush Yu Mang.* Smash Mouth soon realized that besides "Walkin' on the Sun" and "Why Can't We Be Friends," no other singles from their debut would be forthcoming. As Harwell pointed out to *Alternative Press*, "Once radio stations played 'Walkin',' nobody would touch anything else on that record." With this in mind, Smash Mouth resolved to broaden the musical scope of the group's second album, *Astro Lounge,* released in the spring of 1999 and produced by Eric Valentine, who also worked with the band for *Fush Yu Mang.* Not only did the band intend to step beyond the confines of rock, Smash Mouth wanted to make each and every track suitable for pop radio. "With this record, we were like, 'We want five singles,'" Harwell said in an interview with Tim Kenneally in *Spin.* "When we talked about writing it, I'm like, 'Dude, we've gotta make the whole thing radio-playable—like, every song.'"

Critics, including Kenneally, agreed that the group fulfilled such a mission: "The first single, 'All Star,' gushes with hooray-for everybody optimism. Lounge nuances reprised from 'Walkin'' abound, but only a few tracks come within skanking distance of the ska-punk territory they minded on the remainder of *Fush Yu Mang.*" Likewise, Clifford J. Corcoran surmised in an *Alternative Press* review, "Tastefully layered with all kinds of synths, keyboards, vibes and sound effects, *Astro Lounge* features a much more cohesive and compelling eclecticism that stretches from swirling psychedelia to reggae and dub to Blondie-esque new wave and even to Casiotone bossa nova. While not exactly groundbreaking, *Astro Lounge* far exceeds expectations." Before the end of May, "All Star" entered the Billboard top five, and the single was also featured in the film *The Mystery Men* later that summer.

However, Smash Mouth were not without their share of detractors. Within the Bay Area music scene especially, several musicians denounced Smash Mouth as opportunists and careerists. "There's this one guy who, every time I see him, he hisses at me," Camp told Kenneally. And Harwell himself admitted without apology to picking band members who he believed could help Smash Mouth earn popular recognition. But these insults did little to discourage the group. "We built this team and nobody's going to take it away from us," Harwell boasted to Chonin.

Selected discography

Fush Yu Mang, Interscope, 1997.
Astro Lounge, Interscope, 1999.

Sources

Alternative Press, June 1999; August 1999.
BAM (Bay Area Music), May 21, 1999, p. 17.
Billboard, August 30, 1997, p. 9; June 19, 1999.
Entertainment Weekly, June 11, 1999.
Guitar, August 1999.
Guitar World, September 1999.
Los Angeles Times, June 6, 1999; June 14, 1999.
New York Daily News, June 13, 1999.
People, July 19, 1999, p. 37.
Pulse!, August 1999, p. 19.
Request, August 1999.
Rolling Stone, October 30, 1997, p. 80; February 19, 1998, p. 24; June 24, 1999, p. 67; August 6, 1999.
Spin, July 1999; August 1999
Teen People, September 1999.
Time Out, June 24-July 1, 1999.
USA Today, July 13, 1999.

Additional information provided by Interscope Records.

—*Laura Hightower*

Social Distortion

Punk band

For rockabilly punk band Social Distortion, gaining national recognition during the eighties punk era demanded an edge. A self described "hard-ass, macho group," Social Distortion grinded its way through Fullerton, California's, punk movement by doing their own thing while committing themselves to their art. Singer, songwriter, guitarist, and frontman Mike Ness drew from the sounds of fifties musicians such as Johnny Cash, Eddie Cochran, and Chuck Berry, and added to them the raw, explosive angst of punk. That mix, along with a willingness to work hard as a band, eventually put Social Distortion into its own arena. *The Trouser Press Guide to 90's Rock* stated that "Social Distortion was recognized as the sonic template for some of the bands that broke California punk-pop into the big time in 1994."•

Ness and guitarist Dennis Danell founded Social Distortion in 1979 while they were in high school. Claiming that they felt they were more of a social band than a political band, Social Distortion said the name just went along with much of their song writing. They began making music with a philosophy that learning to play the instruments was a priority. Jeffrey Ressner from *Rolling Stone* quoted Ness in 1990 as proclaiming "We were never really part of what we called the forbidden beat, that real thump, thump, thump, one-two-f---- you drumbeat and screaming into the microphone. We always wanted to learn how to sing and play our guitars." Social Distortion live shows initially covered acts such as the Rolling Stones and Creedence Clearwater Revival. Danell commented on their simple, heavy guitar sound in an interview with an Earwig writer, "I credit that to the fact that we grew up in Fullerton, which is where Fender guitars come from. So we'd always been around that, and we always wanted a heavy, vintage kind of tube sound, but as intense as possible. And we try to keep it as simple as we possibly can, and not let other things mask what we're trying to do." Common among punk and alternative groups, the Sex Pistols were a preeminent influence. Ness stated in an interview by *Rolling Stone's* Chris Mundy, "When I heard the Sex Pistols ... those guys sounded like I felt. I fell in love with it."

Social Distortion's first incarnation was completed by Brent Liles on bass and Derek O'Brien on drums and vocals. Their debut, 1983's *Mommy's Little Monster,* was put out amidst Ness' heroin addiction which nearly took his life and wreaked havoc on the career of the band. Liles and O'Brien left the group during those turbulent years, but were replaced by drummer Chris Reece and bassist John Maurer in 1984. Alex Ogg stated in *The Rough Guide to Rock,* "by 1984 Ness's drug problems were devouring most of the band's income, and they practically vanished from view, with only the occasional Los Angeles or San Francisco date to keep any memories alive." Finally in 1988, Ness claimed to have quit his addiction, later telling Chris Mundy of *Rolling Stone* "My life got better the day I stopped...." Their 1988 offering, *Prison Bound,* seemed to be a work created from a feeling of camaraderie with Johnny Cash as it contained a heavy acoustic guitar sound and a significant country influence.

Miraculously surviving the chaos of the early eighties, Social Distortion worked hard during the nineties, putting out their first major label album, *Social Distortion,* along with an EP entitled *Story of My Life...and Other Stories* in 1990. Ness and his fellow band mates did what they had to do to keep things going. Ness painted houses, Maurer worked in a barber shop cutting hair for at least eight months before heading back into the studio for their next project. 1992's *Somewhere Between Heaven and Hell,* a chronicle of life on the streets, broken hearts, punks, addictions, and lost innocence, continued their three-chord, straight-up rock style of expression even while letting up on the savage electric feel of *Social Distortion.*

A collection of singles from their early days in 1981 were gathered, along with a few compilation tracks, for a 1995 release, *Mainliner (Wreckage from the Past).* It was obvious from the previous work that Social Distortion was cutting their own path through the punk landscape. Even while many others were cranking out the hardcore stuff in the early eighties, Social Distortion's rockabilly

For the Record . . .

Members include **Chuck Biscuits**, drums; **Dennis Danell**, guitar; **John Maurer**, bass; **Mike Ness**, vocals, guitar, songwriter.

Group formed in 1979 in Fullerton, CA; recorded several singles in 1981; debut album, *Mommy's Little Monster,* released in 1983; signed with Epic, released *Social Distortion,* 1990; live release, *Live at the Roxy,* released, 1998; Mike Ness' solo release, *Cheating at Solataire,* 1999.

Addresses: *Record company*—Epic Records, 550 Madison Ave., New York, NY 10022.

punk sound was distinctive. After their sensitive and reflective *White Light White Heat White Trash* in 1996, Chuck Biscuits, a former member of such pioneering bands as DOA, the Circle Jerks, Black Flag, and Danzig, was added as the new drummer. Danell commented in an interview with *Miami New Times*' Georgina Cardenas on the group's return to their punk roots for the 1996 release, "We went back to our punk roots because we thought punk was getting lost in the alternative onslaught.... All these alternative bands are supposed to be part of the punk movement, but we just don't see it; we don't feel that what they do has anything to do with punk."

Even though Social Distortion's music has been flavored with vintage rock and roll, the group kept up with modern times by broadcasting a live concert over the Internet. Late in 1996, a sold-out show at the Hollywood Palladium was available for viewing on the Web. Social Distortion captured their live sound from three concerts played in Southern California and released a project in 1998 entitled *Live at the Roxy.* Returning to the small label recording company, their live album was released by Time Bomb.

Despite the commitment and hard work over their 20 year career, Social Distortion has produced only one gold album. Even though the group lacked the exposure of having cover shots on *Rolling Stone* and appearances at the Grammy Awards, Ness seemed to take the band's limited success in stride by stating to Michael Gelfand of Allmusic Zine, "I probably wouldn't go [to the Grammys] anyway, but it's the point. You want the credibility and the acknowledgment." However, he also stated that he was proud of their gold record and he was grateful that he has not had to paint houses for about ten years. Members of the band appeared to be ordinary people with common hobbies and interests. Danell enjoys mountain biking, riding motorcycles, and playing poker. Ness collects '50s atomic paraphernalia and various religious figures. However, Maurer was slightly more unique in his pursuits as he was licensed as a cosmetologist. Also, both Ness and Danell moved to different areas in their life when they fathered children. They said the move was something new and that it did not take anything away from their philosophies; they were just viewing the world with a different perspective.

Some band members took their Social Distortion experience and progressed into other pursuits. In 1995, the group purchased an Orange County, California, recording studio where they recorded their first two albums. The guys were going to give local bands help with establishing themselves. Maurer did some musical work on his own. He started an independent label, Slip Records, which was something he had wanted to do for many years. The label put out work from punk and acid bands such as Hellbound Hayride's *Sinner.* Ness released two solo albums in 1999. The first, a roots-rock project was titled, *Cheating at Solitaire.* The second album was entitled *Under the Influence.* Gelfand said Ness stated "It was very necessary for me to do this record [*Cheating at Solitaire*] to just let that stuff out. I felt it was very bottled up inside me, and it was very therapeutic to get it out." Recording for the roots-rock album was done with old style equipment in order to capture the rockabilly sound as well as possible. Ness hoped that the break from Social Distortion provided by his solo work would refresh him for a return to the studio with the band.

Selected discography

Mommy's Little Monster, 13th Floor, 1983; released Triple X, 1990; released Time Bomb, 1995.
Prison Bound, Restless, 1988; Time Bomb, 1995.
Social Distortion, Epic, 1990.
Story of My Life...and Other Stories, (EP), Epic 1990.
Somewhere Between Heaven and Hell, Epic, 1992.
Mainliner (Wreckage from the Past), Time Bomb, 1995
White Light White Heat White Trash, 550 Music/Epic, 1996
Live at the Roxy, Time Bomb, 1998.

Sources

Books

Robbins, Ira A., editor, *The Trouser Press Guide to '90s Rock,* Fireside/Simon & Schuster, 1997.
musicHound Rock, Visible Ink Press, 1999.

Periodicals

Rolling Stone, May 31, 1990, p. 34; July 9-23, 1992, pp. 32-3.

Online

"Mike Ness: Life Beyone Social Distortion," *Allmusic Zine*, http://www.allmusic.com (September 26, 1999).

Earwig, http://earwig.com (December 9, 1999).

"I Wanna Be Distorted," *Miami NewTimes.com*, http://www.miaminewstimes.com (July 31, 1997).

The Rough Guide to Rock, http://www.roughguides.com (December 9, 1999).

Social Distortion home page, http://www.socialdistortion.com (December 9, 1999).

—Nathan Sweet

Kay Starr

Singer

General Artists Corporation. Reproduced by permission. ©

If Academy Awards were given for transition from one vocal style to another, Kay Starr would win every year with her delivery of country, jazz, blues and popular music. She was born July 21, 1922 in the small rural community of Dougherty, Oklahoma, to Harry and Annie Coll Starks. Harry was a full blooded Iroquois Indian born on a reservation near Buffalo, New York and Annie, a native of Oklahoma, was of Cherokee, Choctaw and Irish descent. Contrary to other stories, Starr was not born on an Indian reservation. When she was three, the family moved to Dallas, Texas where Harry worked at the Texas Automated Sprinkler Company as an installer and Annie raised chickens at their home. When Kay was small she would go to the hen house and standing atop an apple box sing to the chickens that had been gathered in rows at different levels similar to an amphitheater. Her aunt, Nora, heard her singing and entered her in a yo yo contest at radio station WRR where she sang and yo yoed; she won third prize. Starr later competed in a series of talent contests at the Melba Theater and won three times, triggering the station manager to offer her a fifteen minute program of her own, three times a week.

In 1935, her father's work uprooted the family again and they moved to Memphis, Tennessee where she soon landed on country radio station WMPS's *Saturday Night Jamboree*. She sang with Grand Old Opry legend Bob Wills and his Texas Playboys; she was only fifteen. WMPS frequently received fan mail addressed to names like Kathryn Stokes, Starch, Stairs and even Kathryn Stinks and eventually WMPS's management asked Starr and her father to meet with them for the purpose of changing her name to one that listeners could easily remember. They explained the reason to her father and eventually came up with the name "Star". Her parents felt it was inappropriate because God made the star. It was Starr herself who came up with the idea of adding another "R" and the name Kay was chosen after Kathryn was shortened to "Kay."

While attending Technical High School in Memphis, her radio program was heard by Joe Venuti, a popular orchestra leader, who was slated to perform at the famous Peabody Hotel. Venuti's contract called for a girl singer, which he did not have. Venuti visited her parents to obtain permission for her to appear with his orchestra; they agreed, provided she would be accompanied and returned home before midnight since she was only fifteen years old. That same year she briefly appeared with Bob Crosby and his Bobcats on the syndicated *Chesterfield Supper Club* in Detroit, and she also toured Canada with her mother, who posed as her sister. In July of 1939, she also replaced ailing singer, Marion Hutton, who collapsed with exhaustion on the bandstand. The seventeen year old Starr was considered to be a better

For the Record . . .

Born Kathryn La Verne Starks on July 21, 1922 in Dougherty, OK; daughter of Asa Starks, (an employee of the Texas Automatic Sprinkler Company) and Annie, (an employee of the Works Progress Administration (WPA).

Made singing debut on Radio Station WRR, 1932 in Dallas, TX; began singing on Radio Station WREC, 1935 in Memphis, TN; served as a staff vocalist at the station throughout high school; joined Joe Venuti and his orchestra, 1937 at the Peabody Hotel in Memphis; eventually led to assignments with Bob Crosby and Glenn Miller, where she made her first recordings; rejoined Venuti; sang with Wingy Manone's band and later with Charlie Barnet and his orchestra.; joined Capitol Records, 1946 and had a number of top ten hits including "Wheel of Fortune" her theme song; left Capitol in the 1950s; joined RCA and had a number one hit in "Rock and Roll Waltz;" today Starr performs when she wants to have fun and makes appearances from FL to CA.

Awards: Hit Parade Number One Female Performer of the Year; Oklahoma Hall of Fame.

Address: *Management*—Henry Miller, P. O. Box 195 Encino, CA 91426, (818) 905-9077.

singer than Hutton in several ways. Starr also appeared with Glenn Miller's band at Glen Cove, Long Island, New York, and recorded "Baby Me" and "Love, with a Capital You" with the band.

She moved to Los Angeles and rejoined Joe Venuti his orchestra in California, and and later began singing with trumpeter Wingy Monone's band. Bandleader Charlie Barnet hired her away from Monone, replacing vocalist Lena Horne, and she remained with Barnet until 1945. During that time she toured military hospitals and installations around the world and also performed at posh nightclubs in the Los Angeles area, including Mocambo's, Ciro's and El Rancho Vegas. During this time she developed pneumonia and spent six months in an Army hospital. She would eventually lose the use of her voice due to fatigue, overwork, and pneumonia. She was ordered by the doctor to cease talking, whispering, and to abandon singing until she healed. When her voice returned, it was much huskier and tighter.

In 1946 she went solo and was signed on to the newly formed Capitol Records by Dave Dexter after he had heard her sing in a local nightclub. Capitol had a stable of the finest female vocalists in America including Peggy Lee, Jo Stafford, Ella Mae Morse and Margaret Whiting. There Starr met Tennessee Ernie Ford and they recorded duets together. She remained with Capitol and produced such hits a "Bonaparte's Retreat," "Wheel of Fortune," "I'm the Lonesomest Gal in Town," "Half a Photograph," "Allez Vous En," "Crazy," and "Kay's Lament." "Bonaparte's Retreat" was originally an instrumental written by Pee Wee King , the co-author of the Tennessee Waltz. Its lyrics occurred when Starr visited her family in Dougherty,Oklahoma, and her cousin took her to a new "Juke joint" in town. She had a "fiddle song" and asked the manager to pull the record from the juke box. She called Roy Acuff in Nashville, who was the country and western singer and country music publisher, asking that lyrics be added. Acuff subsequently enlisted King's aid and lyrics were added to his instrumental composition. It rose to number four on the charts and nearly a million dollars in records were sold in 1950.

Starr described "Wheel of Fortune" as her favorite of all pieces because it allowed her to have a lovely home in California It also provided an education for her two daughters, Kathy and Donna and the opportunity to sing all over the world and before Presidents. She described recording "Wheel of Fortune" as difficult since the wheel had to emit the right sound to correspond to the lyrics and music that were easily recorded. This 1952 introduction to the pop music field became her theme song and her first gold record.

Other hits followed including "Allez Vous En," the Cole Porter composition from "Can-Can," "Half a Photograph," and her first hit released single "I'm the Lonesomest Gal In Town." In 1952, she recorded a late 1920's song written by Harry Woods, a former Cape Cod, Massachusetts farmer, who had gone to New York after successfully writing "When the Red Red Robin Goes Bob Bob Bobin Along." Wood's song, "Side by Side" had been written in the 1920's depression era and was inspired as a result of the hard times he and his wife had endured while working at the songwriter's Brill Building in New York. The song became a big hit when Starr revived it in 1953.

Starr indicated in an interview that Capitol often treated her as a utility singer and songs were offered to other female singers before being offered to her, and that she was assigned offbeat selections. On one occasion she submitted a list of songs she wanted to sing and the list was given to Peggy Lee and the other female vocalists. When it was returned a line had been drawn through all of them and she felt she was finding songs for them. Other top twenty hits include "Changing Partners," "Man Upstairs," "So Tired," and "If You Love Me." Starr also recorded an English version of Edith Piaf's song "Hymn L'Amour", written for her lover, French boxing champion Marcel Cerdan.

In 1955, she moved to RCA Records, which had a large stable of top male vocalists including Perry Como and Eddie Fisher. The following year she was presented with the sheet music to a song entitled "The Rock and Roll Waltz." When she looked at the sheet music, she first thought the song was a joke since she could not read musical scales. It also appeared to sound like a nursery rhyme. However, "The Rock and Roll Waltz" became her first RCA recording and rose to number one on the charts in the United States and it made it to the top ten in the United Kingdom. It was also considered the first hit by a female vocalist in the newly issued in "Rock and Roll Era".

The 1950s saw a reduction in Starr's musical activities. She wanted to spend more time with her daughter, Kathy However, she began to book engagements in Las Vegas and Lake Tahoe casinos and made guest appearances on numerous major television shows including those of *The Ed Sullivan Show*, *The Perry Como Show*, *The Dinah Shore Show*, and others. In 1959 she renewed her relationship with Capitol Records and since that time has appeared in nightclubs and theaters all over the world as well as appearing on television and in the motion picture *The Lord Don't Play Favorites* with Robert Stack, Buster Keaton and singer Dick Haymes. In recent years she has regularly appeared in revues at Palm Beach, Florida.

Selected discography

All Starr Hits, Capitol.
Big Band Singers, AJAZZ.
Blue Mood, Capitol.
Blue Starr, RCA.
I Cry By Night, Capitol.
In A Blue Mood, Capitol.
Jazz Singer, Capitol.
Kay Starr Country, Crescendo.
Kay Starr in the Forties, Hindsight.
Kay Starr, Jazz Singer, Capitol.
Kay Starr on Stage, Coronet.
Kay Starr Sings, Coronet.
Kay Starr Style, Capitol.
Kay Starr's Again, Capitol.
Losers Weepers, Capitol.
Movin, Capitol.
Movin' On Broadway, Capitol.
Portrait of a Starr, Sunset.
Tears and Heartaches/Old Records, Capitol.
Them Their Eyes, Rondo.
Back to the Roots, GNP Crescendo.
Christmas Jubilee, Vintage Jazz.
Halloween Stomp, Jass.
Kay Starr, The RCA Years, BMG.
Kay Starr, Collector Series, Capitol.
Moonbeams and Steamy Dreams, Stash.
Spotlight on Kay Starr, Capitol.

Sources

Books

Bronson, Fred, *The Billboard Book of Number One Hits*, Billboard Publications Inc. 1992.
Feather, Leonard, *The Encyclopedia of Jazz*, Horizon Press, 1960.
Lax, Roger and Frederick Smith, *The Great Song Thesaurus*,- Oxford University Press 1989.
Maltin, Leonard, *Movie and Video Guide 1995,* Penguin Books Ltd., 1994.
McAleer, David, *The All Music Book of Hit Singles*, Miller Freeman Books, 1994.
Osborne, Jerry, *Rockin Records,* Osborne Publications 1999.
Simon, George T., *Big Bands*, MacMillan Company, 1970.
Stambler, Irwin, *Encyclopedia of Popular Music,* St. Martin's Press, 1966.

Additional information was obtained through an interview with Kay Starr on August 23, 1999; and from liner notes from Gene, *Back to the Roots*, 1995 and *Kay Starr Collectors Series*, 1991.

—*Francis D. McKinley*

Sun Ra

Jazz musician

For a man who claimed citizenship on the planet Saturn, Sun Ra traveled galaxies away from his Alabama roots where he was born Herman (Sonny) Blount. "The Sun" and his Myth Science Arkestra paved the way of the black arts movement in Harlem in the 1960s and carried thousands of international followers into a music and movement uniquely, sometimes bizarrely, his own.

Sun Ra was remembered by many after his death perhaps more for his outlandish performances with his "Arkestra" than for his music itself. He was, in fact, one of the leading jazz artists to emerge after World War II, and he had already been a working musician for nearly 20 years since arriving in Chicago in the 1930s. In the 1950s, Sun Ra's experimental music followed his long evolution from his early years as a piano player in the blues traditions of New Orleans and Chicago—traveling with Wynonie Harris and Fess Whatley to backup for the famous jazz singers Joe Williams and Lavern Baker—and holding his own as bandleader in Chicago's famous Club De Lisa. By that time, Sun Ra began to startle his

Photograph by Jack Vartoogian. Reproduced by permission.

For the Record . . .

Born Herman "Sonny" Blount in 1914 in Birmingham, AL; (died May 30, 1993, in Birmingham, AL); *Education*: Attended Alabama Agricultural and Mechanical University on scholarship; majored in education.

Jazz musician and band leader c. 1935 until his death; worked as backup musician in Nashville and Chicago before forming own ensemble, Sun Ra and His Arkestra, c. 1950; cut over 200 albums on private labels; music was featured in the film *The Cry of Jazz*.

Awards: Liberty Bell citizenship award from the city of Philadelphia, 1990, for body of work; inducted into the Alabama Hall of Fame, State of Alabama.

audiences with his visual appearances as much as with his music. According to Sun Ra's obituary written by Peter Watrous in the *New York Times*, after the musician's death in Birmingham, Alabama, in 1993, "In the mid-1950's, Sun Ra organized a rehearsal band that wore purple blazers, beanies topped by propellers and white gloves when it performed in public." The glittering robes and Egyptian, Space Age-styled headdressess he would don by the end of the 1960s became a part of a total performance which no one else ever seemed to equal.

Sun Ra was born Herman (Sonny) Blount in 1914, in Birmingham, Alabama. Presumably due to Sun Ra's own purposeful lack of clarity, little else is known about his early childhood. As he grew in his own vision, Sun Ra went so far as to claim he had come from Saturn. "People say I'm Herman Blount, but I don't know him," Mark Jacobson quoted in *Esquire*. "That's an imaginary person," Sun Ra said. "Imaginary on Saturn, at least," said Jacobson, "which is where the real Sun Ra comes from." He attended Alabama Agricultural and Mechanical University, but left for Chicago to pursue a life in music. By the late 1960s, he moved his band to Philadelphia, which was still his home base when he died. Sun Ra left no known survivors when he died except for his band, his spiritual legacy, and hundreds of recordings.

In 1970, Tam Fiofori talked to Sun Ra about his music in the May 14, 1970, issue of *Down Beat*. By this time, Sun Ra was in what some called his "experimental" phase. For him, it was not experimental, rather a natural movement toward awareness. "The intergalactic phase of music touches upon many points," began Sun Ra when Fiofori asked him about the special qualities of intergalactic music. "For instance, everything is every thing and outside of that is nothing. So in order to deal with the infinity, I would have to deal with the nothings and the everythings, of which each one has its different potentials. Then, after that, each one has its multi-potentials; and after that each one has its purposelessness, like the whole infinity of the duality everything." To Sun Ra, whose concept dealt with an infinite space where his music traveled, there was "no purpose ... because if purpose is considered by some as an end, then endlessness to others would mean without purpose. Infinity, however purposeless, does not hesitate to sponsor infinity idea-projects."

In that same interview Sun Ra revealed revealed some history of his own early years, and their influence on his later music. "To me, the best point about jazz," he noted, was the "idea or being of jazz," based on the "spontaneous improvisation principle," Sun Ra told Fiofori. "Pure jazz is that which is without preconceived notion, or it is just being, and that's really my definition of jazz." Sun Ra said his idea was a "result of experiences through the years and my acquaintance with jazz from my so-called childhood." He commented that he saw every band in high school, whether known or unknown. "I loved music beyond the stage of liking it," he said. "Some of the bands I heard never got popular and never made hit records, but they were truly natural Black beauty." If some of his music or recordings were not successful according to critics, Sun Ra believed it was because of the notion of what was commercially-viable music hampered their view.

His years in Chicago were the beginning of his renown in the world of blues and jazz. In addition to his connections at the Club Da Lisa, he encountered other jazz artists making their way to fame, including Miles Davis. Later years in New York, where he and his band eventually became fixtures at the famous jazz club Slug's, Sun Ra's newer sound began to emerge. At a club called the Playhouse, he first met Pharoah Sanders who let him play. He also invited Sun Ra to stay in his place in the West Village (not yet the trendy section of Manhattan it would become in the 1980s). Sun Ra told Fiofori that in those days they would "often be playing to an empty house. ... On very cold nights we'd play in overcoats, but I felt that I should always be doing what I was supposed to do on this planet, regardless of whether the planet responded or not." During that time Sanders played with the Arkestra as well. That was 1950s New York, with its avant garde movement in everything from music to art to lifestyles. As Sun Ra put it, they were not talking about space or intergalactic things, but were instead "talking about the avant garde and the New things. That was what was happening when I came to New York. But what I was doing also entered into the picture, as a remote but indirect influence."

While he started out as a pianist, Sun Ra moved into organ, clavioline, celeste, and became the first musician to use synthesizers to capture a new age of music, complete with light show, films and costume. According to Watrous, "no one else in jazz except Dizzy Gillespie," had "come close to that sort of mixture of vaudevillian carnival and musical intelligence." In 1956, he and the Arkestra began recording after years of struggle and performing for nights on end. That year they performed, *Angels and Demons at Play, Sun Ra Visits Planet Earth*, and the Arkestra's "official" debut, *Super-Sonic Jazz*. The title track for the album, *Angels and Demons...*, was actually recorded in 1960 with other tracks including "A Call for All Demons" and "Demons Lullaby," recorded in 1956. Between 1956 and 1960, the group recorded *The Nubians of Plutonia*, in an early tribute to the African heritage he claimed in much of his music and later performances. While his roots in blues and swing were clearly evident throughout a performance or recording, Sun Ra's use of African-style chants and drums emphasized part of the direction of his spiritual journey.

In January of 1992, Jeff Levenson of *Billboard* noted that a newly-formed record label, Evidence Music, put Sun Ra in the center of their operation. Initially, they licensed ten of his titles from Saturn Records, his "vanity" label established and owned by Sun Ra since the 1950s and inactive for decades.

Remembering Sun Ra, Jacobson commented that on a "wintry predawn nearly twenty-five years ago ... down by the turbid East River," he encountered the entire Myth Science Arkestra "dressed in aluminum-foil tunics, flowing scarves, and tight leggings, just as if it were Monday night at Slugs. The Arkestra stood unspeaking, staring up at the cloud-strewn sky, engaged in secret ritual. At the (helio) center of the assemblage, attired in spangled, gold-leafed shower cap, was the Sun himself, Ra." According to Amiri Baraka, in a tribute to Sun Ra in the *African American Review*, in the Summer of 1995, "Ra was so far out because he had the true self-consciousness of the Afro American intellectual artist revolutionary. He knew our historic ideology and socio-political consciousness was freedom." Sun Ra's music has remained controversial even into the twenty-first century. Whether he would take his place in history as one of the great influences of jazz or as someone who heard voices from other planets, Sun Ra made an interesting curve for most critics and fans.

Selected discography

Super-Sonic Jazz, 1956; Evidence, 1992.
Sound of Joy, 1957; Delmark, 1994.
Jazz in Silhouette, 1958; Evidence, 1992.
The Futuristic Sounds of Sun Ra, 1961; Savoy, 1995.
Other Planes of There, 1964; Evidence, 1994.
The Magic City, 1965; Evidence, 1993.
Monorails and Satellites, 1966; Evidence, 1992.
Holiday for Soul Dance, 1969; Evidence, 1992.
Atlantis, 1969; Evidence, 1993.
My Brother the Wind, Vol. 2, 1970; Evidence 1992.
Space Is the Place, 1972; Evidence, 1993.
Strange Celestial Road, Rounder, 1987.
Reflections in Blue, Black Saint, 1987.
Out There a Minute, Blast First, 1989.
Hours After, Black Saint, 1990.
Mayan Temples, Black Saint, 1990.
Sun Song, Delmark, 1991.
Sunrise in Different Dimensions, Hat Hut, 1991.
Cosmic Tones for Mental Therapy/Art Forms of Dimensions Tomorrow, Evidence, 1992.
Sound Sun Pleasure!, Evidence, 1992.
Sun Ra Visits Planet Earth/Interstellar Low Ways, Evidence, 1992.
We Travel the Spaceways/Bad and Beautiful, Evidence, 1992.
Angels and Demons at Play/The Nubians of Plutonia, Evidence, 1993.
Fate in a Pleasant Mood/When the Sun Comes Out, Evidence, 1993.
Somewhere Else, Rounder, 1993.
At the Village Vanguard, Rounder, 1993.
The Singles, Evidence, 1996.

Sources

Books

Campbell, Robert, *The Earthly Recordings, A Sun Ra Discography,* Cadence Jazz Books, 1994.
Cook, Richard, and Brian Morton, *The Penguin Guide to Jazz on Compact Disc,* 1992; 3rd edition, 1998.
Duke Ellington & Anthony Braxton, Duke University Press, December 1999.
George-Warren, Holly, editor, *The Rolling Stone Jazz Record Guide,* Random House, 1999.
Lock, Graham, *Blutopia, Visions of the Future & Revisions of the past in the Work of Sun Ra,*
Szwed, John F., *Space is the Place, The Lives & Times of Sun Ra*, Da Capo Press, Incorporated, 1998.
Trent, Chris, *Another Shade of Blue, Sun Ra on Record,* Stride Publications, 1997.

Periodicals

African American Review, Summer 1995, p. 253.
Billboard, January 25, 1992, p.12.
Down Beat, February 1994, p.161; June 1997, p.40; August 1999, p. 16.
Esquire, September 1993, p.56.
Jet, June 21, 1993.
New York Times, May 31, 1993; October 19, 1996.
Time, June 14, 1993, p.21.

—*Jane Spear*

David Sylvian

Composer, singer

Photograph by Steve Double. Corbis. Reproduced by permission. ©

British musician and ambient pioneer David Sylvian first attained prominence as the lyricist, composer, and vocalist of the high-art pop group Japan. A restless and progressive artist who strived for perfection, Sylvian left the group in 1982 to embark on an impressive solo and collaborative career. Over the years, and in between solo projects, Sylvian worked with other notable musicians, including Ryuichi Sakamoto (composer of classical scores for the films *Last Emperor* and *Little Buddha*), German composer Holger Czukay, and rock guitarist Robert Fripp (of the group King Crimson). In 1999, Sylvian, after a long absence from solo work, resurfaced with his first full-length album in 12 years since 1987's *Secrets of the Beehive.* Critics immediately hailed *Dead Bees on A Cake,* a title which Sylvian, a devout follower of the Buddhist religion, said referred to the concept of egolessness, as perhaps his most important solo record to date.

David Sylvian was born in 1958 in Beckenham, Kent, England, but spent most of his childhood and young adulthood in London. He gravitated toward a career in music early in life, and at age 16, joined a band at school in Catford, South London. As a founding member of the group Japan, a band that critics define as one of the most underrated and extraordinary bands of the late 1970s and early 1980s, Sylvian served as the group's lyricist, composer, and vocalist. Japan's other members included bassist and bass clarinetist Mick Karn (also known as Anthony Michaelides), synthesist Richard Barbieri, and drummer Steve Jansen (Sylvian's brother). While Japan's first two albums resembled the glam-rock style and image found with many pop groups of the late 1970s, their music progressively moved to a unique style that included both Eastern and orchestral influences, as well as early electronica. Consequently, Japan rose in popularity with singles such as "The Art of Parties" and "Ghost" (from the album *Tin Drum*), which reached number five on the British charts in 1982.

Lost Interest in Japan

Just as the band was gaining a wider audience and critical acclaim, Sylvian lost interest in the pop business, and the band broke up in 1982 to pursue other musical avenues. Even years later, Sylvian resisted indulging in the nostalgia of Japan, preferring instead to discuss his future plans as a solo artist and collaborator with other like-minded musicians. "I've come down hard on Japan, because it was difficult to break away from being perceived as part of that line-up. I realise now that I probably never will. But I haven't heard that material since 1982, so my evaluation of it comes through memory of what I thought I'd achieved at that time," he

For the Record . . .

Born in 1958 in Beckenham, Kent, England; married singer/poet Ingrid Chavez, 1992; children: two daughters.

Joined group Japan, c. 1954; Japan disbanded upon the success of their first hit single, "Ghost" from *Tin Dum,* 1982; recorded first single with composer Ryuichi Sakamoto, "BambooMusic/Bamboo Houses," 1982; composed lyrics for Sakamoto's theme music for award-winning film *Merry Christmas, Mr. Lawrence,* released first solo album, *Brilliant Trees,* 1984; released ambitious double album, *Gone to Earth,* 1986; produced jazz-inspired, more acoustic album, *Secrets of the Beehive,* 1987; reunited with members of Japan as Rain Tree Crow, group released self-titled album, 1991; released two albums with rock guitarist Robert Fripp, *The First Day,* 1993, and *Damage,* 1994; moved to Minneapolis, MN, 1992; relocated to Sonoma, CA, 1997; released fourth solo album, *Dead Bees On A Cake,* 1999.

Addresses: *Record company*—Virgin Records, 338 N. Foothill Rd., Beverly Hills, CA 90210. *Manager*—Richard Chadwick, Opium (Arts) Ltd., 49 Portland Rd., London, U.K., W114LJ. *Website*—http://www.virginrecords.com.

told Chris Roberts of the *Daily Telegraph.* Nonetheless, Sylvian continued an ever-maturing personal as well as professional relationship with his former band mates and felt that his friendships with them grew beyond the popular success of Japan in Great Britain.

Soon after the breakup of Japan, Sylvian met and began collaborating with musician Ryuichi Sakamoto, and their professional and personal relationship endured throughout Sylvian's career."Ryuichi has a wealth of knowledge of music of all genres," Sylvian said to John L. Walters in an interview for *Independent.* "He's one of the few people who can apply that knowledge [clicks fingers] like that. You can be sitting in a room with him, working out an arrangement and say 'elements of Debussy would be nice,' and suddenly there they are; and then say, 'not Debussy, Bill Evans,' and there it is. That's very rare, and it all has his signature." In 1982, the two musicians recorded their first single together, "Bamboo Music/ Bamboo Houses." Then in 1984, Sylvian joined his friend for another joint effort when Sakamoto invited him to write and record the lyrics to the theme music from the award-winning film *Merry Christmas, Mr. Lawrence,* released in a vocal version as *Forbidden Colours.* Later, in 1992, Sylvian wrote the lyrics for Sakamoto's single "Heartbeat." Another long-standing relationship, this time with German composer Holger Czukay, resulted in the duo producing two albums together, *Plight and Premonition* in 1988 and *Flux + Mutability* in 1989. Both recordings featured long, lulling instrumentals.

Started Creating Music of His Own

Meanwhile, Sylvian also started to write music of his own. During the first stage of his solo career, he revisited what remained of Japan's dreamy, pop-oriented explorations for 1984's *Brilliant Trees* (which included contributions by Jon Hassell and Holger Czukay), but infused the songs with jazz and world music. In addition, he drew from the inspiration he had recently discovered through Buddhist teachings during his first visit to Tibet. This religion and love for the Tibetan people would influence the artist's musical and personal direction for years to come. Sylvian then explored ambient music with *Alchemy—An Index of Possibilities,* released in 1985 on cassette only, and *Words With Shaman,* an EP drawn from *Alchemy.* His next undertaking, the ambitious double album *Gone to Earth,* arrived in 1986 and included contributors Robert Fripp and Bill Nelson. This work consisted of "semi-conventional songs and languid instrumentals," according to the *Trouser Press Guide to '90s Rock.* Also in 1986, Sylvian released a body of previously unreleased songs entitled *Gone to Earth.* Following this, Sylvian produced a more jazz-inspired and acoustic album entitled *Secrets of the Beehive* in 1987. In 1989, all of these recording became available in one five-CD set called *Weatherbox.*

The next phase of Sylvian's musical career saw a retreat from solo work that spanned over a decade. During this time, Sylvian "felt the need to move away from familiar forms, to stretch as a performer and writer," as he explained to A.D. Amorosi in an interview for *Magnet* magazine. "Simultaneously, I went through an experience that was very difficult to get to grips with—one where I couldn't comprehend it as I was going through it, so I couldn't contend with it in my writing," Sylvian continued. "I though collaboration would provoke a response through which I would recognize what I was living through." Thus, he proceeded to call on the members of his former band for a reunion. However, he declined to record again under the name Japan and settled on calling the cast of musicians Rain Tree Crow. In the studio, the foursome improvised the unrestrained yet highly structured music reminiscent of Japan, exemplified in tracks such as the ethereal "New Moon at Red Deer Wallow," as well as in the illusionary, flowing songs "Every Colour

You Are," "Boat's for Burning," "Blackwater," and "Pocket Full of Change." The group released the collection of work from their session in 1991 entitled *Rain Tree Crow.*

Following his work with Rain Tree Crow, Sylvian accepted an offer to collaborate again with Fripp, joined also by stick player Trey Gunn (who would later join King Crimson), drummer Jerry Marotta, and co-producer and programmer David Bottrill. They released the album *The First Day* in 1993, which the *Trouser Guide to '90s Rock* described as "a fascinating and rewarding dialectic between Fripp's searing, rhythmically intense physicality and Sylvian's cerebral nonchalance" and "an engrossing, invigorating and mind-expanding adventure of sharp teeth and smooth skin." Sylvian and Fripp then teamed again in 1994 to record *Damage,* an album with a quieter overall mood. Whereas the first album centered primarily around Fripp's guitar playing, *Damage* more closely focused on Sylvian's placid keyboard playing and vocals.

Personal difficulties further prevented Sylvian from taking on his next solo album. "It was a debilitating four-year period where I had to work through rather traumatic emotional experiences. A lot came to the surface," he admitted to Amorosi. "I went into analysis... This breakthrough came at the same time I started working with Fripp, which is the same time I met my wife. It was strange because it felt like profound depression. Yet I couldn't pinpoint it to any particular subject matter."

Gained Inspiration

Just prior to initiating his albums with Fripp, Sylvian met his wife Ingrid Chavez while recording with Sakamoto in 1992. Chavez, a singer and poet, co-star of pop singer Prince's 1990 film *Graffiti Bridge,* and co-author of entertainer Madonna's hit single "Justify My Love," had sent Sylvian a tape of her work with the hopes of one day working with the talented musician. Then, when his lyrics written for Sakamoto's single required female vocals, he remembered Chavez's tape. Within two months after their meeting, Sylvian relocated from London to Minneapolis, Minnesota, and the couple married. They later had two daughters and moved to the town of Sonoma, located in California's Napa Valley. Sylvian attributed much of his recovery and ability to progress creatively with *Dead Bees On A Cake* to moving to the United States, discovering his wife, and raising a family. After leaving London, Sylvian told Amorosi, "I felt more comfortable with my sense of alienation... In Minneapolis, I didn't participate in the culture much. It's a very isolated existence, which is easy to do there. I just hung out with the family and the studio I had built into the house. And the new work was borne of that life."

However, the actual making of his solo project would not progress so easily for Sylvian, known for his slow work rate. In all, the album took about eight years to complete; roughly five years of writing the songs and almost three years of recording and studio work. Originally, Sakamato joined Sylvian as co-producer, but as the music went through numerous transformations and time dragged on, Sylvian found himself producing alone. His studio bill grew out of control, and when the money ran out, Sylvian was forced to mix the album (with engineer Dave Kent) in a barn studio in California. While at times Sylvian felt totally defeated, his perseverance paid off with the release of *Dead Bees on A Cake* in the spring of 1999. "For all of that," he told Amorosi, "it became a far more personal album and all the richer for it. In the future, I won't be so quick to hand over the reins."

Like Sylvian, critics also agreed that *Dead Bees On A Cake* extended far beyond his previous solo work. Chris Roberts in the *Daily Telegraph,* for example, concluded that "*Dead Bees On A Cake* is a lush, compelling and poignant a record as diehard fans might have hoped...." The album explored jazz and rhythm and blues alongside more ambient pieces, and lyrically, the songs represented a journey of self-discovery. In addition, Sylvian used samples for the first time during the finishing process. In one instance, he sampled legendary blues guitarist John Lee Hooker for the song "Midnight Sun." Upon the positive reception of Sylvian's 1999 solo project, the musician planned to continue working alone, as well as with other artists "After I've finished working on Ingrid's album, that's actually my next project," he told Martin James of *Future Music* magazine.

Selected discography

Brilliant Trees, U.K. Virgin, 1984.
Alchemy—An Index of Possibilities, U.K. Virgin, 1985.
Words With the Saman EP, U.K. Virgin, 1985.
Gone to Earth, Virgin, 1986.
Secrets of the Beehive, Virgin, 1987.
(With Holger Czukay) *Plight & Premonition,* Venture/Virgin, 1988.
(With Holger Czukay) *Flux + Mutability,* Venture/Virgin, 1989.
Weatherbox, Virgin, 1989.
Brilliant Trees/Words With the Saman, Blue Plate, 1991.
(With Rain Tree Crow) *Rain Tree Crow,* Virgin, 1991.
(With Robert Fripp) *The First Day,* Virgin, 1993.
(With Robert Fripp) *Damage,* Virgin, 1994.
Dead Bees On A Cake, Virgin, 1999.

Sources

Books

Robbins, Ira A., editor, *Trouser Press Guide to '90s Rock,*, Fireside/Simon & Schuster, 1997.

Periodicals

Calgary Sun, April 4, 1999, p. 42; April 14, 1999, p. 66.
Daily Telegraph, March 27, 1999; April 3, 1999.
Independent, March 26, 1999, p. 11.
Future Music, August 1999, pp. 64-5.
Magnet, June/July 1999, p. 26.
Newsday, November 4, 1993, p. 83.
Reuters, August 23, 1996.

Online

"Sylvian Remains One of Music's Innovators," *Virgin Records,* http://www.virginrecords.com (August 23, 1999).
"Years of Memories: an Interview with David Sylvian," *Weatherbox website,* http://web.nl.net/users/K.vanBunningen/music/sylvian/publications/articles/dboac/index.html (August 23, 1999).

—Laura Hightower

Texas

Pop group

Photograph by Steve Jennings. Corbis. Reproduced by permission. ©

With a name like Texas, one would most likely expect to hear the straightforward country and blues-rock tunes or the rolling folk songs often associated with the southwestern state. Despite the images the name implies, Texas, whose members hail from Glasgow, Scotland, also grasp the moody textures of British 1980s pop and American radio rock. Named after the 1985 Wim Wenders film *Paris, Texas* for which Ry Cooder, a folk musician admired by the members of the band, composed the soundtrack, the group took inspiration from blues and folk music and added an overall modern rock feel. "The name Texas causes so many problems," frontwoman Sharleen Spiteri told Neil McCormick in the *Daily Telegraph.* "Sometimes I wonder what possessed us, I really do. But it was pouring with rain in Glasgow, we were sitting there playing a Southern blues twang thing, wishing we really were in Texas... What can I say? It seemed like a great idea at the time." Texas achieved pop-star status in Great Britain with their debut album in 1989, *Southside,* but reached only a limited following of fans in the United States. Throughout the 1990s, the Scottish quintet amassed an even broader audience, selling over ten million records worldwide, although a substantial American fan base continued to elude them. However, critics predicted that with their 1999 release, *The Hush,* Texas would earn greater recognition outside of the United Kingdom and Europe.

Texas formed in 1986 in Glasgow, Scotland, when Spiteri, praised for her deep, soulful voice, met Johnny McElhone, a veteran of the British rock circuit and a member of two former groups, Hipsway and Altered Images. While Hipsway remained a relatively unknown band, Altered Images had considerable chart success in both Britain and the United States during the mid-1980s. McElhone, who played bass guitar for Texas, and Spiteri, who served as the group's lead singer, rhythm guitarist, and occasional pianist, penned a number of songs before recruiting guitarist Ally McErlaine and drummer Stuart Kerr to join the band. Although Spiteri began playing guitar at the age of ten, she claimed she never held aspirations to form or play with a pop/rock ensemble. In fact, until the creation of Texas, Spiteri worked as a hairdresser in Glasgow.

Spiteri remained the dominating force behind Texas's success from the beginning. Labeled by the British press as "the U.K.'s sexiest female," Spiteri displayed a sensual style with her dark hair, pale skin, and slender frame, without appearing as a stereotypical beauty. While many pop groups tend to experience conflicts when one band member receives most of the attention, Texas placed Spiteri in the spotlight on purpose. As the lead singer told McCormick, "We made that decision as a band. I am the most confident about having photo-

For the Record . . .

Members include **Eddie Campbell** (joined group 1989), keyboards; **Richard Hynd** (joined group c. 1991), drums; **Stuart Kerr** (left group c. 1991), drums; **John McElhone**, bass; **Ally McErlaine**, guitar; **Sharleen Spiteri** (born 1968 in Glasgow, Scotland), vocals, rhythm guitar, piano.

Formed group in Glasgow, Scotland, 1986; performed first live show as a group, 1988; signed with Phonogram/ Mercury label, released debut album *Southside*, 1989; released single "Tired Of Being Alone," 1992; released *Ricks Road,* 1993; released *White on Blonde,* 1997; signed with Universal Records, released career highlight *The Hush,* 1999.

Addresses: *Record company*—Universal Records, 1755 Broadway, 7th Fl., New York City, NY 10019; (212)373-0600; fax (212) 247-3954.

graphs taken. They've no desire to do it, no desire to be in the videos." In March of 1988, with Spiteri fronting the band, Texas performed live for the firsttime as a group at a local college in Glasgow. They continued to tour around the United Kingdom extensively before signing with the British record label Phonogram (known as Mercury in the United States). In 1989, after recruiting keyboard player Eddie Campbell, Texas released their debut album entitled *Southside.* The strength of the song "I Don't Want a Lover," which became a top ten British hit single, helped make *Southside* an instant success and launch it to number three on the British charts. Eventually, the album went platinum, selling 1.6 million copies worldwide, even though many critics described the remainder of the record's songs as derivative and bland. In the United States, the album's engaging yet low-key blending of blues, R&B, soul, country-folk, and modern rock only received air play on college radio stations.

After touring across Europe, Richard Hynd replaced Kerr on drums, and Texas released their second effort, 1991's *Mothers Heaven,* an overall improvement on the band's debut release. Maintaining their prior blues undertones brought to the surface by slide-guitar and Spiteri's handsome vocals, the band also introduced more rock and roll influences with their sophomore release. Critics marveled at Spiteri's singing, often comparing her vocal skills to those of Motown legend Diana Ross, country singer Linda Ronstadt, and singer/songwriter Maria McKee, former vocalist for the country-rock group Lone Justice. McKee sang back-up vocals on two songs for *Mothers Heaven,* including the album's title track. "What makes Texas truly special is the singing of Sharleen Spiteri," concluded *People* magazine. "On a song like the gospelized 'Alone with You,' Spiteri moves easily from a prairie-dust roughness to a slippery sexiness." But despite the record's artistic merits, Texas unfortunately fell victim to bad timing with the release of *Mothers Heaven,* and found themselves displaced by the growing popularity of British dance-pop bands. Thus sales for the album, under one million mostly in continental Europe, proved disappointing in comparison to Texas's debut.

However, the group's disappointment was short-lived as they were reinvigorated by the success of their 1992 British Top 20 hit single "Tired Of Being Alone," a cover of an Al Green song. That year, Texas also traveled to the United States for the first time and enjoyed a popular American tour, performing before mainly alternative music audiences. In 1993, Texas released a third album containing 12 songs, the back-to-basics and unpretentious *Ricks Road,* for which the band again won favorable reviews. For this release produced by Paul Fox, Texas settled into a rich groove, featuring songs accented with but not dominated by country, blues, gospel, and rock undertones. The focus of *Ricks Road,* as with the band's first two releases, centered on Spiteri, who gave full voice to such memorable, straightforward songs as "You Owe It All to Me," "You've Got to Live a Little," "Listen To Me," the country twang "So Called Friend," and the rock-inspired "Fade Away." Throughout the album, Texas's influences came to the surface, most notably Spiteri's gritty rock and smooth country-styled vocals, as well as McErlaine's blues-based guitar playing.

For the next few years, Texas took a break from recording but returned in 1997 with *White on Blonde,* the group's second number one album in the United Kingdom. Not since the release of *Southside* had the band witnessed such popular success. For most of the record's songs, Texas chose to drop their American rock and roll sound for a combination of pop-rock, hip-hop, and soul. Spiteri described *White on Blonde* as a "modern soul record," as quoted by Andy Gill in *Independent.* Nevertheless, the same Texas sound came through under the alterations, and the band drew on a variety of styles without letting go of their adult-pop composure. "Hints of ambient electronics, gritty rock and R&B grooves ripple through the lush layers of sound," stated *Los Angeles Times* writer Sandy Masuo, printed in the *Minneapolis Star Tribune.* Masuo further added, "Spiteri shifts effortlessly from bluesy crooning to a forthright folkiness without ever losing her poise." Also taking more chances with *White on Blonde,* Texas produced more ambitious songs such as the dark, moody "Insane" and "Put Your Arms Around Me," both set to stringed instrumentals and a slowed-down beat.

Texas released *The Hush* in the spring of 1999 on Universal Records, and the album soon became considered the group's best collection of songs. The more finely produced effort recorded in a studio in Spiteri's house offered more depth and made Texas seem more like a sophisticated modern soul act. The subtle opening track "In Our Lifetime," for example, gradually develops without sounding predictable, and the album progresses with references to Texas's influences, from R&B singer Marvin Gaye to the classic rock band Fleetwood Mac. In the past, some of Texas's songs had come off as clumsy and underwritten when paired with the grandeur of Spiteri's voice. But with *The Hush,* propelled by drummer Hynd and the soulful rock guitar of McElhone (who also shared production duties), Spiteri shined similar to a member of Motown's the Supremes for "When We Are Together" and delivered the sultry "Tell Me the Answer," a track resembling a lustful Prince tune, with a soft, sexy style. Other noteworthy tracks included the dreamy "Sunday Afternoon," and the pop song "Summer Son," reminiscent of the 1970s group Abba. With plans to return to the United States to promote their latest release, Texas, now based in London, England, seemed certain to attract a more mainstream American audience and surpass the sales of their previous albums.

Selected discography

Southside, Mercury, 1989.
Mothers Heaven, Mercury, 1991.
Ricks Road, Mercury, 1993.
Live From Ricks Road, Mercury, 1994.
White on Blonde, Mercury, 1997.
The Hush, Universal, 1999.

Sources

Books

musicHound Rock: The Essential Album Guide, Visible Ink Press, 1999.

Robbins, Ira A., ed., *Trouser Press Guide to '90s Rock,* Fireside/Simon and Schuster, 1997.

Periodicals

Daily Telegraph, May 8, 1999; August 26, 1999, p. 19.

Dallas Morning News, May 23, 1999, p. 10C.

Entertainment Weekly, May 21, 1999, p. 78.

Independent, January 31, 1997, p. 10; May 9, 1997, p. 13; May 8, 1999, p. 11.

Independent on Sunday, March 23, 1997, p. 15; July 27, 1997, p. 24.

Minneapolis Star Tribune, November 9, 1997, p. 02F.

People, November 11, 1991, p. 25; March 28, 1994, p. 23; July 12, 1999, p. 39.

Rolling Stone, June 10, 1999.

Online

"Texas," *All Music Guide website,* http://allmusic.com (September 22, 1999).

RollingStone.com, http://www.rollingstone.tunes.com (September 22, 1999).

—Laura Hightower

Type O Negative

Metal rock band

Photograph by Joe Giron. Corbis. Reproduced by permission.

With each band member boasting long hair, plenty of tattoos, and prime influences such as the hard-rocking 1970s outfit Black Sabbath, it comes as no surprise that Type O Negative earned labels like "gothic-metal gurus" from the media. However, lead singer and bassist Peter Steele resisted such pigeonholing. "A goth image has been cast upon us by the media because they have to label us something, I guess," Steele suggested to John Roos in an interview for the *Los Angeles Times.* "People think we're vampires. I mean, we may suck, but it's not blood. Seriously, I don't like being called goth because there are more elements to our music than that label suggests. If you're gonna call us something, I prefer 'junk rock' or 'gothadelic.' I think we make music that dead hippies might like." In fact, as Steele proposed, Type O Negative combined elements of metal, industrial, psychedelia, and alternative music, in addition to goth-rock, into their overall sound. Moreover, as stated by the Rolling Stone.com website, "Steele's songcraft supplies Type O Negative with a larger-than-life sound. The rumbling bass lines, thrashing guitar riffs and massive vocalization (paired by the equally massive stature of Steele [who stands six feet, six inches tall]) make this band nearly frightening in its magnitude."

Although Type O Negative first earned a reputation for their brash, speed-metal sound punctuated with vulgar, offensive lyrics, the band would later transform their image. And when the album *Bloody Kisses* arrived in 1993, critics and fans alike seemed surprised to hear Type O Negative abandoning humor and vulgarity and attempting to convey feeling. The change, as Steele told Roos, stemmed largely from Steele's personal influences growing up. "I've always liked really heavy rock music, like Black Sabbath and Iron Butterfly," said Steele. "Yet at the same time, who didn't like the Beatles and Stones? Then I got older, I was into the droning, dreamy sounds of bands like the Cocteau Twins, My Bloody Valentine and Dead Can Dance.... I guess you could say that I like music that's soft on the outside but with a strong, solid foundation. With Type O Negative, we like to sugarcoat our bricks."

Based in New York City, Type O Negative formed in 1990 (some sources say 1989) when Steele left his former band, a cult favorite called Carnivore, to create his own metal group. Building on Carnivore's solid reputation as a hard-hitting speed-metal act, vocalist and bassist Steele enlisted guitarist Kenny Hickey, drummer Johnny Kelly, and keyboardist Josh Silver to continue the tradition. Like Steele, Kenny was influenced by other music besides heavy metal. He grew up in Brooklyn, New York, emulating the guitar styles of John Lennon and Brian May. "I was the kid that tried guitar lessons but lacked discipline. I was just like any other teenage kid

For the Record . . .

Members include **Kenny Hickey**, guitar; **Johnny Kelly**, drums; **Josh Silver**, keyboards; **Peter Steele** (born c. 1963), vocals, bass.

Formed band in New York City, 1990; released debut album *Slow, Deep and Hard*, 1991; released gold status album *Bloody Kisses*, 1993; released *October Rust*, 1996; toured with Ozzfest '97; released *World Coming Down*, which focused on real-life issues and featured a medley of Beatles songs, 1999.

Addresses: *Record company*—Roadrunner Records, 536 Broadway, 4th Flr., New York, NY 10012, (212) 274-7500, fax (212) 334-6921. *Website*—Type O Negative at Roadrunner Records, http://www.roadrun.com/artists/TypeONegative.

looking for a way to express myself and to become more noticeable," the guitarist told Aaron Johnston in a 1997 interview for *Guitar Player.* "I'm more at ease now, and I'm more interested in finding stimulating sounds than blasting away, but for me playing guitar has always been more about emotions than intellectualizing."

After signing with Roadrunner Records, Type O Negative debuted in 1991 with *Slow, Deep and Hard,* an album built around blazing guitar riffs, church organs, and theatrical vocals—not to mention an onslaught of offensive lyrics. One line from the record, for instance, declared, "Hey,don't think I don't know what you're doing, you stupid twat!," as quoted by *Rolling Stone* writer Julia Szabo. Following this, Type O Negative released an EP (also referred to as a Mini-LP by the band's website) with equally objectionable lyrics entitled *Origin of the Feces.* "Since both records featured the lyric 'I know you're [expletive] someone else,' it's safe to say that Type O Negative concerned itself for the most part with vulgar expressions of base emotion and bodily urges," surmised Szabo.

However, Type O Negative seemed to have matured by the time they recorded 1993's *Bloody Kisses,* an album that hit number 200 on the *Billboard* charts well over a year after its release. Singing about nursing a broken heart rather than the above-mentioned indignities, Type O Negative amazed fans and critics alike. Songs such as "Blood and Fire" exemplified the foursome's radical change with lines like "I always thought we'd be together/ And that our love could not be better," as quoted by Szabo. Upon the strength of other tracks including the solemn dirges "Black No. 1" and "Christian Woman," as well as a cover of Seals and Crofts' "Summer Breeze," *Bloody Kisses* gave Type O Negative their first hit album and eventually surpassed gold-status sales.

The band's subsequent album, *October Rust,* appeared in 1996, featuring another cover: Neil Young's "Cinnamon Girl." But Steele insisted that all of the band's cover tracks were played with sincere intentions. "We're not into doing parodies," asserted Steele in his husky voice to Roos. "I'm just taking something I like; I chew it up and spit it out, and then I see how it looks and sounds. It's not a challenge to me to replicate a song note-for-note. I'd much rather put our own style into it by taking a light song and turning it into something heavier." Described by Roos as a "sprawling 15-song, 73-minute epic filled with layers of guitar, keyboard and synthesizer" *October Rust* also featured heartfelt, yet at times brutal and self-destructive tracks such as "Haunted," "Love You to Death," and "Burnt Flowers Fallen." Explaining how he came to write these songs, Steele, the band's primary lyricist, further explained, "I have gotten my heart broken so many times that I've lost count. Any time I've been involved with someone I've cared about, I've suffocated them by caring too much. That's probably why I lost them."

After contributing to the soundtrack *I Know What You Did Last Summer,* issued by Columbia Records in 1997, and drawing in crowds for the Ozzfest '97 tour, Type O Negative released their fourth full-length album entitled *World Coming Down.* Hailed by *Alternative Press* as "One of the Most Anticipated Albums of 1999," according to the band's official website, Steele, who had recently lost several members of his extended family, revealed that most of the songs were "about battling personal demons, missing people you love, and women walking out on us ... and self-pity and chemical addiction." Therefore, when Steele announced "Everyone I Love Is Dead," he was referencing his own personal hardships. Comparing *World Coming Down* to Type O Negative's earlier work, Steele further added, "The band capitalized on a sexual aspect. Now we're trying to move on. I'm too old for heavy metal. I just want to do something unexpected."

And as Steele and Type O Negative had hoped, *World Coming Down* did succeed in taking critics by surprise. As *Washington Post* writer Mark Jenkins noted, "Almost as unexpected [as replacing the monsters and victims of the heavy metal genre with issues of real-life mortality] is the band's growing interest in melody. ... Any band that ends its album with a medley of the Beatles' 'Day

Tripper,' 'If I Needed Someone,' and 'I Want You (She's So Heavy)' is bucking to get evicted from goth-metal's mausoleum." Produced by Steele along with keyboardist Silver, the album still managed to find room for a few goth-inspired tracks, including "White Slavery," which opened with a funeral-like organ, and the title song, which featured a Gregorian-sounding chant.

In addition to creating their own albums, Type O Negative contributed to numerous film soundtracks in addition to *I Know What You Did Last Summer,* such as *Bride of Chucky,* Howard Stern's *Private Parts* (for a version of Status Quo's "Pictures of Matchstick Men" with Ozzy Osbourne on vocals), and the highly-anticipated 1999 film *The Blair Witch Project* (for the song "Haunted," previously recorded for *October Rust*). "Haunted" was again used in an Interplay Productions video game called *Descent 2.* The band also produced a home video entitled *After Dark,* released around 1993.

Selected discography

Slow, Deep and Hard, Roadrunner, 1991.
Origin of the Feces, (EP), Roadrunner, 1992.
Bloody Kisses, Roadrunner, 1993.
October Rust, Roadrunner, 1996.
I Know What You Did Last Summer soundtrack, (contributor),Columbia, 1997.
Private Parts soundtrack, (contributor), Warner Brothers, 1997.
World Coming Down, Roadrunner, 1999.
The Blair Witch Project soundtrack, (contributor), 1999.

Sources

Periodicals

Alternative Press, August 1999.
Billboard, September 21, 1996, p. 63.
Guitar Player, March 1997, pp. 37-43.
Los Angeles Times, February 14, 1997, p. 37; February 22, 1997, p. F, 4:3; July 1, 1997, p. F, 2:3.
Melody Maker, October 9, 1999, p. 39.
Rolling Stone, February 23, 1995, p. 74.
Washington Post, October 22, 1999, p. N14.

Online

"Type O Negative," *Rolling Stone.com,* http://www.rollingstone.tunes.com (December 6, 1999).
"Type O Negative," *Type O Negative at Roadrunner Records*, http://www.roadrun.com/artists/TypeONegative (December 6, 1999).

—Laura Hightower

Tom Waits

Singer, songwriter, actor

Photograph by Lynn Goldsmith. Corbis. Reproduced by permission. ©

Although he has applied his many talents to acting and composing for stage and screen, Tom Waits's performances on albums and in concert have remained his trademark. His rumpled suits, his rough and gravelly voice, and his songs about downtrodden but hopeful characters all make a Waits performance instantly recognizable. Still, there have been changes in Waits's music. Early on, his songs showed the influence of the jazz and blues he had listened to as a child. Over time he became more experimental, showing classical influences and a willingness to use any object that could make a sound as an instrument. Then, after his 1992 album, *Bone Machine,* Waits seemingly stopped recording new materials, releasing only retrospectives and music from movies and musicals. This hiatus ended in 1999 with the release of *Mule Variations,* in which he brought together the various sounds and styles from his entire career.

The way life began for Waits sounds like something that might have happened in one of his songs. He was born in a taxicab outside a hospital in Pomona, California, on December 7, 1949. His parents taught school, but more important for Waits, his father taught him how to build Heathkit radios. On his crystal sets he heard radio programs from around the country, listening to the blues of Ray Charles and Leadbelly, the country music of Johnny Horton and Floyd Cramer, and the rock and roll played by Wolfman Jack. While his musical tastes were forming, so were his literary ones, as he discovered the works of the Beat authors, especially Jack Kerouac and his best-known work, the novel *On the Road.*

Waits took to the road himself, heading to Los Angeles. There he continued his fascination with the lives of the people who populated the city late at night, living on the margins of society. These people became the sources for the songs that he started performing around the city. His appearance on stage meshed with his characters. Dressed in a rumpled old suit and often wearing a porkpie hat, Waits would brandish a cigarette or a drink while telling stories between songs. He became well known on the Los Angeles club circuit, and during a 1969 stint at the Troubadour, a legendary West Hollywood club, he signed a contract with rock manager Herb Cohen. Still, he remained a songwriter and stage performer until 1973, when his first album, *Closing Time,* came out on the Asylum label.

Even though he had signed with a major record company, Waits did not lead the stereotypical life of a rock star. Living in Los Angeles, he roomed at the Tropicana Hotel, a residence more seedy than luxurious. He stayed at similar places when he toured. He explained his reasons to David Fricke of *Rolling Stone*: "I would wind up in these

For the Record . . .

Born Thomas Alan Waits, December 7, 1949, in Pomona, CA (some sources say Whittier); son of Jesse Frank Waits and Alma (Johnson) McMurray, both school teachers; married Kathleen Patricia Brennan (script editor and playwright), August 10, 1980; children: Casey, Kellesimone, and Sullivan.

Began performing in night clubs in Los Angeles and Hollywood, CA, late 1960s; released first album, *Closing Time,* on Asylum, 1973; made film acting debut in *Paradise Alley,* 1978; began writing film scores, 1980; composed, co-produced, and starred in stage musical *Frank's Wild Years,* 1986; collaborated on stage musical *The Black Rider,* 1993; released most commercially successful album, *Mule Variations*, 1999.

Awards: *Rolling Stone* Magazine Music Critics' Picks for best songwriter, 1985; Grammy Award for best alternative album, *Bone Machine,* 1992.

Addresses: *Record company*—Epitaph Records, 2798 W. Sunset Blvd., Los Angeles, CA 90026-2102. *Home*—P. O. Box 498, Valley Ford, CA 94972-0498.

very strange places—these rooms with stains on the wallpaper, foggy voices down the hall, sharing a bathroom with a guy with a hernia. I'd watch TV with old men in the lobby. I knew there was music in those places—and stories. That's what I was looking for." Many of his early gigs were not all that glamorous, either. At one time he found himself performing in front of children in the morning, serving as the opening act for1950s children's television star Buffalo Bob and his famous marionette, Howdy Doody. Even when opening for other rock acts, Waits wasn't comfortable. On a tour with Frank Zappa, Waits had what he described to Fricke as his "first experience with rodeos and hockey arenas.... It was like *Frankenstein,* with the torches, the whole thing."

While the life of a rock and roll star didn't appeal to Waits, his music appealed to many of the stars themselves. Artists such as the Eagles, Bette Midler, and Bruce Springsteen all recorded their own versions of Waits's songs from the 1970s. Waits was prolific throughout the decade, releasing a total of eight albums on Asylum from 1973 through 1981, including *The Heart of Saturday Night* in 1974, *Small Change* in 1977, and *Heart Attack and Vine* in 1980. Steve Huey of allmusic.com summarized Waits's music during this period as "a mix of Beat poetry recited over jazz-trio backing and blues, alcohol-soaked piano and/or orchestral balladry." The 1975 live album *Nighthawks at the Diner* captured the full Waits stage performance, laced with the story telling and one-liners that he interspersed within the musical performances.

Waits's penchant for performing led him into acting. He made his film debut with a small part in the Sylvester Stallone vehicle *Paradise Alley* in 1978. Waits went on to appear in numerous films, working with such respected directors as Robert Altman (*Short Cuts*), Terry Gilliam (*The Fisher King*), Jim Jarmusch (several films, most notably *Down by Law*), and Francis Ford Coppola (several films, including Bram Stoker*'s Dracula*). Working with Jarmusch and Coppola also gave Waits the opportunity to write soundtracks. One collaboration with Coppola also led Waits to one of the most important events of his life and career. While writing the soundtrack for *One From the* Heart, he met script editor Kathleen Brennan. The two married in 1980, and while she changed his life in small ways, such as not allowing him to wear his suits to bed, she also influenced his song writing by encouraging him to open up musically.

Waits's first album after their marriage was 1983's *Swordfishtrombones,* which marked the beginning of a new sound for him, a sound that came out of collaborating with Brennan. He described how she liberated him to Gil Kaufman and Michael Goldberg of *Addicted to* Noise web magazine: "You try to reconcile the fact that you like Collapsing New Buildings and Skip James and Elmer Bernstein and Nick Cave and Beefheart and Eric Satie and all this stuff that you don't know what to do with. I guess it was her that gave me the notion that you can find some reconciliation between these things that you like. That was the beginning, and we've been working together since then." Some of the new elements to appear in Waits's music at this time were the influence of German composer Kurt Weill and the willingness to use sounds made by everyday objects in his arrangements. Waits told Fricke, "I'm the kind of bandleader who when he says, 'Don't forget to bring the Fender,' I mean the fender from the Dodge."

While Waits's music and instruments changed over time, the lyrics of his songs continued to explore the lives of the down-and-out and the dispossessed. Even though the situations may seem bizarre, Waits and Brennan write from everyday life, although they exaggerate a bit. He told Fricke, "If I know three things about my neighbor, I take those, and that's enough for me to goon. Everybody mixes truth and fiction. If you're stuck for a place for a story to go, you make up the part you need." Waits also stressed the importance of making the setting for the song feel authentic in an interview with Jonathan Valania of *Magnet* magazine: "Every song needs to be anatomically correct: You need weather, you need the name of the town, something to eat—every song needs certain ingredients to be balanced."

Still, *Swordfishtrombones* marked a change in the tone of Waits's songs. *musicHound Rock* described the songs from the 1970s as "sentimental in the way people get after a few too many cocktails," but by the time *Bone Machine* was released in 1992, Waits's material was the "most harrowing ever." Even this material, though, appealed to other artists. Rod Stewart scored a hit with his cover of "Downtown Train" from 1985's *Raindogs*. *Bone Machine,* though, brought Waits the most recognition for his work from the recording industry, winning a Grammy for Best Alternative Music Performance. Evidently Waits didn't think much of the award. Jim Jarmusch reported Waits's reaction to Valania: "He flipped out when he got the Grammy. He hated that. 'Alternative to what?! What the hell does that mean?'"

Following *Bone Machine*, Waits turned his attention away from the studio and toward the stage. He had already collaborated with Brennan on the musical *Frank's Wild Years,* the story of an accordion player recalling his life while freezing on a park bench, in 1987. In 1993, Waits teamed with legendary Beat author William Burroughs and composer Robert Wilson on a musical called *The Black Rider,* based on a 19th-century German folk opera about a man who makes a deal with the devil so that he can marry the woman he loves. Waits then worked with Wilson on an operatic adaptation of *Alice in Wonderland.* Waits also kept his hand in composing for movies, collaborating with Brennan on the music of an Oscar-winning animated short subject, *Bunny*, in 1998.

In 1999 Waits released *Mule Variations,* his first album of new material not related to stage or screen work in seven years. Commercially, it was immediately Waits's largest success. Only two of his previous albums had even cracked the *Billboard* top 100, but *Mule Variations* debuted at number 30 on the chart. The album also achieved good critical notices, with many reviews pointing out that all the sounds and styles of Waits's earlier recordings appeared here in various songs. Valania wrote, "*Mule Variations,* his first album in seven years, and possibly his best, finds him moving full circle." As usual, Brennan collaborated with Waits on this album, receiving co-writing credits on two-thirds of the songs. The couple composed on a rented piano in a hotel room, a process that Waits described to Fricke as "a sack race. You learn to move forward together." Reviewing the album in the *Village Voice,* Robert Christgau wrote, "Together they humanize the percussion-battered *Bone Machine* sound, reconstituting his '80s alienation effects into a Delta harshness with more give to it—enough to accommodate a tenderness that's never soft."

Ironically, after all his years of recording for major labels, this most commercially successful of Waits's albums appeared on Epitaph records, an independent company known for its punk rock emphasis. Bradley Bambarger of *Billboard* reported that Waits "wanted to avoid what he calls 'the plantation system of the music business.'" For Waits, remaining independent of the business dealings of major record labels brought the freedom to make the kind of music that he wanted and to take seven years between album releases if he so chose. Addressing the issue of his fans' frustration at having to wait so long to hear a new Tom Waits album, he told Fricke, "It's like looking for your waitress. People get like that with artists. We are a product-oriented society." Waits has defied that kind of expectation throughout his career, never performing the popular sound of the moment. He even defied his fans' expectations when he changed from the derelict lounge singer of the 1970s to the sound experimentalist of the 1980s. And, comparing song writing to fishing, he told Fricke that it didn't matter how frequently he produced new work: "So you don't want to fish for a couple of weeks, a couple of years? The fish will get along fine without you."

Selected discography

with Elektra/Asylum

Closing Time, 1973.
The Heart of Saturday Night, 1974.
Nighthawks at the Diner, 1975.
Small Change, 1976.
Foreign Affairs, 1977.
Blue Valentine, 1978.
Heart Attack and Vine, 1980.
Bounced Checks, 1981.
Asylum Years, 1985.
Anthology, 1985.
The Asylum Years, 1985.

with Columbia

One From the Heart, 1982.

with Island

Swordfishtrombones, 1983.
Rain Dogs, 1985.
Frank's Wild Years, 1987.
Big Time, 1988.
Bone Machine, 1992.

Night on Earth, 1992.
The Black Rider, 1993.
Beautiful Maladies: The Island Years, 1998.

with Epitaph

Mule Variations, 1999.

Sources

Books

Contemporary Musicians, volume 12, Gale Research, Inc., 1994.
musicHound Rock: The Essential Album Guide, Visible Ink Press, 1999.

Periodicals

Billboard, March 20, 1999, p. 11.
Magnet, June/July, 1999, p. 51.
Rolling Stone, June 24, 1999, p. 37.
Village Voice, June 1, 1999, p. 76.

Online

"Tom Waits," *All Music Guide*, http://www.allmusic.com (November 26, 1999).
"Tom Waits '99: The ATN Interview," *Addicted to Noise,* http://www.addict.com (November 26, 1999).

—*Lloyd Hemingway*

Rick Wakeman

Composer, keyboards

Photograph by Lynn Goldsmith. Corbis. Reproduced by permission. ©

For over 30 years, pianist and keyboardist Rick Wakeman has maintained one of the busiest performance and session schedules in modern popular music. Since the mid-1960s, he has performed on an estimated 2,000 tracks and belonged to nearly one dozen bands. At one point in his early career he reportedly completed as many as 18 recording sessions per week. During his youth, Wakeman was immersed in classical piano lessons and musical education until his teen-age years, when he branched out in search of musical venues that appealed more closely to his personal taste. Wakeman is most widely associated with his membership in two popular bands of the 1970s, Strawbs and Yes, although he has also performed in sessions with a diverse list of artists, including Elton John, David Bowie, Cat Stevens, Lou Reed, and Black Sabbath. He has recorded numerous solo albums and composed numerous musical scores.

Wakeman was born Richard Christopher Wakeman in Perivale, Middlesex, England, on May 18, 1949. His parents, Cyril and Mildred Wakeman, sent their son to Wood End Infants School beginning in 1954. Wakeman was a typical child; he joined the Cub Scouts' 1st Scout Troop of Sudbury in 1958, and the following year he graduated to Drayton Manor County Grammar School in West London. He vacationed with his family at Exmouth in Devon every summer, and joined a football team in the early 1960s.

Wakeman studied classical piano from age seven, and became a regular participant—and winner—of musical competitions; he won his first music festival competition in 1960. In 1961 he started a band, called Brother Wakeman and the Clergyman, and in 1962 he abandoned his scout troop for the Boys Brigade at nearby Baptist Church, where he also learned to play the church organ. In 1963 he joined a mediocre (at best) band called the Atlantic Blues, and by 1964, when he first began to study the clarinet, he had evolved into a seasoned young performer. He quit the Atlantic Blues in 1965 and joined a dance band quartet called the Concords, but by 1966 he had formed another band of his own, called Curdled Milk—a takeoff on Eric Clapton's Cream. Additionally, Wakeman established a dance band called the Green Dolphin Trio, and in 1967 he joined the Ronnie Smith Band. During his years with the Ronnie Smith Band, Wakeman became acquainted with a vocalist named Ashley Holt. The two formed a professional bond, and years later Holt was a frequent contributor to Wakeman's solo endeavors.

Though Wakeman's musical interests flourished, he was bored with school and avoided his studies. Eventually he quit school in order to train to become a concert pianist.

For the Record . . .

Born Richard Christopher Wakeman on May 18, 1949 in Middlesex, England; son of Cyril and Mildred W. Wakeman; married Nina Carter, 1983; children: Oliver, Adam, Benjamin (from first marriage); Jemma, Oscar (from second marriage). *Education*: Royal College of Music, London, 1968.

Formed or was a member of several bands as a youth in the 1960s; member of the Strawbs, 1970-71; signed with A&M Records, 1971-80; signed with Charisma Records, 1980; member of Yes, 1971-72 and 1976-80; solo artist, 1973—; toured U.S. with the National Philharmonic Orchestra and Chorus, 1974; composed soundtrack for Ken Russell's *Listztomania*, 1975; toured U.S. with Yes, 1977, 1978, 1979, 1991; toured with Anderson, Bruford, Wakeman, and Howe, 1989—.

Addresses: *Record company*—Atlantic Records, 75 Rockefeller Plaza, New York, NY 10019-6908. *Management*—Bajonor Ltd., Bajonor House, 2 Bridge St., Peel Isle of Man, U.K.

In 1968 he enrolled at London's Royal College of Music where he studied clarinet, orchestration, modern music, and piano. He remained at the college only briefly, but his training there constituted the mainstay of his education in keyboard and composition. By 1969 he grew tired of the classical orientation of the Royal College and left the school to indulge his own musical inclinations. His natural energy and instinctive curiosity kept him on the move; even his membership even in the Ronnie Smith Band became sporadic at best. On two occasions he was in fact dismissed from the group outright. In the wake of his waning relationship with the Ronnie Smith Band, Wakeman joined the Spinning Wheel, a group that performed regularly at the Greyhound Pub in Chadwell-Heath in Essex.

Talent Recognized

Before long he found work at recording studios as a session pianist where his musical talent was readily appreciated. In 1972 he played the eloquent piano background for Cat Stevens's "Morning has Broken," and in 1973 Wakeman played in session for David Bowie on the *Space Oddity* album as a part of the Mellotron soundmaking ensemble. Wakeman was exceptionally deliberate in his approach to music and quickly earned a reputation as "One-Take Wakeman." He performed in sessions with T. Rex and Elton John, and went on to accompany White Plains, Brotherhood of Man, Edison Lighthouse, Black Sabbath, and many others. Michel Bane in *Who's Who in Rock* called Wakeman "perhaps the premier keyboard man in rock."

In 1970 Wakeman abandoned the Spinning Wheel band, and for approximately the next 15 months, performed as a member of Strawbs. Strawbs originated as a folk-rock band, but evolved toward an electric sound when Wakeman joined the group. His initial tour with Strawbs not only took him to Paris, but coincided conveniently with the honeymoon celebration of his first marriage in April of 1970. Wakeman's first recording with Strawbs was a live performance at Queen Elizabeth Hall, called *Just a Collection of Antiques and Curios.* The recording was a breakthrough for Wakeman's career in terms of name recognition. The album featured an extended organ solo by Wakeman on "Where Is This Dream of Your Youth," and Wakeman achieved headliner status. During his brief tenure with Strawbs, Wakeman made one studio recording with the group; that album, called *From the Witchwood,* appeared in 1971.

Solo Career

In August of 1971 Wakeman left Strawbs and joined a group called Yes as a replacement for one of the original band members, Tony Kay. Wakeman's first album with that group was released in early in 1972. The recording, called *Fragile,* drew praise as a classic example of progressive rock, and by 1972, the band was a worldwide sensation. Wakeman played with Yes until 1974 when Patrick Moraz replaced Wakeman who left the group to further his solo career. Wakeman returned to Yes in 1976 and remained with the group until the end of the decade, after which time he continued a sporadic association with the group.

Even during his years with Yes, Wakeman spent a great deal of time in solo recording sessions for A&M Records. His earliest releases received notable reviews and earned gold records. *Six Wives of Henry VIII* was released in January of 1973, and *Journey to the Center of the Earth* appeared in 1974. *Journey,* recorded with the London Symphony Orchestra and narrated by David Hemmings, was an original Wakeman composition, based on the Jules Verne novel by the same name. The recording topped the charts in England, and Wakeman performed the composition at London's Royal Festival Hall on January 18, 1974. He recorded his next album, *Myths and Legends of King Arthur and the Knights of the Round*

Table, with the English Chamber Choir in 1975. *Myths* received mixed reviews, and Wakeman recorded and released a fourth album, *No Earthly Connection,* in 1976, shortly before he rejoined with Yes. His reunion with Yes was encouraged by the resurgence of longer, symphonic renditions by the group, music that was abandoned during Wakeman's absence. The Wakeman charisma was seen especially on their 1977 gold album, *Going for the One,* and their platinum release, *Tormato,* in 1978. According to Irwin Stambler in *Encyclopedia of Pop, Rock Soul,* Wakeman returned to Yes because, "they were back to playing the kind of music they should be playing." Wakeman also recorded two solo albums for A&M during the next few years: *Criminal Record* in 1977, and *Rhapsodies in* 1979.

In 1980 Wakeman left Yes once more and signed with Charisma Records. Later in 1990, he reunited with Yes co-founder Jon Anderson Bruford, to try to reignite Yes. Although the reunion failed to earn critical approval, the music received a warm reception from audiences. In 1989 Wakeman rejoined with his old Yes bandmates to form the group Anderson, Bruford, Wakeman, and Howe. The foursome released an album that sold over a million copies worldwide; they toured extensively that year, and in 1991 their album, *Union,* sold over two million copies worldwide. Wakeman toured extensively throughout the United States with Yes in 1977, 1978, 1979, and again in 1991.

Other Pursuits

Wakeman emerged as a talented composer during the 1970s. In 1975 he contracted to write the soundtrack for *Lisztomania,* a Ken Russell production based on the works of the composer Franz Liszt. Wakeman later wrote a soundtrack for *White Rock,* a documentary of the 1976 Winter Olympics. In 1983 he composed the soundtrack for a film, *Golé,* about World Cup Soccer, and in 1984 he collaborated with Tim Rice to put George Orwell's *1984* to music. Also that year he scored the film *Crimes of Passion;* and earlier, in 1982, he composed the score for *The Burning.* Anthologies of Wakeman's best works were released as albums in 1978, 1981, 1984, and 1994.

Wakeman's intense involvement in his own productions lay at the heart of his genius. Early in his solo career, in 1975, the stress took a toll on his health when he collapsed at the Crystal Palace Bowl following a performance of *Journey to the Center of the Earth.* He wrote his next album, *Myths and Legends of King Arthur,* largely during his recuperation, and in November of that year moved to Switzerland. He returned to England in 1980, following the death of his father. In 1988 Wakeman and his family moved to Isle of Man where he fulfilled a lifelong dream of building his own recording studio.

Even as Wakeman nurtured his career, his family grew. His oldest child, Oliver, was born in 1972, followed by a second son, Adam, in March of 1974. That same year Wakeman toured the United States with the National Philharmonic Orchestra and Chorus, and in 1975 he again toured the United States as a solo artist with his own backup group. Wakeman's third son, Benjamin, was born in February of 1978. In 1983 Wakeman married the former model, Nina Carter; they set up housekeeping in Edinburgh. Their daughter, Jemma, was born in February of 1983. The family moved to Surrey in 1986 shortly before the birth of Wakeman's fourth son, Oscar, in May of that year. Wakeman has involved himself with various athletic clubs over the years, includingthe position of director of the Brentford Football Club in 1979, and as the chairman of Camberley Town Football Club in 1983. Additionally he joined the Peel Golf Club, Isle of Man, in 1984, with a handicap of 16. Wakeman began work on an autobiography, *Say Yes!,* in 1993. In addition to his solo work and continued involvement with Anderson, Bruford, Wakeman, and Howe, Wakeman spent much of his time in the 1990s bonding with his children and working for charity benefits.

Wakeman continually released solo albums throughout the 1990s, including *Black Knights at the Court of Ferdinand IV,* with Mario Fasciano in 1991, and *The Official Bootleg,* a live recording from his 1993 South American tour. In 1994 Wakeman traveled to India; he also made assorted television appearances. He composed *Cirque Surreal* in 1995, a human circus that toured England under the musical direction of his son, Adam Wakeman. Rick Wakeman later signed with EMI Records to reprise *Journey to the Center of the Earth* and spent the remainder of that calendar year in recording sessions associated with that contract. The new *Journey* was released in March of 1999.

Selected discography

Solo

Just a Collection of Antiques and Curios (with Strawbs, recorded live at Queen Elizabeth Hall), 1970.
From the Witchwood (with Strawbs), 1971.
Six Wives of Henry VIII, A&M Records, 1973.
Journey to the Center of the Earth (with the London Symphony Orchestra and narrated by David Hemmings), A&M Records, 1974.
Myths and Legends of King Arthur and the Knights of the Round Table (with the English Chamber Choir), A&M Records, 1975.

No Earthly Connection, A&M Records, 1976.
Criminal Record, A&M Records, 1977.
Rhapsodies, A&M, 1979.
Silent Nights, TBG/President Records, 1985.
Live at the Hammersmith, TBG/President Records, 1985.
The Family Album (with Tony Fernandez), 1987.
Zodiaque, Relativity, 1988.
A Suite of Gods, Relativity, 1988.
Time Machine, President Records, 1988.
Phantom Powers, Ambient Records, 1990.
Aspirant Sunset, Ambient Records, 1990.
Aspirant Sunrise, Roi Digital Records, 1990.
Softsword, King John & the Magna Carta, Roi Digital Records, 1991.
Black Knights at the Court of Ferdinand IV (with Mario Fasciano), 1991
The Official Bootleg (recorded live in South America), 1993.

with Yes

Fragile (included "Roundabout"), 1972.
Close to the Edge, 1972.
Tales from Topographic Oceans, 1973.
Going for the One, 1977.
Tormato, 1978.

with Anderson, Wakeman, Bruford and Howe

Anderson, Wakeman, Bruford and Howe, Arista, 1989.
An Evening of Yes Music Plus, Herald, 1994.

Sources

Books

Bane, Michael, editor, *Who's Who in Rock,* Facts On File, Inc., New York, 1981.
Gammond, Peter, editor, *The Oxford Companion to Popular Music,* Oxford University Press, New York, 1991.
Hardy, Phil and Dave Laing, editors, *Encyclopedia of Rock,* Schirmer Books, New York, 1988.
musicHound Rock: The Essential Album Guide, Visible Ink Press, 1999.
Stambler, Irwin, editor, *Encyclopedia of Pop, Rock & Soul,* revised edition, St. Martin's Press, New York, 1989.

Online

"Rick Wakeman Biography," *Rick Wakeman Website,* http://www.rwcc.com/rwcc/code/biogra.htm (November 26, 1999).

—*Gloria Cooksey*

The Waterboys

Celtic folk-rock band

The Celtic folk-rock group the Waterboys was originally made up of a group of British musicians from England, Ireland, Scotland, and Wales, and was formed under the direction of Mike Scott, considered one of the greatest singers and songwriters in modern music. The musical history of the group was centered around Scott's quest to explore different genres, from Irish folk music to mainstream guitar rock. One song from the band's second album *A Pagan Place*, "The Big Music," was taken as a metaphor for Scott's soul-searching quest, to lose and perhaps find himself in music. As Scott told Neil McCormick in the *Daily Telegraph,* "Music has a life of its own." Thus the Waterboys were credited as the inventors of the "Big Music" sound, as Scott termed it, a style of music that combined the Celtic tradition with stirring rock and passionate, poetic lyrics.

Scott, the group's sole constant leader, was born on December 14, 1958, in Edinburgh, Scotland. His interest in music led him to create a fanzine called *Jungleland,* and he later played in a series of local punk groups. Scott studied English and philosophy in college, a course of study which shaped his regard for the British poets William Blake and William Butler Yeats; their words and symbolic imagery would later inspire the Waterboys' music. Afterwards, he moved his latest group, Edinburgh's highly touted Another Pretty Face, to London. Described as a cross between rocker Bruce Springsteen and the punk band the Clash, Another Pretty Face failed to build a successful career, and after a series of failed singles, the group broke up.

Subsequently, Scott formed the Waterboys in 1981. He chose the name after a line in a Lou Reed song called "The Kids," as well as for his own lyrical fascination with sea imagery, a device that would often recur in his new group's work. After placing a newspaper advertisement calling for musicians, Scott recruited multi-instrumentalist Anthony Thistlethwaite and drummer Kevin Wilkinson for the group's self-titled debut album in 1983. With *The Waterboys,* the ensemble played a spirited combination of stirring rock and Celtic folk, a passionate blend of music that swelled under Scott's unrestrained vocals and colorful guitar playing. Following the release of their follow-up album, 1984's *A Pagan Place,* the Waterboys further solidified their reputation for playing their unique concoction of rock and Celtic folk. Joined now by keyboardist Karl Wallinger and trumpeter Roddy Lorimer, the Waterboys expanded their dramatic sound and delved further into Scott's spiritual ambitions. Although their first two albums were poorly produced, they earned considerable critical praise.

The Waterboys returned in 1985 with *This Is the Sea,* which marked an early peak in the group's career. Musically, the album had something in common with rock and folk, and had eloquent, mystical lyrics that were compared to Yeats. One single, "The Whole of the Moon" seemed destined to become a major hit. However, Scott turned down an opportunity to perform on Great Britain's *Top of the Pops*, a first sign of his stubborn streak that would run throughout the Waterboys' career. He also refused to allow his record company to release singles in multiple formats including 12-inch singles, cassettes, B-sides, and colored vinyl records, which marketing departments viewed as vital to making a record a hit. Then, band member Wallinger decided toleave the Waterboys to form his own group, World Party.

In order to reinvent the Waterboys, Scott and Thistlethwaite relocated in the mid-1980s to County Galway in Ireland. "I learned a lot about being a man living in Ireland," Scott admitted to McCormick regarding his decision to relocate to County Galway. "And I learned a lot about Celtic tradition. It has given me a grounding. It's one of those things: you never appreciate the place you come from. When I was a young man, Scotland was a place to get away from. I had to go to where the bright lights were.... When I went to Ireland all those illusions fell off me. My years in Ireland helped me to rediscover Scotland. Scottish culture is very close to Irish culture. The music is the same, only slightly spikier, and I got all that given back to me."

For the Record . . .

Members include **Colin Blakey,** whistle, flute, organ, piano; **Noel Bridgeman**, drums, percussion; **Guy Chambers** (joined group c. 1988), keyboards; **Jay Dee Daugherty**, drums; **Trevor Hutchinson**, bass, bouzouki; **Roddy Lorimer**, trumpet; **Dave Ruffy** (joined group c. 1988), drums; **Mike Scott** (born Dec. 14, 1958, in Edingurgh, Scotland), vocals, guitar, piano, organ; **Sharon Shannon,** accordion, fiddle; **Anthony Thistlethwaite** (born in Leicester, England), saxophone, mandolin, guitar, keyboards, organ, harmonica; **Karl Wallinger** (left group c. 1985), bass, keyboards; **Marco Weissman** (joined group c. 1988), bass; **Steve Wickham** (born in Ireland, joined group c. 1988), fiddle, organ, vocals; **Kevin Wilkinson** (born June 11, 1958, at Stoke-on-Trent, Staffordshire, England; married Marilyn Fitzgerald, 1986; children: one son, two daughters; committed suicide and died July 17, 1999, at Baydon, Wiltshire, England), drums.

Scott formed the Waterboys, 1981; released debut album *The Waterboys,* 1983, followed by *A Pagan Place,* 1984; released epic album *This Is the Sea,* 1985; relocated to County Galway in Ireland, mid-1980s; released *Fisherman's Blues,* 1988; released *Room to Roam,* 1990; Scott moved to New York City and hired new band members, 1991; released unsuccessful mainstream rock album, *Dream Harder,* and disbanded the Waterboys, 1993;

Addresses: *Record company*—EMI-Capitol Records, 1750 N. Vine St., Hollywood, CA 90028.

By moving, Scott hoped to erase most traces of the group's prior music in favor of a more stripped-down, acoustic folk sound, largely shaped by an important new addition to the lineup, Irish fiddler Steve Wickham. Also joined by three other traditional Irish musicians, drummer Dave Ruffy, keyboardist Guy Chambers, and bassist Marco Weissman, the Waterboys released the acclaimed *Fisherman's Blues* in 1988. Considered a masterpiece from start to finish, *Fisherman's Blues* embraced the Celtic tradition and included the last recorded song written by Scott and Wallinger (with Trevor Hutchinson) entitled "World Party." The album also featured such rollicking songs as "And a Bang on the Ear," "Has Anybody Here Seen Hank?," and "When Will We Be Married?," in addition to a cover of Van Morrison's "Sweet Thing." Scott continued to promote his adopted heritage on the album with the exception of two electric rock tracks, toning down his "Big Music" sound and placing his Celtic passions at the forefront for the group's next release, 1990's *Room to Roam.* Noteworthy tracks from this release, the Waterboys' last album to feature the Irish tradition, included a rendition of "Raggle Taggle Gypsy," the bouncy and romantic "A Man Is in Love," and the slow-moving epiphany "Bigger Picture." A year later, the group released *The Best of the Waterboys '81-'90,* a sampling of their first five albums.

After *Room to Roam,* Scott left Ireland in 1991 for New York City. Here he gathered an entirely new group of musicians to fulfill his next musical ambition: mainstream guitar rock. Despite Scott's newfound passion, most critics agreed that the Waterboys' 1993 release, *Dream Harder,* failed to match the quality of the group's previous work. Thus, perhaps feeling devastated, Scott disbanded the Waterboys for good and moved back to London shortly after the album's release. The final Waterboys album *The Secret Life of the Waterboys: 81-85* came out in 1994, a 15-track collection of outtakes, demos, radio session, concert takes, and remixes from the band's early years.

With the Waterboys behind him, Scott pursued a solo career, releasing *Bring 'Em All In* in 1995. For this project, Scott reverted to his uncluttered folk acoustic style rather than making another attempt at guitar rock. While critics continued to complain about his spiritual preachings and new age idealism (he had since moved to a new age retreat in Scotland called Findhorn Community), they also complemented Scott's effort as his most enjoyable recording since *Fisherman's Blues.* Although more laid-back than the Celtic tradition of the Waterboys, Scott's solo record contained notable songs such as "She Is So Beautiful" and "City Full of Ghosts (Dublin)."

Thistlethwaite, one of Scott's original cohorts, released a solo project as well. Unlike Scott, he moved away from Irish traditionalism with a straight-up Chicago blues album entitled *Aesop Wrote a Fable* in 1995. The work was a mix of original songs and classic blues pieces by artists such as Willie Dixon, Sonny Boy Williamson, Peter Green, and John Mayall. The album included a horn section for three of the songs, and former band mate Wallinger made a guest appearance on piano.

On July 17, 1999, original Waterboys band member Wilkinson took his own life in Staffordshire, England. Survived by his wife Marilyn Fitzgerald, one son, and two daughters, the drummer had played with other big-name bands including China Crisis, Squeeze, Marillion, and Ultravox. He had recently completed a tour of the United States with the pop group the Proclaimers and had turned down an offer to tour with rock legend Bonnie Raitt because he wanted to take time off to spend with his family. In addition to the drums, Wilkinson was also accomplished at playing mandolin, bass, guitar, and bouzouki.

Selected discography

The Waterboys (EP), Ensign/Island, 1983.
The Waterboys, UK Ensign, 1983; Ensign/Chrysalis, 1986.
A Pagan Place, Ensign/Island, 1984; Ensign/Chrysalis, 1987.
This Is the Sea, Ensign/Island, 1986; Ensign/Chrysalis, 1987.
Fisherman's Blues, Ensign/Chrysalis, 1988.
The Best of the Waterboys '81-'90, Ensign/Chrysalis, 1991.
Dream Harder, Geffen, 1993.
The Secret Life of the Waterboys: 81-85, Ensign/Chrysalis, 1994.

Sources

Books

musicHound Rock: The Essential Album Guide, Visible Ink Press, 1999.
Robbins, Ira A., editor, *Trouser Press Guide to '90s Rock,* Fireside/Simon & Schuster, 1997.

Periodicals

Daily Telegraph, September 18, 1997, p. 27.
Independent, July 23, 1999, p. 7.
Independent on Sunday, August 24, 1997, p. 12.
Irish Voice, September 15, 1995; September 26, 1995; October 17, 1995.
Minneapolis Star Tribune, March 9, 1996, p. 10E.

Online

All Music Guide website, http://www.allmusic.com (August 15, 1999).

—*Laura Hightower*

Wilco

Alternative country group

Photograph by Marty Perez. Corbis. Reproduced by permission. ©

When the progressive country band Uncle Tupelo broke apart in 1994, one of the group's cofounders, Jeff Tweedy, along with four other band members, knew that he still wanted to carry on. Thus, Tweedy formed Wilco, a group that held on to its country roots, while at the same time adopting a more pop/rock, commercially appealing sound. After releasing their debut album, 1996's *A.M.*, the group quickly earned a reputation as a no frills rock band, and Tweedy proved his value as a simple, personal, and uncomplicated storyteller.

In 1988, two longtime friends with a passion for traditional country and punk music, who were both natives of Belleville, Illinois, a decaying blue-collar suburb east of St. Louis, Missouri, Jay Farrar and Jeff Tweedy formed Uncle Tupelo. Prior to Uncle Tupelo, the two had formed a punk band, the Primitives, which broke up when Farrar's brother enlisted in the United States Army. Both men shared responsibility for writing music and lyrics, creating a persuasive blend of country punk, an intense style of punk-informed rural music, and were joined by drummer Mike Heidorn (later replaced by Ken Coomer).

The group toured on the Midwestern club circuit for a couple of years before releasing their debut album, *No Depression* in 1990, followed by *Still Feel Gone* in 1991, both for the independent Rockville label. These releases brought the group an instant cult following of both country and rock fans, as well as critical accolades from music magazines such as *Rolling Stone*. Tweedy, who played bass for the group, and Farrar, who served as lead guitarist and vocalist, each provided the group with a distinct sensibility. While Tweedy held the sweeter instincts and a critical interest in music, Farrar added soul to Uncle Tupelo's songs with his grand, indignant voice and pained tone. The group returned in 1992 with a more subdued, acoustic album of traditional folk tunes entitled *March 16-20, 1992,* produced by R.E.M. guitarist Peter Buck, which also earned favorable critical attention. After signing with a major label, Warner Brothers' Sire/Reprise, Uncle Tupelo released *Anodyne* in 1993, considered the group's best album. Here, the group placed country in the background and opted for a more progressive sound.

Despite the band's newfound commercial appeal, major label contract, and growing popularity, Farrar abruptly left Uncle Tupelo in 1994 and formed a new American folk/country group called Son Volt. Neither of the men would elaborate on the exact circumstances of the split, but Tweedy did suggest that "I think it was a personal decision for Jay, but he wasn't very communicative about anything to us, which was fairly normal for

For the Record . . .

Members include **Jay Bennett** (joined band 1995), guitar; **Ken Coomer,** drums; **Bob Egan** (joined band 1996), guitar, fiddle; **Max Johnston** (left band 1996), guitar, vocals, fiddle, mandolin, banjo; **John Stirratt**, bass; **Jeff Tweedy** (born August 25, 1967, in Belleville, IL; married; children: one son, born c. 1996) guitar, vocals.

Formed band in St. Louis, MO, started touring throughout the Midwest, 1994; toured with H.O.R.D.E., released debut album *A.M.,* 1995; released *Being There,* 1996; released *Mermaid Avenue* with Billy Bragg; released *Summer Teeth,* toured worldwide with R.E.M., 1999.

Addresses: *Home*—Chicago, IL. *Record company*—Reprise Records, 3300 Warner Blvd., Burbank, CA 91505-4694. *Website*—http://www.RepriseRec.com.

Jay," as quoted by Alan Sculley in the *St. Louis Post-Dispatch.* "I mean, a lot of things that were used as explanations were fairly contradictory so I wouldn't really be able to comment on it." Even though Tweedy and Farrar had worked together for years, Tweedy further commented that their relationship centered around music, rather than a personal friendship.

From the moment Farrar announced his departure, the remaining members knew that they loved making music together and did not want to stop. Thus, Tweedy took the leading role as guitarist and vocalist and renamed the group Wilco. The former members of Uncle Tupelo, which alsoincluded drummer Coomer, fiddler and mandolin and banjo player Max Johnston, and bassist John Stirratt, were later joined by a second guitarist, Jay Bennett (formerly of the group Titanic Love Affair). After closing the door on Uncle Tupelo, the newly-formed Wilco felt truly liberated. "Certain things, I think, would kind of be tossed out before they ever became a song, just on the idea that it wouldn't really fit in on an Uncle Tupelo record or really didn't work next to Jays songs—things like that," Tweedy told Sculley. Therefore, with a new sense of creative freedom, Wilco seemed determined to include all styles of music into their new band. In 1995, they joined the H.O.R.D.E. (Horizons of Rock Developing Everywhere) tour, playing some old Uncle Tupelo songs, as well as some new songs that later appeared on their debut release.

After relocating to Chicago from St. Louis, Wilco released their first album, *A.M.,* in 1996 on the Sire/Reprise label. For the debut, the group, joined by guest guitarist Brian Henneman of the group the Bottle Rockets, maintained its country roots, but also added more pop and rock influences. Consisting of 13 tracks, 12 of which were written by Tweedy, *A.M.* opens with four solid rock songs, including "Box Full of Letters," which deals with separation (perhaps in regards to Farrar's leaving), and "Casino Queen," a rock song full of unbridled energy. Throughout the rest of the album, the music deepens in scope, moving back and forth between heavier rock songs and mid-tempo ballads, such as the love songs "Pick Up the Change," "That's Not the Issue," "Should've Been in Love," and "Too Far Apart." Bassist and rhythm guitarist Stirratt wrote and sang one song for the album entitled "It's Just That Simple," a tearful, traditional country tune. Later that year, multi-instrumentalist Johnson left Wilco, and fiddler and guitarist Bob Egan joined the band.

The following year, Wilco released their second album, a 19-track double CD entitled *Being There.* Publications such as *Rolling Stone* and the *Los Angeles Times* raved about the group's latest collection, using catch phrases like "album of the year" and "ambitious versatility," and their music saw air play on alternative rock radio stations across the United States. Like their debut, *Being There* included music from several genres, from neo-punk to rockabilly on top of their firm progressive country foundation. For example, the song "Monday" recalled the swinging rock of the Rolling Stones' hit "Brown Sugar," "Outta Mind (Outta Sight)" took inspiration from West Coast 1960s pop, and "Kingpin" boasted the sounds of swaggering country.

The band went back into the studio in 1997 to begin work on their third album. In the meantime, they took time off to work on a project with British folk singer and musician Billy Bragg in Dublin. In 1998, Bragg and Wilco released the critically acclaimed *Mermaid Avenue,* a collection of Woodie Guthrie lyrics for which the musicians wrote their own original music. The concept for the album came about in 1995 when Guthrie's daughter, Nora Guthrie, gave Bragg reams of her father's handwritten song lyrics and asked him to write music for them. Although Guthrie had composed some of the music for the lyrics, he did not have the chance to write the notes down before he died in 1967 following a long battle with a rare nervous disorder called Huntington's chorea. The resulting album, with music co-written by Wilco and Bragg, combined the folk blueprint of Bragg with the soul and genre-bending tendencies of Wilco.

Subsequently, Wilco returned to Chicago to complete recording songs for *Summer Teeth,* released in 1999. A strong 1960s pop element came though in tracks like "I'm Always in Love,""ELT," and "Summer Teeth." However, Tweedy contrasted Wilco's bright pop songs with dark, often disturbing lyrics, although the overall feel of the album was upbeat. "There's a darkness to the lyrical half of the the record and there's an overwhelming brightness to the music," Tweedy informed Curtis Ross in the *Tampa Tribune.* "The effort was to make the record more hopeful as it progressed." Like the group's prior work, *Summer Teeth* received critical praise and further solidified Tweedy's reputation as one of America's most stellar songwriters. Also that year, Wilco toured Europe and the United States, opening for the group R.E.M. in larger arenas and headlining their own show at smaller venues.

Despite Wilco's success after breaking away from Uncle Tupelo, Tweedy insisted that he still remains an ordinary guy. "I'm not some big rock star, but I do run into fans every now and then who think I'm this super-special person... and it's weird, because you can't be who they think you are." Nevertheless, he admitted to acting "freaked out" when he met one of his musical heroes in 1966, when Wilco shared a bill with Johnny Cash at a show in New York City. "I don't know if someone coached him on my name or something, but he actually walked into the room and said, 'Where's Jeff?' and my heart stopped," Tweedy recalled to Thor Christensen of the *Dallas Morning News.* "After you've made a few records, you think you could meet [famous] people and not act goofy. But when I'm around a guy like Johnny Cash, there's no way I can act or talk normally."

Selected discography

A.M., Sire/Reprise, 1995.
Being There, Reprise, 1996.
Mermaid Avenue, (with Billy Bragg), 1998.
Summer Teeth, Reprise, 1999.

Sources

Books

Kingsbury, Paul, editor, *Encyclopedia of Country Music,* Oxford University Press, 1998.
musicHound Rock: The Essential Album Guide, Visible Ink Press, 1999.
Robbins, Ira A., editor, *Trouser Press Guide to '90s Rock,* Fireside/Simon & Schuster, 1997.

Periodicals

Capital Times (Madison, WI), February 5, 1997, p. 1D.
Dallas Morning News, November 3, 1996, p. 1C; November 8, 1996, p. 33A; June 21, 1998, p. 1C.
Independent, April 2, 1999, p. 11.
Independent on Sunday, March 30, 1997.
New Statesman, March 26, 1999.
Newsday, June 13, 1995, p. B02; February 17, 1997, p. B07.
The Record (Bergen County, NJ), June 14, 1995, p. f09.
Rolling Stone, June 24, 1999.
St. Louis Post-Dispatch, March 23, 1995, p. 04G; April 21, 1995, p. 06E; November 2, 1995, p. 11; January 1, 1997, p. 14; August 19, 1999, p. 26.
Spin, May 1999, p. 55.
Tampa Tribune, August 27, 1999, p. 18.
Toronto Sun, April 14, 1999, p. 63.
Wisconsin State Journal, April 8, 1999, p. 16.

Online

Reprise Records, http://www.RepriseRec.com (September 6, 1999).

—Laura Hightower

Mark Wills

Singer

Since the release of his platinum-selling sophomore album, 1998's *Wish You Were Here,* recording artist Mark Wills has remained one of the few new male country musicians to break through in radio. Wills's achievement was evident when three of the record's singles reached number one on country charts. Two years later, the unassuming, yet exuberant performer released *Permanently,* an album he believed would solidify his status in country music. "I wanted this album to show how much I've grown as an artist and as a man," Wills explained, according to his record label, Mercury Nashville. "It was important to me that this album was more diverse than the first two, and I think we accomplished that. I want my fans to know who I am. I'm a sensitive guy, but I also like to have fun. My first album was a good start, I think [the singles] "Jacob's Ladder" and "Places I've Never Seen" gave everyone a taste of my personality. *Wish You Were Here* took that a bit further.... But I think the songs on this album take my music to a new level."

Born Daryl Mark Williams on August 8, 1973, in Cleveland, Tennessee, Wills spent much of his life in his adopted home state of Georgia with his parents, his sister Amy, and foster brother Teo. Wills's parents, Jerry and Shirley Williams, taught their children to enjoy the simple pleasures of life and the value of spending time with family. Despite his later success as a country recording artist, Wills remained close to his roots, living near the Atlanta area club scene where he first took the stage. After learning to play both guitar and drums, Wills spent over five years performing at local night clubs around Atlanta. As the young singer's popularity grew by word of mouth, he eventually landed a record deal with Mercury Records Nashville. In 1996, Wills released his self-titled debut album that spawned two hits, "Jacob's Ladder" and "Places I've Never Been," and exhibited his experience as a club singer. Wills commented that his first album "was a great introduction album and gives more insight into who I am, and where I'm from, and who I want to be, and the songs I want to sing," as quoted by *Billboard* magazine's Jim Bessman. But in spite of Wills's success on the singles charts ("Jacob's Ladder" became a top ten hit on *Billboard*'s Hot Country Singles & Tracks chart), his efforts failed to translate into record sales. "You have such high expectations for your first album and have a couple of hits but no real success in sales," Wills told Bessman. "But I feel that this album [*Wish You Were Here*] will be what I envisioned for the first one."

"A lot of different things came into play when I recorded this album," Wills continued. "I wasn't married then, and now I have a baby on the way, and when I made this album I had a better idea of where I wanted to go as an artist." The singer further stated on his official website, "This album has been compiled of real life. It deals with a lot of real issues." While reviewers such as Bessman noted Wills's "thoughtful maturity uncommon for such a youthful newcomer" evident on *Wish You Were Here,* the singer's follow-up record didn't completely let go of his spirited nature. For example, the title track and other songs contained youthful, upbeat elements that offset the others tracks' adult themes.

Nonetheless, Wills intended for each song on *Wish You Were Here* to carry a message, adding, asquoted by Bessman, "every song on this record is a song that I and the producer [Carson Chamberlain, who also produced Wills's debut] both sat down and said 'I love this song.' There's nothing on it that I didn't like." Such careful attention to each song, in addition to focusing on more grown up life experiences, helped propel Wills into country music stardom. Three singles from the album, including the optimistic love song "I Do (Cherish You)," the soul-searching "Don't Laugh At Me," and the sad, yet hopeful "Wish You Were Here" all climbed to number one on the country charts, the latter holding the top position for three weeks straight. *Wish You Were Here* gave the rising country singer his first certified platinum album.

During the next two years, Wills won and was nominated for numerous honors. He was named 1998's Top New Male Vocalist from the *Country Weekly* Golden Pick

For the Record . . .

Born Daryl Mark Williams on August 8, 1973, in Cleveland, TN; son of Jerry and Shirley Williams; siblings: Amy and Teo (foster brother); married Kim (born c. 1970), a cosmetologist, 1996; one daughter: Mally Ann, born August 26, 1998, in Atlanta, GA.

Started performing in Atlanta at night clubs; signed with Mercury Records Nashville, 1995; released debut album *Mark Wills*, 1996; released *Wish You Were Here*, 1998; toured as part of the George Strait Chevy Truck Country Music Festival, 1999; released *Permanently*, 2000.

Awards: Academy of Country Music Award, Top New Male Vocalist, 1999; *Country Weekly* Golden Pick Awards, Top New Male Vocalist, 1999.

Addresses: *Record company*—Mercury Records Nashville, 66 Music Square West, Nashville, TN 37203, (615) 320-1428, fax (615) 327-4856. *Home*—Kennesaw, GA, near Atlanta. *Website*—The Mark Wills Homepage, http://www.markwills.com.

Awards in May of 1999. "This award means the world to me because it's from the readers," said Wills, according to his official website. "They're the wonderful people you put down their hard-earned money to buy this magazine, to buy my albums, to buy tickets to my shows." Furthermore, the singer picked up his first Academy of Country Music (ACM) award for the year's Top New Male Vocalist, also in May of 1999. In August of 1999, Wills received nominations for three Country Music Association (CMA) awards: Video of the Year for "Don't Laugh At Me," Single of the Year for "Don't Laugh At Me," and Song of the Year for "Don't Laugh At Me" (written by Steve Seskin and Allen Shamblin). Although he did not take home an award that night, he performed at the televised awards ceremony held in mid September.

In early November 1999, Wills performed live at Grand Ole Opry and was a presenter at the Christian Country Music Awards, both in Nashville. Earlier in the year, he toured as part of the George Strait Chevy Truck Country Music Festival, sharing the stage with other popular country stars such as Tim McGraw, the Dixie Chicks, JoDee Messina, Kenny Chesney, and Asleep At The Wheel. That year he not only performed his music for large concerts held in arenas and auditoriums, but also headlined smaller clubs across the U.S., appearing with musicians like Neal McCoy, Terri Clark, and Lila McCann.

January of 2000 brought the release of Wills's third album, *Permanently.* Similar to his musical and emotional progression from his debut to his sophomore effort, the singer felt *Permanently* took his music in a more diverse direction as well. He claimed that some tracks stemmed from his own life experiences. The song "In My Arms," for one, was a tribute to his daughter, Mally Ann, co-written with Monty Criswell and Michael White. Likewise, "Rich Man" discussed the possessions in life, such as love, that Wills himself believed the most important. Other songs included the up-tempo "This Can't Be Love," the heartbreaking "Perfect Conversation," and the blues-inspired title track. According to Mercury Nashville, the first single off the album, "Back At One," written by popular country singer Brian McKnight, almost missed making its way on to *Permanently.* The album was completed when the single was brought to the attention to Luke Lewis, President of Mercury, and Wills. However, Wills and producer Chamberlain insisted on returning to the studio in order to record the song and add it to the album.

In addition to establishing himself as one of the most popular new country recording artists of the late 1990s, Wills also found happiness in his personal life. In 1996, at the same time his debut was climbing the album charts, Wills married his wife Kim, a cosmetologist. The couple had adaughter, Mally Ann, born on August 26, 1998, in Atlanta, shortly after the release of *Wish You Were Here.*

Selected discography

Mark Wills, Mercury, 1996
Wish You Were Here, Mercury, 1998.
Permanently, Mercury, 2000.

Sources

Periodicals

Billboard, April 4, 1998; June 12, 1999.
People, September 21, 1998.

Online

"Mark Wills: *Back at One*," Mark Wills Homepage, http://www.markwills.com (November 29, 1999).

Additional information provided by Mercury Records Nashville.

—*Laura Hightower*

Cumulative Indexes

Cumulative Subject Index

Volume numbers appear in **bold.**

A cappella
Brightman, Sarah **20**
Bulgarian State Female Vocal Choir, The **10**
Golden Gate Quartet **25**
Nylons, The **6**
Sweet Honey In The Rock **26**
Earlier sketch in CM **1**
Take 6 **6**
Zap Mama **14**

Accordion
Buckwheat Zydeco **6**
Chenier, C. J. **15**
Chenier, Clifton **6**
Queen Ida **9**
Richard, Zachary **9**
Rockin' Dopsie **10**
Simien, Terrance **12**
Sonnier, Jo-El **10**
Yankovic, "Weird Al" **7**

Ambient/Rave/Techno
2 Unlimited **18**
Aphex Twin **14**
Chemical Brothers **20**
Deep Forest **18**
Front Line Assembly **20**
Gus Gus **26**
KMFDM **18**
Kraftwerk **9**
Lords of Acid **20**
Man or Astroman? **21**
Orb, The **18**
Propellerheads **26**
Shadow, DJ **19**
Sheep on Drugs **27**
Underworld **26**

Bandoneon
Piazzolla, Astor **18**
Saluzzi, Dino **23**

Banjo
Boggs, Dock **25**
Bromberg, David **18**
Clark, Roy **1**
Crowe, J.D. **5**
Fleck, Bela **8**
Also see New Grass Revival, The
Hartford, John **1**
McCoury, Del **15**
Piazzolla, Astor **18**
Scruggs, Earl **3**
Seeger, Pete **4**
Also see Weavers, The
Skaggs, Ricky **5**
Stanley, Ralph **5**
Watson, Doc **2**

Bass
Brown, Ray **21**
Carter, Ron **14**
Chambers, Paul **18**
Clarke, Stanley **3**
Collins, Bootsy **8**
Dixon, Willie **10**
Fender, Leo **10**
Haden, Charlie **12**
Holland, Dave **27**
Kaye, Carol **22**
Laswell, Bill **14**
Love, Laura **20**
Mann, Aimee **22**
McBride, Christian **17**
McCartney, Paul **4**
Also see Beatles, The
Mingus, Charles **9**
Ndegéocello, Me'Shell **18**
Sting **19**
Earlier sketch in CM **2**
Sweet, Matthew **9**
Was, Don **21**
Also see Was (Not Was)
Watt, Mike **22**
Whitaker, Rodney **20**

Big Band/Swing
Andrews Sisters, The **9**
Arnaz, Desi **8**
Atomic Fireballs, The **27**
Bailey, Pearl **5**
Basie, Count **2**
Beiderbecke, Bix **16**
Bennett, Tony **16**
Earlier sketch in CM **2**
Berrigan, Bunny **2**
Blakey, Art **11**
Brown, Lawrence **23**
Calloway, Cab **6**
Carter, Benny **3**
Chenille Sisters, The **16**
Cherry Poppin' Daddies **24**
Clooney, Rosemary **9**
Como, Perry **14**
Cugat, Xavier **23**
Dorsey Brothers, The **8**
Eckstine, Billy **1**
Eldridge, Roy **9**
Ellington, Duke **2**
Ferguson, Maynard **7**
Fitzgerald, Ella **1**
Fountain, Pete **7**
Getz, Stan **12**
Gillespie, Dizzy **6**
Goodman, Benny **4**
Henderson, Fletcher **16**
Herman, Woody **12**
Hines, Earl "Fatha" **12**
Jacquet, Illinois **17**
James, Harry **11**
Jones, Spike **5**
Jordan, Louis **11**
Krupa, Gene **13**
Lee, Peggy **8**
Madness **27**
McGuire Sisters, The **27**
McKinney's Cotton Pickers **16**
Miller, Glenn **6**
Norvo, Red **12**
Parker, Charlie **5**
Prima, Louis **18**
Puente, Tito **14**
Ray Condo and His Ricochets **26**
Rich, Buddy **13**
Rodney, Red **14**
Roomful of Blues **7**
Scott, Jimmy **14**
Severinsen, Doc **1**
Shaw, Artie **8**
Sinatra, Frank **23**
Earlier sketch in CM **1**
Squirrel Nut Zippers **20**
Stafford, Jo **24**
Strayhorn, Billy **13**
Teagarden, Jack **10**
Torme, Mel **4**
Vaughan, Sarah **2**
Welk, Lawrence **13**
Whiteman, Paul **17**

Bluegrass
Auldridge, Mike **4**
Bluegrass Patriots **22**
Clements, Vassar **18**
Country Gentlemen, The **7**
Crowe, J.D. **5**
Flatt, Lester **3**
Fleck, Bela **8**
Also see New Grass Revival, The
Gill, Vince **7**
Grisman, David **17**
Hartford, John **1**
Krauss, Alison **10**
Louvin Brothers, The **12**
Martin, Jimmy **5**
Also see Osborne Brothers, The
McCoury, Del **15**
McReynolds, Jim and Jesse **12**
Monroe, Bill **1**
Nashville Bluegrass Band **14**
New Grass Revival, The **4**
Northern Lights **19**
O'Connor, Mark **1**
Osborne Brothers, The **8**
Parsons, Gram **7**
Also see Byrds, The
Reverend Horton Heat **19**
Scruggs, Earl **3**
Seldom Scene, The **4**
Skaggs, Ricky **5**
Stanley Brothers, The **17**
Stanley, Ralph **5**
Stuart, Marty **9**
Watson, Doc **2**
Wiseman, Mac **19**

Blues

Allison, Luther **21**
Ayler , Albert **19**
Bailey, Pearl **5**
Baker, Ginger **16**
Also see Cream
Ball, Marcia **15**
Barnes, Roosevelt, "Booba" **23**
Berry, Chuck **1**
Bill Wyman & the Rhythm Kings **26**
Bland, Bobby "Blue" **12**
Block, Rory **18**
Blood, Sweat and Tears **7**
Blues Brothers, The **3**
Boggs, Dock **25**
Broonzy, Big Bill **13**
Brown, Clarence "Gatemouth" **11**
Brown, Ruth **13**
Burdon, Eric **14**
Also see War
Also see Animals
Cale, J. J. **16**
Charles, Ray **24**
Earlier sketch in CM **1**
Clapton, Eric **11**
Earlier sketch in CM **1**
Also see Cream
Also see Yardbirds, The
Collins, Albert **4**
Cray, Robert **8**
Davis, Reverend Gary **18**
Diddley, Bo **3**
Dixon, Willie **10**
Dr. John **7**
Dupree, Champion Jack **12**
Earl, Ronnie **5**
Also see Roomful of Blues
Estes, John **25**
Everlast **27**
Fabulous Thunderbirds, The **1**
Fuller, Blind Boy **20**
Fulson, Lowell **20**
Gatton, Danny **16**
Guy, Buddy **4**
Handy, W. C. **7**
Hart, Alvin Youngblood **27**
Hawkins, Screamin' Jay **8**
Healey, Jeff **4**
Holiday, Billie **6**
Hooker, John Lee **26**
Earlier sketch in CM **1**
Hopkins, Lightnin' **13**
House, Son **11**
Howlin' Wolf **6**
James, Elmore **8**
James, Etta **6**
Jefferson, Blind Lemon **18**
Johnson, Blind Willie **26**
Johnson, Lonnie **17**
Johnson, Robert **6**
Jon Spencer Blues Explosion **18**
Joplin, Janis **3**
King, Albert **2**
King, B. B. **24**
Earlier sketch in CM **1**
King, Freddy **17**
Lang, Jonny **27**
Leadbelly **6**
Led Zeppelin **1**
Lewis, Furry **26**
Little Feat **4**
Little Walter **14**
Lockwood, Robert, Jr. **10**
Mayall, John **7**
McClennan, Tommy **25**
McClinton, Delbert **14**
McDowell, Mississippi Fred **16**
McLean, Dave **24**
McTell, Blind Willie **17**
Memphis Jug Band **25**
Memphis Minnie **25**
Montgomery, Little Brother **26**
Muldaur, Maria **18**
Patton, Charley **11**
Plant, Robert **2**
Also see Led Zeppelin
Professor Longhair **6**
Raitt, Bonnie **23**
Earlier sketch in CM **3**
Redding, Otis **5**
Reed, Jimmy **15**
Rich, Charlie **3**
Robertson, Robbie **2**
Robillard, Duke **2**
Roomful of Blues **7**
Rush, Otis **12**
Shaffer, Paul **13**
Shines, Johnny **14**
Smith, Bessie **3**
Snow, Phoebe **4**
Spann, Otis **18**
Sunnyland Slim **16**
Sykes, Roosevelt **20**
Taj Mahal **6**
Tampa Red **25**
Taylor, Koko **10**
Thornton, Big Mama **18**
Toure, Ali Farka **18**
Turner, Big Joe **13**
Ulmer, James Blood **13**
Van Zandt, Townes **13**
Vaughan, Jimmie **24**
Vaughan, Stevie Ray **1**
Waits, Tom **27**
Earlier sketch in CM **12**
Earlier sketch in CM **1**
Walker, T-Bone **5**
Wallace, Sippie **6**
Washington, Dinah **5**
Waters, Ethel **11**
Waters, Muddy **24**
Earlier sketch in CM **4**
Wells, Junior **17**
Weston, Randy **15**
Whitfield, Mark **18**
Whitley, Chris **16**
Whittaker, Hudson **20**
Williams, Joe **11**
Williamson, Sonny Boy **9**
Wilson, Gerald **19**
Winter, Johnny **5**
Witherspoon, Jimmy **19**
ZZ Top **2**

Cajun/Zydeco

Ball, Marcia **15**
Brown, Clarence "Gatemouth" **11**
Buckwheat Zydeco **6**
Chenier, C. J. **15**
Chenier, Clifton **6**
Doucet, Michael **8**
Landreth, Sonny **16**
Queen Ida **9**
Richard, Zachary **9**
Rockin' Dopsie **10**
Simien, Terrance **12**
Sonnier, Jo-El **10**

Cello

Casals, Pablo **9**
DuPré, Jacqueline **26**
Harrell, Lynn **3**
Holland, Dave **27**
Ma, Yo Yo **24**
Earlier sketch in CM **2**
Rasputina **26**
Rostropovich, Mstislav **17**

Children's Music

Bartels, Joanie **13**
Cappelli, Frank **14**
Chapin, Tom **11**
Chenille Sisters, The **16**
Harley, Bill **7**
Lehrer, Tom **7**
Nagler, Eric **8**
Penner, Fred **10**
Raffi **8**
Rosenshontz **9**
Sharon, Lois & Bram **6**

Christian Music

4Him **23**
Anointed **21**
Ashton, Susan **17**
Audio Adrenaline **22**
Avalon **26**
Champion, Eric **21**
Chapman, Steven Curtis **15**
dc Talk **18**
Duncan, Bryan **19**
Eskelin, Ian **19**
Grant, Amy **7**
Jars of Clay **20**
Joy Electric **26**
Keaggy, Phil **26**
King's X **7**
Newsboys, The **24**
Paris, Twila **16**
Patti, Sandi **7**
Petra **3**
Point of Grace **21**
Rice, Chris **25**
Sixpence None the Richer **26**
Smith, Michael W. **11**
St. James, Rebecca **26**
Stryper **2**
Taylor, Steve **26**
Waters, Ethel **11**

Clarinet

Adams, John **8**
Bechet, Sidney **17**
Braxton, Anthony **12**
Brötzmann, Peter **26**
Byron, Don **22**
Fountain, Pete **7**
Goodman, Benny **4**
Herman, Woody **12**
Russell, Pee Wee **25**
Shaw, Artie **8**
Stoltzman, Richard **24**

Classical

Ameling, Elly **24**
Anderson, June **27**
Anderson, Marian **8**
Argerich, Martha **27**
Arrau, Claudio **1**
Austral, Florence **26**
Baker, Janet **14**
Beecham, Thomas **27**

Bernstein, Leonard **2**
Boulez, Pierre **26**
Boyd, Liona **7**
Bream, Julian **9**
Britten, Benjamin **15**
Bronfman, Yefim **6**
Canadian Brass, The **4**
Carter, Ron **14**
Casals, Pablo **9**
Chang, Sarah **7**
Clayderman, Richard **1**
Cliburn, Van **13**
Copland, Aaron **2**
Davis, Anthony **17**
Davis, Chip **4**
Davis, Colin **27**
DuPré, Jacqueline **26**
Dvorak, Antonin **25**
Fiedler, Arthur **6**
Fleming, Renee **24**
Galway, James **3**
Gardiner, John Eliot **26**
Gingold, Josef **6**
Gould, Glenn **9**
Gould, Morton **16**
Hampson, Thomas **12**
Harrell, Lynn **3**
Hayes, Roland **13**
Hendricks, Barbara **10**
Herrmann, Bernard **14**
Hinderas, Natalie **12**
Horne, Marilyn **9**
Horowitz, Vladimir **1**
Jarrett, Keith **1**
Kennedy, Nigel **8**
Kissin, Evgeny **6**
Kronos Quartet **5**
Kunzel, Erich **17**
Lemper, Ute **14**
Levine, James **8**
Liberace **9**
Ma, Yo Yo **24**
  Earlier sketch in CM **2**
Marsalis, Wynton **6**
Mascagni, Pietro **25**
Masur, Kurt **11**
McNair, Sylvia **15**
McPartland, Marian **15**
Mehta, Zubin **11**
Menuhin, Yehudi **11**
Midori **7**
Mutter, Anne-Sophie **23**
Nyman, Michael **15**
Ott, David **2**
Parkening, Christopher **7**
Pavarotti, Luciano **20**
  Earlier sketch in CM **1**
Perahia, Murray **10**
Perlman, Itzhak **2**
Phillips, Harvey **3**
Pires, Maria João **26**
Quasthoff, Thomas **26**
Rampal, Jean-Pierre **6**
Rangell, Andrew **24**
Rieu, André **26**
Rostropovich, Mstislav **17**
Rota, Nino **13**
Rubinstein, Arthur **11**
Salerno-Sonnenberg, Nadja **3**
Salonen, Esa-Pekka **16**
Schickele, Peter **5**
Schuman, William **10**
Segovia, Andres **6**
Shankar, Ravi **9**
Solti, Georg **13**
Stern, Isaac **7**
Stoltzman, Richard **24**
Sutherland, Joan **13**
Takemitsu, Toru **6**
Temirkanov, Yuri **26**
Thibaudet, Jean-Yves **24**
Tilson Thomas, Michael **24**
Toscanini, Arturo **14**
Upshaw, Dawn **9**
Vanessa-Mae **26**
Vienna Choir Boys **23**
von Karajan, Herbert **1**
Weill, Kurt **12**
Wilson, Ransom **5**
Yamashita, Kazuhito **4**
York, Andrew **15**
Zukerman, Pinchas **4**

Composers

Adams, John **8**
Allen, Geri **10**
Alpert, Herb **11**
Anderson, Wessell **23**
Anka, Paul **2**
Arlen, Harold **27**
Atkins, Chet **5**
Bacharach, Burt **20**
  Earlier sketch in CM **1**
Badalamenti, Angelo **17**
Beiderbecke, Bix **16**
Benson, George **9**
Berlin, Irving **8**
Bernstein, Leonard **2**
Blackman, Cindy **15**
Bley, Carla **8**
Bley, Paul **14**
Boulez, Pierre **26**
Braxton, Anthony **12**
Brickman, Jim **22**
Britten, Benjamin **15**
Brubeck, Dave **8**
Burrell, Kenny **11**
Byrne, David **8**
  Also see Talking Heads
Byron, Don **22**
Cage, John **8**
Cale, John **9**
Casals, Pablo **9**
Clarke, Stanley **3**
Coleman, Ornette **5**
Cooder, Ry **2**
Cooney, Rory **6**
Copeland, Stewart **14**
  Also see Police, The **20**
Copland, Aaron **2**
Crouch, Andraé **9**
Curtis, King **17**
Davis, Anthony **17**
Davis, Chip **4**
Davis, Miles **1**
de Grassi, Alex **6**
Dorsey, Thomas A. **11**
Dvorak, Antonin **25**
Elfman, Danny **9**
Ellington, Duke **2**
Eno, Brian **8**
Enya **6**
Esquivel, Juan **17**
Evans, Bill **17**
Evans, Gil **17**
Fahey, John **17**
Foster, David **13**
Frisell, Bill **15**
Frith, Fred **19**
Galás, Diamanda **16**
Garner, Erroll **25**
Gillespie, Dizzy **6**
Glass, Philip **1**
Golson, Benny **21**
Gould, Glenn **9**
Gould, Morton **16**
Green, Benny **17**
Grusin, Dave **7**
Guaraldi, Vince **3**
Hamlisch, Marvin **1**
Hammer, Jan **21**
Hancock, Herbie **8**
Handy, W. C. **7**
Hargrove, Roy **15**
Harris, Eddie **15**
Hartke, Stephen **5**
Henderson, Fletcher **16**
Herrmann, Bernard **14**
Hunter, Alberta **7**
Ibrahim, Abdullah **24**
Isham, Mark **14**
Jacquet, Illinois **17**
Jarre, Jean-Michel **2**
Jarrett, Keith **1**
Johnson, James P. **16**
Jones, Hank **15**
Jones, Howard **26**
Jones, Quincy **20**
  Earlier sketch in CM **2**
Joplin, Scott **10**
Jordan, Stanley **1**
Kenny G **14**
Kenton, Stan **21**
Kern, Jerome **13**
Kitaro **1**
Kottke, Leo **13**
Lacy, Steve **23**
Lateef, Yusef **16**
Lee, Peggy **8**
Legg, Adrian **17**
Lewis, Ramsey **14**
Lincoln, Abbey **9**
Lloyd, Charles **22**
Lloyd Webber, Andrew **6**
Loesser, Frank **19**
Mancini, Henry **20**
  Earlier sketch in CM **1**
Marsalis, Branford **10**
Marsalis, Ellis **13**
Martino, Pat **17**
Mascagni, Pietro **25**
Masekela, Hugh **7**
McBride, Christian **17**
McPartland, Marian **15**
Menken, Alan **10**
Metheny, Pat **26**
  Earlier sketch in CM **2**
Miles, Ron **22**
Mingus, Charles **9**
Moby **27**
  Earlier sketch in CM **17**
Monk, Meredith **1**
Monk, Thelonious **6**
Montenegro, Hugo **18**
Morricone, Ennio **15**
Morton, Jelly Roll **7**
Mulligan, Gerry **16**
Nascimento, Milton **6**
Newman, Randy **4**
Nyman, Michael **15**
Oldfield, Mike **18**
Orff, Carl **21**

Osby, Greg 21
Ott, David 2
Palmieri, Eddie 15
Parker, Charlie 5
Parks, Van Dyke 17
Perez, Danilo 25
Peterson, Oscar 11
Piazzolla, Astor 18
Ponty, Jean-Luc 8
Porter, Cole 10
Post, Mike 21
Previn, André 15
Puente, Tito 14
Pullen, Don 16
Reich, Steve 8
Reinhardt, Django 7
Ritenour, Lee 7
Roach, Max 12
Rollins, Sonny 7
Rota, Nino 13
Sakamoto, Ryuichi 19
Salonen, Esa-Pekka 16
Sanders, Pharoah 16
Satie, Erik 25
Satriani, Joe 4
Schickele, Peter 5
Schuman, William 10
Shankar, Ravi 9
Shaw, Artie 8
Shorter, Wayne 5
Silver, Horace 19
Solal, Martial 4
Sondheim, Stephen 8
Sousa, John Philip 10
Story, Liz 2
Strauss, Richard 25
Stravinsky, Igor 21
Strayhorn, Billy 13
Styne, Jule 21
Summers, Andy 3
Also see Police, The
Sun Ra 27
Earlier sketch in CM 5
Sylvian, David 27
Takemitsu, Toru 6
Talbot, John Michael 6
Tatum, Art 17
Taylor, Billy 13
Taylor, Cecil 9
Tesh, John 20
Thielemans, Toots 13
Threadgill, Henry 9
Tilson Thomas, Michael 24
Towner, Ralph 22
Tyner, McCoy 7
Vangelis 21
Wakeman, Rick 27
Also see Yes
Was, Don 21
Also see Was (Not Was)
Washington, Grover, Jr. 5
Weill, Kurt 12
Weston, Randy 15
Whelan, Bill 20
Whiteman, Paul 17
Williams, John 9
Wilson, Cassandra 12
Wilson, Cassandra 26
Winston, George 9
Winter, Paul 10
Worrell, Bernie 11
Yanni 11
Yeston, Maury 22
York, Andrew 15
Young, La Monte 16
Zappa, Frank 17
Earlier sketch in CM 1
Zimmerman, Udo 5
Zorn, John 15

Conductors

Bacharach, Burt 20
Earlier sketch CM 1
Beecham, Thomas 27
Bernstein, Leonard 2
Boulez, Pierre 26
Britten, Benjamin 15
Casals, Pablo 9
Copland, Aaron 2
Davies, Dennis Russell 24
Davis, Colin 27
Domingo, Placido 20
Earlier sketch in CM 1
Evans, Gil 17
Fiedler, Arthur 6
Gardiner, John Eliot 26
Gould, Morton 16
Herrmann, Bernard 14
Ibrahim, Abdullah 24
Jarrett, Keith 1
Jones, Hank 15
Kunzel, Erich 17
Levine, James 8
Mancini, Henry 20
Earlier sketch in CM 1
Marriner, Neville 7
Mascagni, Pietro 25
Masur, Kurt 11
Mehta, Zubin 11
Menuhin, Yehudi 11
Nero, Peter 19
Previn, André 15
Rampal, Jean-Pierre 6
Rieu, André 26
Rostropovich, Mstislav 17
Salonen, Esa-Pekka 16
Schickele, Peter 5
Solti, Georg 13
Strauss, Richard
Temirkanov, Yuri 26
Tilson Thomas, Michael 24
Toscanini, Arturo 14
Valdes, Chuco 25
von Karajan, Herbert 1
Welk, Lawrence 13
Williams, John 9
Zukerman, Pinchas 4

Contemporary Dance Music

Abdul, Paula 3
Aphex Twin 14
Bee Gees, The 3
B-52's, The 4
Brown, Bobby 4
Brown, James 2
C + C Music Factory 16
Cherry, Neneh 4
Clinton, George 7
Craig, Carl 19
Deee-lite 9
De La Soul 7
Depeche Mode 5
Earth, Wind and Fire 12
English Beat, The 9
En Vogue 10
Erasure 11
Eurythmics 6
Exposé 4
Fox, Samantha 3
Fun Lovin' Criminals 20
Gang of Four 8
Hammer, M.C. 5
Harry, Deborah 4
Also see Blondie
Ice-T 7
Idol, Billy 3
Jackson, Janet 16
Earlier sketch in CM 3
Jackson, Michael 17
Earlier sketch in CM 1
Also see Jacksons, The
James, Rick 2
Jones, Grace 9
Madonna 16
Earlier sketch in CM 4
Massive Attack 17
Moby 27
Earlier sketch in CM 17
M People 15
New Order 11
Orbital 20
Peniston, CeCe 15
Pet Shop Boys 5
Pizzicato Five 18
Portishead 22
Prince 14
Earlier sketch in CM 1
Queen Latifah 24
Earlier sketch in CM 6
Rodgers, Nile 8
Salt-N-Pepa 6
Shadow, DJ 19
Shamen, The 23
Simmons, Russell 7
Soul II Soul 17
Sugar Ray 22
Summer, Donna 12
Technotronic 5
TLC 15
Tricky 18
2 Unlimited 18
Vasquez, Junior 16
Village People, The 7
Was (Not Was) 6
Waters, Crystal 15
Young M.C. 4

Contemporary Instrumental/New Age

Ackerman, Will 3
Arkenstone, David 20
Clinton, George 7
Collins, Bootsy 8
Davis, Chip 4
De Gaia, Banco 27
de Grassi, Alex 6
Enigma 14
Enya 6
Esquivel, Juan 17
Hedges, Michael 3
Isham, Mark 14
Jarre, Jean-Michel 2
Kitaro 1
Kronos Quartet 5
Legg, Adrian 17
Mogwai 27
Roth, Gabrielle 26
Sete, Bola 26
Story, Liz 2
Summers, Andy 3
Also see Police, The
Tangerine Dream 12
Tesh, John 20

Winston, George **9**
Winter, Paul **10**
Yanni **11**

Cornet
Armstrong, Louis **4**
Beiderbecke, Bix **16**
Cherry, Don **10**
Handy, W. C. **7**
Oliver, King **15**
Vaché, Jr., Warren **22**

Country
Acuff, Roy **2**
Akins, Rhett **22**
Alabama **21**
Earlier sketch in CM **1**
Anderson, John **5**
Arnold, Eddy **10**
Asleep at the Wheel **5**
Atkins, Chet **26**
Atkins, Chet **5**
Auldridge, Mike **4**
Autry, Gene **25**
Earlier sketch in CM **12**
Barnett, Mandy **26**
Bellamy Brothers, The **13**
Berg, Matraca **16**
Berry, John **17**
Black, Clint **5**
BlackHawk **21**
Blue Rodeo **18**
Boggs, Dock **25**
Bogguss, Suzy **11**
Bonamy, James **21**
Boone, Pat **13**
Boy Howdy **21**
Brandt, Paul **22**
Brannon, Kippi **20**
Brooks & Dunn **25**
Earlier sketch in CM **12**
Brooks, Garth **25**
Earlier sketch in CM **8**
Brown, Junior **15**
Brown, Marty **14**
Brown, Tony **14**
Buffett, Jimmy **4**
Byrds, The **8**
Cale, J. J. **16**
Campbell, Glen **2**
Carter, Carlene **8**
Carter, Deana **25**
Carter Family, The **3**
Cash, Johnny **17**
Earlier sketch in CM **1**
Cash, June Carter **6**
Cash, Rosanne **2**
Chapin Carpenter, Mary **25**
Earlier sketch in CM **6**
Chesney, Kenny **20**
Chesnutt, Mark **13**
Clark, Guy **17**
Clark, Roy **1**
Clark, Terri **19**
Clements, Vassar **18**
Cline, Patsy **5**
Coe, David Allan **4**
Collie, Mark **15**
Confederate Railroad **23**
Cooder, Ry **2**
Cowboy Junkies, The **4**
Crawford, Randy **25**
Crowe, J. D. **5**
Crowell, Rodney **8**
Cyrus, Billy Ray **11**
Daniels, Charlie **6**
Davis, Linda **21**
Davis, Skeeter **15**
Dean, Billy **19**
DeMent, Iris **13**
Denver, John **22**
Earlier sketch in CM **1**
Desert Rose Band, The **4**
Diamond Rio **11**
Dickens, Little Jimmy **7**
Diffie, Joe **27**
Earlier sketch CM **10**
Dixie Chicks **26**
Dylan, Bob **21**
Earlier sketch in CM **3**
Earle, Steve **16**
Estes, John **25**
Evans, Sara **27**
Flatt, Lester **3**
Flores, Rosie **16**
Ford, Tennessee Ernie **3**
Foster, Radney **16**
Frizzell, Lefty **10**
Gayle, Crystal **1**
Germano, Lisa **18**
Gill, Vince **7**
Gilley, Mickey **7**
Gilmore, Jimmie Dale **11**
Gordy, Jr., Emory **17**
Greenwood, Lee **12**
Griffith, Nanci **3**
Haggard, Merle **2**
Hall, Tom T. **4**
Hall, Tom T. **26**
Harris, Emmylou **4**
Hartford, John **1**
Hay, George D. **3**
Herndon, Ty **20**
Hiatt, John **8**
Highway 101 **4**
Hill, Faith **18**
Hinojosa, Tish **13**
Howard, Harlan **15**
Jackson, Alan **25**
Earlier sketch in CM **7**
Jennings, Waylon **4**
Jones, George **4**
Judds, The **2**
Keith, Toby **17**
Kentucky Headhunters, The **5**
Kershaw, Sammy **15**
Ketchum, Hal **14**
Kristofferson, Kris **4**
Lamb, Barbara **19**
Lang, kd **25**
Earlier sketch in CM **4**
Lawrence, Tracy **11**
LeDoux, Chris **12**
Lee, Brenda **5**
Little Feat **4**
Little Texas **14**
Lonestar **27**
Louvin Brothers, The **12**
Loveless, Patty **21**
Earlier sketch in CM **5**
Lovett, Lyle **5**
Lynn, Loretta **2**
Lynne, Shelby **5**
Mandrell, Barbara **4**
Mattea, Kathy **5**
Mavericks, The **15**
McBride, Martina **14**
McCann, Lila **26**
McClinton, Delbert **14**
McCoy, Neal **15**
McCready, Mindy **22**
McEntire, Reba **11**
McGraw, Tim **17**
Messina, Jo Dee **26**
Miller, Roger **4**
Milsap, Ronnie **2**
Moffatt, Katy **18**
Monroe, Bill **1**
Montgomery, John Michael **14**
Morgan, Lorrie **10**
Murphey, Michael Martin **9**
Murray, Anne **4**
Nelson, Willie **11**
Earlier sketch in CM **1**
Newton-John, Olivia **8**
Nitty Gritty Dirt Band, The **6**
O'Connor, Mark **1**
Oak Ridge Boys, The **7**
Oslin, K. T. **3**
Owens, Buck **2**
Parnell, Lee Roy **15**
Parsons, Gram **7**
Also see Byrds, The
Parton, Dolly **24**
Earlier sketch in CM **2**
Pearl, Minnie **3**
Pierce, Webb **15**
Price, Ray **11**
Pride, Charley **4**
Rabbitt, Eddie **24**
Earlier sketch in CM **5**
Raitt, Bonnie **3**
Ray Condo and His Ricochets **26**
Raye, Collin **16**
Reeves, Jim **10**
Restless Heart **12**
Rich, Charlie **3**
Richey, Kim **20**
Ricochet **23**
Rimes, LeAnn **19**
Robbins, Marty **9**
Rodgers, Jimmie **3**
Rogers, Kenny **1**
Rogers, Roy **24**
Earlier sketch in CM **9**
Sawyer Brown **27**
Earlier sketch in CM **13**
Scruggs, Earl **3**
Scud Mountain Boys **21**
Seals, Dan **9**
Shenandoah **17**
Skaggs, Ricky **5**
Sonnier, Jo-El **10**
Statler Brothers, The **8**
Stevens, Ray **7**
Stone, Doug **10**
Strait, George **5**
Stuart, Marty **9**
Sweethearts of the Rodeo **12**
Texas Tornados, The **8**
Tillis, Mel **7**
Tillis, Pam **25**
Earlier sketch in CM **8**
Tippin, Aaron **12**
Travis, Merle **14**
Travis, Randy **9**
Tritt, Travis **7**
Tubb, Ernest **4**
Tucker, Tanya **3**
Twain, Shania **17**
Twitty, Conway **6**
Van Shelton, Ricky **5**

Van Zandt, Townes **13**
Wagoner, Porter **13**
Walker, Clay **20**
Walker, Jerry Jeff **13**
Wariner, Steve **18**
Watson, Doc **2**
Wells, Kitty **6**
West, Dottie **8**
White, Lari **15**
Whitley, Keith **7**
Williams, Don **4**
Williams, Hank, Jr. **1**
Williams, Hank, Sr. **4**
Williams, Lucinda **24**
Earlier sketch in CM **10**
Willis, Kelly **12**
Wills, Bob **6**
Wills, Mark **27**
Wynette, Tammy **24**
Earlier sketch in CM **2**
Wynonna **11**
Also see Judds, The
Yearwood, Trisha **25**
Earlier sketch in CM **10**
Yoakam, Dwight **21**
Earlier sketch in CM **1**
Young, Faron **7**

Dobro
Auldridge, Mike **4**
Also see Country Gentlemen, The
Also see Seldom Scene, The
Knopfler, Mark **25**
Also see Dire Straits
Earlier sketch in CM **3**
Whitley, Chris **16**

Drums
Aronoff, Kenny **21**
See **Percussion**
Colaiuta, Vinnie **23**
Parker, Leon **27**
Starr, Ringo **24**

Dulcimer
Ritchie, Jean **4**

Fiddle
MacIsaac, Ashley **21**
See **Violin**

Film Scores
Anka, Paul **2**
Arlen, Harold **27**
Bacharach, Burt **20**
Earlier sketch in CM **1**
Badalamenti, Angelo **17**
Berlin, Irving **8**
Bernstein, Leonard **2**
Blanchard, Terence **13**
Britten, Benjamin **15**
Byrne, David **8**
Also see Talking Heads
Cahn, Sammy **11**
Cliff, Jimmy **8**
Copeland, Stewart **14**
Also see Police, The
Copland, Aaron **2**
Crouch, Andraé **9**
Dibango, Manu **14**
Dolby, Thomas **10**
Donovan **9**
Eddy, Duane **9**
Elfman, Danny **9**
Ellington, Duke **2**
Ferguson, Maynard **7**
Froom, Mitchell **15**
Gabriel, Peter **16**
Earlier sketch in CM **2**
Also see Genesis
Galás, Diamanda **16**
Gershwin, George and Ira **11**
Gould, Glenn **9**
Grusin, Dave **7**
Guaraldi, Vince **3**
Hamlisch, Marvin **1**
Hancock, Herbie **8**
Harrison, George **2**
Hayes, Isaac **10**
Hedges, Michael **3**
Herrmann, Bernard **14**
Isham, Mark **14**
Jones, Quincy **20**
Earlier sketch in CM **2**
Knopfler, Mark **25**
Earlier sketch in CM **3**
Also see Dire Straits
Lennon, John **9**
Also see Beatles, The
Lerner and Loewe **13**
Loesser, Frank **19**
Mancini, Henry **20**
Earlier sketch in CM **1**
Marsalis, Branford **10**
Mayfield, Curtis **8**
McCartney, Paul **4**
Also see Beatles, The
Menken, Alan **10**
Mercer, Johnny **13**
Metheny, Pat **26**
Earlier sketch in CM **2**
Montenegro, Hugo **18**
Morricone, Ennio **15**
Nascimento, Milton **6**
Newman, Randy **27**
Earlier sketch in CM **4**
Nilsson **10**
Nyman, Michael **15**
Parks, Van Dyke **17**
Peterson, Oscar **11**
Porter, Cole **10**
Previn, André **15**
Reznor, Trent **13**
Richie, Lionel **2**
Robertson, Robbie **2**
Rollins, Sonny **7**
Rota, Nino **13**
Sager, Carole Bayer **5**
Sakamoto, Ryuichi **18**
Schickele, Peter **5**
Shankar, Ravi **9**
Taj Mahal **6**
Waits, Tom **27**
Earlier sketch in CM **12**
Earlier sketch in CM **1**
Weill, Kurt **12**
Williams, John **9**
Williams, Paul **26**
Williams, Paul **5**
Willner, Hal **10**
Young, Neil **15**
Earlier sketch in CM **2**

Flugelhorn
Sandoval, Arturo **15**
Mangione, Chuck **23**

Flute
Galway, James **3**
Jethro Tull **8**
Lateef, Yusef **16**
Mangione, Chuck **23**
Mann, Herbie **16**
Najee **21**
Nakai, R. Carlos **24**
Rampal, Jean-Pierre **6**
Ulmer, James Blood **13**
Wilson, Ransom **5**

Folk/Traditional
Altan **18**
America **16**
Anonymous 4 **23**
Arnaz, Desi **8**
Baez, Joan **1**
Belafonte, Harry **8**
Black, Mary **15**
Blades, Ruben **2**
Bloom, Luka **14**
Blue Rodeo **18**
Boggs, Dock **25**
Brady, Paul **8**
Bragg, Billy **7**
Bromberg, David **18**
Buckley, Tim **14**
Buffalo Springfield **24**
Bulgarian State Female Vocal Choir, The **10**
Byrds, The **8**
Campbell, Sarah Elizabeth **23**
Caravan **24**
Carter Family, The **3**
Chandra, Sheila **16**
Chapin, Harry **6**
Chapman, Tracy **20**
Earlier sketch in CM **4**
Chenille Sisters, The **16**
Cherry, Don **10**
Chieftains, The **7**
Childs, Toni **2**
Clannad **23**
Clegg, Johnny **8**
Cockburn, Bruce **8**
Cohen, Leonard **3**
Collins, Judy **4**
Colvin, Shawn **11**
Cotten, Elizabeth **16**
Crosby, David **3**
Also see Byrds, The
Cruz, Celia **22**
Earlier sketch in CM **10**
de Lucia, Paco **1**
DeMent, Iris **13**
Donovan **9**
Dr. John **7**
Drake, Nick **17**
Driftwood, Jimmy **25**
Dylan, Bob **21**
Earlier sketch in CM **3**
Elliot, Cass **5**
Enya **6**
Estefan, Gloria **15**
Earlier sketch in CM **2**
Fahey, John **17**
Fairport Convention **22**
Feliciano, José **10**
Galway, James **3**
Germano, Lisa **18**
Gibson, Bob **23**
Gilmore, Jimmie Dale **11**
Gipsy Kings, The **8**
Gorka, John **18**

Griffin, Patty **24**
Griffith, Nanci **3**
Grisman, David **17**
Guthrie, Arlo **6**
Guthrie, Woody **2**
Hakmoun, Hassan **15**
Hardin, Tim **18**
Harding, John Wesley **6**
Hartford, John **1**
Havens, Richie **11**
Henry, Joe **18**
Hinojosa, Tish **13**
Ian and Sylvia **18**
Ian, Janis **24**
  Earlier sketch in CM **5**
Iglesias, Julio **20**
  Earlier sketch in CM **2**
Incredible String Band **23**
Indigo Girls **20**
  Earlier sketch in CM **3**
Ives, Burl **12**
Khan, Nusrat Fateh Ali **13**
Kingston Trio, The **9**
Klezmatics, The **18**
Kottke, Leo **13**
Kuti, Fela **7**
Ladysmith Black Mambazo **1**
Larkin, Patty **9**
Lavin, Christine **6**
Leadbelly **6**
Lightfoot, Gordon **3**
Los Lobos **2**
Makeba, Miriam **8**
Mamas and the Papas **21**
Masekela, Hugh **7**
McKennitt, Loreena **24**
McLean, Don **7**
Melanie **12**
Mitchell, Joni **17**
  Earlier sketch in CM **2**
Moffatt, Katy **18**
Morrison, Van **24**
  Earlier sketch in CM **3**
Morrissey, Bill **12**
N'Dour, Youssou **6**
Nascimento, Milton **6**
Near, Holly **1**
O'Connor, Sinead **3**
Ochs, Phil **7**
Odetta **7**
Parsons, Gram **7**
  Also see Byrds, The
Paxton, Tom **5**
Pentangle **18**
Peter, Paul & Mary **4**
Pogues, The **6**
Prine, John **7**
Proclaimers, The **13**
Rankins, The **24**
Redpath, Jean **1**
Ritchie, Jean, **4**
Roches, The **18**
Rodgers, Jimmie **3**
Russell, Tom **26**
Sainte-Marie, Buffy **11**
Santana, Carlos **19**
  Earlier sketch in CM **1**
Seeger, Peggy **25**
Seeger, Pete **4**
  Also see Weavers, The
Selena **16**
Shankar, Ravi **9**
Simon and Garfunkel **24**
Simon, Paul **16**
  Earlier sketch in CM **1**
  Also see Simon and Garfunkel
Snow, Pheobe **4**
Steeleye Span **19**
Story, The **13**
Sweet Honey in the Rock **26**
  Earlier sketch in CM **1**
Taj Mahal **6**
Thompson, Richard **7**
Tikaram, Tanita **9**
Toure, Ali Farka **18**
Van Ronk, Dave **12**
Van Zandt, Townes **13**
Vega, Suzanne **3**
Wainwright III, Loudon **11**
Walker, Jerry Jeff **13**
Waterboys, The **27**
Watson, Doc **2**
Weavers, The **8**
Whitman, Slim **19**

Funk
Bambaataa, Afrika **13**
Brand New Heavies, The **14**
Brown, James **2**
Burdon, Eric **14**
  Also see War
  Also see Animals
Clinton, George **7**
Collins, Bootsy **8**
Fishbone **7**
Gang of Four **8**
Jackson, Janet **16**
  Earlier sketch in CM **3**
Khan, Chaka **19**
  Earlier sketch in CM **9**
Mayfield, Curtis **8**
Meters, The **14**
Ohio Players **16**
Parker, Maceo **7**
Prince **14**
  Earlier sketch in CM **1**
Red Hot Chili Peppers, The **7**
Sly and the Family Stone **24**
Stone, Sly **8**
  Also see Sly and the Family Stone
Toussaint, Allen **11**
Worrell, Bernie **11**

Funky
Avery, Teodross **23**
Citizen King **27**
Front 242 **19**
Jamiroquai **21**
Joy Electric **26**
Wu-Tang Clan **19**

Fusion
Anderson, Ray **7**
Avery, Teodross **23**
Beck, Jeff **4**
  Also see Yardbirds, The
Clarke, Stanley **3**
Coleman, Ornette **5**
Corea, Chick **6**
Davis, Miles **1**
Fishbone **7**
Hancock, Herbie **8**
Harris, Eddie **15**
Johnson, Eric **19**
Lewis, Ramsey **14**
Mahavishnu Orchestra **19**
McLaughlin, John **12**
Metheny, Pat **26**
  Earlier sketch in CM **2**
O'Connor, Mark **1**
Ponty, Jean-Luc **8**
Reid, Vernon **2**
Ritenour, Lee **7**
Shorter, Wayne **5**
Summers, Andy **3**
  Also see Police, The
Washington, Grover, Jr. **5**

Gospel
4Him **23**
Anderson, Marian **8**
Armstrong, Vanessa Bell **24**
Baylor, Helen **20**
Boone, Pat **13**
Brown, James **2**
Caesar, Shirley **17**
Carter Family, The **3**
Charles, Ray **24**
  Earlier sketch in CM **1**
Cleveland, James **1**
Cooke, Sam **1**
  Also see Soul Stirrers, The
Crouch, Andraé **9**
Dorsey, Thomas A. **11**
Five Blind Boys of Alabama **12**
Ford, Tennessee Ernie **3**
Franklin, Aretha **17**
  Earlier sketch in CM **2**
Franklin, Kirk **22**
Golden Gate Quartet **25**
Greater Vision **26**
Green, Al **9**
Hawkins, Tramaine **17**
Houston, Cissy **26**
  Earlier sketch in CM **6**
Jackson, Mahalia **8**
Johnson, Blind Willie **26**
Kee, John P. **15**
Knight, Gladys **1**
Little Richard **1**
Louvin Brothers, The **12**
Mighty Clouds of Joy, The **17**
Oak Ridge Boys, The **7**
Oakland Interfaith Gospel Choir **26**
Paris, Twila **16**
Pickett, Wilson **10**
Presley, Elvis **1**
Redding, Otis **5**
Reese, Della **13**
Robbins, Marty **9**
Smith, Michael W. **11**
Soul Stirrers, The **11**
Sounds of Blackness **13**
Staples, Mavis **13**
Staples, Pops **11**
Sweet Honey In The Rock **26**
  Earlier sketch in CM **1**
Take 6 **6**
Waters, Ethel **11**
Watson, Doc **2**
Williams, Deniece **1**
Williams, Marion **15**
Winans, The **12**
Womack, Bobby **5**

Guitar
Abercrombie, John **25**
Ackerman, Will **3**
Adé, King Sunny **18**
Allison, Luther **21**
Alvin, Dave **17**
Atkins, Chet **26**
  Earlier sketch in CM **5**
Autry, Gene **25**
  Earlier sketch in CM **12**

Barnes, Roosevelt "Booba" **23**
Beck **18**
Beck, Jeff **4**
  Also see Yardbirds, The
Belew, Adrian **5**
Benson, George **9**
Berry, Chuck **1**
Berry, John **17**
Block, Rory **18**
Bloom, Luka **14**
Boyd, Liona **7**
Bream, Julian **9**
Bromberg, David **18**
Brooks, Garth **25**
  Earlier sketch in CM **8**
Brötzmann, Caspar **27**
Brown, Junior **15**
Buckingham, Lindsey **8**
  Also see Fleetwood Mac
Burrell, Kenny **11**
Campbell, Glen **2**
Carter, Deana **25**
Chapin-Carpenter, Mary **25**
  Earlier sketch in CM **6**
Chaquico, Craig **23**
Chesney, Kenny **20**
Chesnutt, Mark **13**
Christian, Charlie **11**
Clapton, Eric **11**
  Earlier sketch in CM **1**
  Also see Cream
  Also see Yardbirds, The
Clark, Roy **1**
Cockburn, Bruce **8**
Collie, Mark **15**
Collins, Albert **19**
  Earlier sketch in CM **4**
Cooder, Ry **2**
Cotten, Elizabeth **16**
Cray, Robert **8**
Cropper, Steve **12**
Dale, Dick **13**
Daniels, Charlie **6**
Davis, Reverend Gary **18**
de Grassi, Alex **6**
de Lucia, Paco **1**
Del Rubio Triplets **21**
Denver, John **22**
  Earlier sketch in CM **1**
Di Meola, Al **12**
Dickens, Little Jimmy **7**
Diddley, Bo **3**
DiFranco, Ani **17**
Drake, Nick **17**
Earl, Ronnie **5**
  Also see Roomful of Blues
Eddy, Duane **9**
Ellis, Herb **18**
Emmanuel, Tommy **21**
Etheridge, Melissa **16**
  Earlier sketch in CM **4**
Fahey, John **17**
Fankhauser, Merrell **24**
Feliciano, José **10**
Fender, Leo **10**
Flatt, Lester **3**
Flores, Rosie **16**
Ford, Lita **9**
Frampton, Peter **3**
Fripp, Robert **9**
Frisell, Bill **15**
Frith, Fred **19**
Fuller, Blind Boy **20**
Fulson, Lowell **20**
Garcia, Jerry **4**
  Also see Grateful Dead, The
Gatton, Danny **16**
Gibson, Bob **23**
Gil, Gilberto **26**
Gill, Vince **7**
Gorka, John **18**
Green, Grant **14**
Guy, Buddy **4**
Hackett, Bobby **21**
Haley, Bill **6**
Hall, Tom T. **26**
Hardin, Tim **18**
Harper, Ben **17**
Harrison, George **2**
Hart, Alvin Youngblood **27**
Hatfield, Juliana **12**
  Also see Lemonheads, The
Havens, Richie **11**
Healey, Jeff **4**
Hedges, Michael **3**
Hendrix, Jimi **2**
Hepcat, Harry **23**
Hitchcock, Robyn **9**
Holly, Buddy **1**
Hooker, John Lee **26**
  Earlier sketch in CM **1**
Hopkins, Lightnin' **13**
Howlin' Wolf **6**
Hunter, Charlie **24**
Ives, Burl **12**
Jackson, Alan **25**
  Earlier sketch in CM **7**
James, Elmore **8**
James, Skip **24**
Jean, Wyclef **22**
Jefferson, Blind Lemon **18**
Jewel **25**
Jobim, Antonio Carlos **19**
Johnson, Blind Willie **26**
Johnson, Eric **19**
Johnson, Lonnie **17**
Johnson, Robert **6**
Jordan, Stanley **1**
Keaggy, Phil **26**
Keith, Toby **17**
King, Albert **2**
King, B.B. **24**
  Earlier sketch in CM **1**
King, Freddy **17**
Klugh, Earl **10**
Knopfler, Mark **25**
  Earlier sketch in CM **3**
  Also see Dire Straits
Kottke, Leo **13**
Landreth, Sonny **16**
Lang, Jonny **27**
Larkin, Patty **9**
Leadbelly **6**
Legg, Adrian **17**
Lennon, John **9**
  Also see Beatles, The
Lindley, David **2**
Lockwood, Robert, Jr. **10**
Loeb, Lisa **19**
Lofgren, Nils **25**
Malmsteen, Yngwie **24**
Malone, Russell **27**
Martino, Pat **17**
Matthews, Eric **22**
Mayfield, Curtis **8**
McClinton, Delbert **14**
McCoury, Del **15**
McDowell, Mississippi Fred **16**
McLachlan, Sarah **12**
McLaughlin, John **12**
McLean, Dave **24**
McLennan, Grant **21**
McTell, Blind Willie **17**
Metheny, Pat **26**
  Earlier sketch in CM **2**
Mitchell, Joni **17**
  Earlier sketch in CM **2**
Mo', Keb' **21**
Montgomery, Wes **3**
Morrissey, Bill **12**
Muldaur, Maria **18**
Nugent, Ted **2**
Oldfield, Mike **18**
Owens, Buck **2**
Page, Jimmy **4**
  Also see Led Zeppelin
  Also see Yardbirds, The
Parkening, Christopher **7**
Parnell, Lee Roy **15**
Pass, Joe **15**
Patton, Charley **11**
Perkins, Carl **9**
Petty, Tom **9**
Phair, Liz **14**
Phillips, Sam **12**
Powell, Baden, **23**
Prince **14**
  Earlier sketch in CM **1**
Raitt, Bonnie **23**
  Earlier sketch in CM 1
Redbone, Leon **19**
Reed, Jimmy **15**
Reid, Vernon **2**
  Also see Living Colour
Reinhardt, Django **7**
Richards, Keith **11**
  Also see Rolling Stones, The
Richman, Jonathan **12**
Ritenour, Lee **7**
Robbins, Marty **9**
Robertson, Robbie **2**
Robillard, Duke **2**
Rodgers, Nile **8**
Rush, Otis **12**
Sambora, Richie **24**
  Also see Bon Jovi
Santana, Carlos **19**
  Earlier sketch in CM **1**
Satriani, Joe **4**
Scofield, John **7**
Segovia, Andres **6**
Sete, Bola **26**
Sexsmith, Ron **27**
Sharrock, Sonny **15**
Shepherd, Kenny Wayne **22**
Shines, Johnny **14**
Simon, Paul **16**
  Earlier sketch in CM **1**
  Also see Simon and Garfunkel
Skaggs, Ricky **5**
Springsteen, Bruce **25**
  Earlier sketch in CM **6**
Stills, Stephen **5**
Stuart, Marty **9**
Summers, Andy **3**
  Also see Police, The
Tampa Red **25**
Thielemans, Toots **13**
Thompson, Richard **7**
Tippin, Aaron **12**
Toure, Ali Farka **18**
Towner, Ralph **22**

Townshend, Pete **1**
Travis, Merle **14**
Trynin, Jen **21**
Tubb, Ernest **4**
Ulmer, James Blood **13**
Vai, Steve **5**
Van Ronk, Dave **12**
Vaughan, Jimmie **24**
Also see Fabulous Thunderbirds, The
Vaughan, Stevie Ray **1**
Wachtel, Waddy **26**
Wagoner, Porter **13**
Waits, Tom **27**
Earlier sketch in CM **12**
Earlier sketch in CM **1**
Walker, Jerry Jeff **13**
Walker, T-Bone **5**
Walsh, Joe **5**
Also see Eagles, The
Wariner, Steve **18**
Waters, Muddy **24**
Earlier sketch in CM **4**
Watson, Doc **2**
Weller, Paul **14**
White, Lari **15**
Whitfield, Mark **18**
Whitley, Chris **16**
Whittaker, Hudson **20**
Wilson, Brian **24**
Also see Beach Boys, The
Winston, George **9**
Winter, Johnny **5**
Wiseman, Mac **19**
Wray, Link **17**
Yamashita, Kazuhito **4**
Yoakam, Dwight **21**
Earlier sketch in CM **1**
York, Andrew **15**
Young, Neil **15**
Earlier sketch in CM **2**
Zappa, Frank **17**
Earlier sketch in CM **1**

Harmonica
Barnes, Roosevelt, "Booba" **23**
Dylan, Bob **3**
Guthrie, Woody **2**
Horton, Walter **19**
Lewis, Huey **9**
Little Walter **14**
McClinton, Delbert **14**
Musselwhite, Charlie **13**
Reed, Jimmy **15**
Thielemans, Toots **13**
Waters, Muddy **24**
Earlier sketch in CM **4**
Wells, Junior **17**
Williamson, Sonny Boy **9**
Wonder, Stevie **17**
Earlier sketch in CM **2**
Young, Neil **15**
Earlier sketch in CM **2**

Heavy Metal
AC/DC **4**
Aerosmith **22**
Earlier sketch in CM **1**
Alice in Chains **10**
Anthrax **11**
Black Sabbath **9**
Blue Oyster Cult **16**
Cinderella **16**
Circle Jerks **17**
Danzig **7**
Deep Purple **11**
Def Leppard **3**
Dokken **16**
Faith No More **7**
Fear Factory **27**
Fishbone **7**
Ford, Lita **9**
Guns n' Roses **2**
Iron Maiden **10**
Judas Priest **10**
Kilgore **24**
King's X **7**
Kiss **25**
Earlier sketch in CM **5**
L7 **12**
Led Zeppelin **1**
Megadeth **9**
Melvins **21**
Metallica **7**
Mötley Crüe **1**
Motörhead **10**
Nugent, Ted **2**
Osbourne, Ozzy **3**
Pantera **13**
Petra **3**
Queensryche **8**
Reid, Vernon **2**
Also see Living Colour
Reznor, Trent **13**
Roth, David Lee **1**
Also see Van Halen
Sepultura **12**
Skinny Puppy **17**
Slayer **10**
Soundgarden **6**
Spinal Tap **8**
Stryper **2**
Suicidal Tendencies **15**
Tool **21**
Type O Negative **27**
Warrant **17**
Wendy O. Williams and The Plasmatics **26**
White Zombie **17**
Whitesnake **5**

Humor
Borge, Victor **19**
Coasters, The **5**
Dr. Demento **23**
Jones, Spike **5**
Lehrer, Tom **7**
Pearl, Minnie **3**
Russell, Mark **6**
Sandler, Adam **19**
Schickele, Peter **5**
Shaffer, Paul **13**
Spinal Tap **8**
Stevens, Ray **7**
Yankovic, "Weird Al" **7**

Inventors
Fender, Leo **10**
Harris, Eddie **15**
Paul, Les **2**
Teagarden, Jack **10**
Theremin, Leon **19**

Jazz
Abercrombie, John **25**
Adderly, Cannonball **15**
Allen, Geri **10**
Allison, Mose **17**
Anderson, Ray **7**
Armstrong, Louis **4**
Art Ensemble of Chicago **23**
Avery, Teodross **23**
Bailey, Mildred **13**
Bailey, Pearl **5**
Baker, Anita **9**
Baker, Chet **13**
Baker, Ginger **16**
Also see Cream
Barbieri, Gato **22**
Basie, Count **2**
Bechet, Sidney **17**
Beiderbecke, Bix **16**
Belle, Regina **6**
Bennett, Tony **16**
Earlier sketch in CM **2**
Benson, George **9**
Berigan, Bunny **2**
Blackman, Cindy **15**
Blakey, Art **11**
Blanchard, Terence **13**
Bley, Carla **8**
Bley, Paul **14**
Blood, Sweat and Tears **7**
Brand New Heavies, The **14**
Braxton, Anthony **12**
Bridgewater, Dee Dee **18**
Brötzmann, Peter **26**
Brown, Clifford **24**
Brown, Lawrence **23**
Brown, Ray **21**
Brown, Ruth **13**
Brubeck, Dave **8**
Burrell, Kenny **11**
Burton, Gary **10**
Calloway, Cab **6**
Canadian Brass, The **4**
Carter, Benny **3**
Also see McKinney's Cotton Pickers
Carter, Betty **6**
Carter, James **18**
Carter, Regina **22**
Carter, Ron **14**
Chambers, Paul **18**
Charles, Ray **24**
Earlier sketch in CM **1**
Cherry, Don **10**
Christian, Charlie **11**
Clarke, Stanley **3**
Clements, Vassar **18**
Clooney, Rosemary **9**
Cole, Holly **18**
Cole, Nat King **3**
Coleman, Ornette **5**
Coltrane, John **4**
Connick, Harry, Jr. **4**
Corea, Chick **6**
Crawford, Randy **25**
Davis, Anthony **17**
Davis, Miles **1**
DeJohnette, Jack **7**
Di Meola, Al **12**
Dietrich, Marlene **25**
Dirty Dozen **23**
Eckstine, Billy **1**
Eldridge, Roy **9**
Also see McKinney's Cotton Pickers
Ellington, Duke **2**
Ellis, Herb **18**
Evans, Bill **17**
Evans, Gil **17**
Ferguson, Maynard **7**
Ferrell, Rachelle **17**
Fitzgerald, Ella **1**
Five Iron Frenzy **26**

Flanagan, Tommy 16
Fleck, Bela 8
Also see New Grass Revival, The
Fountain, Pete 7
Frisell, Bill 15
Galway, James 3
Garner, Erroll 25
Getz, Stan 12
Gillespie, Dizzy 6
Goodman, Benny 4
Gordon, Dexter 10
Grappelli, Stephane 10
Green, Benny 17
Green, Grant 14
Guaraldi, Vince 3
Hackett, Bobby 21
Haden, Charlie 12
Hampton, Lionel 6
Hancock, Herbie 25
Earlier sketch in CM 8
Hardcastle, Paul 20
Hargrove, Roy 15
Harris, Eddie 15
Harris, Teddy 22
Hawkins, Coleman 11
Hawkins, Erskine 19
Hedges, Michael 3
Henderson, Fletcher 16
Henderson, Joe 14
Herman, Woody 12
Hines, Earl "Fatha" 12
Hirt, Al 5
Holiday, Billie 6
Holland, Dave 27
Horn, Shirley 7
Horne, Lena 11
Humes, Helen 19
Hunter, Alberta 7
Hunter, Charlie 24
Ibrahim, Abdullah 24
Incognito 16
Isham, Mark 14
Israel "Cachao" Lopez 14
Jackson, Milt 15
Jacquet, Illinois 17
James, Boney 21
James, Harry 11
Jarreau, Al 1
Jarrett, Keith 1
Jensen, Ingrid 22
Jobim, Antonio Carlos 19
Johnson, James P. 16
Johnson, Lonnie 17
Jones, Elvin 9
Jones, Hank 15
Jones, Philly Joe 16
Jones, Quincy 20
Earlier sketch in CM 2
Jones, Thad 19
Jordan, Stanley 1
Kennedy, Nigel 8
Kenny G 14
Kenton, Stan 21
Kirk, Rahsaan Roland 6
Kitt, Eartha 9
Klugh, Earl 10
Krall, Diana 27
Kronos Quartet 5
Krupa, Gene 13
Laine, Cleo 10
Lateef, Yusef 16
Lee, Peggy 8
Lewis, Ramsey 14
Lincoln, Abbey 9
Lloyd, Charles 22
Lovano, Joe 13
Mahavishnu Orchestra 19
Mahogany, Kevin 26
Malone, Russell 27
Mancini, Henry 20
Earlier sketch in CM 1
Mangione, Chuck 23
Manhattan Transfer, The 8
Mann, Herbie 16
Marsalis, Branford 10
Marsalis, Ellis 13
Marsalis, Wynton 20
Earlier sketch in CM 6
Martino, Pat 17
Masekela, Hugh 7
McBride, Christian 17
McCorkle, Susannah 27
McFerrin, Bobby 3
McKinney's Cotton Pickers 16
McLaughlin, John 12
McPartland, Marian 15
McRae, Carmen 9
Metheny, Pat 26
Earlier sketch in CM 2
Mingus, Charles 9
Monk, Thelonious 6
Montgomery, Wes 3
Morgan, Frank 9
Morton, Jelly Roll 7
Mulligan, Gerry 16
Najee 21
Nascimento, Milton 6
Navarro, Fats 25
Norvo, Red 12
O'Day, Anita 21
Oliver, King 15
Palmer, Jeff 20
Palmieri, Eddie 15
Parker, Charlie 5
Parker, Leon 27
Parker, Maceo 7
Pass, Joe 15
Paul, Les 2
Payton, Nicholas 27
Pepper, Art 18
Perez, Danilo 25
Peterson, Oscar 11
Ponty, Jean-Luc 8
Powell, Bud 15
Previn, André 15
Professor Longhair 6
Puente, Tito 14
Pullen, Don 16
Ralph Sharon Quartet 26
Rampal, Jean-Pierre 6
Redman, Joshua 25
Earlier sketch in CM 12
Reeves, Dianne 16
Reid, Vernon 2
Also see Living Colour
Reinhardt, Django 7
Rich, Buddy 13
Roach, Max 12
Roberts, Marcus 6
Robillard, Duke 2
Rodney, Red 14
Rollins, Sonny 7
Russell, Pee Wee 25
Saluzzi, Dino
Sanborn, David 1
Sanders, Pharoah 16
Sandoval, Arturo 15
Santana, Carlos 19
Earlier sketch in CM 1
Schuur, Diane 6
Scofield, John 7
Scott, Jimmy 14
Scott-Heron, Gil 13
Severinsen, Doc 1
Sharrock, Sonny 15
Shaw, Artie 8
Shaw, Woody 27
Shorter, Wayne 5
Silver, Horace 19
Simone, Nina 11
Solal, Martial 4
Strayhorn, Billy 13
Summers, Andy 3
Also see Police, The
Sun Ra 27
Earlier sketch in CM 5
Take 6 6
Tatum, Art 17
Taylor, Billy 13
Taylor, Cecil 9
Teagarden, Jack 10
Terry, Clark 24
Thielemans, Toots 13
Threadgill, Henry 9
Torme, Mel 4
Tucker, Sophie 12
Turner, Big Joe 13
Turtle Island String Quartet 9
Tyner, McCoy 7
Ulmer, James Blood 13
US3 18
Valdes, Chuco 25
Vaughan, Sarah 2
Walker, T-Bone 5
Washington, Dinah 5
Washington, Grover, Jr. 5
Weather Report 19
Webb, Chick 14
Weston, Randy 15
Whitaker, Rodney 20
Whiteman, Paul 17
Whitfield, Mark 18
Whittaker, Rodney 19
Williams, Joe 11
Wilson, Cassandra 12
Wilson, Cassandra 26
Wilson, Nancy 14
Winter, Paul 10
Witherspoon, Jimmy 19
Young, La Monte 16
Young, Lester 14
Zorn, John 15

Juju
Adé, King Sunny 18

Keyboards, Electric
Aphex Twin 14
Bley, Paul 14
Brown, Tony 14
Chemical Brothers 20
Corea, Chick 6
Davis, Chip 4
Dolby, Thomas 10
Eno, Brian 8
Foster, David 13
Froom, Mitchell 15
Hammer, Jan 21
Hancock, Herbie 25
Hancock, Herbie 8
Hardcastle, Paul 20
Jackson, Joe 22
Earlier sketch in CM 4
Jarre, Jean-Michel 2

Jones, Booker T. **8**
Kitaro **1**
Man or Astroman? **21**
Orbital **20**
Palmer, Jeff **20**
Sakamoto, Ryuichi **19**
Shaffer, Paul **13**
Sun Ra **27**
Earlier sketch in CM **5**
Wakeman, Rick **27**
Also see Yes
Waller, Fats **7**
Winwood, Steve **2**
Also see Spencer Davis Group
Also see Traffic
Wonder, Stevie **17**
Earlier sketch in CM **2**
Worrell, Bernie **11**
Yanni **11**

Liturgical Music
Cooney, Rory **6**
Talbot, John Michael **6**

Mandolin
Bromberg, David **18**
Grisman, David **17**
Hartford, John **1**
Lindley, David **2**
Monroe, Bill **1**
Skaggs, Ricky **5**
Stuart, Marty **9**

Musicals
Allen, Debbie **8**
Allen, Peter **11**
Andrews, Julie **4**
Andrews Sisters, The **9**
Bacharach, Burt **20**
Earlier sketch in CM **1**
Bailey, Pearl **5**
Baker, Josephine **10**
Berlin, Irving **8**
Brightman, Sarah **20**
Brown, Ruth **13**
Buckley, Betty **16**
Earlier sketch in CM **1**
Burnett, Carol **6**
Carter, Nell **7**
Channing, Carol **6**
Chevalier, Maurice **6**
Crawford, Michael **4**
Crosby, Bing **6**
Curry, Tim **3**
Davis, Sammy, Jr. **4**
Day, Doris **24**
Garland, Judy **6**
Gershwin, George and Ira **11**
Hamlisch, Marvin **1**
Horne, Lena **11**
Johnson, James P. **16**
Jolson, Al **10**
Kern, Jerome **13**
Laine, Cleo **10**
Lerner and Loewe **13**
Lloyd Webber, Andrew **6**
LuPone, Patti **8**
Masekela, Hugh **7**
Menken, Alan **10**
Mercer, Johnny **13**
Moore, Melba **7**
Patinkin, Mandy **20**
Earlier sketch in CM **3**
Peters, Bernadette **27**
Earlier sketch in CM **7**
Porter, Cole **10**
Robeson, Paul **8**
Rodgers, Richard **9**
Sager, Carole Bayer **5**
Shaffer, Paul **13**
Sondheim, Stephen **8**
Styne, Jule **21**
Waters, Ethel **11**
Weill, Kurt **12**
Yeston, Maury **22**

Oboe
Lateef, Yusef **16**

Opera
Adams, John **8**
Ameling, Elly **24**
Anderson, June **27**
Anderson, Marian **8**
Austral, Florence **26**
Baker, Janet **14**
Bartoli, Cecilia **12**
Battle, Kathleen **6**
Blegen, Judith **23**
Bocelli, Andrea **22**
Bumbry, Grace **13**
Caballe, Monserrat **23**
Callas, Maria **11**
Carreras, José **8**
Caruso, Enrico **10**
Copeland, Stewart **14**
Also see Police, The
Cotrubas, Ileana **1**
Davis, Anthony **17**
Domingo, Placido **20**
Earlier sketch in CM **1**
Fleming, Renee **24**
Freni, Mirella **14**
Gershwin, George and Ira **11**
Graves, Denyce **16**
Hampson, Thomas **12**
Hendricks, Barbara **10**
Hoppner, Ben **23**
Herrmann, Bernard **14**
Horne, Marilyn **9**
McNair, Sylvia **15**
Norman, Jessye **7**
Pavarotti, Luciano **20**
Earlier sketch in CM **1**
Price, Leontyne **6**
Quasthoff, Thomas **26**
Sills, Beverly **5**
Solti, Georg **13**
Sutherland, Joan **13**
Te Kanawa, Kiri **2**
Toscanini, Arturo **14**
Upshaw, Dawn **9**
von Karajan, Herbert **1**
Weill, Kurt **12**
Zimmerman, Udo **5**

Percussion
Aronoff, Kenny **21**
Baker, Ginger **16**
Also see Cream
Blackman, Cindy **15**
Blakey, Art **11**
Burton, Gary **10**
Collins, Phil **20**
Earlier sketch in CM **2**
Also see Genesis
Copeland, Stewart **14**
Also see Police, The
DeJohnette, Jack **7**
Hampton, Lionel **6**
Henley, Don **3**
Jones, Elvin **9**
Jones, Philly Joe **16**
Jones, Spike **5**
Krupa, Gene **13**
Mo', Keb' **21**
N'Dour, Youssou **6**
Otis, Johnny **16**
Palmieri, Eddie **15**
Parker, Leon **27**
Puente, Tito **14**
Rich, Buddy **13**
Roach, Max **12**
Sheila E. **3**
Starr, Ringo **10**
Also see Beatles, The
Walden, Narada Michael **14**
Webb, Chick **14**

Piano
Allen, Geri **10**
Allison, Mose **17**
Amos, Tori **12**
Argerich, Martha **27**
Arrau, Claudio **1**
Bacharach, Burt **20**
Earlier sketch in CM **1**
Ball, Marcia **15**
Basie, Count **2**
Berlin, Irving **8**
Blake, Eubie **19**
Bley, Carla **8**
Bley, Paul **14**
Borge, Victor **19**
Brendel, Alfred **23**
Brickman, Jim **22**
Britten, Benjamin **15**
Bronfman, Yefim **6**
Brubeck, Dave **8**
Bush, Kate **4**
Carpenter, Richard **24**
Also see Carpenters
Charles, Ray **24**
Earlier sketch in CM **1**
Clayderman, Richard **1**
Cleveland, James **1**
Cliburn, Van **13**
Cole, Nat King **3**
Collins, Judy **4**
Collins, Phil **20**
Earlier sketch in CM **2**
Also see Genesis
Connick, Harry, Jr. **4**
Crouch, Andraé **9**
Davies, Dennis Russell **24**
DeJohnette, Jack **7**
Domino, Fats **2**
Dr. John **7**
Dupree, Champion Jack **12**
Ellington, Duke **2**
Esquivel, Juan **17**
Evans, Bill **17**
Evans, Gil **17**
Feinstein, Michael **6**
Ferrell, Rachelle **17**
Flack, Roberta **5**
Flanagan, Tommy **16**
Frey, Glenn **3**
Galás, Diamanda **16**
Garner, Erroll **25**
Glass, Philip **1**
Gould, Glenn **9**
Green, Benny **17**

Grusin, Dave 7
Guaraldi, Vince 3
Hamlisch, Marvin 1
Hancock, Herbie 25
Earlier sketch in CM 8
Harris, Teddy 22
Helfgott, David 19
Henderson, Fletcher 16
Hinderas, Natalie 12
Hines, Earl "Fatha" 12
Horn, Shirley 7
Hornsby, Bruce 25
Earlier sketch in CM 3
Horowitz, Vladimir 1
Ibrahim, Abdullah 24
Jackson, Joe 22
Earlier sketch in CM 4
James, Skip 24
Jarrett, Keith 1
Joel, Billy 12
Earlier sketch in CM 2
John, Elton 20
Earlier sketch in CM 3
Johnson, James P. 16
Jones, Hank 15
Jones, Howard 26
Joplin, Scott 10
Kenton, Stan 21
Kissin, Evgeny 6
Krall, Diana 27
Levine, James 8
Lewis, Jerry Lee 2
Lewis, Ramsey 14
Liberace 9
Little Richard 1
Manilow, Barry 2
Marsalis, Ellis 13
Matthews, Eric 22
McPartland, Marian 15
McRae, Carmen 9
Milsap, Ronnie 2
Mingus, Charles 9
Monk, Thelonious 6
Montgomery, Little Brother 26
Morton, Jelly Roll 7
Nero, Peter 19
Newman, Randy 27
Earlier sketch in CM 4
Palmieri, Eddie 15
Perahia, Murray 10
Perez, Danilo 25
Peterson, Oscar 11
Pires, Maria João 26
Post, Mike 21
Powell, Bud 15
Pratt, Awadagin 19
Previn, André 15
Professor Longhair 6
Puente, Tito 14
Pullen, Don 16
Rangell, Andrew 24
Rich, Charlie 3
Roberts, Marcus 6
Rubinstein, Arthur 11
Russell, Mark 6
Schickele, Peter 5
Sedaka, Neil 4
Shaffer, Paul 13
Solal, Martial 4
Solti, Georg 13
Spann, Otis 18
Story, Liz 2
Strayhorn, Billy 13
Sunnyland Slim 16
Sykes, Roosevelt 20
Tatum, Art 17
Taylor, Billy 13
Taylor, Cecil 9
Thibaudet, Jean-Yves 24
Tilson Thomas, Michael 24
Tyner, McCoy 7
Valdes, Chuco 25
Vangelis 21
Waits, Tom 27
Earlier sketch in CM 12
Earlier sketch in 1
Waller, Fats 7
Weston, Randy 15
Wilson, Brian 24
Also see Beach Boys, The
Wilson, Cassandra 12
Winston, George 9
Winwood, Steve 2
Also see Spencer Davis Group
Also see Traffic
Wonder, Stevie 17
Earlier sketch in CM 2
Young, La Monte 16

Piccolo
Galway, James 3

Pop
10,000 Maniacs 3
A-ha 22
Abba 12
Abdul, Paula 3
Adam Ant 13
Adams, Bryan 20
Earlier sketch in CM 2
Adams, Oleta 17
Air Supply 22
All Saints 25
All-4-One 17
Alpert, Herb 11
America 16
Amos, Tori 12
Anderson, Laurie 25
Earlier sketch in CM 1
Andrews Sisters, The 9
Arden, Jann 21
Arena, Tina 21
Armatrading, Joan 4
Arnold, Eddy 10
Artifacts 23
Astley, Rick 5
Atari Teenage Riot 27
Atkins, Chet 5
Atomic Fireballs, The 27
Avalon, Frankie 5
B-52's, The 4
Bacharach, Burt 20
Earlier sketch in CM 1
Backstreet Boys 21
Badu, Erykah 26
Bailey, Pearl 5
Baker, Arthur 23
Bananarama 22
Bangles 22
Basia 5
Bauhaus 27
Beach Boys, The 1
Beatles, The 2
Beaver Brown Band, The 3
Bee Gees, The 3
Belly 16
Bennett, Tony 16
Earlier sketch in CM 2
Benson, George 9
Benton, Brook 7
Beta Band, The 27
Better Than Ezra 19
Blige, Mary J. 15
Blink 182 27
Blondie 27
Earlier sketch in CM 14
Blood, Sweat and Tears 7
Blue Rodeo 18
BoDeans, The 20
Earlier sketch in CM 3
Bolton, Michael 4
Boo Radleys, The 21
Booker T. & the M.G.'s 24
Boone, Pat 13
Boston 11
Bowie, David 23
Earlier sketch in CM 1
Boyz II Men 15
Bragg, Billy 7
Branigan, Laura 2
Braxton, Toni 17
Brickell, Edie 3
Brooks, Garth 25
Earlier sketch in CM 8
Brown, Bobby 4
Brown, Foxy 25
Browne, Jackson 3
Bryson, Peabo 11
Buckingham, Lindsey 8
Also see Fleetwood Mac
Buckley, Tim 14
Buffett, Jimmy 4
Burdon, Eric 14
Also see War
Also see Animals
Burroughs, William S. 26
Cabaret Voltaire 18
Campbell, Glen 2
Campbell, Tevin 13
Captain Beefheart and the Magic Band 26
Cardigans 19
Carey, Mariah 20
Earlier sketch in CM 6
Carlisle, Belinda 8
Carmichael, Hoagy 27
Carnes, Kim 4
Carpenter, Richard 24
Also see Carpenters
Carpenters 13
Case, Peter 13
Chandra, Sheila 16
Chapin, Harry 6
Chapin-Carpenter, Mary 25
Earlier sketch in CM 6
Chapman, Tracy 20
Earlier sketch in CM 4
Charlatans, The 13
Charles, Ray 24
Earlier sketch in CM 1
Checker, Chubby 7
Cher 1
Also see Sonny and Cher
Cherry, Neneh 4
Cherry Poppin' Daddies 24
Chicago 3
Chilton, Alex 10
Clapton, Eric 11
Earlier sketch in CM 1
Also see Cream
Also see Yardbirds, The
Clayderman, Richard 1
Clooney, Rosemary 9

Coasters, The **5**
Cocker, Joe **4**
Cocteau Twins, The **12**
Cole, Lloyd **9**
Cole, Nat King **3**
Cole, Natalie **21**
Earlier sketch in CM **1**
Cole, Paula **20**
Collins, Judy **4**
Collins, Phil **20**
Earlier sketch in CM **2**
Also see Genesis
Color Me Badd **23**
Colvin, Shawn **11**
Commodores, The **23**
Como, Perry **14**
Connick, Harry, Jr. **4**
Cooke, Sam **1**
Also see Soul Stirrers, The
Cope, Julian **16**
Cornershop **24**
Costello, Elvis **12**
Earlier sketch in CM **2**
Cranberries, The **14**
Crash Test Dummies **14**
Crenshaw, Marshall **5**
Croce, Jim **3**
Crosby, David **3**
Also see Byrds, The
Crow, Sheryl **18**
Crowded House **12**
Cure, The **20**
Earlier sketch in CM **3**
D'Arby, Terence Trent **3**
Daltrey, Roger **3**
Also see Who, The
Darin, Bobby **4**
Dave Clark Five, The **12**
Davies, Ray **5**
Davis, Sammy, Jr. **4**
Davis, Skeeter **15**
Day, Doris **24**
Dayne, Taylor **4**
DeBarge, El **14**
Del Amitri **18**
Del Rubio Triplets **21**
Denver, John **1**
Depeche Mode **5**
Des'ree **24**
Earlier sketch in CM **15**
Devo **13**
Diamond, Neil **1**
Dietrich, Marlene **25**
Dion **4**
Dion, Celine **25**
Earlier sketch in CM **12**
Doc Pomus **14**
Donovan **9**
Doobie Brothers, The **3**
Doors, The **4**
Droge, Pete **24**
Dubstar **22**
Duran Duran **4**
Dylan, Bob **21**
Earlier sketch in CM **3**
Eagles, The **3**
Earth, Wind and Fire **12**
Easton, Sheena **2**
Edmonds, Kenneth "Babyface" **12**
Electric Light Orchestra **7**
Elfman, Danny **9**
Elliot, Cass **5**
Also see Mamas and the Papas
En Vogue **10**
Enigma **14**
Estefan, Gloria **15**
Earlier sketch in CM **2**
Eurythmics **6**
Everly Brothers, The **2**
Everything But The Girl **15**
Exposé **4**
Fabian **5**
Fatboy Slim **22**
Feliciano, José **10**
Ferguson, Maynard **7**
Ferry, Bryan **1**
Fiedler, Arthur **6**
Fine Young Cannibals **22**
Fisher, Eddie **12**
Fitzgerald, Ella **1**
Flack, Roberta **5**
Fleetwood Mac **5**
Fogelberg, Dan **4**
Fordham, Julia **15**
Foster, David **13**
Four Tops, The **11**
Fox, Samantha **3**
Frampton, Peter **3**
Francis, Connie **10**
Franklin, Aretha **17**
Earlier sketch in CM **2**
Frey, Glenn **3**
Also see Eagles, The
Garbage **25**
Garfunkel, Art **4**
Also see Simon and Garfunkel
Gaye, Marvin **4**
Gayle, Crystal **1**
Geldof, Bob **9**
Genesis **4**
Gershwin, George and Ira **11**
Gibson, Deborah **24**
Earlier sketch in CM **1**
See Gibson, Debbie
Gift, Roland **3**
Gil, Gilberto **26**
Gin Blossoms **18**
Ginsberg, Allen **26**
Go-Go's, The **24**
Gong **24**
Goodman, Benny **4**
Gordy, Berry, Jr. **6**
Grant, Amy **7**
Grebenshikov, Boris **3**
Green, Al **9**
Guthrie, Arlo **6**
Hall & Oates **6**
Hammer, M.C. **5**
Hancock, Herbie **8**
Hanson **20**
Harding, John Wesley **6**
Harrison, George **2**
Also see Beatles, The
Harry, Deborah **4**
Also see Blondie
Hawkins, Sophie B. **21**
Healey, Jeff **4**
Henley, Don **3**
Also see Eagles, The
Herman's Hermits **5**
Hill, Lauryn **25**
Hitchcock, Robyn **9**
Holland-Dozier-Holland **5**
Hootie and the Blowfish **18**
Horne, Lena **11**
Hornsby, Bruce **25**
Earlier sketch in CM **3**
Houston, Cissy **26**
Earlier sketch in CM **6**
Houston, Whitney **25**
Earlier sketch in CM **8**
Human League, The **17**
Humperdinck, Engelbert **19**
Ian, Janis **24**
Earlier sketch in CM **5**
Idol, Billy **3**
Iglesias, Julio **20**
Earlier sketch in CM **2**
Imbruglia, Natalie **27**
Incubus **23**
Indigo Girls **20**
Earlier sketch in CM **3**
Ingram, James **11**
Ink Spots, The **23**
Isaak, Chris **6**
Isley Brothers, The **8**
Jackson, Janet **16**
Earlier sketch in CM **3**
Jackson, Joe **22**
Earlier sketch in CM **4**
Jackson, Michael **17**
Earlier sketch in CM **1**
Also see Jacksons, The
Jacksons, The **7**
Jam, Jimmy, and Terry Lewis **11**
James **12**
James, Harry **11**
James, Rick **2**
Jarreau, Al **1**
Jayhawks, The **15**
Jefferson Airplane **5**
Jesus Jones **23**
Jewel **25**
Jodeci **13**
Joel, Billy **12**
Earlier sketch in CM **2**
Johansen, David **7**
John, Elton **20**
Earlier sketch in CM **3**
Johnston, Freedy **20**
Jolson, Al **10**
Jones, Howard **26**
Jones, Quincy **20**
Earlier sketch in CM **2**
Jones, Rickie Lee **4**
Jones, Tom **11**
Joplin, Janis **3**
Joy Electric **26**
Kaye, Carol **22**
Keaggy, Phil **26**
Khan, Chaka **19**
Earlier sketch in CM **9**
King, Ben E. **7**
King, Carole **6**
Kiss **25**
Earlier sketch in CM **5**
Kitt, Eartha **9**
Knight, Gladys **1**
Knopfler, Mark **25**
Earlier sketch in CM **3**
Also see Dire Straits
Kool & the Gang **13**
Kraftwerk **9**
Kristofferson, Kris **4**
LaBelle, Patti **8**
Lang, kd **25**
Earlier sketch in CM **4**
Lauper, Cyndi **11**
Lee, Brenda **5**
Leiber and Stoller **14**
Lemper, Ute **14**
Lennon, John **9**
Also see Beatles, The

Lennon, Julian **26**
Earlier sketch in CM **2**
Lennox, Annie **18**
Also see Eurythmics
Lewis, Huey **9**
Liberace **9**
Lightfoot, Gordon **3**
Lightning Seeds **21**
Lisa Lisa **23**
Loeb, Lisa **19**
Logan, Jack **27**
Loggins, Kenny **20**
Earlier sketch in CM **3**
Lovett, Lyle **5**
Lowe, Nick **25**
Earlier sketch in CM **6**
Lush **13**
Lynne, Jeff **5**
MacColl, Kirsty **12**
Madness **27**
Madonna **16**
Earlier sketch in CM **4**
Mamas and the Papas **21**
Mancini, Henry **20**
Earlier sketch in CM **1**
Manhattan Transfer, The **8**
Manilow, Barry **2**
Marley, Bob **3**
Marley, Ziggy **3**
Marsalis, Branford **10**
Marshall, Amanda **27**
Martin, Dean **1**
Martin, George **6**
Martin, Mary **27**
Martin, Ricky **26**
Marx, Richard **21**
Earlier sketch in CM **3**
Mathis, Johnny **2**
Mazzy Star **17**
McCartney, Paul **4**
Also see Beatles, The
McFerrin, Bobby **3**
McGuire Sisters, The **27**
McLachlan, Sarah **12**
McLean, Don **7**
McLennan, Grant **21**
Medley, Bill **3**
Melanie **12**
Merchant, Natalie **25**
Merman, Ethel **27**
Michael, George **9**
Midler, Bette **8**
Mighty Mighty Bosstones **20**
Mike & the Mechanics **17**
Miller, Mitch **11**
Miller, Roger **4**
Milli Vanilli **4**
Mills Brothers, The **14**
Minnelli, Liza **19**
Mitchell, Joni **17**
Earlier sketch in CM **2**
Mojave 3 **26**
Money, Eddie **16**
Monica **26**
Monkees, The **7**
Montand, Yves **12**
Moore, Chante **21**
Morcheeba **25**
Morissette, Alanis **19**
Morrison, Jim **3**
Morrison, Van **24**
Earlier sketch in CM **3**
Morrissey **10**
Mouskouri, Nana **12**
Moyet, Alison **12**
Murray, Anne **4**
Myles, Alannah **4**
'N Sync **25**
Neville, Aaron **5**
Also see Neville Brothers, The
Neville Brothers, The **4**
New Kids on the Block **3**
Newman, Randy **27**
Earlier sketch in CM **4**
Newton, Wayne **2**
Newton-John, Olivia **8**
Nicks, Stevie **25**
Also see Fleetwood Mac
Earlier sketch in CM **2**
Nilsson **10**
Nitty Gritty Dirt Band **6**
No Doubt **20**
Nyro, Laura **12**
O'Connor, Sinead **3**
Oak Ridge Boys, The **7**
Ocasek, Ric **5**
Ocean, Billy **4**
Odds **20**
Oldfield, Mike **18**
Orchestral Manoeuvres in the Dark **21**
Orlando, Tony **15**
Orton, Beth **26**
Osborne, Joan **19**
Osmond, Donny **3**
Page, Jimmy **4**
Also see Led Zeppelin
Also see Yardbirds, The
Page, Patti **11**
Parks, Van Dyke **17**
Parsons, Alan **12**
Parton, Dolly **2**
Pendergrass, Teddy **3**
Peniston, CeCe **15**
Penn, Michael **4**
Pet Shop Boys **5**
Peter, Paul & Mary **4**
Phillips, Sam **12**
Piaf, Edith **8**
Pizzicato Five **18**
Plant, Robert **2**
Also see Led Zeppelin
Pointer Sisters, The **9**
Porter, Cole **10**
Prefab Sprout **15**
Presley, Elvis **1**
Priest, Maxi **20**
Prince **14**
Earlier sketch in CM **1**
Proclaimers, The **13**
Prodigy **22**
Propellerheads **26**
Pulp **18**
Queen **6**
R.E.M. **25**
Earlier sketch in CM **5**
Rabbitt, Eddie **24**
Earlier sketch in CM **5**
Raitt, Bonnie **23**
Earlier sketch in CM **3**
Rea, Chris **12**
Redding, Otis **5**
Reddy, Helen **9**
Reeves, Martha **4**
Also see Martha and the Vandellas
Republica **20**
Richard, Cliff **14**
Richie, Lionel **2**
Riley, Teddy **14**
Robbins, Marty **9**
Robinson, Smokey **1**
Rogers, Kenny **1**
Rolling Stones **23**
Earlier sketch in CM **3**
Ronstadt, Linda **2**
Roots, The **27**
Ross, Diana **1**
Also see Supremes, The
Roth, David Lee **1**
Also see Van Halen
Roxette **23**
Ruffin, David **6**
RuPaul **20**
Sade **2**
Sager, Carole Bayer **5**
Sainte-Marie, Buffy **11**
Sanborn, David **1**
Seal **14**
Seals & Crofts **3**
Seals, Dan **9**
Secada, Jon **13**
Sedaka, Neil **4**
Selena **16**
Shaffer, Paul **13**
Shamen, The **23**
Sheep on Drugs **27**
Sheila E. **3**
Shirelles, The **11**
Shonen Knife **13**
Siberry, Jane **6**
Simon, Carly **22**
Earlier sketch in CM **4**
Simon, Paul **16**
Earlier sketch in CM **1**
Also see Simon and Garfunkel
Sinatra, Frank **23**
Earlier sketch in CM **1**
Sixpence None the Richer **26**
Smiths, The **3**
Snow, Pheobe **4**
Sobule, Jill **20**
Sonny and Cher **24**
Soul Coughing **21**
Sparks **18**
Spector, Phil **4**
Spice Girls **22**
Springfield, Dusty **20**
Springfield, Rick **9**
Springsteen, Bruce **25**
Earlier sketch in CM **6**
Squeeze **5**
Stafford, Jo **24**
Stansfield, Lisa **9**
Starr, Kay **27**
Starr, Ringo **24**
Earlier sketch in CM **10**
Steely Dan **5**
Stereolab **18**
Stevens, Cat **3**
Stewart, Rod **20**
Earlier sketch in CM **2**
Also see Faces, The
Stills, Stephen **5**
Sting **19**
Earlier sketch in CM **2**
Also see Police, The
Stockwood, Kim **26**
Story, The **13**
Straw, Syd **18**
Streisand, Barbra **2**
Suede **20**
Summer, Donna **12**
Sundays, The **20**

Supremes, The **6**
Surfaris, The **23**
Sweat, Keith **13**
Sweet, Matthew **9**
SWV **14**
Sylvian, David **27**
Talk Talk **19**
Talking Heads **1**
Taylor, James **25**
  Earlier sketch in CM **2**
Taylor, Steve **26**
Tears for Fears **6**
Teenage Fanclub **13**
Temptations, The **3**
Texas **27**
The The **15**
They Might Be Giants **7**
Thomas, Irma **16**
Three Dog Night **5**
Tiffany **4**
Tikaram, Tanita **9**
Timbuk 3 **3**
TLC **15**
Toad the Wet Sprocket **13**
Tony! Toni! Toné! **12**
Torme, Mel **4**
Townshend, Pete **1**
  Also see Who, The
Turner, Tina **1**
  Also see Ike & Tina Turner
Valli, Frankie **10**
Vandross, Luther **2**
Vanessa-Mae **26**
Vega, Suzanne **3**
Velocity Girl **23**
Vinton, Bobby **12**
Walsh, Joe **5**
Warnes, Jennifer **3**
Warwick, Dionne **2**
Was (Not Was) **6**
Washington, Dinah **5**
Waters, Crystal **15**
Watley, Jody **26**
  Earlier sketch in CM **9**
Webb, Jimmy **12**
Weird Al" Yankovic **7**
Weller, Paul **14**
Who, The **3**
Williams, Andy **2**
Williams, Dar **21**
Williams, Deniece **1**
Williams, Joe **11**
Williams, Lucinda **24**
  Earlier sketch in CM **10**
Williams, Paul **26**
  Earlier sketch in CM **5**
Williams, Robbie **25**
Williams, Vanessa **10**
Williams, Victoria **17**
Wilson, Brian **24**
  Also see Beach Boys, The
Wilson, Jackie **3**
Wilson Phillips **5**
Winwood, Steve **2**
  Also see Spencer Davis Group
  Also see Traffic
Womack, Bobby **5**
Wonder, Stevie **17**
  Earlier sketch in CM **2**
Young M.C. **4**
Young, Neil **15**
  Earlier sketch in CM **2**

Producers
Ackerman, Will **3**
Afanasieff, Walter **26**
Albini, Steve **15**
Alpert, Herb **11**
Austin, Dallas **16**
Baker, Anita **9**
Bass, Ralph **24**
Benitez, Jellybean **15**
Brown, Junior **15**
Brown, Tony **14**
Browne, Jackson **3**
Burnett, T Bone **13**
Cale, John **9**
Clark, Dick **25**
  Earlier sketch in CM **2**
Clarke, Stanley **3**
Clinton, George **7**
Collins, Phil **2**
  Also see Genesis
Combs, Sean "Puffy" **25**
  Earlier sketch in CM **16**
Costello, Elvis **2**
Cropper, Steve **12**
Crowell, Rodney **8**
Dixon, Willie **10**
Dolby, Thomas **10**
Dr. Dre **15**
  Also see N.W.A.
Dupri, Jermaine **25**
  Earlier sketch in CM **2**
Edmonds, Kenneth "Babyface" **12**
Enigma **14**
Eno, Brian **8**
Ertegun, Ahmet **10**
Ertegun, Nesuhi **24**
Foster, David **13**
Fripp, Robert **9**
Froom, Mitchell **15**
Gabler, Milton **25**
Gordy, Jr., Emory **17**
Gray, F. Gary **19**
Grusin, Dave **7**
Hardcastle, Paul **20**
Jackson, Millie **14**
Jam, Jimmy, and Terry Lewis **11**
Jones, Booker T. **8**
Jones, Quincy **20**
  Earlier sketch in CM **2**
Jordan, Montell **26**
Krasnow, Bob **15**
Lanois, Daniel **8**
Laswell, Bill **14**
Leiber and Stoller **14**
Lillywhite, Steve **13**
Lynne, Jeff **5**
Marley, Rita **10**
Martin, George **6**
Master P **22**
Mayfield, Curtis **8**
McKnight, Brian **22**
McLaren, Malcolm **23**
Miller, Mitch **11**
Osby, Greg **21**
Parks, Van Dyke **17**
Parsons, Alan **12**
Post, Mike **21**
Prince **14**
  Earlier sketch in CM **1**
Queen Latifah **24**
  Earlier sketch in CM **6**
Riley, Teddy **14**
Robertson, Robbie **2**
Rodgers, Nile **8**
Rubin, Rick **9**
Rundgren, Todd **11**
Shocklee, Hank **15**
Simmons, Russell **7**
Skaggs, Ricky **5**
Spector, Phil **4**
Sure!, Al B. **13**
Sweat, Keith **13**
Too $hort **16**
Toussaint, Allen **11**
Tricky **18**
Vandross, Luther **2**
Vasquez, Junior **16**
Vig, Butch **17**
Wachtel, Waddy **26**
Walden, Narada Michael **14**
Was, Don **21**
Watt, Mike **22**
Wexler, Jerry **15**
Whelan, Bill **20**
Willner, Hal **10**
Wilson, Brian **24**
  Also see Beach Boys, The
Winbush, Angela **15**
Woods-Wright, Tomica **22**

Promoters
Clark, Dick **25**
  Earlier sketch in CM **2**
Geldof, Bob **9**
Graham, Bill **10**
Hay, George D. **3**
Simmons, Russell **7**

Ragtime
Johnson, James P. **16**
Joplin, Scott **10**

Rap
2Pac **17**
Anthony, Marc **19**
Arrested Development **14**
Austin, Dallas **16**
Bambaataa, Afrika **13**
Basehead **11**
Beastie Boys **25**
  Earlier sketch in CM **8**
Biz Markie **10**
Black Sheep **15**
Bone Thugs-N-Harmony **18**
Busta Rhymes **18**
Campbell, Luther **10**
Cherry, Neneh **4**
Combs, Sean "Puffy **25**
  Earlier sketch in CM **16**
Common **23**
Coolio **19**
Cypress Hill **11**
Das EFX **14**
De La Soul **7**
Digable Planets **15**
Digital Underground **9**
DJ Jazzy Jeff and the Fresh Prince **5**
DMX **25**
Dr. Dre **15**
  Also see N.W.A.
Dupri, Jermaine **25**
Eazy-E **13**
  Also see N.W.A.
EPMD **10**
Eric B. and Rakim **9**
Evans, Faith **25**
Franti, Michael **16**
Fugees, The **17**

Gang Starr **13**
Geto Boys, The **11**
Goodie Mob **24**
Grandmaster Flash **14**
Gravediggaz **23**
Hammer, M.C. **5**
Heavy D **10**
House of Pain **14**
Ice Cube **25**
  Earlier sketch in CM **10**
Ice-T **7**
Insane Clown Posse **22**
Jackson, Millie **14**
Kane, Big Daddy **7**
Kid 'n Play **5**
Kid Rock **27**
Knight, Suge **15**
Kool Moe Dee **9**
Kris Kross **11**
KRS-One **8**
L.L. Cool J. **5**
Last Poets **21**
Love, G. **24**
Mase **27**
Master P **22**
MC 900 Ft. Jesus **16**
MC Breed **17**
MC Eiht **27**
MC Lyte **8**
MC Serch **10**
N.W.A. **6**
Nas **19**
Naughty by Nature **11**
Notorious B.I.G. **20**
P.M. Dawn **11**
Pharcyde, The **17**
Public Enemy **4**
Queen Latifah **24**
  Earlier sketch in CM **6**
Rage Against the Machine **18**
Riley, Teddy **14**
Rubin, Rick **9**
Run-D.M.C. **25**
  Earlier sketch in CM **4**
Salt-N-Pepa **6**
Scott-Heron, Gil **13**
Shaggy **19**
Shanté **10**
Shocklee, Hank **15**
Simmons, Russell **7**
Sir Mix-A-Lot **14**
Slick Rick **27**
Smith, Will **26**
Snoop Doggy Dogg **17**
Snow **23**
Spearhead **19**
Special Ed **16**
Sure!, Al B. **13**
TLC **15**
Tone-L c **3**
Too $hort **16**
Tribe Called Quest, A **8**
Tricky **18**
US3 **18**
Usher **23**
Vanilla Ice **6**
Wu-Tang Clan **19**
Yo Yo **9**
Young M.C. **4**

Record Company Executives
Ackerman, Will **3**
Alpert, Herb **11**
Blackwell, Chris **26**
Brown, Tony **14**
Busby, Jheryl **9**
Chess, Leonard **24**
Combs, Sean "Puffy" **25**
  Earlier sketch in CM **16**
Davis, Chip **4**
Davis, Clive **14**
Ertegun, Ahmet **10**
Foster, David **13**
Gabriel, Peter **16**
  Earlier sketch in CM **2**
  Also see Genesis
Geffen, David **8**
Gordy, Berry, Jr. **6**
Hammond, John **6**
Harley, Bill **7**
Harrell, Andre **16**
Jam, Jimmy, and Terry Lewis **11**
Knight, Suge **15**
Koppelman, Charles **14**
Krasnow, Bob **15**
LiPuma, Tommy **18**
Madonna **16**
  Earlier sketch in CM **4**
Marley, Rita **10**
Martin, George **6**
Mayfield, Curtis **8**
Mercer, Johnny **13**
Miller, Mitch **11**
Mingus, Charles **9**
Near, Holly **1**
Ostin, Mo **17**
Penner, Fred **10**
Phillips, Sam **5**
Reznor, Trent **13**
Rhone, Sylvia **13**
Robinson, Smokey **1**
Rubin, Rick **9**
Simmons, Russell **7**
Spector, Phil **4**
Teller, Al **15**
Too $hort **16**
Wexler, Jerry **15**
Woods-Wright, Tomica **22**

Reggae
Bad Brains **16**
Big Mountain **23**
Black Uhuru **12**
Burning Spear **15**
Cliff, Jimmy **8**
Dube, Lucky **17**
Inner Circle **15**
Israel Vibration **21**
Marley, Bob **3**
Marley, Rita **10**
Marley, Ziggy **3**
Mystic Revealers **16**
Skatalites, The **18**
Sly and Robbie **13**
Steel Pulse **14**
Third World **13**
Tosh, Peter **3**
UB40 **4**
Wailer, Bunny **11**

Rhythm and Blues/Soul
Aaliyah **21**
Abdul, Paula **3**
Adams, Oleta **17**
Alexander, Arthur **14**
All-4-One **17**
Austin, Dallas **16**
Badu, Erykah **26**
Baker, Anita **9**
Baker, LaVern **25**
Ball, Marcia **15**
Ballard, Hank **17**
Basehead **11**
Belle, Regina **6**
Benét, Eric **27**
Berry, Chuck **1**
Blackstreet **23**
Bland, Bobby "Blue" **12**
Blessid Union of Souls **20**
Blige, Mary J. **15**
Blues Brothers, The **3**
Bolton, Michael **4**
Booker T. & the M.G.'s **24**
Boyz II Men **15**
Brandy **19**
Braxton, Toni **17**
Brown, James **16**
  Earlier sketch in CM **2**
Brown, Ruth **13**
Brownstone **21**
Bryson, Peabo **11**
Burdon, Eric **14**
  Also see War
  Also see Animals
Busby, Jheryl **9**
C + C Music Factory **16**
Campbell, Tevin **13**
Carey, Mariah **20**
  Earlier sketch in CM **6**
Carr, James **23**
Charles, Ray **24**
  Earlier sketch in CM **1**
Cole, Natalie **21**
  Earlier sketch in CM **1**
Color Me Badd **23**
Commodores, The **23**
Cooke, Sam **1**
  Also see Soul Stirrers, The
Crawford, Randy **25**
Cropper, Steve **12**
Curtis, King **17**
D'Angelo **20**
D'Arby, Terence Trent **3**
DeBarge, El **14**
Des'ree **24**
  Earlier sketch in CM **15**
Dibango, Manu **14**
Diddley, Bo **3**
Domino, Fats **2**
Dr. John **7**
Dru Hill **25**
Earth, Wind and Fire **12**
Edmonds, Kenneth "Babyface" **12**
En Vogue **10**
Evora, Cesaria **19**
Fabulous Thunderbirds, The **1**
Four Tops, The **11**
Fox, Samantha **3**
Franklin, Aretha **17**
  Earlier sketch in CM **2**
Gaye, Marvin **4**
Gill, Johnny **20**
Gordy, Berry, Jr. **6**
Green, Al **9**
Guthrie, Gwen **26**
Hall & Oates **6**
Hayes, Isaac **10**
Hill, Lauryn **25**
Holland-Dozier-Holland **5**
Houston, Whitney **25**
  Earlier sketch in CM **8**
Howland, Don **24**

Hurt, Mississippi John **24**
Ike and Tina Turner **24**
Incognito **16**
Ingram, James **11**
Isley Brothers, The **8**
Jackson, Freddie **3**
Jackson, Janet **3**
Jackson, Michael **17**
  Earlier sketch in CM **1**
  Also see Jacksons, The
Jackson, Millie **14**
Jacksons, The **7**
Jam, Jimmy, and Terry Lewis **11**
James, Etta **6**
Jodeci **13**
John, Willie **25**
Jones, Booker T. **8**
Jones, Grace **9**
Jones, Quincy **20**
  Earlier sketch CM **2**
Jordan, Louis **11**
Jordan, Montell **26**
Kelly, R. **19**
Khan, Chaka **19**
  Earlier sketch CM **9**
King, B. B. **24**
  Earlier sketch in CM **1**
King, Ben E. **7**
Knight, Gladys **1**
Kool & the Gang **13**
LaBelle, Patti **8**
Los Lobos **2**
Love, G. **24**
Martha and the Vandellas **25**
Maxwell **22**
Mayfield, Curtis **8**
McKnight, Brian **22**
McPhatter, Clyde **25**
Medley, Bill **3**
Meters, The **14**
Milli Vanilli **4**
Mills, Stephanie **21**
Mo', Keb' **21**
Monica **26**
Monifah **24**
Moore, Chante **21**
Moore, Melba **7**
Morrison, Van **24**
  Earlier sketch in CM **3**
Ndegéocello, Me'Shell **18**
Neville, Aaron **5**
  Also see Neville Brothers, The
Neville Brothers, The **4**
O'Jays, The **13**
Ocean, Billy **4**
Ohio Players **16**
Otis, Johnny **16**
Pendergrass, Teddy **3**
Peniston, CeCe **15**
Perry, Phil **24**
Pickett, Wilson **10**
Platters, The **25**
Pointer Sisters, The **9**
Price, Lloyd **25**
Priest, Maxi **20**
Prince **14**
  Earlier sketch in CM **1**
Rainey, Ma **22**
Rawls, Lou **19**
Redding, Otis **5**
Reese, Della **13**
Reeves, Martha **4**
Richie, Lionel **2**
Riley, Teddy **14**
Robinson, Smokey **1**
Ross, Diana **1**
  Also see Supremes, The
Ruffin, David **6**
  Also see Temptations, The
Sam and Dave **8**
Scaggs, Boz **12**
Secada, Jon **13**
Shai **23**
Shanice **14**
Shirelles, The **11**
Shocklee, Hank **15**
Silk **26**
Sledge, Percy **15**
Sly & the Family Stone **24**
Soul II Soul **17**
Spinners , The **21**
Stansfield, Lisa **9**
Staples, Mavis **13**
Staples, Pops **11**
Stewart, Rod **20**
  Earlier sketch in CM **2**
  Also see Faces, The
Stone, Sly **8**
Subdudes, The **18**
Supremes, The **6**
  Also see Ross, Diana
Sure!, Al B. **13**
Sweat, Keith **13**
SWV **14**
Temptations, The **3**
Third World **13**
Thomas, Irma **16**
Thornton, Big Mama **18**
TLC **15**
Tony! Toni! Toné! **12**
Toussaint, Allen **11**
Turner, Tina **1**
  Also see Ike & Tina Turner
Vandross, Luther **24**
  Earlier sketch in CM **2**
Was (Not Was) **6**
Waters, Crystal **15**
Watley, Jody **26**
  Earlier sketch in CM **9**
Wexler, Jerry **15**
White, Karyn **21**
Williams, Deniece **1**
Williams, Vanessa **10**
Wilson, Jackie **3**
Winans, The **12**
Winbush, Angela **15**
Womack, Bobby **5**
Wonder, Stevie **17**
  Earlier sketch in CM **2**
Zhane **22**

Rock
10,000 Maniacs **3**
311 **20**
AC/DC **4**
Adam Ant **13**
Adams, Bryan **20**
  Earlier sketch in CM **2**
Aerosmith **22**
  Earlier sketch in CM **3**
Afghan Whigs **17**
Alarm **2**
Albini, Steve **15**
Alexander, Arthur **14**
Alice in Chains **10**
Alien Sex Fiend **23**
Allman Brothers, The **6**
Alvin, Dave **17**
America **16**
American Music Club **15**
Animals **22**
Anthrax **11**
Aquabats **22**
Archers of Loaf **21**
Art of Noise **22**
Audio Adrenaline **22**
Aztec Camera **22**
Babes in Toyland **16**
Bad Brains **16**
Bad Company **22**
Badfinger **23**
Baker, Ginger **16**
  Also see Cream
Ballard, Hank **17**
Band, The **9**
Barenaked Ladies **18**
Barlow, Lou **20**
  Also see Sebadoh
Basehead **11**
Beach Boys, The **1**
Beastie Boys, The **25**
  Earlier sketch in CM **8**
Beat Farmers, The **23**
Beatles, The **2**
Beaver Brown Band, The **3**
Beck **18**
Beck, Jeff **4**
  Also see Yardbirds, The
Belew, Adrian **5**
Belly **16**
Ben Folds Five **20**
Benatar, Pat **8**
Berry, Chuck **1**
Bettie Serveert **17**
Bevis Frond **23**
Biafra, Jello **18**
Big Audio Dynamite **18**
Big Head Todd and the Monsters **20**
Bill Wyman & the Rhythm Kings **26**
Bjork **16**
Black Crowes, The **7**
Black Flag **22**
Black, Frank **14**
Black Sabbath **9**
Blackman, Cindy **15**
Blind Melon **21**
Blink 182 **27**
Blondie **27**
  Earlier sketch in CM **14**
Blood, Sweat and Tears **7**
Blue Oyster Cult **16**
Blue Rodeo **18**
Blues Traveler **15**
Blur **17**
BoDeans, The **20**
  Earlier sketch in CM **3**
Bon Jovi **10**
Boston **11**
Bowie, David **23**
  Earlier sketch in CM **1**
Brad **21**
Bragg, Billy **7**
Breeders **19**
Brickell, Edie **3**
Brötzmann, Caspar **27**
Browne, Jackson **3**
Buckingham, Lindsey **8**
  Also see Fleetwood Mac
Buckley, Tim **14**
Buffalo Springfield **24**
Buffalo Tom **18**
Built to Spill **27**

Burdon, Eric **14**
Also see War
Also see Animals
Burnett, T Bone **13**
Bush **18**
Butthole Surfers **16**
Buzzcocks, The **9**
Byrds, The **8**
Byrne, David **8**
Also see Talking Heads
Cake **27**
Cale, J. J. **16**
Earlier sketch in CM **9**
Camel **21**
Captain Beefheart and the Magic Band **26**
Earlier sketch in CM **10**
Caravan **24**
Cardigans **19**
Cars, The **20**
Catherine Wheel **18**
Cave, Nick **10**
Charlatans, The **13**
Charm Farm **20**
Cheap Trick **12**
Cher **1**
Also see Sonny and Cher
Chicago **3**
Chumbawamba **21**
Church, The **14**
Cinderella **16**
Circle Jerks, The **17**
Citizen King **27**
Clapton, Eric **11**
Earlier sketch in CM **1**
Also see Cream
Also see Yardbirds, The
Clash, The **4**
Clemons, Clarence **7**
Clinton, George **7**
Coasters, The **5**
Cochrane , Tom **22**
Cocker, Joe **4**
Collective Soul **16**
Collins, Phil **2**
Also see Genesis
Compulsion **23**
Congo Norvell **22**
Cooder, Ry **2**
Also see Captain Beefheart and His Magic Band
Cooke, Sam **1**
Also see Soul Stirrers, The
Cooper, Alice **8**
Cope, Julian **16**
Costello, Elvis **12**
Earlier sketch in CM **2**
Cougar, John(ny)
See Mellencamp, John
Counting Crows **18**
Cracker **12**
Cramps, The **16**
Cranberries, The **14**
Crash Test Dummies **14**
Cream **9**
Creedence Clearwater Revival **16**
Crenshaw, Marshall **5**
Crosby, David **3**
Also see Byrds, The
Crosby, Stills, and Nash **24**
Crow, Sheryl **18**
Crowded House **12**
Cult, The **16**
Cure, The **20**
Earlier sketch in CM **3**
Curry, Tim **3**
Curve **13**
D Generation **26**
D'Arby, Terence Trent **3**
Dale, Dick **13**
Daltrey, Roger **3**
Also see Who, The
Damon and Naomi **25**
Dandy Warhols, The
Daniels, Charlie **6**
Danzig **7**
Dave Clark Five, The **12**
Dave Matthews Band **18**
Davies, Ray **5**
dc Talk **18**
de Burgh, Chris **22**
Dead Can Dance **16**
Dead Milkmen **22**
Deep Purple **11**
Def Leppard **3**
Deftones **22**
Del Amitri **18**
Depeche Mode **5**
Devo **13**
Diddley, Bo **3**
DiFranco, Ani **17**
Dinosaur Jr. **10**
Dire Straits **22**
Doc Pomus **14**
Dog's Eye View **21**
Dokken **16**
Doobie Brothers, The **3**
Doors, The **4**
Dreamtheater **23**
Dropkick Murphys **26**
Duran Duran **4**
Dylan, Bob **3**
Eagles, The **3**
Echobelly **21**
Eddy, Duane **9**
Einstürzende Neubauten **13**
Electric Light Orchestra **7**
Elliot, Cass **5**
Emerson, Lake & Palmer/Powell **5**
Emmet Swimming **24**
English Beat, The **9**
Eno, Brian **8**
Erickson, Roky **16**
Escovedo, Alejandro **18**
Etheridge, Melissa **16**
Earlier sketch in CM **4**
Eurythmics **6**
Everclear **18**
Extreme **10**
Faces, The **22**
Fairport Convention **22**
Faith No More **7**
Faithfull, Marianne **14**
Fall, The **12**
Fear Factory **27**
Ferry, Bryan **1**
fIREHOSE **11**
Fishbone **7**
Five Iron Frenzy **26**
Flaming Lips **22**
Fleetwood Mac **5**
Flores, Rosie **16**
Fogelberg, Dan **4**
Fogerty, John **2**
Also see Creedence Clearwater Revival
Foo Fighters **20**
Ford, Lita **9**
Foreigner **21**
Fountains of Wayne **26**
Four Seasons, The **24**
Fox, Samantha **3**
Frampton, Peter **3**
Frankie Lymon and The Teenagers **24**
Franti, Michael **16**
Frey, Glenn **3**
Also see Eagles, The
Front 242 **19**
Froom, Mitchell **15**
Fu Manchu **22**
Fuel **27**
Fugazi **13**
Gabriel, Peter **16**
Earlier sketch in CM **2**
Also see Genesis
Gang of Four **8**
Garcia, Jerry **4**
Also see Grateful Dead, The
Gatton, Danny **16**
Gene Loves Jezebel **27**
Genesis **4**
Geraldine Fibbers **21**
Ghost **24**
Gift, Roland **3**
Gin Blossoms **18**
Glitter, Gary **19**
Goo Goo Dolls, The **16**
Graham, Bill **10**
Grant Lee Buffalo **16**
Grateful Dead **5**
Grebenshikov, Boris **3**
Green Day **16**
Griffin, Patty **24**
Guess Who **23**
Guided By Voices **18**
Guns n' Roses **2**
Gus Gus **26**
Gwar **13**
Hagar, Sammy **21**
Hagen, Nina **25**
Hall & Oates **6**
Harper, Ben **17**
Harrison, George **2**
Also see Beatles, The
Harry, Deborah **4**
Also see Blondie
Harvey, Polly Jean **11**
Hassman, Nikki **26**
Hatfield, Juliana **12**
Also see Lemonheads, The
Healey, Jeff **4**
Heart **1**
Helmet **15**
Hendrix, Jimi **2**
Henley, Don **3**
Also see Eagles, The
Henry, Joe **18**
Hiatt, John **8**
Hodgson, Roger **26**
Also see Supertramp
Hole **14**
Holland-Dozier-Holland **5**
Hooters **20**
Hootie and the Blowfish **18**
Idol, Billy **3**
Imperial Teen **26**
INXS **21**
Earlier sketch in CM **2**
Iron Maiden **10**
Isaak, Chris **6**
Jackson, Joe **22**
Earlier sketch in CM **4**
Jackyl **24**
Jagger, Mick **7**
Also see Rolling Stones, The

Jam, The **27**
Jane's Addiction **6**
Jars of Clay **20**
Jayhawks, The **15**
Jefferson Airplane **5**
Jesus and Mary Chain, The **10**
Jesus Lizard **19**
Jethro Tull **8**
Jett, Joan **3**
Jimmie's Chicken Shack **22**
Joel, Billy **12**
Earlier sketch in CM **2**
Johansen, David **7**
John, Elton **20**
Earlier sketch in CM **3**
Jon Spencer Blues Explosion **18**
Joplin, Janis **3**
Journey **21**
Joy Division **19**
Judas Priest **10**
Kennedy, Nigel **8**
Kid Rock **27**
Kidjo, Anjelique **17**
King Crimson **17**
King Missile **22**
Kinks, The **15**
Kiss **25**
Earlier sketch in CM **5**
KMFDM **18**
Knopfler, Mark **25**
Earlier sketch in CM **3**
Also see Dire Straits
Korn **20**
Kravitz, Lenny **26**
Earlier sketch in CM **5**
L7 **12**
Landreth, Sonny **16**
Led Zeppelin **1**
Lee, Ben **26**
Leiber and Stoller **14**
Lemonheads, The **12**
Lennon, John **9**
Also see Beatles, The
Lennon, Julian **26**
Earlier sketch in CM **2**
Less Than Jake **22**
Letters to Cleo **22**
Limp Bizkit **27**
Lindley, David **2**
Linkous, Mark **26**
Lit **27**
Little Feat **4**
Little Texas **14**
Live **14**
Living Colour **7**
Lofgren, Nils **25**
Logan, Jack **27**
Loggins, Kenny **20**
Earlier sketch in CM **3**
Los Lobos **2**
Love and Rockets **15**
Love Spit Love **21**
Lowe, Nick **25**
Earlier sketch in CM **6**
Luna **18**
Luscious Jackson **27**
Earlier sketch in CM **19**
Lush **13**
Lydon, John **9**
Also see Sex Pistols, The
Lynne, Jeff **5**
Lynyrd Skynyrd **9**
M People **27**
MacIsaac, Ashley **21**
Madder Rose **17**
Manic Street Preachers **27**
Marilyn Manson **18**
Martin, George **6**
Marx, Richard **3**
Matchbox 20 **27**
MC5, The **9**
McCartney, Paul **4**
Also see Beatles, The
McClinton, Delbert **14**
McKee, Maria **11**
McMurtry, James **10**
Meat Loaf **12**
Meat Puppets, The **13**
Megadeth **9**
Mekons, The **15**
Mellencamp, John **20**
Earlier sketch in CM **2**
Metallica **7**
Midnight Oil **11**
Mighty Mighty Bosstones **20**
Mike & the Mechanics **17**
Miller, Steve **2**
Ministry **10**
Moby Grape **12**
Mogwai **27**
Mojave 3 **26**
Money, Eddie **16**
Moody Blues, The **18**
Morphine **16**
Morrison, Jim **3**
Also see Doors, The
Morrison, Van **24**
Earlier sketch in CM **3**
Mötley Crüe **1**
Motörhead **10**
Mould, Bob **10**
Mudhoney **16**
Muldaur, Maria **18**
Murphy, Peter **22**
Myles, Alannah **4**
Nelson, Rick **2**
New York Dolls **20**
Newman, Randy **4**
Newsboys, The **24**
Nicks, Stevie **25**
Earlier sketch in CM **2**
Also see Fleetwood Mac
Nirvana **8**
NRBQ **12**
Nugent, Ted **2**
O'Connor, Sinead **3**
Oasis **16**
Ocasek, Ric **5**
Offspring **19**
Ono, Yoko **11**
Orbison, Roy **2**
Orgy **27**
Osbourne, Ozzy **3**
Our Lady Peace **22**
Page, Jimmy **4**
Also see Led Zeppelin
Also see Yardbirds, The
Palmer, Robert **2**
Pantera **13**
Parker, Graham **10**
Parker, Maceo **7**
Parsons, Alan **12**
Parsons, Gram **7**
Also see Byrds, The
Pavement **14**
Pearl Jam **12**
Pearls Before Swine **24**
Pennywise **27**
Pere Ubu **17**
Perkins, Carl **9**
Petty, Tom **9**
Also see Tom Petty and the Heartbreakers
Phillips, Sam **5**
Phish **25**
Earlier sketch in CM **13**
Pigface **19**
Pink Floyd **2**
Pixies, The **21**
Placebo **27**
Plant, Robert **2**
Also see Led Zeppelin
Pogues, The **6**
Poi Dog Pondering **17**
Poison **11**
Police, The **20**
Pop, Iggy **23**
Earlier sketch in CM **1**
Presley, Elvis **1**
Pretenders, The **8**
Pretty Things, The **26**
Primal Scream **14**
Primus **11**
Prince **14**
Earlier sketch in CM **1**
Prine, John **7**
Proclaimers, The **13**
Prong **23**
Pulp **18**
Quasi **24**
Queen **6**
Queensryche **8**
Quicksilver Messenger Service **23**
R.E.M. **25**
Earlier sketch in CM **5**
Radiohead **24**
Rage Against the Machine **18**
Raitt, Bonnie **23**
Earlier sketch in CM **3**
Rammstein **25**
Ramones, The **9**
Rasputina **26**
Red Hot Chili Peppers, The **7**
Redd Kross **20**
Reed, Lou **16**
Earlier sketch in CM **1**
Also see Velvet Underground, The
Reef **24**
Reid, Vernon **2**
Also see Living Colour
REO Speedwagon **23**
Replacements, The **7**
Residents, The **14**
Reverend Horton Heat **19**
Reznor, Trent **13**
Richards, Keith **11**
Also see Rolling Stones, The
Richman, Jonathan **12**
Robertson, Robbie **2**
Rolling Stones, The **23**
Earlier sketch in CM **3**
Rollins, Henry **11**
Roth, David Lee **1**
Also see Van Halen
Rubin, Rick **9**
Rundgren, Todd **11**
Rush **8**
Rusted Root **26**
Ryder, Mitch **11**
Sambora, Richie **24**
Also see Bon Jovi
Santana, Carlos **19**
Earlier sketch in CM **1**

Satriani, Joe **4**
Scaggs, Boz **12**
Scorpions, The **12**
Screaming Trees **19**
Scud Mountain Boys **21**
Seal **14**
Sebadoh **26**
Seger, Bob **15**
Sepultura **12**
Sex Pistols, The **5**
Shadows, The **22**
Shaffer, Paul **13**
Shannon, Del **10**
Shocked, Michelle **4**
Shonen Knife **13**
Shudder to Think **20**
Silver Apples **23**
Silverchair **20**
Simon and Garfunkel **24**
Simon, Carly **22**
  Earlier sketch in CM **4**
Simon, Paul **16**
  Earlier sketch in CM **1**
  Also see Simon and Garfunkel
Simple Minds **21**
Siouxsie and the Banshees **8**
Skinny Puppy **17**
Skunk Anansie **27**
Slayer **10**
Sleater-Kinney **20**
Smash Mouth **27**
Smashing Pumpkins **13**
Smith, Patti **17**
  Earlier sketch in CM **1**
Smithereens, The **14**
Smiths, The **3**
Social Distortion **27**
  Earlier sketch in CM **19**
Son Volt **21**
Sonic Youth **26**
  Earlier sketch in CM **9**
Soul Asylum **10**
Soundgarden **6**
Sparks **18**
Specials, The **21**
Spector, Phil **4**
Spencer Davis Group **19**
Spin Doctors **14**
Spinal Tap **8**
Spirit **22**
Sponge **18**
Springsteen, Bruce **25**
  Earlier sketch in CM **6**
Squeeze **5**
Starr, Ringo **24**
  Earlier sketch in CM **10**
  Also see Beatles, The
Steeleye Span **19**
Steely Dan **5**
Steppenwolf **20**
Stevens, Cat **3**
Stewart, Rod **20**
  Earlier sketch in CM **2**
  Also see Faces, The
Stills, Stephen **5**
  Also see Buffalo Springfield
  Also see Crosby, Stills and Nash
Sting **19**
  Earlier sketch in CM **2**
  Also see Police, The
Stone Roses, The **16**
Stone, Sly **8**
  Also see Sly & the Family Stone
Stone Temple Pilots **14**
Straw, Syd **18**
Stray Cats, The **11**
Stryper **2**
Sublime **19**
Sugarcubes, The **10**
Suicidal Tendencies **15**
Summers, Andy **3**
  Also see Police, The
Superdrag **23**
Supertramp **25**
Surfin' Pluto **24**
T. Rex **11**
Taylor, Mick
  Also see Beatles, The
Taylor, Steve **26**
Tears for Fears **6**
Teenage Fanclub **13**
Television **17**
Tesla **15**
Texas Tornados, The **8**
The The **15**
They Might Be Giants **7**
Thin Lizzy **13**
Third Eye Blind **25**
Thompson, Richard **7**
Three Dog Night **5**
Throwing Muses **15**
Timbuk 3 **3**
Toad the Wet Sprocket **13**
Tom Petty and the Heartbreakers **26**
Tool **21**
Townshend, Pete **1**
  Also see Who, The
Traffic **19**
Tragically Hip, The **18**
Treadmill Trackstar **21**
Trynin, Jen **21**
Tsunami **21**
Turner, Tina **1**
  Also see Ike & Tina Turner
Tuxedomoon **21**
Type O Negative **27**
U2 **12**
  Earlier sketch in CM **2**
Ulmer, James Blood **13**
Underworld **26**
Unitt, Victor
  Also see Beatles, The
Urge Overkill **17**
Uriah Heep **19**
Vai, Steve **5**
Valens, Ritchie **23**
Valli, Frankie **10**
Van Halen **25**
  Earlier sketch in CM **8**
Vaughan, Jimmie **24**
Vaughan, Stevie Ray **1**
Velvet Underground, The **7**
Ventures **19**
Veruca Salt **20**
Verve Pipe, The **20**
Verve, The **18**
Vincent, Gene **19**
Violent Femmes **12**
Waits, Tom **27**
  Earlier sketch in CM **12**
  Earlier sketch in CM **1**
Wakeman, Rick **27**
  Also see Yes
Wallflowers, The **20**
Walsh, Joe **5**
  Also see Eagles, The
War **14**
Warrant **17**
Waterboys, The **27**
Weezer **20**
Weller, Paul **14**
Wendy O. Williams and The Plasmatics **26**
Westerberg, Paul **26**
White Zombie **17**
Whitesnake **5**
Whitley, Chris **16**
Who, The **3**
Wilson, Brian **24**
  Also see Beach Boys, The
Winter, Johnny **5**
Winwood, Steve **2**
  Also see Spencer Davis Group
  Also see Traffic
Wolf, Peter **25**
Wray, Link **17**
Wyatt, Robert **24**
X **11**
XTC **26**
  Earlier sketch in CM **10**
Yardbirds, The **10**
Yes **8**
Yo La Tengo **24**
Young, Neil **15**
  Earlier sketch in CM **2**
Zappa, Frank **17**
  Earlier sketch in CM **1**
Zevon, Warren **9**
Zombies, The **23**
ZZ Top **2**

Rock and Roll Pioneers

Ballard, Hank **17**
Berry, Chuck **1**
Clark, Dick **25**
  Earlier sketch in CM **2**
Darin, Bobby **4**
Diddley, Bo **3**
Dion **4**
Domino, Fats **2**
Eddy, Duane **9**
Everly Brothers, The **2**
Francis, Connie **10**
Glitter, Gary **19**
Haley, Bill **6**
Hawkins, Screamin' Jay **8**
Holly, Buddy **1**
James, Etta **6**
Jordan, Louis **11**
Lewis, Jerry Lee **2**
Little Richard **1**
Nelson, Rick **2**
Orbison, Roy **2**
Otis, Johnny **16**
Paul, Les **2**
Perkins, Carl **9**
Phillips, Sam **5**
Presley, Elvis **1**
Professor Longhair **6**
Sedaka, Neil **4**
Shannon, Del **10**
Shirelles, The **11**
Spector, Phil **4**
Twitty, Conway **6**
Valli, Frankie **10**
Wilson, Jackie **3**
Wray, Link **17**

Saxophone

Adderly, Cannonball **15**
Anderson, Wessell **23**
Ayler , Albert **19**
Barbieri, Gato **22**

Bechet, Sidney **17**
Braxton, Anthony **12**
Brötzmann, Peter **26**
Carter, Benny **3**
Also see McKinney's Cotton Pickers
Carter, James **18**
Chenier, C. J. **15**
Clemons, Clarence **7**
Coleman, Ornette **5**
Coltrane, John **4**
Curtis, King **17**
Desmond, Paul **23**
Dibango, Manu **14**
Getz, Stan **12**
Golson, Benny **21**
Gordon, Dexter **10**
Harris, Eddie **15**
Hawkins, Coleman **11**
Henderson, Joe **14**
Herman, Woody **12**
Hodges, Johnny **24**
Jacquet, Illinois **17**
James, Boney **21**
Kenny G **14**
Kirk, Rahsaan Roland **6**
Koz, Dave **19**
Lacy, Steve **23**
Lateef, Yusef **16**
Lloyd, Charles **22**
Lopez, Israel "Cachao" **14**
Lovano, Joe **13**
Marsalis, Branford **10**
Morgan, Frank **9**
Mulligan, Gerry **16**
Najee **21**
Osby, Greg **21**
Parker, Charlie **5**
Parker, Maceo **7**
Pepper, Art **18**
Redman, Joshua **25**
Earlier sketch in CM **12**
Rollins, Sonny **7**
Russell, Pee Wee **25**
Sanborn, David **1**
Sanders, Pharoah **16**
Shorter, Wayne **5**
Threadgill, Henry **9**
Washington, Grover, Jr. **5**
Winter, Paul **10**
Young, La Monte **16**
Young, Lester **14**
Zorn, John **15**

Sintir
Hakmoun, Hassan **15**

Songwriters
2Pac **17**
Acuff, Roy **2**
Adams, Bryan **20**
Earlier sketch in CM **2**
Adams, Yolanda **23**
Afanasieff, Walter **26**
Aikens, Rhett **22**
Albini, Steve **15**
Alexander, Arthur **14**
Allen, Peter **11**
Allison, Mose **17**
Alpert, Herb **11**
Alvin, Dave **17**
Amos, Tori **12**
Anderson, John **5**
Anka, Paul **2**
Armatrading, Joan **4**
Atkins, Chet **26**
Earlier sketch in CM **5**
Autry, Gene **25**
Earlier sketch in CM **12**
Bacharach, Burt **20**
Earlier sketch in CM **1**
Badu, Erykah **26**
Baez, Joan **1**
Baker, Anita **9**
Barlow, Lou **20**
Basie, Count **2**
Belew, Adrian **5**
Benét, Eric **27**
Benton, Brook **7**
Berg, Matraca **16**
Berlin, Irving **8**
Berry, Chuck **1**
Bjork **16**
Also see Sugarcubes, The
Black, Clint **5**
Black, Frank **14**
Blades, Ruben **2**
Blige, Mary J. **15**
Bloom, Luka **14**
Brady, Paul **8**
Bragg, Billy **7**
Brandt, Paul **22**
Brickell, Edie **3**
Brokop, Lisa **22**
Brooks, Garth **25**
Earlier sketch in CM **8**
Brown, Bobby **4**
Brown, James **16**
Earlier sketch in CM **2**
Brown, Junior **15**
Brown, Marty **14**
Browne, Jackson **3**
Buckingham, Lindsey **8**
Also see Fleetwood Mac
Buckley, Jeff **22**
Buckley, Tim **14**
Buffett, Jimmy **4**
Burdon, Eric **14**
Also see War
Also see Animals
Burnett, T Bone **13**
Burning Spear **15**
Burroughs, William S. **26**
Bush, Kate **4**
Byrne, David **8**
Also see Talking Heads
Cahn, Sammy **11**
Cale, J. J. **16**
Earlier sketch in CM **9**
Also see Cale, John
Calloway, Cab **6**
Campbell, Sarah Elizabeth **23**
Captain Beefheart and His Magic Band **26**
Earlier sketch in CM **10**
Cardwell, Joi **22**
Carlisle, Bob **22**
Carmichael, Hoagy **27**
Carter, Carlene **8**
Carter, Deana **25**
Cash, Johnny **17**
Earlier sketch in CM **1**
Cash, Rosanne **2**
Chandra, Sheila **16**
Chapin, Harry **6**
Chapin-Carpenter, Mary **25**
Earlier sketch in CM **6**
Chapman, Steven Curtis **15**
Chapman, Tracy **4**
Chaquico, Craig **23**
Also see Jefferson Starship
Charles, Ray **24**
Earlier sketch in CM **1**
Chenier, C. J. **15**
Childs, Toni **2**
Chilton, Alex **10**
Clapton, Eric **11**
Earlier sketch in CM **1**
Also see Cream
Also see Yardbirds, The
Clark, Guy **17**
Clements, Vassar **18**
Cleveland, James **1**
Clinton, George **7**
Cochrane, Tom **23**
Cockburn, Bruce **8**
Cohen, Leonard **3**
Cole, Lloyd **9**
Cole, Nat King **3**
Collie, Mark **15**
Collins, Albert **4**
Collins, Judy **4**
Collins, Phil **2**
Also see Genesis
Cooder, Ry **2**
Cooke, Sam **1**
Also see Soul Stirrers, The
Cooper, Alice **8**
Cope, Julian **16**
Costello, Elvis **12**
Earlier sketch in CM **2**
Cotten, Elizabeth **16**
Crenshaw, Marshall **5**
Croce, Jim **3**
Cropper, Steve **12**
Crosby, David **3**
Also see Byrds, The
Crow, Sheryl **18**
Crowe, J. D. **5**
Crowell, Rodney **8**
Daniels, Charlie **6**
Davies, Ray **5**
Also see Kinks, the
de Burgh, Chris **22**
DeBarge, El **14**
DeMent, Iris **13**
Denver, John **22**
Earlier sketch in CM **1**
Des'ree **24**
Earlier sketch in CM **15**
Diamond, Neil **1**
Diddley, Bo **3**
Diffie, Joe **27**
Earlier sketch in CM **10**
Difford, Chris
See Squeeze
DiFranco, Ani **17**
Dion **4**
Dixon, Willie **10**
DMX **25**
Doc Pomus **14**
Domino, Fats **2**
Donovan **9**
Dorsey, Thomas A. **11**
Doucet, Michael **8**
Drake, Nick **17**
Dube, Lucky **17**
Dulli, Greg **17**
See Afghan Whigs, The
Dylan, Bob **21**
Earlier sketch in CM **3**
Earle, Steve **16**
Earlier sketch in CM **1**
Edmonds, Kenneth "Babyface" **12**
Elfman, Danny **9**
Ellington, Duke **2**

Emmanuel, Tommy **21**
English, Michael **23**
Enigma **14**
Erickson, Roky **16**
Ertegun, Ahmet **10**
Escovedo, Alejandro **18**
Estefan, Gloria **15**
Earlier sketch in CM **2**
Etheridge, Melissa **16**
Earlier sketch in CM **4**
Evans, Sara **27**
Everlast **27**
Faithfull, Marianne **14**
Ferry, Bryan **1**
Flack, Roberta **5**
Flatt, Lester **3**
Fogelberg, Dan **4**
Fogerty, John **2**
Also see Creedence Clearwater Revival
Fordham, Julia **15**
Foster, David **13**
Frampton, Peter **3**
Franti, Michael **16**
Frey, Glenn **3**
Also see Eagles, The
Fripp, Robert **9**
Frizzell, Lefty **10**
Gabriel, Peter **16**
Earlier sketch in CM **2**
Also see Genesis
Garcia, Jerry **4**
Also see Grateful Dead, The
Gaye, Marvin **4**
Geldof, Bob **9**
Gershwin, George and Ira **11**
Gibson, Bob **23**
Gibson, Debbie **24**
Earlier sketch in CM **1**
Also see Gibson, Deborah
Gift, Roland **3**
Gill, Vince **7**
Gilley, Mickey **7**
Goffin-King **24**
Gold, Julie **22**
Goodman, Benny **4**
Gordy, Berry, Jr. **6**
Gorka, John **18**
Grant, Amy **7**
Green, Al **9**
Greenwood, Lee **12**
Griffin, Patty **24**
Griffith, Nanci **3**
Guthrie, Arlo **6**
Guthrie, Gwen **26**
Guthrie, Woodie **2**
Guy, Buddy **4**
Hagen, Nina **25**
Haggard, Merle **2**
Hall, Tom T. **26**
Earlier sketch in CM **4**
Hamlisch, Marvin **1**
Hammer, M.C. **5**
Hancock, Herbie **25**
Earlier sketch in CM **8**
Hardin, Tim **18**
Harding, John Wesley **6**
Harley, Bill **7**
Harper, Ben **17**
Harris, Emmylou **4**
Harrison, George **2**
Also see Beatles, The
Harry, Deborah **4**
Also see Blondie
Hartford, John **1**
Hatfield, Juliana **12**
Also see Lemonheads, The
Hawkins, Screamin' Jay **8**
Hayes, Isaac **10**
Healey, Jeff **4**
Hedges, Michael **3**
Hendrix, Jimi **2**
Henley, Don **3**
Also see Eagles, The
Henry, Joe **18**
Hiatt, John **8**
Hill, Lauryn **25**
Hinojosa, Tish **13**
Hitchcock, Robyn **9**
Holly, Buddy **1**
Hornsby, Bruce **25**
Earlier sketch in CM **3**
Howard, Harlan **15**
Ian, Janis **24**
Earlier sketch in CM **5**
Ice Cube **25**
Earlier sketch in CM **10**
Ice-T **7**
Idol, Billy **3**
Imbruglia, Natalie **27**
Isaak, Chris **6**
Jackson, Alan **25**
Earlier sketch in CM **7**
Jackson, Janet **16**
Earlier sketch in CM **3**
Jackson, Joe **22**
Earlier sketch in CM **4**
Jackson, Michael **17**
Earlier sketch in CM **1**
Also see Jacksons, The
Jackson, Millie **14**
Jagger, Mick **7**
Also see Rolling Stones, The
Jam, Jimmy, and Terry Lewis **11**
James, Rick **2**
Jarreau, Al **1**
Jennings, Waylon **4**
Jett, Joan **3**
Jewel **25**
Joel, Billy **12**
Earlier sketch in CM **2**
Johansen, David **7**
John, Elton **20**
Earlier sketch in CM **3**
Johnson, Lonnie **17**
Jones, George **4**
Jones, Quincy **20**
Earlier sketch in CM **2**
Jones, Rickie Lee **4**
Joplin, Janis **3**
Jordan, Montell **26**
Kane, Big Daddy **7**
Kee, John P. **15**
Keith, Toby **17**
Kelly, R. **19**
Ketchum, Hal **14**
Khan, Chaka **19**
Earlier sketch in CM **9**
King, Albert **2**
King, B. B. **24**
Earlier sketch in CM **1**
King, Ben E. **7**
King, Carole **6**
King, Freddy **17**
Knopfler, Mark **25**
Earlier sketch in CM **3**
Also see Dire Straits
Kottke, Leo **13**
Kravitz, Lenny **26**
Earlier sketch in CM **5**
Kristofferson, Kris **4**
L.L. Cool J **5**
Landreth, Sonny **16**
Lang, K. D. **25**
Earlier sketch in CM **4**
Larkin, Patty **9**
Lavin, Christine **6**
LeDoux, Chris **12**
Lee, Ben **26**
Lee, Peggy **8**
Lehrer, Tom **7**
Leiber and Stoller **14**
Lennon, John **9**
Also see Beatles, The
Lennon, Julian **26**
Earlier sketch in CM **2**
Lewis, Huey **9**
Lightfoot, Gordon **3**
Linkous, Mark **26**
Little Richard **1**
Loeb, Lisa **23**
Logan, Jack **27**
Loggins, Kenny **20**
Earlier sketch in CM **3**
Love, Laura **20**
Loveless, Patty **5**
Lovett, Lyle **5**
Lowe, Nick **25**
Earlier sketch in CM **6**
Lydon, John **9**
Also see Sex Pistols, The
Lynn, Loretta **2**
Lynne, Jeff **5**
Lynne, Shelby **5**
MacColl, Kirsty **12**
Madonna **16**
Earlier sketch in CM **4**
Manilow, Barry **2**
Mann, Aimee **22**
Mann, Billy **23**
Marley, Bob **3**
Marley, Ziggy **3**
Marshall, Amanda **27**
Marx, Richard **3**
Mattea, Kathy **5**
Mayfield, Curtis **8**
MC 900 Ft. Jesus **16**
MC Breed **17**
McCartney, Paul **4**
Also see Beatles, The
McClinton, Delbert **14**
McCorkle, Susannah **27**
McCoury, Del **15**
McCulloch, Ian **23**
McLachlan, Sarah **12**
McLaren, Malcolm **23**
McLean, Don **7**
McLennan, Grant **21**
McMurtry, James **10**
McTell, Blind Willie **17**
Medley, Bill **3**
Melanie **12**
Mellencamp, John **20**
Earlier sketch in CM **2**
Also see John Cougar Mellencamp
Mercer, Johnny **13**
Merchant, Natalie **25**
Also see 10,000 Maniacs
Messina, Jo Dee **26**
Michael, George **9**
Miller, Roger **4**
Miller, Steve **2**
Milsap, Ronnie **2**
Mitchell, Joni **17**
Earlier sketch in CM **2**
Moffatt, Katy **18**

Morrison, Jim **3**
Morrison, Van **24**
Earlier sketch in CM **3**
Morrissey **10**
Morrissey, Bill **12**
Morton, Jelly Roll **7**
Mould, Bob **10**
Moyet, Alison **12**
Nascimento, Milton **6**
Ndegéocello, Me'Shell **18**
Near, Holly **1**
Nelson, Rick **2**
Nelson, Willie **11**
Earlier sketch in CM **1**
Newman, Randy **27**
Earlier sketch in CM **4**
Nicks, Stevie **25**
Earlier sketch in CM **2**
Also see Fleetwood Mac
Nilsson **10**
Nugent, Ted **2**
Nyro, Laura **12**
O'Connor, Sinead **3**
Ocasek, Ric **5**
Ocean, Billy **4**
Ochs, Phil **7**
Odetta **7**
Orbison, Roy **2**
Orton, Beth **26**
Osbourne, Ozzy **3**
Oslin, K. T. **3**
Owens, Buck **2**
Page, Jimmy **4**
Also see Led Zeppelin
Also see Yardbirds, The
Palmer, Robert **2**
Paris, Twila **16**
Parker, Graham **10**
Parks, Van Dyke **17**
Parnell, Lee Roy **15**
Parsons, Gram **7**
Also see Byrds, The
Parton, Dolly **24**
Earlier sketch in CM **2**
Paul, Les **2**
Paxton, Tom **5**
Peniston, CeCe **15**
Penn, Michael **4**
Perkins, Carl **9**
Petty, Tom **9**
Also see Tom Petty and the Heartbreakers
Phair, Liz **14**
Phillips, Sam **12**
Pickett, Wilson **10**
Plant, Robert **2**
Also see Led Zeppelin
Pop, Iggy **23**
Porter, Cole **10**
Price, Lloyd **25**
Prince **14**
Earlier sketch in CM **1**
Prine, John **7**
Professor Longhair **6**
Rabbitt, Eddie **24**
Earlier sketch in CM **5**
Raitt, Bonnie **23**
Earlier sketch in CM **3**
Rea, Chris **12**
Redding, Otis **5**
Reddy, Helen **9**
Reed, Lou **16**
Earlier sketch in CM **1**
Also see Velvet Underground, The
Reid, Vernon **2**
Also see Living Colour
Rice, Chris **25**
Rich, Charlie **3**
Richards, Keith **11**
Also see Rolling Stones, The
Richey, Kim **20**
Richie, Lionel **2**
Richman, Jonathan **12**
Riley, Teddy **14**
Ritchie, Jean **4**
Robbins, Marty **9**
Robertson, Robbie **2**
Robillard, Duke **2**
Robinson, Smokey **1**
Rodgers, Jimmie **3**
Rodgers, Richard **9**
Roth, David Lee **1**
Also see Van Halen
Russell, Mark **6**
Ryder, Mitch **23**
Sade **2**
Sager, Carole Bayer **5**
Sangare, Oumou **22**
Satriani, Joe **4**
Scaggs, Boz **12**
Scott-Heron, Gil **13**
Scruggs, Earl **3**
Seal **14**
Seals, Dan **9**
Secada, Jon **13**
Sedaka, Neil **4**
Seeger, Pete **4**
Also see Weavers, The
Seger, Bob **15**
Sexsmith, Ron **27**
Shannon, Del **10**
Sheila E. **3**
Shepherd, Kenny Wayne **22**
Shocked, Michelle **4**
Siberry, Jane **6**
Simon, Carly **22**
Earlier sketch in CM **4**
Simon, Paul **16**
Earlier sketch in CM **1**
Also see Simon and Garfunkel
Skaggs, Ricky **5**
Sledge, Percy **15**
Smith, Patti **17**
Earlier sketch in CM **1**
Smith, Will **26**
Snoop Doggy Dogg **17**
Sondheim, Stephen **8**
Spector, Phil **4**
Springsteen, Bruce **25**
Earlier sketch in CM **6**
St. James, Rebecca **26**
Stanley, Ralph **5**
Starr, Ringo **10**
Also see Beatles, The
Stevens, Cat **3**
Stevens, Ray **7**
Stewart, Rod **20**
Earlier sketch in CM **2**
Also see Faces, The
Stills, Stephen **5**
Sting **19**
Earlier sketch in CM **2**
Also see Police, The
Stockwood, Kim **26**
Strait, George **5**
Straw, Syd **18**
Streisand, Barbra **2**
Stuart, Marty **9**
Styne, Jule **21**
Summer, Donna **12**
Summers, Andy **3**
Also see Police, The
Sure!, Al B. **13**
Sweat, Keith **13**
Sweet, Matthew **9**
Taj Mahal **6**
Taupin, Bernie **22**
Taylor, James **25**
Earlier sketch in CM **2**
Taylor, Koko **10**
Taylor, Steve **26**
Thompson, Richard **7**
Thornton, Big Mama **18**
Tikaram, Tanita **9**
Tillis, Mel **7**
Tillis, Pam **25**
Earlier sketch in CM **8**
Tippin, Aaron **12**
Tone-L c **3**
Torme, Mel **4**
Tosh, Peter **3**
Toussaint, Allen **11**
Townshend, Pete **1**
Also see Who, The
Travis, Merle **14**
Travis, Randy **9**
Treadmill Trackstar **21**
Tricky **18**
Tritt, Travis **7**
Trynin, Jen **21**
Tubb, Ernest **4**
Twain, Shania **17**
Twitty, Conway **6**
Vai, Steve **5**
Also see Whitesnake
Van Ronk, Dave **12**
Van Shelton, Ricky **5**
Van Zandt, Townes **13**
Vandross, Luther **24**
Earlier sketch in CM **2**
Vega, Suzanne **3**
Wachtel, Waddy **26**
Wagoner, Porter **13**
Waits, Tom **27**
Earlier sketch in CM **12**
Earlier sketch in CM **1**
Walden, Narada Michael **14**
Walker, Jerry Jeff **13**
Walker, T-Bone **5**
Waller, Fats **7**
Walsh, Joe **5**
Also see Eagles, The
Wariner, Steve **18**
Warren, Diane **21**
Waters, Crystal **15**
Waters, Muddy **24**
Earlier sketch in CM **4**
Watley, Jody **26**
Earlier sketch in CM **9**
Watt, Mike **22**
Webb, Jimmy **12**
Weill, Kurt **12**
Weller, Paul **14**
West, Dottie **8**
Westerberg, Paul **26**
White, Karyn **21**
White, Lari **15**
Whitley, Chris **16**
Whitley, Keith **7**
Williams, Dar **21**
Williams, Deniece **1**
Williams, Don **4**
Williams, Hank, Jr. **1**
Williams, Hank, Sr. **4**

Williams, Lucinda **24**
  Earlier sketch in CM **10**
Williams, Paul **26**
  Earlier sketch in CM **5**
Williams, Victoria **17**
Wills, Bob **6**
Wilson, Brian **24**
  Also see Beach Boys, The
Winbush, Angela **15**
Winter, Johnny **5**
Winwood, Steve **2**
  Also see Spencer Davis Group
  Also see Traffic
Womack, Bobby **5**
Wonder, Stevie **17**
  Earlier sketch in CM **2**
Wray, Link **17**
Wyatt, Robert **24**
Wynette, Tammy **24**
  Earlier sketch in CM **2**
Yearwood, Trisha **25**
  Earlier sketch in CM **10**
Yoakam, Dwight **21**
  Earlier sketch in CM **1**
Young, Neil **15**
  Earlier sketch in CM **2**
Zappa, Frank **17**
  Earlier sketch in CM **1**
Zevon, Warren **9**

Trombone
Anderson, Ray **7**
Brown, Lawrence **23**
Miller, Glenn **6**
Teagarden, Jack **10**
Turre, Steve **22**

Trumpet
Alpert, Herb **11**
Armstrong, Louis **4**
Baker, Chet **13**
Berigan, Bunny **2**
Blanchard, Terence **13**
Brown, Clifford **24**
Cherry, Don **10**
Coleman, Ornette **5**
Davis, Miles **1**
Eldridge, Roy **9**
  Also see McKinney's Cotton Pickers
Ferguson, Maynard **7**
Gillespie, Dizzy **6**
Hargrove, Roy **15**
Hawkins, Erskine **19**
Hirt, Al **5**
Isham, Mark **14**
James, Harry **11**
Jensen, Ingrid **22**
Jones, Quincy **20**
  Earlier sketch in CM **2**
Jones, Thad **19**
Loughnane, Lee **3**
Marsalis, Wynton **20**
  Earlier sketch in CM **6**
Masekela, Hugh **7**
Matthews, Eric **22**
Mighty Mighty Bosstones **20**
Miles, Ron **22**
Navarro, Fats **25**
Oliver, King **15**
Payton, Nicholas **27**
Rodney, Red **14**
Sandoval, Arturo **15**
Severinsen, Doc **1**
Shaw, Woody **27**
Terry, Clark **24**

Tuba
Phillips, Harvey **3**

Vibraphone
Burton, Gary **10**
Hampton, Lionel **6**
Jackson, Milt **15**
Norvo, Red **12**

Viola
Menuhin, Yehudi **11**
Zukerman, Pinchas **4**

Violin
Acuff, Roy **2**
Anderson, Laurie **25**
  Earlier sketch in CM **1**
Bell, Joshua **21**
Bromberg, David **18**
Carter, Regina **22**
Chang, Sarah **7**
Clements, Vassar **18**
Coleman, Ornette **5**
Cugat, Xavier **23**
Daniels, Charlie **6**
Doucet, Michael **8**
Germano, Lisa **18**
Gingold, Josef **6**
Grappelli, Stephane **10**
Hartford, John **1**
Kennedy, Nigel **8**
Krauss, Alison **10**
Lamb, Barbara **19**
Marriner, Neville **7**
Menuhin, Yehudi **11**
Midori **7**
Mutter, Anne-Sophie **23**
O'Connor, Mark **1**
Perlman, Itzhak **2**
Ponty, Jean-Luc **8**
Rieu, André **26**
Salerno-Sonnenberg, Nadja **3**
Skaggs, Ricky **5**
Stern, Isaac **7**
Vanessa-Mae **26**
Whiteman, Paul **17**
Wills, Bob **6**
Zukerman, Pinchas **4**

Cumulative Musicians Index

Volume numbers appear in **bold.**

10,000 Maniacs **3**
2 Unlimited **18**
23, Richard
See Front 242
2Pac **17**
Also see Digital Underground
3-D
See Massive Attack
311 **20**
4Him **23**
A-ha **22**
Aaliyah **21**
Abba **12**
Abbott, Jacqueline
See Beautiful South
Abbott, Jude
See Chumbawamba
Abbruzzese, Dave
See Pearl Jam
Abdul, Paula **3**
Abercrombie, Jeff
See Fuel
Abercrombie, John **25**
Abong, Fred
See Belly
Abrahams, Mick
See Jethro Tull
Abrams, Bryan
See Color Me Badd
Abrantes, Fernando
See Kraftwerk
AC/DC **4**
Ace of Base **22**
Ackerman, Will **3**
Acland, Christopher
See Lush
Acuff, Roy **2**
Acuna, Alejandro
See Weather Report
Adam Ant **13**
Adamendes, Elaine
See Throwing Muses
Adams, Bryan **20**
Earlier sketch in CM **2**
Adams, Clifford
See Kool & the Gang
Adams, Craig
See Cult, The
Adams, Donn
See NRBQ
Adams, John **8**
Adams, Mark
See Specials, The
Adams, Oleta **17**
Adams, Terry
See NRBQ
Adams, Victoria
See Spice Girls
Adams, Yolanda **23**
Adcock, Eddie
See Country Gentleman, The
Adderly, Cannonball **15**
Adderly, Julian
See Adderly, Cannonball
Adé, King Sunny **18**
Adler, Steven
See Guns n' Roses
Aerosmith **22**
Earlier sketch in CM **3**
Afanasieff, Walter **26**
Afghan Whigs **17**
Afonso, Marie
See Zap Mama
AFX
See Aphex Twin
Agust, Daniel
See Gus Gus
Air Supply **22**
Aitchison, Dominic
See Mogwai
Ajile
See Arrested Development
Akingbola, Sola
See Jamiroquai
Akins, Rhett **22**
Alabama **21**
Earlier sketch in CM **1**
Alan, Skip
See Pretty Things, The
Alarm **22**
Albarn, Damon
See Blur
Albert, Nate
See Mighty Mighty Bosstones
Alberti, Dorona
See KMFDM
Albini, Steve **15**
Albuquerque, Michael de
See Electric Light Orchestra
Alder, John
See Gong
See Pretty Things, The
Alexakis, Art
See Everclear
Alexander, Arthur **14**
Alexander, Tim "Herb"
See Primus
Alexander, Tim
See Asleep at the Wheel
Ali
See Tribe Called Quest, A
Alice in Chains **10**
Alien Sex Fiend **23**
Alkema, Jan Willem
See Compulsion
All Saints **25**
All-4-One **17**
Allcock, Martin
See Fairport Convention
See Jethro Tull
Allen, April
See C + C Music Factory
Allen, Chad
See Guess Who
Allen, Daevid
See Gong
Allen, Dave
See Gang of Four
Allen, Debbie **8**
Allen, Duane
See Oak Ridge Boys, The
Allen, Geri **10**
Allen, Johnny Ray
See Subdudes, The
Allen, Papa Dee
See War
Allen, Peter **11**
Allen, Red
See Osborne Brothers, The
Allen, Rick
See Def Leppard
Allen, Ross
See Mekons, The
Allen, Wally
See Pretty Things, The
Allison, Luther **21**
Allison, Mose **17**
Allman Brothers, The **6**
Allman, Chris
See Greater Vision
Allman, Duane
See Allman Brothers, The
Allman, Gregg
See Allman Brothers, The
Allsup, Michael Rand
See Three Dog Night
Alpert, Herb **11**
Alphonso, Roland
See Skatalites, The
Alsing, Pelle
See Roxette
Alston, Andy
See Del Amitri
Alston, Shirley
See Shirelles, The
Altan **18**
Alvin, Dave **17**
Also see X
Am, Svet
See KMFDM
Amato, Dave
See REO Speedwagon
Amedee, Steve
See Subdudes, The
Ameling, Elly **24**
Ament, Jeff
See Pearl Jam
America **16**
American Music Club **15**
Amon, Robin
See Pearls Before Swine
Amos, Tori **12**
Anastasio, Trey
See Phish
Anderson, Al
See NRBQ

Anderson, Andy
See Cure, The
Anderson, Brett
See Suede
Anderson, Cleave
See Blue Rodeo
Anderson, Emma
See Lush
Anderson, Gladstone
See Skatalites, The
Anderson, Ian
See Jethro Tull
Anderson, Jhelisa
See Shamen, The
Anderson, John **5**
Anderson, Jon
See Yes
Anderson, June **27**
Anderson, Keith
See Dirty Dozen Brass Band
Anderson, Laurie **25**
Earlier sketch in CM **1**
Anderson, Marian **8**
Anderson, Pamela
See Incognito
Anderson, Ray **7**
Anderson, Signe
See Jefferson Airplane
Anderson, Wessell **23**
Andersson, Benny
See Abba
Andes, Mark
See Spirit
Andes, Matt
See Spirit
Andes, Rachel
See Spirit
Andrews, Barry
See XTC
Andrews, Christopher
See Mojave 3
Andrews, Julie **4**
Andrews, Laverne
See Andrews Sisters, The
Andrews, Mark
See Dru Hill,
Andrews, Maxene
See Andrews Sisters, The
Andrews, Patty
See Andrews Sisters, The
Andrews, Revert
See Dirty Dozen Brass Band
Andrews Sisters, The **9**
Andy, Horace
See Massive Attack
Anger, Darol
See Turtle Island String Quartet
Angus, Colin
See Shamen, The
Animals, The **22**
Anka, Paul **2**
Anointed **21**
Anonymous 4 **23**
Anonymous, Rodney
See Dead Milkmen
Anselmo, Philip
See Pantera
Ant, Adam
See Adam Ant
Anthony, Larry
See Dru Hill
Anthony, Marc **19**
Anthony, Michael
See Van Halen
Anthony, Michael
See Massive Attack
Anthrax **11**
Anton, Alan
See Cowboy Junkies, The
Antoni, Mark De Gli
See Soul Coughing
Antunes, Michael
See Beaver Brown Band, The
Aphex Twin **14**
Appice, Vinnie
See Black Sabbath
Appleton, Natalie
See All Saints
Appleton, Nicole
See All Saints
Aqua Velvets **23**
Aquabats, The **22**
Araya, Tom
See Slayer
Archers of Loaf **21**
Arden, Jann **21**
Ardolino, Tom
See NRBQ
Arellano, Rod
See Aquabats, The
Arena, Tina **21**
Argent, Rod
See Zombies, The
Argerich, Martha **27**
Arkenstone, David **20**
Arlen, Harold **27**
Arm, Mark
See Mudhoney
Armatrading, Joan **4**
Armerding, Jake
See Northern Lights
Armerding, Taylor
See Northern Lights
Armstrong, Billie Joe
See Green Day
Armstrong, Louis **4**
Armstrong, Vanessa Bell **24**
Arnaz, Desi **8**
Arni, Stefan
See Gus Gus
Arnold, Eddy **10**
Arnold, Kristine
See Sweethearts of the Rodeo
Aronoff, Kenny **21**
Arrau, Claudio **1**
Arrested Development **14**
Art Ensemble of Chicago, The **23**
Art of Noise **22**
Arthurs, Paul
See Oasis
Artifacts **23**
Ash, Daniel
See Bauhaus
Ash, Daniel
See Love and Rockets
Ashcroft, Richard
See Verve, The
Ashford, Rosalind
See Martha and the Vandellas
Ashley, Bob
See Guess Who
Ashton, John
See Psychedelic Furs
Ashton, Susan **17**
Asleep at the Wheel **5**
Astbury, Ian
See Cult, The
Astley, Rick **5**
Aston, Jay "J"
See Gene Loves Jezebel
Aston, Michael
See Gene Loves Jezebel
Astro
See UB40
Asuo, Kwesi
See Arrested Development
Atari Teenage Riot **27**
Atkins, Chet **26**
Earlier sketch in CM **5**
Atkins, Martin
See Pigface
Atkinson, Paul
See Zombies, The
Atkinson, Sweet Pea
See Was (Not Was)
Atomic Fireballs, The **27**
Audio Adrenaline **22**
Auf Der Maur, Melissa
See Hole
Augustyniak, Jerry
See 10,000 Maniacs
Auldridge, Mike **4**
Also see Country Gentlemen, The
Also see Seldom Scene, The
Austin, Cuba
See McKinney's Cotton Pickers
Austin, Dallas **16**
Austral, Florence **26**
Autry, Gene **25**
Earlier sketch in CM **12**
Avalon **26**
Avalon, Frankie **5**
Avery, Eric
See Jane's Addiction
Avery, Teodross **23**
Avory, Mick
See Rolling Stones, The
Avory, Mick
See Kinks, The
Ayers, Kevin
See Gong
Aykroyd, Dan
See Blues Brothers, The
Ayler, Albert **19**
Ayres, Ben
See Cornershop
Azorr, Chris
See Cherry Poppin' Daddies
Aztec Camera **22**
B, Daniel
See Front 242
B-52's, The **4**
B-Real
See Cypress Hill
Baah, Reebop Kwaku
See Traffic
Babatunde, Don
See Last Poets
Babes in Toyland **16**
Babjak, James
See Smithereens, The
Babyface
See Edmonds, Kenneth "Babyface"
Bacchus, Richard
See D Generation
Bacharach, Burt **20**
Earlier sketch in CM **1**
Bachman, Eric
See Archers of Loaf
Bachman, Randy
See Guess Who
Backstreet Boys **21**

Bad Brains **16**
Bad Company **22**
Bad Livers, The **19**
Badalamenti, Angelo **17**
Badfinger **23**
Badger, Pat
 See Extreme
Badrena, Manola
 See Weather Report
Badu, Erykah **26**
Baez, Joan **1**
Bailey, Keith
 See Gong
Bailey, Mildred **13**
Bailey, Pearl **5**
Bailey, Phil
 See Earth, Wind and Fire
Bailey, Victor
 See Weather Report
Baker, Anita **9**
Baker, Arthur **23**
Baker, Bobby
 See Tragically Hip, The
Baker, Chet **13**
Baker, Dale
 See Sixpence None the Richer
Baker, Ginger **16**
 Also see Cream
Baker, Janet **14**
Baker, Jon
 See Charlatans, The
Baker, Josephine **10**
Baker, LaVern **25**
Balakrishnan, David
 See Turtle Island String Quartet
Balch, Bob
 See Fu Manchu
Balch, Michael
 See Front Line Assembly
Baldes, Kevin
 See Lit
Baldursson, Sigtryggur
 See Sugarcubes, The
Baldwin, Donny
 See Starship
Baliardo, Diego
 See Gipsy Kings, The
Baliardo, Paco
 See Gipsy Kings, The
Baliardo, Tonino
 See Gipsy Kings, The
Balin, Marty
 See Jefferson Airplane
Ball, Marcia **15**
Ballard, Florence
 See Supremes, The
Ballard, Hank **17**
Balsley, Phil
 See Statler Brothers, The
Baltes, Peter
 See Dokken
Balzano, Vinnie
 See Less Than Jake
Bambaataa, Afrika **13**
Bamonte, Perry
 See Cure, The
Bananarama **22**
Bancroft, Cyke
 See Bevis Frond
Band, The **9**
Bangles, The **22**
Banks, Nick
 See Pulp
Banks, Peter
 See Yes
Banks, Tony
 See Genesis
Baptiste, David Russell
 See Meters, The
Barbarossa, Dave
 See Republica
Barbata, John
 See Jefferson Starship
Barber, Keith
 See Soul Stirrers, The
Barbero, Lori
 See Babes in Toyland
Barbieri, Gato **22**
Bardens, Peter
 See Camel
Barenaked Ladies **18**
Bargeld, Blixa
 See Einstürzende Neubauten
Bargeron, Dave
 See Blood, Sweat and Tears
Barham, Meriel
 See Lush
Barile, Jo
 See Ventures, The
Barker, Paul
 See Ministry
Barker, Travis Landon
 See Aquabats, The
Barker, Travis
 See Blink 182
Barlow, Barriemore
 See Jethro Tull
Barlow, Lou **20**
 Also see Dinosaur Jr.
 Also see Sebadoh
Barlow, Tommy
 See Aztec Camera
Barnes, Danny
 See Bad Livers, The
Barnes, Micah
 See Nylons, The
Barnes, Roosevelt "Booba" **23**
Barnett, Mandy **26**
Barnwell, Duncan
 See Simple Minds
Barnwell, Ysaye Maria
 See Sweet Honey in the Rock
Barr, Al
 See Dropkick Murphys
Barr, Ralph
 See Nitty Gritty Dirt Band, The
Barre, Martin
 See Jethro Tull
Barrere, Paul
 See Little Feat
Barrett, (Roger) Syd
 See Pink Floyd
Barrett, Dicky
 See Mighty Mighty Bosstones
Barrett, Robert "T-Mo"
 See Goodie Mob
Barron, Christopher
 See Spin Doctors
Barrow, Geoff
 See Portishead
Barson, Mike
 See Madness
Bartels, Joanie **13**
Bartholomew, Simon
 See Brand New Heavies, The
Bartoli, Cecilia **12**
Barton, Lou Ann
 See Fabulous Thunderbirds, The
Barton, Rick
 See Dropkick Murphys
Bartos, Karl
 See Kraftwerk
Basehead **11**
Basher, Mick
 See X
Basia **5**
Basie, Count **2**
Bass, Colin
 See Camel
Bass, Lance
 See 'N Sync
Bass, Ralph **24**
Batchelor, Kevin
 See Big Mountain
 See Steel Pulse
Batel, Beate
 See Einstürzende Neubauten
Batiste, Lionel
 See Dirty Dozen Brass Band
Batoh, Masaki
 See Ghost
 See Pearls Before Swine
Battin, Skip
 See Byrds, The
Battle, Kathleen **6**
Bauer, Judah
 See Jon Spencer Blues Explosion
Bauhaus **27**
Baumann, Peter
 See Tangerine Dream
Bautista, Roland
 See Earth, Wind and Fire
Baxter, Adrian
 See Cherry Poppin' Daddies
Baxter, Jeff
 See Doobie Brothers, The
Bayer Sager, Carole
 See Sager, Carole Bayer
Baylor, Helen **20**
Baynton-Power, David
 See James
Bazilian, Eric
 See Hooters
Beach Boys, The **1**
Beale, Michael
 See Earth, Wind and Fire
Beard, Annette
 See Martha and the Vandellas
Beard, Frank
 See ZZ Top
Beasley, Paul
 See Mighty Clouds of Joy, The
Beastie Boys **25**
 Earlier sketch in CM **8**
Beat Farmers **23**
Beatles, The **2**
Beauford, Carter
 See Dave Matthews Band
Beautiful South **19**
Beauvoir, Jean
 See Wendy O. Williams and The Plasmatics
Beaver Brown Band, The **3**
Bechdel, John
 See Fear Factory
Bechet, Sidney **17**
Beck **18**
Beck, Jeff **4**
 Also see Yardbirds, The
Beck, William
 See Ohio Players
Becker, Walter
 See Steely Dan

Beckford, Theophilus
See Skatalites, The
Beckley, Gerry
See America
Bedford, Mark
See Madness
Bee Gees, The **3**
Beech, Wes
See Wendy O. Williams and The Plasmatics
Beecham, Thomas **27**
Beers, Garry Gary
See INXS
Behler, Chuck
See Megadeth
Beiderbecke, Bix **16**
Belafonte, Harry **8**
Belew, Adrian **5**
Also see King Crimson
Belfield, Dennis
See Three Dog Night
Bell, Andy
See Erasure
Bell, Brian
See Weezer
Bell, Burton C.
See Fear Factory
Bell, Carl
See Fuel
Bell, Chris
See Gene Loves Jezebel
Bell, Derek
See Chieftains, The
Bell, Eric
See Thin Lizzy
Bell, Jayn
See Sounds of Blackness
Bell, Joshua **21**
Bell, Melissa
See Soul II Soul
Bell, Robert "Kool
See Kool & the Gang
Bell, Ronald
See Kool & the Gang
Bell, Taj
See Charm Farm
Belladonna, Joey
See Anthrax
Bellamy Brothers, The **13**
Bellamy, David
See Bellamy Brothers, The
Bellamy, Howard
See Bellamy Brothers, The
Belle, Regina **6**
Bello, Elissa
See Go-Go's, The
Bello, Frank
See Anthrax
Belly **16**
Belove, David
See Oakland Interfaith Gospel Choir
Belushi, John
See Blues Brothers, The
Ben Folds Five **20**
Benante, Charlie
See Anthrax
Benatar, Pat **8**
Benckert, Vicki
See Roxette
Benedict, Scott
See Pere Ubu
Benét, Eric **27**
Bengry, Peter
See Cornershop
Benitez, Jellybean **15**
Bennett, Brian
See Shadows, The
Bennett, Tony **16**
Earlier sketch in CM **2**
Bennett-Nesby, Ann
See Sounds of Blackness
Benson, George **9**
Benson, Ray
See Asleep at the Wheel
Benson, Renaldo "Obie"
See Four Tops, The
Bentley, Jay
See Circle Jerks
Bentley, John
See Squeeze
Benton, Brook **7**
Bentyne, Cheryl
See Manhattan Transfer, The
Berenyi, Miki
See Lush
Berg, Matraca **16**
Bergeson, Ben
See Aquabats, The
Berggren, Jenny
See Ace of Base
Berggren, Jonas
See Ace of Base
Berggren, Linn
See Ace of Base
Berigan, Bunny **2**
Berkely, Anthony (Poetic the Grym Reaper)
See Gravediggaz
Berlin, Irving **8**
Berlin, Liz
See Rusted Root
Berlin, Steve
See Los Lobos
Bernal, Steve
See Poi Dog Pondering
Berndt, Jay
See Kilgore
Bernstein, Leonard **2**
Berry, Bill
See R.E.M.
Berry, Chuck **1**
Berry, John **17**
Berry, Robert
See Emerson, Lake & Palmer/Powell
Berryhill, Bob
See Surfaris, The
Bert, Bob
See Sonic Youth
Bessant, Jack
See Reef
Best, Nathaniel
See O'Jays, The
Best, Pete
See Beatles, The
Beta Band, The **27**
Betha, Mason
See Mase
Bettencourt, Nuno
See Extreme
Better Than Ezra **19**
Bettie Serveert **17**
Bettini, Tom
See Jackyl
Betts, Dicky
See Allman Brothers, The
Bevan, Bev
See Black Sabbath
Also see Electric Light Orchestra
Bevis Frond **23**
Bezozi, Alan
See Dog's Eye View
Biafra, Jello **18**
Big Audio Dynamite **18**
Big Head Todd and the Monsters **20**
Big Mike
See GetoBoys, The
Big Money Odis
See Digital Underground
Big Mountain **23**
Bigham, John
See Fishbone
Bill Wyman & the Rhythm Kings **26**
Bin Hassan, Umar
See Last Poets
Bingham, John
See Fishbone
Binks, Les
See Judas Priest
Biondo, George
See Steppenwolf
Birchfield, Benny
See Osborne Brothers, The
Bird
See Parker, Charlie
Birdsong, Cindy
See Supremes, The
Birdstuff
See Man or Astroman?
Biscuits, Chuck
See Danzig
Also see Social Distortion
Also see Circle Jerks
Bishop, Michael
See Gwar
Biz Markie **10**
BizzyBone
See Bone Thugs-N-Harmony
Bjelland, Kat
See Babes in Toyland
Bjork, Brant
See Fu Manchu
Björk **16**
Also see Sugarcubes, The
Black, Clint **5**
Black Crowes, The **7**
Black Flag **22**
Black Francis
See Black, Frank
Black, Frank **14**
Black, Jimmy Carl "India Ink"
See Captain Beefheart and His Magic Band
Black, Mary **15**
Black Sabbath **9**
Black Sheep **15**
Black Uhuru **12**
Black, Vic
See C + C Music Factory
BlackHawk **21**
Blackman, Cindy **15**
Blackman, Tee-Wee
See Memphis Jug Band
Blackmore, Ritchie
See Deep Purple
Blackstreet **23**
Blackwell, Chris **26**
Blackwood, Sarah
See Dubstar
Bladd, Stephen Jo
See J. Geils Band
Blades, Ruben **2**
Blair, Ron
See Tom Petty and the Heartbreakers
Blake, Eubie **19**
Blake, Norman
See Teenage Fanclub

Blake, Tim
See Gong
Blakely, Paul
See Captain Beefheart and His Magic Band
Blakey, Art **11**
Blakey, Colin
See Waterboys, The
Blanchard, Terence **13**
Bland, Bobby "Blue" **12**
Blatt, Melanie
See All Saints
Blegen, Jutith **23**
Blessid Union of Souls **20**
Bley, Carla **8**
Bley, Paul **14**
Blige, Mary J. **15**
Blind Melon **21**
Blink 182 **27**
Block, Norman
See Rasputina
Block, Rory **18**
Blondie **14**
Blondie **27**
Blood, Dave
See Dead Milkmen
Blood, Sweat and Tears **7**
Bloom, Eric
See Blue Oyster Cult
Bloom, Luka **14**
Blount, Herman "Sonny"
See Sun Ra
Blue, Buddy
See Beat Farmers
Blue Oyster Cult **16**
Blue Rodeo **18**
Bluegrass Patriots **22**
Blues, "Joliet" Jake
See Blues Brothers, The
Blues Brothers, The **3**
Blues, Elwood
See Blues Brothers, The
Blues Traveler **15**
Blunstone, Colin
See Zombies, The
Blunt, Martin
See Charlatans, The
Blur **17**
Bob, Tim
See Rage Against the Machine
Bocelli, Andrea **22**
BoDeans, The **20**
Earlier sketch in CM **3**
Boff, Richard
See Chumbawamba
Bogaert, Jo
See Technotronic
Bogdan, Henry
See Helmet
Boggs, Dock **25**
Bogguss, Suzy **11**
Bogle, Bob
See Ventures, The
Bohannon, Jim
See Pearls Before Swine
Bolade Casel, Nitanju
See Sweet Honey in the Rock
Bolan, Marc
See T. Rex
Bolton, Michael **4**
Bon Jovi **10**
Bon Jovi, Jon
See Bon Jovi
Bonamy, James **21**
Bone Thugs-N-Harmony **18**
Bonebrake, D. J.
See X
Bonham, John
See Led Zeppelin
Bonnecaze, Cary
See Better Than Ezra
Bonner, Leroy "Sugarfoot"
See Ohio Players
Bono
See U2
Bono, Sonny
See Sonny and Cher
Bonsall, Joe
See Oak Ridge Boys, The
Boo Radleys, The **21**
Booker T. & the M.G.'s **24**
Books
See Das EFX
Boone, Pat **13**
Booth, Tim
See James
Boquist, Dave
See Son Volt
Boquist, Jim
See Son Volt
Bordin, Mike
See Faith No More
Borg, Bobby
See Warrant
Borge, Victor **19**
Borland, Wes
See Limp Bizkit
Borowiak, Tony
See All-4-One
Bostaph, Paul
See Slayer
Bostek, James
See Atomic Fireballs, The
Boston **11**
Boston, Mark "Rockette Morton"
See Captain Beefheart and His Magic Band
Bostrom, Derrick
See Meat Puppets, The
Bottum, Roddy
See Faith No More
Also see Imperial Teen
Bouchard, Albert
See Blue Oyster Cult
Bouchard, Joe
See Blue Oyster Cult
Bouchikhi, Chico
See Gipsy Kings, The
Boulez, Pierre **26**
Bowen, Jimmy
See Country Gentlemen, The
Bowens, Sir Harry
See Was (Not Was)
Bowie, David **23**
Earlier sketch in CM **1**
Bowie, Lester
See Art Ensemble of Chicago, The
Bowman, Steve
See Counting Crows
Box, Mick
See Uriah Heep
Boy Howdy **21**
Boyd, Brandon
See Incubus
Boyd, Eadie
See Del Rubio Triplets
Boyd, Elena
See Del Rubio Triplets
Boyd, Liona **7**
Boyd, Milly
See Del Rubio Triplets
Boyle, Doug
See Caravan
Boyz II Men **15**
Bozulich, Carla
See Geraldine Fibbers
Brad **21**
Bradbury, John
See Specials, The
Bradbury, Randy
See Pennywise
Bradfield, James Dean
See Manic Street Preachers
Bradshaw, Tim
See Dog's Eye View
Bradstreet, Rick
See Bluegrass Patriots
Brady, Paul **8**
Bragg, Billy **7**
Braithwaite, Stuart
See Mogwai
Bramah, Martin
See Fall, The
Brand New Heavies, The **14**
Brandt, Paul **22**
Brandy **19**
Branigan, Laura **2**
Brannon, Kippi **20**
Brantley, Junior
See Roomful of Blues
Braxton, Anthony **12**
Braxton, Toni **17**
Bream, Julian **9**
Breeders **19**
Brendel, Alfred **23**
Brennan, Ciaran
See Clannad
Brennan, Maire
See Clannad
Brennan, Paul
See Odds
Brennan, Pol
See Clannad
Brenner, Simon
See Talk Talk
Brevette, Lloyd
See Skatalites, The
Brickell, Edie **3**
Brickman, Jim **22**
Bridgeman, Noel
See Waterboys, The
Bridgewater, Dee Dee **18**
Briggs, David
See Pearls Before Swine
Briggs, James Randall
See Aquabats, The
Briggs, Vic
See Animals, The
Bright, Garfield
See Shai
Bright, Ronnie
See Coasters, The
Brightman, Sarah **20**
Briley, Alex
See Village People, The
Brindley, Paul
See Sundays, The
Britt, Michael
See Lonestar
Britten, Benjamin **15**
Brittingham, Eric
See Cinderella
Brix
See Fall, The
Brockenborough, Dennis
See Mighty Mighty Bosstones

Brockie, Dave
See Gwar
Brokop, Lisa **22**
Bromberg, David **18**
Bronfman, Yefim **6**
Brooke, Jonatha
See Story, The
Brooker, Gary
See Bill Wyman & the Rhythm Kings
Brookes, Jon
See Charlatans, The
Brookes, Steve
See Jam, The
Brooks & Dunn **25**
Earlier sketch in CM **12**
Brooks, Baba
See Skatalites, The
Brooks, DJ
See Citizen King
Brooks, Garth **25**
Earlier sketch in CM **8**
Brooks, Leon Eric "Kix" III
See Brooks & Dunn,
Brooks, Stuart
See Pretty Things, The
Broonzy, Big Bill **13**
Brotherdale, Steve
See Joy Division
Also see Smithereens, The
Brötzmann, Caspar **27**
Brötzmann, Peter **26**
Broudie, Ian
See Lightning Seeds
Brown, Bobby **4**
Brown, Brooks
See Cherry Poppin' Daddies
Brown, Clarence "Gatemouth" **11**
Brown, Clifford **24**
Brown, Donny
See Verve Pipe, The
Brown, Duncan
See Stereolab
Brown, Foxy **25**
Brown, George
See Kool & the Gang
Brown, Greg
See Cake
Brown, Harold
See War
Brown, Heidi
See Treadmill Trackstar
Brown, Ian
See Stone Roses, The
Brown, James **16**
Earlier sketch in CM **2**
Brown, Jimmy
See UB40
Brown, Junior **15**
Brown, Lawrence **23**
Brown, Marty **14**
Brown, Melanie
See Spice Girls
Brown, Mick
See Dokken
Brown, Morris
See Pearls Before Swine
Brown, Norman
See Mills Brothers, The
Brown, Rahem
See Artifacts
Brown, Ray **21**
Brown, Ruth **13**
Brown, Selwyn "Bumbo"
See Steel Pulse
Brown, Steven
See Tuxedomoon
Brown, Tim
See Boo Radleys, The
Brown, Tony **14**
Browne, Jackson **3**
Also see Nitty Gritty Dirt Band, The
Brownstein, Carrie
See Sleater-Kinney
Brownstone **21**
Brubeck, Dave **8**
Bruce, Dustan
See Chumbawamba
Bruce, Jack
See Cream
Bruce, Joseph Frank
See Insane Clown Posse
Bruford, Bill
See King Crimson
Also see Yes
Bruno, Gioia
See Exposé
Bruster, Thomas
See Soul Stirrers, The
Bryan, David
See Bon Jovi
Bryan, Karl
See Skatalites, The
Bryan, Mark
See Hootie and the Blowfish
Bryant, Elbridge
See Temptations, The
Bryant, Jeff
See Ricochet
Bryant, Junior
See Ricochet
Bryson, Bill
See Desert Rose Band, The
Bryson, David
See Counting Crows
Bryson, Peabo **11**
Buchanan, Wallis
See Jamiroquai
Buchholz, Francis
See Scorpions, The
Buchignani, Paul
See Afghan Whigs
Buck, Mike
See Fabulous Thunderbirds, The
Buck, Peter
See R.E.M.
Buck, Robert
See 10,000 Maniacs
Buckingham, Lindsey **8**
Also see Fleetwood Mac
Buckler, Rick
See Jam, The
Buckley, Betty **16**
Earlier sketch in CM **1**
Buckley, Jeff **22**
Buckley, Tim **14**
Buckwheat Zydeco **6**
Budgie
See Siouxsie and the Banshees
Buerstatte, Phil
See White Zombie
Buffalo Springfield **24**
Buffalo Tom **18**
Buffett, Jimmy **4**
Built to Spill **27**
Bulgarian State Radio and Television Female Vocal Choir, The
See Bulgarian State Female Vocal Choir, The
Bulgarian State Female Vocal Choir, The **10**
Bulgin, Lascelle
See Israel Vibration
Bulloch, Martin
See Mogwai
Bullock, Craig "DJ Homicide"
See Sugar Ray
Bumbry, Grace **13**
Bumpus, Cornelius
See Doobie Brothers, The
Bunker, Clive
See Jethro Tull
Bunkley, John
See Atomic Fireballs, The
Bunnell, Dewey
See America
Bunskoeke, Herman
See Bettie Serveert
Bunton, Emma
See Spice Girls
Burch, Curtis
See New Grass Revival, The
Burchill, Charlie
See Simple Minds
Burden, Ian
See Human League, The
Burdon, Eric **14**
Also see War
Also see Animals, The
Burgess, Paul
See Camel
Burgess, Tim
See Charlatans, The
Burke, Clem
See Blondie
Burke, Clem
See Blondie
Burkum, Tyler
See Audio Adrenaline
Burnett, Carol **6**
Burnett, T Bone **13**
Burnette, Billy
See Fleetwood Mac
Burnham, Hugo
See Gang of Four
Burning Spear **15**
Burns, Barry
See Mogwai
Burns, Bob
See Lynyrd Skynyrd
Burns, Karl
See Fall, The
Burr, Clive
See Iron Maiden
Burrell, Boz
See Bad Company
Burrell, Kenny **11**
Burrell, Raymond "Boz"
See King Crimson
Burroughs, William S. **26**
Burse, Charlie
See Memphis Jug Band
Burse, Robert
See Memphis Jug Band,
Burton, Cliff
See Metallica
Burton, Gary **10**
Burton, Tim
See Mighty Mighty Bosstones
Busby, Jheryl **9**
Bush **18**
Bush, Dave
See Fall, The
Bush, John
See Anthrax

Bush, Kate **4**
Bush, Sam
See New Grass Revival, The
Bushwick, Bill
See Geto Boys, The
Busta Rhymes **18**
Butler, Bernard
See Suede
Butler, Richard
See Love Spit Love
Also see Psychedelic Furs
Butler, Terry "Geezer"
See Black Sabbath
Butler, Tim
See Love Spit Love
Also see Psychedelic Furs
Butterfield, Paul **23**
Butterfly
See Digable Planets
Butthole Surfers **16**
Buttrey, Kenneth
See Pearls Before Swine
Buynak, John
See Rusted Root
Buzzcocks, The **9**
Byers, Roddy
See Specials, The
Byrds, The **8**
Byrne, David **8**
Also see Talking Heads
Byrne, Dermot
See Altan
Byrom, Larry
See Steppenwolf
Byron, David
See Uriah Heep
Byron, Don **22**
Byron, Lord T.
See Lords of Acid
C + C Music Factory **16**
Caballe, Monserrat **23**
Cabaret Voltaire **18**
Cachao
See Lopez, Israel "Cachao"
Cadogan, Kevin
See Third Eye Blind
Caesar, Shirley **17**
Cafferty, John
See Beaver Brown Band, The
Caffey, Charlotte
See Go-Go's, The
Cage, John **8**
Cahn, Sammy **11**
Cain, Jonathan
See Journey
Cake **27**
Calderon, Mark
See Color Me Badd
Cale, J. J. **16**
Earlier sketch in CM **9**
Also see Velvet Underground, The
Cale, John
See Cale, J. J.
Calhoun, Will
See Living Colour
California, Randy
See Spirit
Calire, Mario
See Wallflowers, The
Callahan, Ken
See Jayhawks, The
Callahan, Ray
See Wendy O. Williams and The Plasmatics
Callas, Maria **11**
Callis, Jo
See Human League, The
Calloway, Cab **6**
Camel **21**
Cameron, Clayton
See Ralph Sharon Quartet
Cameron, Duncan
See Sawyer Brown
Cameron, G. C.
See Spinners, The
Cameron, Matt
See Soundgarden
Cameron, Timothy
See Silk
Camp, Greg
See Smash Mouth
Campbell, Ali
See UB40
Campbell, Eddie
See Texas
Campbell, Glen **2**
Campbell, Kerry
See War
Campbell, Luther **10**
Campbell, Martyn
See Lightning Seeds
Campbell, Mike
See Tom Petty and the Heartbreakers
Campbell, Phil
See Motörhead
Campbell, Robin
See UB40
Campbell, Sarah Elizabeth **23**
Campbell, Tevin **13**
Canadian Brass, The **4**
Cantrell, Jerry
See Alice in Chains
Canty, Brendan
See Fugazi
Capaldi, Jim
See Traffic
Cappelli, Frank **14**
Cappos, Andy
See Built to Spill
Captain Beefheart and the Magic Band **26**
Earlier sketch in CM **10**
Caravan **24**
Carbonara, Paul
See Blondie
Cardigans **19**
Cardwell, Joi **22**
Carey, Danny
See Tool
Carey, Mariah **20**
Earlier sketch in CM **6**
Carlisle, Belinda **8**
Also see Go-Go's, The
Carlisle, Bob **22**
Carlos, Bun E.
See Cheap Trick
Carlos, Don
See Black Uhuru
Carlson, Paulette
See Highway 101
Carmichael, Hoagy **27**
Carnes, Kim **4**
Carpenter, Bob
See Nitty Gritty Dirt Band, The
Carpenter, Karen
See Carpenters, The
Carpenter, Richard **24**
Also see Carpenters, The
Carpenter, Stephen
See Deftones
Carpenters, The **13**
Carr, Ben
See Mighty Mighty Bosstones
Carr, Eric
See Kiss
Carr, James **23**
Carr, Martin
See Boo Radleys, The
Carr, Teddy
See Ricochet
Carrack, Paul
See Mike & the Mechanics
Also see Squeeze
Carreras, José **8**
Carrigan, Andy
See Mekons, The
Carroll, Earl "Speedo"
See Coasters, The
Carruthers, John
See Siouxsie and the Banshees
Cars, The **20**
Carter, A. P.
See Carter Family, The
Carter, Anita
See Carter Family, The
Carter, Benny **3**
Also see McKinney's Cotton Pickers
Carter, Betty **6**
Carter, Carlene **8**
Carter, Deana **25**
Carter Family, The **3**
Carter, Helen
See Carter Family, The
Carter, James **18**
Carter, Janette
See Carter Family, The
Carter, Jimmy
See Five Blind Boys of Alabama
Carter, Joe
See Carter Family, The
Carter, June Cash **6**
Also see Carter Family, The
Carter, Maybell
See Carter Family, The
Carter, Nell **7**
Carter, Nick
See Backstreet Boys
Carter, Regina **22**
Carter, Ron **14**
Carter, Sara
See Carter Family, The
Carthy, Martin
See Steeleye Span
Caruso, Enrico **10**
Cary, Justin
See Sixpence None the Richer
Casady, Jack
See Jefferson Airplane
Casale, Bob
See Devo
Casale, Gerald V.
See Devo
Casals, Pablo **9**
Case, Peter **13**
Casey, Ken
See Dropkick Murphys
Cash, Johnny **17**
Earlier sketch in CM **1**
Cash, Rosanne **2**
Cassidy, Ed
See Spirit
Catallo, Chris
See Surfin' Pluto
Catallo, Gene
See Surfin' Pluto

Cates, Ronny
See Petra
Catherall, Joanne
See Human League, The
Catherine Wheel **18**
Caustic Window
See Aphex Twin
Cauty, Jimmy
See Orb, The
Cavalera, Igor
See Sepultura
Cavalera, Max
See Sepultura
Cave, Nick **10**
Cavoukian, Raffi
See Raffi
Cazares, Dino
See Fear Factory
Cease, Jeff
See Black Crowes, The
Cervenka, Exene
See X
Cetera, Peter
See Chicago
Chamberlin, Jimmy
See Smashing Pumpkins
Chambers, Guy
See Waterboys, The
Chambers, Martin
See Pretenders, The
Chambers, Paul **18**
Chambers, Terry
See XTC
Champion, Eric **21**
Chan, Spencer
See Aqua Velvets
Chance, Slim
See Cramps, The
Chancellor, Justin
See Tool
Chandler, Chas
See Animals, The
Chandra, Sheila **16**
Chaney, Jimmy
See Jimmie's Chicken Shack
Chang, Sarah **7**
Channing, Carol **6**
Chapin Carpenter, Mary **25**
Earlier sketch in CM **6**
Chapin, Harry **6**
Chapin, Tom **11**
Chapman, Steven Curtis **15**
Chapman, Tony
See Rolling Stones, The
Chapman, Tracy **20**
Earlier sketch in CM **4**
Chaquico, Craig **23**
Also see Jefferson Starship
Charlatans, The **13**
Charles, Ray **24**
Earlier sketch in CM **1**
Charles, Yolanda
See Aztec Camera
Charm Farm **20**
Chasez, Joshua Scott "JC"
See 'N Sync
Che Colovita, Lemon
See Jimmie's Chicken Shack
Chea, Alvin "Vinnie"
See Take 6
Cheap Trick **12**
Cheatam, Aldolphus "Doc"
See McKinney's Cotton Pickers
Checker, Chubby **7**
Cheeks, Julius
See Soul Stirrers, The
Chemical Brothers **20**
Cheng, Chi
See Deftones
Chenier, C. J. **15**
Chenier, Clifton **6**
Chenille Sisters, The **16**
Cher **1**
Also see Sonny and Cher
Cherone, Gary
See Extreme
Cherone, Gary
See Van Halen
Cherry, Don **10**
Cherry, Neneh **4**
Cherry Poppin' Daddies **24**
Chesney, Kenny **20**
Chesnutt, Mark **13**
Chess, Leonard **24**
Chevalier, Maurice **6**
Chevron, Phillip
See Pogues, The
Chicago **3**
Chieftains, The **7**
Childress, Ross
See Collective Soul
Childress Saxton, Shirley
See Sweet Honey in the Rock
Childs, Toni **2**
Chilton, Alex **10**
Chimes, Terry
See Clash, The
Chin, Tony
See Big Mountain
Chisholm, Melanie
See Spice Girls
Chopmaster J
See Digital Underground
Chrisman, Andy
See 4Him
Christ, John
See Danzig
Christian, Charlie **11**
Christina, Fran
See Fabulous Thunderbirds, The
Also see Roomful of Blues
Chuck D
See Public Enemy
Chumbawamba **21**
Chung, Mark
See Einstürzende Neubauten
Church, Kevin
See Country Gentlemen, The
Church, The **14**
Churilla, Scott
See Reverend Horton Heat
Ciccone, Don
See Four Seasons, The
Cieka, Rob
See Boo Radleys, The
Cinderella **16**
Cinelu, Mino
See Weather Report
Cipollina, John
See Quicksilver Messenger Service
Circle Jerks, The **17**
Cissell, Ben
See Audio Adrenaline
Citizen King **27**
Clannad **23**
Clapton, Eric **11**
Earlier sketch in CM **1**
Also see Cream
Also see Yardbirds, The
Clark, Alan
See Dire Straits
Clark, Dave
See Dave Clark Five, The
Clark, Dick **25**
Earlier sketch in CM **2**
Clark, Gene
See Byrds, The
Clark, Graham
See Gong
Clark, Guy **17**
Clark, Keith
See Circle Jerks, The
Clark, Mike
See Suicidal Tendencies
Clark, Roy **1**
Clark, Steve
See Def Leppard
Clark, Terri **19**
Clark, Tony
See Blessid Union of Souls
Clarke, "Fast" Eddie
See Motörhead
Clarke, Bernie
See Aztec Camera
Clarke, Michael
See Byrds, The
Clarke, Stanley **3**
Clarke, Vince
See Depeche Mode
Also see Erasure
Clarke, William
See Third World
Clash, The **4**
Clayderman, Richard **1**
Claypool, Les
See Primus
Clayton, Adam
See U2
Clayton, Sam
See Little Feat
Clayton-Thomas, David
SeeBlood, Sweat and Tears
Clean, Dean
See Dead Milkmen
Cleaves, Jessica
See Earth, Wind and Fire
Clegg, Johnny **8**
Clements, Vassar **18**
Clemons, Clarence **7**
Cleveland, James **1**
Cliburn, Van **13**
Cliff, Jimmy **8**
Clifford, Douglas Ray
See Creedence Clearwater Revival
Cline, Nels
See Geraldine Fibbers
Cline, Patsy **5**
Clinton, George **7**
Clivilles, Robert
See C + C Music Factory
Clooney, Rosemary **9**
Close, Bill
See Dropkick Murphys
Cloud, Jeff
See Joy Electric
Clouser, Charlie
See Prong
Coasters, The **5**
Cobain, Kurt
See Nirvana
Cobham, Billy
See Mahavishnu Orchestra
Cochran, Bobby
See Steppenwolf

Cochrane, Tom **23**
Cockburn, Bruce **8**
Cocker, Jarvis
See Pulp
Cocker, Joe **4**
Cocking, William "Willigan"
See Mystic Revealers
Coco the Electronic Monkey Wizard
See Man or Astroman?
Cocteau Twins, The **12**
Codenys, Patrick
See Front 242
Codling, Neil
See Suede
Cody, John
See Ray Condo and His Ricochets
Coe, David Allan **4**
Coffey, Jeff
See Butthole Surfers
Coffey, Jr., Don
See Superdrag
Coffie, Calton
See Inner Circle
Cohen, Jeremy
See Turtle Island String Quartet
Cohen, Leonard **3**
Cohen, Porky
See Roomful of Blues
Colaiuta, Vinnie **23**
Colbourn, Chris
See Buffalo Tom
Cole, David
See C + C Music Factory
Cole, Holly **18**
Cole, Lloyd **9**
Cole, Nat King **3**
Cole, Natalie **21**
Earlier sketch in CM **1**
Cole, Paula **20**
Cole, Ralph
See Nylons, The
Coleman, Helen
See Sweet Honey in the Rock
Coleman, Kevin
See Smash Mouth
Coleman, Michael
See Seldom Scene, The
Coleman, Ornette **5**
Coles, Dennis "Ghostface Killer"
See Wu-Tang Clan
Collective Soul **16**
Collen, Phil
See Def Leppard
Colletti, Dominic
See Bevis Frond
Colley, Dana
See Morphine
Collie, Mark **15**
Collingwood, Chris
See Fountains of Wayne
Collins, Albert **19**
Earlier sketch in CM **4**
Collins, Allen
See Lynyrd Skynyrd
Collins, Bootsy **8**
Collins, Chris
See Dream Theater
Collins, Judy **4**
Collins, Mark
See Charlatans, The
Collins, Mel
See Camel
See King Crimson
Collins, Phil **20**
Earlier sketch in CM **2**
Also see Genesis
Collins, Rob
See Charlatans, The
Collins, William
See Collins, Bootsy
Colomby, Bobby
See Blood, Sweat and Tears
Color Me Badd **23**
Colt, Johnny
See Black Crowes, The
Coltrane, John **4**
Colvin, Shawn **11**
Colwell, David
See Bad Company
Combs, Sean "Puffy" **25**
Earlier sketch in CM **16**
Comess, Aaron
See Spin Doctors
Commodores, The **23**
Common **23**
Como, Perry **14**
Compulsion **23**
Condo, Ray
See Ray Condo and His Ricochets
Confederate Railroad **23**
Congo Norvell **22**
Conneff, Kevin
See Chieftains, The
Connelly, Chris
See KMFDM
See Pigface
Conner, Gary Lee
See Screaming Trees
Conner, Van
See Screaming Trees
Connick, Harry, Jr. **4**
Connolly, Pat
See Surfaris, The
Connors, Marc
See Nylons, The
Conti, Neil
See Prefab Sprout
Conway, Billy
See Morphine
Conway, Gerry
See Pentangle
Cooder, Ry **2**
Also see Captain Beefheart and His Magic Band
Cook, David Kyle
See Matchbox 20
Cook, Greg
See Ricochet
Cook, Jeffrey Alan
See Alabama
Cook, Paul
See Sex Pistols, The
Cook, Stuart
See Creedence Clearwater Revival
Cook, Wayne
See Steppenwolf
Cooke, Sam **1**
Also see Soul Stirrers, The
Cool, Tre
See Green Day
Cooley, Dave
See Citizen King
Coolio **19**
Coomes, Sam
See Quasi
Cooney, Rory **6**
Cooper, Alice **8**
Cooper, Jason
See Cure, The
Cooper, Martin
See Orchestral Manoeuvres in the Dark
Cooper, Michael
See Third World
Cooper, Paul
See Nylons, The
Cooper, Ralph
See Air Supply
Coore, Stephen
See Third World
Cope, Julian **16**
Copeland, Stewart **14**
Also see Police, The
Copland, Aaron **2**
Copley, Al
See Roomful of Blues
Corea, Chick **6**
Corella, Doug
See Verve Pipe, The
Corgan, Billy
See Smashing Pumpkins
Corina, Sarah
See Mekons, The
Cornelius, Robert
See Poi Dog Pondering
Cornell, Chris
See Soundgarden
Cornershop **24**
Cornick, Glenn
See Jethro Tull
Corrigan, Brianna
See Beautiful South
Cosper, Kina
See Brownstone
Costello, Elvis **12**
Earlier sketch in CM **2**
Coté, Billy
See Madder Rose
Cotoia, Robert
See Beaver Brown Band, The
Cotrubas, Ileana **1**
Cotten, Elizabeth **16**
Cotton, Caré
See Sounds of Blackness
Cotton, Jeff "Antennae Jimmy Siemens"
See Captain Beefheart and His Magic Band
Cougar, John(ny)
See Mellencamp, John
Coughlan, Richard
See Caravan
Counting Crows **18**
Country Gentlemen, The **7**
Coury, Fred
See Cinderella
Coutts, Duncan
See Our Lady Peace
Coverdale, David
See Whitesnake **5**
Cowan, John
See New Grass Revival, The
Cowboy Junkies, The **4**
Cox, Andy
See English Beat, The
Also see Fine Young Cannibals
Cox, Terry
See Pentangle
Coxon, Graham
See Blur
Coyne, Mark
See Flaming Lips
Coyne, Wayne
See Flaming Lips
Crack, Carl
See Atari Teenage Riot
Cracker **12**
Craig, Albert
See Israel Vibration

Craig, Carl **19**
Crain, S. R.
See Soul Stirrers, The
Cramps, The **16**
Cranberries, The **14**
Craney, Mark
See Jethro Tull
Crash Test Dummies **14**
Crawford, Dave Max
See Poi Dog Pondering
Crawford, Ed
See fIREHOSE
Crawford, Michael **4**
Crawford, Randy **25**
Crawford, Steve
See Anointed
Crawford-Greathouse, Da'dra
See Anointed
Cray, Robert **27**
Cray, Robert **8**
Creach, Papa John
See Jefferson Starship
Creager, Melora
See Rasputina
Cream **9**
Creedence Clearwater Revival **16**
Creegan, Andrew
See Barenaked Ladies
Creegan, Jim
See Barenaked Ladies
Crenshaw, Marshall **5**
Cretu, Michael
See Enigma
Criss, Peter
See Kiss,
Crissinger, Roger
See Pearls Before Swine
Croce, Jim **3**
Crofts, Dash
See Seals & Crofts
Cronin, Kevin
See REO Speedwagon
Cropper, Steve **12**
Also see Booker T. & the M.G.'s
Crosby, Bing **6**
Crosby, David **3**
Also see Byrds, The
Also see Crosby, Stills, and Nash
Crosby, Stills, and Nash **24**
Cross, Bridget
See Velocity Girl
Cross, David
See King Crimson
Cross, Mike
See Sponge
Cross, Tim
See Sponge
Crouch, Andraé **9**
Crover, Dale
See Melvins
Crow, Sheryl **18**
Crowded House **12**
Crowe, J. D. **5**
Crowell, Rodney **8**
Crowley, Martin
See Bevis Frond
Cruikshank, Gregory
See Tuxedomoon
Cruz, Celia **22**
Earlier sketch in CM **10**
Cuddy, Jim
See Blue Rodeo
Cuffee, Ed
See McKinney's Cotton Pickers
Cugat, Xavier **23**
Culp, Dennis
See Five Iron Frenzy
Cult, The **16**
Cumming, Graham
See Bevis Frond
Cummings, Burton
See Guess Who
Cummings, Danny
See Dire Straits
Cummings, David
See Del Amitri
Cummings, John
See Mogwai
Cunniff, Jill
See Luscious Jackson
Cunningham, Abe
See Deftones
Cunningham, Ruth
See Anonymous 4
Cuomo, Rivers
See Weezer
Cure, The **20**
Earlier sketch in CM **3**
Curl, Langston
See McKinney's Cotton Pickers
Curless, Ann
See Exposé
Curley, John
See Afghan Whigs
Curran, Ciaran
See Altan
Currie, Justin
See Del Amitri
Currie, Kevin
See Supertramp
Currie, Steve
See T. Rex
Curry, Tim **3**
Curtis, Ian
See Joy Division
Curtis, King **17**
Curve **13**
Custance, Mickey
See Big Audio Dynamite
Cuthbert, Scott
See Everclear
Cutler, Chris
See Pere Ubu
Cypress Hill **11**
Cyrus, Billy Ray **11**
D Generation **26**
D.J. Lethal
See House of Pain
D.J. Minutemix
See P.M. Dawn
D'Amour, Paul
See Tool
D'Angelo **20**
D'Angelo, Greg
See Anthrax
D'Arby, Terence Trent **3**
Dachert, Peter
See Tuxedomoon
Dacus, Donnie
See Chicago
Dacus, Johnny
See Osborne Brothers, The
Daddy G
See Massive Attack
Daddy Mack
See Kris Kross
Daellenbach, Charles
See Canadian Brass, The
Dahlheimer, Patrick
See Live
Daisley, Bob
See Black Sabbath
Dale, Dick **13**
Daley, Richard
See Third World
Dall, Bobby
See Poison
Dallin, Sarah
See Bananarama
Dalton, John
See Kinks, The
Dalton, Nic
See Lemonheads, The
Daltrey, Roger **3**
Also see Who, The
Damiani, Victor
See Cake
Dammers, Jerry
See Specials, The
Damon and Naomi **25**
Dando, Evan
See Lemonheads, The
Dandy Warhols **22**
Danell, Dennis
See Social Distortion
Danell, Dennis
See Social Distortion
Daniels, Charlie **6**
Daniels, Jack
See Highway 101
Daniels, Jerry
See Ink Spots
Danko, Rick
See Band, The
Danny Boy
See House of Pain
Danzig **7**
Danzig, Glenn
See Danzig
Darin, Bobby **4**
Darling, Eric
See Weavers, The
Darriau, Matt
See Klezmatics, The
Darvill, Benjamin
See Crash Test Dummies
Das EFX **14**
Daugherty, Jay Dee
See Waterboys, The
Daugherty, Jay Dee
See Church, The
Daulne, Marie
See Zap Mama
Dave Clark Five, The **12**
Dave, Doggy
See Lords of Acid
Dave Matthews Band **18**
Davenport, N'Dea
See Brand New Heavies, The
Davidson, Lenny
See Dave Clark Five, The
Davie, Hutch
See Pearls Before Swine
Davies, Dave
See Kinks, The
Davies, Dennis Russell **24**
Davies, James
See Jimmie's Chicken Shack
Davies, Ray **5**
Also see Kinks, The
Davies, Richard
See Supertramp

Davies, Saul
See James
Davis, Anthony **17**
Davis, Brad
See Fu Manchu
Davis, Chip **4**
Davis, Clive **14**
Davis, Colin **27**
Davis, Gregory
See Dirty Dozen Brass Band
Davis, Jody
See Newsboys, The
Davis, John
See Superdrag
Davis, Jonathan
See Korn
Davis, Linda **21**
Davis, Michael
See MC5, The
Davis, Miles **1**
Davis, Reverend Gary **18**
Davis, Sammy, Jr. **4**
Davis, Santa
See Big Mountain
Davis, Skeeter **15**
Davis, Spencer
See Spencer Davis Group
Davis, Steve
See Mystic Revealers
Davis, Zelma
See C + C Music Factory
Dawdy, Cheryl
See Chenille Sisters, The
Dawn, Sandra
See Platters, The
Day, Doris **24**
Dayne, Taylor **4**
dc Talk **18**
de Albuquerque, Michael
See Electric Light Orchestra
de Burgh, Chris **22**
de Coster, Jean Paul
See 2 Unlimited
de Grassl, Alex **6**
de la Rocha, Zack
See Rage Against the Machine
de Lucia, Paco **1**
de Prume, Ivan
See White Zombie
de Young, Joyce
See Andrews Sisters, The
De Borg, Jerry
See Jesus Jones
De Gaia, Banco **27**
De La Luna, Shai
See Lords of Acid
De La Soul **7**
De Lisle, Paul
See Smash Mouth
De Meyer, Jean-Luc
See Front 242
De Oliveria, Laudir
See Chicago
Deacon, John
See Queen
Dead Can Dance **16**
Dead Milkmen **22**
Deakin, Paul
See Mavericks, The
Deal, Kelley
See Breeders
Deal, Kim
See Breeders
Also see Pixies, The
Dean, Billy **19**
DeBarge, El **14**
Dee, Mikkey
See Dokken
Also see Motörhead
Deee-lite **9**
Deep Forest **18**
Deep Purple **11**
Def Leppard **3**
Deftones **22**
DeGarmo, Chris
See Queensryche
Deibert, Adam Warren
See Aquabats, The
Deily, Ben
See Lemonheads, The
DeJohnette, Jack **7**
Del Amitri **18**
Del Mar, Candy
See Cramps, The
Del Rubio Triplets **21**
Delaet, Nathalie
See Lords of Acid
DeLeo, Dean
See Stone Temple Pilots
DeLeo, Robert
See Stone Temple Pilots
Delonge, Tom
See Blink 182
DeLorenzo, Victor
See Violent Femmes
Delp, Brad
See Boston
DeMent, Iris **13**
Demeski, Stanley
See Luna
Demos, Greg
See Guided By Voices
Dempsey, Michael
See Cure, The
Denison, Duane
See Jesus Lizard
Dennis, Garth
See Black Uhuru
Denny, Sandy
See Fairport Convention
Densmore, John
See Doors, The
Dent, Cedric
See Take 6
Denton, Sandy
See Salt-N-Pepa
Denver, John **22**
Earlier sketch in CM **1**
Depeche Mode **5**
Derakh, Amir
See Orgy
Derosier, Michael
See Heart
Des'ree **24**
Earlier sketch in CM **15**
Desaulniers, Stephen
See Scud Mountain Boys
Deschamps, Kim
See Blue Rodeo
Desert Rose Band, The **4**
Desjardins, Claude
See Nylons, The
Desmond, Paul **23**
Destri, Jimmy
See Blondie
Deupree, Jerome
See Morphine
Deutrom, Mark
See Melvins
Deutsch, Stu
See Wendy O. Williams and The Plasmatics
DeVille, C. C.
See Poison
Devito, Nick
See Four Seasons, The
Devito, Tommy
See Four Seasons, The
Devo **13**
Devoto, Howard
See Buzzcocks, The
DeWitt, Lew C.
See Statler Brothers, The
Dexter X
See Man or Astroman?
di Fiore, Vince
See Cake
Di Meola, Al **12**
Di'anno, Paul
See Iron Maiden
Diagram, Andy
See James
Diamond "Dimebag" Darrell
See Pantera
Diamond, Mike "Mike D"
See Beastie Boys, The
Diamond, Neil **1**
Diamond Rio **11**
Dibango, Manu **14**
Dick, Magic
See J. Geils Band
Dickens, Little Jimmy **7**
Dickerson, B.B.
See War
Dickinson, Paul Bruce
See Iron Maiden
Dickinson, Rob
See Catherine Wheel
Diddley, Bo **3**
Dietrich, Marlene **25**
Diffie, Joe **27**
Earlier sketch in CM **10**
Difford, Chris
See Squeeze
DiFranco, Ani **17**
Digable Planets **15**
Diggle, Steve
See Buzzcocks, The
Diggs, Robert "RZA" (Prince Rakeem)
See Gravediggaz
See Wu-Tang Clan
Digital Underground **9**
Dillon, James
See Built to Spill
Dilworth, Joe
See Stereolab
DiMant, Leor
See House of Pain
DiMucci, Dion
See Dion
DiNizo, Pat
See Smithereens, The
Dinning, Dean
See Toad the Wet Sprocket
Dinosaur Jr. **10**
Dio, Ronnie James
See Black Sabbath
Dion **4**
Dion, Celine **25**
Earlier sketch in CM **12**
Dire Straits **22**
Dirks, Michael
See Gwar
Dirnt, Mike
See Green Day

Dirty Dozen Brass Band **23**
DiSpirito, Jim
See Rusted Root
Dittrich, John
See Restless Heart
Dixie Chicks **26**
Dixon, George W.
See Spinners, The
Dixon, Jerry
See Warrant
Dixon, Willie **10**
DJ Domination
See Geto Boys, The
DJ Fuse
See Digital Underground
DJ Jazzy Jeff and the Fresh Prince **5**
DJ Muggs
See Cypress Hill
DJ Premier
See Gang Starr
DJ Ready Red
See Geto Boys, The
DJ Terminator X
See Public Enemy
DMC
See Run DMC
DMX **25**
Doc Pomus **14**
Doe, John
See X
Dog's Eye View **21**
Dogbowl
See King Missile
Doherty, Denny
See Mamas and the Papas
Dokken **16**
Dokken, Don
See Dokken
Dolby, Monica Mimi
See Brownstone
Dolby, Thomas **10**
Dolenz, Micky
See Monkees, The
Dombroski, Vinnie
See Sponge
Domingo, Placido **20**
Earlier sketch in CM **1**
Dominici, Charlie
See Dream Theater
Domino, Fats **2**
Don, Rasa
See Arrested Development
Donahue, Jerry
See Fairport Convention
Donahue, Jonathan
See Flaming Lips
Donald, Tony
See Simple Minds
Donelly, Tanya
See Belly
Also see Breeders
Also see Throwing Muses
Donohue, Tim
See Cherry Poppin' Daddies
Donovan **9**
Donovan, Bazil
See Blue Rodeo
Donovan, Jim
See Rusted Root
Doobie Brothers, The **3**
Doodlebug
See Digable Planets
Doors, The **4**
Dorge, Michel (Mitch)
See Crash Test Dummies
Dorney, Tim
See Republica
Dorough, Bob
See Pearls Before Swine
Dorough, Howie
See Backstreet Boys
Dorsey Brothers, The **8**
Dorsey, Jimmy
See Dorsey Brothers, The
Dorsey, Thomas A. **11**
Dorsey, Tommy
See Dorsey Brothers, The
Doth, Anita
See 2 Unlimited
Dott, Gerald
See Incredible String Band
Doucet, Michael **8**
Doucette, Paul John
See Matchbox 20
Doughty, M.
See Soul Coughing
Doughty, Neal
See REO Speedwagon
Douglas, Jerry
See Country Gentlemen, The
Dowd, Christopher
See Fishbone
Dowling, Dave
See Jimmie's Chicken Shack
Downes, Geoff
See Yes
Downey, Brian
See Thin Lizzy
Downie, Gordon
See Tragically Hip, The
Downing, K. K.
See Judas Priest
Doyle, Candida
See Pulp
Dozier, Lamont
See Holland-Dozier-Holland
Dr. Demento **23**
Dr. Dre **15**
Also see N.W.A.
Dr. John **7**
Dragge, Fletcher
See Pennywise
Drake, Nick **17**
Drake, Steven
See Odds
Drayton, Leslie
See Earth, Wind and Fire
Dream Theater **23**
Dreja, Chris
See Yardbirds, The
Dres
See Black Sheep
Drew, Dennis
See 10,000 Maniacs
Driftwood, Jimmy **25**
Droge, Pete **24**
Dropkick Murphys **26**
Drozd, Stephen
See Flaming Lips
Dru Hill **25**
Drumbago,
See Skatalites, The
Drumdini, Harry
See Cramps, The
Drummond, Don
See Skatalites, The
Drummond, Tom
See Better Than Ezra
Dryden, Spencer
See Jefferson Airplane
Dryer, Debroah
See Skunk Anansie
Dubbe, Berend
See Bettie Serveert
Dube, Lucky **17**
Dubstar **22**
Dudley, Anne
See Art of Noise
Duffey, John
See Country Gentlemen, The
Also see Seldom Scene, The
Duffy, Billy
See Cult, The
Duffy, Martin
See Primal Scream
Dufresne, Mark
See Confederate Railroad
Duggan, Noel
See Clannad
Duggan, Paidraig
See Clannad
Duke, John
See Pearls Before Swine
Dukowski, Chuck
See Black Flag
Dulli, Greg
See Afghan Whigs
Dumont, Tom
See No Doubt
Dunbar, Aynsley
See Jefferson Starship
Also see Journey
Also see Whitesnake
Dunbar, Sly
See Sly and Robbie
Duncan, Bryan **19**
Duncan, Gary
See Quicksilver Messenger Service
Duncan, Steve
See Desert Rose Band, The
Duncan, Stuart
See Nashville Bluegrass Band
Dunham, Nathanel "Brad"
See Five Iron Frenzy
Dunlap, Slim
See Replacements, The
Dunn, Donald "Duck"
See Booker T. & the M.G.'s
Dunn, Holly **7**
Dunn, Larry
See Earth, Wind and Fire
Dunn, Ronnie Gene
See Brooks & Dunn
Dunning, A.J.
See Verve Pipe, The
DuPré, Jacqueline **26**
Dupree, Champion Jack **12**
Dupree, Jesse James
See Jackyl
Dupri, Jermaine **25**
Duran Duran **4**
Durante, Mark
See KMFDM
Duritz, Adam
See Counting Crows
Durrill, Johnny
See Ventures, The
Durst, Fred
See Limp Bizkit
Dutt, Hank
See Kronos Quartet
Dutton, Garrett
See G. Love
Dvorak, Antonin **25**

Dyble, Judy
See Fairport Convention
Dylan, Bob **21**
Earlier sketch in CM **3**
Dylan, Jakob
See Wallflowers, The
D'Amour, Paul
See Tool
E., Sheila
See Sheila E.
Eacrett, Chris
See Our Lady Peace
Eagles, The **3**
Earl, Ronnie **5**
Also see Roomful of Blues
Earle, Steve **16**
Also see Afghan Whigs
Early, Ian
See Cherry Poppin' Daddies
Earth, Wind and Fire **12**
Easton, Elliot
See Cars, The
Easton, Sheena **2**
Eazy-E **13**
Also see N.W.A.
Echeverria, Rob
See Helmet
Echobelly **21**
Eckstine, Billy **1**
Eddy, Duane **9**
Eden, Sean
See Luna
Edge, Graeme
See Moody Blues, The
Edge, The
See U2
Edmonds, Kenneth "Babyface" **12**
Edmonton, Jerry
See Steppenwolf
Edson, Richard
See Sonic Youth
Edwards, Dennis
See Temptations, The
Edwards, Edgar
See Spinners, The
Edwards, Gordon
See Kinks, The
See Pretty Things, The
Edwards, John
See Spinners , The
Edwards, Johnny
See Foreigner
Edwards, Leroy "Lion"
See Mystic Revealers
Edwards, Mark
See Aztec Camera
Edwards, Michael James
See Jesus Jones
Edwards, Mike
See Electric Light Orchestra
Edwards, Nokie
See Ventures, The
Edwards, Skye
See Morcheeba
Efrem, Towns
See Dirty Dozen Brass Band
Ehran
See Lords of Acid
Eid, Tamer
See Emmet Swimming
Einheit, F.M.
See KMFDM
Einheit
See Einstürzende Neubauten
Einstürzende Neubauten **13**
Einziger, Michael
See Incubus
Eisenstein, Michael
See Letters to Cleo
Eitzel, Mark
See American Music Club
Ekberg, Ulf
See Ace of Base
Eklund, Greg
See Everclear
El-Hadi, Sulieman
See Last Poets
Eldon, Thór
See Sugarcubes, The
Eldridge, Ben
See Seldom Scene, The
Eldridge, Roy **9**
Also see McKinney's Cotton Pickers
Electric Light Orchestra **7**
Elfman, Danny **9**
Elias, Hanin
See Atari Teenage Riot
Elias, Manny
See Tears for Fears
Ellefson, Dave
See Megadeth
Ellington, Duke **2**
Elliot, Cass **5**
Also see Mamas and the Papas
Elliott, Dennis
See Foreigner
Elliott, Doug
See Odds
Elliott, Joe
See Def Leppard
Ellis, Art
See Pearls Before Swine
Ellis, Bobby
See Skatalites, The
Ellis, Herb **18**
Ellis, Ingrid
See Sweet Honey in the Rock
Ellis, Terry
See En Vogue
Ellison, Rahsaan
See Oakland Interfaith Gospel Choir
Elmore, Greg
See Quicksilver Messenger Service
ELO
See Electric Light Orchestra
Ely, John
See Asleep at the Wheel
Ely, Vince
See Cure, The
Also see Psycedelic Furs
Emerson, Bill
See Country Gentlemen, The
Emerson, Darren
See Underworld
Emerson, Keith
See Emerson, Lake & Palmer/Powell
Emerson, Lake & Palmer/Powell **5**
Emery, Jill
See Hole
Emmanuel, Tommy **21**
Emmet Swimming **24**
Empire, Alec
See Atari Teenage Riot
En Vogue **10**
Endo, Nic
See Atari Teenage Riot
English Beat, The **9**
English, Michael **23**
English, Richard
See Flaming Lips
Enigma **14**
Eno, Brian **8**
Enos, Bob
See Roomful of Blues
Enright, Pat
See Nashville Bluegrass Band
Entwistle, John
See Who, The
Enya **6**
Also see Clannad
EPMD **10**
Epstein, Howie
See Tom Petty and the Heartbreakers
Erasure **11**
Eric B.
See Eric B. and Rakim
Eric B. and Rakim **9**
Erickson, Roky **16**
Erikson, Duke
See Garbage
Erlandson, Eric
See Hole
Erner, Jeff "The Shark"
See Dropkick Murphys
Errico, Greg
See Sly & the Family Stone
Also see Quicksilver Messenger Service
Erskine, Peter
See Weather Report
Ertegun, Ahmet **10**
Ertegun, Nesuhi **24**
Erwin, Emily
See Dixie Chicks
Esch, En
See KMFDM
Also see Pigface
Escovedo, Alejandro **18**
Eshe, Montsho
See Arrested Development
Eskelin, Ian **19**
Esler-Smith, Frank
See Air Supply
Esquivel, Juan **17**
Estefan, Gloria **15**
Earlier sketch in CM **2**
Estes, Sleepy John **25**
Estrada, Roy
See Little Feat
Also see Captain Beefheart and His Magic Band
Etheridge, Melissa **16**
Earlier sketch in CM **4**
Eurythmics **6**
Evan, John
See Jethro Tull
Evans, Bill **17**
Evans, Dick
See U2
Evans, Faith **25**
Evans, Gil **17**
Evans, Mark
See AC/DC
Evans, Sara **27**
Evans, Shane
See Collective Soul
Evans, Tom
See Badfinger
Everclear **18**
Everlast **27**
Also see House of Pain
Everly Brothers, The **2**
Everly, Don
See Everly Brothers, The

Everly, Phil
See Everly Brothers, The
Everman, Jason
See Soundgarden
Everything But The Girl **15**
Evora, Cesaria **19**
Ewen, Alvin
See Steel Pulse
Exkano, Paul
See Five Blind Boys of Alabama
Exposé **4**
Extreme **10**
Ezell, Ralph
See Shenandoah
Fabian **5**
Fabulous Thunderbirds, The **1**
Faces, The **22**
Fadden, Jimmie
See Nitty Gritty Dirt Band, The
Fagan, Don
See Steely Dan
Fahey, John **17**
Fahey, Siobhan
See Bananarama
Fairport Convention **22**
Fairs, Jim
See Pearls Before Swine
Faith No More **7**
Faithfull, Marianne **14**
Fakir, Abdul "Duke"
See Four Tops, The
Falconer, Earl
See UB40
Fall, The **12**
Fallon, David
See Chieftains, The
Fältskog, Agnetha
See Abba
Fambrough, Henry
See Spinners, The
Fame, Georgie
See Bill Wyman & the Rhythm Kings
Fankhauser, Merrell **24**
Farley, J. J.
See Soul Stirrers, The
Farndon, Pete
See Pretenders, The
Farrar, Jay
See Son Volt
Farrar, John
See Shadows, The
Farrell, Frank
See Supertramp
Farrell, Perry
See Jane's Addiction
Farris, Dionne
See Arrested Development
Farris, Tim
See Israel Vibration
Farriss, Andrew
See INXS
Farriss, Jon
See INXS
Farriss, Tim
See INXS
Fast
See Fun Lovin' Criminals
Fatboy Slim **22**
Fatone, Joey
See 'N Sync
Fay, Bob
See Sebadoh
Fay, Johnny
See Tragically Hip, The
Fay, Martin
See Chieftains, The
Fear Factory **27**
Fearnley, James
See Pogues, The
Fehlmann, Thomas
See Orb, The
Feinstein, Michael **6**
Fela
See Kuti, Fela
Felber, Dean
See Hootie and the Blowfish
Felder, Don
See Eagles, The
Feldman, Eric Drew
See Pere Ubu
Also see Captain Beefheart and His Magic Band
Feliciano, José **10**
Fender, Freddy
See Texas Tornados, The
Fender, Leo **10**
Fennell, Kevin
See Guided By Voices
Fennelly, Gere
See Redd Kross
Fenwick, Ray
See Spencer Davis Group
Ferguson, Doug
See Camel
Ferguson, Jay
See Spirit
Ferguson, Keith
See Fabulous Thunderbirds, The
Ferguson, Maynard **7**
Ferguson, Neil
See Chumbawamba
Ferguson, Steve
See NRBQ
Ferrell, Rachelle **17**
Ferrer, Frank
See Love Spit Love
Ferry, Bryan **1**
Ficca, Billy
See Television
Fiedler, Arthur **6**
Fielder, Jim
See Blood, Sweat and Tears
Fields, Johnny
See Five Blind Boys of Alabama
Fieldy
See Korn
Fier, Anton
See Pere Ubu
Finch, Jennifer
See L7
Fine Young Cannibals **22**
Finer, Jem
See Pogues, The
Fink, Jr., Rat
See Alien Sex Fiend
Finn, Micky
See T. Rex
Finn, Neil
See Crowded House
Finn, Tim
See Crowded House
fIREHOSE **11**
Fishbone **7**
Fisher, Brandon
See Superdrag
Fisher, Eddie **12**
Fisher, Jerry
See Blood, Sweat and Tears
Fisher, John "Norwood"
See Fishbone
Fisher, Phillip "Fish"
See Fishbone
Fisher, Roger
See Heart
Fishman, Jon
See Phish
Fitzgerald, Ella **1**
Fitzgerald, Kevin
See Geraldine Fibbers
Five Blind Boys of Alabama **12**
Five Iron Frenzy **26**
Flack, Roberta **5**
Flaming Lips **22**
Flanagan, Tommy **16**
Flannery, Sean
See Cherry Poppin' Daddies
Flansburgh, John
See They Might Be Giants
Flatt, Lester **3**
Flavor Flav
See Public Enemy
Flea
See Red Hot Chili Peppers, The
Fleck, Bela **8**
Also see New Grass Revival, The
Fleetwood Mac **5**
Fleetwood, Mick
See Fleetwood Mac
Fleischmann, Robert
See Journey
Fleming, Renee **24**
Flemons, Wade
See Earth, Wind and Fire
Flesh-N-Bone
See Bone Thugs-N-Harmony
Fletcher, Andy
See Depeche Mode
Fletcher, Guy
See Dire Straits
Flint, Keith
See Prodigy
Flores, Rosie **16**
Floyd, Heather
See Point of Grace
Flür, Wolfgang
See Kraftwerk
Flynn, Pat
See New Grass Revival, The
Fogelberg, Dan **4**
Fogerty, John **2**
Also see Creedence Clearwater Revival
Fogerty, Thomas
See Creedence Clearwater Revival
Folds, Ben
See Ben Folds Five
Foley
See Arrested Development
Foo Fighters **20**
Forbes, Derek
See Simple Minds
Forbes, Graham
See Incredible String Band
Ford, Frankie
See Pretty Things, The
Ford, Lita **9**
Ford, Marc
See Black Crowes, The
Ford, Penny
See Soul II Soul
Ford, Robert "Peg"
See Golden Gate Quartet
Ford, Tennessee Ernie **3**

Fordham, Julia **15**
Foreigner **21**
Foreman, Chris
 See Madness
Forrester, Alan
 See Mojave 3
Forsi, Ken
 See Surfaris, The
Forte, Juan
 See Oakland Interfaith Gospel Choir
Fortune, Jimmy
 See Statler Brothers, The
Fortus, Richard
 See Love Spit Love
Fossen, Steve
 See Heart
Foster, David **13**
Foster, Malcolm
 See Pretenders, The
Foster, Paul
 See Soul Stirrers, The
Foster, Radney **16**
Fountain, Clarence
 See Five Blind Boys of Alabama
Fountain, Pete **7**
Fountains of Wayne **26**
Four Seasons, The **24**
Four Tops, The **11**
FourHim **23**
Fowler, Bruce "Fossil Fowler"
 See Captain Beefheart and His Magic Band
Fox, Lucas
 See Motörhead
Fox, Oz
 See Stryper
Fox, Samantha **3**
Foxton, Bruce
 See Jam, The
Foxwell Baker, Iain Richard
 See Jesus Jones
Foxx, Leigh
 See Blondie
Frame, Roddy
 See Aztec Camera
Frampton, Peter **3**
Francis, Black
 See Pixies, The
Francis, Connie **10**
Francis, Mike
 See Asleep at the Wheel
Franke, Chris
 See Tangerine Dream
Frankenstein, Jeff
 See Newsboys, The
Frankie Lymon and The Teenagers **24**
Franklin, Aretha **17**
 Earlier sketch in CM **2**
Franklin, Elmo
 See Mighty Clouds of Joy, The
Franklin, Kirk **22**
Franklin, Larry
 See Asleep at the Wheel
Franklin, Melvin
 See Temptations, The
Franti, Michael **16**
 Also see Spearhead
Frantz, Chris
 See Talking Heads
Fraser, Elizabeth
 See Cocteau Twins, The
Frater, Shaun
 See Fairport Convention
Frazier, Stan
 See Sugar Ray
Fredriksson, Marie
 See Roxette
Freese, Josh
 See Suicidal Tendencies
Frehley, Ace
 See Kiss
Freiberg, David
 See Quicksilver Messenger Service
 Also see Jefferson Starship
French, Frank
 See Cake
French, John "Drumbo"
 See Captain Beefheart and His Magic Band
French, Mark
 See Blue Rodeo
Freni, Mirella **14**
Freshwater, John
 See Alien Sex Fiend
Frey, Glenn **3**
 Also see Eagles, The
Fricker, Sylvia
 See Ian and Sylvia
Friedman, Marty
 See Megadeth
Friel, Tony
 See Fall, The
Fripp, Robert **9**
 Also see King Crimson
Frisell, Bill **15**
Frishmann, Justine
 See Suede
Frith, Fred **19**
Frizzell, Lefty **10**
Froese, Edgar
 See Tangerine Dream
Front 242 **19**
Front Line Assembly **20**
Froom, Mitchell **15**
Frusciante, John
 See Red Hot Chili Peppers, The
Fu Manchu **22**
Fuel **27**
Fugazi **13**
Fugees, The **17**
Fulber, Rhys
 See Front Line Assembly
Fuller, Blind Boy **20**
Fuller, Craig
 See Little Feat
Fuller, Jim
 See Surfaris, The
Fulson, Lowell **20**
Fun Lovin' Criminals **20**
Funahara, O. Chosei
 See Wendy O. Williams and The Plasmatics
Fuqua, Charlie
 See Ink Spots
Furay, Richie
 See Buffalo Springfield
Furler, Peter
 See Newsboys, The
Furr, John
 See Treadmill Trackstar
Furuholmen, Magne
 See A-ha
Futter, Brian
 See Catherine Wheel
G. Love **24**
Gabay, Yuval
 See Soul Coughing
Gabler, Milton **25**
Gabriel, Peter **16**
 Earlier sketch in CM **2**
 Also see Genesis
Gadler, Frank
 See NRBQ
Gaffney, Eric
 See Sebadoh
Gagliardi, Ed
 See Foreigner
Gahan, Dave
 See Depeche Mode
Gaines, Steve
 See Lynyrd Skynyrd
Gaines, Timothy
 See Stryper
Galás, Diamanda **16**
Gale, Melvyn
 See Electric Light Orchestra
Galea, Darren
 See Jamiroquai
Gallagher, Liam
 See Oasis
Gallagher, Noel
 See Oasis
Gallup, Simon
 See Cure, The
Galore, Lady
 See Lords of Acid
Galway, James **3**
Gambill, Roger
 See Kingston Trio, The
Gamble, Cheryl "Coko"
 See SWV
Gane, Tim
 See Stereolab
Gang of Four **8**
Gang Starr **13**
Gannon, Craig
 See Aztec Camera
Gano, Gordon
 See Violent Femmes
Garbage **25**
Garcia, Dean
 See Curve
Garcia, Jerry **4**
 Also see Grateful Dead, The
Garcia, Leddie
 See Poi Dog Pondering
Gardiner, John Eliot **26**
Gardner, Carl
 See Coasters, The
Gardner, Suzi
 See L7
Garfunkel, Art **4**
 Also see Simon and Garfunkel
Garland, Judy **6**
Garner, Erroll **25**
Garnes, Sherman
 See Frankie Lymon and The Teenagers
Garrett, Amos
 See Pearls Before Swine
Garrett, Peter
 See Midnight Oil
Garrett, Scott
 See Cult, The
Garvey, Steve
 See Buzzcocks, The
Gaskill, Jerry
 See King's X
Gates, Jimmy Jr.
 See Silk
Gatton, Danny **16**
Gaudio, Bob
 See Four Seasons, The
Gaudreau, Jimmy
 See Country Gentlemen, The
Gaugh, "Bud" Floyd, IV
 See Sublime

Gavurin, David
See Sundays, The
Gay, Marc
See Shai
Gayden, Mac
See Pearls Before Swine
Gaye, Marvin **4**
Gayle, Crystal **1**
Gaynor, Adam
See Matchbox 20
Gaynor, Mel
See Simple Minds
Gayol, Rafael "Danny"
See BoDeans
Geary, Paul
See Extreme
Gee, Rosco
See Traffic
Geffen, David **8**
Geils, J.
See J. Geils Band
Geldof, Bob **9**
Gene Loves Jezebel **27**
Genensky, Marsha
See Anonymous 4
Genesis **4**
Gentling, Matt
See Archers of Loaf
Gentry, Teddy Wayne
See Alabama
George, Lowell
See Little Feat
George, Rocky
See Suicidal Tendencies
Georges, Bernard
See Throwing Muses
Georgiev, Ivan
See Tuxedomoon
Geraldine Fibbers **21**
Germano, Lisa **18**
Gerrard, Lisa
See Dead Can Dance
Gershwin, George and Ira **11**
Gessle, Per
See Roxette
Geto Boys, The **11**
Getz, Stan **12**
Ghost **24**
Giammalvo, Chris
See Madder Rose
Gianni, Angelo
See Treadmill Trackstar
Gibb, Barry
See Bee Gees, The
Gibb, Maurice
See Bee Gees, The
Gibb, Robin
See Bee Gees, The
Gibbins, Mike
See Badfinger
Gibbons, Beth
See Portishead
Gibbons, Billy
See ZZ Top
Gibbons, Ian
See Kinks, The
Giblin, John
See Simple Minds
Gibson, Bob **23**
Gibson, Debbie
See Gibson, Deborah
Gibson, Deborah **24**
Earlier sketch in CM **1**
Gibson, Wilf
Gifford, Alex
See Propellerheads
See Electric Light Orchestra
Gifford, Katharine
See Stereolab
Gifford, Peter
See Midnight Oil
Gift, Roland **3**
Also see Fine Young Cannibals
Gil, Gilberto **26**
Gilbert, Gillian
See New Order
Gilbert, Nicole Nicci
See Brownstone
Gilbert, Ronnie
See Weavers, The
Gilbert, Simon
See Suede
Giles, Michael
See King Crimson
Gilkyson, Tony
See X
Gill, Andy
See Gang of Four
Gill, Janis
See Sweethearts of the Rodeo
Gill, Johnny **20**
Gill, Pete
See Motörhead
Gill, Vince **7**
Gillan, Ian
See Deep Purple
Also see Black Sabbath
Gillespie, Bobby
See Jesus and Mary Chain, The
Also see Primal Scream
Gillespie, Dizzy **6**
Gilley, Mickey **7**
Gillian, Ian
See Black Sabbath
Gillies, Ben
See Silverchair
Gillingham, Charles
See Counting Crows
Gilmore, Jimmie Dale **11**
Gilmour, David
See Pink Floyd
Gilvear, Marcus
See Gene Loves Jezebel
Gin Blossoms **18**
Gingold, Josef **6**
Ginn, Greg
See Black Flag
Ginsberg, Allen **26**
Gioia
See Exposé
Gipp, Cameron "Big Gipp"
See Goodie Mob
Gipsy Kings, The **8**
Giraudy, Miquitte
See Gong
Gittleman, Joe
See Mighty Mighty Bosstones
Glabicki, Michael
See Rusted Root
Glascock, John
See Jethro Tull
Glaser, Gabby
See Luscious Jackson
Glass, Eddie
See Fu Manchu
Glass, Philip **1**
Glasscock, John
See Jethro Tull
Glenn, Gary
See Silk
Glennie, Jim
See James
Glitter, Gary **19**
Glover, Corey
See Living Colour
Glover, Roger
See Deep Purple
Go-Go's, The **24**
Gobel, Robert
See Kool & the Gang
Godchaux, Donna
See Grateful Dead, The
Godchaux, Keith
See Grateful Dead, The
Godfrey, Paul
See Morcheeba
Godfrey, Ross
See Morcheeba
Goettel, Dwayne Rudolf
See Skinny Puppy
Goffin, Gerry
See Goffin-King
Goffin-King **24**
Gogin, Toni
See Sleater-Kinney
Goh, Rex
See Air Supply
Gold, Julie **22**
Golden Gate Quartet **25**
Golden, William Lee
See Oak Ridge Boys, The
Golding, Lynval
See Specials, The
Goldsmith, William
See Foo Fighters
Goldstein, Jerry
See War
Golson, Benny **21**
Gong **24**
Goo Goo Dolls, The **16**
Gooden, Ramone Pee Wee
See Digital Underground
Goodie Mob **24**
Goodman, Benny **4**
Goodman, Jerry
See Mahavishnu Orchestra
Goodridge, Robin
See Bush
Gordon, Dexter **10**
Gordon, Dwight
See Mighty Clouds of Joy, The
Gordon, Jay
See Orgy
Gordon, Jim
See Traffic
Gordon, Kim
See Sonic Youth
Gordon, Mike
See Phish
Gordon, Nina
See Veruca Salt
Gordy, Berry, Jr. **6**
Gordy, Emory, Jr. **17**
Gore, Martin
See Depeche Mode
Gorham, Scott
See Thin Lizzy
Gorka, John **18**
Gorman, Christopher
See Belly
Gorman, Steve
See Black Crowes, The

Gorman, Thomas
See Belly
Gosling, John
See Kinks, The
Gossard, Stone
See Brad
Also see Pearl Jam
Goswell, Rachel
See Mojave 3
Gott, Larry
See James
Goudreau, Barry
See Boston
Gould, Billy
See Faith No More
Gould, Glenn **9**
Gould, Morton **16**
Goulding, Steve
See Gene Loves Jezebel
See Poi Dog Pondering
Grable, Steve
See Pearls Before Swine
Gracey, Chad
See Live
Gradney, Ken
See Little Feat
Graffety-Smith, Toby
See Jamiroquai
Graham, Bill **10**
Graham, Glen
See Blind Melon
Graham, Johnny
See Earth, Wind and Fire
Graham, Larry
See Sly & the Family Stone
Gramm, Lou
See Foreigner
Gramolini, Gary
See Beaver Brown Band, The
Grandmaster Flash **14**
Grant, Amy **7**
Grant, Bob
See The Bad Livers
Grant Lee Buffalo **16**
Grant, Lloyd
See Metallica
Grappelli, Stephane **10**
Grateful Dead, The **5**
Gratzer, Alan
See REO Speedwagon
Gravatt, Eric
See Weather Report
Gravediggaz **23**
Graves, Denyce **16**
Gray, David
See Spearhead
Gray, Del
See Little Texas
Gray, Ella
See Kronos Quartet
Gray, F. Gary **19**
Gray, James
See Blue Rodeo
Gray, James
See Spearhead
Gray, Luther
See Tsunami
Gray, Tom
See Country Gentlemen, The
Also see Seldom Scene, The
Gray, Walter
See Kronos Quartet
Gray, Wardell
See McKinney's Cotton Pickers
Greater Vision **26**
Grebenshikov, Boris **3**
Grech, Rick
See Traffic
Greco, Paul
See Chumbawamba
Green, Al **9**
Green, Benny **17**
Green, Carlito "Cee-lo"
See Goodie Mob
Green, Charles
See War
Green, David
See Air Supply
Green Day **16**
Green, Grant **14**
Green, James
See Dru Hill
Green, Peter
See Fleetwood Mac
Green, Susaye
See Supremes, The
Green, Willie
See Neville Brothers, The
Greene, Karl Anthony
See Herman's Hermits
Greenhalgh, Tom
See Mekons, The
Greensmith, Domenic
See Reef
Greenspoon, Jimmy
See Three Dog Night
Greentree, Richard
See Beta Band, The
Greenwood, Al
See Foreigner
Greenwood, Colin
See Radiohead
Greenwood, Gail
See Belly
Greenwood, Jonny
See Radiohead
Greenwood, Lee **12**
Greenwood,Colin
See Radiohead
Greer, Jim
See Guided By Voices
Gregg, Paul
See Restless Heart
Gregory, Bryan
See Cramps, The
Gregory, Dave
See XTC
Gregory, Troy
See Prong
Greller, Al
See Yo La Tengo
Grey, Charles Wallace
See Aquabats, The
Grice, Gary "The Genius"
See Wu-Tang Clan
Griffin, A.C. "Eddie"
See Golden Gate Quartet
Griffin, Bob
See BoDeans, The
Griffin, Kevin
See Better Than Ezra
See NRBQ
Griffin, Mark
See MC 900 Ft. Jesus
Griffin, Patty **24**
Griffin, Rodney
See Greater Vision
Griffith, Nanci **3**
Grigg, Chris
See Treadmill Trackstar
Grisman, David **17**
Grohl, Dave
See Nirvana
Also see Foo Fighters
Grotberg, Karen
See Jayhawks, The
Groucutt, Kelly
See Electric Light Orchestra
Grove, George
See Kingston Trio, The
Grover, Charlie
See Sponge
Grundy, Hugh
See Zombies, The
Grusin, Dave **7**
Guaraldi, Vince **3**
Guard, Dave
See Kingston Trio, The
Gudmundsdottir, Björk
See Björk
Also see Sugarcubes, The
Guerin, John
See Byrds, The
Guess Who **23**
Guest, Christopher
See Spinal Tap
Guided By Voices **18**
Gunn, Trey
See King Crimson
Guns n' Roses **2**
Gunther, Cornell
See Coasters, The
Gunther, Ric
See Bevis Frond
Guru
See Gang Starr
Gus Gus **26**
Guss, Randy
See Toad the Wet Sprocket
Gustafson, Steve
See 10,000 Maniacs
Gut, Grudrun
See Einstürzende Neubauten
Guthrie, Arlo **6**
Guthrie, Gwen **26**
Guthrie, Robin
See Cocteau Twins, The
Guthrie, Woody **2**
Guy, Billy
See Coasters, The
Guy, Buddy **4**
Guyett, Jim
See Quicksilver Messenger Service
Gwar **13**
H.R.
See Bad Brains
Hacke, Alexander
See Einstürzende Neubauten
Hackett, Bobby **21**
Hackett, Steve
See Genesis
Haden, Charlie **12**
Hadjopulos, Sue
See Simple Minds
Hagar, Regan
See Brad
Hagar, Sammy **21**
Also see Van Halen
Hagen, Nina **25**
Haggard, Merle **2**
HaHa, Jimi
See Jimmie's Chicken Shack

Hakim, Omar
See Weather Report
Hakmoun, Hassan **15**
Hale, Simon
See Incognito
Haley, Bill **6**
Haley, Mark
See Kinks, The
Haley, Paige
See Orgy
Halford, Rob
See Judas Priest
Hall & Oates **6**
Hall, Bruce
See REO Speedwagon
Hall, Daryl
See Hall & Oates
Hall, John S.
See King Missile
Hall, Lance
See Inner Circle
Hall, Randall
See Lynyrd Skynyrd
Hall, Terry
See Specials, The
Hall, Tom T. **26**
Earlier sketch in CM **4**
Hall, Tony
See Neville Brothers, The
Halliday, Toni
See Curve
Halliwell, Geri
See Spice Girls
Halstead, Neil
See Mojave 3
Ham, Pete
See Badfinger
Hamer, Harry
See Chumbawamba
Hamilton, Arnold (Frukwan da Gatekeeper)
See Gravediggaz
Hamilton, Frank
See Weavers, The
Hamilton, Katie
See Treadmill Trackstar
Hamilton, Milton
See Third World
Hamilton, Page
See Helmet
Hamilton, Tom
See Aerosmith
Hamlisch, Marvin **1**
Hammer, Jan **21**
Also see Mahavishnu Orchestra
Hammer, M.C. **5**
Hammerstein, Oscar
See Rodgers, Richard
Hammett, Kirk
See Metallica
Hammon, Ron
See War
Hammond, John **6**
Hammond-Hammond, Jeffrey
See Jethro Tull
Hampson, Sharon
See Sharon, Lois & Bram
Hampson, Thomas **12**
Hampton, Lionel **6**
Hancock, Herbie **25**
Earlier sketch in CM **8**
Handley, Jerry
See Captain Beefheart and His Magic Band
Handy, W. C. **7**
Hanley, Kay
See Letters to Cleo
Hanley, Steve
See Fall, The
Hanna, Jeff
See Nitty Gritty Dirt Band, The
Hannan, Patrick
See Sundays, The
Hanneman, Jeff
See Slayer
Hannibal, Chauncey "Black"
See Blackstreet
Hannon, Frank
See Tesla
Hansen, Mary
See Stereolab
Hanson **20**
Hanson, Isaac
See Hanson
Hanson, Paul (Prince Paul A.K.A. Dr. Strange)
See Gravediggaz
Hanson, Taylor
See Hanson
Hanson, Zachary
See Hanson
Hardcastle, Paul **20**
Hardin, Eddie
See Spencer Davis Group
Hardin, Geraldine
See Sweet Honey in the Rock
Hardin, Tim **18**
Harding, John Wesley **6**
Hardson, Tre "Slimkid"
See Pharcyde, The
Hargreaves, Brad
See Third Eye Blind
Hargrove, Kornell
See Poi Dog Pondering
Hargrove, Roy **15**
Harkelroad, Bill "Zoot Horn Rollo"
See Captain Beefheart and His Magic Band
Harket, Morten
See A-ha
Harley, Bill **7**
Harley, Wayne
See Pearls Before Swine
Harms, Jesse
See REO Speedwagon
Harper, Ben **17**
Harper, Raymond
See Skatalites, The
Harrell, Andre **16**
Harrell, Lynn **3**
Harrington, Ayodele
See Sweet Honey in the Rock
Harrington, Carrie
See Sounds of Blackness
Harrington, David
See Kronos Quartet
Harris, Addie "Micki"
See Shirelles, The
Harris, Damon Otis
See Temptations, The
Harris, Eddie **15**
Harris, Emmylou **4**
Harris, Evelyn Maria
See Sweet Honey in the Rock
Harris, Gerard
See Kool & the Gang
Harris, James
See Echobelly
Harris, Jet
See Shadows, The
Harris, Joey
See Beat Farmers
Harris, Kevin
See Dirty Dozen Brass Band
Harris, Lee
See Talk Talk
Harris, Mark
See 4Him
Harris, Mary
See Spearhead
Harris, Nigel
See Jam, The
Harris, R. H.
See Soul Stirrers, The
Harris, Steve
See Iron Maiden
Harris, Teddy **22**
Harrison, George **2**
Also see Beatles, The
Harrison, Jerry
See Talking Heads
Harrison, Nigel
See Blondie
Harrison, Richard
See Stereolab
Harry, Deborah **4**
Also see Blondie
Hart, Alvin Youngblood **27**
Hart, Chuck
See Surfin' Pluto
Hart, Douglas
See Jesus and Mary Chain, The
Hart, Hattie
See Memphis Jug Band
Hart, Lorenz
See Rodgers, Richard
Hart, Mark
See Crowded House
Hart, Mark
See Supertramp
Hart, Mickey
See Grateful Dead, The
Hart, Robert
See Bad Company
Hart, Tim
See Steeleye Span
Hartford, John **1**
Hartke, Stephen **5**
Hartley, Matthieu
See Cure, The
Hartman, Bob
See Petra
Hartman, John
See Doobie Brothers, The
Hartnoll, Paul
See Orbital
Hartnoll, Phil
See Orbital
Harvey, Bernard "Touter"
See Inner Circle
Harvey, Philip "Daddae"
See Soul II Soul
Harvey, Polly Jean **11**
Harvie, Iain
See Del Amitri
Harwell, Steve
See Smash Mouth
Harwood, Justin
See Luna
Haseltine, Dan
See Jars of Clay
Hashian
See Boston
Haskell, Gordon
See King Crimson
Haskins, Kevin
See Bauhaus
See Love and Rockets

Haslinger, Paul
See Tangerine Dream
Hassan, Norman
See UB40
Hassman, Nikki
See Avalon
Hastings, Jimmy
See Caravan
Hastings, Pye
See Caravan
Hatfield, Juliana **12**
Also see Lemonheads, The
Hauser, Tim
See Manhattan Transfer, The
Havens, Richie **11**
Hawes, Dave
See Catherine Wheel
Hawkes, Greg
See Cars, The
Hawkins, Coleman **11**
Hawkins, Erskine **19**
Hawkins, Lamont "U-God"
See Wu-Tang Clan
Hawkins, Nick
See Big Audio Dynamite
Hawkins, Richard (Dick)
See Gene Loves Jezebel
Hawkins, Roger
See Traffic
Hawkins, Screamin' Jay **8**
Hawkins, Sophie B. **21**
Hawkins, Taylor
See Foo Fighters
Hawkins, Tramaine **17**
Hawkins, Xian
See Silver Apples
Hay, George D. **3**
Hayden, Victor "The Mascara Snake"
See Captain Beefheart and His Magic Band
Hayes, Gordon
See Pearls Before Swine
Hayes, Isaac **10**
Hayes, Roland **13**
Haynes, Gibby
See Butthole Surfers
Haynes, Warren
See Allman Brothers, The
Hays, Lee
See Weavers, The
Hayward, David Justin
See Moody Blues, The
Hayward, Richard
See Little Feat
Headliner
See Arrested Development
Headon, Topper
See Clash, The
Healey, Jeff **4**
Heard, Paul
See M People
Heard, Paul
See M People
Hearn, Kevin
See Barenaked Ladies
Heart **1**
Heath, James
See Reverend Horton Heat
Heaton, Paul
See Beautiful South
Heavy D **10**
Hecker, Robert
See Redd Kross
Hedford, Eric
See Dandy Warhols
Hedges, Eddie
See Blessid Union of Souls
Hedges, Michael **3**
Heggie, Will
See Cocteau Twins, The
Heidorn, Mike
See Son Volt
Heitman, Dana
See Cherry Poppin' Daddies
Helfgott, David **19**
Hell, Richard
See Television
Hellauer, Susan
See Anonymous 4
Hellerman, Fred
See Weavers, The
Helliwell, John
See Supertramp
Helm, Levon
See Band, The
Also see Nitty Gritty Dirt Band, The
Helmet **15**
Hemingway, Dave
See Beautiful South
Hemmings, Paul
See Lightning Seeds
Henderson, Andy
See Echobelly
Henderson, Billy
See Spinners, The
Henderson, Fletcher **16**
Henderson, Joe **14**
Hendricks, Barbara **10**
Hendrix, Jimi **2**
Henley, Don **3**
Also see Eagles, The
Henrit, Bob
See Kinks, The
Henry, Bill
See Northern Lights
Henry, Joe **18**
Henry, Kent
See Steppenwolf
Henry, Nicholas "Drummie"
See Mystic Revealers
Hensley, Ken
See Uriah Heep
Hepcat, Harry **23**
Hepner, Rich
See Captain Beefheart and His Magic Band
Heppner, Ben **23**
Herdman, Bob
See Audio Adrenaline
Herman, Maureen
See Babes in Toyland
Herman, Tom
See Pere Ubu
Herman, Woody **12**
Herman's Hermits **5**
Herndon, Mark Joel
See Alabama
Herndon, Ty **20**
Heron, Mike
See Incredible String Band
Herrera, R. J.
See Suicidal Tendencies
Herrera, Raymond
See Fear Factory
Herrlin, Anders
See Roxette
Herrmann, Bernard **14**
Herron, Cindy
See En Vogue
Hersh, Kristin
See Throwing Muses
Hester, Paul
See Crowded House
Hetfield, James
See Metallica
Hetson, Greg
See Circle Jerks, The
Heveroh, Ben
See Oakland Interfaith Gospel Choir
Hewitt, Bobby
See Orgy
Hewitt, Steve
See Placebo
Hewson, Paul
See U2
Hexum, Nick
See 311
Hiatt, John **8**
Hickey, Kenny
See Type O Negative
Hickman, Johnny
See Cracker
Hicks, Chris
See Restless Heart
Hicks, Sheree
See C + C Music Factory
Hidalgo, David
See Los Lobos
Higgins, Jimmy
See Altan
Higgins, Terence
See Dirty Dozen Brass Band
Highway 101 **4**
Hijbert, Fritz
See Kraftwerk
Hill, Brendan
See Blues Traveler
Hill, Dusty
See ZZ Top
Hill, Faith **18**
Hill, Ian
See Judas Priest
Hill, Lauryn **25**
Also see Fugees, The
Hill, Scott
See Fu Manchu
Hill, Stuart
See Shudder to Think
Hillage, Steve
See Orb, The
Also see Gong
Hillier, Steve
See Dubstar
Hillman, Bones
See Midnight Oil
Hillman, Chris
See Byrds, The
See Desert Rose Band, The
Hinderas, Natalie **12**
Hinds, David
See Steel Pulse
Hines, Earl "Fatha" **12**
Hines, Gary
See Sounds of Blackness
Hinojosa, Tish **13**
Hirst, Rob
See Midnight Oil
Hirt, Al **5**
Hitchcock, Robyn **9**
Hitchcock, Russell
See Air Supply
Hitt, Bryan
See REO Speedwagon
Hodge, Alex
See Platters, The

Hodges, Johnny **24**
Hodgson, Roger **26**
Also see See Supertramp
Hodo, David
See Village People, The
Hoenig, Michael
See Tangerine Dream
Hoerig, Keith
See Five Iron Frenzy
Hoffman, Ellen
See Oakland Interfaith Gospel Choir
Hoffman, Guy
See BoDeans, The
Also see Violent Femmes
Hoffman, Kristian
See Congo Norvell
Hoffman, Sam
See Captain Beefheart and His Magic Band
Hoffs, Susanna
See Bangles, The
Hogan, Mike
See Cranberries, The
Hogan, Noel
See Cranberries, The
Hoke, Jim
See NRBQ
Holder, Gene
See Yo La Tengo
Hole **14**
Holiday, Billie **6**
Holland, Brian
See Holland-Dozier-Holland
Holland, Bryan "Dexter"
See Offspring
Holland, Dave **27**
Holland, Dave
See Judas Priest
Holland, Eddie
See Holland-Dozier-Holland
Holland, Julian "Jools"
See Squeeze
Holland-Dozier-Holland **5**
Hollis, Mark
See Talk Talk
Hollister, Dave
See Blackstreet
Holly, Buddy **1**
Holmes, Malcolm
See Orchestral Manoeuvres in the Dark
Holmstrom, Peter
See Dandy Warhols
Holt, David Lee
See Mavericks, The
Homme, Josh
See Screaming Trees
Honeyman, Susie
See Mekons, The
Honeyman-Scott, James
See Pretenders, The
Hood, David
See Traffic
Hook, Peter
See Joy Division
Also see New Order
Hooker, John Lee **26**
Earlier sketch in CM **1**
Hooks, Rosie Lee
See Sweet Honey in the Rock
Hoon, Shannon
See Blind Melon
Hooper, Nellee
See Soul II Soul
Also see Massive Attack
Hooters **20**
Hootie and the Blowfish **18**
Hope, Gavin
See Nylons, The
Hopkins, Doug
See Gin Blossoms
Hopkins, Lightnin' **13**
Hopkins, Nicky
See Quicksilver Messenger Service
Hoppus, Mark
See Blink 182
Hopwood, Keith
See Herman's Hermits
Horn, Shirley **7**
Horn, Trevor
See Yes
Horne, Lena **11**
Horne, Marilyn **9**
Horner, Jessica
See Less Than Jake
Hornsby, Bruce **25**
Earlier sketch in CM **3**
Horovitz, Adam "King Ad-Rock"
See Beastie Boys
Horowitz, Vladimir **1**
Horton, Jeff
See Northern Lights
Horton, Walter **19**
Hossack, Michael
See Doobie Brothers, The
Houari, Rachid
See Gong
House, Kenwyn
See Reef
House of Pain **14**
House, Son **11**
Houston, Cissy **26**
Earlier sketch in CM **6**
Houston, Whitney **25**
Earlier sketch in CM **8**
Howard, Harlan **15**
Howe, Brian
See Bad Company
Howe, Steve
See Yes
Howell, Porter
See Little Texas
Howland, Don **24**
Howlett, Liam
See Prodigy
Howlett, Mike
See Gong
Howlin' Wolf **6**
Hubbard, Greg "Hobie"
See Sawyer Brown
Hubbard, Gregg "Hobie"
See Sawyer Brown
Hubbard, Preston
See Fabulous Thunderbirds, The
Also see Roomful of Blues
Huber, Connie
See Chenille Sisters, The
Hubrey, Georgia
See Yo La Tengo
Hudson, Earl
See Bad Brains
Hudson, Garth
See Band, The
Hudson, Ian
See Gene Loves Jezebel
Huey
See Fun Lovin' Criminals
Huffman, Doug
See Boston
Hughes, Bruce
See Cracker
Hughes, Bruce
See Poi Dog Pondering
Hughes, Glenn
See Black Sabbath
Hughes, Glenn
See Village People, The
Hughes, Leon
See Coasters, The
Huld, Hafdis
See Gus Gus
Human League, The **17**
Humes, Helen **19**
Humperdinck, Engelbert **19**
Humphreys, Paul
See Orchestral Manoeuvres in the Dark
Hunt, Darryl
See Pogues, The
Hunter, Alberta **7**
Hunter, Charlie **24**
Hunter, Jason "The Rebel INS" (Inspectah Deckk)
See Wu-Tang Clan
Hunter, Mark
See James
Hunter, Shepherd "Ben"
See Soundgarden
Hurley, George
See fIREHOSE
Hurst, Ron
See Steppenwolf
Hurt, Mississippi John **24**
Hutchence, Michael
See INXS
Hutchings, Ashley
See Fairport Convention
Also see Steeleye Span
Hutchinson, Trevor
See Waterboys, The
Huth, Todd
See Primus
Hütter, Ralf
See Kraftwerk
Hutton, Danny
See Three Dog Night
Huxley, Rick
See Dave Clark Five, The
Hyatt, Aitch
See Specials, The
Hyde, Karl
See Underworld
Hyde, Michael
See Big Mountain
Hyman, Jerry
See Blood, Sweat and Tears
Hyman, Rob
See Hooters
Hynd, Richard
See Texas
Hynde, Chrissie
See Pretenders, The
Hyslop, Kenny
See Simple Minds
Ian and Sylvia **18**
Ian, Janis **24**
Earlier sketch in CM **5**
Ian, Scott
See Anthrax
Ibbotson, Jimmy
See Nitty Gritty Dirt Band, The
Ibold, Mark
See Pavement
Ibrahim, Abdullah **24**
Ice Cube **25**
Earlier sketch in CM **10**
Also see N.W.A

Ice-T **7**
Idol, Billy **3**
Iglesias, Enrique **27**
Iglesias, Julio **20**
Earlier sketch in CM **2**
Iha, James
See Smashing Pumpkins
Ike and Tina Turner **24**
Illsley, John
See Dire Straits
Imbruglia, Natalie **27**
Imperial Teen **26**
Incognito **16**
Incredible String Band **23**
Incubus **23**
Indigo Girls **20**
Earlier sketch in CM **3**
Inez, Mike
See Alice in Chains
Infante, Frank
See Blondie
Ingber, Elliot "Winged Eel Fingerling"
See Captain Beefheart and His Magic Band
Inge, Edward
See McKinney's Cotton Pickers
Ingram, Jack
See Incredible String Band
Ingram, James **11**
Ink Spots **23**
Inner Circle **15**
Innes, Andrew
See Primal Scream
Innis, Dave
See Restless Heart
Insane Clown Posse **22**
Interior, Lux
See Cramps, The
INXS **21**
Earlier sketch in CM **2**
Iommi, Tony
See Black Sabbath
Iron Maiden **10**
Irons, Jack
See Red Hot Chili Peppers, The
Isaak, Chris **6**
Isabelle, Jeff
See Guns n' Roses
Isacsson, Jonas
See Roxette
Isham, Mark **14**
Isles, Bill
See O'Jays, The
Isley Brothers, The **8**
Isley, Ernie
See Isley Brothers, The
Isley, Marvin
See Isley Brothers, The
Isley, O'Kelly, Jr.
See Isley Brothers, The
Isley, Ronald
See Isley Brothers, The
Isley, Rudolph
See Isley Brothers, The
Israel Vibration **21**
Ives, Burl **12**
Ivey, Michael
See Basehead
Ivins, Michael
See Flaming Lips
J, David
See Bauhaus
See Love and Rockets
J. Geils Band **25**
J.
See White Zombie
Jabs, Matthias
See Scorpions, The
Jackson 5, The
See Jacksons, The
Jackson, Al
See Booker T. & the M.G.'s
Jackson, Alan **25**
Earlier sketch in CM **7**
Jackson, Clive
See Ray Condo and His Ricochets
Jackson, Eddie
See Queensryche
Jackson, Freddie **3**
Jackson, Jackie
See Jacksons, The
Jackson, Janet **16**
Earlier sketch in CM **3**
Jackson, Jermaine
See Jacksons, The
Jackson, Joe **22**
Earlier sketch in CM **4**
Jackson, Karen
See Supremes, The
Jackson, Mahalia **8**
Jackson, Marlon
See Jacksons, The
Jackson, Michael **17**
Earlier sketch in CM **1**
Also see Jacksons, The
Jackson, Millie **14**
Jackson, Milt **15**
Jackson, Pervis
See Spinners , The
Jackson, Quentin
See McKinney's Cotton Pickers
Jackson, Randy
See Jacksons, The
Jackson, Tito
See Jacksons, The
Jacksons, The **7**
Jackyl **24**
Jacobs, Christian Richard
See Aquabats The
Jacobs, Jeff
See Foreigner
Jacobs, Parker
See Aquabats, The
Jacobs, Walter
See Little Walter
Jacox, Martin
See Soul Stirrers, The
Jacquet, Illinois **17**
Jade 4U
See Lords of Acid
Jaffee, Rami
See Wallflowers, The
Jagger, Mick **7**
Also see Rolling Stones, The
Jairo T.
See Sepultura
Jalal
See Last Poets
Jam, Jimmy
See Jam, Jimmy, and Terry Lewis
Jam, Jimmy, and Terry Lewis **11**
Jam Master Jay
See Run DMC
Jam, The **27**
James **12**
James, Alex
See Blur
James, Andrew "Bear"
See Midnight Oil
James, Boney **21**
James, Cheryl
See Salt-N-Pepa
James, David
See Alien Sex Fiend
James, David
See Spearhead
James, Doug
See Roomful of Blues
James, Elmore **8**
James, Etta **6**
James, Harry **11**
James, Jesse
See Jackyl
James, John
See Newsboys, The
James, Onieda
See Spearhead
James, Richard
See Aphex Twin
James, Richey
See Manic Street Preachers
James, Rick **2**
James, Ruby
See Aztec Camera
James, Skip **24**
James, Sylvia
See Aztec Camera
Jamiroquai **21**
Jamison, Le Le
See Spearhead
Jane's Addiction **6**
Janovitz, Bill
See Buffalo Tom
Jansch, Bert
See Pentangle
Jardine, Al
See Beach Boys, The
Jarman, Joseph
See Art Ensemble of Chicago, The
Jarobi
See Tribe Called Quest, A
Jarre, Jean-Michel **2**
Jarreau, Al **1**
Jarrett, Irwin
See Third World
Jarrett, Keith **1**
Jars of Clay **20**
Jasper, Chris
See Isley Brothers, The
Jaworski, Al
See Jesus Jones
Jay, Miles
See Village People, The
Jayhawks, The **15**
Jayson, Mackie
See Bad Brains
Jazzie B
See Soul II Soul
Jean, Wyclef **22**
Also see Fugees, The
Jeanrenaud, Joan Dutcher
See Kronos Quartet
Jeczalik, Jonathan
See Art of Noise
Jefferson Airplane **5**
Jefferson, Blind Lemon **18**
Jefferson Starship
See Jefferson Airplane
Jemmott, Gerald
See Pearls Before Swine
Jenifer, Darryl
See Bad Brains
Jenkins, Barry
See Animals, The

Jenkins, Gary
See Silk
Jenkins, Stephan
See Third Eye Blind
Jennings, Greg
See Restless Heart
Jennings, Waylon **4**
Jensen, Ingrid **22**
Jerry, Jah
See Skatalites, The
Jessee, Darren
See Ben Folds Five
Jessie, Young
See Coasters, The
Jesus and Mary Chain, The **10**
Jesus Jones **23**
Jesus Lizard **19**
Jethro Tull **8**
Jett, Joan **3**
Jewel **25**
Jimbo
See Reverend Horton Heat
Jimenez, Flaco
See Texas Tornados, The
Jimmie's Chicken Shack **22**
Joannou, Chris
See Silverchair
Jobim, Antonio Carlos **19**
Jobson, Edwin
See Jethro Tull
Jodeci **13**
Joel, Billy **12**
Earlier sketch in CM **2**
Joel, Phil
See Newsboys, The
Johansen, David
See New York Dolls
Johansen, David **7**
Johanson, Jai Johanny
See Allman Brothers, The
Johansson, Glenn
See Echobelly
Johansson, Lars-Olof
See Cardigans
John, Elton **20**
Earlier sketch in CM **3**
John, Little Willie **25**
John Spencer Blues Explosion **18**
Johns, Daniel
See Silverchair
Johnson, Alphonso
See Weather Report
Johnson, Blind Willie **26**
Johnson, Bob
See Steeleye Span
Johnson, Brian
See AC/DC
Johnson, Courtney
See New Grass Revival, The
Johnson, Danny
See Steppenwolf
Johnson, Daryl
See Neville Brothers, The
Johnson, Eric
See Archers of Loaf
Johnson, Eric **19**
Johnson, Gene
See Diamond Rio
Johnson, Gerry
See Steel Pulse
Johnson, James P. **16**
Johnson, Jerry
See Big Mountain
Johnson, Lonnie **17**
Johnson, Matt
See The The
Johnson, Mike
See Dinosaur Jr.
Johnson, Patricia
See Sweet Honey in the Rock
Johnson, Ralph
See Earth, Wind and Fire
Johnson, Robert **6**
Johnson, Scott
See Gin Blossoms
Johnson, Shirley Childres
See Sweet Honey in the Rock
Johnson, Tamara "Taj"
See SWV
Johnson, Willie
See Golden Gate Quartet
Johnston, Bruce
See Beach Boys, The
Johnston, Freedy **20**
Johnston, Howie
See Ventures, The
Johnston, Sonnie
See Five Iron Frenzy
Johnston, Tom
See Doobie Brothers, The
JoJo
See Jodeci
Jolly, Bill
See Butthole Surfers
Jolson, Al **10**
Jon Spencer Blues Explosion **18**
Jones, Adam
See Tool
Jones, Benny
See Dirty Dozen Brass Band
Jones, Booker T. **8**
Also see Booker T. & the M.G.'s
Jones, Brian
See Rolling Stones, The
Jones, Busta
See Gang of Four
Jones, Claude
See McKinney's Cotton Pickers
Jones, Darryl
See Rolling Stones, The
Jones, Davy
See Monkees, The
Jones, Denise
See Point of Grace
Jones, Elvin **9**
Jones, Geoffrey
See Sounds of Blackness
Jones, George **4**
Jones, Grace **9**
Jones, Hank **15**
Jones, Howard **26**
Jones, Jab
See Memphis Jug Band
Jones, Jamie
See All-4-One
Jones, Jim
See Pere Ubu
Jones, John Paul
See Led Zeppelin
Jones, Kendall
See Fishbone
Jones, Kenny
See Faces, The
Jones, Kenny
See Who, The
Jones, Marshall
See Ohio Players
Jones, Maxine
See En Vogue
Jones, Mic
See Big Audio Dynamite
Also see Clash, The
Jones, Michael
See Kronos Quartet
Jones, Mick
See Foreigner
Jones, Mick
See Clash, The
Jones, Orville
See Ink Spots
Jones, Philly Joe **16**
Jones, Quincy **20**
Earlier sketch in CM **2**
Jones, Randy
See Village People, The
Jones, Rickie Lee **4**
Jones, Robert "Kuumba"
See Ohio Players
Jones, Robin
See Beta Band, The
Jones, Ronald
See Flaming Lips
Jones, Russell "Ol Dirdy Bastard"
See Wu-Tang Clan
Jones, Sandra "Puma"
See Black Uhuru
Jones, Simon
See Verve, The
Jones, Spike **5**
Jones, Stacy
See Letters to Cleo
Also see Veruca Salt
Jones, Steve
See Sex Pistols, The
Jones, Terry
See Point of Grace
Jones, Thad **19**
Jones, Tom **11**
Jones, Will "Dub"
See Coasters, The
Jonsson, Magnus
See Gus Gus
Joplin, Janis **3**
Joplin, Scott **10**
Jordan, Lonnie
See War
Jordan, Louis **11**
Jordan, Montell **26**
Jordan, Stanley **1**
Jorgenson, John
See Desert Rose Band, The
Joseph, Charles
See Dirty Dozen Brass Band
Joseph, Kirk
See Dirty Dozen Brass Band
Joseph-I, Israel
See Bad Brains
Josephmary
See Compulsion
Jourgensen, Al
See Ministry
Journey **21**
Joy Division **19**
Joy Electric **26**
Joyce, Mike
See Buzzcocks, The
See Smiths, The
Judas Priest **10**
Judd, Naomi
See Judds, The
Judd, Wynonna
See Judds, The
Also see Wynonna

Judds, The **2**
Juhlin, Dag
See Poi Dog Pondering
Jukebox
See Geto Boys, The
Jungle DJ "Towa" Towa
See Deee-lite
Jurado, Jeanette
See Exposé
Justman, Seth
See J. Geils Band
K-Ci
See Jodeci
Kabongo, Sabine
See Zap Mama
Kahlil, Aisha
See Sweet Honey in the Rock
Kain, Gylan
See Last Poets
Kakoulli, Harry
See Squeeze
Kale, Jim
See Guess Who
Kalligan, Dick
See Blood, Sweat and Tears
Kamanski, Paul
See Beat Farmers
Kaminski, Mik
See Electric Light Orchestra
Kamomiya, Ryo
See Pizzicato Five
Kanal, Tony
See No Doubt
Kanawa, Kiri Te
See Te Kanawa, Kiri
Kane, Arthur
See New York Dolls
Kane, Big Daddy **7**
Kane, Nick
See Mavericks, The
Kannberg, Scott
See Pavement
Kantner, Paul
See Jefferson Airplane
Kaplan, Ira
See Yo La Tengo
Karajan, Herbert von
See von Karajan, Herbert
Karges, Murphy
See Sugar Ray
Kath, Terry
See Chicago
Kato, Nash
See Urge Overkill
Katunich, Alex
See Incubus
Katz, Simon
See Jamiroquai
Katz, Steve
See Blood, Sweat and Tears
Kaukonen, Jorma
See Jefferson Airplane
Kavanagh, Chris
See Big Audio Dynamite
Kay Gee
See Naughty by Nature
Kay, Jason
See Jamiroquai
Kay, John
See Steppenwolf
Kaye, Carol **22**
Kaye, Tony
See Yes
Keaggy, Phil **26**
Kean, Martin
See Stereolab
Keane, Sean
See Chieftains, The
Kee, John P. **15**
Keelor, Greg
See Blue Rodeo
Keenan, Maynard James
See Tool
Keene, Barry
See Spirit
Keifer, Tom
See Cinderella
Keitaro
See Pizzicato Five
Keith, Jeff
See Tesla
Keith, Toby **17**
Kelly, Betty
See Martha and the Vandellas
Kelly, Charlotte
See Soul II Soul
Kelly, Ed
See Oakland Interfaith Gospel Choir
Kelly, Johnny
See Type O Negative
Kelly, Kevin
See Byrds, The
Kelly, Matt
See Dropkick Murphys
Kelly, R. **19**
Kelly, Rashaan
See US3
Kelly, Sean
See Sixpence None the Richer
Kelly, Terrance
See Oakland Interfaith Gospel Choir
Kemp, Rick
See Steeleye Span
Kendrick, David
See Devo
Kendricks, Eddie
See Temptations, The
Kennedy, Delious
See All-4-One
Kennedy, Frankie
See Altan
Kennedy, Nigel **8**
Kenner, Doris
See Shirelles, The
Kenny, Bill
See Ink Spots
Kenny, Clare
See Aztec Camera
Kenny G **14**
Kenny, Herb
See Ink Spots
Kent, Julia
See Rasputina
Kenton, Stan **21**
Kentucky Headhunters, The **5**
Kern, Jerome **13**
Kerr, Jim
See Simple Minds
Kerr, Scott
See Five Iron Frenzy
Kerr, Stuart
See Texas
Kershaw, Sammy **15**
Ketchum, Hal **14**
Key, Cevin
See Skinny Puppy
Keyser, Alex
See Echobelly
Khan, Chaka **19**
Earlier sketch in CM **9**
Khan, Nusrat Fateh Ali **13**
Khan, Praga
See Lords of Acid
Kibble, Mark
See Take 6
Kibby, Walter
See Fishbone
Kick, Johnny
See Madder Rose
Kid 'n Play **5**
Kid Rock **27**
Kidjo, Anjelique **17**
Kiedis, Anthony
See Red Hot Chili Peppers, The
Kilbey, Steve
See Church, The
Kilbourn, Duncan
See Psychedelic Furs
Kilgallon, Eddie
See Ricochet
Kilgore **24**
Killian, Tim
See Kronos Quartet
Kimball, Jennifer
See Story, The
Kimball, Jim
See Jesus Lizard
Kimble, Paul
See Grant Lee Buffalo
Kinard, Tulani Jordan
See Sweet Honey in the Rock
Kincaid, Jan
See Brand New Heavies, The
Kinchla, Chan
See Blues Traveler
Kinde, Geoff
See Atomic Fireballs, The
King Ad-Rock
See Horovitz, Adam
King, Albert **2**
King, Andy
See Hooters
King, B.B. **24**
Earlier sketch in CM **1**
King, Ben E. **7**
King, Bob
See Soul Stirrers, The
King, Carole **6**
Also see Goffin-King
King Crimson **17**
King, Ed
See Lynyrd Skynyrd
King, Freddy **17**
King, Jon
See Gang of Four
King, Jr., William
See Commodores, The
King, Kerry
See Slayer
King Missile **22**
King, Philip
See Lush
King, William Jr.
See Commodores, The
King's X **7**
Kingins, Duke
See Atomic Fireballs, The
Kingston Trio, The **9**
Kinks, The **15**
Kinney, Sean
See Alice in Chains
Kirk, Rahsaan Roland **6**

Kirk, Richard H.
See Cabaret Voltaire
Kirke, Simon
See Bad Company
Kirkland, Mike
See Prong
Kirkpatrick, Chris
See 'N Sync
Kirkwood, Cris
See Meat Puppets, The
Kirkwood, Curt
See Meat Puppets, The
Kirtley, Peter
See Pentangle
Kirwan, Danny
See Fleetwood Mac
Kiss **25**
Earlier sketch in CM **5**
Kisser, Andreas
See Sepultura
Kissin, Evgeny **6**
Kitaro **1**
Kitsos, Nick
See BoDeans
Kitt, Eartha **9**
Kjartansson, Siggi
See Gus Gus
Klein, Danny
See J. Geils Band
Klein, Jon
See Siouxsie and the Banshees
Klezmatics, The **18**
Klugh, Earl **10**
Kmatsu, Bravo
See Pizzicato Five
KMFDM **18**
Knight, Gladys **1**
Knight, Jon
See New Kids on the Block
Knight, Jordan
See New Kids on the Block
Knight, Larry
See Spirit
Knight, Peter
See Steeleye Span
Knight, Suge **15**
Knighton, Willie "Khujo"
See Goodie Mob
Knopfler, David
See Dire Straits
Knopfler, Mark **25**
Earlier sketch in CM **3**
Also see Dire Straits
Know, Dr.
See Bad Brains
Knowledge
See Digable Planets
Knox, Nick
See Cramps, The
Knox, Richard
See Dirty Dozen Brass Band
Knudsen, Keith
See Doobie Brothers, The
Konietzko, Sascha
See KMFDM
Konishi, Yasuharu
See Pizzicato Five
Konto, Skip
See Three Dog Night
Kool & the Gang **13**
Kool Moe Dee **9**
Kooper, Al
See Blood, Sweat and Tears
Koppelman, Charles **14**
Koppes, Peter
See Church, The
Korn **20**
Kottke, Leo **13**
Kotzen, Richie
See Poison
Kowalczyk, Ed
See Live
Koz, Dave **20**
Kraftwerk **9**
Krakauer, David
See Klezmatics, The
Krall, Diana **27**
Kramer, Joey
See Aerosmith
Kramer, Wayne
See MC5, The
Krasnow, Bob **15**
Krause, Bernie
See Weavers, The
Krauss, Alison **10**
Krauss, Scott
See Pere Ubu
Kravitz, Lenny **26**
Earlier sketch in CM **5**
Krawits, Michael
See Pearls Before Swine
Krayzie Bone
See Bone Thugs-N-Harmony
Krazy Drayz
See Das EFX
Kretz, Eric
See Stone Temple Pilots
Kreutzman, Bill
See Grateful Dead, The
Krieger, Robert
See Doors, The
Kriesel, Greg "Greg K."
See Offspring
Kris Kross **11**
Kristofferson, Kris **4**
Krizan, Anthony
See Spin Doctors
Kronos Quartet **5**
Kropp, Mike
See Northern Lights
KRS-One **8**
Krukowski, Damon
See Damon and Naomi
Krupa, Gene **13**
Krusen, Dave
See Pearl Jam
Kruspe, Richard
See Rammstein
Kulak, Eddie
See Aztec Camera
Kulick, Bruce
See Kiss
Kunkel, Bruce
See Nitty Gritty Dirt Band, The
Kunzel, Erich **17**
Kurdziel, Eddie
See Redd Kross
Kurihara, Michio
See Ghost
Kuti, Fela **7**
L.L. Cool J. **5**
L7 **12**
LaBar, Jeff
See Cinderella
LaBelle, Patti **8**
LaBrie, James
See Dream Theater
Lack, Steve
See Veruca Salt
Lacy, Steve **23**
Lady Miss Kier
See Deee-lite
Ladybug
See Digable Planets
Ladysmith Black Mambazo **1**
Lafalce, Mark
See Mekons, The
Lagerburg, Bengt
See Cardigans, The
Laine, Cleo **10**
Laine, Denny
See Moody Blues, The
Laird, Rick
See Mahavishnu Orchestra
Lake, Greg
See Emerson, Lake & Palmer/Powell
Also see King Crimson
LaKind, Bobby
See Doobie Brothers, The
Lally, Joe
See Fugazi
LaLonde, Larry "Ler"
See Primus
Lamb, Brabara **19**
Lamb, Michael
See Confederate Railroad
Lamble, Martin
See Fairport Convention
Lamm, Robert
See Chicago
Lampkin, Troy
See Oakland Interfaith Gospel Choir
Lancaster, Brian
See Surfin' Pluto
Landers, Paul
See Rammstein
Landreth, Sonny **16**
Lane, Jani
See Warrant
Lane, Jay
See Primus
Lane, Ronnie
See Faces, The
Lanegan, Mark
See Screaming Trees
lang, k. d. **25**
Earlier sketch in CM **4**
Lang, Jonny **27**
Langan, Gary
See Art of Noise
Langford, Jon
See Mekons, The
Langford, Willie
See Golden Gate Quartet
Langley, John
See Mekons, The
Langlois, Paul
See Tragically Hip, The
Langosch, Paul
See Ralph Sharon Quartet
Langston, Leslie
See Throwing Muses
Lanier, Allen
See Blue Oyster Cult
Lanker, Dustin
See Cherry Poppin' Daddies
Lanois, Daniel **8**
LaPread, Ronald
See Commodores, The
Larkin, Patty **9**
Larson, Chad Albert
See Aquabats, The
Larson, Nathan
See Shudder to Think

Last Poets **21**
Laswell, Bill **14**
Lataille, Rich
See Roomful of Blues
Lateef, Yusef **16**
Latimer, Andrew
See Camel
Laughner, Peter
See Pere Ubu
Lauper, Cyndi **11**
Laurence, Lynda
See Supremes, The
Lavin, Christine **6**
Lavis, Gilson
See Squeeze
Lawler, Feargal
See Cranberries, The
Lawnge
See Black Sheep
Lawrence, Tracy **11**
Lawry, John
See Petra
Laws, Roland
See Earth, Wind and Fire
Lawson, Doyle
See Country Gentlemen, The
Layzie Bone
See Bone Thugs-N-Harmony
Le Bon, Simon
See Duran Duran
Le Mystère des VoixBulgares
See Bulgarian State Female Vocal Choir, The
Leadbelly **6**
Leadon, Bernie
See Eagles, The
Also see Nitty Gritty Dirt Band, The
Lear, Graham
See REO Speedwagon
Leary, Paul
See Butthole Surfers
Leavell, Chuck
See Allman Brothers, The
LeBon, Simon
See Duran Duran
Leckenby, Derek "Lek"
See Herman's Hermits
Led Zeppelin **1**
Ledbetter, Huddie
See Leadbelly
LeDoux, Chris **12**
Lee, Ben **26**
Lee, Beverly
See Shirelles, The
Lee, Brenda **5**
Lee, Buddy
See Less Than Jake
Lee, Buddy
See McKinney's Cotton Pickers
Lee, Garret
See Compulsion
Lee, Geddy
See Rush
Lee, Peggy **8**
Lee, Pete
See Gwar
Lee, Sara
See Gang of Four
Lee, Stan
See Incredible String Band
Lee, Tommy
See Mötley Crüe
Lee, Tony
See Treadmill Trackstar
Leeb, Bill
See Front Line Assembly
Leen, Bill
See Gin Blossoms
Leese, Howard
See Heart
Legg, Adrian **17**
Legowitz, Herr
See Gus Gus
Leherer, Keith "Lucky"
See Circle Jerks
Lehrer, Tom **7**
Leiber and Stoller **14**
Leiber, Jerry
See Leiber and Stoller
LeMaistre, Malcolm
See Incredible String Band
Lemmy
See Motörhead
Lemonheads, The **12**
Lemper, Ute **14**
Lenear, Kevin
See Mighty Mighty Bosstones
Lenners, Rudy
See Scorpions, The
Lennon, John **9**
Also see Beatles, The
Lennon, Julian **26**
Earlier sketch in CM **2**
Lennox, Annie **18**
Also see Eurythmics
Leonard, Glenn
See Temptations, The
Lerner, Alan Jay
See Lerner and Loewe
Lerner and Loewe **13**
Lesh, Phil
See Grateful Dead, The
Leskiw, Greg
See Guess Who
Leslie, Chris
See Fairport Convention
Less Than Jake **22**
Lessard, Stefan
See Dave Matthews Band
Lethal, DJ
See Limp Bizkit
Letters to Cleo **22**
Levene, Keith
See Clash, The
Levert, Eddie
See O'Jays, The
Leverton, Jim
See Caravan
Levin, Tony
See King Crimson
Levine, James **8**
Levy, Andrew
See Brand New Heavies, The
Levy, Ron
See Roomful of Blues
Lewis, Furry **26**
Lewis, Hambone
See Memphis Jug Band
Lewis, Huey **9**
Lewis, Ian
See Inner Circle
Lewis, Jerry Lee **2**
Lewis, Marcia
See Soul II Soul
Lewis, Michael
See Quicksilver Messenger Service
Lewis, Mike
See Yo La Tengo
Lewis, Otis
See Fabulous Thunderbirds, The
Lewis, Peter
See Moby Grape
Lewis, Ramsey **14**
Lewis, Roger
See Dirty Dozen Brass Band
See Inner Circle
Lewis, Roger
Lewis, Roy
See Kronos Quartet
Lewis, Samuel K.
See Five Blind Boys of Alabama
Lewis, Shaznay T.
See All Saints
Lewis, Terry
See Jam, Jimmy, and Terry Lewis
Lhote, Morgan
See Stereolab
Li Puma, Tommy **18**
Libbea, Gene
See Nashville Bluegrass Band
Liberace **9**
Liberty, Earl
See Circle Jerks
Licht, David
See Klezmatics, The
Lifeso'n, Alex
See Rush
Lightfoot, Gordon **3**
Lightning Seeds **21**
Ligon, Willie Joe
See Mighty Clouds of Joy, The
Liles, Brent
See Social Distortion
Lilienstein, Lois
See Sharon, Lois & Bram
Lilker, Dan
See Anthrax
Lilley, John
See Hooters
Lillywhite, Steve **13**
Limp Bizkit **27**
Lincoln, Abbey **9**
Lindberg, Jim
See Pennywise
Lindemann, Till
See Rammstein
Lindes, Hal
See Dire Straits
Lindley, David **2**
Lindner, Michael
See Aqua Velvets
Linkous, Mark **26**
Linna, Miriam
See Cramps, The
Linnell, John
See They Might Be Giants
Lipsius, Fred
See Blood, Sweat and Tears
Lisa, Lisa **23**
Lit **27**
Little Feat **4**
Little, Keith
See Country Gentlemen, The
Little, Levi
See Blackstreet
Little Richard **1**
Little Texas **14**
Little Walter **14**
Littrell, Brian
See Backstreet Boys
Live **14**
Living Colour **7**

Llanas, Sam
See BoDeans
Llanas, Sammy
See BoDeans, The
Lloyd, Charles **22**
Lloyd, Richard
See Television
Lloyd Webber, Andrew **6**
Lo Fidelity All Stars **27**
Locke, John
See Spirit
Locking, Brian
See Shadows, The
Lockwood, Robert, Jr. **10**
Lodge, John
See Moody Blues, The
Loeb, Lisa **23**
See sketch in CM **19**
Loesser, Frank **19**
Loewe, Frederick
See Lerner and Loewe
Loewenstein, Jason
See Sebadoh
Lofgren, Nils **25**
Logan, Jack **27**
Loggins, Kenny **20**
Earlier sketch in CM **3**
Lombardo, Dave
See Slayer
London, Frank
See Klezmatics, The
Lonestar **27**
Lopes, Lisa "Left Eye"
See TLC
Lopez, Israel "Cachao" **14**
Lopez, Jennifer **27**
Lord, Jon
See Deep Purple
Lords of Acid **20**
Lorenz, Flake
See Rammstein
Loria, Steve
See Spirit
Lorimer, Roddy
See Waterboys, The
Lorson, Mary
See Madder Rose
Los Lobos **2**
Los Reyes
See Gipsy Kings, The
Loughnane, Lee
See Chicago
Louison, Steve
See Massive Attack
Louris, Gary
See Jayhawks, The
Louvin Brothers, The **12**
Louvin, Charlie
See Louvin Brothers, The
Louvin, Ira
See Louvin Brothers, The
Lovano, Joe **13**
Love and Rockets **15**
Love, Courtney
See Hole
Love, Gerry
See Teenage Fanclub
Love, Laura **20**
Love, Mike
See Beach Boys, The
Love, Rollie
See Beat Farmers
Love Spit Love **21**
Loveless, Patty **21**
Earlier sketch in CM **5**
Lovering, David
See Cracker
Also see Pixies, The
Lovett, Lyle **5**
Lowe, Chris
See Pet Shop Boys
Lowe, Nick **25**
Earlier sketch in CM **6**
Lowe, Victoria
See Tuxedomoon
Lowell, Charlie
See Jars of Clay
Lowery, David
See Cracker
Lozano, Conrad
See Los Lobos
Lucas, Gary
See Captain Beefheart and His Magic Band
Lucas, Trevor
See Fairport Convention
Luccketta, Troy
See Tesla
Lucia, Paco de
See de Lucia, Paco
Luciano, Felipe
See Last Poets
Luke
See Campbell, Luther
Lukin, Matt
See Mudhoney
Luna **18**
Lupo, Pat
See Beaver Brown Band, The
LuPone, Patti **8**
Luscious Jackson **27**
Earlier sketch in CM **19**
Lush **13**
Luttell, Terry
See REO Speedwagon
Lydon, John **9**
Also see Sex Pistols, The
Lyfe, DJ
See Incubus
Lymon, Frankie
See Frankie Lymon and The Teenagers
Lynch, David
See Platters, The
Lynch, Dermot
See Dog's Eye View
Lynch, George
See Dokken
Lynch, Laura
See Dixie Chicks
Lynch, Stan
See Tom Petty and the Heartbreakers
Lyngstad, Anni-Frid
See Abba
Lynn, Lonnie Rashid
See Common
Lynn, Loretta **2**
Lynne, Jeff **5**
Also see Electric Light Orchestra
Lynne, Shelby **5**
Lynott, Phil
See Thin Lizzy
Lynyrd Skynyrd **9**
Lyons, Leanne "Lelee"
See SWV
M People **27**
Earlier sketch in CM **15**
M.C. Hammer
See Hammer, M.C.
M.C. Ren
See N.W.A.
Ma, Yo-Yo **24**
Earlier sketch in CM **2**
MacColl, Kirsty **12**
MacDonald, Barbara Kooyman
See Timbuk 3
MacDonald, Eddie
See Alarm
MacDonald, Pat
See Timbuk **3**
Macfarlane, Lora
See Sleater-Kinney
MacGowan, Shane
See Pogues, The
MacIsaac, Ashley **21**
Mack Daddy
See Kris Kross
MacKaye, Ian
See Fugazi
Mackey, Steve
See Pulp
MacNeil, Michael
See Simple Minds
MacPherson, Jim
See Breeders
Macy, Robin
See Dixie Chicks
Madan, Sonya Aurora
See Echobelly
Madder Rose **17**
Madness **27**
Madonna **16**
Earlier sketch in CM **4**
Mael, Ron
See Sparks
Mael, Russell
See Sparks
Magehee, Marty
See 4Him
Maghostut, Malachi Favors
See Art Ensemble of Chicago, The
Maginnis, Tom
See Buffalo Tom
Magnie, John
See Subdudes, The
Magoogan, Wesley
See English Beat, The
Mahavishnu Orchestra **19**
Maher, John
See Buzzcocks, The
Mahogany, Kevin **26**
Mahoney, Tim
See 311
Maida, Raine
See Our Lady Peace
Maillard, Carol
See Sweet Honey in the Rock
Maimone, Tony
See Pere Ubu
Maines, Natalie
See Dixie Chicks
Maïtra, Shyamal
See Gong
Majewski, Hank
See Four Seasons, The
Makeba, Miriam **8**
Malcolm, Hugh
See Skatalites, The
Malcolm, Joy
See Incognito
Male, Johnny
See Republica
Malherbe, Didier
See Gong
Malin, Jesse
See D Generation

Malins, Mike
See Goo Goo Dolls, The
Malkmus, Stephen
See Pavement
Malley, Matt
See Counting Crows
Mallinder, Stephen
See Cabaret Voltaire
Malmsteen, Yngwie **24**
Malo, Raul
See Mavericks, The
Malone, Russell **27**
Malone, Tom
See Blood, Sweat and Tears
Malone, Tommy
See Subdudes, The
Mamas and the Papas **21**
Man or Astroman? **21**
Mancini, Henry **20**
Earlier sketch in CM **1**
Mandrell, Barbara **4**
Maness, J. D.
See Desert Rose Band, The
Mangione, Chuck **23**
Manhattan Transfer, The **8**
Manic Street Preachers **27**
Manilow, Barry **2**
Mann, Aimee **22**
Mann, Billy **23**
Mann, Herbie **16**
Manninger, Hank
See Aqua Velvets
Manson, Shirley
See Garbage
Manuel, Richard
See Band, The
Manzarek, Ray
See Doors, The
March, Kevin
See Shudder to Think
Marie, Buffy Sainte
See Sainte Marie, Buffy
Marilyn Manson **18**
Marini, Lou, Jr.
See Blood, Sweat and Tears
Marker, Steve
See Garbage
Marks, Toby
See De Gaia, Banco
Marley, Bob **3**
Marley, Rita **10**
Marley, Ziggy **3**
Marr, Johnny
See Smiths, The
Also see The The
Marriner, Neville **7**
Mars, Chris
See Replacements, The
Mars, Derron
See Less Than Jake
Mars, Mick
See Mötley Crüe
Marsalis, Branford **10**
Marsalis, Ellis **13**
Marsalis, Wynton **20**
Earlier sketch in CM **6**
Marsh, Ian Craig
See Human League, The
Marshal, Cornel
See Third World
Marshall, Amanda **27**
Marshall, Jenell
See Dirty Dozen Brass Band
Marshall, Steve
See Gene Loves Jezebel
Martensen, Vic
See Captain Beefheart and His Magic Band
Martha and the Vandellas **25**
Martin, Barbara
See Supremes, The
Martin, Barrett
See Screaming Trees
Martin, Carl
See Shai
Martin, Christopher
See Kid 'n Play
Martin, Dean **1**
Martin, Dewey
See Buffalo Springfield
Martin, George **6**
Martin, Greg
See Kentucky Headhunters, The
Martin, Jim
See Faith No More
Martin, Jimmy **5**
Also see Osborne Brothers, The
Martin, Johnney
See Mighty Clouds of Joy, The
Martin, Mary **27**
Martin, Phonso
See Steel Pulse
Martin, Ricky **26**
Martin, Ronnie
See Joy Electric
Martin, Sennie
See Kool & the Gang
Martin, Tony
See Black Sabbath
Martinez, Anthony
See Black Flag
Martinez, Cliff
See Captain Beefheart and His Magic Band
Martinez, S. A.
See 311
Martini, Jerry
See Sly & the Family Stone
Martino, Pat **17**
Martsch, Doug
See Built to Spill
Marvin, Hank B.
See Shadows, The
Marx, Richard **21**
Earlier sketch in CM **3**
Mascagni, Pietro **25**
Mascis, J
See Dinosaur Jr.
Masdea, Jim
See Boston
Mase **27**
Masekela, Hugh **7**
Maseo, Baby Huey
See De La Soul
Masi, Nick
See Four Seasons, The
Mason, Dave
See Traffic
Mason, Nick
See Pink Floyd
Mason, Stephen
See Beta Band, The
Mason, Steve
See Jars of Clay
Mason, Terry
See Joy Division
Masse, Laurel
See Manhattan Transfer, The
Massey, Bobby
See O'Jays, The
Massi, Nick
See Four Seasons, The
Massive Attack **17**
Mastelotto, Pat
See King Crimson
Master P **22**
Masur, Kurt **11**
Matchbox 20 **27**
Material
See Laswell, Bill
Mathis, Johnny **2**
Mathus, Jim
See Squirrel Nut Zippers
Matlock, Glen
See Sex Pistols, The
Mattacks, Dave
See Fairport Convention
Mattea, Kathy **5**
Matthews Band, Dave
See Dave Matthews Band
Matthews, Chris
See Shudder to Think
Matthews, Dave
See Dave Matthews Band
Matthews, Eric **22**
Matthews, Ian
See Fairport Convention
Matthews, Quinn
See Butthole Surfers
Matthews, Scott
See Butthole Surfers
Matthews, Simon
See Jesus Jones
Maunick, Bluey
See Incognito
Maurer, John
See Social Distortion
Mavericks, The **15**
Maxwell **22**
Maxwell, Charmayne
See Brownstone
Maxwell, Tom
See Squirrel Nut Zippers
May, Brian
See Queen
May, Phil
See Pretty Things, The
Mayall, John **7**
Mayfield, Curtis **8**
Mays, Odeen, Jr.
See Kool & the Gang
Mazelle, Kym
See Soul II Soul
Mazibuko, Abednigo
See Ladysmith Black Mambazo
Mazibuko, Albert
See Ladysmith Black Mambazo
Mazzola, Joey
See Sponge
Mazzy Star **17**
MC 900 Ft. Jesus **16**
MC Breed **17**
MC Clever
See Digital Underground
MC Eiht **27**
MC Eric
See Technotronic
MC Lyte **8**
MC Serch **10**
MC5, The **9**
MCA
See Yauch, Adam
McAloon, Martin
See Prefab Sprout
McAloon, Paddy
See Prefab Sprout

McArthur, Keith
See Spearhead
McBrain, Nicko
See Iron Maiden
McBrayer, Jody
See Avalon
MCBreed **17**
McBride, Christian **17**
McBride, Martina **14**
McCabe, Nick
See Verve, The
McCabe, Zia
See Dandy Warhols
McCall, Renee
See Sounds of Blackness
McCann, Lila **26**
McCarrick, Martin
See Siouxsie and the Banshees
McCarroll, Tony
See Oasis
McCartney, Paul **4**
Also see Beatles, The
McCarty, Jim
See Yardbirds, The
McCary, Michael S.
See Boyz II Men
McClary, Thomas
See Commodores, The
McClennan, Tommy **25**
McClinton, Delbert **14**
McCluskey, Andy
See Orchestral Manoeuvres in the Dark
McColgan, Mike
See Dropkick Murphys
McCollum, Rick
See Afghan Whigs
McConnell, Page
See Phish
McCook, Tommy
See Skatalites, The
McCorkle, Susannah **27**
McCoury, Del **15**
McCowin, Michael
See Mighty Clouds of Joy, The
McCoy, Neal **15**
McCracken, Chet
See Doobie Brothers, The
McCrea, John
See Cake
McCready, Mike
See Pearl Jam
McCready, Mindy **22**
McCulloch, Andrew
See King Crimson
McCullough, Danny
See Animals, The
McCuloch, Ian **23**
McCurdy, Xan
See Cake
McCutcheon, Ian
See Mojave 3
McD, Jimmy
See Jimmie's Chicken Shack
McDaniel, Chris
See Confederate Railroad
McDaniels, Darryl "D"
See Run DMC
McDermott, Brian
See Del Amitri
McDonald, Ian
See Foreigner
Also see King Crimson
McDonald, Jeff
See Redd Kross
McDonald, Michael
See Doobie Brothers, The
McDonald, Richie
See Lonestar
McDonald, Steven
See Redd Kross
McDorman, Joe
See Statler Brothers, The
McDougall, Don
See Guess Who
McDowell, Hugh
See Electric Light Orchestra
McDowell, Mississippi Fred **16**
McElhone, John
See Texas
McEntire, Reba **11**
McErlaine, Ally
See Texas
McEuen, John
See Nitty Gritty Dirt Band, The
McFarlane, Elaine
See Mamas and the Papas
McFee, John
See Doobie Brothers, The
McFerrin, Bobby **3**
McFessel, Sean
See Cake
McGee, Brian
See Simple Minds
McGee, Jerry
See Ventures, The
McGeoch, John
See Siouxsie and the Banshees
McGinley, Raymond
See Teenage Fanclub
McGinniss, Will
See Audio Adrenaline
McGrath, Mark
See Sugar Ray
McGraw, Tim **17**
McGuigan, Paul
See Oasis
McGuinn, Jim
See McGuinn, Roger
McGuinn, Roger
See Byrds, The
McGuinness
See Lords of Acid
McGuire, Christine
See McGuire Sisters, The
McGuire, Dorothy
See McGuire Sisters, The
McGuire, Mike
See Shenandoah
McGuire, Phyllis
See McGuire Sisters, The
McGuire Sisters, The **27**
McIntosh, Robbie
See Pretenders, The
McIntyre, Joe
See New Kids on the Block
McJohn, Goldy
See Steppenwolf
McKagan, Duff
See Guns n' Roses
McKay, Al
See Earth, Wind and Fire
McKay, John
See Siouxsie and the Banshees
McKean, Michael
See Spinal Tap
McKee , Julius
See Dirty Dozen Brass Band
McKee, Maria **11**
McKeehan, Toby
See dc Talk
McKenna, Greg
See Letters to Cleo
McKennitt, Loreena **24**
McKenzie, Christina "Licorice"
See Incredible String Band
McKenzie, Derrick
See Jamiroquai
McKenzie, Scott
See Mamas and the Papas
McKernan, Ron "Pigpen"
See Grateful Dead, The
McKinney, William
See McKinney's Cotton Pickers
McKinney's Cotton Pickers **16**
McKnight, Brian **22**
McKnight, Claude V. III
See Take 6
McLachlan, Sarah **12**
McLagan, Ian
See Faces, The
McLaren, Malcolm **23**
McLaughlin, John **12**
Also see Mahavishnu Orchestra
McLean, A. J.
See Backstreet Boys
McLean, Dave **24**
McLean, Don **7**
McLean, John
See Beta Band, The
McLennan, Grant **21**
McLeod, Rory
See Roomful of Blues
McLoughlin, Jon
See Del Amitri
McMackin, Bryon
See Pennywise
McMeel, Mickey
See Three Dog Night
McMurtry, James **10**
McNabb, Travis
See Better Than Ezra
McNair, Sylvia **15**
McNeilly, Mac
See Jesus Lizard
McNew, James
See Yo La Tengo
McPartland, Marian **15**
McPhatter, Clyde **25**
McPherson, Graham "Suggs"
See Madness
McQuillar, Shawn
See Kool & the Gang
McRae, Carmen **9**
McReynolds, Jesse
See McReynolds, Jim and Jesse
McReynolds, Jim
See McReynolds, Jim and Jesse
McReynolds, Jim and Jesse **12**
McShane, Ronnie
See Chieftains, The
McShee, Jacqui
See Pentangle
McTell, Blind Willie **17**
McVie, Christine
See Fleetwood Mac
McVie, John
See Fleetwood Mac
McWhinney, James
See Big Mountain
McWhinney, Joaquin
See Big Mountain
Mdletshe, Geophrey
See Ladysmith Black Mambazo

Meat Loaf **12**
Meat Puppets, The **13**
Medley, Bill **3**
Medlock, James
 See Soul Stirrers, The
Meehan, Tony
 See Shadows, The
Megadeth **9**
Mehldau, Brad **27**
Mehta, Zubin **11**
Meine, Klaus
 See Scorpions, The
Meisner, Randy
 See Eagles, The
Mekons, The **15**
Melanie **12**
Melax, Einar
 See Sugarcubes, The
Mellencamp, John **20**
 Earlier sketch in CM **2**
Melvins **21**
Memphis Jug Band **25**
Memphis Minnie **25**
Mendel, Nate
 See Foo Fighters
Mengede, Peter
 See Helmet
Menken, Alan **10**
Menuhin, Yehudi **11**
Menza, Nick
 See Megadeth
Mercer, Johnny **13**
Merchant, Jimmy
 See Frankie Lymon and The Teenagers
Merchant, Natalie **25**
 Also see 10,000 Maniacs
Mercier, Peadar
 See Chieftains, The
Mercury, Freddie
 See Queen
Merman, Ethel **27**
Mertens, Paul
 See Poi Dog Pondering
Mesaros, Michael
 See Smithereens, The
Messecar, Dek
 See Caravan
Messina, Jim
 See Buffalo Springfield
Messina, Jo Dee **26**
Metallica **7**
Meters, The **14**
Methembu, Russel
 See Ladysmith Black Mambazo
Metheny, Pat **26**
 Earlier sketch in CM **2**
Meyer, Eric
 See Charm Farm
Meyers, Augie
 See Texas Tornados, The
Mhaonaigh, Mairead Ni
 See Altan
Michael, George **9**
Michaels, Bret
 See Poison
Michel, Luke
 See Emmet Swimming
Michel, Prakazrel "Pras"
 See Fugees, The
Michiles, Malcolm
 See Citizen King
Middlebrook, Ralph "Pee Wee"
 See Ohio Players
Middleton, Mark
 See Blackstreet
Midler, Bette **8**
Midnight Oil **11**
Midori **7**
Mighty Clouds of Joy, The **17**
Mighty Mighty Bosstones **20**
Mike & the Mechanics **17**
Mike D
 See Diamond, Michael
Mikens, Dennis
 See Smithereens, The
Mikens, Robert
 See Kool & the Gang
Milchem, Glenn
 See Blue Rodeo
Miles, Chris
 See Northern Lights
Miles, Richard
 See Soul Stirrers, The
Miles, Ron **22**
Millar, Deborah
 See Massive Attack
Miller, Charles
 See War
Miller, Glenn **6**
Miller, Jacob "Killer" Miller
 See Inner Circle
Miller, Jerry
 See Moby Grape
Miller, Kevin
 See Fuel
Miller, Mark
 See Sawyer Brown
Miller, Mitch **11**
Miller, Rice
 See Williamson, Sonny Boy
Miller, Robert
 See Supertramp
Miller, Roger **4**
Miller, Steve **2**
Milli Vanilli **4**
Mills Brothers, The **14**
Mills, Donald
 See Mills Brothers, The
Mills, Fred
 See Canadian Brass, The
Mills, Harry
 See Mills Brothers, The
Mills, Herbert
 See Mills Brothers, The
Mills, John, Jr.
 See Mills Brothers, The
Mills, John, Sr.
 See Mills Brothers, The
Mills, Mike
 See R.E.M.
Mills, Sidney
 See Steel Pulse
Mills, Stephanie **21**
Milsap, Ronnie **2**
Milton, Doctor
 See Alien Sex Fiend
Mingus, Charles **9**
Ministry **10**
Minnelli, Liza **19**
Miss Kier Kirby
 See Lady Miss Kier
Mitchell, Alex
 See Curve
Mitchell, John
 See Asleep at the Wheel
Mitchell, Joni **17**
 Earlier sketch in CM **2**
Mitchell, Keith
 See Mazzy Star
Mitchell, Mitch
 See Guided By Voices
Mitchell, Roscoe
 See Art Ensemble of Chicago, The
Mittoo, Jackie
 See Skatalites, The
Mize, Ben
 See Counting Crows
Mizell, Jay "Jam Master Jay"
 See Run DMC
Mo', Keb' **21**
Moby **27**
 Earlier sketch in CM **17**
Moby Grape **12**
Modeliste, Joseph "Zigaboo"
 See Meters, The
Moerlen, Pierre
 See Gong
Moffatt, Katy **18**
Moginie, Jim
 See Midnight Oil
Mogwai **27**
Mohr, Todd
 See Big Head Todd and the Monsters
Mojave 3 **26**
Molko, Brian
 See Placebo
Molland, Joey
 See Badfinger
Molloy, Matt
 See Chieftains, The
Moloney, Paddy
 See Chieftains, The
Monarch, Michael
 See Steppenwolf
Money B
 See Digital Underground
Money, Eddie **16**
Monica **26**
Monifah **24**
Monk, Meredith **1**
Monk, Thelonious **6**
Monkees, The **7**
Monroe, Bill **1**
Montana, Country Dick
 See Beat Farmers
Montand, Yves **12**
Montenegro, Hugo **18**
Montgomery, John Michael **14**
Montgomery, Little Brother **26**
Montgomery, Wes **3**
Monti, Steve
 See Curve
Montoya, Craig
 See Everclear
Montrose, Ronnie **22**
Moody Blues, The **18**
Moon, Doug
 See Captain Beefheart and His Magic Band
Moon, Keith
 See Who, The
Mooney, Tim
 See American Music Club
Moore, Alan
 See Judas Priest
Moore, Angelo
 See Fishbone
Moore, Archie
 See Velocity Girl
Moore, Chante **21**
Moore, Johnny "Dizzy"
 See Skatalites, The
Moore, Kevin
 See Dream Theater

Moore, LeRoi
See Dave Matthews Band
Moore, Melba **7**
Moore, Sam
See Sam and Dave
Moore, Sean
See Manic Street Preachers
Moore, Thurston
See Sonic Youth
Morand, Grace
See Chenille Sisters, The
Moraz, Patrick
See Moody Blues, The
Also see Yes
Morcheeba **25**
Moreira, Airto
See Weather Report
Morello, Tom
See Rage Against the Machine
Moreno, Chino
See Deftones
Moreve, Rushton
See Steppenwolf
Morgan, Frank **9**
Morgan, John Russell
See Steppenwolf
Morgan, Lorrie **10**
Morissette, Alanis **19**
Morley, Pat
See Soul Asylum
Morphine **16**
Morricone, Ennio **15**
Morris, Keith
See Circle Jerks, The
Morris, Kenny
See Siouxsie and the Banshees
Morris, Nate
See Boyz II Men
Morris, Roger
See Psychedelic Furs
Morris, Stephen
See Joy Division
Also see New Order
Also see Pogues, The
Morris, Wanya
See Boyz II Men
Morrison, Bram
See Sharon, Lois & Bram
Morrison, Claude
See Nylons, The
Morrison, Jim **3**
Also see Doors, The
Morrison, Sterling
See Velvet Underground, The
Morrison, Van **24**
Earlier sketch in CM **3**
Morrissett, Paul
See Klezmatics, The
Morrissey **10**
Also see Smiths, The
Morrissey, Bill **12**
Morrissey, Steven Patrick
See Morrissey
Morton, Everett
See English Beat, The
Morton, Jelly Roll **7**
Morvan, Fab
See Milli Vanilli
Mosbaugh, Garth
See Nylons, The
Mosely, Chuck
See Faith No More
Moser, Scott "Cactus"
See Highway 101
Mosher, Ken
See Squirrel Nut Zippers
Mosley, Bob
See Moby Grape
Moss, Jason
See Cherry Poppin' Daddies
Mothersbaugh, Bob
See Devo
Mothersbaugh, Mark
See Devo
Mötley Crüe **1**
Motörhead **10**
Motta, Danny
See Roomful of Blues
Mould, Bob **10**
Moulding, Colin
See XTC
Mounfield, Gary
See Stone Roses, The
Mouquet, Eric
See Deep Forest
Mouskouri, Nana **12**
Mouzon, Alphonse
See Weather Report
Moye, Famoudou Don
See Art Ensemble of Chicago, The
Moyet, Alison **12**
Moyse, David
See Air Supply
Mr. Dalvin
See Jodeci
Mudhoney **16**
Mueller, Karl
See Soul Asylum
Muir, Jamie
See King Crimson
Muir, Mike
See Suicidal Tendencies
Muldaur, Maria **18**
Mulholland, Dave
See Aztec Camera
Mullen, Larry, Jr.
See U2
Mullen, Mary
See Congo Norvell
Mulligan, Gerry **16**
Murcia, Billy
See New York Dolls
Murdock, Roger
See King Missile
Murph
See Dinosaur Jr.
Murphey, Michael Martin **9**
Murphy, Brigid
See Poi Dog Pondering
Murphy, Dan
See Soul Asylum
Murphy, John
See Gene Loves Jezebel
Murphy, Michael
See REO Speedwagon
Murphy, Peter
See Bauhaus
Murphy, Peter **22**
Murray, Anne **4**
Murray, Dave
See Iron Maiden
Murray, Dee
See Spencer Davis Group
Murray, Jim
See Quicksilver Messenger Service
Mushroom
See Massive Attack
Musselwhite, Charlie **13**
Mustaine, Dave
See Megadeth
Also see Metallica
Mutter, Anne-Sophie **23**
Mwelase, Jabulane
See Ladysmith Black Mambazo
Mydland, Brent
See Grateful Dead, The
Myers, Alan
See Devo
Myles, Alannah **4**
Mystic Revealers **16**
Myung, John
See Dream Theater
'N Sync **25**
N.W.A. **6**
N'Dour, Youssou **6**
Na'dirah
See Arrested Development
Naftalin, Mark
See Quicksilver Messenger Service
Nagler, Eric **8**
Najee **21**
Nakai, R. Carlos **24**
Nakamura, Tetsuya "Tex"
See War
Nakatami, Michie
See Shonen Knife
Nana
See Rasputina
Narcizo, David
See Throwing Muses
Nas **19**
Nascimento, Milton **6**
Nash, Graham
See Crosby, Stills, and Nash
Nash, Leigh
See Sixpence None the Richer
Nashville Bluegrass Band **14**
Nastanovich, Bob
See Pavement
Naughty by Nature **11**
Navarro, David
See Jane's Addiction
Navarro Fats **25**
Nawasadio, Sylvie
See Zap Mama
Ndegéocello, Me'Shell **18**
Ndugu
See Weather Report
Near, Holly **1**
Neel, Johnny
See Allman Brothers, The
Negron, Chuck
See Three Dog Night
Negroni, Joe
See Frankie Lymon and The Teenagers
Neil, Chris
See Less Than Jake
Neil, Vince
See Mötley Crüe
Nelson, Brett
See Built to Spill
Nelson, Brian
See Velocity Girl
Nelson, David
See Last Poets
Nelson, Errol
See Black Uhuru
Nelson, Gabe
See Cake
Nelson, Nate
See Platters, The
Nelson, Rick **2**

Nelson, Shara
See Massive Attack
Nelson, Willie **11**
Earlier sketch in CM **1**
Nero, Peter **19**
Nesbitt, John
See McKinney's Cotton Pickers
Nesmith, Mike
See Monkees, The
Ness, Mike
See Social Distortion
Netson, Brett
See Built to Spill
Neufville, Renee
See Zhane
Neumann, Kurt
See BoDeans
Nevarez, Alfred
See All-4-One
Neville, Aaron **5**
Also see Neville Brothers, The
Neville, Art
See Meters, The
Also see Neville Brothers, The
Neville Brothers, The **4**
Neville, Charles
See Neville Brothers, The
Neville, Cyril
See Meters, The
Also see Neville Brothers, The
Nevin, Brian
See Big Head Todd and the Monsters
New Grass Revival, The **4**
New Kids on the Block **3**
New Order **11**
New Rhythm and Blues Quartet
See NRBQ
New York Dolls **20**
Newman, Randy **27**
Earlier sketch in CM **4**
Newmann, Kurt
See BoDeans, The
Newsboys, The **24**
Newson, Arlene
See Poi Dog Pondering
Newsted, Jason
See Metallica
Newton, Paul
See Uriah Heep
Newton, Wayne **2**
Newton-Davis, Billy
See Nylons, The
Newton-John, Olivia **8**
Nibbs, Lloyd
See Skatalites, The
Nicholas, James Dean "J.D."
See Commodores, The
Nicholls, Geoff
See Black Sabbath
Nichols, Gates
See Confederate Railroad
Nichols, Todd
See Toad the Wet Sprocket
Nickerson, Charlie
See Memphis Jug Band
Nicks, Stevie **25**
Earlier sketch in CM **2**
Also see Fleetwood Mac
Nico
See Velvet Underground, The
Nicol, Simon
See Fairport Convention
Nicolette
See Massive Attack
Nielsen, Rick
See Cheap Trick
Nikleva, Steven
See Ray Condo and His Ricochets
Nilija, Robert
See Last Poets
Nilsson **10**
Nilsson, Harry
See Nilsson
Nirvana **8**
Nisbett, Steve "Grizzly"
See Steel Pulse
Nishino, Kohji
See Ghost
Nitty Gritty Dirt Band, The **6**
No Doubt **20**
Nobacon, Danbert "The Cat"
See Chumbawamba
Nocentelli, Leo
See Meters, The
Nolan, Jerry
See New York Dolls
Nomiya, Maki
See Pizzicato Five
Noone, Peter "Herman"
See Herman's Hermits
Norica, Sugar Ray
See Roomful of Blues
Norman, Jessye **7**
Norman, Jimmy
See Coasters, The
Norman, Patrick
See Rusted Root
Norris, Jean
See Zhane
Northern Lights **19**
Northey, Craig
See Odds
Norum, John
See Dokken
Norvell, Sally
See Congo Norvell
Norvo, Red **12**
Notorious B.I.G. **20**
Novoselic, Chris
See Nirvana
Nowell, Bradley James
See Sublime
NRBQ **12**
Nugent, Ted **2**
Nunn, Bobby
See Coasters, The
Nutter, Alice
See Chumbawamba
Nylons, The **6**
Nyman, Michael **15**
Nyolo, Sally
See Zap Mama
Nyro, Laura **12**
O'Brien, Darrin Kenneth
See Snow
O'Brien, Derek
See Social Distortion
O'Brien, Dwayne
See Little Texas
O'Brien, Ed
See Radiohead
O'Brien, Marty
See Kilgore
O'Bryant, Alan
See Nashville Bluegrass Band
O'Connell, Chris
See Asleep at the Wheel
O'Connor, Billy
See Blondie
O'Connor, Daniel
See House of Pain
O'Connor, Mark **1**
O'Connor, Sinead **3**
O'Day, Anita **21**
O'Donnell, Roger
See Cure, The
O'Hagan, Sean
See Stereolab
O'Hare, Brendan
See Mogwai
See Teenage Fanclub
O'Jays, The **13**
O'Reagan, Tim
See Jayhawks, The
O'Riordan, Cait
See Pogues, The
O'Riordan, Dolores
See Cranberries, The
Oak Ridge Boys, The **7**
Earlier sketch in CM **4**
Oakes, Richard
See Suede
Oakey, Philip
See Human League, The
Oakland Interfaith Gospel Choir **26**
Oakley, Berry
See Allman Brothers, The
Oasis **16**
Oates, John
See Hall & Oates
Ocasek, Ric **5**
Also see Cars, The
Ocean, Billy **4**
Oceans, Lucky
See Asleep at the Wheel
Ochs, Phil **7**
Odds **20**
Odetta **7**
Odmark, Matt
See Jars of Clay
Offspring, The **19**
Ofwerman, Clarence
See Roxette
Ofwerman, Staffan
See Roxette
Ogino, Kazuo
See Ghost
Ogletree, Mike
See Simple Minds
Ogre, Nivek
See Pigface
See Skinny Puppy
Ohanian, David
See Canadian Brass, The
Ohio Players **16**
Oje, Baba
See Arrested Development
Olafsson, Bragi
See Sugarcubes, The
Olander, Jimmy
See Diamond Rio
Olaverra, Margot
See Go-Go's, The
Olde-Wolbers, Christian
See Fear Factory
Oldfield, Mike **18**
Oldham, Jack
See Surfaris, The
Oldham, Sean
See Cherry Poppin' Daddies
Olds, Brent
See Poi Dog Pondering
Oliver, Joe
See Oliver, King

Oliver, King **15**
Olsdal, Stefan
See Placebo
Olson, Jeff
See Village People, The
Olson, Mark
See Jayhawks, The
Olsson, Nigel
See Spencer Davis Group
Onassis, Blackie
See Urge Overkill
Ono, Yoko **11**
Opokuwaa, Akua
See Sweet Honey in the Rock
Orange, Walter "Clyde"
See Commodores, The
Orb, The **18**
Orbison, Roy **2**
Orbital **20**
Orchestral Manoeuvres in the Dark **21**
Orff, Carl **21**
Orgy **27**
Orlando, Tony **15**
Örn, Einar
See Sugarcubes, The
Örnolfsdottir, Margret
See Sugarcubes, The
Orr, Benjamin
See Cars, The
Orr, Casey
See Gwar
Orrall, Frank
See Poi Dog Pondering
Ortega, Leonor "Jeff"
See Five Iron Frenzy
Ortega, Micah
See Five Iron Frenzy
Orton, Beth **26**
Orzabal, Roland
See Tears for Fears
Osborne, Bob
See Osborne Brothers, The
Osborne Brothers, The **8**
Osborne, Buzz
See Melvins
Osborne, Joan **19**
Osborne, Sonny
See Osborne Brothers, The
Osbourne, Ozzy **3**
Also see Black Sabbath
Osby, Greg **21**
Oskar, Lee
See War
Oslin, K. T. **3**
Osman, Mat
See Suede
Osmond, Donny **3**
Ostin, Mo **17**
Otis, Johnny **16**
Ott, David **2**
Otto, John
See Limp Bizkit
Our Lady Peace **22**
Outler, Jimmy
See Soul Stirrers, The
Owen, Randy Yeuell
See Alabama
Owens, Buck **2**
Owens, Campbell
See Aztec Camera
Owens, Henry
See Golden Gate Quartet
Owens, Ricky
See Temptations, The
Oyewole, Abiodun
See Last Poets
P.M. Dawn **11**
Page, Jimmy **4**
Also see Led Zeppelin
Also see Yardbirds, The
Page, Patti **11**
Page, Steven
See Barenaked Ladies
Paice, Ian
See Deep Purple
Paliotta, Cherie
See Avalon
Palmer, Bruce
See Buffalo Springfield
Palmer, Carl
See Emerson, Lake & Palmer/Powell
Palmer, Clive
See Incredible String Band
Palmer, David
See Jethro Tull
Palmer, Jeff **20**
Palmer, Keeti
See Prodigy
Palmer, Phil
See Dire Straits
Palmer, Richard
See Supertramp
Palmer, Robert **2**
Palmer-Jones, Robert
See King Crimson
Palmieri, Eddie **15**
Paluzzi, Jimmy
See Sponge
Pamer, John
See Tsunami
Pankow, James
See Chicago
Panter, Horace
See Specials, The
Pantera **13**
Papach, Leyna
See Geraldine Fibbers
Pappas, Tom
See Superdrag
Parazaider, Walter
See Chicago
Paris, Twila **16**
Park, Cary
See Boy Howdy
Park, Larry
See Boy Howdy
Parkening, Christopher **7**
Parker, Charlie **5**
Parker, Graham **10**
Parker, Kris
See KRS-One
Parker, Leon **27**
Parker, Maceo **7**
Parker, Tom
See Animals, The
Parkin, Chad
See Aquabats, The
Parks, Van Dyke **17**
Parnell, Lee Roy **15**
Parsons, Alan **12**
Parsons, Dave
See Bush
Parsons, Gene
See Byrds, The
Parsons, Gram **7**
Also see Byrds, The
Parsons, Ted
See Prong
Parsons, Tony
See Iron Maiden
Parton, Dolly **24**
Earlier sketch in CM **2**
Partridge, Andy
See XTC
Parvo, Carpella
See Rasputina
Pasemaster, Mase
See De La Soul
Pash, Jim
See Surfaris, The
Pasillas, Jose
See Incubus
Pass, Joe **15**
Passons, Michael
See Avalon
Pastorius, Jaco
See Weather Report
Paterson, Alex
See Orb, The
Patinkin, Mandy **20**
Earlier sketch CM **3**
Patti, Sandi **7**
Patton, Charley **11**
Patton, Mike
See Faith No More
Paul, Alan
See Manhattan Transfer, The
Paul III, Henry
See BlackHawk
Paul, Les **2**
Paul, Vinnie
See Pantera
Paulo, Jr.
See Sepultura
Pavarotti, Luciano **20**
Earlier sketch in CM **1**
Pavement **14**
Pavia, John
See Four Seasons, The
Paxton, Tom **5**
Payne, Bill
See Little Feat
Payne, Scherrie
See Supremes, The
Payton, Denis
See Dave Clark Five, The
Payton, Lawrence
See Four Tops, The
Payton, Nicholas **27**
Pearl Jam **12**
Pearl, Minnie **3**
Pearls Before Swine **24**
Pearson, Dan
See American Music Club
Peart, Neil
See Rush
Pedersen, Herb
See Desert Rose Band, The
Peduzzi, Larry
See Roomful of Blues
Peek, Dan
See America
Peeler, Ben
See Mavericks, The
Pegg, Dave
See Fairport Convention
Also see Jethro Tull
Pegrum, Nigel
See Steeleye Span
Pelletier, Mike
See Kilgore
Pence, Jeff
See Blessid Union of Souls

Pendergrass, Teddy **3**
Pendleton, Brian
See Pretty Things, The
Pengilly, Kirk
See INXS
Peniston, CeCe **15**
Penn, Michael **4**
Penner, Fred **10**
Pennywise **27**
Pentangle **18**
Pepper, Art **18**
Perahia, Murray **10**
Pere Ubu **17**
Peretz, Jesse
See Lemonheads, The
Perez, Danilo **25**
Perez, Louie
See Los Lobos
Perkins, Carl **9**
Perkins, John
See XTC
Perkins, Percell
See Five Blind Boys of Alabama
Perkins, Steve
See Jane's Addiction
Perko, Lynn
See Imperial Teen
Perlman, Itzhak **2**
Perlman, Marc
See Jayhawks, The
Pernice, Joe
See Scud Mountain Boys
Perry, Brendan
See Dead Can Dance
Perry, Doane
See Jethro Tull
Perry, Joe
See Aerosmith
Perry, John G.
See Caravan
Perry, Phil **24**
Perry, Steve
See Cherry Poppin' Daddies
Perry, Steve
See Journey
Perry, Virgshawn
See Artifacts
Persson, Nina
See Cardigans
Pet Shop Boys **5**
Peter, Paul & Mary **4**
Peters, Bernadett **27**
Earlier sketch in CM **7**
Peters, Dan
See Mudhoney
Peters, Joey
See Grant Lee Buffalo
Peters, Mike
See Alarm
Petersen, Chris
See Front Line Assembly
Peterson, Debbi
See Bangles, The
Peterson, Garry
See Guess Who
Peterson, Oscar **11**
Peterson, Vicki
See Bangles, The
Petersson, Tom
See Cheap Trick
Petra **3**
Petri, Tony
See Wendy O. Williams and The Plasmatics
Petrucci, John
See Dream Theater
Petty, Tom **26**
Earlier sketch in CM **9**
Also see Tom Petty and the Heartbreakers
Pfaff, Kristen
See Hole
Phair, Liz **14**
Phantom, Slim Jim
See Stray Cats, The
Pharcyde, The **17**
Phelps, Doug
See Kentucky Headhunters, The
Phelps, Ricky Lee
See Kentucky Headhunters, The
Phife
See Tribe Called Quest, A
Phil, Gary
See Boston
Philbin, Greg
See REO Speedwagon
Philips, Anthony
See Genesis
Phillips, Chris
See Squirrel Nut Zippers
Phillips, Chynna
See Wilson Phillips
Phillips, Glenn
See Toad the Wet Sprocket
Phillips, Grant Lee
See Grant Lee Buffalo
Phillips, Harvey **3**
Phillips, John
See Mamas and the Papas
Phillips, Mackenzie
See Mamas and the Papas
Phillips, Michelle
See Mamas and the Papas
Phillips, Sam **12**
Phillips, Sam **5**
Phillips, Shelley
See Point of Grace
Phillips, Simon
See Judas Priest
Phish **25**
Earlier sketch in CM **13**
Phungula, Inos
See Ladysmith Black Mambazo
Piaf, Edith **8**
Piazzolla, Astor **18**
Picciotto, Joe
See Fugazi
Piccolo, Greg
See Roomful of Blues
Pickerel, Mark
See Screaming Trees
Pickering, Michael
See M People
Pickering, Mike
See M People
Pickett, Wilson **10**
Pierce, Charlie
See Memphis Jug Band
Pierce, Marvin "Merv"
See Ohio Players
Pierce, Webb **15**
Pierson, Kate
SeeB-52's, The
Pigface **19**
Pilatus, Rob
See Milli Vanilli
Pilson, Jeff
See Dokken
Pinder, Michael
See Moody Blues, The
Pine, Courtney
See Soul II Soul
Pink Floyd **2**
Pinkus, Jeff
See Butthole Surfers
Pinnick, Doug
See King's X
Pires, Maria João **26**
Pirner, Dave
See Soul Asylum
Pirroni, Marco
See Siouxsie and the Banshees
Pixies, The **21**
Pizzicato Five **18**
Placebo **27**
Plakas, Dee
See L7
Plant, Robert **2**
Also see Led Zeppelin
Platters, The **25**
Pleasant, Alvin
See Carter Family, The
Ploog, Richard
See Church, The
Plouf, Scott
See Built to Spill
Pogues, The **6**
Poi Dog Pondering **17**
Poindexter, Buster
See Johansen, David
Point of Grace **21**
Pointer, Anita
See Pointer Sisters, The
Pointer, Bonnie
See Pointer Sisters, The
Pointer, June
See Pointer Sisters, The
Pointer, Ruth
See Pointer Sisters, The
Pointer Sisters, The **9**
Poison **11**
Poison Ivy
See Rorschach, Poison Ivy
Poland, Chris
See Megadeth
Polce, Tom
See Letters to Cleo
Polci, Gerry
See Four Seasons, The
Police, The **20**
Pollard, Jim
See Guided By Voices
Pollard, Robert, Jr.
See Guided By Voices
Pollard, Russ
See Sebadoh
Pollock, Courtney Adam
See Aquabats. The
Polygon Window
See Aphex Twin
Pomus, Doc
See Doc Pomus
Ponty, Jean-Luc **8**
Also see Mahavishnu Orchestra
Pop, Iggy **23**
Earlier sketch in CM **1**
Popoff, A. Jay
See Lit
Popoff, Jeremy
See Lit
Popper, John
See Blues Traveler
Porter, Cole **10**
Porter, George, Jr.
See Meters, The
Porter, Jody
See Fountains of Wayne

Porter, Tiran
See Doobie Brothers, The
Portishead **22**
Portman-Smith, Nigel
See Pentangle
Portnoy, Mike
See Dream Theater
Posdnuos
See De La Soul
Post, Louise
See Veruca Salt
Post, Mike **21**
Potter, Janna
See Avalon
Potts, Sean
See Chieftains, The
Povey, John
See Pretty Things, The
Powell, Baden **23**
Powell, Billy
See Lynyrd Skynyrd
Powell, Bud **15**
Powell, Cozy
See Emerson, Lake & Palmer/Powell
Powell, Kobie
See US3
Powell, Paul
See Aztec Camera
Powell, William
See O'Jays, The
Powers, Kid Congo
See Congo Norvell
Also see Cramps, The
Prater, Dave
See Sam and Dave
Pratt, Awadagin **19**
Prefab Sprout **15**
Presley, Elvis **1**
Pretenders, The **8**
Pretty Things, The **26**
Previn, André **15**
Price, Alan
See Animals, The
Price, Leontyne **6**
Price, Lloyd **25**
Price, Louis
See Temptations, The
Price, Mark
See Archers of Loaf
Price, Ray **11**
Price, Rick
See Electric Light Orchestra
Pride, Charley **4**
Priest, Maxi **20**
Prima, Louis **18**
Primal Scream **14**
Primettes, The
See Supremes, The
Primus **11**
Prince **14**
Earlier sketch in CM **1**
Prince Be
See P.M. Dawn
Prince, Prairie
See Journey
Prince, Vivian
See Pretty Things, The
Prine, John **7**
Prior, Maddy
See Steeleye Span
Proclaimers, The **13**
Prodigy **22**
Professor Longhair **6**
Prong **23**
Propatier, Joe
See Silver Apples
Propellerheads **26**
Propes, Duane
See Little Texas
Prout, Brian
See Diamond Rio
Psychedelic Furs **23**
Public Enemy **4**
Puccini, Giacomo **25**
Puente, Tito **14**
Puff Daddy
See Combs, Sean "Puffy"
Pullen, Don **16**
Pulp **18**
Pulsford, Nigel
See Bush
Pusey, Clifford "Moonie"
See Steel Pulse
Pyle, Andy
See Kinks, The
Pyle, Artemis
See Lynyrd Skynyrd
Pyle, Pip
See Gong
Pyro, Howie
See D Generation
Q-Tip
See Tribe Called Quest, A
Quaife, Peter
See Kinks, The
Quasi **24**
Quasthoff, Thomas **26**
Queen **6**
Queen Ida **9**
Queen Latifah **24**
Earlier sketch in CM **6**
Queensryche **8**
Querfurth, Carl
See Roomful of Blues
Quicksilver Messenger Service **23**
R.E.M. **25**
Earlier sketch in CM **5**
Rabbitt, Eddie **24**
Earlier sketch in CM **5**
Rabin, Trevor
See Yes
Radiohead **24**
Raekwon
See Wu-Tang Clan
Raffi **8**
Rage Against the Machine **18**
Raheem
See GetoBoys, The
Rainey, Ma **22**
Rainey, Sid
See Compulsion
Rainford, Simone
See All Saints
Rainwater, Keech
See Lonestar
Raitt, Bonnie **23**
Earlier sketch in CM **3**
Rakim
See Eric B. and Rakim
Raleigh, Don
See Squirrel Nut Zippers
Ralph Sharon Quartet **26**
Ralphs, Mick
See Bad Company
Rammstein **25**
Ramone, C. J.
See Ramones, The
Ramone, Dee Dee
See Ramones, The
Ramone, Joey
See Ramones, The
Ramone, Johnny
See Ramones, The
Ramone, Marky
See Ramones, The
Ramone, Ritchie
See Ramones, The
Ramone, Tommy
See Ramones, The
Ramones, The **9**
Rampal, Jean-Pierre **6**
Ramsay, Andy
See Stereolab
Ranaldo, Lee
See Sonic Youth
Randall, Bobby
See Sawyer Brown
Raney, Jerry
See Beat Farmers
Rangell, Andrew **24**
Ranglin, Ernest
See Skatalites, The
Ranken, Andrew
See Pogues, The
Rankin, Cookie
See Rankins, The
Rankin, Heather
See Rankins, The
Rankin, Jimmy
See Rankins, The
Rankin, John Morris
See Rankins, The
Rankin, Raylene
See Rankins, The
Ranking, Roger
See English Beat, The
Rankins, The **24**
Rapp, Tom
See Pearls Before Swine
Rarebell, Herman
See Scorpions, The
Rasboro, Johnathen
See Silk
Rasputina **26**
Rat Fink, Jr.
See Alien Sex Fiend
Ravel, Maurice **25**
Raven, Paul
See Prong
Rawls, Lou **19**
Ray, Amy
See Indigo Girls
Ray Condo and His Ricochets **26**
Raybon, Marty
See Shenandoah
Raye, Collin **16**
Raymonde, Simon
See Cocteau Twins, The
Raynor, Scott
See Blink 182
Rea, Chris **12**
Read, John
See Specials, The
Reagon, Bernice Johnson
See Sweet Honey in the Rock
Red Hot Chili Peppers, The **7**
Redbone, Leon **19**
Redd Kross **20**
Redding, Otis **5**
Reddy, Helen **9**
Redman, Don
See McKinney's Cotton Pickers
Redman, Joshua **25**
Earlier sketch in CM **12**

Redpath, Jean **1**
Redus, Richard
See Captain Beefheart and His Magic Band
Reece, Chris
See Social Distortion
Reed, Herbert
See Platters, The
Reed, Jimmy **15**
Reed, Lou **16**
Earlier sketch in CM **1**
Also see Velvet Underground, The
Reef **24**
Reese, Della **13**
Reese, Joey
See Wendy O. Williams and The Plasmatics
Reeves, Dianne **16**
Reeves, Jim **10**
Reeves, Lois
See Martha and the Vandellas
Reeves, Martha **4**
Also see Martha and the Vandellas
Regan, Julianne
See Gene Loves Jezebel
Reich, Steve **8**
Reid, Charlie
See Proclaimers, The
Reid, Christopher
See Kid 'n Play
Reid, Craig
See Proclaimers, The
Reid, Delroy "Junior"
See Black Uhuru
Reid, Don
See Statler Brothers, The
Reid, Ellen Lorraine
See Crash Test Dummies
Reid, Harold
See Statler Brothers, The
Reid, Janet
See Black Uhuru
Reid, Jim
See Jesus and Mary Chain, The
Reid, Lou
See Seldom Scene, The
Reid, Vernon **2**
Also see Living Colour
Reid, William
See Jesus and Mary Chain, The
Reifman, William
See KMFDM
Reinhardt, Django **7**
Reininger, Blaine
See Tuxedomoon
Reitzell, Brian
See Redd Kross
Relf, Keith
See Yardbirds, The
Renbourn, John
See Pentangle
Reno, Ronnie
See Osborne Brothers, The
REO Speedwagon **23**
Replacements, The **7**
Republica **20**
Residents, The **14**
Restless Heart **12**
Revell, Adrian
See Jamiroquai
Reverend Horton Heat **19**
Rex
See Pantera
Reyes, Andre
See Gipsy Kings, The
Reyes, Canut
See Gipsy Kings, The
Reyes, Nicolas
See Gipsy Kings, The
Reynolds, Nick
See Kingston Trio, The
Reynolds, Robert
See Mavericks, The
Reynolds, Sheldon
See Earth, Wind and Fire
Reznor, Trent **13**
Rhodes, Nick
See Duran Duran
Rhodes, Philip
See Gin Blossoms
Rhodes, Todd
See McKinney's Cotton Pickers
Rhone, Sylvia **13**
Rice, Chris **25**
Rich, Buddy **13**
Rich, Charlie **3**
Rich, John
See Lonestar
Richard, Cliff **14**
Richard, Zachary **9**
Richards, Edward
See Shamen, The
Richards, Keith **11**
Also see Rolling Stones, The
Richardson, Geoffrey
See Caravan
Richardson, Kevin
See Backstreet Boys
Richey, Kim **20**
Richie, Lionel **2**
Also see Commodores, The
Richling, Greg
See Wallflowers, The
Richman, Jonathan **12**
Richrath, Gary
See REO Speedwagon
Rick, Dave
See King Missile
Ricochet **23**
Riebling, Scott
See Letters to Cleo
Rieckermann, Ralph
See Scorpions, The
Riedel, Oliver
See Rammstein
Rieflin, William
See Ministry
See Pigface
Rieu, André **26**
Riles, Kelly
See Velocity Girl
Riley, Kristian
See Citizen King
Riley, Teddy "Street" **14**
See Blackstreet
Riley, Timothy Christian
See Tony! Toni! Toné!
Rimes, LeAnn **19**
Rippon, Steve
See Lush
Ritchie, Brian
See Violent Femmes
Ritchie, Jean **4**
Ritchie, John Simon
See Sid Vicious
Ritchie, Robert
See Kid Rock
Ritenour, Lee **7**
Rivers, Sam
See Limp Bizkit
Rizzo, Joe
See D Generation
Rizzo, Peter
See Gene Loves Jezebel
Roach, Max **12**
Roback, David
See Mazzy Star
Robbins, Charles David
See BlackHawk
Robbins, Marty **9**
Roberts, Brad
See Crash Test Dummies
Roberts, Brad
See Gwar
Roberts, Dan
See Crash Test Dummies
Roberts, Ken
See Charm Farm
Roberts, Marcus **6**
Roberts, Nathan
See Flaming Lips
Robertson, Brian
See Motörhead
Also see Thin Lizzy
Robertson, Ed
See Barenaked Ladies
Robertson, Robbie **2**
Also see Band, The
Robeson, Paul **8**
Robi, Paul
See Platters, The
Robie, Milton
See Memphis Jug Band
Robillard, Duke **2**
Also see Roomful of Blues
Robinson, Arnold
See Nylons, The
Robinson, Chris
See Black Crowes, The
Robinson, Cynthia
See Sly & the Family Stone
Robinson, David
See Cars, The
Robinson, Dawn
See En Vogue
Robinson, Louise
See Sweet Honey in the Rock
Robinson, Prince
See McKinney's Cotton Pickers
Robinson, R.B.
See Soul Stirrers, The
Robinson, Rich
See Black Crowes, The
Robinson, Romye "Booty Brown"
See Pharcyde, The
Robinson, Smokey **1**
Roche, Maggie
See Roches, The
Roche, Suzzy
See Roches, The
Roche, Terre
See Roches, The
Roches, The **18**
Rockenfield, Scott
See Queensryche
Rocker, Lee
See Stray Cats, The
Rockett, Rikki
See Poison
Rockin' Dopsie **10**
Rodford, Jim
See Kinks, The
Rodgers, Jimmie **3**
Rodgers, Nile **8**
Rodgers, Paul
See Bad Company

Rodgers, Richard **9**
Rodney, Red **14**
Rodriguez, Rico
See Skatalites, The
Also see Specials, The
Rodriguez, Sal
See War
Roe, Marty
See Diamond Rio
Roeder, Klaus
See Kraftwerk
Roeser, Donald
See Blue Oyster Cult
Roeser, Eddie "King"
See Urge Overkill
Roessler, Kira
See Black Flag
Roger, Ranking
See English Beat, The
Rogers, Dan
See Bluegrass Patriots
Rogers, Kenny **1**
Rogers, Norm
See Jayhawks, The
Rogers, Roy **24**
Earlier sketch in CM **9**
Rogers, Willie
See Soul Stirrers, The
Rogerson, Roger
See Circle Jerks
Roland, Dean
See Collective Soul
Roland, Ed
See Collective Soul
Rolie, Gregg
See Journey
Rolling Stones, The **23**
Earlier sketch in CM **3**
Rollins, Henry **11**
Also see Black Flag
Rollins, Sonny **7**
Rollins, Winston
See Jamiroquai
Romanelli, Chris "Junior"
See Wendy O. Williams and The Plasmatics
Romano, Ruben
See Fu Manchu
Romm, Ronald
See Canadian Brass, The
Ronstadt, Linda **2**
Roomful of Blues **7**
Roots, The **27**
Roper, Dee Dee
See Salt-N-Pepa
Roper, Reese
See Five Iron Frenzy
Roper, Todd
See Cake
Rorschach, Poison Ivy
See Cramps, The
Rosas, Cesar
See Los Lobos
Rose, Axl
See Guns n' Roses
Rose, Felipe
See Village People, The
Rose, Johanna Maria
See Anonymous 4
Rose, Michael
See Black Uhuru
Rosen, Gary
See Rosenshontz
Rosen, Peter
See War
Rosenshontz **9**
Rosenthal, Jurgen
See Scorpions, The
Rosenthal, Phil
See Seldom Scene, The
Ross, Diana **1**
Also see Supremes, The
Ross, Malcolm
See Aztec Camera
Rossdale, Gavin
See Bush
Rossi, John
See Roomful of Blues
Rossington, Gary
See Lynyrd Skynyrd
Rossy, Jose
See Weather Report
Rostill, John
See Shadows, The
Rostropovich, Mstislav **17**
Rota, Nino **13**
Roth, C. P.
See Blessid Union of Souls
Roth, David Lee **1**
Also see Van Halen
Roth, Gabrielle **26**
Roth, Ulrich
See Scorpions, The
Rotheray, Dave
See Beautiful South
Rotsey, Martin
See Midnight Oil
Rotten, Johnny
See Lydon, John
Also see Sex Pistols, The
Rourke, Andy
See Smiths, The
Rowberry, Dave
See Animals, The
Rowe, Dwain
See Restless Heart
Rowe, Simon
See Mojave 3
Rowlands, Bruce
See Fairport Convention
Rowlands, Tom
See Chemical Brothers
Rowntree, Dave
See Blur
Roxette **23**
Roy, Jimmy
See Ray Condo and His Ricochets
Rubin, Mark
See Bad Livers, The
Rubin, Rick **9**
Rubinstein, Arthur **11**
Rucker, Darius
See Hootie and the Blowfish
Rudd, Phillip
See AC/DC
Rue, Caroline
See Hole
Ruffin, David **6**
Also see Temptations, The
Ruffin, Tamir
See Dru Hill
Ruffy, Dave
See Waterboys, The
Ruffy, Dave
See Aztec Camera
Run DMC **25**
Earlier sketch in CM **4**
Run
See Run DMC
Rundgren, Todd **11**
RuPaul **20**
Rush **8**
Rush, Otis **12**
Rushlow, Tim
See Little Texas
Russell, Alecia
See Sounds of Blackness
Russell, Graham
See Air Supply
Russell, John
See Steppenwolf
Russell, Mark **6**
Russell, Mike
See Shudder to Think
Russell, Pee Wee **25**
Russell, Tom **26**
Rusted Root **26**
Rutherford, Mike
See Genesis
Also see Mike & the Mechanics
Rutsey, John
See Rush
Ryan, David
See Lemonheads, The
Ryan, Mark
See Quicksilver Messenger Service
Ryan, Mick
See Dave Clark Five, The
Rybska, Agnieszka
See Rasputina
Ryder, Mitch **23**
Earlier sketch in CM **11**
Ryland, Jack
See Three Dog Night
Rzeznik, Johnny
See Goo Goo Dolls, The
Sabo, Dave
See Bon Jovi
Sade **2**
Sadier, Laetitia
See Stereolab
Saffery, Anthony
See Cornershop
Saffron,
See Republica
Sage, Danny
See D Generation
Sager, Carole Bayer **5**
Sahm, Doug
See Texas Tornados, The
Saint-Saëns, Camille **25**
Sainte-Marie, Buffy **11**
Sakamoto, Ryuichi **19**
Salazar, Arion
See Third Eye Blind
Salerno-Sonnenberg, Nadja **3**
Saliers, Emily
See Indigo Girls
Salisbury, Peter
See Verve, The
Also see Pizzicato Five
Salmon, Michael
See Prefab Sprout
Saloman, Nick
See Bevis Frond
Salonen, Esa-Pekka **16**
Salt-N-Pepa **6**
Saluzzi, Dino **23**
Sam and Dave **8**
Sambora, Richie **24**
Also see Bon Jovi
Sammy, Piazza
See Quicksilver Messenger Service

Sampson, Doug
See Iron Maiden
Sams, Dean
See Lonestar
Samuelson, Gar
See Megadeth
Samwell-Smith, Paul
See Yardbirds, The
Sanborn, David **1**
Sanchez, Michel
See Deep Forest
Sanctuary, Gary
See Aztec Camera
Sanders, Pharoah **16**
Sanders, Ric
See Fairport Convention
Sanders, Steve
See Oak Ridge Boys, The
Sandler, Adam **19**
Sandman, Mark
See Morphine
Sandoval, Arturo **15**
Sandoval, Hope
See Mazzy Star
Sands, Aaron
See Jars of Clay
Sanford, Gary
See Aztec Camera
Sangare, Oumou **22**
Sanger, David
See Asleep at the Wheel
Santana, Carlos **19**
Earlier sketch in CM **1**
Santiago, Herman
See Frankie Lymon and The Teenagers
Santiago, Joey
See Pixies, The
Saraceno, Blues
See Poison
Sargent, Gray
See Ralph Sharon Quartet
Sasaki, Mamiko
See Pulp
Satchell, Clarence "Satch"
See Ohio Players
Satie, Erik **25**
Satriani, Joe **4**
Savage, Rick
See Def Leppard
Savage, Scott
See Jars of Clay
Sawyer Brown **27**
Earlier sketch in CM **13**
Sawyer, Phil
See Spencer Davis Group
Saxa
See English Beat, The
Saxon, Stan
See Dave Clark Five, The
Scaccia, Mike
See Ministry
Scaggs, Boz **12**
Scaggs, Shawn
See Atomic Fireballs, The
Scallions, Brett
See Fuel
Scanlon, Craig
See Fall, The
Scarface
See Geto Boys, The
Schelhaas, Jan
See Camel
Also see Caravan
Schellenbach, Kate
See Luscious Jackson
Schemel, Patty
See Hole
Schenker, Michael
See Scorpions, The
Schenker, Rudolf
See Scorpions, The
Schenkman, Eric
See Spin Doctors
Schermie, Joe
See Three Dog Night
Scherpenzeel, Ton
See Camel
Schickele, Peter **5**
Schlesinger, Adam
See Fountains of Wayne
Schlitt, John
See Petra
Schloss, Zander
See Circle Jerks, The
Schmelling, Johannes
See Tangerine Dream
Schmid, Daniel
See Cherry Poppin' Daddies
Schmit, Timothy B.
See Eagles, The
Schmoovy Schmoove
See Digital Underground
Schneider, Christoph
See Rammstein
Schneider, Florian
See Kraftwerk
Schneider, Fred III
See B-52's, The
Schnitzler, Conrad
See Tangerine Dream
Schock, Gina
See Go-Go's, The
Scholten, Jim
See Sawyer Brown
Scholz, Tom
See Boston
Schon, Neal
See Journey
Schramm, Dave
See Yo La Tengo
Schrody, Erik
See House of Pain
Also see Everlast
Schroyder, Steve
See Tangerine Dream
Schulman, Mark
See Foreigner
Schulz, Guenter
See KMFDM
Schulzberg, Robert
See Placebo
Schulze, Klaus
See Tangerine Dream
Schuman, William **10**
Schuur, Diane **6**
Schwartz, Will
See Imperial Teen
Sclavunos, Jim
See Congo Norvell
Scofield, John **7**
Scorpions, The **12**
Scott, George
See Five Blind Boys of Alabama
Scott, Howard
See War
Scott, Jimmy **14**
Scott, Mike
See Waterboys, The
Scott, Ronald Belford "Bon"
See AC/DC
Scott, Sherry
See Earth, Wind and Fire
Scott-Heron, Gil **13**
Screaming Trees **19**
Scruggs, Earl **3**
Scud Mountain Boys **21**
Seal **14**
Seales, Jim
See Shenandoah
Seals & Crofts **3**
Seals, Brady
See Little Texas
Seals, Dan **9**
Seals, Jim
See Seals & Crofts
Seaman, Ken
See Bluegrass Patriots
Sears, Pete
See Jefferson Starship
Sebadoh **26**
Secada, Jon **13**
Secrest, Wayne
See Confederate Railroad
Sedaka, Neil **4**
See Smiths, The
Seeger, Peggy **25**
Seeger, Pete **4**
Also see Weavers, The
Seger, Bob **15**
Segovia, Andres **6**
Seidel, Martie
See Dixie Chicks
Seldom Scene, The **4**
Selena **16**
Selway, Phil
See Radiohead
Sen Dog
See Cypress Hill
Senior, Milton
See McKinney's Cotton Pickers
Senior, Russell
See Pulp
Sensi
See Soul II Soul
Sepultura **12**
Seraphine, Daniel
See Chicago
Sermon, Erick
See EPMD
Sete, Bola **26**
Setzer, Brian
See Stray Cats, The
Severin, Steven
See Siouxsie and the Banshees
Severinsen, Doc **1**
Sex Pistols, The **5**
Sexsmith, Ron **27**
Sexton, Chad
See 311
Seymour, Neil
See Crowded House
Shabalala, Ben
See Ladysmith Black Mambazo
Shabalala, Headman
See Ladysmith Black Mambazo
Shabalala, Jockey
See Ladysmith Black Mambazo
Shabalala, Joseph
See Ladysmith Black Mambazo
Shabo, Eric
See Atomic Fireballs, The
Shade, Will
See Memphis Jug Band
Shadow, DJ **19**

Shadows, The **22**
Shaffer, James
See Korn
Shaffer, Paul **13**
Shaggy **19**
Shaggy 2 Dope
See Insane Clown Possee
Shai **23**
Shakespeare, Robbie
See Sly and Robbie
Shakur, Tupac
See 2Pac
Shallenberger, James
See Kronos Quartet
Shamen, The **23**
Shane, Bob
See Kingston Trio, The
Shanice **14**
Shankar, Ravi **9**
Shannon, Del **10**
Shannon, Sarah
See Velocity Girl
Shannon, Sharon
See Waterboys, The
Shanté **10**
Shapiro, Jim
See Veruca Salt
Shapiro, Lee
See Four Seasons, The
Shapps, Andre
See Big Audio Dynamite
Sharon, Lois & Bram **6**
Sharon, Ralph
See Ralph Sharon Quartet
Sharp, Dave
See Alarm
Sharp, Laura
See Sweet Honey in the Rock
Sharpe, Matt
See Weezer
Sharrock, Chris
See Lightning Seeds
Sharrock, Sonny **15**
Shaw, Adrian
See Bevis Frond
Shaw, Artie **8**
Shaw, Martin
See Jamiroquai
Shaw, Woody **27**
Shea, Tom
See Scud Mountain Boys
Shearer, Harry
See Spinal Tap
Sheehan, Bobby
See Blues Traveler
Sheehan, Fran
See Boston
Sheep on Drugs **27**
Sheila E. **3**
Shellenberger, Allen
See Lit
Shelley, Peter
See Buzzcocks, The
Shelley, Steve
See Sonic Youth
Shenandoah **17**
Shepherd, Hunter "Ben"
See Soundgarden
Shepherd, Kenny Wayne **22**
Sheppard, Rodney
See Sugar Ray
Sherba, John
See Kronos Quartet
Sherinian, Derek
See Dream Theater
Sherman, Jack
See Red Hot Chili Peppers, The
Shines, Johnny **14**
Shirelles, The **11**
Shirley, Danny
See Confederate Railroad
Shively, William
See Big Mountain
Shives, Andrew
See Fear Factory
Shock G
See Digital Underground
Shocked, Michelle **4**
Shocklee, Hank **15**
Shogren, Dave
See Doobie Brothers, The
Shonen Knife **13**
Shontz, Bill
See Rosenshontz
Shorter, Wayne **5**
Also see Weather Report
Shovell
See M People
Shuck, Ryan
See Orgy
Shudder to Think **20**
Siberry, Jane **6**
Sice
See Boo Radleys, The
Sidelnyk, Steve
See Aztec Camera
Siebenberg, Bob
See Supertramp
Siegal, Janis
See Manhattan Transfer, The
Sikes, C. David
See Boston
Silk **26**
Sills, Beverly **5**
Silva, Kenny Jo
See Beaver Brown Band, The
Silver Apples **23**
Silver, Horace **19**
Silver, Josh
See Type O Negative
Silverchair **20**
Silveria, David
See Korn
Simeon
See Silver Apples
Simien, Terrance **12**
Simins, Russell
See Jon Spencer Blues Explosion
Simmons, Gene
See Kiss
Simmons, Joe "Run"
See Run DMC
Simmons, Patrick
See Doobie Brothers, The
Simmons, Russell **7**
Simmons, Trinna
See Spearhead
Simms, Nick
See Cornershop
Simon and Garfunkel **24**
Simon, Carly **22**
Earlier sketch in CM **4**
Simon, Paul **16**
Earlier sketch in CM **1**
Also see Simon and Garfunkel
Simone, Nina **11**
Simonon, Paul
See Clash, The
Simons, Ed
See Chemical Brothers
Simple Minds **21**
Simpson, Denis
See Nylons, The
Simpson, Derrick "Duckie"
See Black Uhuru
Simpson, Mel
See US3
Simpson, Ray
See Village People, The
Simpson, Rose
See Incredible String Band
Sims, David William
See Jesus Lizard
Sims, Matt
See Citizen King
Sims, Neil
See Catherine Wheel
Sin, Will
See Shamen, The
Sinatra, Frank **23**
Earlier sketch in CM **1**
Sinclair, David
See Camel
See Caravan
Sinclair, Gord
See Tragically Hip, The
Sinclair, Richard
See Camel
See Caravan
Sinfield, Peter
See King Crimson
Singer, Eric
See Black Sabbath
Singer, Eric
See Kiss
Singh, Talvin
See Massive Attack
Singh, Tjinder
See Cornershop
Sioux, Siouxsie
See Siouxsie and the Banshees
Siouxsie and the Banshees **8**
Sir Mix-A-Lot **14**
Sir Rap-A-Lot
See Geto Boys, The
Sirois, Joe
See Mighty Mighty Bosstones
Siverton
See Specials, The
Sixpence None the Richer **26**
Sixx, Nikki
See Mötley Crüe
Sixx, Roger
See Less Than Jake
Skaggs, Ricky **5**
Also see Country Gentlemen, The
Skatalites, The **18**
Skeete, Beverley
See Bill Wyman & the Rhythm Kings
Skeoch, Tommy
See Tesla
Skillings, Muzz
See Living Colour
Skinny Puppy **17**
Sklamberg, Lorin
See Klezmatics, The
Skoob
See Das EFX
Skunk Anansie **27**
Slash
See Guns n' Roses
Slayer **10**
Sleater-Kinney **20**
Sledd, Dale
See Osborne Brothers, The

Sledge, Percy **15**
Sledge, Robert
See Ben Folds Five
Slick, Grace
See Jefferson Airplane
Slick Rick **27**
Slijngaard, Ray
See 2 Unlimited
Sloan, Eliot
See Blessid Union of Souls
Slocum, Matt
See Sixpence None the Richer
Slovak, Hillel
See Red Hot Chili Peppers, The
Sly & the Family Stone **24**
Sly and Robbie **13**
Sly, Randy "Ginger"
See Atomic Fireballs, The
Small, Heather
See M People
Smalls, Derek
See Spinal Tap
Smart, Terence
See Butthole Surfers
Smash, Chas
See Madness
Smash Mouth **27**
Smashing Pumpkins **13**
Smear, Pat
See Foo Fighters
Smith, Adrian
See Iron Maiden
Smith, Bessie **3**
Smith, Brad
See Blind Melon
Smith, Chad
See Red Hot Chili Peppers, The
Smith, Charles
See Kool & the Gang
Smith, Clifford "Method Man"
See Wu-Tang Clan
Smith, Curt
See Tears for Fears
Smith, Debbie
See Curve
See Echobelly
Smith, Fran
See Hooters
Smith, Fred
See Blondie
Smith, Fred
See MC5, The
Smith, Fred
See Television
Smith, Garth
See Buzzcocks, The
Smith, James, "Smitty"
See Three Dog Night
Smith, Joe
See McKinney's Cotton Pickers
Smith, Kevin
See dc Talk
Smith, Mark E.
See Fall, The
Smith, Michael W. **11**
Smith, Mike
See Dave Clark Five, The
Smith, Parrish
See EPMD
Smith, Patti **17**
Earlier sketch in CM **1**
Smith, Rick
See Underworld
Smith, Robert
See Spinners, The
Smith, Robert
See Cure, The
Also see Siouxsie and the Banshees
Smith, Shawn
See Brad
Smith, Smitty
See Three Dog Night
Smith, Steve
See Journey
Smith, Tweed
See War
Smith, Wendy
See Prefab Sprout
Smith, Will **26**
Also see DJ Jazzy Jeff and the Fresh Prince
Smithereens, The **14**
Smiths, The **3**
Smyth, Gilli
See Gong
Smyth, Joe
See Sawyer Brown
Sneed, Floyd Chester
See Three Dog Night
Snoop Doggy Dogg **17**
Snouffer, Alex "Alex St. Clair"
See Captain Beefheart and His Magic Band
Snow **23**
Snow, Don
See Squeeze
Snow, Phoebe **4**
Snyder, Richard "Midnight Hatsize Snyder"
See Captain Beefheart and His Magic Band
Soan, Ashley
See Del Amitri
Sobule, Jill **20**
Social Distortion **27**
Earlier sketch in CM **19**
Solal, Martial **4**
Soloff, Lew
See Blood, Sweat and Tears
Solti, Georg **13**
Son Volt **21**
Sondheim, Stephen **8**
Sonefeld, Jim
See Hootie and the Blowfish
Sonic Youth **26**
Earlier sketch in CM **9**
Sonnenberg, Nadja Salerno
See Salerno-Sonnenberg, Nadja
Sonni, Jack
See Dire Straits
Sonnier, Jo-El **10**
Sonny and Cher **24**
Sorum, Matt
See Cult, The
Sosa, Mercedes **3**
Soucie, Michael
See Surfin' Pluto
Soul Asylum **10**
Soul Coughing **21**
Soul II Soul **17**
Soul Stirrers, The **11**
Soundgarden **6**
Sounds of Blackness **13**
Sousa, John Philip **10**
Southerland, Bill
See Kilgore
Spampinato, Joey
See NRBQ
Spampinato, Johnny
See NRBQ
Spann, Otis **18**
Sparks **18**
Sparks, Donita
See L7
Spearhead **19**
Special Ed **16**
Specials, The **21**
Spector, Phil **4**
Speech
See Arrested Development
Spellman, Jim
See Velocity Girl
Spence, Alexander "Skip"
See Jefferson Airplane
Also see Moby Grape
Spence, Cecil
See Israel Vibration
Spence, Skip
See Spence, Alexander "Skip"
Spencer Davis Group **19**
Spencer, Jeremy
See Fleetwood Mac
Spencer, Jim
See Dave Clark Five, The
Spencer, Jon
See Jon Spencer Blues Explosion
Spencer, Thad
See Jayhawks, The
Spice Girls **22**
Spin Doctors **14**
Spinal Tap **8**
Spindt, Don
See Aqua Velvets
Spinners, The **21**
Spirit **22**
Spiteri, Sharleen
See Texas
Spitz, Dan
See Anthrax
Spitz, Dave
See Black Sabbath
Sponge **18**
Spring, Keith
See NRBQ
Springfield, Dusty **20**
Springfield, Rick **9**
Springsteen, Bruce **25**
Earlier sketch in CM **6**
Sproule, Daithi
See Altan
Sprout, Tobin
See Guided By Voices
Squeeze **5**
Squire, Chris
See Yes
Squire, John
See Stone Roses, The
Squires, Rob
See Big Head Todd and the Monsters
Squirrelu Nut Zippers **20**
St. Hubbins, David
See Spinal Tap
St. James, Rebecca **26**
St. John, Mark
See Kiss
St. Marie, Buffy
See Sainte-Marie, Buffy
St. Nicholas, Nick
See Steppenwolf
Stacey, Peter "Spider"
See Pogues, The
Stacy, Jeremy
See Aztec Camera
Staehely, Al
See Spirit
Staehely, J. Christian
See Spirit

Stafford, Jo **24**
Stahl, Franz
See Foo Fighters
Staley, Layne
See Alice in Chains
Staley, Tom
See NRBQ
Stanier, John
See Helmet
Stanley, Ian
See Tears for Fears
Stanley, Paul
See Kiss
Stanley, Ralph **5**
Stansfield, Lisa **9**
Staples, Mavis **13**
Staples, Neville
See Specials, The
Staples, Pops **11**
Starcrunch
See Man or Astroman?
Starkey, Kathryn La Verne
See Starr, Kay
Starkey, Richard
See Starr, Ringo
Starks, Tia Juana
See Sweet Honey in the Rock
Starling, John
See Seldom Scene, The
Starr, Kay **27**
Starr, Mike
See Alice in Chains
Starr, Ringo **24**
Earlier sketch in CM **10**
Also see Beatles, The
Starship
See Jefferson Airplane
Statler Brothers, The **8**
Stax, John
See Pretty Things, The
Stead, David
See Beautiful South
Steaks, Chuck
See Quicksilver Messenger Service
Stebbins, Jone
See Imperial Teen
Steel, John
See Animals, The
Steel Pulse **14**
Steele, Billy
See Sounds of Blackness
Steele, David
See English Beat, The
Also see Fine Young Cannibals
Steele, Jeffrey
See Boy Howdy
Steele, Michael
See Bangles, The
Steele, Peter
See Type O Negative
Steeleye Span **19**
Steely Dan **5**
Stefani, Gwen
See No Doubt
Stefansson, Baldur
See Gus Gus
Steier, Rick
See Warrant
Stein, Chris
See Blondie
Steinberg, Lewis
See Booker T. & the M.G.'s
Steinberg, Sebastian
See Soul Coughing
Stephenson, Van Wesley
See BlackHawk
Steppenwolf **20**
Sterban, Richard
See Oak Ridge Boys, The
Stereolab **18**
Sterling, Lester
See Skatalites, The
Stern, Isaac **7**
Steve
See Fun Lovin' Criminals
Stevens, Cat **3**
Stevens, Ray **7**
Stevens, Roger
See Blind Melon
Stevens, Vol
See Memphis Jug Band
Stevenson, Bill
See Black Flag
Stevenson, Don
See Moby Grape
Stevenson, James
See Gene Loves Jezebel
Steward, Pat
See Odds
Stewart, Dave
See Eurythmics
Stewart, Derrick "Fatlip"
See Pharcyde, The
Stewart, Freddie
See Sly & the Family Stone
Stewart, Ian
See Rolling Stones, The
Stewart, Jamie
See Cult, The
Stewart, John
See Kingston Trio, The
Stewart, Larry
See Restless Heart
Stewart, Rex
See McKinney's Cotton Pickers
Stewart, Rod **20**
Earlier sketch in CM **2**
Also see Faces, The
Stewart, Sylvester
See Sly & the Family Stone
Stewart, Tyler
See Barenaked Ladies
Stewart, Vaetta
See Sly & the Family Stone
Stewart, William
See Third World
Stewart, Winston "Metal"
See Mystic Revealers
Stiff, Jimmy
See Jackyl
Stills, Stephen **5**
See Buffalo Springfield
Also see Crosby, Stills, and Nash
Sting **19**
Earlier sketch in CM **2**
Also see Police, The
Stinson, Bob
See Replacements, The
Stinson, Tommy
See Replacements, The
Stipe, Michael
See R.E.M.
Stockman, Shawn
See Boyz II Men
Stockwood, Kim **26**
Stoll
See Clannad
See Big Mountain
Stoller, Mike
See Leiber and Stoller
Stoltz, Brian
See Neville Brothers, The
Stoltzman, Richard **24**
Stonadge, Gary
See Big Audio Dynamite
Stone, Curtis
See Highway 101
Stone, Doug **10**
Stone Roses, The **16**
Stone, Sly **8**
Stone Temple Pilots **14**
Stookey, Paul
See Peter, Paul & Mary
Story, Liz **2**
Story, The **13**
Stotts, Richie
See Wendy O. Williams and The Plasmatics
Stradlin, Izzy
See Guns n' Roses
Strain, Sammy
See O'Jays, The
Strait, George **5**
Stratton, Dennis
See Iron Maiden
Strauss, Richard **25**
Stravinsky, Igor **21**
Straw, Syd **18**
Stray Cats, The **11**
Strayhorn, Billy **13**
Street, Richard
See Temptations, The
Streisand, Barbra **2**
Strickland, Keith
See B-52's, The
Stringer, Gary
See Reef
Strummer, Joe
See Clash, The
Stryper **2**
Stuart, Mark
See Audio Adrenaline
Stuart, Marty **9**
Stuart, Peter
See Dog's Eye View
Stubbs, Levi
See Four Tops, The
Styne, Jule **21**
Sub Commander Ras I Zulu
See Spearhead
Subdudes, The **18**
Sublime **19**
Such, Alec Jon
See Bon Jovi
Suede **20**
Sugar Ray **22**
Sugarcubes, The **10**
Suicidal Tendencies **15**
Sulley, Suzanne
See Human League, The
Sullivan, Jacqui
See Bananarama
Sullivan, Kirk
See 4Him
Summer, Donna **12**
Summer, Mark
See Turtle Island String Quartet
Summers, Andy **3**
Also see Police, The
Sumner, Bernard
See Joy Division
Also see New Order
Sun Ra **27**
Earlier sketch in CM **5**

Sundays, The **20**
Sunnyland Slim **16**
Super DJ Dmitry
See Deee-lite
Superdrag **23**
Supertramp **25**
Supremes, The **6**
Sure!, Al B. **13**
Surfaris, The **23**
Surfin' Pluto **24**
Sutcliffe, Stu
See Beatles, The
Sutherland, Joan **13**
Svenigsson, Magnus
See Cardigans
Svensson, Peter
See Cardigans
Svigals, Alicia
See Klezmatics, The
Swarbrick, Dave
See Fairport Convention
Sweat, Keith **13**
Sweet Honey In The Rock **26**
Earlier sketch in CM **1**
Sweet, Matthew **9**
Sweet, Michael
See Stryper
Sweet, Robert
See Stryper
Sweethearts of the Rodeo **12**
Swing, DeVante
See Jodeci
SWV **14**
Sykes, John
See Whitesnake
Sykes, Roosevelt **20**
Sylvain, Sylvain
See New York Dolls
Sylvian, David **27**
T. Rex **11**
Tabac, Tony
See Joy Division
Tabor, Ty
See King's X
Tackett, Fred
See Little Feat
Tadlock, Tom
See Tuxedomoon
TAFKAP (The Artist Formerly Known as Prince)
See Prince
Taggart, Jeremy
See Our Lady Peace
Tait, Michael
See dc Talk
Taj Mahal **6**
Tajima, Takao
See Pizzicato Five
Takac, Robby
See Goo Goo Dolls, The
Takanami
See Pizzicato Five
Take 6 **6**
Takemitsu, Toru **6**
Takizawa, Taishi
See Ghost
Talbot, John Michael **6**
Talcum, Joe Jack
See Dead Milkmen
Talk Talk **19**
Talking Heads **1**
Tampa Red **25**
Tandy, Richard
See Electric Light Orchestra
Tangerine Dream **12**
Taree, Aerle
See Arrested Development
Tate, Geoff
See Queensryche
Tatum, Art **17**
Taupin, Bernie **22**
Taylor, Aaron
See MC Eiht
Taylor, Andy
See Duran Duran
Taylor, Billy **13**
Taylor, Cecil **9**
Taylor, Chad
See Live
Taylor, Courtney
See Dandy Warhols
Taylor, Dan
See Silver Apples
Taylor, Dave
See Pere Ubu
Taylor, Dick
See Rolling Stones, The
Taylor, Earl
See Country Gentlemen, The
Taylor, James **25**
Earlier sketch in CM **2**
Taylor, James "J.T."
See Kool & the Gang
Taylor, John
See Duran Duran
Taylor, Johnnie
See Soul Stirrers, The
Taylor, Koko **10**
Taylor, Leroy
See Soul Stirrers, The
Taylor, Melvin
See Ventures, The
Taylor, Mick
See Rolling Stones, The
Also see Pretty Things, The
Taylor, Philip "Philthy Animal"
See Motörhead
Taylor, Roger
See Duran Duran
Taylor, Roger Meadows
See Queen
Taylor, Steve
See Ray Condo and His Ricochets
Taylor, Steve **26**
Taylor, Teresa
See Butthole Surfers
Taylor, Zola
See Platters, The
Te Kanawa, Kiri **2**
Teagarden, Jack **10**
Tears for Fears **6**
Technotronic **5**
Teenage Fanclub **13**
Television **17**
Teller, Al **15**
Temirkanov, Yuri **26**
Tempesta, John
See White Zombie
Temple, Michelle
See Pere Ubu
Temptations, The **3**
Tench, Benmont
See Tom Petty and the Heartbreakers
Tennant, Neil
See Pet Shop Boys
Tepper, Jeff "Morris"
See Captain Beefheart and His Magic Band
Terminator X
See Public Enemy
Terrell, Jean
See Supremes, The
Terry, Boyd
See Aquabats, The
Terry, Clark **24**
Tesh, John **20**
Tesla **15**
Texas **27**
Texas Tornados, The **8**
Thacker, Rocky
See Shenandoah
Thain, Gary
See Uriah Heep
Thayil, Kim
See Soundgarden
The The **15**
Theremin, Leon **19**
They Might Be Giants **7**
Thibaudet, Jean-Yves **24**
Thielemans, Toots **13**
Thin Lizzy **13**
Third Eye Blind **25**
Third World **13**
Thirsk, Jason
See Pennywise
Thistlethwaite, Anthony
See Waterboys, The
Thomas, Alex
See Earth, Wind and Fire
Thomas, David
See Take 6
Thomas, David Clayton
See Clayton-Thomas, David
Thomas, David
See Pere Ubu
Thomas, Dennis "D.T."
See Kool & the Gang
Thomas, George "Fathead"
See McKinney's Cotton Pickers
Thomas, Irma **16**
Thomas, John
See Captain Beefheart and His Magic Band
Thomas, Mickey
See Jefferson Starship
Thomas, Olice
See Five Blind Boys of Alabama
Thomas, Ray
See Moody Blues, The
Thomas, Richard
See Jesus and Mary Chain, The
Thomas, Rob
See Matchbox 20
Thomas, Rozonda "Chilli"
See TLC
Thompson, Chester
See Weather Report
Thompson, Danny
See Pentangle
Thompson, Dennis
See MC5, The
Thompson, Dougie
See Supertramp
Thompson, Lee
See Madness
Thompson, Les
See Nitty Gritty Dirt Band, The
Thompson, Mayo
See Pere Ubu
Thompson, Porl
See Cure, The
Thompson, Richard
See Fairport Convention
Thompson, Richard **7**
Thomson, Kristin
See Tsunami

Thoranisson, Biggi
See Gus Gus
Thorn, Christopher
See Blind Melon
Thorn, Stan
See Shenandoah
Thorn, Tracey
See Everything But The Girl
Also see Massive Attack
Thornalley, Phil
See Cure, The
Thornburg, Lee
See Supertramp
Thornhill, Leeroy
See Prodigy
Thornton, Big Mama **18**
Thornton, Kevin "KT"
See Color Me Badd
Thornton, Willie Mae
See Thornton, Big Mama
Threadgill, Henry **9**
Three Dog Night **5**
Throwing Muses **15**
Thunders, Johnny
See New York Dolls
Tickner, George
See Journey
Tiffany **4**
Tikaram, Tanita **9**
Tilbrook, Glenn
See Squeeze
Tiller, Mary
See Anointed
Tilley, Sandra
See Martha and the Vandellas
Tillis, Mel **7**
Tillis, Pam **25**
Earlier sketch in CM **8**
Tilson Thomas, Michael **24**
Timberlake, Justin
See 'N Sync
Timbuk 3 **3**
Timmins, Margo
See Cowboy Junkies, The
Timmins, Michael
See Cowboy Junkies, The
Timmins, Peter
See Cowboy Junkies, The
Timms, Sally
See Mekons, The
Tinsley, Boyd
See Dave Matthews Band
Tippin, Aaron **12**
Tipton, Glenn
See Judas Priest
TLC **15**
Toad the Wet Sprocket **13**
Toback, Jeremy
See Brad
Todd, Andy
See Republica
Tolhurst, Laurence
See Cure, The
Tolland, Bryan
See Del Amitri
Toller, Dan
See Allman Brothers, The
Tolliver, T.C.
See Wendy O. Williams and The Plasmatics
Tolson, Peter
See Pretty Things, The
Tom Petty and the Heartbreakers **26**
Tone-Loc **3**
Tong, Winston
See Tuxedomoon
Tontoh, Frank
See Aztec Camera
Tony K
See Roomful of Blues
Tony Williams **6**
Tony! Toni! Toné! **12**
Too $hort **16**
Toohey, Dan
See Guided By Voices
Took, Steve Peregrine
See T. Rex
Tool **21**
Toomey, Jenny
See Tsunami
Topham, Anthony "Top"
See Yardbirds, The
Tork, Peter
See Monkees, The
Torme, Mel **4**
Torres, Hector "Tico"
See Bon Jovi
Toscanini, Arturo **14**
Tosh, Peter **3**
Toure, Ali Farka **18**
Tourish, Ciaran
See Altan
Toussaint, Allen **11**
Towner, Ralph **22**
Townes, Jeffery
See DJ Jazzy Jeff and the Fresh Prince
Towns, Efrem
See Dirty Dozen Brass Band
Townshend, Pete **1**
Also see Who, The
Traffic **19**
Tragically Hip, The **18**
Trammell, Mark
See Greater Vision
Travers, Brian
See UB40
Travers, Mary
See Peter, Paul & Mary
Travis, Merle **14**
Travis, Randy **9**
Treach
See Naughty by Nature
Treadmill Trackstar **21**
Tribe Called Quest, A **8**
Tricky **18**
Tricky
See Massive Attack
Trimble, Vivian
See Luscious Jackson
Trimble, Vivien
See Luscious Jackson
Trimm, Rex
See Cherry Poppin' Daddies
Tripp, Art "Art Marimba"
See Captain Beefheart and His Magic Band
Tritsch, Christian
See Gong
Tritt, Travis **7**
Trotter, Kera
See C + C Music Factory
Trucks, Butch
See Allman Brothers, The
Trugoy the Dove
See De La Soul
Trujillo, Robert
See Suicidal Tendencies
Truman, Dan
See Diamond Rio
Trynin, Jen **21**
Tsunami **21**
Tubb, Ernest **4**
Tubridy, Michael
See Chieftans, The
Tucker, Corin
See Sleater-Kinney
Tucker, Moe
See Velvet Underground, The
Tucker, Sophie **12**
Tucker, Tanya **3**
Tucker, William
See Ministry
Also see Pigface
Tufnel, Nigel
See Spinal Tap
Tull, Bruce
See Scud Mountain Boys
Turbin, Neil
See Anthrax
Turgon, Bruce
See Foreigner
Turner, Big Joe **13**
Turner, Elgin "Masta Killa"
See Wu-Tang Clan
Turner, Erik
See Warrant
Turner, Ike
See Ike and Tina Turner
Turner, Joe Lynn
See Deep Purple
Turner, Mike
See Our Lady Peace
Turner, Sonny
See Platters, The
Turner, Steve
See Mudhoney
Turner, Tina **1**
Also see Ike and Tina Turner
Turpin, Will
See Collective Soul
Turre, Steve **22**
Turtle Island String Quartet **9**
Tutton, Bill
See Geraldine Fibbers
Tutuska, George
See Goo Goo Dolls, The
Tuxedomoon **21**
Twain, Shania **17**
Twist, Nigel
See Alarm
Twitty, Conway **6**
Tyagi, Paul
See Del Amitri
Tyler, Steve
See Aerosmith
Tyner, McCoy **7**
Tyner, Rob
See MC5, The
Type O Negative **27**
Tyson, Ian
See Ian and Sylvia
Tyson, Ron
See Temptations, The
U2 **12**
Earlier sketch in CM **2**
UB40 **4**
Ulmer, James Blood **13**
Ulrich, Lars
See Metallica
Ulvaeus, Björn
See Abba
Um Romao, Dom
See Weather Report
Underworld **26**
Unitt, Victor
See Pretty Things, The

Unruh, N. U.
See Einstürzende Neubauten
Uosikkinen, David
See Hooters
Upshaw, Dawn **9**
Urge Overkill **17**
Uriah Heep **19**
US3 **18**
Usher **23**
Utley, Adrian
See Portishead
Utsler, Joseph
See Insane Clown Possee
Vaché, Jr., Warren **22**
Vachon, Chris
See Roomful of Blues
Vai, Steve **5**
Also see Whitesnake
Valdès, Chucho **25**
Valens, Ritchie **23**
Valenti, Dino
See Quicksilver Messenger Service
Valentine, Gary
See Blondie
Valentine, Gary
See Blondie
Valentine, Hilton
See Animals, The
Valentine, Kathy
See Go-Go's, The
Valentine, Rae
See War
Valenzuela, Jesse
See Gin Blossoms
Valli, Frankie **10**
Also see Four Seasons, The
Valory, Ross
See Journey
van Dijk, Carol
See Bettie Serveert
van Lieshout, Lars
See Tuxedomoon
Van Gelder, Nick
See Jamiroquai
Van Halen **25**
Earlier sketch in CM **8**
Van Halen, Alex
See Van Halen
Van Halen, Edward
See Van Halen
Van Hook, Peter
See Mike & the Mechanics
Van Rensalier, Darnell
See Shai
Van Ronk, Dave **12**
Van Shelton, Ricky **5**
Van Vliet, Don "Captain Beefheart"
See Captain Beefheart and His Magic Band
Van Zandt, Townes **13**
Van Zant, Johnny
See Lynyrd Skynyrd
Van Zant, Ronnie
See Lynyrd Skynyrd
Vandenburg, Adrian
See Whitesnake
Vander Ark, Brian
See Verve Pipe, The
Vander Ark, Brad
See Verve Pipe, The
Vandross, Luther **24**
Earlier sketch in CM **2**
Vanessa-Mae **26**
Vangelis **21**
Vanilla Ice **6**
Vasquez, Junior **16**
Vaughan, Jimmie **24**
Also see Fabulous Thunderbirds, The
Vaughan, Sarah **2**
Vaughan, Stevie Ray **1**
Vedder, Eddie
See Pearl Jam
Vega, Bobby
See Quicksilver Messenger Service
Vega, Suzanne **3**
Velocity Girl **23**
Velvet Underground, The **7**
Ventures, The **19**
Verdecchio, Andy
See Five Iron Frenzy
Verlaine, Tom
See Television
Verta-Ray, Matt
See Madder Rose
Veruca Salt **20**
Verve Pipe, The **20**
Verve, The **18**
Vettese, Peter-John
See Jethro Tull
Vicious, Sid
See Sex Pistols, The
Also see Siouxsie and the Banshees
Vickrey, Dan
See Counting Crows
Victor, Tommy
See Prong
Vienna Choir Boys **23**
Vig, Butch **17**
Also see Garbage
Village People, The **7**
Vincent, Gene **19**
Vincent, Vinnie
See Kiss
Vinnie
See Naughty by Nature
Vinton, Bobby **12**
Violent Femmes **12**
Violent J
See Insane Clown Posse
Virtue, Michael
See UB40
Visser, Peter
See Bettie Serveert
Vito, Rick
See Fleetwood Mac
Vitous, Mirslav
See Weather Report
Voelz, Susan
See Poi Dog Pondering
Volz, Greg
See Petra
von Karajan, Herbert **1**
Von, Eerie
See Danzig
Vox, Bono
See U2
Vudi
See American Music Club
Waaktaar, Pal
See A-ha
Wachtel, Waddy **26**
Wade, Adam
See Shudder to Think
Wade, Chrissie
See Alien Sex Fiend
Wade, Nik
See Alien Sex Fiend
Wadenius, George
See Blood, Sweat and Tears
Wadephal, Ralf
See Tangerine Dream
Wagoner, Faidest
See Soul Stirrers, The
Wagoner, Porter **13**
Wahlberg, Donnie
See New Kids on the Block
Wailer, Bunny **11**
Wainwright III, Loudon **11**
Waits, Tom **27**
Earlier sketch in CM **1**
Earlier sketch in CM **12**
Wakeling, David
See English Beat, The
Wakeman, Rick **27**
Also see Yes
Walden, Narada Michael **14**
Waldroup, Jason
See Greater Vision
Walford, Britt
See Breeders
Walker, Clay **20**
Walker, Colin
See Electric Light Orchestra
Walker, Ebo
See New Grass Revival, The
Walker, Jerry Jeff **13**
Walker, T-Bone **5**
Wallace, Bill
See Guess Who
Wallace, Ian
See King Crimson
Wallace, Richard
See Mighty Clouds of Joy, The
Wallace, Sippie **6**
Waller, Charlie
See Country Gentlemen, The
Waller, Dave
See Jam, The
Waller, Fats **7**
Wallflowers, The **20**
Wallinger, Karl
See Waterboys, The
Wallinger, Karl **11**
Wallis, Larry
See Motörhead
Walls, Chris
See Dave Clark Five, The
Walls, Denise "Nee-C"
See Anointed
Walls, Greg
See Anthrax
Walsh, Joe **5**
Also see Eagles, The
Walsh, Marty
See Supertramp
Walters, Richard
See Slick Rick
Walters, Robert "Patch"
See Mystic Revealers
War **14**
Ward, Andy
See Bevis Frond
See Camel
Ward, Bill
See Black Sabbath
Ward, Michael
See Wallflowers, The
Also see Black Sabbath
Ware, Martyn
See Human League, The
Wareham, Dean
See Luna
Wariner, Steve **18**

Warner, Les
See Cult, The
Warnes, Jennifer **3**
Warrant **17**
Warren, Diane **21**
Warren, George W.
See Five Blind Boys of Alabama
Warren, Mervyn
See Take 6
Warwick, Clint
See Moody Blues, The
Warwick, Dionne **2**
Was (Not Was) **6**
Was, David
See Was (Not Was)
Was, Don **21**
Also see Was (Not Was)
Wash, Martha
See C + C Music Factory
Washington, Chester
See Earth, Wind and Fire
Washington, Dinah **5**
Washington, Grover, Jr. **5**
Wasserman, Greg "Noodles"
See Offspring
Waterboys, The **27**
Waters, Crystal **15**
Waters, Ethel **11**
Waters, Muddy **24**
Earlier sketch in CM **4**
Waters, Roger
See Pink Floyd
Watkins, Christopher
See Cabaret Voltaire
Watkins, Tionne "T-Boz"
See TLC
Watley, Jody **26**
Earlier sketch in CM **9**
Watson, Doc **2**
Watson, Guy
See Surfaris, The
Watson, Ivory
See Ink Spots
Watt, Ben
See Everything But The Girl
Watt, Mike **22**
Also see fIREHOSE
Watters, Sam
See Color Me Badd
Watts, Bari
See Bevis Frond
Watts, Charlie
See Rolling Stones, The
Watts, Eugene
See Canadian Brass, The
Watts, Lou
See Chumbawamba
Watts, Raymond
See KMFDM
Watts, Todd
See Emmet Swimming
Weather Report **19**
Weaver, Louie
See Petra
Weavers, The **8**
Webb, Chick **14**
Webb, Jimmy **12**
Webb, Paul
See Talk Talk
Webber, Andrew Lloyd
See Lloyd Webber, Andrew
Webber, Mark
See Pulp
Webster, Andrew
See Tsunami
Wedgwood, Mike
See Caravan
Wedren, Craig
See Shudder to Think
Weezer **20**
Weider, John
See Animals, The
Weiland, Scott
See Stone Temple Pilots
Weill, Kurt **12**
Weir, Bob
See Grateful Dead, The
Weiss, Janet
See Sleater-Kinney
Also see Quasi
Weissman, Marco
See Waterboys, The
Welch, Bob
See Fleetwood Mac
Welch, Brian
See Korn
Welch, Bruce
See Shadows, The
Welch, Mcguinness
See Fleetwood Mac
Also see Lords of Acid
Welch, Sean
See Beautiful South
Welk, Lawrence **13**
Weller, Paul
See Jam, The
Weller, Paul **14**
Wells, Cory
See Three Dog Night
Wells, Junior **17**
Wells, Kitty **6**
Welnick, Vince
See Grateful Dead, The
Welsh, Alan
See Aztec Camera
Welty, Ron
See Offspring
Wenberg, Erik
See Emmet Swimming
Wendy O. Williams and The Plasmatics **26**
Wertz, Jenn
See Rusted Root
West, Brian
See Cherry Poppin' Daddies
West, Dottie **8**
West, Steve
See Pavement
Westerberg, Paul **26**
Also see Replacements, The
Weston, Randy **15**
Weston
See Orb, The
Wetton, John
See King Crimson
Wexler, Jerry **15**
Weymouth, Tina
See Talking Heads
Whalen, Katharine
See Squirrel Nut Zippers
Whalley, Dennis
See Captain Beefheart and His Magic Band
Wharton, Dianaruthe
See Sweet Honey in the Rock
Wheat, Brian
See Tesla
Wheeler, Audrey
See C + C Music Factory
Wheeler, Caron
See Soul II Soul
Wheeler, Harriet
See Sundays, The
Wheeler, Robert
See Pere Ubu
Whelan, Bill **20**
Whelan, Gavan
See James
Whitaker, Rodney **20**
Whitaker, Yolanda
See Yo Yo
White, Alan
See Oasis
See Yes
White, Barry **6**
White, Billy
See Dokken
White, Chris
See Dire Straits
See Zombies, The
White, Clarence
See Byrds, The
White, Dave
See Warrant
White, Dennis
See Charm Farm
See Dokken
White, Freddie
See Earth, Wind and Fire
White, Karyn **21**
White, Lari **15**
White, Mark
See Mekons, The
White, Mark
See Spin Doctors
White, Maurice
See Earth, Wind and Fire
White, Ralph
See Bad Livers, The
White, Roland
See Nashville Bluegrass Band
White, Verdine
See Earth, Wind and Fire
White, Will
See Propellerheads
White Zombie **17**
Whitehead, Donald
See Earth, Wind and Fire
Whiteman, Paul **17**
Whitesnake **5**
Whitfield, Mark **18**
Whitford, Brad
See Aerosmith
Whitley, Chris **16**
Whitley, Keith **7**
Whitman, Slim **19**
Whittaker, Hudson **20**
Whitten, Chris
See Dire Straits
Whitwam, Barry
See Herman's Hermits
Who, The **3**
Wichnewski, Stephen
See Yo La Tengo
Wickham, Steve
See Waterboys, The
Widenhouse, Je
See Squirrel Nut Zippers
Wiedlin, Jane
See Go-Go's, The
Wiggins, Dwayne
See Tony! Toni! Toné!
Wiggins, Raphael
See Tony! Toni! Toné!
Wiggs, Josephine
See Breeders

Wikso, Ron
See Foreigner
Wilborn, Dave
See McKinney's Cotton Pickers
Wilburn, Ishmael
See Weather Report
Wilco **27**
Wilcox, Imani
See Pharcyde, The
Wilde, Phil
See 2 Unlimited
Wilder, Alan
See Depeche Mode
Wildwood, Michael
See D Generation
Wilk, Brad
See Rage Against the Machine
Wilkeson, Leon
See Lynyrd Skynyrd
Wilkie, Chris
See Dubstar
Wilkinson, Geoff
See US3
Wilkinson, Keith
See Squeeze
Wilkinson, Kevin
See Waterboys, The
Williams, Andy **2**
Williams, Boris
See Cure, The
Williams, Cliff
See AC/DC
Williams, Dana
See Diamond Rio
Williams, Dar **21**
Williams, Deniece **1**
Williams, Don **4**
Williams, Eric
See Blackstreet
Williams, Fred
See C + C Music Factory
Williams, Hank, Sr. **4**
Williams, Hank, Jr. **1**
Williams, James "Diamond"
See Ohio Players
Williams, Joe **11**
Williams, John **9**
Williams, Lamar
See Allman Brothers, The
Williams, Lucinda **24**
Earlier sketch in CM **10**
Williams, Marion **15**
Williams, Milan
See Commodores, The
Williams, Otis
See Temptations, The
Williams, Paul **26**
Earlier sketch in CM **5**
Williams, Paul
See Temptations, The
Williams, Phillard
See Earth, Wind and Fire
Williams, Robbie **25**
Williams, Robert
See Captain Beefheart and His Magic Band
Williams, Terry
See Dire Straits
Williams, Tony
See Platters, The
Williams, Vanessa **10**
Williams, Victoria **17**
Williams, Walter
See O'Jays, The
Williams, Wendy O.
See Wendy O. Williams and The Plasmatics
Williams, Wilbert
See Mighty Clouds of Joy, The
Williams, William Elliot
See Artifacts
Williams, Yasmeen
See Sweet Honey in the Rock
Williamson, Gloria
See Martha and the Vandellas
Williamson, Robin
See Incredible String Band
Williamson, Sonny Boy **9**
Willie D.
See Geto Boys, The
Willis, Clarence "Chet"
See Ohio Players
Willis, Kelly **12**
Willis, Larry
See Blood, Sweat and Tears
Willis, Pete
See Def Leppard
Willis, Rick
See Foreigner
Willis, Victor
See Village People, The
Willner, Hal **10**
Wills, Aaron (P-Nut)
See 311
Wills, Bob **6**
Wills, Mark **27**
Wills, Rick
See Bad Company
Willson-Piper, Marty
See Church, The
Wilmot, Billy "Mystic"
See Mystic Revealers
Wilson, Anne
See Heart
Wilson, Brian **24**
Also see Beach Boys, The
Wilson, Carl
See Beach Boys, The
Wilson, Carnie
See Wilson Phillips
Wilson, Cassandra **26**
Earlier sketch in CM **12**
Wilson, Chris
See Love Spit Love
Wilson, Cindy
See B-52's, The
Wilson, Dennis
See Beach Boys, The
Wilson, Don
See Ventures, The
Wilson, Eric
See Sublime
Wilson, Gerald **19**
Wilson, Jackie **3**
Wilson, Kim
See Fabulous Thunderbirds, The
Wilson, Mary
See Supremes, The
Wilson, Nancy **14**
Also see Heart
Wilson, Orlandus
See Golden Gate Quartet
Wilson, Patrick
See Weezer
Wilson Phillips **5**
Wilson, Ransom **5**
Wilson, Ricky
See B-52's, The
Wilson, Robin
See Gin Blossoms
Wilson, Ron
See Surfaris, The
Wilson, Shanice
See Shanice
Wilson, Wendy
See Wilson Phillips
Wilson-James, Victoria Soul II Soul
Also see Shamen, The
Wilton, Michael
See Queensryche
Wimpfheimer, Jimmy
See Roomful of Blues
Winans, Carvin
See Winans, The
Winans, Marvin
See Winans, The
Winans, Michael
See Winans, The
Winans, Ronald
See Winans, The
Winans, The **12**
Winbush, Angela **15**
Winfield, Chuck
See Blood, Sweat and Tears
Winston, George **9**
Winter, Johnny **5**
Winter, Kurt
See Guess Who
Winter, Paul **10**
Winthrop, Dave
See Supertramp
Winwood, Muff
See Spencer Davis Group
Winwood, Steve **2**
Also see Spencer Davis Group
Also see Traffic
Wire, Nicky
See Manic Street Preachers
Wiseman, Bobby
See Blue Rodeo
Wiseman, Mac **19**
WishBone
See Bone Thugs-N-Harmony
Withers, Pick
See Dire Straits
Witherspoon, Jimmy **19**
Wolf, Peter
See J. Geils Band
Wolfe, Gerald
See Greater Vision
Wolstencraft, Simon
See Fall, The
Womack, Bobby **5**
Wonder, Stevie **17**
Earlier sketch in CM **2**
Wood, Chris
See Traffic
Wood, Danny
See New Kids on the Block
Wood, Ron
See Faces, The
Also see Rolling Stones, The
Wood, Roy
See Electric Light Orchestra
Woodgate, Dan
See Madness
Woods, Gay
See Steeleye Span
Woods, Terry
See Pogues, The
See Steeleye Span
Woods-Wright, Tomica **22**
Woodson, Ollie
See Temptations, The
Woodward, Keren
See Bananarama

Woody, Allen
See Allman Brothers, The
Woolfolk, Andrew
See Earth, Wind and Fire
Worley, Chris
See Jackyl
Worley, Jeff
See Jackyl
Worrell, Bernie **11**
Wray, Link **17**
Wreede, Katrina
See Turtle Island String Quartet
Wren, Alan
See Stone Roses, The
Wretzky, D'Arcy
See Smashing Pumpkins
Wright, Adrian
See Human League, The
Wright, David "Blockhead"
See English Beat, The
Wright, Heath
See Ricochet
Wright, Hugh
See Boy Howdy
Wright, Jimmy
See Sounds of Blackness
Wright, Norman
See Country Gentlemen, The
Wright, Rick
See Pink Floyd
Wright, Simon
See AC/DC
Wright, Tim
See Pere Ubu
Wu-Tang Clan **19**
Wurzel
See Motörhead
Wyatt, Robert **24**
Wyman, Bill
See Rolling Stones, The
Also see Bill Wyman & the Rhythm Kings
Wynette, Tammy **24**
Earlier sketch in CM **2**
Wynne, Philippe
See Spinners, The
Wynonna **11**
Also see Judds, The
X **11**
Xefos, Chris
See King Missile
XTC **26**
Earlier sketch in CM **10**
Ya Kid K
See Technotronic
Yale, Brian
See Matchbox 20
Yamamoto, Hiro
See Soundgarden
Yamano, Atsuko
See Shonen Knife
Yamano, Naoko
See Shonen Knife
Yamashita, Kazuhito **4**
Yamauchi, Tetsu
See Faces, The
Yamazaki, Iwao
See Ghost
Yang, Naomi
See Damon and Naomi
Yankovic, "Weird Al" **7**
Yanni **11**
Yardbirds, The **10**
Yarrow, Peter
See Peter, Paul & Mary
Yates, Bill
See Country Gentlemen, The
Yauch, Adam
See Beastie Boys, The
Yearwood, Trisha **25**
Earlier sketch in CM **10**
Yella
See N.W.A.
Yes **8**
Yeston, Maury **22**
Yo La Tengo **24**
Yo Yo **9**
Yoakam, Dwight **21**
Earlier sketch in CM **1**
Yoot, Tukka
See US3
York, Andrew **15**
York, John
See Byrds, The
York, Pete
See Spencer Davis Group
Yorke, Thom E.
See Radiohead
Young, Adrian
See No Doubt
Young, Angus
See AC/DC
Young, Brian
See Fountains of Wayne
Young, Faron **7**
Young, Fred
See Kentucky Headhunters, The
Young, Gary
See Pavement
Young, Grant
See Soul Asylum
Young, Jeff
See Megadeth
Young, La Monte **16**
Young, Lester **14**
Young M.C. **4**
Young, Malcolm
See AC/DC
Young, Neil **15**
Earlier sketch in CM **2**
Also see Buffalo Springfield
Young, Paul
See Mike & the Mechanics
Young, Richard
See Kentucky Headhunters, The
Young, Robert "Throbert"
See Primal Scream
Youth, Todd
See D Generation
Youtz, Raif
See Built to Spill
Yow, David
See Jesus Lizard
Yseult, Sean
See White Zombie
Yule, Doug
See Velvet Underground, The
Zander, Robin
See Cheap Trick
Zankey, Glen
See Bluegrass Patriots
Zap Mama **14**
Zappa, Frank **17**
Earlier sketch in CM **1**
Zawinul, Josef
See Weather Report
Zender, Stuart
See Jamiroquai
Zevon, Warren **9**
Zhane **22**
Zilinskas, Annette
See Bangles, The
Zimmerman, Udo **5**
Zombie, Rob
See White Zombie
Zombies, The **23**
Zoom, Billy
See X
Zorn, John **15**
Zoyes, Dino
See Charm Farm
Zuccaro, Steve
See Charm Far
Zukerman, Pinchas **4**
Zulu, Ras I
See Spearhead
ZZ Top **2**